P9-DUG-289

# Central
# Australia
## Adelaide to Darwin

Darwin to
Uluru
(p145)

Adelaide &
South Australia
(p48)

THIS EDITION WRITTEN AND RESEARCHED BY

Charles Rawlings-Way, Meg Worby,

Lindsay Brown

## PLAN YOUR TRIP

## ON THE ROAD

Jul 201

# Contents

## UNDERSTAND

## SURVIVAL
## GUIDE

# Welcome to Central Australia

*Explore Australia's epic heartland: from the cold Southern Ocean, through South Australia's wine valleys, beyond Uluru in the central desert and into the tropical Top End.*

## National Parks

Central Australia is flush with iconic natural landscapes. Whether it's counting pelicans in the Coorong, ogling the crags of the Flinders Ranges, ticking Uluru and Kata Tjuta off your 'must-see' list, paddling the gorges at Nitmiluk, or marvelling over ancient Aboriginal rock art in Kakadu, the national parks here are nothing short of astonishing. Planning your journey around them is the perfect way to experience the outrageous diversity of this ancient region.

## Wine & Food

It seems unnecessary to introduce South Australia as one of the world's key wine producers, but indeed it is! Big-ticket regions such as the Barossa Valley, McLaren Vale and the Coonawarra have been bottling blockbuster reds for decades, while boutique areas such as the Clare Valley and Adelaide Hills are self-assured viticultural success stories. Hungry? Along the road you'll find gourmet cheeses, fabulous organic beef and lamb, multicultural food markets, buzzy eat streets and seafood worth jumping out of the boat for. Don't miss trying some classic outback game (emu, crocodile, kangaroo or camel, anyone?) and Aboriginal bush tucker: traditional native fruits, herbs and meats.

## Indigenous Culture

You'll find Aboriginal culture more accessible and mainstream in central Australia than it is in east-coast cities. This isn't just by virtue of numbers – Australia-wide indigenous people comprise around 2.5% of the population; in the Northern Territory it's closer to 30% – but it also illustrates how indigenous people themselves interact with the tourist market here. Right across SA and the NT you can take an indigenous-run tour, shop for Aboriginal art, catch an indigenous cultural performance or festival, visit galleries, hear Aboriginal Dreaming stories and try some bush tucker.

## Cities & Towns

When you conjure up images of central Australia, Adelaide and Darwin mightn't leap into your consciousness. But they should! All sandstone orderliness, Adelaide remains at Australia's cultural high-water mark, unleashing a torrent of creative energy through its amazing festivals, arts scene, pubs and foodie culture. Darwin is an anything-goes northern upstart, fuelled by a current natural-gas boom: like the apartment towers going up, this is a city on the rise. In between are kooky outback outposts, hip wine towns and vacant desert pit-stops.

## Why We Love Central Australia

By Charles Rawlings-Way & Meg Worby, Coordinating Authors

Meg first saw Uluru when she was three, but Charles didn't visit the outback until he was 30-something, on a trip with Meg. Climbing down off the *Ghan* train in Alice Springs, we exchanged looks that said, respectively, 'See what I mean?' and, '*Ohh*, now I get it!'. The air out here is charged with desert ions; the night sky is milky with stars – outback camping is an unmissable experience. And then there's our ongoing love affair with South Australia's wineries, pubs, beaches, festivals...and our home among the Adelaide Hills stringybarks.

**For more about our authors, see p296**

Above: Uluru (p227)

# Central Australia

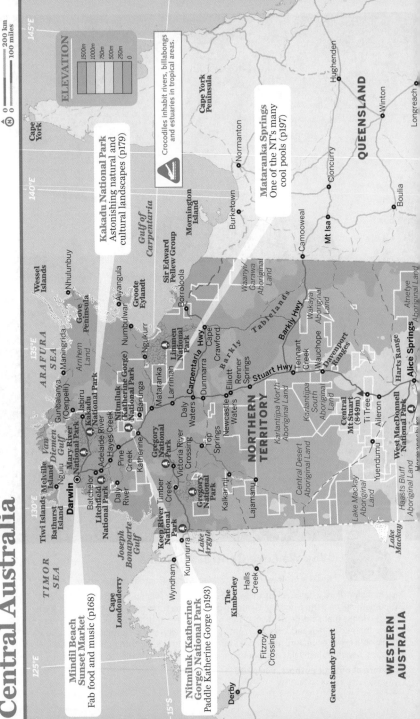

Mindil Beach Sunset Market
Fab food and music (p168)

Kakadu National Park
Astonishing natural and cultural landscapes (p179)

Crocodiles inhabit rivers, billabongs and estuaries in tropical areas.

Mataranka Springs
One of the NT's many cool pools (p197)

Nitmiluk (Katherine Gorge) National Park
Paddle Katherine Gorge (p193)

ELEVATION

| 1500m |
| 1000m |
| 750m |
| 500m |
| 250m |
| 0 |

0    200 km
0    100 miles

**Kings Canyon & Watarrka National Park**
A unique outback oasis (p220)

**Uluru-Kata Tjuta National Park**
Two natural wonders (p223)

**The Ghan**
Adelaide to Darwin by rail (p283)

**Oodnadatta Track**
Adventurous 615km outback detour (p143)

**Ikara (Wilpena Pound)**
Remarkable Flinders Ranges rock formations (p135)

**Adelaide Central Market**
Multicultural downtown foodie delights (p55)

**McLaren Vale Wine Region**
One of SA's brilliant wine regions (p82)

**Kangaroo Island**
Wildlife, wilderness and fine edibles (p90)

## ROAD DISTANCES (km)

Note: Distances are approximate

| | Alice Springs | Darwin | Katherine | Mt Gambier | Port Augusta | Tennant Ck |
|---|---|---|---|---|---|---|
| Alice Springs | 1524 | | | | | |
| Darwin | 3020 | 1496 | | | | |
| Katherine | 2702 | 1178 | 318 | | | |
| Mt Gambier | 430 | 1960 | 3460 | 3150 | | |
| Port Augusta | 300 | 1224 | 2720 | 2402 | 750 | |
| Tennant Ck | 2032 | 508 | 988 | 670 | 2470 | 1732 |

| | Adelaide | Alice Springs | Darwin | Katherine | Mt Gambier | Port Augusta |

# Central Australia's
# Top 12

## Kakadu National Park, NT

**1** Kakadu (p179) is more than a nature reserve: it's an adventure into a natural and cultural landscape like no other. Weathered by successive seasons of Wet and Dry, the sandstone ramparts of Kakadu, and neighbouring Arnhem Land, have sheltered humans for eons, and an extraordinary legacy of rock art remains. Represented are mysterious figures of the Dreaming, hunting stories, zoological diagrams, and 'contact art' – records of visitors from Indonesia and more recent European colonists. Kakadu's Ubirr and Nourlangie galleries are of World Heritage significance and accessible to all.

Below left: Jim Jim Falls (p185)

## Uluru-Kata Tjuta National Park, NT

**2** Australia's most recognised natural wonder, Uluru (Ayers Rock; p227), draws pilgrims from around the world like moths to a big red flame. No matter how many postcard images you have seen, nothing prepares you for the Rock's immense presence, character-pitted epidermis and spiritual gravitas. Not far away is a mystical clutch of stone siblings known as Kata Tjuta (the Olgas; p228). Deeply cleaved with narrow gorges and decorated with tufts of vegetation, these 36 pink-red domes majestically flaunt their curves and blush intensely at sunset.

Below right: Uluru

RICHARD I'ANSON / GETTY IMAGES ©

ANDREW WATSON / GETTY IMAGES ©

## Adelaide Central Market, SA

**3** Lift the lid on multi-cultural Adelaide with a visit to the city's world-class food market (p55). Beneath one vast roof you'll find cheesewrights, pasta stalls, delis, locally farmed fruit-and-veg, yogurt shops, family-run seafood vendors and sausage stands that have been here for decades. Italian, Greek, German, French, Hungarian...it's crowded, in-your-face trading, but never intimidating or claustrophobic. Right next door is Adelaide's Chinatown: hit the foodcourts for a steaming laksa, forage for a new mobile-phone cover, or settle in for a Friday-night beer.

## Wine Regions, SA

**4** If you're into wine, get into SA. Persecuted Lutherans on the run from Prussia and Silesia first had the bright idea of planting vines here. Lo-and-behold – one of the world's great wine societies was born! Coonawarra (p104) cabernet sauvignon, Barossa Valley (p112) and McLaren Vale (p82) shiraz, Adelaide Hills (p78) sauvignon blanc, Clare Valley (p117) riesling... The quality is sky-high, and the experience of wobbling between cellar doors and their adjunct restaurants and B&Bs is an indulgent delight.
Left: Vineyard, McLaren Vale

## Nitmiluk (Katherine Gorge) National Park, NT

**5** Paddling a canoe upstream, through one gorge and then another, leaving the crowds behind, you will be drawn into the silence of these towering cliffs, which squeeze the waters of the Katherine River. Take a break on a sandy river beach; walk up to a viewpoint, or take helicopter flight for an eagle-eye view. The surrounding Nitmiluk National Park (p193) has even more to offer such as the Jatbula Trail, a five-day walk from the Gorge to the wonderful Leliyn (Edith Falls).

## Kings Canyon & Watarrka National Park, NT

**6** Central Australia's lesser-known geological wonder lies isolated within the low George Gill Ranges between Alice Springs and Uluru. Yet it is still a jaw-dropping spectacle. Centuries of changing climates have sliced the canyon (p220) out of the reddish sandstone like a knife through butter. The 100m-high walls are extraordinarily smooth. Above the canyon rim are fascinating 'beehive' formations, while beneath the cliffs permanent water-holes nourish rare plants and shy animals.

## Kangaroo Island, SA

**7** 'KI' (p90) makes a delightful detour from mainland SA's tourist trail. Just a 45-minute ferry chug across the Backstairs Passage from Cape Jervis, the island (the 131st-biggest island in the world, don'tcha know – about half the size of Crete!) is a haven for wildlife, wineries, rock formations and wild ocean beaches. The ferry tickets are pricey and the locals are begging for progress, but we like KI the way it is: unspoiled, untouristy and unso-phisticated in the best possible way.

Right: Lighthouse, Cape du Couedic (p98)

6

CLAVER CARROLL / GETTY IMAGES ©

DAVID WALL PHOTO / GETTY IMAGES ©

## The Ghan, SA & NT

**8** The legendary *Ghan* (p283) – named after central Australia's pioneering Afghan cameleers – is one of the world's great railway journeys. Begun in 1877, the old line from Marree to Alice Springs suffered from wash-outs and shoddy construction before a shiny new line replaced it in 1980. The Alice-to-Darwin section followed in 2004: now there's 2979km and 42 hours of track between Adelaide and Darwin. The *Ghan* isn't cheap or fast, but the experience of rolling through the vast, flat expanse of central Australia's deserts is magical.

## Oodnadatta Track, SA

**9** Feeling adventurous? Take a two-day trip along SA's Oodnadatta Track (p143) – an unsealed 615km desert drive between Marree in the northern Flinders Ranges and Marla on the main Adelaide–Darwin Stuart Hwy. There's plenty of history and natural heritage here: threadbare railway towns, remarkable old pubs, natural springs, the astonishing Lake Eyre... But the drive itself is the true reward – an essential Australian desert-heart experience. You'll need a 4WD to do it justice.
Above: *Planehenge* (p144), by Robin Cooke with thanks to the Arabuna people

## Plunge Pools & Hot Springs, NT

**10** Step into a glossy tourist brochure and take the plunge into an Eden-like rock pool complete with sparkling waterfall and surrounding foliage. Litchfield National Park is renowned for its shimmering cascades and gin-clear pools teeming with fish. Katherine (p189), Berry Springs (p175), Mataranka (p197) and Bitter Springs (p197) are just some of the easily accessible hot springs where rock-heated spring water bubbles to the surface.

Below: Florence Falls (p176)

## Mindil Beach Sunset Market, NT

**11** As the sun dips behind the coconut palms every Thursday and Sunday evening during the Dry season, Darwin locals and tourists migrate to Mindil Beach (p168). Old-hands arrive with picnic tables, chairs and eskies (coolboxes) to claim their favourite spots. People mingle among the smoking food carts, fire-twirlers, live music and craft stalls bulging with indigenous art. But it's the food stalls that attract the biggest queues – just about every cuisine is represented.

10

## Ikara (Wilpena Pound), SA

**12** The geologic highlight of SA's Flinders Ranges is Wilpena Pound (p135), known to the area's Adnyamathanha people as Ikara. The local campground is shaded by native pines, the Wilpena resort is attractive and affordable, and there are bushwalks to suit everyone from overachievers to the terminally lazy. But the real lure is Ikara itself: an astonishing formation of purple-brown rock escarpments encircling a vast, dusty bowl full of arid scrub, homestead ruins and wandering emus. On a camera-wielding flight or a picturesque hike, the Pound is seriously scenic.

# Need to Know

**For more information, see Survival Guide (p261)**

**Currency**
Australian dollar ($)

**Language**
English

**Money**
ATMs widely available, especially in larger cities and towns. Credit card and Eftpos purchases accepted in most hotels and restaurants.

**Visas**
All visitors to Australia need a visa (except New Zealanders). Apply online for a three-month ETA or eVisitor Visa, or standard 12-month Tourist Visa.

**Mobile Phones**
European phones work on Australia's network, but not most American or Japanese phones. Use global roaming or a local SIM card.

**Time**
Central Standard Time (CST) = GMT/UTC plus 9.5 hours. South Australia observes Central Daylight Time (CDT) in summer (GMT/UTC plus 10.5 hours).

## When to Go

Darwin
● GO Jun–Aug

Alice Springs
● GO May–Jul

Adelaide
● GO Feb–Apr

Kingscote
GO Jan–Mar ●

Mt Gambier
● GO Dec–Feb

Desert; dry climate
Dry climate
Tropical climate; wet, dry seasons
Warm to hot summers, mild winters

### High Season
(Dec–Feb)

➡ Summertime: local holidays, busy beaches and cricket on the TV.

➡ SA accommodation prices jump by 25%.

➡ High Season is winter (June to August) in the deserts and tropical north – warm days, low humidity.

### Shoulder
(Sep–Nov)

➡ Warm sun, clear skies, shorter queues.

➡ Local business people are relaxed, gearing up for (SA) or recovering from (NT) peak tourist trade.

➡ Autumn (March to May) is also shoulder season – particularly atmospheric around Adelaide.

### Low Season
(Jun–Aug)

➡ Cool rainy days down south (few tourists); clear sunny skies up north (many tourists).

➡ Restaurants and attractions keep shorter hours in SA.

➡ Winter is peak season in Uluru and Kakadu: accommodation prices leap 25%.

# Useful Websites

**Lonely Planet** (www.lonely planet.com/australia) Destination information, hotel bookings, traveller forum and more.

**Bureau of Meteorology** (www.bom.gov.au) Weather forecasts and warnings.

**South Australian Tourism Commission** (www.southaustralia.com) SA accommodation, activities, events, tours and transport.

**Travel NT** (www.travelnt.com) NT travel guide.

**Department of Environment, Water & Natural Resources** (www.environment.sa.gov.au/parks) SA national parks info.

**Parks & Wildlife Commission** (www.parksandwildlife.nt.gov.au) NT national parks info.

# Important Numbers

Australian phone numbers have two-digit area codes followed by eight-digit numbers. Drop the initial 0 calling Australia from overseas.

| | |
|---|---|
| **Country code** | ☑61 |
| **International access code** | ☑0011 |
| **Emergency (ambulance, fire, police)** | ☑000 |
| **Outback NT road conditions** | ☑1800 246 199 |
| **Directory assistance** | ☑1223 |

# Exchange Rates

| | | |
|---|---|---|
| **Canada** | C$1 | $0.97 |
| **China** | CNY1 | $0.15 |
| **Euro zone** | €1 | $1.23 |
| **Japan** | ¥100 | $1.21 |
| **New Zealand** | NZ$1 | $0.79 |
| **UK** | UK£1 | $1.55 |
| **USA** | US$1 | $0.96 |

**For current exchange rates see www.xe.com.**

# Daily Costs

## Budget less than $150

➡ Dorm bed: $25–$35 per night

➡ Double room in pub/budget hotel: $80

➡ Budget pizza or pasta main course: $15

➡ Adelaide or Darwin bus ride: $3–$5

## Midrange $150–250

➡ Double room in midrange hotel/motel: $100–$200

➡ Midrange restaurant main course with glass of wine: $28

➡ Small-car hire per day: $35

➡ Short taxi ride: $25

## Top End more than $250

➡ Double room in top-end hotel: from $200

➡ Top-end restaurant main course with glass of wine: $45

➡ Nightclub admission: $10 to $15

➡ 4WD hire per day: from $100

# Opening Hours

We've provided high-season opening hours; hours generally decrease in low season. Some outback businesses close altogether in summer.

**Banks** 9.30am to 4pm Monday to Thursday; to 5pm Friday

**Cafes** 7am to 5pm

**Pubs & Bars** noon to 11pm; later Thursday to Saturday

**Restaurants** noon to 2pm and 6pm to 8pm; later in cities

**Shops** 9am to 5pm Monday to Friday, to noon or 5pm Saturday

# Arriving in Central Australia

**Adelaide Airport (ADL; p77)** Pre-booked private **SkyLink** (p77) minibuses connect the airport with the city ($10; 6am to 11.30pm). Public **Adelaide Metro** (p77) JetBuses ply the same route ($3 to $5; 5am to 11pm). Taxis charge around $25 into the city (15 minutes).

**Darwin Airport (DRW; p150)** private **Darwin Airport Shuttle** (p170) minibuses connect the airport with the city ($15; 24 hours); pre-booking recommended. Taxis charge around $30 into the city (15 minutes).

# Getting Around

Central Australia is vast: buses and trains shuttle you between the major centres, but you'll be getting behind the wheel for most other destinations.

**Car & 4WD** To explore central Australia properly you'll need your own wheels (4WDs for outback tracks). There are car-hire outlets in cities and most large towns. Drive on the left.

**Bus** Useful, affordable, regular connections between major centres: good for covering long distances on a budget.

**Train** Expensive, infrequent long-distance routes: more for romance and scenery than expedience.

For much more on **transport**, see p274.

# First Time: The Red Centre

**For more information, see Survival Guide (p261)**

## Checklist

➡ Make sure your passport is valid for at least six months past your arrival date.

➡ Check the airline baggage restrictions.

➡ Inform your debit/credit card company.

➡ Arrange for appropriate travel insurance (p267).

➡ Check if you can use your mobile/cell phone (p270).

## What to Pack

➡ Sturdy walking shoes – there are many excellent walks, long and short.

➡ Warm clothes – the desert nights are surprisingly cold in winter.

➡ Hat, sunglasses and sunscreen.

➡ Water bottle.

➡ Australian electrical adapter.

## Top Tips for Your Trip

➡ On long drives don't forget to stop the car regularly to reboot your brain. Outside the confines of the car you'll find revitalizing fresh air and some of Australia's friendliest characters to meet and greet.

➡ Avoid driving at night. The empty landscape teems with car-wrecking kangaroos at night, while cattle find the sun-warmed roads a fine place to rest on a cold desert night.

## What to Wear

It will be of no surprise to learn that the theme is casual; however, it is not a free-for-all and many dining and entertainment venues will require covered shoes or sandals (no flip-flops or singlets). The central deserts are very cold in winter, with sub-zero temperatures at night. As soon as the sun sets winter woolies are needed. Sensible and stylish under the outback sun is the broad-brimmed hat and, if you are travelling in summer, bring swimwear to cool off in the waterholes and swimming pools.

## Sleeping

During the peak season (June to August) it is best to book accommodation to avoid disappointment. See p262 for more accommodation information.

➡ **Roadhouses** One-stop shops along the highways where you can fuel up and get a meal, a drink, and a bed. Standards range from basic dongas with share facilities to modern motel rooms. Campsites are also usually available.

➡ **Caravan Parks** Most caravan parks have cabins in addition to the caravan and camping sites. The best also have swimming pools, licensed restaurants and camp kitchens.

➡ **Hostels** Only found in Alice Springs, hostels tend to be highly social affairs ideal for young travellers looking to meet others and find work.

➡ **Hotels & Motels** At the tourist hotspots (Yulara, Alice Springs, Kings Canyon) you will find quality four-star hotels. Pub accommodation is usually very basic and motels are typically clean, convenient and conventional.

## Money

ATMs are mostly restricted to the big centres and tourist hot-spots, however there are several ATMs in roadhouses along the Stuart Hwy. Most ATMs accept cards issued by other banks and are linked to international networks. Most businesses have Eftpos (Electronic Funds Transfer at Point of Sale) facilities for your credit and debit card. American Express and Diners Club credit cards are not as widely accepted as Mastercard and Visa and will often incur a greater fee.

**For more information, see p268.**

## Bargaining

Gentle haggling is fairly common in weekend markets, second-hand shops and often when purchasing arts and crafts from the artist. It's common practice to ask for a discount on expensive items when paying cash (not that you are guaranteed to get one). In most other instances you are expected to pay the stated price.

## Tipping

➡ **Hotels** Not usually expected

➡ **Restaurants** For excellent table service tip 5% to 10%

➡ **Taxis** Not expected, but the drivers will appreciate you rounding up the fare

Standley Chasm (p218)

## Etiquette

➡ **Greetings** Usually a simple 'G'day' or 'Howzitgoin?' suffices. Shake hands with men or women when meeting for the first time. Australian's expect a firm handshake with eye contact. However, when visiting an Aboriginal community this can be seen as overbearing. Here, a soft clasp with little arm movement, and virtually no eye contact can be expected. The best advice is to take it as it comes and respond in like manner.

➡ **Shout** Australians like to take it in turn to buy ('shout') a round of drinks for the group and everyone is expected to take part.

➡ **Alcohol** Check whether alcohol rules apply when visiting a community. You may be breaking the law even with unopened bottles in your vehicle.

## Eating

➡ **Restaurants** The Centre has a small selection of fine-dining restaurants found within the better hotels in Alice Springs and Yulara. Here you will get the chance to sample bush herbs and marsupial meat in addition to more familiar European fare. Also, Alice Springs has a handful of Asian restaurants.

➡ **Roadhouses** More of a necessity than a recommendation, roadhouse fare (think burgers and steaks) suffers from the tyranny of distance, whereby fresh ingredients and reliable cooks are hard to source. Nevertheless, there are some pearls.

PLAN YOUR TRIP FIRST TIME: THE RED CENTRE

# If You Like...

## Beaches

Bookending central Australia to the north and south are long, convoluted coastlines studded with beautiful beaches. In South Australia you can surf and swim; Northern Territory beaches are better suited to sitting and reading.

**Snelling Beach** On Kangaroo Island's sheltered north coast is this gem: take a dip or snooze under an umbrella. (p97)

**Pondalowie Bay** Some of SA's best surf peels into Pondalowie, on the southern tip of Yorke Peninsula. (p123)

**Glenelg Beach** Adelaide's big city beach is all white sand, pubs, boutiques, bakeries, bikinis... (p59)

**Ninety Mile Beach** Fronting the Southern Ocean in Coorong National Park (SA) is this surf beach. Bring your 4WD. (p100)

**Mindil Beach** Darwin's Mindil Beach Sunset Market happens behind the dunes: but the beach is a beaut spot to chew a few satay sticks. (p168)

**Carrickalinga Beach** Southeast of Adelaide is this under-populated 2km beach: good fishing, winter beachcombing and aquamarine summer swimming. (p85)

## Wine Regions

Wine is hard-wired in South Australia's DNA; and even if you're more of a beer boffin, your visit here will undoubtedly involve dipping into a wine region or three.

**Barossa Valley** More than 80 wineries in this German-settled enclave, home to some of Australia's greatest reds. (p112)

**Clare Valley** Clare Valley riesling rocks! Skillogalee is our fave, with a fab cellar-door restaurant that makes life feel somehow more agreeable. (p117)

**Coonawarra** Cabernet sauvignon is the name of Coonawarra's game, with 100-year-old vines as thick as your leg. (p104)

**Adelaide Hills** Cool-climate grapes (sauvignon blanc, pinot noir) dapple the slopes in Adelaide's backyard. (p78)

**McLaren Vale** Famously weighty shiraz grows an hour south of Adelaide, with a string of beaut beaches nearby. (p82)

**Langhorne Creek** Lesser-light Langhorne features small vineyards bottling superb SA reds. (p82)

## Indigenous Experiences

Aboriginal culture is more accessible in SA and the NT than anywhere else in Australia. Tours, performances, art galleries, shops, festivals... All mainstream tourist experiences!

**Uluru-Kata Tjuta National Park** Tour the big pebbles and understand their importance to local indigenous people. (p223)

**Animal Tracks** Tours through Kakadu's famous Aboriginal rock-art galleries and wetlands, departing from Darwin or Jabiru. (p179)

**Gunbalanya** Visit Gunbalanya (Oenpelli), a small Aboriginal community in remote Arnhem Land. (p187)

**Bookabee Tours** Aboriginal-run day tours of Adelaide, plus longer jaunts into the Flinders Ranges. (p62)

---

### IF YOU LIKE... OUTBACK DETOURS

Take a drive off the Stuart Hwy to Roper Bar, then down the Nathan River Road through Limmen National Park to Borroloola. Superb fishing and remote camping ahoy!

**Tandanya National Aboriginal Cultural Institute** Catch a didgeridoo demo or a Torres Strait Islander cultural performance in downtown Adelaide. (p57)

**Barunga Festival** NT Aboriginal cultural and sports festival near Katherine. Music dance, arts, story-telling, crafts, football and spear throwing. (p160)

PLAN YOUR TRIP IF YOU LIKE...

## Wildlife

You'll see a whole lotta native wildlife on your central Australian road trip: emus, goannas, snakes, koalas, seals, parrots, frill-necked lizards, cockatoos, dolphins... And that's before you hit the wildlife parks!

**Alice Springs Desert Park** Sure, the desert is damn hot, but there's plenty of wildlife living here. Don't miss the birds of prey. (p203)

**Seal Bay Conservation Park** On Kangaroo Island (SA) is Seal Bay, home to a malodorous colony of Australian sea lions. (p97)

**Territory Wildlife Park** Meet the residents of wetlands, woodlands and monsoon vine forests just south of Darwin. (p175)

**Adelaide River Jumping Crocodiles** Ever seen a 5m croc propel itself out of a river and snatch a hunk of meat? (p175)

**Whale Watching** Seeing a southern right whale breaching is unforgettable. Scan the seas off Victor Harbor or Ceduna in SA. (p52)

**Cleland Wildlife Park** Accessible, well-run Adelaide Hills park: cuddle a koala and chase a wallaby. (p80)

**(Top)** Frill-necked lizard
**(Bottom)** Seal Bay Conservation Park (p97)

## Arts Festivals

The best arts festivals aren't always the ones with the loftiest ambitions. Sure, go highbrow if you like, but central Australia also celebrates the off-beat and the downright ridiculous.

**Adelaide Festival of the Arts** The big one with the big names: became an annual event in 2012. (p24)

**Alice Springs Beanie Festival** Alice is hot: donning a beanie (woolly hat) isn't the first thing that springs to mind... Lots of local arts and crafts. (p208)

**Alice Desert Festival** The desert delivers offbeat cinema, street art, bush foods and arts-and-crafts. (p25)

**Darwin Festival** The Top End's best theatre, lit, music, cabaret, comedy and visual arts. Expect a big Aboriginal and Asian focus. (p25)

**Adelaide Fringe** Hip, off-kilter and unfailingly entertaining, Adelaide's Fringe is second only to Edinburgh's. (p24)

**Adelaide Writers' Week** Sit in a shady marquee and listen to some wordsmiths say some words. (p62)

## Natural Wonders

Big rocks, gaping chasms, wildlife-rich billabongs, lurid lakes and astonishing caves: central Australia wrote the book on wonders of the natural realm.

**Uluru (Ayres Rock)** Sure, you've seen it on TV, but you'll still do a double-take when you spy it on the horizon. (p227)

**Kata Tjuta** The tallest of these 36 jaw-droppingly big boulders is actually higher than Uluru. (p228)

**Remarkable Rocks** Forget marsupials – the real lure on SA's Kangaroo Island are these spectacular weather-gouged rocks. Remarkable! (p98)

**Yellow Water Wetlands** Kakadu National Park's famed wetlands are fertile, fecund and festooned with wildlife. (p185)

**Blue Lake** The undisputed highlight of Mt Gambier in southeastern SA is this 75m-deep lake, which turns ludicrously blue in summer. (p102)

**Naracoorte Caves** World Heritage-listed limestone caves in southeastern SA. Kudos if you can find any 'Dave Attenborough woz here' graffiti. (p105)

## Markets

To market, to market, to buy a fat...[insert gourmet/boutique item of choice]. Right across central Australia you'll find fabulous markets to blow your dollars at: food, produce and arts-and-crafts.

**Central Market** A true Adelaide highlight, Central Market is a food-lover's paradise (p55).

**Parap Village Market** In suburban Darwin is this unexpected, claustrophobic Asian street mart complete with smoky aisles and tropical flowers. (p168)

**Mindil Beach Sunset Market** Darwin during the Dry? Tail the crowds to this famed evening market: food, live music and loads of fun. (p168)

**Gilles Street Market** Hip fashion and design in downtown Adelaide at this monthly market (twice monthly in summer). (p59)

**Willunga Farmers Market** On the doorstep of SA's McLaren Vale Wine Region is Willunga, a cute-as-a-button sandstone town with a pumping Saturday-morning market. (p85)

## Quirky Small Towns

'Woah...how do people live out here?!' Not an uncommon thought in remote central Australia. But isolation breeds small towns with community spirit, quirkiness, charm and (usually) a good pub.

**William Creek** On SA's Oodnadatta Track is William Creek. There's not much here: an airstrip, a petrol pump and an amazing old pub. (p143)

**Wycliffe Well** On the Stuart Hwy 380km north of Alice in the NT, Wycliffe Well is a UFO-spotting hotspot. (p201)

**Coober Pedy** With its subterranean, opal-obsessed locals, Coober Pedy in SA is truly one of a kind. (p139)

**Melrose** Two pubs, a national park, a derelict brewery and inexplicable gravitas: is Melrose SA's perfect small town? (p132)

**Daly Waters** The pub here claims to be the NT's oldest (1893). 120 years later it's still a worthy pit stop. (p199)

### IF YOU LIKE... EAT STREETS

Big cities and eating-out: it's a symbiotic relationship, with the best restaurants often keeping close company. In Adelaide head for Rundle St or Gouger St; in Darwin it's Mitchell St.

Remarkable Rocks (p98)

**Aileron** Yes, it's a thing on a wing, but this wee NT blip associates more readily with 'Naked Charlie Quartpot'. (p202)

## Bushwalking

If the sun's not scorching and the heavens aren't delivering a deluge, there are some brilliant bushwalks in central Australia. Just get your timing right!

**Uluru Base Walk** Take your time on this lap of Uluru: for such a monstrous monolith the atmosphere is surprisingly intimate. (p227)

**Heysen Trail** Tackle SA's epic 1200km Heysen Trail, from the Flinders Ranges to the Fleurieu Peninsula, or maybe just part of it. (p54)

**Valley of the Winds** A 7.4km loop weaving through Kata Tjuta's wondrous rock-scapes. (p228)

**Jatbula Trail** An intense, five-day jaunt through 66km of Nitmiluk National Park. (p194)

**Barrk Walk** Challenging 12km day-walk through the Nourlangie area in Kakadu National Park. (p185)

**Waterfall Gully Track** Traipse past waterfalls on the way up/down the surprisingly perky Mt Lofty (710m) behind Adelaide. (p60)

# Month by Month

## January

January yawns into action as central Australia recovers from its Christmas hangover... But then everyone realises: 'Hey, summer holidays!' South Australia and the central deserts are hot and dry; the Top End is hot and wet. SA locals head to the Adelaide Oval to watch cricket.

### 🏃 Tour Down Under

(www.tourdownunder.com. au) SA's six-stage version of the Tour de France. People line the streets to watch the lycra-clad lads whizz past, with picnic rugs, champagne and Euro vibes.

## February

February is central Australia's warmest month: hot and sticky in the Wet season up north, while much of SA swelters in dry desert heat. Locals go back to work or to the beach.

### 🍷 Crush

(www.crushfestival.com.au) Fine wine and music at this Adelaide Hills festival, billing itself as the 'stylish alternative'. Our advice: pick your winery and stay put – racing the crowds from winery to winery ain't stylish.

## March

March is harvest time in SA's vineyards, and in recent years it has been just as hot as January and February. Festival time in Adelaide: international visitors drag the city onto the world stage.

### 🎭 Adelaide Festival of Arts

(www.adelaidefestival.com. au) Culture vultures absorb international and Australian dance, drama, opera and theatre performances at this ultra-classy annual event. Australia's biggest multi-arts event.

### 🎭 Adelaide Fringe

(www.adelaidefringe.com. au) This festival features all the acts that don't make the cut (or simply don't want to) for the highbrow Adelaide Festival of Arts. Comedy, music, theatre, buskers and the hyperactive Garden of Unearthly Delights. Second only to the Edinburgh Fringe.

### ☆ WOMADelaide

(www.womadelaide.com. au) Annual festival of world music, arts, food and dance, held over four days in Adelaide's luscious Botanic Park. Eight stages and more than 400 world-music acts: very family friendly, and you can get a cold beer too.

### ☆ Clipsal 500

(www.clipsal500.com.au) Mulleted bogans rejoice as Adelaide's city streets become a four-day Holden-versus-Ford racing track. High-pitched engine whine resonates through the suburbs.

## April

The Adelaide Hills are atmospheric as European trees turn golden then maroon. Up north the rain is abating and the desert temperatures are manageable. Easter = pricey accommodation everywhere.

### 🍷 Barossa Vintage Festival

(www.barossavintagefestival.com.au) Biennial festival (odd-numbered years) with processions, maypole dancing, traditional dinners and muchos Barossa Valley wine (...shoot for a sip of Penfolds famous 'Grange').

## May

The Dry season begins in the Northern Territory: relief from humidity and returning tourists. This is a great time to visit Uluru, before the tour buses arrive in droves.

### 🐋 Whale Watching

Along the SA coast, migrating southern right and humpback whales come close to shore to feed, breed and calf. The whales are here between May and October; see them at Victor Harbor and west of Ceduna.

## June

Winter begins: peak season in the tropical Top End and central deserts. Waterfalls and outback tracks are accessible (accommodation prices less so). Chilly across SA.

### ☆ Adelaide Cabaret Festival

(www.adelaidecabaret.com) Unique cabaret festival supporting local and interstate music and theatre. Everything from stockings-and-suspenders burlesque shows to intimate concerts by top crooners.

### 🍴 Sea & Vines Festival

(www.mclarenvale.info) Wine, seafood and live music in McLaren Vale (SA) wineries over the June long weekend. Can get insanely crowded: book your transport and accommodation many moons in advance.

## July

Pubs with open fires, cosy coffee shops and empty beaches down south; packed markets, tours and accommodation up north. Pack warm clothes for anywhere south of Alice Springs.

### ☆ Darwin Cup Carnival

(www.darwinturfclub.org.au) Darwin's Fannie Bay racecourse erupts with six days of thundering hoofs and fine-lookin' folk. Wear your shiny shoes and your best hat.

### NAIDOC Week

(www.naidoc.org.au) The National Aboriginal & Islander Day Observance Committee conducts performances, exhibitions and talks in communities around SA and the NT.

## August

Southerners, sick of winter's grey-sky drear, head north for some sun. Last chance to visit the outback and tropical Top End before things get too hot or wet (or both). Kakadu, anyone?

### SALA Festival

(www.salafestival.com) The South Australian Living Artists Festival zooms in on contemporary art (no dusty old canvasses here). Look for SALA posters in cafes/bars/theatres/pubs around the state.

### Darwin Festival

(www.darwinfestival.org.au) Two weeks of theatre, comedy, cabaret, dance, music, food and workshops – an artistic cavalcade! A focus on Aboriginal, Asian and outdoor events.

### Alice Desert Festival

(www.alicedesertfestival.com.au) Central Australian visual arts, music, dancing, exhibitions and street performers. Runs right through September, spilling into October.

## September

Spring heralds a rampant bloom of wildflowers across outback SA, especially in the majestic Flinders Ranges. It's cool and windy down south; starting to get hot and sticky up north.

### 🏃 Henley-on-Todd Regatta

(www.henleyontodd.com. au) Alice Springs' iconic 'boat' races on the (usually) bone-dry Todd River. Watch from the riverbanks, or build your own boat and join in.

### ☆ Royal Adelaide Show

(www.theshow.com.au) A major seven-day agricultural festa. How many prize bulls, tattooed carnies and blue-singleted sheep shearers can you handle?

## October

The weather avoids extremes everywhere: a good time to go camping. After the football and before the cricket, sports fans twiddle their thumbs... But there's always wine and food!

### 🍷 Riverland Wine & Food Festival

(www.riverlandwineand foodfestival.com) Sample Riverland food and drink in Berri, on the banks of the mighty, meandering Murray River (Australia's Mississippi).

## November

'Stinger' (jellyfish) season across coastal NT. Hooray for swimming pools! Warm spring SA days tease city workers with a hint of summer.

### 🎆 Feast Festival

(www.feast.org.au) Annual gay and lesbian festival in Adelaide, with film, cabaret, music, forums, theatre and literature (and a few feasts).

### ☆ Adelaide Christmas Pageant

(www.cupageant.com.au) An Adelaide institution – floats, bands and marching troupes hijack the city streets for a day in November. Kitsch, hokey, outmoded? Yes, but the kids love it.

## December

Ring the bell, school's out! Holidays begin two weeks before Christmas. Darwin and Adelaide fill with shoppers and the weather is hot. Up north it's monsoon season: afternoon thunderstorms bring pelting rain.

### 🎆 Lights of Lobethal

(www.lightsoflobethal.com. au) Get a wholesome dose of Christmas with a dusk drive through Lobethal, a Germanic Adelaide Hills' town festooned with fairy lights.

# Itineraries

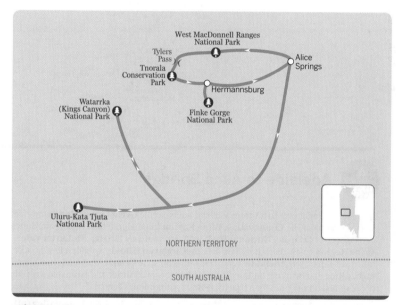

## 3 WEEKS The Red Centre

Getting to Australia's red desert heart is half the fun: hop on an internal flight from the east coast, jump on the legendary train the *Ghan* from either Darwin or Adelaide, or tackle the Stuart Hwy from the north or south. But whichever conveyance you choose, you'll be confronted by one of Australia's great truths: this place is gargantuan! Travel in winter to beat the heat.

**Alice Springs** (p202; just 'Alice' to her friends) will come as sweet relief if you've been clocking up the desert highway miles. Enjoy the trappings of civilisation for a while, but don't dally: there are national parks out there waiting to be explored!

**Uluru-Kata Tjuta National Park** (p223) is a must-see, but **Finke Gorge National Park** (p219) is for serious 4WD-ers. More accessible is the **Watarrka (Kings Canyon) National Park** (p220) and **West MacDonnel Ranges National Park** (p217).

For a real taste of outback driving, head for **Tylers Pass** (p217) in the 'West Macs', from where you can view the crater of **Tnorala Conservation Park** (p219). From here, if you've got a 4WD, take the 'inner loop' road down to **Hermannsburg** (p219) and back to Alice on Larapinta Dr – but be prepared for some devilish road corrugations!

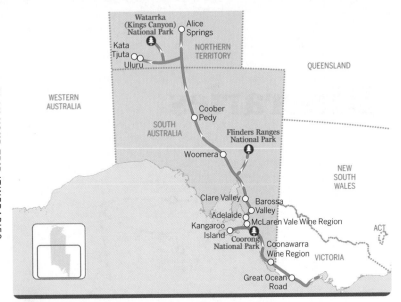

## Adelaide to Alice Springs

**4 WEEKS**

If you're hoofing it over to SA from Victoria, super-scenic **Great Ocean Road** conveniently spits you out near the **Coonawarra Wine Region** (p104). From here explore the dunes and lagoons of **Coorong National Park** (p99), sip your way through **McLaren Vale Wine Region** (p82), then either hop over to **Kangaroo Island** (p90) for a few days, or roll into festival-frenzied **Adelaide** (p54). Don't miss a trip to Central Market for lunch, and a night eating and drinking on Rundle St. If it's hot, cool off inside the estimable Art Galley of SA, or hop on the tram for a beachy swim at palindromic Glenelg.

More wine! About an hour north of Adelaide is the old-school **Barossa Valley** (p112; big reds); and about two hours north is the boutiquey **Clare Valley** (p117) with its world-class riesling, cottagey B&Bs and old stone mining towns.

Continuing north, raggedy **Flinders Ranges National Park** (p131) jags up from the semi-desert like a rust-coloured mirage. Rich in indigenous culture, the Flinders – the heart of which is the amazing Ikara (Wilpena Pound) – will etch itself into your memory. Hit the Stuart Hwy and journey north to the mildly spooky rocket-testing town **Woomera** (p139) and the opal-tinged dugouts of **Coober Pedy** (p139).

Trucking north, you'll enter the Simpson Desert and cross into the NT. The Lasseter Hwy turn-off takes you to weighty, eye-popping **Uluru** (p227) and the mesmerising **Kata Tjuta** (p228) rock formations. You've seen the photos and the TV shows, but there's nothing quite like seeing an Uluru sunset firsthand.

About 300km north of Uluru, the spectacular, vertigo-inducing **Watarrka (Kings Canyon) National Park** (p220) rewards intrepid travellers with scenic walks into and around the rim of this gaping desert chasm. Finish up in the desert oasis of **Alice Springs** (p202), in the heart of the steep-sided MacDonnell Ranges. Alice has plenty to keep you busy for a few days: the excellent Alice Springs Desert Park, some classy restaurants or just a soak in a swimming pool as you gear-up for the next leg of your journey (the Stuart Hwy drive or *Ghan* train ride to Darwin, or an internal flight if you're time-poor).

Top: Flinders Ranges
National Park (p131)
Bottom: Outdoor dining,
Rundle St, Adelaide

KYLIE MCLAUGHLIN / GETTY IMAGES ©

PLAN YOUR TRIP ITINERARIES

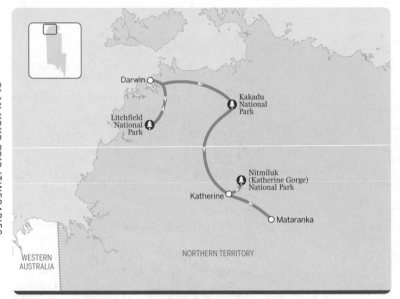

# Darwin, Kakadu & Katherine

**2 WEEKS**

Gone are the days when **Darwin** (p151) was a brawling frontier town full of fishermen, miners and truck drivers blowing off steam. These days there seem to be more backpackers here than anyone else, and Darwin is very multicultural, as a visit to the fabulous Mindil Beach Sunset Market will confirm. Grab some Thai stir-fry, Indonesian beef rendang, a Malaysian laksa or a Greek souvlaki and head for the beach.

While you're in Darwin, don't miss the outdoor Deckchair Cinema in the dry season, and the outstanding Aboriginal and Cyclone Tracy exhibits at the Museum & Art Gallery of the Northern Territory. Also worth a look is the atmospheric Saturday-morning Parap Village Market, crammed with tropical produce and food stalls, followed by a night on Mitchell St, where a free-wheelin', anything-goes vibe confirms Darwin's rep as a hedonistic haven (...depending on your mood, you might want to head for bed before or around 1am, after which things can get messy). Shopping-wise, the commercial galleries in Darwin are great for making an informed, ethical purchase of some Aboriginal art.

A few hours south on the Stuart Hwy you'll run into some superb national parks. **Litchfield National Park** (p176) is famous for its plummeting waterfalls, bushwalks and cooling swimming holes – so welcoming on a hot day. From here, backtrack 50km north then head east into World Heritage-listed **Kakadu National Park** (p179), a wetland of international significance with amazing rock outcrops dappled with equally amazing, millennia-old Aboriginal rock art. Check out the Kakadu wildlife too: crocs, lizards, snakes, brolgas, jabirus, barramundi and flocks of raucous birdlife.

Further south is **Nitmiluk (Katherine Gorge) National Park** (p193), where the Katherine River cuts its way through 13 jagged ravines. Take a walk, a swim, a scenic flight, or paddle a canoe to find an isolated spot for lunch. **Katherine** (p189) is the regional 'big-smoke': there's not a lot going on here, but it's a good place to stock-up for your road trip or take a dip in some thermal springs. Continuing south, there are also thermal springs at **Mataranka** (p197) – soak off the road dust in a (free!) naturally-heated swimming hole and wonder what the folks back home are doing this afternoon.

Plan Your Trip

# Your Outback Trip

Australia's outback starts somewhere 'beyond the black stump'. Exactly where that is, is a little hard to pin down on a map. But you'll know you are there when the sky yawns enormously wide, the horizon is unnervingly empty, and the sparse inhabitants you encounter are incomparably resilient and distinctively Australian. Globalised sameness is yet to fully infiltrate the outback and so the enduring indigenous culture, unique wildlife and intriguing landscape awaits the modern day adventurer.

## About the Outback

The Australian outback is a vast, imprecise region extending out from the centre of the continent. While most Australians live on the coast, that thin green fringe of the continent is hardly typical of this enormous land mass. Inland is the desert soul of Australia.

Weather patterns vary from region to region – from sandy arid deserts to semi-arid scrublands to tropical savannah – but you can generally rely on hot sunny days, starry night skies and mile after mile of unbroken horizon.

### When to Go

**Best Times**

June through August is when southeastern Australia (where most of the population lives) is sniffling through rainy, cloudy winter days, the outback comes into its own. Rain isn't unheard of in central Australia – in fact there's been a hell of a lot of it in recent years – but clear skies, moderate daytime temperatures, cold nights and good driving conditions are the norm.

September and October is spring and is also a prime time to head into the outback, especially if you're into wildflowers. The MacDonnell Ranges near Alice Springs and the Flinders Ranges in northern South

## The Best...

### Season
**Winter** (June to August) Mild days, cool nights and low humidity.

### Things to Pack
Sunscreen, sunglasses, a hat, insect repellent, plenty of water and some good tunes for the car stereo.

### Outback Track
**Oodnadatta Track** (p143) 620km of red dust, emus, lizards, salt lakes and historic railroad remnants.

### Indigenous Culture
**Kakadu National Park** (p179) Head into the tropical Top End wilderness for ancient rock art and cultural tours run by indigenous guides.

### Outback National Park
**Uluru-Kata Tjuta National Park** (p223) Iconic Uluru (Ayres Rock) is simply unmissable, while nearby Kata Tjuta is less well known but just as impressive.

# Outback Tracks: Off the Beaten Road

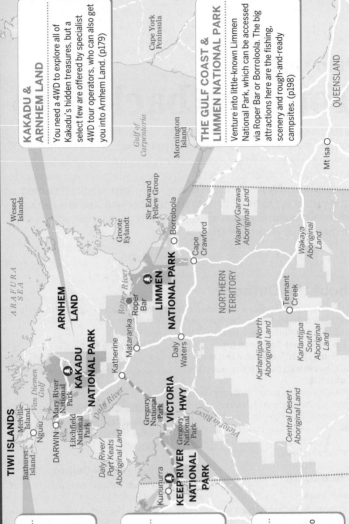

## TIWI ISLANDS

Leave the car far behind and venture across the waters to Bathurst Island to experience Tiwi Island culture with its fascinating history and unique art. (p171)

## KEEP RIVER NATIONAL PARK

A little-visited yet rewarding detour on the way to northern WA. Keep River National Park features Aboriginal art, wildlife, short walks and stunning sandstone formations. (p196)

## VICTORIA RIVER REGION

The Victoria Hwy travels through legendary cattle country, much of it returning to nature as national park. Detours lead off the highway and onto 4WD tracks boasting remote camps under big skies. (p196)

## KAKADU & ARNHEM LAND

You need a 4WD to explore all of Kakadu's hidden treasures, but a select few are offered by specialist 4WD tour operators, who can also get you into Arnhem Land. (p179)

## THE GULF COAST & LIMMEN NATIONAL PARK

Venture into little-known Limmen National Park, which can be accessed via Roper Bar or Borroloola. The big attractions here are the fishing, scenery and rough-and-ready campsites. (p198)

## DESERT TRACKS

The famous cross-desert routes – the Birdsville, Oodnadatta and Strzelecki Tracks – should not be taken lightly. Well-prepared travellers are rewarded with pioneering history, big skies and unparalleled solitude. (p143)

## FLINDERS RANGES

Getting off the tarmac is the best way to explore the Flinders and the only way to get into the Gammon Ranges. Experience Aboriginal heritage, mining relics and magnificent scenery. (p131)

## RED CENTRE WAY

Link iconic central Australia – the gorges of the MacDonnell Ranges, the gape of Kings Canyon, and the splendor of Uluru and Kata Tjuta – by taking this road less travelled. (p219)

WESTERN AUSTRALIA

Lake Mackay Aboriginal Land

Gibson Desert

Great Victoria Desert

Nullarbor Plain

Eucla

STRZELECKI TRACK

Innamincka Regional Reserve

Birdsville

BIRDSVILLE TRACK

Simpson Desert

Atnetye Aboriginal Land

Pmere Nyente Aboriginal Land

Prner Ulperre Ingwemime Aboriginal Land

Simpson Desert Regional Reserve

Strzelecki Regional Reserve

Vulkathunha-Gammon Ranges National Park

FLINDERS RANGES

Port Augusta

Lake Eyre National Park

Lake Eyre North

Lake Eyre South

Lake Torrens

OODNADATTA TRACK

SOUTH AUSTRALIA

Coober Pedy

Marla

Lake Gairdner

Alice Springs

Finke Gorge National Park

MacDonnell Ranges

Haasts Bluff Aboriginal Land

Kings Canyon

Petermann Aboriginal Land

Uluru-Kata Tjuta National Park

RED CENTRE WAY

Pitjantjatjara Aboriginal Land

Tallaringa Conservation Park

Maralinga Tjarutja Aboriginal Land

Conservation Park

Nullarbor Regional Reserve

Yalata Aboriginal Land

Nullarbor National Park

Yellabinna Regional Reserve

Ceduna

Great Australian Bight

Lake Mackay

### OUTBACK ROAD SHOW

On many outback highways you'll see thundering road trains: huge trucks (a prime mover plus two, three or four trailers) some more than 50m long. These things don't move over for anyone, and it's like a scene out of *Mad Max* having one bear down on you at 120km/h. When you see a road train approaching on a narrow bitumen road, slow down and pull over – if the truck has to put its wheels off the road to pass you, the resulting barrage of stones will almost certainly smash your windscreen. When trying to overtake one, allow plenty of room (about a kilometre) to complete the manoeuvre. Road trains throw up a lot of dust on dirt roads, so if you see one coming it's best to just pull over and stop until it's gone past.

And while you're on outback roads, don't forget to give the standard bush wave to oncoming drivers – it's simply a matter of lifting the index finger off the steering wheel to acknowledge your fellow motorist.

Australia explode with colourful blooms, all the more dazzling in contrast with red-orange desert sands.

### Avoid

Central Australia heats up over summer (December through February) – temperatures approaching 50°C have been recorded in some desert towns – but that's just part of the picture. With the heat comes dusty roads, overheating cars, driver fatigue, irritating flies and the need to carry extra water everywhere you go. In the Top End the build-up to the Wet season is uncomfortably humid, and the eventual monsoon can see many a road cut and dirt roads made impassable for weeks at a time.

## Planes, Trains or Automobiles?

**Air** If you want to access the outback without a long drive, the major airlines fly into Alice Springs and Yulara (for the central deserts) and Darwin (for the tropical Top End), departing from Perth,

Adelaide and the major east-coast cities. From Darwin or Alice you can join a guided tour or hire a 4WD and off you go.

**Train** Unlike much of the world, train travel in Australia is neither affordable nor expedient. It's something you do for a special occasion or for the sheer romance of trains, not if you want to get anywhere in a hurry. That said, travelling on the *Indian Pacific* between Perth and Sydney or the legendary *Ghan* between Adelaide and Darwin takes you through parts of the country you wouldn't see otherwise, and it certainly makes for a leisurely holiday. Train travel is also a good way to beat the heat if you're travelling in summer. So if you have time on your side, and you can afford it, give it a try because it could be perfect for you.

**Car** You can drive through the Red Centre from Darwin to Adelaide with detours to Uluru and Kakadu and more without ever leaving sealed roads. However, if you really want to see outback Australia, there are plenty of side routes that breathe new life into the phrase 'off the beaten track'. Driving in the outback has its challenges – immense distances and occasionally difficult terrain – but it's ultimately the most rewarding and intimate way to experience Australia's 'dead heart' (rest assured, it's alive and kicking!).

## Essential Outback

### The Red Centre: Alice Springs, Uluru & Kings Canyon

From Alice Springs it's a six-hour drive to Uluru-Kata Tjuta National Park. Alice is a surprising oasis: big enough to have some great places to eat and stay, as well as some social problems. Uluru is to tourists what half a watermelon is to ants at a picnic: people from all over the globe swarm to and from this monolith at all times of the day. But it's still a remarkable find. The local Anangu people would prefer that you didn't climb it. Kings Canyon, north of Uluru, is a spectacular chasm carved into the rugged landscape.

### The Stuart Highway: Adelaide to Darwin

In either direction, from the north or south, this is one of Australia's greatest road trips: 3020km of red desert sands, flat scrublands and galloping roadside emus. Make sure you stop at spookily pock-marked Coober Pedy – the opal-mining capital of the world – and detour to Uluru on your way to the Alice. Nitmiluk (Katherine Gorge) National

## OUTBACK DRIVING & SAFETY CHECKLIST

You need to be particularly organised and vigilant when travelling in the outback, especially on remote sandy tracks, due to the lack of water, long distances between fuel stops and isolation. Here are a few tips:

### Communication

➡ Report your route and schedule to the police, a friend or relative.

➡ Mobile phones are useless if you travel off the highway. Consider hiring a satellite phone, high-frequency (HF) radio transceiver equipped to pick up Royal Flying Doctor Service bases, or emergency position-indicating radio beacon (EPIRB).

➡ In an emergency, stay with your vehicle; it's easier to spot than you are, and you won't be able to carry a heavy load of water very far.

➡ If you do become stranded, consider setting fire to a spare tyre (let the air out first). The pall of smoke will be visible for miles.

### Your Vehicle

➡ Have your vehicle serviced and checked before you leave.

➡ Load the vehicle evenly, with heavy items inside and light items on the roof rack.

➡ Consider carrying spare fuel in an appropriate container.

➡ Carry essential tools: a spare tyre (two is preferable), fan belt, radiator hose, tyre-pressure gauge and air pump, and a shovel.

➡ An off-road jack might be handy, as will a snatchem strap or tow rope for quick extraction when you're stuck (useful if there's another vehicle to pull you out).

### Supplies & Equipment

➡ Carry plenty of water: in warm weather allow 5L per person per day and an extra amount for the radiator, carried in several containers.

➡ Bring plenty of food in case of a breakdown.

➡ Carry a first-aid kit, maps, a torch with spare batteries, a compass, and a GPS.

### Weather & Road Conditions

➡ Check road conditions before travelling: roads that are passable in the Dry (March to October) can disappear beneath water during the Wet.

➡ Don't attempt to cross flooded bridges or causeways unless you're sure of the depth, and of any road damage hidden underwater.

### Dirt-Road Driving

➡ Inflate your tyres to the recommended levels for the terrain you're travelling on; on desert sand, deflate your tyres to 20-25psi to avoid getting bogged. Don't forget to re-inflate them when you leave the sand.

➡ Reduce speed on unsealed roads as braking distances increase.

➡ Dirt roads are often corrugated: keeping an even speed is the best approach.

➡ Dust on outback roads can obscure vision, so stop and wait for it to settle.

➡ Choose a low gear for steep inclines and the lowest gear for steep declines. Use the brake sparingly and don't turn sideways on a hill.

### Road Hazards

➡ Take a rest every few hours: driver fatigue is an all-too-common problem.

➡ Wandering cattle, sheep, emus, kangaroos, camels etc make driving fast a dangerous prospect. Take care and avoid nocturnal driving, as this is often when native animals come out. Many car-hire companies prohibit night-time driving.

➡ Road trains are an ever-present menace on the main highways. Give them a wide berth, they're much bigger than you!

Park is also en route, a photogenic series of sheer rocky gorges and waterholes. Kakadu National Park is next, with World Heritage listed tropical wetlands. When you get to Darwin, reward yourself with a cold beer and some nocturnal high jinks on Mitchell St.

### The Tropics:
### Darwin, Kakadu & Katherine

The outback in the tropical Top End is a different experience to the deserts further south. Here, the wet and dry seasons determine how easy it is to get from A to B. In the Wet, roads become impassable and crocodiles move freely through the wetlands. But before you cancel your plans, this is also a time of abundance and great natural beauty in the national parks – plus Kakadu resorts approach half-price! Darwin isn't really an outback town these days, especially in the Dry when backpackers from around the world fill the bars and Mindil Beach market. Katherine, three hours to the south, is much more 'country', and the jumping-off point for the astonishing Nitmiluk (Katherine Gorge) National Park.

### The Victoria Highway:
### Katherine to the Kimberley

The Victoria Highway is a significant section of the epic Savannah Way from Cairns to Broome, the classic 'across-the-top' route. Leaving Katherine it winds through classic cattle country, where farms can be as big as small European countries. There are 4WD and hiking opportunities, outback campsites, rock art, national parks, red gorges and crocodiles. And this region boasts some of the Top End's best barramundi fishing. The immense Gregory National Park, a former cattle station, is best explored with 4WD, however, in the Dry a 2WD will get you into most of the historic sites, campgrounds and Keep River National Park near the border with Western Australia.

## Facilities

Outback roadhouses emerge from the desert heat haze with surprising regularity. It always pays to calculate the distance to the next fuel stop, but even on the remote Oodnadatta Track you'll find petrol and cold beer every few hundred kilometres. Most roadhouses (many of them open 24 hours) sell fuel and have attached restaurants where you can get a decent steak and a fry-up feed. Just don't expect an epicurean experience. There's often accommodation for road-weary drivers out the back – including campsites, air-conditioned motel-style rooms, and basic cabins.

## Resources

**Tourism NT** (www.travelnt.com) Bountiful info about the Northern Territory outback. Also produces *The Essential NT Drive Guide*, a terrific booklet with driving distances, national parks, and outback info and advice for 2WD and 4WD travellers.

**Parks & Wildlife NT** (www.nt.gov.au/parks) General advice on the NT's fabulous national parks: access, walking tracks, and camping etc.

**South Australian Tourism Commission** (www.southaustralia.com) The lowdown on the South Australian outback, from the Flinders Ranges to Coober Pedy.

**Department of Environment, Water & Natural Resources** (www.environment.sa.gov.au) Advice, maps and camping permits for SA's national parks.

**Parks Australia** (www.environment.gov.au/parks) Extensive information about the federally administered Kakadu and Uluru-Kata Tjuta National Parks.

### PERMITS FOR ABORIGINAL LAND

In the outback, if you plan on driving through pastoral stations and Aboriginal communities you may need to get permission first. This is for your safety; many travellers have tackled this rugged landscape on their own and required complicated rescues after getting lost or breaking down.

Permits are issued by various Aboriginal land-management authorities; see destination chapters for details. Processing applications can take anywhere from a few minutes to a few days.

## OUTBACK CYCLING

Pedalling your way through the outback is not something to tackle lightly, and certainly not something you'd even consider in summer. But you do see the odd wiry, suntanned soul pushing their panniers along the Stuart Hwy between Adelaide and Darwin. Availability of drinking water is the main concern: isolated water sources (bores, tanks, creeks etc) shown on maps may be dry or undrinkable. Make sure you've got the necessary spare parts and bike-repair knowledge. Check with locals if you're heading into remote areas, and always tell someone where you're headed. And if you make it through, try for a book deal – this is intrepid travel defined.

## Organised Tours

If you don't feel like doing all the planning and driving, a guided tour is a great way to experience the outback. These range from beery backpacker jaunts between outback pubs, to indigenous cultural tours and multiday bushwalking treks into remote wilderness.

## Outback Tracks

The Australian outback is criss-crossed by sealed highways, but one of the more interesting ways to get from A to B is by taking a detour along historic cattle and rail routes. While you may not necessarily need a 4WD to tackle some of these roads, the rugged construction of these vehicles makes for a much more comfortable drive. Whatever the vehicle, you will need to be prepared for the isolation and lack of facilities.

Don't attempt the tougher routes during the hottest part of the year (December to February, inclusive); apart from the risk of heat exhaustion, simple mishaps can lead to tragedy in these conditions. There's also no point going anywhere on outback dirt roads if there's been recent flooding.

### Red Centre Way & Mereenie Loop Road

Starting in Alice Springs this well-used track is an alternative route to the big attractions of the Red Centre. The route initially follows the sealed Larapinta and Namatjira Drives skirting the magnificent MacDonnell Ranges to Glen Helen Gorge. Beyond Glen Helen the route meets the Mereenie Loop Road. This is where things get interesting. The Mereenie Loop road requires a permit ($3.50) and is usually so heavily corrugated that it will rattle a conventional 2WD until it finds its weak spot. This is the rugged short cut to Kings Canyon, Watarrka National Park, and from Kings Canyon the sealed Luritja Road connects to the Lasseter Highway and Uluru-Kata Tjuta National Park.

### Oodnadatta Track

Mostly running parallel to the old *Ghan* railway line through outback SA, this iconic track is fully bypassed by the sealed Stuart Hwy to the west. Using this track, it's 429km from Marree to Oodnadatta, then another 216km to the Stuart Hwy at Marla. As long as there is no rain, any well-prepared conventional vehicle should be able to manage this fascinating route, but a 4WD will do it in comfort.

### Birdsville Track

Spanning 517km from Marree in SA to Birdsville just across the border of Queensland, this old droving trail is one of Australia's best-known outback routes - although it's not known for spectacular and varying scenery. Again it's feasible to travel it in a well-prepared, conventional vehicle but not recommended. Don't miss a beer at the Birdsville Hotel!

### Strzelecki Track

This track covers much of the same territory through SA as the Birdsville Track. Starting south of Marree at Lyndhurst, it reaches Innamincka 460km northeast and close to the Queensland border. It was at Innamincka that the explorers Burke and Wills died. A 4WD is a safe bet, even though this route has been much improved due to work on the Moomba gas fields.

### Nathan River Road

This road, which resembles a farm track in parts, is a scenic section of the Savannah Way, a cobbled together route which winds all the way from Cairns to Broome. This particular section traverses some remote country along the western edge of the Gulf of Carpentaria between Roper Bar and Borroloola, much of it protected within Limmen National Park. A high-clearance vehicle is a must and carrying two spare tyres is recommended because of the frequent sharp rocks. Excellent camping beside barramundi- and crocodile-filled streams and waterholes is the main attraction here.

## Tanami Track

Turning off the Stuart Hwy just north of Alice Springs, this 1000km route runs northwest across the Tanami Desert to Halls Creek in WA. The road has received extensive work so conventional vehicles are normally OK, although there are sandy stretches on the WA side and it can be very corrugated if it hasn't been graded recently. Get advice on road conditions in Alice Springs.

## Plenty & Sandover Highways

These remote routes run east from the Stuart Hwy, north of Alice Springs, to Boulia or Mt Isa in Queensland. The Plenty Highway skirts the northern fringe of the Simpson Desert and offers the chance of gemstone fossicking in the Harts Range. The Sandover Hwy offers a memorable if monotonous experience in remote touring. It is a novelty to see another vehicle. Both roads are not to be taken lightly; they are often very rough going with little water and with sections that are very infrequent-

ly used. Signs of human habitation are rare and facilities are few and far between.

## Finke & Old Andado Tracks

The Finke Track (the first part of which is the Old South Rd) follows the route of the old *Ghan* railway (long since dismantled) between Alice Springs and the Aboriginal settlement of Finke (Aputula). Along the way you can call into Chambers Pillar Historical Reserve to view the colourful sandstone tower. From Finke the road heads east along the Goyder Creek, a tributary of the Finke River, before turning north towards Andado Station and, 18km further, the homestead. At Old Andado the track swings north for the 321km trip to Alice. The Old Andado Track winds its way through the Simpson Desert to link the Old Andado Homestead with Alice Springs. On the way you pass the Mac Clark Conservation Reserve, which protects a stand of rare waddy trees. A high-clearance 4WD is definitely recommended and you should be equipped with high-frequency (HF) radio or emergency position-indicating radio beacon (EPIRB).

## Simpson Desert

The route crossing the Simpson Desert from Mt Dare, near Finke, to Birdsville is a real test of both driver and vehicle. A 4WD is definitely required on the unmaintained tracks and you should be in a party of at least three vehicles equipped with sat phones, HF radio and/or EPIRB.

Plan Your Trip

# South Australian Wine & Food

South Australian wine and food are its great achievement, its allure and its saving grace. Adelaide has the culinary and viticultural punch of a heavyweight. Beyond the city you'll find fresher seafood, smoother shiraz, stinkier cheddar and fatter strawberries than anywhere else in this hemisphere – and that's just for lunch!

## Where to Go

### Barossa & Clare Valleys

Close enough to be kissing cousins but far enough apart to conjure up very different wine-region experiences, these two valleys are probably the first regions that spring to mind when anyone mentions South Australian wine. Just an hour from Adelaide, the **Barossa Valley** (www.barossa.com) represents SA's old-school Germanic establishment, with day-trippers galore and iconic names such as Penfolds and Henschke ruling the roost (actually, Henschke is 10km over the hill in Eden Valley, but close enough). Big, ballsy Australian red wine is what you're here for.

An hour north, the **Clare Valley** (www.clarevalley.com.au) is a more intimate, cloistered overnighter, with myriad stone B&Bs dating from the late 1800s and cool-climate valley folds producing world-class riesling. The **Riesling Trail** (www.south australiantrails.com) is an easy-does-it bike track meandering through the vineyards.

### McLaren Vale

Just an hour south of Adelaide, **McLaren Vale** (www.mclarenvale.info) is an agrarian patchwork landscape, vineyards and almond groves patterning the sun-baked slopes of the Willunga Escarpment as it

## Best Wineries

**Deviation Road** (p80) Unpretentious Adelaide Hills winery doing cool climate drops to warm your heart.

**Alpha Box & Dice** (p84) Quirky McLaren Vale outfit bottling luscious blends and shiraz.

**Majella Wines** (p105) Classy Coonawarra cabernet made by fourth-generation locals.

**Rockford Wines** (p114) Gorgeous old stone cellar door off the beaten path in the Barossa.

**Pikes** (p119) A big angry fish? Hard to imagine as you sip into a summery riesling in the Clare Valley.

## Best Places to Eat

**Central Market** (p72) Fill your Adelaide picnic hamper with cheese, salami, pasta, seafood, yogurt, nuts, mushrooms, pickles, bratwursts...

**Press** (p66) Book way ahead for a seat in Adelaide's most 'now' food room.

**Russell's Pizza** (p85) Showcasing Fleurieu Peninsula produce on big rustic pizzas. In Willunga.

**Flying Fish Cafe** (p88) The best of SA seafood right on the Encounter Coast. In Port Elliot.

**Ferment Asian** (p115) If you perfer red duck curry to bratwursts, this Barossa Valley food room will be your saviour.

levels out down to shimmering Gulf St Vincent. This gorgeous place – a kind of fantastical new-world Tuscany – produces some of the best shiraz you'll ever smack across your lips, and has a progressive vibe. You won't find much that's quaint or cottagey here – the mood and is more celebratory, decadent and contemporary, with some fab restaurants, cafes and markets in among the vines rows.

## Coonawarra

Practical, no-fuss **Coonawarra** (www.coona warra.org) is far enough from both Adelaide and Melbourne to rule it out as a day-trip or easy overnighter. People live here rather than pass through: the resultant wine trade is hard-working, utilitarian and often family-run, exploiting the area's fertile *terra rossa* soils and producing super-silky cabernet sauvignon. Penola is the region's service town – an affable country hamlet with a decent pub, a couple of good eateries and Australia's only saint – one-time resident school teacher Saint Mary MacKillop – presiding over the grape biz with imagined ambivalence.

## Lesser-known Wine Regions

Ever heard of wines from Padthaway, Kangaroo Island, the Adelaide Hills, the Riverland, Currency Creek or Langhorne Creeks? Maybe not. The wine in these regions veer between nascent and surprisingly well established, producing everything from chardonnay to sparking shiraz.

➡ **Padthaway** (www.padthawaywineregion. com; such a romantic-sounding word!) isn't far from the Coonawarra, but with a tad more altitude and frosty nights it does a mean chardonnay to go with the local cab sav. There are a lot of vineyards here, but not many cellar doors.

➡ **Kangaroo Island** (www.tourkangarooisland. com.au/foodandwine/wine.aspx) There are half-a-dozen wineries on 'KI', the oldest of which dates from the distant 1990s. But that means they're free from the binds of expectation! Expect flinty sauvignon blanc and sunny chardonnay.

➡ **Adelaide Hills** (www.adelaidehillswine.com. au) Actually, you might have heard of wines from the Adelaide Hills: awesome cool-climate chardonnay, pinot noir, shiraz, sauvignon blanc and more interesting pinot grigio, pinot gris and

viognier vintages. Plenty of classy cellar doors, and just 20 minutes up the hill from Adelaide.

➡ **Riverland** (www.riverlandwine.org.au) Around Renmark and Barmera is one of Australia's largest wine-growing regions, but one with almost no hype or wine tourism trade. It's all about volume here, with endless acres of vines irrigated by the Murray River. Not many cellar doors, but some great bargains to be had.

➡ **Currency & Langhorne Creeks** Inland from Goolwa on the Fleurieu Peninsula, **Currency Creek** (www.currencycreekwineregion.com. au) is one of SA's oldest wine regions, but it still feels like a well-kept secret. The same applies to nearby **Langhorne Creek** (www.langhornewine. com.au): both areas are compact and accessible yet remarkably untouristy. Swing through midweek and you'll have them all to yourself. Impressive shiraz, to say the least.

# Where to Stay

➡ **For festivals** The Barossa Valley seems to have a major event of one kind of another every month. Lots of music and German heritage on display.

➡ **For romantic B&Bs** Cuddle up in an 1880s stone cottage in the Clare Valley, with DIY bacon-and-eggs for breakfast.

➡ **For foodie culture** McLaren Vale brings the foodies down from Adelaide: farmers markets, winery restaurants and cafes conspire to keep them sober.

➡ **For a day-trip from Adelaide** Head for the Adelaide Hills, just 20 minutes up the freeway from the city. Old German towns, savvy wineries, cafes and cosy pubs.

➡ **For winery work** The Coonawarra is gritty, dirt-under-the-fingernails wine country, with seasonal pruning and picking work aplenty.

---

### BEST WINERY RESTAURANTS

➡ **Skillogallee** (p119), Clare Valley

➡ **Dudley Cellar Door** (p94), Kangaroo Island

➡ **d'Arenberg** (p84), McLaren Vale

➡ **Coriole** (p84), McLaren Vale

➡ **Banrock Station Wine & Wetland Centre** (p109), Riverland

# When to Go

➡ **For crowd-free cellar doors** Winter (June to August) is the right time for empty cellar doors with attentive vingnerons.

➡ **For festivals** Summer (December to February) sees plenty of crooners among the vines.

➡ **For vineyard photogenics** Autumn vine colours (April and May) are hard to beat, but in winter (June to August) mists creeping along vine rows paint a compelling picture.

➡ **For winery work** Grape picking season is autumn (March to May); pruning season is early winter (June and July).

# What to Eat

From oysters to honey and brie to blueberries, tasting the local fare is one of the true pleasures of travel in SA.

## Seafood

Love seafood? Love SA. Kangaroo Island (being an island) is one of the best places to try the local product. King George whiting is the best of the sea's bounty – not a big fish, but succulent and flavoursome, best served simply with parsley and lemon. To the southeast, Robe, Kingston SE and Port MacDonnell have large fishing fleets heading out from shore for crayfish (aka lobster). If you're into oysters, head straight for the Eyre Peninsula: the calm, shallow waters off

### TIME FOR A BEER?

Of course, not everyone is into wine, and given South Australia's long hot summers it's no surprise that beer is big business here. For such a successful mainstream brand, Coopers (p59), the all-conquering Adelaide brewery, bottles surprisingly interesting and largely preservative-free beers. Take a tour of the shiny brewery vats and pipes (with tastings afterwards) or rock into pretty much any pub in Adelaide for a cold Pale Ale.

Beyond Adelaide there are some brilliant SA microbreweries, studded belligerently in the middle of wine regions and in unexpected small-town locations. A few of our faves:

➡ **McLaren Vale Beer Company** (p83) The original rebel, this outfit is a McLaren Vale institution these days, with a natty beer bistro at the Vale Inn and serious sales figures around the country. Fab Vale Ale.

➡ **Barossa Brewing Company** (www.barossabrewingcompany.com; Mill St, Greenock; ☺by appointment) In little Greenock, near Nuriootpa in the Barossa, these guys brew lagers and ales in accordance with the German Purity Law of 1516. Pious!

➡ **Lobethal Bierhaus** (p82) Backed by Lobethal's longstanding German heritage, this cool factory conversion in the Adelaide Hills is a beaut spot for a beer. Work your way through from the pilsener to yeasty hefeweizen and hearty Red Truck porter.

➡ **Goodieson Brewery** (www.goodiesonbrewery.com.au; 194 Sand Rd, McLaren Vale; ☺11am-5.30pm) Run by a beer-loving couple, Goodieson flies in the face of McLaren Vale's endless shiraz with a citrusy pilsener, thick stout, light pale ale and nutty seasonal Christmas ale.

➡ **Woolshed Brewery** (www.woolshedbrewery.com.au; Wilkinson Rd, Murtho, via Renmark; ☺by appointment) Near Renmark in the Riverland, newcomer Woolshed – a zero-waste brewer – has been making a splash with its Amazon Ale, an easy-drinking pale ale.

➡ **Steam Exchange Brewery** (p89) Down in the wharf in Goolwa, these guys have been making seaworthy brews for a while now: stout, dark ale, pale ale, and a rather astonishing double-chocolate vanilla-bourbon porter.

Coffin Bay and Ceduna are bivalve hotbeds. Oysterfest (p129) happens every September in Ceduna. Back towards Adelaide, Port Lincoln has a big rep for big tuna, and the big tuna-fishing fleet that lines the town's coffers.

## Cheese

Cheese, glorious cheese! There's plenty of the good stuff (at great prices) at Adelaide's Central Market (p55), or head for the Adelaide Hills where the Woodside Cheese Wrights (p81) specialises in delightfully gloopy soft cheeses. Nearby in Hahndorf, Udder Delights (p80) (ha-ha) is a cool cafe with a dedicated cheese-tasting counter. In picture-perfect Angaston in the Barossa Valley, follow your nose to the marvellous Barossa Valley Cheese Company (p116), where sublime feta, brie and even haloumi vie for your affections. In McLaren Vale township you'll find Blessed Cheese (p83), purveyor of all things cheesy. Inland from here near Mt Compass, **Alexandrina Cheese Company** (www.alexandrinacheese. com.au; Sneyd Rd, Mt Jagged via Mt Compass; ⊙noon-5pm Mon-Fri, 10am-4.30pm Sat & Sun) is an old-fashioned cheese maker with individually named Jersey cows (and super cheddar).

## Honey

An anomaly of natural quarantine, Kangaroo Island is home to the purest strain of Ligurian bees in the world (purer, even, than the busy bees in Liguria itself). Imported for their hard-working ways and passive temperament, they've survived here for decades without generic interference from mainland Australian bees. The honey they produce, sourced from native wildflowers and eucalyptus blooms, is divine. Try some at the low-key Clifford's Honey Farm (p97) (which also does honey ice-cream!), or the more touristy Island Beehive (p95).

## Fruit & Nuts

Need a bit of a health infusion? Tee-up a bowlful of plump Adelaide Hills strawberries. At Beerenberg Strawberry Farm (p79) in Hahndorf you can pick your own

between November and May. While we're talking vitamin C, it would be simply remiss to venture along the Murray River without sampling some Riverland citrus fruit. Berri is the orange-juice capital of the known universe. Further south on the peaty plateaus of the Fleurieu Peninsula, load up on blueberries at the **Blueberry Patch** (☑08-8556 9100; www.blueberrypatch. com.au; Nangkita Rd, Mt Compass; ⊙by appointment Dec-Feb). In nearby Willunga, the prevailing passion is for almonds. The **Almond Blossom Festival** (www.willunga festivals.com) happens here in the last week of July. Willunga is also home to the best farmers market in SA, such as the logically named Willunga Farmers Market (p85).

## Outback Delicacies

Competing with truckstop burgers and steaks, offbeat tucker has found a foothold in outback SA. At pubs and diners along the way you'll find camel schnitzels, emu patties, kangaroo sausages and fillets (which are delicious cooked rare, and served with a red wine and pepper glaze), and even crocodile (imported from the Northern Territory). A one-stop-shop for all of the above is the famed Prairie Hotel (p137) in Parachilna in the northern Flinders Ranges. And while you're in the Flinders, make sure you try a quandong pie – the preferred format for consuming these bittersweet native bush cherries (which taste a bit like rhubarb). Head for the Quandong Café (p134) in Quorn, or the Copley Bush Bakery & Quandong Cafe (p137).

Plan Your Trip
# Travel with Children

Travelling with children in central Australia can be joyous – camping, bushwalks, stargazing, swimming, wildlife spotting... Only extreme temperatures, humidity and long distances conspire to spoil the party. But if you can beat the heat, this isn't a place where you'll encounter much urban menace, pollution or tedious queuing.

## Central Australia for Kids

### On The Road

As anyone with kids knows, getting from A to B is the biggest threat to having a good time. Both A and B are fine once you get there, but the long road-tripping hours in between can be hell on wheels.

For babies and toddlers, time your drives with established sleep times: once they're asleep the hypnotic lull of tyres-on-asphalt can keep them that way for hours. For older kids, there's something to be said for technological distractions in the back seat: portable DVD players or Play Station–type games (with headphones!) can help pass the kilometres, and books-on-CD (available at ABC Shops) are suited to long drives. Factor in regular pitstops, and bring plenty of snacks, colouring books and crayons, sticker albums, drink bottles... And a good game of 'I Spy With My Little Eye' never goes astray.

Have a read of Lonely Planet's *Travel With Children* for some more ideas.

### At The Hotel

When you're knee-high to a grasshopper, staying at a hotel is an adventure. Kids aren't fussed about interior design, fluffy

## Best Regions for Kids

### Kangaroo Island
Yes, there are roos here. Plus wild goanna, echidnas, seals, dolphins, cockatoos and eagles.

### Kakadu National Park
One word: crocodiles. Plus jabirus, turtles, lizards and gaggling flocks of birds.

### Fleurieu Peninsula
Fantastic swimming beaches, farmers markets and fresh fish-and-chip dinners.

### Uluru-Kata Tjuta National Park
Aboriginal culture and excellent short walks around Uluru and through the monumental boulders of Kata Tjuta.

### Adelaide
Playgrounds, parklands, safe-swimming beaches, food markets, Adelaide Zoo, and dinosaur bones in the South Australian Museum.

### Darwin
Fish-feeding, tropical wildlife parks, an outdoor cinema, and satay sticks at Mindil Beach Sunset Markets.

PLAN YOUR TRIP TRAVEL WITH CHILDREN

## CHILDREN'S HIGHLIGHTS

### Wildlife Encounters

**Alice Springs Desert Park** (p203) Many desert species are nocturnal (too hot during the day!). This brilliant park offers a chance to see them in action.

**Seal Bay Conservation Park** (p97) An up-close encounter with Australian sea lions, on a tour or self-guided boardwalk stroll.

**Territory Wildlife Park** (p175) A really sophisticated park, with fantastic recreated environments. Don't miss the birds of prey.

**Jumping Crocs** (p175) The kids will never forget seeing a 5m saltie propel itself out of the Adelaide River to chomp a dead chicken.

### Swimming Spots

**Litchfield National Park** (p176) Take a dip in a cool, clear tropical pool below a waterfall – the stuff of fantasy.

**Port Willunga Beach** (p85) Safe swimming an hour south of Adelaide, with a fish-and-chip kiosk for lunch.

**Glenelg Beach** (p59) Adelaide's biggest and busiest beach is on one end of the city's only tram line: make a day trip of it!

**Wave Lagoon** (p154) You can't swim in the sea around Darwin (stingers and crocs), so hit the surf at this waterfront wave pool.

**Mataranka Thermal Springs** (p197) Free thermal swimming holes bubbling up an hour south of Katherine.

bath robes, Italian tapware or the dated tropical-flower print on the bed linen. The key requirements are facilities-based: swimming pools, playgrounds, games rooms, in-house movies, children's menus and the presence of other kids top the list of priorities. If it means your kids will be happier, try to suspend any ingrained hotel snobberies and stay somewhere where the little ones will be well catered for.

## Planning

➡ You'll find public toilets with family rooms where you can go to feed babies or change nappies in most shopping centres. As anywhere, children should be accompanied in all public toilets, including shopping centres.

➡ Motels and some caravan parks often have playgrounds and swimming pools, and can supply cots and baby baths. Top-end hotels and some (but not all) midrange hotels often accommodate children for free, but B&Bs are often child-free zones.

➡ For babysitting, check under Baby Sitters and Child Care Centres in the local *Yellow Pages*, or phone the local council for a list. Dial-An-

Angel (p61) provides nannies and babysitters in Adelaide. In Darwin, try **All Taken Care Of** (☑0450 341 309; www.alltakencareof.com.au).

➡ Child prices (and family rates) apply for most tours, sight admission fees, and air, bus and train transport, with some discounts as high as 50% off. However, the definition of 'child' can vary from under 12 to under 18 years old.

➡ Heat is a problem while travelling in central Australia, especially in summer, with relentless desert sun and high humidity in the Top End. Time your visit for winter (which is high season!), or make sure the kids are enshrouded in big floppy hats, SPF 30+ sunscreen and sunglasses. Always carry plenty of water and drink it regularly.

➡ Medical services here are of a high standard, with items such as baby-food formula and nappies widely available from pharmacies and supermarkets (plan ahead if heading to remote regions).

➡ Major hire-car companies can supply booster seats, for which you'll be charged around $25 for up to three days' use, with an additional daily fee for longer periods.

# Regions at a Glance

Central Australia is vast and utterly diverse: it's hard to carve it into bite-sized regions for travel consumption. But here goes!

Kick things off in Adelaide: festival-addicted and riddled with fab places to eat and drink. Fanning out from here you'll find impressive wine regions, brilliant beaches and wildlife-spotting opportunities. In the South Australian outback are desolate desert tracks, quirky towns and astonishing national parks.

In the tropical Top End, Darwin is a hip hub with great markets, breezy restaurants and kooky festivals. Don't miss adventures, wildlife encounters and Aboriginal cultural experiences on the Tiwi Islands, in Arnhem Land and in Kakadu and Nitmiluk national parks. Further south in the desert is arty/festive Alice Springs, launch pad for visits to iconic Uluru, Kata Tjuta and Kings Canyon.

## Adelaide

Festivals
Eating
Drinking

### Mad March

Every March Adelaide erupts with festivals: visual arts, music, theatre, busking and the growl of V8 engines. The question is, why do it all at once?

### Eat Streets

Peckish? Hit Rundle St or Gouger St for Thai, Argentinian, vegetarian, Chinese, Mod Oz, Italian, pub grub, or Indian. And don't miss the foodie aisles of Central Market and Chinatown's buzzy foodcourts.

### Perfect Pubs

Adelaide is supposedly the 'City of Churches', but for every steeple there's a temple of tipple. The best ones are free-wheeling booze-rooms doing their own thing: the Exeter, the Wheatsheaf and the Grace Emily.

p54

## Adelaide to the Outback

Wine Regions
Wildlife
Coastline

### Up & Coming Wine Regions

Big-time wine regions encircle Adelaide: Barossa Valley, Clare Valley, McLaren Vale, but how about Langhorne Creek, Mt Benson, Currency Creek, Southern Fleurieu and the Adelaide Hills? All lesser-known regions.

### Kangaroo Island Critters

'KI' is overrun with goannas, cockatoos, snakes, koalas, echidnas and (predictably) kangaroos. Offshore are whales, seals, dolphins, and King George whiting on your hook.

### Beaut Beaches

Explore SA's beaches: try Carrickalinga on the Fleurieu Peninsula (swimming), Locks Well on the Eyre Peninsula (fishing) and Pennington Bay on KI (surfing).

p78

# Outback SA

**National Parks**
**Outback Towns**
**Desert Tracks**

## Flinders Ranges National Park

The Flinders Ranges loom large in russet, purple and brown: super-scenic, desert-edge ridgelines awash with arid scrub and native pines. Don't miss incredible Ikara (Wilpena Pound).

## Coober Pedy

Locals in opal-crazed Coober Pedy beat the desert heat in underground houses, dreaming of deposits of the 'fire in the stone' that will one day make them rich.

## Oodnadatta Track

Belting across 615km of desert between the Flinders Ranges and the Stuart Hwy is this historic route: red dust, emus, skittering lizards and last-gasp towns remembering the railway that once ran through here.

p138

# Darwin

**Markets**
**Eating & Drinking**
**Festivals**

## Mindil Beach Sunset Market

Don't miss famous Mindil Beach Sunset Market: arts, crafts and the weird and wonderful are here, but it's the tropical produce and sizzling food stalls that steal the show.

## Al Fresco Darwin

Darwin's tropical climate blossoms at sunset. Outdoor bars and restaurants line Cullen Bay Marina and Stokes Wharf, but why stay on land? Several vessels offer sunset drinks and dinner cruises.

## Beer Can Regatta

Darwin celebrates its notorious rep for beer consumption by building an armada of 'vessels' for the Beer Can Regatta. Arts festivals occur, but it's this family-fun day that grabs the attention.

p151

# Darwin to Katherine

**Indigenous Culture**
**Wildlife**
**Adventure**

## Kakadu & the Tiwi Islands

Tour Kakadu National Park's ancient rock-art galleries with an Aboriginal guide, or take a bush-tucker tour. From Darwin, hop over to the Tiwi Islands for the Tiwi Grand Final.

## Crocodiles & Birds

Cruise Top End rivers and billabongs where crocs lurk and see massive flocks of water birds, colourful parrots and stately jabirus.

## Arnhem Land, Kakadu & Nitmiluk

Explore western Arnhem Land in a 4WD, venture deep into Kakadu National Park to remote Jim Jim Falls and Twin Falls, or paddle the gorgeous gorges of Nitmiluk National Park.

p171

# Alice Springs to Uluru

**National Parks**
**Indigenous Culture**
**Festivals**

## Uluru, Kata Tjuta & Kings Canyon

It's a long haul to get here, but it's worth it! Visit stupendous Uluru and Kata Tjuta, or explore the awesome gorge of Kings Canyon in Wataarka National Park.

## Art in the Alice

The Red Centre is home to the renowned Desert Art Movement: learn the stories behind these dazzling paintings and make an informed purchase in Alice Springs.

## Alice Springs Festivals

Not to be outdone for quirkiness, Alice Springs is home to the world's only dry-river yacht race – the Henley-on-Todd Regatta – and the town stops for its annual Camel Cup.

p202

# On the Road

# Adelaide & South Australia

## Off The Beaten Track

➡ Port Lincoln (p126)

➡ Oodnadatta Track (p143)

➡ Melrose (p132)

➡ Burra (p122)

## Best Places to Stay

➡ Port Elliot Beach House YHA (p88)

➡ Stirling Hotel (p81)

➡ Wilpena Pound Resort (p136)

➡ Marion Bay Motel (p123)

➡ Largs Pier Hotel (p65)

## Why Go?

Escape the east-coast frenzy in relaxed South Australia (SA). The driest state on the driest continent, SA beats the heat by celebrating life's finer things: fine landscapes, fine festivals, fine food and (...OK, forget the other three) fine wine.

Adelaide is a chilled-out, gracious city offering world-class festivals, restaurants, pubs and a hedonistic arts scene. A day trip away, McLaren Vale and the Barossa and Clare Valleys are long-established wine regions. Further afield are the watery wilds of the Limestone Coast, and the Murray River, curling Mississippi-like towards the sea. Kangaroo Island's wildlife, forests and seafood await just offshore.

To the west, Yorke Peninsula and Eyre Peninsula are off the beaten track: both beachy, slow-paced detours. Wheeling into the Flinders Ranges, wheat fields give way to arid cattle stations beneath ochre-coloured peaks. Further north, eccentric outback towns such as Woomera and Coober Pedy emerge from the dead-flat desert haze.

## When to Go

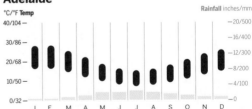

**Adelaide**

**Feb–Mar** Adelaide's festival season hits its straps: Fringe and WOMADelaide are highlights.

**Apr–May** Low autumn sunsets and russet-red grapevines: harvest is in the air.

**Sep** Football finals time: yell yourself silly in the stands, beer and pie in hand(s).

# History

South Australia was declared a province on 28 December 1836, when the first British colonists landed at Holdfast Bay (current-day Glenelg). The first governor, Captain John Hindmarsh, named the state capital Adelaide, after the wife of the British monarch, William IV. While the eastern states struggled with the stigma of convict society, SA's colonists were free citizens – a fact to which many South Australians will happily draw your attention.

The founders based the colony on a utopian 19th-century ideal of social engineering. Land was sold at set prices by the British government to help establish mainly young, skilled married couples; the concept was that equal numbers of men and women, free from religious and political persecution, would create an egalitarian new order.

Between 1838 and 1841, 800 German farmers and artisans (many persecuted Lutherans from Prussia) arrived and settled Hahndorf in the Adelaide Hills – now the best preserved German village in the state. Many more followed over the next decade, bringing vine cuttings with them – SA's famous vineyards began to take root.

The young colony's early progress was slow – only British government funds saved it from bankruptcy – but it became self-supporting by the mid-1840s and self-governing by 1856. Following the successful crossing of the continent by local explorers, SA won the contract to lay the Overland Telegraph from Port Augusta to Darwin, connecting Australia to the world by telegram (1872) and, later, telephone. Following a long recession in the late 19th century, the government became the first to introduce income tax – a fact to which South Australians are hesitant to draw your attention...

SA has maintained its socially progressive creed: trade unions were legalised in 1876; women were permitted to stand for parliament in 1894; and the state was one of the first places in the world to give women the vote, and the first state in Australia to outlaw racial and gender discrimination, legalise abortion and decriminalise gay sex.

## Indigenous Adelaide & South Australia

SA offers up some great opportunities to learn about Aboriginal cultures and beliefs. Some of the best include the indigenous-run Bookabee Tours (p53) of Adelaide and the Flinders Ranges, Yorke Peninsula cultural tours run by Adjahdura Land (p120), and Adelaide's Tandanya National Aboriginal Cultural Institute (p57). Also in Adelaide is the Australian Aboriginal Cultures Gallery in the South Australian Museum (p55).

SA's best-known Aboriginal language is Pitjantjatjara (also known as Pitjantjara), which is spoken throughout the Anangu-Pitjantjarjara Aboriginal Lands of northern SA, down almost to the Great Australian Bight. The traditional language of the Adelaide area is Kaurna. Many Kaurna-derived place names have survived around the city: Aldinga comes from *Ngultingga,* Onkaparinga from *Ngangkiparringga,* and Noarlunga from *Nurlungga.* The Adelaide Hills region is Peramangk country.

The Coorong, in Ngarrindjeri country, is a complex series of dunes and salt pans separated from the sea by the long, thin Younghusband Peninsula. It takes its name from the Ngarrindjeri word *kurangh,* meaning 'long neck'. According to the Ngarrindjeri, their Dreaming ancestor, Ngurundjeri, created the Coorong and the Murray River.

The iconic Ikara (Wilpena Pound), a natural basin in Flinders Ranges National Park, is sacred to the Adnyamathanha people, who have lived in the area for more than 15,000 years. Dreaming stories tell of two *akurra* (giant snakes) who coiled around Ikara during an initiation ceremony, creating a whirlwind and devouring the participants. The snakes were so full after their feast they couldn't move, and willed themselves to die, thus creating the landmark.

In 1966, SA became the first state to grant Aboriginal people title to their land. In the early 1980s most of the land west of the Stuart Hwy and north of the railway to Perth was transferred to Aboriginal ownership. Cultural clashes still sometimes occur, however, exemplified by the politically and culturally divisive Hindmarsh Bridge controversy in the 1990s, which pitted Aboriginal beliefs against development.

## National Parks

Around 22% of SA's land area is under some form of official conservation management, including national parks, recreation parks, conservation parks and wildlife reserves. The Department of Environment, Water & Natural Resources (DEWNR; www.environment.sa.gov.au) manages the state's conservation areas and sells park passes and camping

# Adelaide & South Australia Highlights

**1** Sniff out the ripest cheese, fullest fruit and strongest coffee at Adelaide's **Central Market** (p55).

**2** Swirl, nose and quaff your way through **McLaren Vale** (p82), our favourite SA wine region.

**3** Trundle past pelicans, dunes and lagoons in **Coorong National Park** (p99).

**4** Listen to the seals snort on **Kangaroo Island** (p90).

**5** Hike up to the lofty, desolate rim of **Ikara (Wilpena Pound**; p135) in the Flinders Ranges National Park.

**6** Catch a cricket match or some AFL football at the redesigned **Adelaide Oval** (p56).

**7** Noodle for opals in the moonscape mullock at **Coober Pedy** (p139).

**8** Slurp down a dozen briny oysters at **Coffin Bay** (p128).

**9** Scout for passing whales off **Victor Harbor** (p86) or **Head of Bight** (p130) west of Ceduna.

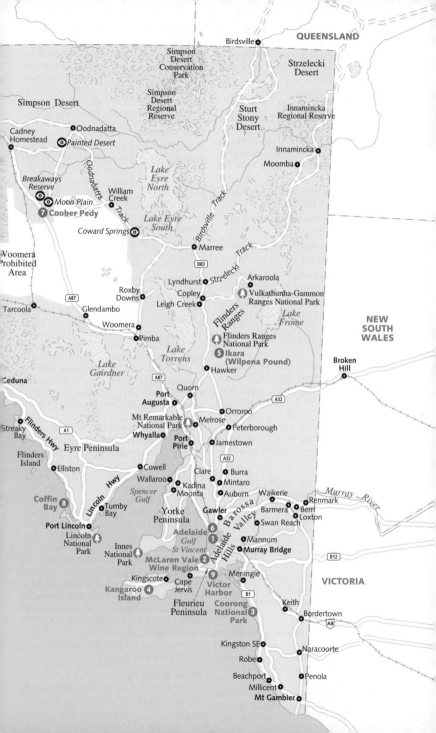

QUEENSLAND

Simpson Desert Conservation Park

Strzelecki Desert

Simpson Desert

Birdsville

Simpson Desert Regional Reserve

Sturt Stony Desert

Innamincka Regional Reserve

Cadney Homestead

*Painted Desert*

Innamincka

Moomba

*Lake Eyre North*

*Oodnadatta*

William Creek

*Breakaways Reserve*

*Moon Plain*

**7** **Coober Pedy**

*Lake Eyre South*

*Coward Springs*

Birdsville Track

Woomera Prohibited Area

A87

Marree

B83

Strzelecki Track

Tarcoola

Glendambo

Roxby Downs

Lyndhurst

Copley

Leigh Creek

Arkaroola

Vulkathunha-Gammon Ranges National Park

*Flinders Ranges*

*Lake Frome*

NEW SOUTH WALES

Woomera

Pimba

*Lake Torrens*

Flinders Ranges National Park

**5** **Ikara (Wilpena Pound)**

Ceduna

*Lake Gairdner*

A87

Hawker

Quorn

Broken Hill

**Port Augusta**

Orroroo

A32

Streaky Bay

*Flinders Hwy*

A1

Mt Remarkable National Park

Melrose

Peterborough

Flinders Island

Elliston

Eyre Peninsula

**Whyalla**

Port Pirie

Jamestown

A32

Cowell

*Lincoln Hwy*

Wallaroo

*Spencer Gulf*

Kadina

Moonta

Clare

Burra

Mintaro

Auburn

Waikerie

*Murray River*

Renmark

**Coffin Bay** **8**

Tumby Bay

Yorke Peninsula

**Gawler**

*Barossa Valley*

Barmera

Berri

Loxton

**Port Lincoln**

Lincoln National Park

Innes National Park

**McLaren Vale Wine Region**

**Adelaide**

**6**

**1**

Swan Reach

*Adelaide Gulf St Vincent*

**2**

*Adelaide Hills*

Mannum

**Murray Bridge**

B12

Kingscote

**Kangaroo Island** **4**

Cape Jervis

**9**

**Victor Harbor**

Meningie

Fleurieu Peninsula

**Coorong National Park** **3**

VICTORIA

Keith

B1

Bordertown

A8

Kingston SE

Naracoorte

Robe

Beachport

Penola

Millicent

**Mt Gambier**

permits. A 'Two Month Holiday Pass' ($40 per vehicle; $70 including camping) covers entry to most of SA's parks, excluding the desert parks and Flinders Chase on Kangaroo Island.

## Wine Regions

Let's cut to the chase: we all know why you're here. South Australian wines are arguably the best in the world, and there's no shortage of wine regions – both established and emerging – in which to taste them. The key players:

➜ **Adelaide Hills** Impressive cool-climate wines in Adelaide's backyard.

➜ **Barossa Valley** Old-school estates and famous reds.

➜ **Clare Valley** Niche riesling vintages and cosy weekend retreats.

➜ **Coonawarrra** Lip-smacking cabernet sauvignon on the Limestone Coast plains.

➜ **McLaren Vale** Awesome shiraz and vine-covered hillsides rolling down to the ocean.

## Activities

With hills, beaches, forests, deserts and wide-open spaces, there's pretty much nothing you can't do in SA (well, apart from skiing...). The Trails SA (www.southaustral iantrails.com) website is chockers with information on activities, including horse riding, canoeing, bushwalking, cycling and diving, with safety tips, maps and useful links.

### Bushwalking

SA's national parks and conservation areas have thousands of kilometres of marked trails traversing eye-popping wilderness. Around Adelaide there are walks to suit all abilities in the Mt Lofty Ranges, including trails in Belair National Park and Morialta Conservation Park; see www.environment. sa.gov.au/parks for details.

In the Flinders Ranges there are outstanding walks in Mt Remarkable National Park and Flinders Ranges National Park.

### Diving

This ain't the Great Barrier Reef, but it's still an ace place to don your flippers and tanks and check out leafy sea dragons, seals, nudibranchs, sponge beds, dolphins and endemic species.

Off the Gulf St Vincent coast, top dive sites include Second Valley, Rapid Bay jetty, Cape Jervis and the ex-destroyer **HMAS Hobart** (www.exhmashobart.com.au), which was scuttled off Yankalilla Bay in 2002. Other good dive sites include the Yorke Peninsula jetties and the reefs off Port Lincoln. Freshwater cave diving around Mount Gambier is also fantastic. Contact the **Scuba Divers Federation of SA** (www.sdfsa.net) for more info.

### Rock Climbing

Rock spiders keen on 10m to 15m cliffs can clamber over the gorges in Morialta Conservation Park and Onkaparinga River Recreation Park, both on the outskirts of Adelaide. More-advanced climbers should head for the Flinders Ranges: SA's premier cliff is at Moonarie on the southeastern side of Wilpena Pound – 120m! Buckaringa Gorge, close to Quorn and Hawker, is another fave for the more daring. Contact the **Climbing Club of South Australia** (www.climbingclubsouthaus tralia.asn.au) for info.

### Swimming & Surfing

Uncrowded, white-sand swimming beaches stretch right along the SA coast; the safest for swimming are along the Gulf St Vincent and Spencer Gulf coasts. Anywhere exposed to the Southern Ocean and the Backstairs Passage (between Kangaroo Island and the mainland) may have strong rips and undertows. If you're after that all-over-tan look, head for the nudie southern end of Maslin Beach, 40km south of Adelaide.

The SA coast is pummelled by rolling Southern Ocean swells. Pennington Bay has the most consistent surf on Kangaroo Island, while Pondalowie Bay on the Yorke Peninsula has the state's strongest breaks. Other hot spots are scattered between Port Lincoln on the Eyre Peninsula and the famous Cactus Beach in the far west. Closer to Adelaide, the beaches around Port Elliot have accessible surf, with swells often holding around 2m; other gnarly breaks are Waitpinga Beach and Parsons Beach, 12km southwest of Victor Harbor.

The best surfing season is March to June, when the northerlies blow. See www.south australia.com/regions/fleurieu-peninsula-surfing.aspx for info, and www.surfsouthoz. com for surf reports.

You can take surfing lessons and hire gear on the Fleurieu Peninsula.

### Whale Watching

Between May and October, migrating southern right whales cruise within a few hundred metres of SA shores as they head to/from their Great Australian Bight breeding grounds. Once prolific, southern right whales suffered unrestrained slaughter during the 19th century, which reduced the whale population from 100,000 to just a few hundred by 1935. Although an endangered species, they are fighting back and the population worldwide may now be as high as 7000.

Key spots for whale watching include Victor Harbor and Head of Bight beyond Ceduna on the far west coast.

To find out about current whale action call the **Whale Information Hotline** (☑1900 942 537), or contact the South Australian Whale Centre in Victor Harbor.

## Tours

Whatever your persuasion or destination, there's probably a SA tour to suit you. There are plenty of tours in and around Adelaide, including day trips to the Adelaide Hills, Fleurieu Peninsula, Murray River and the Barossa and Clare Valleys.

Further afield, outback tours usually include the Flinders Ranges and Coober Pedy, some continuing north to Alice Springs and Uluru in the Northern Territory. Some of the prime movers:

**Adventure Tours**                    WILDERNESS
(☑08-8132 8230, 1800 068 886; www.adventure tours.com.au) Wide range of bus tours around SA and interstate, including trips from Adelaide to Alice Springs and Uluru, Darwin and Kakadu National Park, Kangaroo Island and the Great Ocean Road. Seven days Adelaide to Alice costs $1020; 14 days Adelaide to Darwin is $2113.50.

**Bookabee Tours**                    INDIGENOUS
(☑08-8235 9954; www.bookabee.com.au) Indigenous-run cultural tours to the Flinders Ranges. Two-/three-/four-/five-day tours cost $995/1520/2025/2500.

**Earth Adventure**                    KAYAKING
(☑08-8165 2024; www.earthadventure.com.au) Short and long kayaking and canoeing trips around SA waters, from the Port River at Port Adelaide to the Murray River, Kangaroo Island and Coffin Bay.

**Groovy Grape**                    GUIDED TOUR
(☑1800 661 177; www.groovygrape.com.au) Small-group tours including a three-day trip from Melbourne to Adelaide via the Great Ocean Road ($425), and seven days from

Adelaide to Alice Springs via the Flinders Ranges, Coober Pedy and Uluru ($975). Includes meals, camping and national park entry fees. Kangaroo Island and Barossa Valley tours also available.

**Heading Bush**                    WILDERNESS
(☑1800 639 933; www.headingbush.com) Rugged, small-group, 10-day Adelaide to Alice Springs expeditions are $1995 all inclusive. Stops include the Flinders Ranges, Coober Pedy, Simpson Desert, Aboriginal communities, Uluru and West MacDonnell Ranges. Yorke Peninsula and dedicated Flinders Ranges tours also available.

**Swagabout Tours**                    WILDERNESS
(☑0408 845 378; www.swagabouttours.com.au) Dependable small-group tours with the option of staying in hotels or camping under the stars. The all-inclusive five- to 10-day Adelaide–Alice Springs trips (per day camping/hotels around $300/500) take in the Clare Valley, Flinders Ranges, Oodnadatta Track, Dalhousie Springs and Uluru. Also runs dedicated trips to the Clare Valley, Kangaroo Island and Eyre Peninsula.

## ℹ Information

**South Australian Visitor Information Centre** (Map p56; ☑1300 764 227; www.south australia.com; 108 North Tce, Adelaide; ⏰9am-5pm Mon-Fri, 9am-2pm Sat, 10am-3pm Sun) Abundantly stocked with info (including fab regional booklets) on Adelaide and SA.

**Department of Environment, Water & Natural Resources** (DEWNR; Map p56; ☑08-8124 4972; www.environment.sa.gov.au; Level 1, 100 Pirie St, Adelaide; ⏰9am-5pm Mon-Fri) Maps and parks information.

**Royal Automobile Association of South Australia** (RAA; Map p56; ☑08-8202 4600; www. raa.net; 41 Hindmarsh Sq, Adelaide; ⏰8.30am-5pm Mon-Fri, 9am-noon Sat) Auto advice and plenty of maps.

## ℹ Getting There & Around

### AIR

International, interstate and regional flights service Adelaide Airport (p77), 7km west of the city centre. The usual car-rental suspects all have desks here. Major airlines include:

**Jetstar** (www.jetstar.com.au) Direct flights between Adelaide and Perth, Darwin, Cairns, Brisbane, Sydney and Melbourne.

**Qantas** (www.qantas.com.au) Direct flights between Adelaide and Perth, Alice Springs, Darwin, Cairns, Brisbane, Sydney, Canberra and Melbourne.

## TAKE THE LONG WAY HOME

South Australia has three epic long-distance trails for hiking and cycling:

**Heysen Trail** (www.heysentrail.asn.au) Australia's longest walking trail: 1200km between Cape Jervis on the Fleurieu Peninsula and Parachilna Gorge in the Flinders Ranges. Access points along the way make it ideal for half- and full-day walks. Note that due to fire restrictions, some sections of the trail are closed between December and April.

**Kidman Trail** (www.kidmantrail.org.au) A 10-section cycling and walking trail between Willunga on the Fleurieu Peninsula and Kapunda north of the Barossa Valley.

**Mawson Trail** (www.southaustralian trails.com) A 900km bike trail between Adelaide and Blinman in the Flinders Ranges, via the Adelaide Hills and Clare Valley.

**Regional Express** (Rex; www.regionalexpress.com.au) Flies from Adelaide to regional centres around SA, including Kingscote (from $110, 35 minutes), Coober Pedy (from $235, two hours), Ceduna (from $180, 1½ hours), Mount Gambier (from $200, 1¼ hours), Port Lincoln (from $100, 50 minutes) and Whyalla ($135, 50 minutes).

**Tiger Airways** (www.tigerairways.com.au) Direct flights between Adelaide and Melbourne.

**Virgin Australia** (www.virginaustralia.com) Direct flights between Adelaide and Perth, Brisbane, Sydney, Canberra and Melbourne.

### BUS

Buses are usually the cheapest way of getting from A to B in SA, and the bus companies have more comprehensive networks than the rail system. Adelaide Central Bus Station (p77) has ticket offices and terminals for all major interstate and statewide services. For online bus timetables see the **Bus SA** (www.bussa.com.au) website.

The major long-haul operators:

**Firefly Express** (1300 730 740; www.fireflyexpress.com.au) Buses between Adelaide and Melbourne (from $65, 11 hours), continuing to Sydney.

**Greyhound Australia** (1300 473 946; www.greyhound.com.au) Services between Adelaide and Melbourne (from $56, 11 hours) continuing to Sydney; and Adelaide and Alice Springs (from $190, 20 hours) continuing to Darwin.

**Premier Stateliner** (08-8415 5555; www.premierstateliner.com.au) State-wide bus services.

**V/Line** (1800 800 007; www.vline.com.au) Bus and bus/train services between Adelaide and Melbourne (from $50, 12 hours).

### CAR & MOTORCYCLE

If you're driving between Adelaide and Melbourne, make sure you go via the Great Ocean Road (www.visitvictoria.com) between Torquay and Warrnambool in Victoria – one of the best coastal drives in the world, with awesome views and more twists and turns than a Hitchcock plot.

To hitch a ride (sharing petrol costs) or buy a secondhand car, check out hostel noticeboards.

The Great Ocean Road route is considerably longer than the inland route via Horsham (around 960km and 12 hours versus 730km and eight hours), but it's worth it.

### TRAIN

Interstate trains run by **Great Southern Rail** (13 21 47; www.gsr.com.au) grind into the Adelaide Parklands Terminal (p77), 1km southwest of the city centre. The following trains depart from Adelaide regularly:

**The Ghan** To Alice Springs (seat/sleeper $431/1190, 19 hours)

**The Ghan** To Darwin ($842/2290, 47 hours)

**The Indian Pacific** To Perth ($553/1750, 39 hours)

**The Indian Pacific** To Sydney ($375/850, 25 hours)

**The Overland** To Melbourne (from $116, 11 hours)

# ADELAIDE

POP 1.29 MILLION

Sophisticated, cultured, neat casual – this is the self-image Adelaide projects, a nod to the days of free colonisation without the 'penal colony' taint. Adelaidians may remind you of their convict-free status, but the city's stuffy, affluent origins did more to inhibit development than promote it. Bogged down in the old-school doldrums and painfully short on charisma, this was a pious, introspective place.

But these days things are different. Multicultural flavours infuse Adelaide's restaurants; there's a pumping pub, arts and live-music scene; and the city's festival calendar has vanquished dull Saturday nights. And, of course, there's the local wine. Residents flush with hedonism at the prospect of a punchy McLaren Vale shiraz or summer-scented Clare riesling.

That said, a subtle conservatism remains. 'What school did you go to?' is a common salvo from those unsure of your place in the social hierarchy, while countercultural urges bubble up through Adelaide's countless sex shops, kung-fu dojos and huge bottle shops.

Just down the tram tracks is beachy Glenelg, Adelaide with its guard down and boardshorts up; and Port Adelaide, a historic enclave slowly developing into SA's version of Fremantle. Inland, Adelaide's winking plains rise to the Adelaide Hills, just 12 minutes up the freeway. The Hills' gorgeous valley folds, old-fangled towns and cool-climate vineyards are all close at hand.

## ⊙ Sights

### ⊙ Central & North Adelaide

★Central Market                                    MARKET
(Map p56; www.adelaidecentralmarket.com.au; Gouger St; ⊙7am-5.30pm Tue, 9am-5.30pm Wed & Thu, 7am-9pm Fri, 7am-3pm Sat) Satisfy both obvious and obscure culinary cravings at the 250-odd stalls in Adelaide's superb Central Market. A sliver of salami from the Mettwurst Shop, a sliver of English stilton from the Smelly Cheese Shop, a tub of blueberry yoghurt from the Yoghurt Shop – you name it, it's here. Good luck making it out without eating anything. Adelaide's Chinatown is right next door.

★Art Gallery of
South Australia                                    GALLERY
(Map p56; www.artgallery.sa.gov.au; North Tce; ⊙10am-5pm) FREE Spend a few hushed hours in the vaulted, parquetry-floored gallery that represents the big names in Australian art. Permanent exhibitions include Australian, modern Australian, contemporary Aboriginal, Asian, Islamic and European art (19 bronze Rodins!). Progressive temporary exhibitions occupy the basement. Free guided tours (11am and 2pm daily) and lunchtime talks (12.30pm daily).

★South Australian Museum                           MUSEUM
(Map p56; www.samuseum.sa.gov.au; North Tce; ⊙10am-5pm) FREE Digs into Australia's natural history with special exhibits on whales and Antarctic explorer Sir Douglas Mawson, and an Aboriginal Cultures Gallery displaying artefacts of the Ngarrindjeri people of the Coorong and lower Murray. The giant squid is the undisputed highlight of the free tours (11am weekdays, 2pm and 3pm weekends). There's a cool cafe here too.

Adelaide Zoo                                       ZOO
(Map p66; www.zoossa.com.au; Frome Rd; adult/child/family $31.50/18/85; ⊙9.30am-5pm) Around 1800 exotic and native mammals, birds and reptiles roar, growl and screech at Adelaide's wonderful zoo, which opened in 1883. There are free walking tours halfhourly (plus a slew of longer and overnight tours focusing on specific environments and species), feeding sessions and a children's

---

## ADELAIDE IN...

### Two Days

If you're here at Festival, WOMADelaide or Fringe time, lap it up. Otherwise, kick-start your day at the Central Market (p55) then wander through the Adelaide Botanic Garden (p56), finishing up at the National Wine Centre (p56). After a few bohemian beers at the Exeter (p72) hotel, have a ritzy dinner on Rundle St. Next day, visit the South Australian Museum (p55) and then see if the Bradman Collection Museum at the Adelaide Oval (p56) has reopened. Check out Tandanya National Aboriginal Cultural Institute (p57) before riding the tram to Glenelg for a swim and fish and chips on the sand.

### Four Days

Follow the two-day itinerary – perhaps slotting in the Art Gallery of South Australia (p55) and Jam Factory Contemporary Craft & Design Centre (p59) – then pack a picnic basket of Central Market produce and take a day trip out to the nearby Adelaide Hills, McLaren Vale or Barossa Valley wine regions. Next day, truck out to the museums and historic pubs of Port Adelaide, then catch a band at the Grace Emily Hotel (p72) back in the city, before dinner on Gouger St.

ADELAIDE & SOUTH AUSTRALIA ADELAIDE

# Central Adelaide

zoo. Until Wang Wang and Funi – Australia's only giant pandas – arrived in 2009 (pandemonium!), the major drawcard was the Southeast Asian rainforest exhibit.

You can take a river cruise to the zoo from the Festival Centre on Popeye (p60).

**National Wine Centre of Australia** WINERY
(Map p66; www.wineaustralia.com.au; cnr Botanic & Hackney Rds; ☉9am-5pm) FREE Check out the free self-guided, interactive **Wine Discovery Journey** exhibition, paired with tastings of Australian wines (from $10), at this very sexy wine centre (actually a research facility for the University of Adelaide, more than a visitor centre per se). You will gain an insight into the issues winemakers contend with, and even have your own virtual vintage rated. Free 30-minute tours run at 11.30am daily. Friday-evening 'uncorked' drinks happen at 4.30pm, and here's a cool cafe here too.

**Adelaide Botanic Garden** GARDENS
(Map p66; www.botanicgardens.sa.gov.au; North Tce; ☉7.15am-sunset Mon-Fri, from 9am Sat & Sun, Bicentennial Conservatory 10am-4pm) FREE Meander, jog or chew through your trashy airport novel in these lush city-fringe gardens. Highlights include a restored 1877 palm house, the waterlily pavilion (housing the gigantic *Victoria amazonica*), a cycad collection and the fabulous steel-and-glass arc of the **Bicentennial Conservatory**, which re-creates a tropical rainforest. Free 1½-hour guided walks depart from the Schomburgk Pavilion at 10.30am daily.

**Adelaide Oval** LANDMARK
(Map p66; ☎08-8300 3800; www.cricketsa.com.au; King William Rd, North Adelaide; tour adult/child $10/5; ☉tour 10am Mon-Fri) Hailed as the world's prettiest cricket ground, the Adelaide Oval hosts interstate and international cricket matches in summer, plus South Australian National Football League

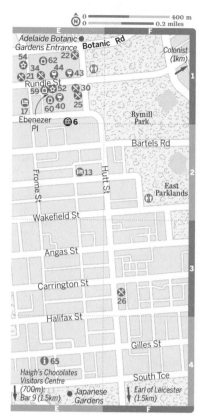

there are interactive displays on living with the land, as well as galleries, gifts and a cafe. There are didgeridoo or Torres Strait Islander **cultural performances** (adult/child $5/3, ⊙noon Tue-Sun), pre-booked group **tours** (tours $5-10), plus indigenous short-film and documentary screenings in the theatre.

**Migration Museum**                                          MUSEUM
(Map p66; www.migrationmuseum.com.au; 82 Kintore Ave; ⊙10am-5pm Mon-Fri, 1-5pm Sat & Sun) This engaging social-history museum tells the story of the many migrants who have made SA their home. The museum has info on 100-plus nationalities (as opposed to individuals) in its database, along with some poignant personal stories. Occupies the site of a former Aboriginal boarding school and destitute asylum.

**West Terrace Cemetery**                                  CEMETERY
(Map p56; www.aca.sa.gov.au; West Tce; ⊙6.30am-6pm Nov-Apr, 6.30am-8.30pm May-Oct) **FREE** Driven-by and overlooked by most Adelaidians, this amazing old cemetery (established in 1837, and now with 150,000 residents) makes a serene and fascinating detour. The 2km self-guided **Heritage Highlights Interpretive Trail** meanders past 29 key sites; collect collect a brochure at the West Tce entrance.

**Adelaide Gaol**                                             MUSEUM
(Map p66; ☑08-8231 4062; www.adelaidegaol.org.au; 18 Gaol Rd, Thebarton; adult/child/family $13/8/32, with guided tour $17/11/48, ghost tours $28; ⊙10am-5pm Sun-Fri, last entry 3.30pm, guided tours 11am, noon & 1pm Sun, ghost tours sunset Thu-Sat) Only decommissioned in 1988, this old lock-up has a grim vibe, but its displays of homemade bongs, weapons and escape devices are amazing. Commentary tapes are available for self-guided tours (included in the admission price). Bookings are required for **guided tours** and adults-only **ghost tours**.

**Haigh's Chocolates**
**Visitors Centre**                                             TOUR
(Map p70; ☑08-8372 7070; www.haighschocolates.com; 154 Greenhill Rd, Parkside; ⊙8.30am-5.30pm Mon-Fri, 9am-5pm Sat, tours 11am, 1pm & 2pm Mon-Sat) **FREE** If you've got a chocolate problem, get guilty at this iconic factory. Free **tours** take you through the chocolate life-cycle from cacao nut to hand-dipped truffle (with samples if you're good). Tour bookings essential.

(SANFL) football games in winter. A wholesale redevelopment is underway (www.adelaideovalredevelopment.com.au), which will boost seating capacity to 50,000 and bring national Australian Football League (AFL) games here. A bronze **statue of 'the Don'** (Sir Donald Bradman) cracks a cover drive out the front. When there are no games happening you can take a two-hour **tour**, departing from the northern gates on Pennington Tce. Call or check the website for tour details. Note that the **Bradman Collection Museum** is on ice until the redevelopment is complete.

**Tandanya National**
**Aboriginal Cultural Institute**              GALLERY
(Map p56; ☑08-8224 3200; www.tandanya.com.au; 253 Grenfell St; ⊙10am-5pm) Tandanya offers an insight into the culture of the local Kaurna people, whose territory extends south to Cape Jervis and north to Port Wakefield. Inside the cultural institute

# Central Adelaide

**Adelaide Parklands** GARDENS

The city and ritzy North Adelaide are surrounded by a broad band of parklands. Colonel William Light, Adelaide's controversial planner, came up with the concept, which has been both a blessing and a curse for the city. Pros: heaps of green space, clean air and sports grounds for the kids. Cons: bone-dry in summer, perverts loitering and a sense that the city is cut off from its suburbs.

Don't miss the **Japanese Gardens** on South Tce and the **statue of Colonel William Light** overlooking the gleaming city office towers from Montefiore Hill.

**Gilles Street Market**                   MARKET
(Map p56; www.gillesstreetmarket.com.au; 91 Gilles St, Gilles Street Primary School; ☉10am-4pm 3rd Sun of the month) Kids' clothes, fashion, arts, crafts and hubbub take over an East End school grounds. Open twice-monthly during summer.

**Jam Factory Contemporary**
**Craft & Design Centre**                  GALLERY
(Map p56; www.jamfactory.com.au; 19 Morphett St; ☉10am-5pm Mon-Sat, from 1pm Sun) `FREE` Quality contemporary local arts and crafts, plus workshops and a hell-hot glass-blowing studio (watch from the balcony above) turning out gorgeous glass.

**Australian**
**Experimental Art Foundation**           GALLERY
(AEAF; Map p56; www.aeaf.org.au; cnr Morphett St & North Tce, Lion Arts Centre; ☉11am-5pm Tue-Fri, from 2pm Sat) `FREE` A focus on innovation, with a hip bookshop specialising in film, architecture, culture and design.

## ◉ Inner Suburbs

**Coopers Brewery**                        BREWERY
(Map p70; ☎08-8440 1800; www.coopers.com.au; 461 South Rd, Regency Park; 1½hr tours per person $22; ☉tours 1pm Tue-Fri) You can't possibly come to Adelaide without entertaining thoughts of touring Coopers Brewery. Tours take you through the brewhouse, bottling hall and history museum, where you can get stuck into samples of stouts, ales and lagers (some of which are carbon neutral). Bookings required; minimum age 18. The brewery is in the northern suburbs – grab a cab, or walk 1km from Islington train station.

**Penfolds Magill Estate Winery**          WINERY
(Map p70; ☎08-8301 5569; www.penfolds.com.au; 78 Penfolds Rd, Magill; tastings free-$50; ☉10am-5pm) This 100-year-old winery is home to Australia's best-known wine – the legendary Grange. Taste the product at the cellar door, dine at the restaurant, take the **Heritage Tour** ($15), or steel your wallet for the **Great Grange Tour** ($150). Tour bookings are essential.

## ◉ Glenelg

Glenelg, or 'the Bay' – the site of SA's colonial landing – is Adelaide at its most 'LA'. Glenelg's beach faces towards the west, and as the sun sinks into the sea, the pubs and bars burgeon with surfies, backpackers and sun-damaged sexagenarians. The tram rumbles in from the city, past the Jetty Rd shopping strip to the alfresco cafes around Moseley Sq.

Take the tram to Glenelg from the city or bus 167, 168 or 190.

**Glenelg Visitor**
**Information Centre**            TOURIST INFORMATION
(☎08-8294 5833; www.glenelgsa.com.au; Shop 22, Marina Pier, Holdfast Shores, Glenelg; ☉9am-4.30pm Mon-Fri, 10am-3pm Sat, 10am-2pm Sun) The visitor centre has the local low-down, incuding info on local diving and sailing opportunities.

**Bay Discovery Centre**                   MUSEUM
(Map p70; www.baydiscovery.com.au; Moseley Sq, Town Hall; admission gold coin donation; ☉10am-5pm summer, 10am-4pm winter) This low-key museum in Glenelg's 1887 Town Hall building depicts the social history of Glenelg from colonisation to today, and addresses the plight of the local Kaurna people, who lost both their land and voice. Don't miss the relics dredged up from the original pier, and the spooky old sideshow machines.

## ◉ Port Adelaide

Bogged in boganity for decades, Port Adelaide – 15km northwest of the city – is in the midst of gentrification, morphing its warehouses into art spaces and museums, and its brawl-house pubs into boutique beer emporia. Things are (slowly) on the up!

Adelaide's solitary tram line is rumoured to be extending to Port Adelaide at some stage. Until then, bus 150 will get you here from North Tce, or you can take the train.

**Port Adelaide Visitor**
**Information Centre**            TOURIST INFORMATION
(☎08-8405 6560, 1800 629 888; www.portenf.sa.gov.au; 66 Commercial Rd; Port Walks gold coin donation; ☉9am-5pm, Port Walks 2pm Thu & Sun; ☎) This helpful visitor centre books guided **Port Walks** around the heritage area, and stocks brochures on self-guided history and heritage-pub walks, plus the enticements of neighbouring Semaphore. Activities include dolphin cruises and kayaking.

### South Australian Maritime Museum
MUSEUM

(Map p70; www.samaritimemuseum.com.au; 126 Lipson St; adult/child/family $10/5/25; ⊙ 10am-5pm daily, lighthouse 10am-2pm Sun-Fri) This salty cache is the oldest of its kind in Australia. Highlights include the iconic Port Adelaide Lighthouse ($1 on its own, or included in museum admission), busty figureheads made everywhere from Londonderry to Quebec, shipwreck and explorer displays, and a computer register of early migrants.

### National Railway Museum
MUSEUM

(Map p70; www.natrailmuseum.org.au; Lipson St Sth; adult/child/family $12/6/32; ⊙ 10am-5pm) Trainspotters rejoice! A delightfully nerdy museum crammed with railway memorabilia. The bookshop stocks as much *Thomas the Tank Engine* merch as you can handle.

### South Australian Aviation Museum
MUSEUM

(Map p70; www.saam.org.au; 66 Lipson St; adult/child/family $9/4.50/22; ⊙ 10.30am-4.30pm) This collection of retired old birds (and rockets from Woomera) roosts in an old hangar in the Port Adelaide back streets.

### Fishermen's Wharf Market
MARKET

(Map p70; www.fishermenswharfmarkets.com.au; Black Diamond Sq; ⊙ 9am-5pm Sun) If you're visiting the Port on a Sunday, this waterside, two-level indoor market has antiques, bric-a-brac and crappy collectables.

## 🏃 Activities

### Cycling & Walking

Adelaide is pancake flat – perfect for cycling and walking (if it's not too hot!). You can take your bike on trains any time, but not buses. **Trails SA** (www.southaustraliantrails.com) offers loads of cycling- and hiking-trail info: pick up its *40 Great South Australian Short Walks* brochure.

There are free guided walks in the Adelaide Botanic Gardens, plus self-guided city walks detailed in brochures from the South Australian Visitor & Travel Centre. The riverside **Linear Park Trail** is a 40km walking/cycling path running from Glenelg to the foot of the Adelaide Hills, mainly along the River Torrens. Another popular hiking trail is the steep **Waterfall Gully Track** (three hours return) up to Mt Lofty Summit and back.

### Eagle Mountain Bike Park
PARK

(Map p70; www.bikesa.asn.au; Mt Barker Rd, Leawood Gardens; ⊙ dawn-dusk) **FREE** Mountain bikers should check out the Eagle Mountain Bike Park in the Adelaide Hills, which has 21km of trails. Check the website for directions.

### Bicycle SA
BICYCLE HIRE

(Map p56; ☑ 08-8168 9999; www.bikesa.asn.au; 111 Franklin St; ⊙ 9am-5pm) Free 'Adelaide City Bikes' (bring your driver's licence or passport), plus cycling maps and advice.

### Bikeabout
CYCLING TOURS

(☑ 0413 525 733; www.bikeabout.com.au) Barnstorming one-day 'Radelaide' mountain-bike sessions (from $130), plus mountain-bike hire (from $30 per day) and tours through the Barossa Valley, McLaren Vale and Clare Valley wine regions.

### Escapegoat
CYCLING TOURS

(☑ 08-8121 8112; www.escapegoat.com.au) Ride from the 710m Mt Lofty Summit down to Adelaide ($90), or take a day trip through McLaren Vale by bike ($120). Flinders Ranges bike trips also available.

### Glenelg Bicycle Hire
BICYCLE HIRE

(Map p70; ☑ 08-8376 1934; www.glenelgbicyclehire.com.au; 71 Broadway, Norfolk Motor Inn, Glenelg South) Cruise 'The Bay' on a mountain bike (per day $40) or tandem (per day $65).

### Linear Park Hire
BICYCLE HIRE

(Map p66; ☑ 0400 596 065; Elder Park; bikes per day $30; ⊙ 9am-5pm) Bike hire, with helmets and locks.

### Water Activities

Adelaide gets *reeeeally* hot in summer. Hit the beach at Glenelg, or try any other activity that gets you out on the water. For more options, check out **Popeye** (Map p66; www.thepopeye.com.au; return adult/child $12/6, one-way $4/2; ⊙ 10am-4pm) river cruises and Captain Jolley's Paddle Boats (p61).

### Adelaide Aquatic Centre
SWIMMING

(Map p66; www.cityofadelaide.com.au; Jeffcott Rd, North Adelaide; casual swim adult/child/family $7.50/6/21; ⊙ 6am-9pm Mon-Fri, 7am-7pm Sat & Sun) The closest pool to the city, with indoor swimming and diving pools, and the usual gym, sauna and spa stuff.

### Adventure Kayaking SA
KAYAKING

(☑ 08-8295 8812; www.adventurekayak.com.au; tours per adult/child from $50/25, kayak hire per

## ADELAIDE FOR CHILDREN

The free monthly paper **Adelaide's Child** (www.adelaideschild.com.au), available at cafes and libraries, is largely advertorial but contains comprehensive events listings. *Adelaide for Kids: A Guide for Parents*, by James Muecke, has comprehensive details and is available at bookshops.

There are few kids who won't love the **tram ride** from the city down to Glenelg (kids under five ride for free!). You may have trouble getting them off the tram – the lure of a splash in the shallows at the **beach** followed by some fish and chips on the lawn should do the trick.

During school holidays, the South Australian Museum (p55), **State Library of South Australia** (☑08-8207 7250; www.slsa.sa.gov.au; cnr North Tce & Kintore Ave, 1st fl; ☉10am-8pm Mon-Wed & Fri, to 6pm Thu & Fri, to 5pm Sat & Sun), Art Gallery of South Australia (p55), Adelaide Zoo (p55) and Adelaide Botanic Garden (p56) run inspired kid-and family-oriented programs with accessible and interactive general displays. The Art Gallery also runs a **START at the Gallery** kids' program (tours, music, activities) from noon to 3pm on the first Sunday of the month.

Down on the River Torrens, **Captain Jolley's Paddle Boats** (Map p66; www.captainjolleyspaddleboats.com; Elder Park; hire per 30min $15; ☉9.30am-6pm daily summer, 10am-4pm Sat & Sun winter) make a satisfying splash.

Live out the kids' (or perhaps your own) *Charlie and the Chocolate Factory* fantasies on a tour at Haigh's Chocolates Visitors Centre (p57). Not the best for young diets, perhaps, but the chocolates sure are Wonka-worthy.

In Port Adelaide, you can check out the Maritime Museum (p60), National Railway Museum (p60) or South Australian Aviation Museum (p60), or set sail on a **dolphin-spotting cruise**.

**Dial-An-Angel** (☑08-8267 3700, 1300 721 111; www.dialanangel.com.au) provides nannies and babysitters to all areas.

3hr adult/child $45/30) 🚣 Family-friendly guided kayak tours around the Port River estuary (dolphins, mangroves, shipwrecks). Also offers kayak hire.

**Temptation Sailing**  DOLPHIN WATCHING
(Map p70; ☑0412 811 838; www.dolphinboat.com.au; Holdfast Shores Marina, Glenelg; 3½hr dolphin watch/swim $68/98) 🚣 Eco-accredited catamaran cruises to watch or swim with dolphins. There are twilight and 1½-hour day cruises too.

**Dolphin Explorer Cruises**  DOLPHIN WATCHING
(Map p70; ☑08-8447 2366; www.dolphinexplorer.com.au; Commercial Rd, Port Adelaide; 2hr cruises from adult/child $10/6; ☉daily) 🚣 Cruises depart from Port Adelaide's Fishermen's Wharf to ogle the local bottlenose dolphins. Lots of cruise-and-dine options also available.

**Adelaide Scuba**  DIVING
(Map p70; ☑08-8294 7744; www.adelaidescuba.com.au; Patawalonga Frontage, Glenelg North; ☉9am-5.30pm Mon-Fri, 8am-5pm Sat & Sun) Hires out snorkelling gear (per day $30) and runs local dives (single/double dive $65/130).

**Adelaide Gondola**  BOATING
(Map p66; ☑08-8358 1800; www.adelaidegondola.com.au; War Memorial Dr, North Adelaide; 4 people per 40 min $110) Maybe if you squint...no, it still doesn't look like Venice. But cruising the River Torrens may still float your boat. You can even order a bottle of wine!

## 🖙 Tours

A great way to see Adelaide is to circle around the main sights on the **free city buses** (see p77). Beyond the city, day tours cover the Adelaide Hills, Fleurieu Peninsula, Barossa Valley and Clare Valley. Note that one-day trips to the Flinders Ranges and Kangaroo Island tend to be rushed and not great value for money.

**Adelaide's Top Food & Wine Tours**  FOOD & WINE
(☑08-8386 0888; www.topfoodandwinetours.com.au) Uncovers SA's gastronomic soul with dawn ($65 including breakfast) and morning ($50) tours of the buzzing Central Market where stallholders introduce their produce. Adelaide Hills, McLaren Vale, Barossa and Clare Valley tours also available.

**LOCAL KNOWLEDGE**

## ADELAIDE ARTS & FESTIVALS

Emma Fey, Development Manager at the Art Gallery of South Australia, filled us in on some highlights of Adelaide's festival calender and arts scene.

### Festival Season

The Adelaide Festival, the Fringe Festival, Adelaide Writers' Week and the Clipsal 500 (V8 race) all happen around February/March. Energy breeds energy: everyone is out and about and the weather's good. I can't think of anywhere else where you can see alternative Fringe-dwellers next to racing enthusiasts. The people-watching is great!

### Art in the City

The Art Gallery of South Australia is in the middle of the North Tce precinct (next to the museum, the university, between the city and the river). The gallery has recently refurbished and rehung its Elder and Melrose wings, and is engaging a wider audience – especially young people and children with a new dedicated art-making space called 'The Studio'. There are also contemporary art spaces popping up in little laneways around the precinct.

### Best Free Events

All sorts of amazing free events appear around the city, especially during the Adelaide Festival. Guerilla street art teamed with pop-up dining experiences, the sensational Adelaide Festival Club Barrio (late-night club) and the Art Gallery of SA's free daily programs.

**Bookabee Tours**                    INDIGENOUS
(☑08-8235 9954; www.bookabee.com.au) Indigenous-run half-/full-day city tours ($105/205) focusing on bush foods in the Adelaide Botanic Gardens, Tandanya National Aboriginal Cultural Institute and the South Australian Museum. A great insight into Kaurna culture. Longer outback tours also available.

**Adelaide Sightseeing**              GUIDED TOUR
(☑1300 769 762; www.adelaidesightseeing.com.au) Runs a city highlights tour ($62) including North Tce, Glenelg, Haigh's Chocolates and the Adelaide Oval (among other sights). Central Market, Barossa Valley, McLaren Vale, Adelaide Hills and Kangaroo Island tours also available (among other destinations).

**Enjoy Adelaide**                    GUIDED TOUR
(☑08-8332 1401; www.enjoyadelaide.com.au) Half-day city highlights tour ($45) with diversions to Mt Lofty Summit and Hahndorf. Barossa Valley tours also available.

**Integrity Tours**                   GUIDED TOUR
(☑0402 120 361, 08-8382 9755; www.integrity toursandcharter.com.au) Adelaide city-lights evening tours ($64), plus half-/full-day tours to the Adelaide Hills (from $59/89) and full-day McLaren Vale/Fleurieu Peninsula explorations (from $89).

**Gray Line**                         GUIDED TOUR
(☑1300 858 687; www.grayline.com.au) Half-day city tours with a river cruise ($86) or tram ride and seaside lunch at Glenelg ($93). Adelaide Zoo and Adelaide Hills add-ons also available.

## Festivals & Events

**Tour Down Under**                   CYCLING
(www.tourdownunder.com.au) The world's best cyclists sweating in their lycra: six races through SA towns, with the grand finale in Adelaide in January.

**Adelaide Fringe**                   ARTS
(www.adelaidefringe.com.au) This annual independent arts festival in February and March is second only to the Edinburgh Fringe. Funky, unpredictable and downright hilarious.

**Adelaide Festival**                 ARTS
(www.adelaidefestival.com.au) Top-flight international and Australian dance, drama, opera, literature and theatre performances in March. Don't miss the Northern Lights along North Tce – old sandstone buildings ablaze with lights – and the Barrio late-night club.

**Clipsal 500**                       MOTORSPORT
(www.clipsal500.com.au) Rev-heads flail their mullets as Adelaide's streets become a four-day Holden versus Ford racing track in March.

### WOMADelaide
MUSIC

(www.womadelaide.com.au) One of the world's best live-music events, with more than 300 musicians and performers from around the globe. In March.

### Adelaide Cabaret Festival
CABARET

(www.adelaidecabaretfestival.com) The only one of its kind in the country. Held in June.

### South Australian Living Artists Festival
ARTS

(SALA; www.salafestival.com.au) Progressive exhibitions and displays across town in August (expired artists not allowed).

### Adelaide Guitar Festival
MUSIC

(www.adelaideguitarfestival.com.au) Annual axe-fest with a whole lotta rock, classical, country, blues and jazz. In August.

### City to Bay
FUN RUN

(www.city-bay.org.au) In September, the annual 12km fun run from the city to Glenelg; much sweat and cardiac duress.

### Royal Adelaide Show
AGRICULTURAL

(www.theshow.com.au) The agricultural, the horticultural and plenty of showbags. In September.

### OzAsia Festival
CULTURAL

(www.ozasiafestival.com.au) Food, arts, conversation, music and the mesmerising Moon Lantern Festival. In September.

### SANFL Grand Final
FOOTBALL

(www.sanfl.com.au) September is the zenith of the local Aussie Rules football season.

### Christmas Pageant
CULTURAL

(www.cupageant.com.au) An Adelaide institution for 70-plus years – kitschy floats, bands and marching troupes occupy city streets for a day in November.

### Feast Festival
GAY & LESBIAN

(www.feast.org.au) Three weeks in November in Adelaide, with a carnival, theatre, dialogue and dance.

## 🛏 Sleeping

Most of Adelaide's budget accommodation is in the city centre, but in a town this easy to navigate, staying outside the CBD is viable. North Adelaide is under the flight path, but it's otherwise low-key. For beachside accommodation, try Glenelg. 'Motel Alley' is along Glen Osmond Rd, the main southeast city access road. See www.bandbfsa.com.au for B&B listings.

## 🛏 Central Adelaide

### My Place
HOSTEL $

(Map p56; ☑ 08-8221 5299; www.adelaidehostel.com.au; 257 Waymouth St; dm/d incl breakfast from $26/68; P❋@🤏) The antithesis of the big formal operations, My Place has a welcoming, personal vibe and is just a stumble from the Grace Emily, arguably Adelaide's best pub! There's a cosy TV room, barbecue terrace above the street, beach-bus in summer, and regular pizza and pub nights – great for solo travellers.

### Adelaide Central YHA
HOSTEL $

(Map p56; ☑ 08-8414 3010; www.yha.com.au; 135 Waymouth St; dm from $29, d without/with bathroom from $79/95; P❋@🤏) The YHA isn't known for its gregariousness, but you'll get plenty of sleep in the spacious and comfortable rooms here. This is a seriously schmick hostel with great security, roomy kitchen and lounge area and immaculate bathrooms. A real step up from the average backpackers around town. Parking $10 per day.

### Majestic Roof Garden Hotel
HOTEL $$$

(Map p56; ☑ 08-8100 4400; www.majestichotels.com.au; 55 Frome St; d from $200; P❋@🤏) Everything looks new in this Japanese-themed place – a speck of dirt would feel lonely. Book a room facing Frome St for a balcony and the best views, or take a bottle of wine up to the rooftop garden to watch the sunset. Good walk-in and last-minute rates; parking from $18 per day.

### Hotel Metropolitan
HOTEL $

(Map p56; ☑ 08-8231 5471; www.hotelmetro.com.au; 46 Grote St; s/tw/d from $55/85/90) Knocked up in 1883, the Metropolitan pub is still looking pretty. Its 26 rooms upstairs feature stripy linen, high ceilings, little flat-screen TVs and various bedding configurations. 'It used to be quite an experience staying here...' says the barman, raising his eyebrows. We're not sure what he meant, but these days you can expect a decent budget sleep in a beaut city location. Shared bathrooms.

### Hotel Richmond
HOTEL $$

(Map p56; ☑ 08-8215 4444; www.hotelrichmond.com.au; 128 Rundle Mall; d from $165; P❋🤏) This opulent hotel in a grand 1920s building in the middle of Rundle Mall has mod-minimalist rooms with king-sized beds, marble bathrooms and American oak and Italian furnishings. Oh, and that hotel rarity – opening windows. Rates include breakfast, movies and papers. Parking from $16 per day.

**Clarion Hotel Soho** HOTEL $$
(Map p56; ☑08-8412 5600; www.clarionhotelsoho.
com.au; 264 Flinders St; d $145-590; P ❋ 🕸 🕯 )
Attempting to conjure up the vibe of Lon-
don's Soho district, these 30 very plush
suites (some with spas, most with balconies)
are complemented by sumptuous linen, 24-
hour room service, iPod docks, Italian mar-
ble bathrooms, jet pool and a fab restaurant.
Rates take a tumble midweek. Parking is
available from $15.

**Hostel 109** HOSTEL $
(Map p56; ☑08-8223 1771, 1800 099 318; www.
hostel109.com; 109 Carrington St; dm/s/d/tr
$30/60/80/99; ❋ @ 🕯 ) A small, well-run
hostel in a quiet corner of town, with a cou-
ple of little balconies over the street and a
cosy kitchen/communal area. Spotlessly
clean and super-friendly, with lockers, travel
info, good security and gas cooking. The
only negative: rooms open onto light wells
rather than the outside world.

**Quest on Sturt** APARTMENTS $$$
(Map p56; ☑08-8416 4200; www.questapart
ments.com.au; 14 Sturt St; 1-/2-/3-bed apt from
$200/210/250; P ❋ 🕯 ) Almost a mini-suburb
within the CBD, this tight enclave of two-
storey, multicoloured apartments wins point
for location (utterly central), security and
privacy. Various online deals include breakfast, free internet, free parking, a bottle of
wine etc. Good for urbanite families.

**Backpack Oz** HOSTEL $
(Map p56; ☑1800 633 307, 08-8223 3551; www.
backpackoz.com.au; cnr Wakefield & Pulteney Sts;
dm/s/d from $25/55/65; ❋ @ 🕯 ) It doesn't
look like much externally, but this converted
pub (the old Orient Hotel) strikes the right
balance between party and placid. There are
spacious dorms and an additional no-frills
guesthouse over the road (good for couples),
and guests can still get a coldie and shoot
some pool in the bar. Communal area; free
barbecue on Wednesday.

**Adelaide City Park Motel** MOTEL $$
(Map p56; ☑08-8223 1444; www.citypark.com.
au; 471 Pulteney St; d without/with bathroom from
$99/120, tr/f from $160/210; P ❋ 🕯 ) Immacu-
late bathrooms, leather lounges, winsome
French prints and an easy walk to the Hutt
St restaurants. Free parking, DVDs and
wireless internet, too. Ask about the apart-
ments on the way to Glenelg (one- and two-
bedroom units $175 to $225).

**Adelaide Backpackers Inn** HOSTEL $
(Map p56; ☑1800 099 318, 08-8223 6635;
www.abpi.com.au; 112 Carrington St; dm/s/d/tr
$27/60/70/99; ❋ @ 🕯 ) A relaxed and sur-
prisingly decent place filling out an 1841 pub
(the ol' Horse & Jockey) that's had a recent
facelift (new bathrooms, fridges, carpets,
washing machines, snappy paint colours
etc). Handy to Hutt and Rundle Sts.

**Shakespeare
International Backpackers** HOSTEL $
(Map p56; ☑1800 556 889, 08-8231 7655; www.
shakeys.com.au; 123 Waymouth St; dm/s/d from
$26/80/80; ❋ @ 🕯 ) Rambling through an
old downtown pub (1879), laid-back Shakeys
has friendly staff, a serious stainless-steel
kitchen, free linen and a balcony over the
street (look down on the suits and count
your blessings). There was a new bar/travel
desk being built downstairs when we visited.

## 🛏 North Adelaide

**Greenways Apartments** APARTMENTS $$
(Map p66; ☑08-8267 5903; www.greenwaysapart
ments.com; 41-45 King William Rd, North Adelaide;
1-/2-/3-bedroom apt $120/150/190; P ❋ 🕯 )
These 1938 apartments ain't flash (floral
tiles and rude 1970s laminates), but if you
have a pathological hatred of 21st-century
open-plan 'lifestyles', then Greenways is for
you! And where else can you stay in clean,
perfectly operational apartments so close to
town at these rates? A must for cricket fans,
the Adelaide Oval is a lofted hook shot away –
book early for Test matches.

**Minima Hotel** HOTEL $$
(Map p66; ☑08-8334 7766; www.majestichotels.
com.au; 146 Melbourne St, North Adelaide; d from
$100; P ❋ @ ) A spaceship has landed in ye
olde North Adelaide! Just a few years old,
Minima offers compact but super-stylish
rooms in a winning Melbourne St location.
Check-in is DIY – use the touch screen in
the lobby. Limited parking $9.50 per night.

**Princes Lodge Motel** MOTEL $
(Map p66; ☑08-8267 5566; www.princeslodge.
com.au; 73 LeFevre Tce, North Adelaide; s/d/f incl
breakfast from $65/85/145; P ❋ 🕯 ) In a grand
1913 house overlooking the parklands, this
friendly, eclectic lodge has high ceilings, new
TVs and a certain faded grandeur. Close to
the chichi North Adelaide restaurants and
within walking distance of the city. Great
value with heaps of character. The budget

rooms in the old coachhouse out the back are a steal.

### Tynte Street Apartments    APARTMENTS $$

(Map p66; ☑ 08-8334 7783; www.majestichotels. com.au; 82 Tynte St, North Adelaide; d/1-bedroom apt from $125/175, extra adult $20; P ❄ 🖥) These post-modern, red-brick, self-contained apartments on a tree-lined street near the O'Connell St cafes and pubs, sleeping three. Check-in is 1km away at 9 Jerningham St. Free parking to boot.

### O'Connell Inn    MOTEL $$

(Map p66; ☑ 08-8239 0766; www.oconnellinn.com. au; 197 O'Connell St, North Adelaide; d from $150; P ❄ 🖥) It's absurdly difficult to find a decent motel in Adelaide (most are mired in the '90s'), but this one makes a reasonable fist of the new century. It's smallish, friendly, affordable and in a beaut location – handy for forays north to the Barossa, Clare, Flinders etc.

## Inner Suburbs

### Levi Park Caravan Park    CARAVAN PARK $

(Map p70; ☑ 08-8344 2209; www.levipark.com.au; 1a Harris Rd, Vale Park; unpowered/powered sites from $33/35, cabins/apt from $102/145; ❄ @ 🖥) This leafy, grassy Torrens-side park is 5km from town and loaded with facilities, including tennis courts and a palm-fringed cricket oval. Apartments are in the restored Vale House, purportedly Adelaide's oldest residence!

### Adelaide Caravan Park    CARAVAN PARK $

(Map p66; ☑ 08-8363 1566; www.adelaidecaravan park.com.au; 46 Richmond St, Hackney; powered sites $36-40, cabins & units $119-166; ❄ @ 🖥 ⛖) A compact, no-frills park on the River Torrens, rather surprisingly slotted in on a quiet street 2km northeast of the city centre. Clean and well run, with a bit of green grass if it's not too far into summer.

## Glenelg & Beach Suburbs

### Glenelg Holiday & Corporate Letting

(☑ 0417 083 634, 08-8376 1934; www.glenelgholi day.com.au; ❄) and **Glenelg Letting Agency** (Map p70; ☑ 08-8294 9666; www.baybeachfront. com.au; ❄) offer self-contained beachside apartments in Glenelg from around $140 per night.

### ★ Largs Pier Hotel    HOTEL $$

(Map p70; ☑ 08-8449 5666; www.largspierhotel. com.au; 198 Esplanade, Largs Bay; d/apt from $159/199; P) Wow, what a surprise! In the otherwise subdued beach suburb of Largs Bay, 5km north of Port Adelaide, is this 130-year-old, three-storey wedding-cake hotel. A bucket of money has been poured into it over recent years, and it's looking great: sky-high ceilings, big beds, taupe-and-chocolate colours and beach views. There's also a low-slung wing of motel rooms off to one side, and apartments across the street.

### Glenelg Beach Hostel    HOSTEL $

(Map p70; ☑ 08-8376 0007, 1800 359 181; www. glenelgbeachhostel.com.au; 1-7 Moseley St, Glenelg; dm/s/d/f from $25/60/70/110; @ 🖥) A couple of streets back from the beach, this beaut old terrace (1879) is Adelaide's budget golden child. Fan-cooled rooms maintain period details and are bunk-free. There's cold Coopers in the basement bar (live music on weekends), open fireplaces, lofty ceilings, girls-only dorms and a courtyard garden. Book *waaay* in advance in summer.

### Seawall Apartments    APARTMENTS $$$

(Map p70; ☑ 08-8295 1197; www.seawallapart ments.com.au; 21-25 South Esplanade, Glenelg; 1-/2-/3-/4-bed apts from $200/270/380/430; P ❄ 🖥) Readers recommend this renovated row of old houses, a five-minute wander along the sea wall from Mosely Sq in Glenelg. They really didn't need a gimmick – the location seals the deal – but the facades are festooned with kitsch nautical paraphernalia (nets, boats, oars, shark jaws...). Inside the apartments are roomy, contemporary and immaculate.

### Adelaide Shores    CARAVAN PARK $

(Map p70; ☑ 08-8355 7320, 1800 444 567; www.ad elaideshores.com.au; 1 Military Rd, West Beach; powered sites $36-57, 1-/2-bed cabins from $87/134; P ❄ @ ⛖) Hunkered-down behind the West Beach dunes with a walking/cycling track extending to Glenelg (3.4km) in one direction and Henley Beach (3.5km) in the other, this is a choice spot in summer. There are lush sites, glistening amenities and passing dolphins.

### Stamford Grand Hotel    HOTEL $$$

(Map p70; ☑ 08-8376 1222; www.stamford.com. au; Moseley Sq, Glenelg; d city/ocean views from $200/250; P ❄ @ 🖥 ⛖) The first Glenelg edifice to scrape the sky with any real authority, this plush, pink-hued hotel overlooks

# North Adelaide

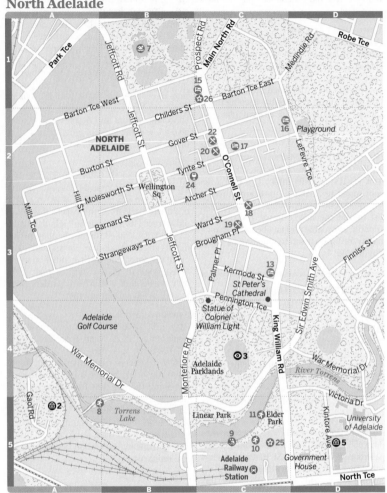

Gulf St Vincent. Dinner, bed and breakfast packages are decent value; good off-season rates. Just sidestep the faux gold-leaf embellishments and chesterfields in the lobby. Parking from $15.

## ✖ Eating

Foodies flock to West End hot spots like Gouger St (pronounced 'Goo-jer'), China-town and food-filled Central Market. There are some great pubs here too. Artsy, alternative Hindley St – Adelaide's dirty little secret – has a smattering of good eateries. In the East End, Rundle St and Hutt St offer al-fresco cafes and people-watching. North Adelaide's Melbourne and O'Connell Sts have a healthy spread of bistros, provedores and pubs.

## ✖ West End

**Press**          MODERN AUSTRALIAN **$$$**
(Map p56; ☑08-8211 8048; www.pressfoodand wine.com.au; 40 Waymouth St; mains $16-46; ⊙noon-9pm Mon-Sat) The best of an emerging strip of restaurants on office-heavy Way-mouth St. Super-stylish (brick, glass, lem-on-coloured chairs) and not afraid of offal

pastry) and anchovies stuffed with Manzanillo olives, washed down with some sparkling sangria. Magic.

### Lucia's Pizza & Spaghetti Bar    ITALIAN $

(Map p56; www.lucias.com.au; 2 Western Mall, Central Market; meals $8-13; ☺7am-4pm Mon-Thu & Sat, to 9pm Fri) This little slice of Italy has been around since Lucia was a lot younger. All her pasta, sauces and pizzas are authentically homemade – perfection any time of day. If you like what you're eating, you can buy fresh pasta next door at Lucia's Fine Foods.

### Village Indian    INDIAN $$

(Map p56; ☎08-8212 2536; www.thevillagerestaurant.com.au; 125 Gouger St; mains $14-29; ☺noon-2.30pm Tue-Fri, 5.30-9pm Tue-Sun; ✍) Taking on Jasmin for bragging rights as Adelaide's best Indian restaurant, the Village (all smooth service, nice knives and balloon-like wine glasses) offers some unusual subcontinental offerings. Try the Kashmiri Goat Yakhni (simmered in yoghurt, aniseed and cardamon) or Moreton Bay Bug masala. Busy Gouger St location.

### Evergreen    CHINESE $

(Map p56; ☎08-8212 1686; 31 Moonta St; yum cha $5-19; ☺11am-3pm Mon-Sat, 5pm-late Mon-Sun; ✍) A few steps away from the Gouger St fray, Chinatown's Evergreen has rapidly earned a rep for great yum cha. There are a staggering 182 items on the menu (everything from eggplant hotpot to stir-fried ginger scallops), plus a passable wine list and paper tablecloths so you can get messy.

### Jerusalem
### Sheshkabab House    MIDDLE EASTERN $

(Map p56; ☎08-8212 6185; 131 Hindley St; mains $10-15; ☺11.30am-2.30pm & 5.30-10pm Tue-Sat, 4-10pm Sun; ✍) A skinny Hindley St room that's been here forever, serving magnificent Middle Eastern and Lebanese delights: falafels, hummus, tabouleh, tahini and (of course) sheshkababs. The plastic furniture and draped tent material are appropriately tacky.

### Ying Chow    CHINESE $$

(Map p56; 114 Gouger St; mains $11-17; ☺noon-2.45pm Fri, 5pm-12.45am daily) This fluoro-lit, bossy-staffed eatery is a culinary gem, serving cuisine styled from the Guangzhou region, such as 'BBC' (bean curd, broad beans and Chinese chutney) and steamed duck with salty sauce. It gets packed – with queues out the door (no bookings) – but it's worth the wait.

pan-fried lamb's brains, grilled calf's tongue) or things raw (beef carpaccio, gravlax salmon) and confit (duck leg, onion, olives). Try the house-made spicy beef sausages, or the tasting menu ($68 per person).

### Mesa Lunga    MEDITERRANEAN $$

(Map p56; ☎08-8410 7617; www.mesalunga.com; cnr Gouger & Morphett Sts; tapas $4-14, mains $16-28; ☺noon-3pm Fri, noon-late Sun, 6pm-late Tue-Sat) In a fishbowl corner room with a sexy dark-wood wine wall, sassy Mesa Lunga serves tapas and quality pizzas. Order some *gamba* (black-salted prawn and chorizo in

# North Adelaide

## ◉ Sights
1 Adelaide Botanic Garden......................F5
2 Adelaide Gaol ...........................................A5
3 Adelaide Oval............................................C4
4 Adelaide Zoo..............................................E4
5 Migration Museum ................................ D5
6 National Wine Centre of
  Australia...................................................F5

## ◍ Activities, Courses & Tours
7 Adelaide Aquatic Centre.......................B1
8 Adelaide Gondola.....................................A5
9 Captain Jolley's Paddle
  Boats ...................................................... C5
10 Linear Park Hire ..................................... C5
11 Popeye ....................................................... C5

## 🛏 Sleeping
12 Adelaide Caravan Park...........................F3
13 Greenways Apartments.........................C3

14 Minima Hotel..............................................E2
15 O'Connell Inn............................................. C1
16 Princes Lodge Motel ..............................C2
17 Tynte Street Apartments......................C2

## 🍴 Eating
18 d'Artagnan.................................................C3
19 Good Life ...................................................C3
20 IGA North Adelaide ................................C2
21 Lion Hotel .................................................. E2
22 Royal Oak ..................................................C2
23 Store.............................................................E2

## 🍷 Drinking & Nightlife
24 Daniel O'Connell .....................................B2

## 🎭 Entertainment
25 Adelaide Festival Centre ......................C5
   Moonlight Cinema...........................(see 1)
26 Piccadilly Cinema ................................... C1

# ✗ East End

**★ Galaxy Lartay** CAFE $
(Map p56; 31 East Tce; mains $7-15; ⊙noon-4pm Tue-Sun; ☑) In a lovely old red-brick East End shopfront, our new favourite Adelaide cafe keeps sketchy opening hours – but don't let that stop you from wandering by to see if they're open. The vibe is arty, hippie, retro and communal: expect big servings of tarts, quiches, curries and pies, plus creative juices, lassis and solid coffee. And you can get a beer here too!

**Zen Kitchen** VIETNAMESE $
(Map p56; www.zenkitchen.com.au; Unit 7, Tenancy 2, Renaissance Arc; mains $6-14; ⊙11am-4pm Mon-Thu, to 8pm Fri, to 3pm Sat) Superb, freshly constructed cold rolls, *pho* soups and super-crunchy barbecue pork bread rolls, eat-in or take away. Wash it all down with a cold coconut milk or a teeth-grindingly strong Vietnamese coffee with sugary condensed milk. Authentic, affordable and absolutely delicious.

**Jasmin Indian Restaurant** INDIAN $$
(Map p56; ☑08-8223 7837; www.jasmin.com.au; 31 Hindmarsh Sq, basement; mains $26-29; ⊙noon-2.30pm Thu & Fri, 5.30-9pm Tue-Sat) Magical North Indian curries and consummately professional staff (they might remember your name from when you ate here in 2006). There's nothing too surprising about the

menu, but it's done to absolute perfection. Bookings essential.

**Botanic Café** ITALIAN $$
(Map p56; ☑08-8232 0626; www.botanicristorante. com; 4 East Tce; mains $25-40; ⊙noon-3pm Tue-Fri, 6pm-late Thu-Sat) Order from a seasonal menu of quality SA produce in this linen-crisp, modern Italian eatery opposite the Adelaide Botanic Gardens. Offerings might include goats-cheese tartlets with pear chutney, or pappardelle with braised lamb shank and thyme *ragu*. The tasting menu (two courses and a glass of wine for $25) is a steal. Great bar next door, too.

**Amalfi Pizzeria Ristorante** ITALIAN $$
(Map p56; ☑08-8223 1948; 29 Frome St; mains $16-26; ⊙noon-2.30pm Mon-Fri, 6-9pm Mon-Sat) What a classic! Authentic pizza and pasta with bentwood chairs, terrazzo floors, specials scribbled on a chalkboard, sleep-defeating coffee and imagined Mafioso mutterings in the back room.

**Sosta** ARGENTINEAN $$$
(Map p56; ☑08-8232 6799; www.sostaargen tiniankitchen.com.au; 291 Rundle St; tapas $16-26, mains $33-45; ⊙noon-2.30pm Mon-Fri, 6-9.30pm daily) Beef, lamb, pork, chicken, fish...vegetarians run for the hills! Sosta's aged 1kg T-bone steaks are legendary. With crisp white tablecloths and blood-brown floorboards, it's an elegant place to launch your nocturnal East End foray.

**Vego & Lovin' It**                    VEGETARIAN $
(Map p56; 240 Rundle St, Level 1; meals $7-13; ⊗10am-3pm Mon-Fri; 🖋) Get your weekly vitamin dose disguised in a scrumptious vegie burger, wrap or focaccia at this artsy upstairs kitchen. Dreadlocked urban renegades order 'extra alfalfa but no hummus'. Has the cool mosaic sign been fixed yet?

**Lemongrass Thai Bistro**                    THAI $$
(Map p56; 🖋08-8223 6627; www.lemongrassthai bistro.com.au; 289 Rundle St; mains $16-26; ⊗11.30am-3pm Mon-Fri, 5pm-late daily; 🖋) Affordable, breezy Thai joint right in the Rundle St mix. Mango and coconut chicken, red curry beef (or kangaroo!), clattering chairs and chilli chatter.

---

## 🍴 North Adelaide

**Store**                    CAFE, BISTRO $$
(Map p66; 🖋08-8361 6999; www.thestore.com.au; 157 Melbourne St; breakfast $8-19, mains $15-28; ⊗7am-3pm daily, 5.30-9pm Thu-Sun; 🖋) Some much-needed hipness in stuffy North Adelaide, Store is a combo of casual Parisian bistro and jazzy cafe. The decor is retro-kitsch (Art Nouveau posters, stag horns, Tretchikoff prints), while on your plate you can expect rapid-fire pastas, risottos, burgers and classy fish, chicken and beef dishes, none of which will break the bank. Impressive wine list, too.

**d'Artagnan**                    BISTRO $$$
(Map p66; 🖋08-8267 6688; www.dartagnan.net. au; 26 O'Connell St; mains $34-42; ⊗6pm-midnight Tue-Sat) Looking like a transplanted tavern from the era of King Louis XIII (all moody mirrors, velvet, dark wood, candles and chandeliers), d'Artagnan is bravely pushing the boundaries of the Adelaide dining experience (places you can eat after 9pm are almost unheard of). Expect meaty mains cooked with Franco flair. No sign of the other musketeers...

**Royal Oak**                    PUB $$
(Map p66; 🖋08-8267 2488; www.royaloakhotel. com.au; 123 O'Connell St; mains $12-34; ⊗8am-noon Sat & Sun, noon-3pm & 6-9.30pm daily) Winning pub grub at this enduring (and endearing) local: steak sangers, vegie lasagne, lamb-shank pie, eggs Florentine and French toast with maple syrup (not all at once). Quirky retro vibe; live jazz/indie-rock Tuesday, Wednesday, Friday and Sunday.

**Lion Hotel**                    PUB $$$
(Map p66; 🖋08-8367 0222; www.thelionhotel. com; 161 Melbourne St; mains $30-40; ⊗noon-3pm Mon-Fri & Sun, 6-10pm Mon-Sat) Off to one side of this upmarket boozer (all big screens, beer terraces and business types) is a sassy restaurant with a cool retro interior and romantic vibes. Hot off the menu are luscious Coorong Angus steaks, market fish and corn-fed chicken breasts, served with very un-pubby professionalism. Breakfast next door in the bar (mains $10 to $26).

---

## 🍴 Inner Suburbs

**Bar 9**                    CAFE $
(Map p70; 🖋08-8373 1108; www.bar9.com.au; 96 Glen Osmond Rd, Parkside; mains $11-17; ⊗7.30am-4pm Mon-Fri, 8.30am-2pm Sat & Sun) If you're serious about coffee, this bean barn – a short

---

### WEST END PUB GRUB

Wander the West End backstreets for some great-value pub food.

**Edinburgh Castle** (Map p56; 🖋08-8231 1435; www.edinburghcastlehotel.com; 233 Currie St; mains from $10; ⊗noon-2pm & 6-8pm Tue-Sun; 🖋) Super cheap $10 menu (the students love it) featuring schnitzels, burgers, vegie lasagne, and beer-battered whiting. Live original bands most nights.

**Prince Albert** (Map p56; 🖋08-8212 7912; www.princealberthotel.com.au; 254 Wright St; mains $10-20; ⊗noon-2.30pm & 6-8.30pm) Cheap pub grub that looms large: steaks, rissoles, burgers, hanging-off-the-plate schnitzels and signature West End sausages. Below-the-belt body piercings not a prerequisite.

**Hotel Wright Street** (Map p56; 🖋08-8211 8000; www.hotelwrightstreet.com.au; 88 Wright St; mains $17-28; ⊗8am-noon Sat & Sun, noon-3pm & 5.30-9pm daily) Mod-industrial renovations, cruising gay guys, makeup-caked cougars and kooky DJs. Oh yeah, and great fish and chips, steaks and schnitzels too.

hop southeast of the city centre – is for you. Food is almost secondary here: the hipster, cardigan-wearing customers are too busy discussing the coffee specials board to eat. But if you are hungry, Bar 9 does a mean bacon-and-eggs, vanilla bircher muesli and creamy mushrooms on toast.

**Earl of Leicester** PUB $$
(Map p70; ☑ 08-8271 5700; www.earl.com.au; 85 Leicester St, Parkside; mains $17-34; ☺ noon-3pm & 6-9pm) Hidden in the suburban Parkside backstreets is this atmospheric old blue-stone pub (1886), serving a winning combo of crafty beers and huge schnitzels. The

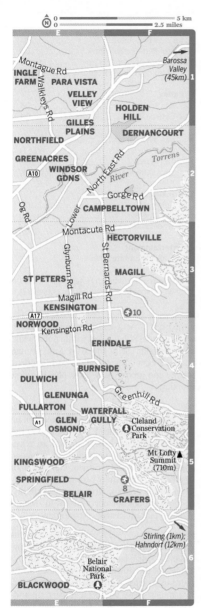

### Café de Vili's                                    FAST FOOD $

(Map p70; www.vilis.com; 2-14 Manchester St, Mile End Sth; meals $3-14; ⊕24hr) Vili's pies are a South Australian institution. Next to its factory, just west of the West End, is this all-night diner, serving equally iconic 'pie floaters' (a meat pie floating in pea soup, topped with mashed potato, gravy and sauce – outstanding!), plus sausage rolls, pasties, burgers, pancakes, cooked breakfasts, custard tarts, donuts...

## ✖ Glenelg

### Cafe Zest                                        CAFE $

(Map p70; ☑ 08-8295 3599; www.zestcafegallery. com.au; 2a Sussex St; meals $5-20; ⊕7.30am-5.30pm; 🗷) This cafe-gallery fills a tiny crack between buildings, but its laid-back vibe and brilliant breakfasts more than compensate for any shortcomings in size. Baguettes and bagels are crammed with creative combos, or you can banish your hangover with some 'Zesty Eggs': on buttered toast with seeded mustard, orange zest cream and smoked salmon. Great coffee, arty staff, and vegetarian specials too.

### Good Life                                      PIZZERIA $$

(Map p70; ☑ 08-8376 5900; www.goodlifepizza. com; cnr Jetty Rd & Moseley St, Level 1; pizzas $14-39; ⊕noon-2.30pm Tue-Fri & Sun, 6pm-late daily; 🗷) 🍃 At this brilliant organic pizzeria above the Jetty Rd tram-scape, thin crusts are stacked with tasty toppings like free-range roast duck, Spencer Gulf 'monster' prawns and spicy Angaston salami. *Ahhh,* life is good... Also has a branch in the city (Map p56; ☑ 08-8223 2618; 170 Hutt St; ⊕noon-2.30pm Mon-Fri, 6pm-late daily; 🗷) 🍃 and North Adelaide (Map p66; ☑ 08-8267 3431; Shop 5, 11 O'Connell St, North Adelaide; ⊕noon-2.30pm Tue-Fri, 6pm-late daily; 🗷) 🍃.

### Thuy-Linh                                    VIETNAMESE $$

(Map p70; ☑ 08-8295 5746; 168c Jetty Rd; mains $15-19, banquets per person from $24; ⊕11.30am-2.30pm Tue-Fri, 5-10pm Tue-Sun) Astonishingly unpretentious Vietnamese/Chinese eatery at the city end of Jetty Rd. Don't expect too much from the interior design – just super-attentive service and a swathe of fresh seafood, meat and noodle delights.

### Zucca Greek Mezze                                GREEK $$$

(Map p70; ☑ 08-8376 8222; www.zucca.com.au; Shop 5, Marina Pier, Holdfast Shores; mezze $5-21, mains $32-45; ⊕noon-3pm & 6pm-late) Spartan

'Liar's Bar' theme (focusing on the misdemeanours of Clinton, Skase, Bond et al) is a bit '90s, but it's what's on your plate/in your glass that counts.

# Greater Adelaide

linen, marina views, super service and a contemporary menu of tapas-style mezze plates – you wouldn't find anything this classy on Santorini. The grilled Cyprian haloumi with sweetened raisins and salty pistachio crumble are sublime.

### Self-Catering

**Central Market**                    MARKET $
(Map p56; www.adelaidecentralmarket.com.au; Gouger St; ⊙7am-5.30pm Tue, 9am-5.30pm Wed & Thu, 7am-9pm Fri, 7am-3pm Sat) This place is an exercise in sensory bombardment: a barrage of smells, colours and yodelling stallholders selling fresh vegetables, breads, cheeses, seafood and gourmet produce. There are cafes, hectic food courts and a supermarket here as well.

**IGA North Adelaide**          SUPERMARKET $
(Map p66; www.iga.net.au; 113 O'Connell St, North Adelaide; ⊙8am-10pm) Look for the nifty deli/butcher counter out the front.

**Woolworths**                SUPERMARKET $
(Map p56; www.woolworths.com.au; 80 Rundle Mall; ⊙7am-9pm Mon-Fri, 7am-5pm Sat, 11am-5pm Sun)

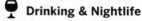

## 🍷 Drinking & Nightlife

### Pubs & Bars
For a true Adelaide experience, head for the bar and order a schooner of Coopers – the

local brew – or a glass of SA's impressive wine. Rundle St has a few iconic pubs, while along Hindley St in the West End, grunge and red-light sleaze collide with student energy and groovy bars. Most bars close on Monday.

**★Exeter**                          PUB
(Map p56; ☎08-8223 2623; www.theexeter.com.au; 246 Rundle St; ⊙11am-late) The best pub in the city, this legendary boozer attracts an eclectic mix of postwork, punk and uni drinkers, shaking the day off their backs. Pull up a stool or a table in the grungy beer garden and settle in for the evening. Original music nightly; no pokies. Book for curry nights in the upstairs restaurant (usually Wednesdays).

**Grace Emily**                      PUB
(Map p56; www.graceemilyhotel.com.au; 232 Waymouth St; ⊙4pm-late) Duking it out with the Exeter for the title of 'Adelaide's Best Pub' (it pains us to separate the two) the 'Gracie' has live music most nights, featuring up-and-coming Australian acts. Inside it's all kooky '50s-meets-voodoo decor, open fires and great beers. Regular cult cinema and open mic nights; no pokies. Look for the UFO on the roof.

**Wheatsheaf**                       PUB
(Map p70; www.wheatsheafhotel.com.au; 39 George St, Thebarton; ⊙11am-midnight Mon-Fri,

noon-midnight Sat, noon-9pm Sun; 🐾) A hidden gem under the flight path in industrial Thebarton, with an artsy crowd of students, jazz musos, lesbians, punks and rockers. Tidy beer garden, live music, open fires and rumours of a new kitchen opening soon. Great beer list.

**Cork Wine Cafe**                WINE BAR

(Map p56; www.facebook.com/corkwinecafe; 61a Gouger St; ⊙4pm-midnight Mon-Thu, 3pm-1am Fri & Sat, 4pm-10pm Sun; 🐾) A down-sized Frenchie hole-in-the-wall wine bar, unexpected among the fluoro-lit Chinese restaurants along this stretch of Gouger St. Well-worn floorboards, bentwood chairs, absinthe posters...perfect for a quick vino before dinner (see fluoro-lit Chinese restaurants, above).

**Udaberri**                BAR

(Map p56; www.udaberri.com.au; 11-13 Leigh St; ⊙4pm-late Tue-Thu, 3pm-late Fri, 6pm-late Sat) Taking a leaf out of the Melbourne book on laneway boozing, Udaberri is a little hole-in-the-wall bar on compact Leigh St, serving Spanish wines by the glass, a few good beers on tap and pintxos (Basque bar snacks) like oysters, cheeses, *jamon* and tortillas. Why aren't there more bars like this in Adelaide?

**Casablabla**                BAR

(Map p56; www.casablabla.com; 12 Leigh St; ⊙4pm-late Tue-Fri, 6pm-late Sat) Billing itself as a 'multicultural tapas lounge bar', Casablabla covers a lot of bases but does it well. The atmosphere is eclectic: exotic art (a bit of Morocco, a bit of Bali, a bit of Brazil), hookah pipes, fish tanks, burnt-orange walls... Sip cocktails in the middle of it all and tune in to reggae, funk, soul and jazz.

**Belgian Beer Café**                THEME BAR

(Map p56; www.oostende.com.au; 27-29 Ebenezer Pl; ⊙11am-midnight Sun-Thu, 11am-2am Fri & Sat) There's shiny brass, sexy staff, much presluicing of glasses and somewhere upwards of 26 imported Belgian superbrews (we lost count...). Order some *moules-frites* to go with your *weiss* beer. Off Rundle St.

**Apothecary 1878**                WINE BAR

(Map p56; www.theapothecary1878.com.au; 118 Hindley St; ⊙5pm-late Tue-Sat) Classy coffee and wine at this gorgeous chemist-turned-bar. Medicine cabinets, bentwood chairs and Parisian marble-topped tables. Perfect first-date territory.

**Colonist**                PUB

(Map p70; www.colonist.com.au; 44 The Parade, Norwood; ⊙9am-late) Funky countercultural boozing on Norwood's otherwise mainstream Parade. Wonderfully well-worn, and bedecked in Gustav Klimt–style murals. Packed after Norwood FC (Aussie Rules football) games empty out from the ground across the road.

**Universal Wine Bar**                WINE BAR

(Map p56; www.universalwinebar.com.au; 285 Rundle St; ⊙noon-late) A snappy crowd clocks in to this stalwart bar to select from 400-plus South Australian and international wines, and a menu (mains $19 to $36) packed with SA produce. 'The scene is very Italian', says the barman.

**Daniel O'Connell**                PUB

(Map p66; www.danieloconnell.com.au; 165 Tynte St, North Adelaide; ⊙11am-midnight) An 1881 Irish pub without a whiff of kitsch Celtic cash-in: just great Guinness, open fires, acoustic music and a house-sized pepper tree in the beer garden (166 years old and counting).

**Distill**                COCKTAIL BAR

(Map p56; www.distillhealth.com.au; 286 Rundle St; ⊙noon-2.30am Tue, Wed, Fri & Sun, 5pm-late Thu & Sat) Super-sassy Rundle St bar with a tight dress code (to the nines) and a kickin' organic cocktail list. Cheese boards and pizzas are available, but no-one here looks like they eat anything with any regularity.

**Pier One Bar**                BAR

(Map p70; www.glenelgpier.com.au; 18 Holdfast Promenade, Glenelg; ⊙noon-midnight Mon-Thu, noon-2am Fri, 11am-2am Sat & Sun) A cavernous mainstream sports bar with voyeuristic beach views and fold-back windows for when the sea breeze drops. As many screens as staff (a lot of each), and raucous Sunday sessions.

---

**ⓘ PINT OF COOPERS PLEASE!**

Things can get confusing at the bar in Adelaide. Aside from 200ml (7oz) 'butchers' – the choice of old men in dim, sticky-carpet pubs – there are three main beer sizes: 285ml (10oz) 'schooners' (pots or middies elsewhere in Australia), 425ml (15oz) 'pints' (schooners elsewhere) and 568ml (20oz) 'imperial pints' (traditional English pints). Now, go forth and order with confidence!

## Clubs

Online, check out www.onion.com.au. Cover charges can be anything from free to $15, depending on the night. Most clubs close Monday to Wednesday.

### Zhivago                                          CLUB
(Map p56; www.zhivago.com.au; 54 Currie St; ⊙9pm-late Fri-Sun) At the pick of the West End clubs (there are quite a few of 'em – some are a bit moron-prone), Zhivago's DJs pump out everything from reggae and dub to quality house. Popular with the 18 to 25 dawn patrol.

### RedLove                                         CLUB
(Map p56; www.redlove.com.au; Level 1, 170 Pulteney St; ⊙4pm-late Fri, 9pm-late Sat) This cool upstairs club used to be a pool hall (lots of elbow room). Spinning old-school RnB, funk and house to a 25-to-35 kinda crowd (old enough to remember the '90s, young enough not to have to hurry home to the babysitter).

### Lotus Lounge                                    CLUB
(Map p56; www.lotuslounge.net.au; 268 Morphett St; ⊙6pm-late Tue-Sat) We like the signage here – a very minimal fluoro martini glass with a flashing olive. Inside it's a glam lounge with cocktails, quality beers and Adelaide dolls cuttin' the rug. Expect queues around the corner on Saturday nights.

### HQ Complex                                      CLUB
(Map p56; www.hqcomplex.com.au; 1 North Tce; ⊙8pm-late Wed & Sat) Adelaide's biggest club fills five big rooms with shimmering sound and light. Night-time is the right time on Saturdays – the biggest (and trashiest) club night in town. Retro Wednesdays.

### Mars Bar                                        CLUB
(Map p56; www.themarsbar.com.au; 120 Gouger St; ⊙9pm-late Thu-Sat) The lynchpin of Adelaide's nocturnal gay and lesbian scene, always-busy Mars Bar features glitzy decor, flashy clientele and OTT drag shows.

## ☆ Entertainment

Artsy Adelaide has a rich cultural life that stacks up favourably with much larger cities. For big-ticket event bookings:

**BASS** (☎13 12 46; www.bass.net.au)

**Moshtix** (☎1300 438 849; www.moshtix.com.au)

**Venue Tix** (☎08-8225 8888; www.venuetix.com.au)

### Adelaide Now
(www.adelaidenow.com.au) City-wide events, cinema and gallery details.

### Adelaide Review
(www.adelaidereview.com.au) Theatre and gallery listings.

### Adelaide Theatre Guide
(www.theatreguide.com.au) Booking details, venues and reviews for comedy, drama and musicals.

### Music SA
(www.musicsa.com.au) All-genre online musical listings.

## Live Music

With serious musical pedigree (from Cold Chisel to Bon Scott and the Audreys), Adelaide knows how to kick out the jams! The free street-press papers *Rip It Up* (www.ripitup.com.au) and *dB* (www.dbmagazine.com.au) – available from record shops, pubs and cafes – have band and DJ listings and reviews. Cover charges vary with acts.

### ★ Governor Hindmarsh Hotel          LIVE MUSIC
(Map p70; www.thegov.com.au; 59 Port Rd, Hindmarsh; ⊙11am-late) Ground Zero for live music in Adelaide, 'The Gov' hosts some legendary local and international acts. The odd Irish band fiddles around in the bar, while the main venue features rock, folk, jazz, blues, salsa, reggae and dance. A huge place with an inexplicably personal vibe. Good food, too.

### Grace Emily                              LIVE MUSIC
(Map p56; www.graceemilyhotel.com.au; 232 Waymouth St) West End alt-rock, country and acoustic, plus open-mic nights. Are the Bastard Sons of Ruination playing tonight?

### Jive                                     LIVE MUSIC
(Map p56; www.jivevenue.com; 181 Hindley St; ⊙varies) In a converted theatre, Jive caters to an off-beat crowd of student types who like their tunes funky, left-field and removed from the mainstream. A sunken dance floor = great views from the bar!

### Wheatsheaf                               LIVE MUSIC
(Map p70; www.wheatsheafhotel.com.au; 39 George St, Thebarton; ⊙11am-midnight Mon-Fri, noon-midnight Sat, noon-9pm Sun) Eclectic offerings (acoustic, blues, country...and a brilliant beer list) in the semi-industrial Thebarton wastelands. Don't let the flightpath sonics put you off.

### Exeter
LIVE MUSIC

(Map p56; www.theexeter.com.au; 246 Rundle St; ☺11am-late) The East End's rockin' soul: original indie bands, electronica and acoustic in the undercover beer garden.

### Fowlers Live
LIVE MUSIC

(Map p56; www.fowlerslive.com.au; 68 North Tce; ☺varies) Inside the former Fowler Flour Factory, this 500-capacity venue is a devilish temple of hard rock, punk and metal.

### Jazz Adelaide
LIVE MUSIC

(www.jazz.adelaide.onau.net)       Finger-snappin' za-bah-dee-dah.

### Adelaide Symphony Orchestra
ORCHESTRA

(Map p56; www.aso.com.au) Online listings for the estimable ASO.

## Cinemas

Check out www.my247.com.au/adelaide/cinemas for movie listings. Tickets generally cost around adult/child $19/13 (cheaper on Tuesdays).

### Palace Nova Eastend Cinemas
CINEMA

(Map p56; ☐08-8232 3434; www.palacenova.com; 250 & 251 Rundle St; ☺10am-midnight) Facing-off across Rundle St, both these cinema complexes screen 'sophisticated cinema': new-release art-house, foreign-language and independent films as well as some mainstream flicks. Fully licensed, too.

### Moonlight Cinema
CINEMA

(Map p66; ☐1300 551 908; www.moonlight.com.au; Botanic Gardens; ☺mid-Dec–mid-Feb) In summer, pack a picnic and mosquito repellent, and spread out on the lawn to watch old and new classics under the stars. 'Gold Grass' tickets secure you a prime-viewing beanbag and cost a little more.

### Piccadilly Cinema
CINEMA

(Map p66; ☐08-8267 1500; www.wallis.com.au; 181 O'Connell St, North Adelaide) A beaut old art-deco cinema on the main North Adelaide strip, with a sexily curved street frontage and chevron-shaped windows spangled across the facade. It screens mostly mainstream releases.

### Mercury Cinema
CINEMA

(Map p56; ☐08-8410 0979; www.mercurycinema.org.au; 13 Morphett St, Lion Arts Centre) The Mercury screens art-house releases, and is home to the Adelaide Cinémathèque (classic, cult and experimental flicks).

## Theatre & Comedy

### Adelaide Festival Centre
PERFORMING ARTS

(Map p66; www.adelaidefestivalcentre.com.au; King William Rd; ☺varies) The hub of performing arts in SA, this crystalline white Festival Centre opened in June 1973, four proud months before the Sydney Opera House! The State Theatre Company (www.statetheatrecompany.com.au) is based here.

### Adelaide Entertainment Centre
CONCERT VENUE

(Map p70; www.theaec.net; 98 Port Rd, Hindmarsh; ☺varies) Around 12,000 bums on seats for everyone from the Wiggles to Stevie Wonder.

### Rhino Room
COMEDY

(Map p56; www.rhinoroom.com.au; 13 Frome St; ☺7.30pm-late Mon, Thu & Fri) Live stand-up acts from around Australia and overseas on Thursday and Friday nights, plus open-mic comedy on Mondays.

## Sport

As most Australian cities do, Adelaide hangs its hat on the successes of its sporting teams. In the Australian Football League (AFL; www.afl.com.au), the Adelaide Crows and Port Adelaide Power have sporadic success (and will be playing at the Adelaide Oval from 2014). Suburban Adelaide teams compete in the South Australian National Football League (SANFL; www.sanfl.com.au). The football season runs from March to September.

In the National Basketball League (NBL; www.nbl.com.au), the Adelaide 36ers have been a force for decades. In soccer's A League (www.a-league.com.au), Adelaide United are usually competitive. In summer, under the auspices of Cricket SA (www.cricketsa.com.au), the Redbacks play one-day and multiday state matches at the Adelaide Oval. The Redbacks re-brand as the Adelaide Strikers in the national T20 Big Bash (www.bigbash.com.au) competition.

## 🔒 Shopping

Shops and department stores (Myer, David Jones et al) line Rundle Mall. The beautiful old arcades running between the mall and Grenfell St retain their original splendour, and house eclectic little shops. Rundle St and the surrounding lanes are home to boutique and retro clothing shops.

### ★Title
BOOKS, MUSIC

(Map p56; www.titlespace.com; 2/15 Vaughan Pl; ☺10am-6pm Mon-Thu & Sat, 10am-9pm Fri, 11am-

5pm Sun) Lefty, arty and subversive in the best possible way, Title is the place to find that elusive Miles Davis disc or Charles Bukowski poetry compilation.

### Imprints Booksellers                    BOOKS
(Map p56; www.imprints.com.au; 107 Hindley St; ☺9am-6pm Mon & Tue, 9am-9pm Wed-Fri, 9am-5pm Sat, 11am-5pm Sun) The best bookshop in Adelaide in the worst location (in the thick of the Hindley St strip-club fray)? Jazz, floorboards, Persian rugs and occasional live readings and book launches.

### Midwest Trader          CLOTHING, ACCESSORIES
(Map p56; www.midwesttrader.com.au; Shop 1 & 2 Ebenezer Pl; ☺10am-6pm Mon-Thu & Sat, 10am-9pm Fri, noon-5pm Sun) Stocks a toothy range of punk, rock, skate and rockabilly gear. Its sister store Old Midwest (Map p56; www.midwesttrader.com.au/old-midwest; 7 Ebeneezer Pl; ☺10am-6pm Mon-Thu & Sat, 10am-9pm Fri, noon-5pm Sun) across the street sells awesome American vintage.

### Urban Cow Studio                    DESIGN
(Map p56; www.urbancow.com.au; 11 Frome St; ☺10am-6pm Mon-Thu, 10am-9pm Fri, 10am-5pm Sat, noon-5pm Sun) ✐ The catch cry here is 'Handmade in Adelaide' – a brilliant assortment of paintings, jewellery, glassware, ceramics and textiles, plus there's a gallery upstairs. Their 'Heaps Good' T-shirts are appropriately pro-SA on a hot summer's afternoon.

### Jurlique                          COSMETICS
(Map p56; www.jurlique.com.au; Shop 2Ga, 50 Rundle Mall Plaza, Rundle Mall; ☺9am-6pm Mon-Thu, 9am-9pm Fri, 9am-5pm Sat, 11am-5pm Sun) An international success story, SA's own Jurlique sells fragrant skincare products (some Rosewater Balancing Mist, anyone?) that are pricey but worth every cent.

### T'Arts                            DESIGN
(Map p56; www.tartscollective.com.au; 10g Gays Arcade, Adelaide Arcade, Rundle Mall; ☺10am-5pm Mon-Sat) ✐ Textiles, jewellery, bags, cards and canvasses from a 35-member local arts co-op. Meet the artists in-store.

### Map Shop                            MAPS
(Map p56; www.mapshop.net.au; 6-10 Peel St; ☺9.30am-5pm Mon-Fri, 9am-12.30pm Sat) Maps, charts and guides for walking, hiking and touring, plus GPS sales and advice.

# ℹ Information

## EMERGENCY
**Ambulance** (☎emergency 000, nonemergency 1300 881 700; www.saambulance.com.au)
**Fire** (☎emergency 000, nonemergency 08-8204 3600; www.mfs.sa.gov.au)
**Lifeline** (☎13 11 14; www.lifeline.org.au; ☺24hr) Crisis support.
**Police** (☎emergency 000, nonemergency 13 14 44; www.sapolice.sa.gov.au)
**RAA Emergency Roadside Assistance** (☎13 11 11; www.raa.net)

## INTERNET ACCESS
**Arena Internet Café** (264 Rundle St, Level 1; ☺11am-midnight Mon-Thu, 10am-late Fri-Sun)
**Internet Coffee** (53 Hindley St; ☺7am-8pm Mon-Fri, 8am-7pm Sat, open later Dec-Feb)

## MEDIA
Adelaide's daily tabloid is the parochial *Advertiser*, though the *Age*, *Australian* and *Financial Review* are also widely available.
**Adelaide Review** (www.adelaidereview.com.au) Highbrow articles, culture and arts. Free fortnightly.
**Blaze** (www.gaynewsnetwork.com.au) Gay-and-lesbian street press.
**dB** (www.dbmagazine.com.au) Local street press; loaded with music info.
**Rip it Up** (www.ripitup.com.au) Rival street press to dB; buckets of music info.

## MEDICAL SERVICES
**Emergency Dental Service** (☎08-8222 8222; www.sadental.sa.gov.au)
**Midnight Pharmacy** (13 West Tce; ☺7am-midnight Mon-Sat, 9am-midnight Sun)
**Royal Adelaide Hospital** (☎08-8222 4000; www.rah.sa.gov.au; 275 North Tce; ☺24hr) Emergency department (not for blisters!) and STD clinic.
**Women's & Children's Hospital** (☎08-8161 7000; www.cywhs.sa.gov.au; 72 King William Rd, North Adelaide; ☺24hr) Emergency and sexual-assault services.

## MONEY
**American Express** (www.americanexpress.com; Citi Centre Arcade, Rundle Mall; ☺9am-5pm Mon-Fri, to noon Sat) Foreign currency exchange.
**Travelex** (www.travelex.com.au; Beehive Corner, Rundle Mall; ☺9am-5.30pm Mon-Fri, to 5pm Sat) Foreign currency exchange.

## POST
**Adelaide General Post Office** (GPO; www.auspost.com.au; 141 King William St; ☺8.30am-5.30pm Mon-Fri)

**Post Office** (www.auspost.com.au; 61 North Tce; ◷9am-5pm Mon-Fri)

### TOURIST INFORMATION

The South Australian Visitor Information Centre (p53) is a valuable resource.

**Adelaide Visitor Information Centre Rundle Mall** (Map p56; ☑08-8203 7611; www.south australia.com; Rundle Mall; ◷10am-5pm Mon-Fri, 10am-4pm Sat & Sun) Adelaide-specific information, and free city-centre walking tours at 9.30am Monday to Friday. At the King William St end of the mall.

**Disability Information & Resource Centre** (DIRC; Map p56; ☑08-8236 0555, 1300 305 558; www.dircsa.org.au; 195 Gilles St; ◷9am-5pm Mon-Fri) Info on accommodation, venues and travel for people with disabilities.

**Women's Information Service** (Map p56; ☑08-8303 0590, 1800 188 158; www.wis.sa.gov.au; Ground Fl, 91-97 Grenfell St, Chesser House; ◷10am-4pm Mon, Tue, Thu & Fri)

## ❶ Getting There & Away

### AIR

**Adelaide Airport** (ADL; ☑08-8308 9211; www.aal.com.au; 1 James Schofield Dr, Adelaide Airport) is connected by regular flights to most Australian capitals and many regional centres. See Getting There & Around (p53) for airline info.

### BUS

**Adelaide Central Bus Station** (www.sa.gov.au; 85 Franklin St; ◷6am-9.30pm) has ticket offices and terminals for all major interstate and statewide services. See Getting There & Around (p54) for more info.

### CAR & MOTORCYCLE

The major international car-rental companies have offices at Adelaide Airport and in the city. Note that some companies don't allow vehicles to be taken to Kangaroo Island. Local operators include:

**Acacia Car Rentals** (www.acaciacarrentals.com.au; 91 Sir Donald Bradman Dr, Hilton; ◷8am-5pm Mon-Fri, 8am-noon Sat) Cheap rentals for travel within a 100km radius of Adelaide; scooter hire available.

**Access Rent-a-Car** (www.accessrentacar.com; 464 Port Rd, West Hindmarsh; ◷8am-6pm Mon-Fri, 8am-noon Sat & Sun) Kangaroo Island travel permitted.

**Cut Price Car & Truck Rentals** (www.cutprice.com.au; cnr Sir Donald Bradman Dr & South Rd, Mile End; ◷7.30am-5pm Mon-Fri, 8am-3pm Sat & Sun) 4WD hire available.

**Koala Car Rentals** (www.koalarentals.com.au; 41 Sir Donald Bradman Dr, Mile End; ◷7.30am-5pm Mon-Fri, 8am-3pm Sat & Sun)

### TRAIN

Adelaide's interstate train terminal is **Adelaide Parklands Terminal** (www.gsr.com.au; Railway Tce, Keswick; ◷6am-1.30pm Mon, Wed & Fri, 7am-6.30pm Tue, 9am-7pm Thu, 5.15-6.30pm Sat, 8.30am-7pm Sun), 1km southwest of the city centre. See Getting There & Around (p54) for details.

## ❶ Getting Around

### TO/FROM THE AIRPORT & TRAIN STATION

Pre-booked private **SkyLink** (☑1300 383 783; www.skylinkadelaide.com) minibuses connect the airport and the train station with the city (one-way $10; 6am to 11.30pm). Public Adelaide Metro JetBuses (p77) ply the same route ($3 to $5; 5am to 11pm).

Taxis charge around $25 into the city (15 minutes). Many hostels will pick you up and drop you off if you're staying with them.

### BICYCLE

With a valid passport or driver's licence you can borrow an 'Adelaide City Bike' (for free!) from **Bicycle SA** (☑08-8168 9999; www.bikesa.asn.au; 111 Franklin St; ◷9am-5pm). Helmet and lock provided.

Down at the beach, hire a bike from **Glenelg Bicycle Hire** (☑08-8376 1934; www.glenelgbicyclehire.com.au; 71 Broadway, Norfolk Motor Inn, Glenelg South; per day $40; ◷9am-5pm).

### PUBLIC TRANSPORT

**Adelaide Metro** (☑1300 311 108; www.adelaidemetro.com.au; cnr King William & Currie Sts; ◷8am-6pm Mon-Fri, 9am-5pm Sat, 11am-4pm Sun) provides timetables and sells tickets for Adelaide's integrated bus, train and tram network.

Tickets can also be purchased on board, at staffed train stations and in delis and news agents. Ticket types include day trip ($9.10), two-hour peak ($4.90) and two-hour off-peak ($3) tickets. Peak travel time is before 9am and after 3pm. Kids under five ride free!

### Bus

Adelaide's buses are clean and reliable. Most services start around 6am and run until midnight. Additional services:

**99C City Loop Bus** (www.adelaidemetro.com.au; ◷8.30am-9.30pm Mon-Fri, 9am-5.30pm Sat, 10am-5.30pm Sun) Adelaide Metro's free 99C City Loop Bus runs clockwise and anti-clockwise around the CBD fringe from Adelaide Train Station on North Tce, passing the Central Market en route. Every 20 minutes weekdays; every 30 minutes Friday night and weekends.

**Adelaide Connector Bus** (www.cityofadelaide.com.au; ◷8am-6pm Mon-Thu, 8am-9pm Fri, 10am-5pm Sat & Sun) Adelaide City Council runs this free service, looping around the CBD and North Adelaide. There are two hourly services – Blue and Red – plying the same route in opposite directions. Key stops include the Adelaide Zoo, Rundle Mall, Hutt St, Central Market, Hindley St, North Tce and O'Connell St.

**After Midnight Buses** (www.adelaidemetro. com.au; ☺midnight-5am Sat) Adelaide Metro's After Midnight buses run select standard routes but have an 'N' preceding the route number on their displays. Standard ticket prices apply.

### Train

Adelaide's hokey old diesel trains depart from **Adelaide Railway Station** (North Tce), plying five suburban routes (Belair, Gawler, Grange, Noarlunga and Outer Harbour). Trains generally run between 6am and midnight (some services start at 4.30am).

### Tram

Adelaide state-of-the-art trams rumble to/from Moseley Sq in Glenelg, through Victoria Sq in the city and along North Tce to the Adelaide Entertainment Centre. Trams run approximately every seven or eight minutes on weekdays (every 15 minutes on weekends) from 6am to midnight daily. Standard ticket prices apply, but the section between South Tce and the Adelaide Entertainment Centre is free.

### TAXI

**Adelaide Independent Taxis** (☎13 22 11, wheelchair-access cabs 1300 360 940; www. aitaxis.com.au)
**Adelaide Transport** (☎08-8212 1861; www. adelaidetransport.com.au) Minibus taxis for four or more people.
**Suburban Taxis** (☎13 10 08; www.suburban taxis.com.au)
**Yellow Cabs** (☎13 22 27; www.yellowcabgroup. com.au)

# ADELAIDE HILLS

When the Adelaide plains are desert-hot in the summer months, the Adelaide Hills (technically the Mt Lofty Ranges) are always a few degrees cooler, with crisp air, woodland shade and labyrinthine valleys. Early colonists built stately summer houses around Stirling and Aldgate, and German settlers escaping religious persecution also arrived, infusing towns such as Hahndorf and Lobethal with European values and architecture.

The Hills make a brilliant day trip from Adelaide: hop from town to town (all with at least one pub), passing carts of fresh produce for sale, stone cottages, olive groves and wineries along the way.

Online, go to www.visitadelaidehills.com. au, and www.adelaidehillswine.com.au for cellar-door listings.

## ❶ Getting There & Around

**Adelaide Metro** (www.adelaidemetro.com. au) runs buses between the city and most Hills towns. The 864 and 864F city–Mt Barker buses stop at Stirling, Aldgate and Hahndorf. The 823 runs from Crafers to Mt Lofty Summit and Cleland Wildlife Park; the 830F runs from the city to Oakbank, Woodside and Lobethal.

Alternatively, there are a few good Hills daytour options departing Adelaide (see p61).

# Hahndorf

POP 1810

Like the Rocks in Sydney, and Richmond near Hobart, Hahndorf is a 'ye olde worlde' colonial enclave that trades ruthlessly on its history: it's something of a kitsch parody of itself.

That said, Hahndorf is undeniably pretty, with Teutonic sandstone architecture, European trees, and flowers overflowing from half wine barrels. And it *is* interesting: Australia's oldest surviving German settlement (1839), founded by 50 Lutheran families fleeing religious persecution in Prussia. Hahndorf was placed under martial law during WWI, and its name changed to 'Ambleside' (renamed Hahndorf in 1935). It's also slowly becoming less kitsch and more cool: there are a few good cafes here now, and on a sunny day the main street is positively lively.

## ◉ Sights & Activities

**Hahndorf Academy
& Heritage Museum**                    MUSEUM
(www.hahndorfacademy.org.au; 68 Main St, Hahndorf; ☺10am-5pm; ♿) The 1857 building houses an art gallery with rotating exhibitions and original sketches by Sir Hans Heysen, the famed landscape artist and Hahndorf homeboy (ask about tours of his nearby former studio, The Cedars). The museum depicts the lives of early German settlers, with churchy paraphernalia, dour dresses and farm equipment. The Adelaide Hills Visitor Information Centre (p80) is here too.

**Hahndorf Walking Tours**          WALKING TOUR
(☎0477 288 011; hahndorfwalkingtours@gmail. com; per person from $10; ☺10am Sat & 2pm Sun,

# Adelaide Hills

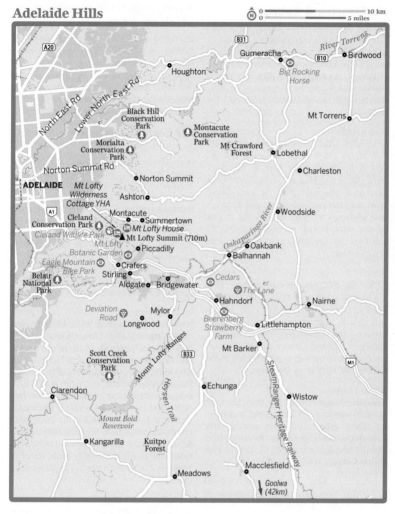

extra tours Oct-Apr) Departing the Hahndorf Academy, these 90-minute, 2km history-soaked walks are a great way to get a feel for the old town. Bookings essential.

**The Lane** WINERY
(☎08-8388 1250; www.thelane.com.au; Ravenswood Lane, Hahndorf; ⊙10am-4pm Mon-Thu, 10am-5pm Fri-Sun) Wow! What a cool building, and what a setting! Camera-conducive views and contemporary varietals (viognier,

pinot grigio, pinot gris), plus an outstanding restaurant (book for lunch).

**Beerenberg Strawberry Farm** STRAWBERRY FARM
(☎08-8388 7272; www.beerenberg.com.au; Mount Barker Rd, Hahndorf; strawberry picking per adult/child $3/free, strawberries per kg from $9.50; ⊙9am-5pm, last entry 4.15pm) Pick your own strawberries between November and May from this famous, family-run farm, also big-noted for its plethora of jams, chutneys and sauces.

## 🛏 Sleeping & Eating

Hit the **German Arms Hotel** (☑ 08-8388 7013; www.germanarmshotel.com.au; 69 Main St; mains $16-29; ⊙ 8.30am-9pm) or **Hahndorf Inn** (☑ 08-8388 7063; www.hahndorfinn.com.au; 35 Main St; mains $17-32; ⊙ 11am-9pm Mon-Fri, 8am-9pm Sat & Sun) for German-style brat-wursts, schnitzels and strudels. See also The Lane (p79).

**Rockbare Retreat**                    APARTMENT $$$
(☑ 08-8388 7155; www.rockbare.com.au; 102 Main St; per 2/4/8 people $400/400/520; ❄) Behind Rockbare cellar door is this reno-vated former-restaurant – brilliant value for groups. Sleeping eight, the stone-walled apartment has two bathrooms and an indus-trial kitchen, and is all decked out in chic urbane colours with exposed timbers, ab-stract art and breakfast provisions for your first morning.

**Manna**                                  MOTEL $$
(☑ 08-8388 1000; www.themanna.com.au; 25 & 35a Main St; d without/with spa from $160/220, 2-bedroom apt from $220; ❄ 🛜 🐾) The Manna is a stylish, contemporary maze of motel suites on the main street, spread over two addresses. The older (more affordable) units occupy a refurbished, exposed-brick motel complex set back from the street.

**Udder Delights**                          CAFE $
(www.udderdelights.com.au; 91a Main St; meals $11-18; ⊙ 9am-5pm; 🍴) This udderly delight-ful cheese cellar/cafe serves salads, tarts, pies, soups, cakes, generous cheese platters and the best coffee this side of Stirling. Free cheese tastings, too.

**Haus**                          CAFE, WINE BAR $$
(☑ 08-8388 7555; www.haushahndorf.com.au; 38 Main St; breakfast & lunch mains $13-28, dinner $25-33; ⊙ 7.30am-11pm) Haus brings some ur-ban hip to the Hills. Rustic-style pizzas are laden with local smallgoods, and the wine list is huge (lots of Hills drops). Also on of-fer are baguettes, pasta, burgers, salads and quiches. Good coffee, too.

## ❶ Information

**Adelaide Hills Visitor Information Centre**
(☑ 08-8388 1185, 1800 353 323; www.visit adelaidehills.com.au; 68 Main St; ⊙ 9am-5pm Mon-Fri, 10am-4pm Sat & Sun) The usual barrage of brochures, plus accommodation bookings and internet access. Pick up its *Short Winery Trail* map if you're thirsty.

# Stirling Area

The photogenic little villages of old-school Stirling (population 2870) and one-horse Aldgate (population 3350) are famed for their bedazzling autumn colours, thanks to the deciduous trees the early residents saw fit to seed. Oddly, Aldgate has also been home to both Bon Scott and Mel Gibson over the years.

## ◉ Sights & Activities

**Cleland Wildlife Park**                    ZOO
(www.clelandwildlifepark.sa.gov.au; 365 Mt Lofty Summit Rd, Crafers; adult/child/family $20/10/50; ⊙ 9.30am-5pm, last entry 4.30pm) Within the steep **Cleland Conservation Park** (www.en vironment.sa.gov.au; ⊙ 24hr), this place lets you interact with all kinds of Australian beasts. There are keeper talks and feeding sessions throughout the day, and you can have your mugshot taken with a koala ($30, 2pm to 4pm). There's a cafe here too. From the city, take bus 864 or 864F from Grenfell St to Crafers for connecting bus 823 to the park.

**Mt Lofty Summit**                    LOOKOUT
(www.environment.sa.gov.au/parks; Mt Lofty Sum-mit Rd, Crafers; ⊙ 24hr) From Cleland Wildlife Park you can bushwalk (2km) or drive up to Mt Lofty Summit (a surprising 710m), which has views across Adelaide. **Mt Lofty Summit Visitor Information Centre** (☑ 08-8370 1054; www.mtloftysummit.com; ⊙ 9am-5pm) has info on local attractions and **walking tracks**, in-cluding the steep Waterfall Gully Track (8km return, 2½ hours) and Mt Lofty Botanic Gar-dens Loop Trail (7km loop, two hours). The video of the Ash Wednesday bushfires of 16 February 1983 is harrowing. There's a snazzy cafe here.

**Mt Lofty Botanic Garden**              GARDENS
(www.botanicgardens.sa.gov.au; gates on Mawson Dr & Lampert Rd, Crafers; ⊙ 8.30am-4pm Mon-Fri, 10am-5pm Sat & Sun) 𝐅𝐑𝐄𝐄 From Mt Lofty, truck south 1.5km to the cool-climate slopes of the botanic garden. Nature trails wind past a lake, exotic temperate plants, native stringybark forest and bodacious rhododendron blooms. Free guided walks depart the Lampert Rd car park at 10.30am on Thursdays from Septem-ber to October and March to May.

**Deviation Road**                          WINERY
(www.deviationroad.com; 214 Scott Creek Rd, Long-wood; ⊙ 10am-5pm) Nothing deviant about the wines here: sublime pinot noir, substan-tial shiraz, zingy pinot gris and a very decent

bubbly, too. Grab a cheese platter and wind down in the afternoon in the sun.

**Stirling Markets** MARKET
(www.stirlingmarket.com.au; Druids Ave, Stirling; ⊙10am-4pm 4th Sun of the month) This lively market takes over oak-lined Druids Ave in Stirling: much plant-life, busking, pies, cakes and Hills knick-knackery (not many druids...).

## 🛏 Sleeping & Eating

**Mt Lofty House** HISTORIC HOTEL $$$
(⊘08-8339 6777; www.mtloftyhouse.com.au; 74 Summit Rd, Crafers; d from $229; 🏵🐾🌊) Proprietarily poised above Mt Lofty Botanic Garden (*awesome* views), this 1850s baronial mansion has lavish heritage rooms and garden suites, plus an upmarket restaurant (also with killer views). The perfect honeymooner or dirty weekender.

**Mt Lofty Wilderness Cottage YHA** CABIN $$
(⊘08-8414 3000; www.yha.com.au; Mt Lofty Summit Rd, Crafers; per night $140) A short detour off the road on the steep flanks of Mt Lofty, this 1880 stone cottage was originally a shepherd's hut. Today it's a basic, self-contained, two-bedroom cabin sleeping eight, with peek-a-boo views of Adelaide through the eucalypts. Minuimun two-night stay.

⭐**Stirling Hotel** PUB, BOUTIQUE HOTEL $$
(⊘08-8339 2345; www.stirlinghotel.com.au; 52 Mt Barker Rd, Stirling; mains $16-38; ⊙noon-3pm & 6-9pm Mon-Fri, 8am-9pm Sat & Sun) The owners spent so much money tarting up this gorgeous old dame, it's a wonder they can pay the staff. A runaway success, the free-flowing bistro (classy pub grub) and romantic restaurant (upmarket regional cuisine) are always packed.

Upstairs are five elegant, contemporary suites (doubles from $220), three of which have open fireplaces (for winter) and breezy balconies (for summer). All have flat-screen TVs, quality linen and luxe bathrooms you'll actually want to spend time in.

**Organic Market & Café** CAFE $
(www.organicmarket.com.au; 5 Druids Ave, Stirling; meals $8-18; ⊙8.30am-5pm; 🐾) 🌿 Rejecting Stirling's pompous tendencies, hirsute Hills types flock to this vibrant, hippie cafe. It's the busiest spot in town – and rightly so. The food's delicious and everything's made with love. Gorge on bruschetta, plump savoury muffins, great coffee and wicked Portuguese custard tarts.

# Oakbank & Woodside

Strung-out Oakbank (population 450), lives for the annual **Oakbank Easter Racing Carnival** (www.oakbankracingclub.com.au), said to be the greatest picnic race meeting in the world. It's a two-day festival of equine splendour, risqué dresses and 18-year-olds who can't hold their liquor.

Agricultural Woodside (population 1830) has a few enticements for galloping gourmands. **Woodside Cheese Wrights** (www.woodsidecheese.com.au; 22 Henry St, Woodside; tastings free, cheeses from $4; ⊙10am-4pm) is a passionate and unpretentious gem producing classic, artisan and experimental cheeses (soft styles a speciality) from locally grazing sheep and cows. Stock up on rocky road, scorched almonds and appallingly realistic chocolate cow pats at **Melba's Chocolate & Confectionery Factory** (www.melbaschocolates.com; 22 Henry St, Woodside; tastings free, chocolates from $2; ⊙9am-4.30pm).

# Gumeracha, Birdwood & Lobethal

A scenic drive from Adelaide to Birdwood leads through the Torrens River Gorge to Gumeracha (population 400), a hardy hillside town with a pub at the bottom (making it hard to roll home). The main lure here is climbing the 18.3m-high **Big Rocking Horse** (www.thetoyfactory.com.au; Birdwood Rd, Gumeracha; admission $2; ⊙9am-5pm), which doesn't actually rock, but is unusually tasteful as far as Australia's 'big' tourist attractions go.

Behind an impressive 1852 flour mill in Birdwood (population 1130), the **National Motor Museum** (⊘08-8568 4000; www.history.sa.gov.au; Shannon St, Birdwood; adult/child/family $12/5/30; ⊙9am-5pm) has a collection of immaculate vintage and classic cars (check out the DeLorean!) and motorcycles. The museum marks the finishing line for September's **Bay to Birdwood** (www.baytobirdwood.com.au): a convoy of classic cars chugging up from the city.

Nearby is Lobethal (population 1660), established by Lutheran Pastor Fritzsche and his followers in 1842. Like Hahndorf, Lobethal was renamed during WWI and 'Tweedale' was the rather unfortunate choice. It hits its straps during the **Lights of Lobethal** (www.lightsoflobethal.com.au) Christmas festival in December. Repair to the Lobethal Bierhaus (🖂 08-8389 5570; www.bierhaus.com.au; 3a Main St, Lobethal; ⊙noon-10pm Fri & Sat, noon-6pm Sun) for some serious microbrewed concoctions.

# FLEURIEU PENINSULA

Patterned with vineyards, olive groves and almond plantations running down to the sea, the Fleurieu (pronounced *floo*-ree-oh) is Adelaide's weekend playground. The McLaren Vale Wine Region is booming, producing gutsy reds (salubrious shiraz) to rival those from the Barossa Valley (actually, we think McLaren Vale wins hands down). Further east, the Fleurieu's Encounter Coast is an engaging mix of surf beaches, historic towns and whales cavorting offshore.

Online, see www.fleurieupeninsula.com.au.

# McLaren Vale

POP 2910

Flanked by the wheat-coloured Willunga Scarp and encircled by vines, McLaren Vale is just 40 minutes south of Adelaide. Servicing the wine industry, it's an energetic, utilitarian town that's not much to look at, but has some great eateries.

## ◉ Sights & Activities

Most people come to McLaren Vale to cruise the wineries. You could spend days doing nothing else!

It seems like most of Adelaide gets tizzied-up and buses down to the annual Sea & Vines Festival (www.southaustralia.com/info.aspx?id=9001064) over the June long weekend. Local wineries cook up seafood, splash wine around and host live bands.

Shiraz Trail                                    CYCLING
An up-tempo way to get the McLaren Vale vibe is to explore this 8km walking/cycling track, running along an old railway line between McLaren Vale and Willunga. Hire a bike from Oxygen Cycles (🖂 08-8323 7345; www.oxygencycles.com; 143 Main Rd; bike hire per half/full day $15/40; ⊙10am-6pm Tue-Fri, 9am-5pm Sat, 11am-4pm Sun); ask the visitor information centre for a map.

## ☞ Tours

You can also organise McLaren Vale tours departing Adelaide (see p61).

Bums on Seats                              GUIDED TOUR
(🖂 0438 808 253; www.bumsonseats.com.au; per person from $75) McLaren Vale and Fleurieu day tours for small groups.

Chook's Little Winery Tours      GUIDED TOUR
(🖂 0414 922 200; www.chookslittlewinerytours.com.au; per person from $90) Small-group tours visiting some of the lesser-known boutique McLaren Vale wineries.

McLaren Vale Tours                      GUIDED TOUR
(🖂 0414 784 666; www.mclarenvaletours.com.au) Customised, locally-run tours around McLaren Vale and the Fleurieu; call for prices.

---

**WORTH A TRIP**

### CURRENCY CREEK & LANGHORNE CREEK WINERIES

Once slated as the capital of SA, Currency Creek, 10km north of Goolwa, is now content with producing award-winning wines. Currency Creek Winery (🖂 08-8555 4069; www.currencycreekwinery.com.au; Winery Rd, Currency Creek; ⊙10am-5pm) has 160 acres under vine (brilliant cabernet sauvignon) plus a fab restaurant (mains $18 to $32, open noon to 3pm Thursday to Sunday and 6pm to 9pm Friday and Saturday). Bookings advised.

Further north, 16km east of Strathalbyn, Langhorne Creek is one of Australia's oldest wine-growing regions (www.langhornewine.com.au), producing shiraz, cabernet sauvignon and chardonnay. A couple of the 20-plus wineries here:

➡ Bleasdale Winery (www.bleasdale.com.au; Wellington Rd, Langhorne Creek; ⊙10am-5pm) The district's first winery, with a large range, historic cellars and an old redgum lever press.

➡ Bremerton (www.bremerton.com.au; Strathalbyn Rd, Langhorne Creek; ⊙10am-5pm) Run by two sisters, Bremerton is an innovative operator in an old-school region. Top chardonnay and shiraz.

# Fleurieu Peninsula

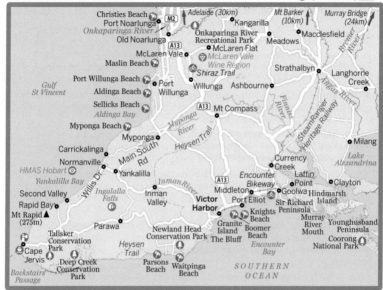

**Wine Diva Tours** GUIDED TOUR
(☑ 08-8323 9806; www.winedivatours.com.au; per person from $150) Upmarket half- or full-day wine tours in Mercedes-driven comfort.

## 🛏 Sleeping & Eating

You can also eat at some of McLaren Vale's cellar doors; see the McLaren Vale Wineries boxed text (p84).

**Red Poles** B&B $$
(☑ 08-8323 8994; www.redpoles.com.au; 190 McMurtrie Rd; d without/with bathroom $115/125; ❄🛜) Nooked away in a bushy enclave, eccentric Red Poles is a great place to stay (and eat!). Aim for the rustic en-suite room – it's bigger than its two counterparts. Order up a saltbush lamb salad (mains $27 to $33, serving noon to 3pm Wednesday to Friday, from 9.30am Saturday and Sunday), and check out some local artwork while you wait. Live music Sunday afternoons.

**McLaren Vale**
**Lakeside Caravan Park** CARAVAN PARK $
(☑ 08-8323 9255; www.mclarenvale.net; 48 Field St; unpowered/powered/en-suite sites $29/34/44, cabins $115-135; ❄🛜) A short walk from town, this park by an artificial lake (any water this summer?) is as affordable as McLaren Vale accommodation gets. There's a camp kitch-

en, pool, spa, tennis court and trashy book exchange. Good winter rates. The Shiraz Trail runs right past.

**McLaren Vale**
**Motel & Apartments** MOTEL, APARTMENT $$
(☑ 08-8323 8265, 1800 631 817; www.mclaren valemotel.com.au; cnr Main Rd & Caffrey St; s/d/f/apt from $120/145/150/250; ❄@🛜🏊) A digestive walk from main-street restaurants, this cheery motel has been around since the '80s but is still in good shape. There are solid doubles, new studio apartments and family suites, plus a pool fringed by scruffy-looking palms.

**Vale Inn** MODERN AUSTRALIAN $$
(☑ 08-8323 8769; www.mvbeer.com; 190 McMurtrie Rd; mains $16-28; ☉10am-6pm Mon, Thu & Sun, 10am-9pm Fri & Sat) This old vine-covered inn has been reborn as a beery bar/bistro. McLaren Vale Beer Co is based here: don't leave without trying its much-awarded Vale Ale, or the meaty Vale Dark or smooth Vale IPA. Food-wise it's zingy pizzas (try the duck, Spanish onion and brie), curries, steaks and seafood.

**Blessed Cheese** CAFE $
(www.blessedcheese.com.au; 150 Main Rd; mains $7-21; ☉8am-4.30pm Mon-Thu, 8am-5pm Fri-

**DON'T MISS**

## MCLAREN VALE WINERIES

If the Barossa Valley is SA wine's old-school, then McLaren Vale is the upstart teenager smoking cigarettes behind the shed and stealing nips from dad's port bottle. The gorgeous vineyards around here have a Tuscan haze in summer, rippling down to a calm coastline that's similarly Ligurian. This is shiraz country – solid, punchy and seriously good.

**Alpha Box & Dice** (www.alphaboxdice.com.au; Lot 50 Olivers Rd; ☺10am-5pm Fri-Sun) One out of the box, this refreshing little gambler wins top billing for interesting blends, funky retro furnishings, quirky labels and laid-back staff.

**Coriole** (www.coriole.com; Chaffeys Rd; ☺10am-5pm Mon-Fri, 11am-5pm Sat & Sun) Take your regional tasting platter out into the garden of this beautiful cottage cellar door (1860), made lovelier by a swill of Redstone shiraz or flagship chenin blanc.

**d'Arenberg** (☎08-8329 4888; www.darenberg.com.au; Osborn Rd; ☺10am-5pm) 'd'Arry's' relaxes atop a hillside and enjoys fine views. The wine labels are part of the character of this place: the Dead Arm shiraz and the Broken Fishplate sauvignon blanc are our faves. Book for lunch.

**Wirra Wirra** (www.wirrawirra.com; McMurtrie Rd; ☺10am-5pm Mon-Sat, 11am-5pm Sun) This barnlike 1894 cellar door has a grassy picnic area, and there's a roaring fire inside in winter. Sample reasonably priced stickies (dessert wines) and the popular Church Block red blend.

**Chapel Hill** (www.chapelhillwine.com.au; 1 Chapel Hill Rd; ☺11am-5pm) At the top of the hill is this restored 1865 chapel with panoramic vineyard and ocean views. The Vicar shiraz will banish your piety.

Sun) This blessed cafe cranks out great coffee, croissants, wraps, salads, tarts, burgers, cheese platters, murderous cakes and funky sausage rolls. The menu changes every couple of days, always with an emphasis on local produce. The aromas emanating from the cheese counter are deliciously stinky.

**Barn**　　　　　MODERN AUSTRALIAN $$
(☎08-8323 8618; www.thebarnbistro.com.au; tapas $6-16, mains $26-36) Retro-mod prints and furniture adorn this 1840s cottage bistro, which quadruples-up as a cellar door, art gallery and wine bar. Mains are fishy and meaty, done with contemporary flair, or settle in for some tapas and a glass or two of good local stuff.

## ☆ Entertainment

**Black Cockatoo Arthouse**　CINEMA, LIVE MUSIC
(☎08-8323 9294; www.blackcockatooarthouse. blogspot.com; 1 Park St; admission free-$15; ☺varies) In a nondescript warehouse behind the police station, Black Cockatoo Arthouse is an independent, nonprofit art space with cinema, live music, DJs and exhibitions.

## ❶ Information

**McLaren Vale & Fleurieu Visitor Information Centre** (☎08-8323 9944; www.mclarenvale. info; 796 Main Rd; ☺9am-5pm Mon-Fri, 10am-4pm Sat & Sun) At the northern end of McLaren Vale. Winery info, plus accommodation assistance and Sealink bus/ferry bookings for Kangaroo Island.

## ❶ Getting There & Away

Regular **Adelaide Metro** (www.adelaidemetro. com.au) suburban trains run between Adelaide and Noarlunga (one hour). From here, buses 751 and 753 run to McLaren Vale and Willunga (45 minutes). Regular Adelaide Metro ticket prices apply.

## Willunga

POP 2260

A one-horse town with three pubs (a winning combo!), artsy Willunga took off in 1840 when high-quality slate was discovered nearby and exported across Australia. Today, the town's early buildings along sloping High St are occupied by gourmet eateries and galleries. The Kidman Trail (p54) kicks off here.

## ⊙ Sights & Activities

**Willunga Farmers Market**  MARKET
(www.willungafarmersmarket.com; Willunga Town Sq; ⊙8am-12.30pm Sat) Heavy on the organic, the bespoke and the locally-sourced, Willunga Farmers Market is on Saturday mornings on the corner of High St and Main Rd.

**Willunga Slate Museum**  MUSEUM
(www.nationaltrust.org.au/sa/willunga-slatemuseum; 61 High St; adult/child $5/free; ⊙1-4pm Tue, Sat & Sun) At the top end of Willunga's ascending high street is this cluster of old stone buildings, which at various times have housed a police station, a courthouse, a prison and a boys school. These days the emphasis is on Willunga's slate-mining history and the Cornish miners who did all the dirty work.

## 🛏 Sleeping & Eating

**Willunga House B&B**  B&B $$$
(☎08-8556 2467; www.willungahouse.com.au; 1 St Peters Tce; d incl breakfast $210-280; ✱ 🖲 ≋) If you're looking for a real treat, this graceful, two-storey 1850 mansion off the main street is for you: Baltic-pine floorboards, Italian cherry-wood beds, open fires, indigenous art and a swimming pool. Breakfast is a feast of organic muesli, fruit salad and poached pears, followed by cooked delights.

**Russell's Pizza**  PIZZA $$
(☎08-8556 2571; 13 High St; pizzas from $24; ⊙6-9pm Fri & Sat) It may look like a ramshackle chicken coop, but Russell's is the place to be on weekends for sensational wood-fired pizza. No-one minds the wait for a meal (which could be an hour) – it's all about the atmosphere. It's super popular, so book way ahead.

**Fino**  MODERN AUSTRALIAN $$
(☎08-8556 4488; www.fino.net.au; 8 Hill St; mains $18-48; ⊙noon-3pm Tue-Sun, 6.30-9pm Fri & Sat) A regular on 'Australia's Top 100 Restaurants' lists and with a cabinet full of regional awards for both food and wine, Fino is fine indeed. It's a low-key conversion of a slate-floored stone cottage, with a small, simple menu of small, simple dishes, sourced locally as much as possible. The Berkshire pork shoulder with coleslaw is a winner.

## ℹ Information

**Willunga Environment Centre** (☎08-8556 4188; www.willungaenviro.org.au; 18 High St; ⊙10am-3pm Mon-Fri, 9am-1pm Sat) Basic tourist info and details on local flora and fauna.

# Gulf St Vincent Beaches

There are some ace swimming beaches (but no surf) along the Gulf St Vincent coastline, extending from suburban **Christies Beach** onto **Maslin Beach**, the southern end of which is a nudist and a gay hang-out. Maslin is 45 minutes from Adelaide by car – just far enough to escape the sprawling shopping centres and new housing developments trickling south from the city.

**Port Willunga** is home to the eternally busy, cliff-top seafood shack the **Star of Greece** (☎08-8557 7420; www.starofgreececafe.com.au; 1 The Esplanade, Port Willunga; mains $28-34; ⊙noon-3pm Wed-Sun, 5.30pm-9pm Fri & Sat), named after a shipwreck: funky decor, great staff and a sunny outdoor patio. We asked the waiter where the whiting was caught: he looked out across the bay and said, 'See that boat out there?'. There's a takeaway kiosk too (snacks $5 to $10, open 10am to 3pm).

On the highway above **Sellicks Beach** is a classily renovated 1858 pub, the **Victory Hotel** (☎08-8556 3083; www.victoryhotel.com.au; Main South Rd, Sellicks Beach; mains $17-34; ⊙noon-3pm & 6-9pm). There are awesome views of the silvery gulf, a cheery, laid-back vibe and a beaut beer garden. Factor in inspired meals, an impressive cellar and wines by the glass and you'll be feeling victorious. Three B&B cabins too (doubles from $150).

Keep on trucking south to cute little **Yankalilla**, which has the regional **Yankalilla Bay Visitor Information Centre** (☎08-8558 0240; www.yankalilla.sa.gov.au; 163 Main South Rd, Yankalilla; ⊙9am-5pm Mon-Fri, 10am-4pm Sat & Sun). There's a small local history **museum** (adult/child $3/1) out the back (look for the radar antenna from the scuttled *HMAS Hobart*, now a nearby dive site offshore). Also in 'Yank' is quirky **Lilla's Cafe** (☎08-8558 2525; www.lillascafe.com.au; 163 Main South Rd, Yankalilla; mains $15-25; ⊙8.30am-4pm Sun-Tue & Thu, 8.30am-9pm Fri & Sat) – perfect for coffee and cake or generous wood-fired pizzas on Friday and Saturday nights. Jenny the donkey will finish off anything you can't eat.

About 60km south of Adelaide is **Carrickalinga**, which has a gorgeous arc of white sandy beach: it's a very chilled spot with no shops. For supplies and accommodation, head to neighbouring **Normanville**, which has a rambling pub, a supermarket, a couple of caravan parks and the **Jetty Food Store** (☎08-8558 2537; www.jettyfoodstore.com; 48a Main Rd; meals $8-16; ⊙7.30am-5.30pm). The motto here is 'Coastal food hunted and gathered for you'. Grab an organic coffee, a dozen Kangaroo Island oysters, some locally caught fish and chips, or raid the fridge for gourmet cheeses, dips and olives. About 10km out of Normanville along Hay Flat Rd are the picturesque little Ingalalla Falls (follow the signs from the Yankalilla side of town).

There's not much at Cape Jervis, 107km from Adelaide, other than the Kangaroo Island ferry terminal, and the start point for the Heysen Trail (p54). Nearby, Deep Creek Conservation Park (www.environment.sa.gov.au; per car $10) has sweeping coastal views, a wicked waterfall, man-size yakkas *(Xanthorrhoea semiplana tateana)*, sandy beaches, kangaroos, kookaburras and bush camping areas (per car from $13).

Off the road to Deep Creek Conservation Park are the curved roofs of the superb Ridgetop Retreats (☑08-8598 4169; www.southernoceanretreats.com.au; d $245): three corrugated-iron-clad, self-contained luxury units in the bush, with wood heaters, leather lounges and stainless-steel benchtops.

# Victor Harbor

POP 11,500

The biggest town on the Encounter Coast is Victor Harbor (yes, that's the correct spelling: blame one of SA's poorly schooled early Surveyor Generals). It's a raggedy, brawling holiday destination with three huge pubs and migrating whales offshore. In November the grassy foreshore runs rampant with teenage school-leavers blowing off hormones at the Schoolies Festival (www.schooliesfestival.com.au).

## ◉ Sights & Activities

South Australian Whale Centre     MUSEUM
(☑08-8551 0750; www.sawhalecentre.com; 2 Railway Tce; adult/child/family $8/4/20; ⊙10.30am-5pm) Victor Harbor is on the migratory path of southern right whales (May to October). The multilevel South Australian Whale Centre has impressive whale displays (including a big stinky skull) and can give you the low-down on where to see them. Not whale season? Check out the big mammals in the new 3D-cinema.

Horse-drawn Tram     TRAM
(www.horsedrawntram.com.au; return adult/child/family $8/6/22; ⊙hourly 10am-4pm) Just offshore is the boulder-strewn Granite Island,

connected to the mainland by a 632m causeway built in 1875. You can walk to the island, but it's more fun to take the 1894 double-decker tram pulled by a big clydesdale. Tickets available from the driver or visitor information centre.

Encounter Bikeway     CYCLING
(www.tourismvictorharbor.com.au/walks_trails.html) The much-wheeled Encounter Bikeway extends 30km from Victor Harbor to Laffin Point beyond Goolwa. The visitors centre stocks maps; hire a bike from Victor Harbor Cycle Skate Bay Rubber (☑08-8552 1417; www.victorharborcycles.com; 73 Victoria St; bike hire per 4/8 hr $30/40; ⊙9am-5pm Mon & Wed-Fri, 10am-3pm Sat & Sun).

Big Duck     BOAT TOUR
(☑0405 125 312; www.thebigduck.com.au; 30min tours adult/child/family $35/25/110, 1hr $55/45/180) Do a lap of Granite Island and check out seals, dolphins and whales (but sadly not many penguins these days) on the rigid inflatable Big Duck boat. Call for times and bookings.

Encounter Coast Discovery Centre     MUSEUM
(www.nationaltrust.org.au/sa; 2 Flinders Pde; adult/child/family $5/3/13; ⊙1-4pm) Inside Victor's 1866 Customs House on the foreshore, this National Trust museum has interesting local-history displays from pre-European times to around 1900: whaling, railways, shipping and local Aboriginal culture. Good for a rainy day.

## 🛏 Sleeping & Eating

Anchorage     GUESTHOUSE $$
(☑08-8552 5970; www.anchorageseafronthotel.com; 21 Flinders Pde; s/d/apt from $55/100/250; ⊚) This grand old seafront guesthouse is the pick of the local crop. Immaculately maintained, great-value rooms open off long corridors. Most rooms face the beach, and some have a balcony (you'd pay through the nose for this in Sydney!). The cheapest rooms are view-free and share bathrooms. The cafe-bar downstairs is a winner.

Victor Harbor
Holiday & Cabin Park     CARAVAN PARK $
(☑08-8552 1949; www.victorharborholiday.com.au; 19 Bay Rd; unpowered/powered sites $30/36, vans/cabins from $52/85; ✸@⊚) The friendliest operation in town, with tidy facilities, free barbecues and a rambling grassed area to pitch a tent on. Runs rings around Victor's other caravan parks.

**Nino's** CAFE $$

(☑08-8552 3501; www.ninoscafe.com.au; 17 Albert Pl; mains $15-33; ⊙10am-10pm Mon-Thu, 10am-midnight Fri-Sun) Nino's cafe has been here since 1974, but it manages to put a contemporary sheen on downtown VH. Hip young staff and a mod interior set the scene for gourmet pizzas, pasta, salads, risottos and meaty Italian mains. Good coffee, cakes and takeaways, too.

**Anchorage Cafe** MODERN AUSTRALIAN $$

(☑08-8552 5970; www.anchorageseafronthotel.com; 21 Flinders Pde; tapas $7-14, mains $16-35; ⊙8-11am, noon-2.30pm & 5.30-8.30pm) This salty sea cave at the Anchorage hotel has an old whaling boat for a bar and a Med/Mod Oz menu (baguettes, pizzas, souvlaki) peppered with plenty of seafood. There's great coffee, tapas and cakes, plus Euro beers and a breezy terrace on which to drink them.

## ℹ Information

**Victor Harbor Visitor Information Centre** (☑1800 557 094, 08-8551 0777; www.tourismvictorharbor.com.au; Foreshore; ⊙9am-5pm) Handles tour and accommodation bookings. Stocks the *Beaches on the South Coast* brochure if you feel like a swim, and the *Old Port Victor* history walk brochure.

## ℹ Getting There & Away

### BUS

**Premier Stateliner** (www.premierstateliner.com.au) runs buses to Victor Harbor from Adelaide ($22, 1¾ hours, one to three daily) continuing to Goolwa.

### TRAIN

On the first and third Sundays from June to November inclusive, **SteamRanger Heritage Railway** (☑1300 655 991; www.steamranger.org.au) operates the *Southern Encounter* (adult/child return $69/36) tourist train from Mt Barker in the Adelaide Hills to Victor Harbor via Strathalbyn, Goolwa and Port Elliot. The *Cockle Train* (adult/child return $28/14) runs along the Encounter Coast between Victor Harbor and Goolwa via Port Elliot every Sunday and Wednesday, and daily during school holidays.

## Port Elliot

POP 3100

About 8km east of Victor Harbor, historic (and today, rather affluent) Port Elliot is set back from **Horseshoe Bay**, an orange-sand arc with gentle surf and good swimming.

Norfolk Island pines reach for the sky, and there are whale-spotting updates posted on the pub wall. If there are whales around, wander out to **Freemans Knob** lookout at the end of the Strand and peer through the free telescope.

## 🏃 Activities

**Commodore Point**, at the eastern end of Horseshoe Bay, and nearby **Boomer Beach** and **Knights Beach** have reliable waves for experienced surfers. The beach at otherwise missable **Middleton**, the next town towards Goolwa, also has solid breaks. You can learn to surf (around $40 for a two-hour lesson, including gear) with **South Coast Surf Academy** (☑0414 341 545; www.danosurf.com.au) and **Surf & Sun** (☑1800 786 386; www.surfandsun.com.au).

History buffs should look for the *Walk Into History at Port Elliot* pamphlet (try Goolwa Visitor Information Centre (p90)) detailing a couple of history walks around town.

**Big Surf Australia** SURFING

(☑08-8554 2399; info@bigsurfaustralia.com; 24 Goolwa Rd, Middleton; surfboards/bodyboards/wetsuits per day $30/20/15; ⊙9am-5pm) For surf-gear hire, check out Big Surf Australia in Middleton.

OFF THE BEATEN TRACK

### RAPID BAY

About 15km south of Normanville, follow the signs past bald hills and farmhouse ruins to Rapid Bay. In the 1950s this was a boomtown, the local limestone quarry shipping 60,000 tonnes of lime per month from the enormous jetty. Production ceased in 1981; since then Rapid Bay has assumed a gothic, ghost-town atmosphere. Empty '50s villas and workers' quarters line the streets, and the local shop (closed) has signs advertising soft drinks they don't make anymore. The jetty (recently rebuilt; www.rapidbayjetty.org) has become a popular fishing and diving site.

Rapid Bay was also the site of Adelaide founder Colonel William Light's first landing in SA in 1836, in his ship the *Rapid*. There's a stone down by the shore with 'WL 1836' carved into it.

**Port Elliot Bike & Leisure Hire** BICYCLE HIRE
(📞0448 370 007; www.portelliotbikeleisurehire.
myob.net; 85-87 Hill St; per day $40) Pick up a
mountain bike and hit the Encounter Bikeway (p86), running through Port Elliot to
Goolwa (15km east) and Victor Harbor (7km
west).

## 🛏 Sleeping & Eating

★ **Port Elliot Beach House YHA** HOSTEL $
(📞08-8554 1885; www.yha.com.au; 13 The Strand;
dm/d/f from $28/90/125; ✳@) Built in 1910
(the old Arcadia Hotel), this sandstone
beauty has sweeping views across the Port
Elliot coastline. If you can drag your eyes
away from the view, you'll find polished
floorboards and contemporary colours
splashed around. It's a classy fit-out, and the
only backpackers on the Fleurieu Peninsula.
Surf lessons are almost mandatory, and the
Flying Fish Cafe is 200m away.

**Port Elliot Holiday Park** CARAVAN PARK $
(📞08-8554 2134; www.portelliotholidaypark.com.
au; Port Elliot Rd; powered sites/cabins/units/
cottages from $33/90/115/150; ✳@📶) In an
unbeatable position behind the Horseshoe
Bay dunes (it can be a touch windy), this
5-hectare park, with lush grass and healthy-
looking trees has all the requisite facilities,
including a shiny camp kitchen and all-
weather barbecue area. Prices plummet in
winter.

**Royal Family Hotel** PUB $
(📞08-8554 2219; www.royalfamilyhotel.com.au;
32 North Tce; s/d $50/65) It's doubtful that
Prince Chuck has ever stayed here, but if he
did he'd find surprisingly decent pub rooms
with clean shared bathrooms, a TV lounge
and balcony over the main street. Downstairs the bistro serves counter meals fit for
a king (mains $16 to $30, serving noon to
2pm and 6pm to 8pm).

**Flying Fish Cafe** MODERN AUSTRALIAN $$
(📞08-8554 3504; www.flyingfishcafe.com.au; 1
The Foreshore; takeaways $10-15, mains $20-40;
⊙9-11am Sat & Sun, noon-3pm daily, 6-9pm Fri &
Sat) Sit down for lunch and you'll find your-
self here all day – the views of Horseshoe
Bay are sublime. Otherwise grab some qual-
ity takeaway of Coopers-battered flathead
and chips and head back to the sand. At
night things get a little classier, with à-la-
carte mains that focus on independent SA
producers.

**Cockles on North** CAFE, MODERN AUSTRALIAN $
(📞08-8554 3187; www.cocklescafe.com.au; 4/33
North Tce; mains $10-19; ⊙7.30am-4pm; 📶) A
bright, breezy, open-sided foodie haunt with
a huge deck overlooking the main strip. Ex-
pect good coffee, all-day breakfasts, snazzy
desserts and mains such as felafels, corn frit-
ters with avocado and smoked salmon, and
king-prawn pasta.

## ❶ Getting There & Away

**Premier Stateliner** (www.premierstateliner.
com.au) has daily bus services between Ad-
elaide and Port Elliot ($22, two hours, one to
three daily), via Victor Harbor and continuing to
Goolwa.

# Goolwa
POP 6500

Much more low-key and elegant than kissing-
cousin Victor Harbor, Goolwa is an unas-
suming town where the rejuvenated Murray
River empties into the sea. Beyond the dunes
is a fantastic beach with ranks of breakers
rolling in from the ocean, same as it ever
was... The **South Australian Wooden Boat
Festival** (www.woodenboatfestival.com.au) at-
tracts boating enthusiasts here in February
in odd-numbered years.

---

### BUILDING BRIDGES (NOT...)

First proposed in 1988, construction of the Hindmarsh Island Bridge at Goolwa was
opposed by Ngarrindjeri women who had concerns about the spiritual and cultural sig-
nificance of the site. A series of court battles ensued, pitting Aboriginal beliefs against
development, culminating in a royal commission (1995) that ruled that the claims
of Aboriginal 'secret women's business' were fabricated. Further court appeals were
launched, and in August 2001 the Federal Court overturned the royal commission, find-
ing the Ngarrindjeri claims to be legitimate. Unfortunately, this vindication came five
months after the bridge was officially opened. The decade-long furore was a step back-
wards for reconciliation; the bridge remains a source of contention.

## ⊙ Sights & Activities

At **Goolwa Beach** a boardwalk traverses the dunes looking out at the barrelling surf: **Goolwa Barrells** (☑08-85555422; www.barrells urf.com.au; 10c Cadell St; hire per day longboard/bodyboard/wetsuit $25/10/15; ☉9.30am-5.30pm) has surfboard hire. You can learn to surf with **Ocean Living Surf School** (☑0487 921 232; www.olsurfschool.com.au; 2/4hr lesson $35/65).

The coastal **Encounter Bikeway** (www. tourismvictorharbor.com.au/walks_trails.html) runs for 30km between Goolwa and Victor Harbor (maps available at the Goolwa visitor centre).

### Steam Exchange Brewery BREWERY
(☑08-8555 3406; www.steamexchange.com.au; Goolwa Wharf; tastings $3; ☉10am-5pm Wed-Sun) Down on the wharf, the Steam Exchange Brewery is a locally-run brewery, turning out manly stouts and ales. Sip a Southerly Buster Dark Ale and look out over the rippling river. Is the whiskey distillery up-and-running yet? Small tasting fee; group tours by arrangement.

### Canoe the Coorong CANOEING
(☑0424 826 008; www.canoethecoorong.com; adult/child $135/85) 🚣 Full-day paddles around the Coorong and Murray River mouth departing Goolwa. Includes lunch and a bush-tucker walk through the dunes.

### Spirit of the Coorong CRUISE
(☑08-8555 2203, 1800 442 203; www.coo rongcruises.com.au; Goolwa Wharf) 🚣 Spirit of the Coorong runs eco-cruises on the Murray and into the Coorong National Park, including lunch and guided walks. The four-hour Coorong Discovery Cruise (adult/child $84/62) runs on Thursdays all year, plus Mondays from October to May. The six-hour Coorong Adventure Cruise ($98/67) runs on Sundays all year, plus Wednesdays from October to May. There's also a two-hour Murray Mouth Cruise ($35/18) on Saturdays from October to April. Bookings essential.

### Goolwa Riverboat Centre CRUISE
(☑08-8555 2108, 1300 466 592; www.oscar-w. info; Goolwa Wharf; adult/child/family $20/8/48; ☉varies) Check out the Murray River on a one-hour paddle-steamer ride aboard the 130-year-old *Oscar W*. It's hard to imagine now, but in 1875 there were 127 riverboats plying the river between here and NSW! Call for times and bookings.

## 🛏 Sleeping

Holiday rentals in and around Goolwa are managed by **LJ Hooker** (☑08-8555 1785; www.ljh.com.au/goolwa; 25 Cadell St) and the **Professionals** (☑08-8555 2122; www.goolwa professionals.com.au; 1 Cadell St), both of whom have houses for as little as $80 per night (though most are around $130) and good weekly rates.

### Australasian BOUTIQUE HOTEL $$$
(☑08-8555 1088; www.australasian1858.com; 1 Porter St; d incl breakfast from $325; ✲🗻) This gorgeous 1858 stone hotel at the head of Goolwa's main street has been reborn as a sassy B&B, with a sequence of Japanese-inspired decks and glazed extensions and an upmarket dining room. The five plush suites all have views, and the breakfast will make you want to wake up here again. Two-night minimum.

### Jackling Cottage B&B B&B $$
(☑08-8555 3489; www.goolwaheritagecottages. com; 18 Oliver St; B&B d from $195, holiday rental 2 nights $330; ✲) A lovely old 1860s cottage on a nondescript Goolwa backstreet (just ignore the petrol station across the road), surrounded by rambling roses and limestone walls. Two bedrooms, sleeping four – good for families or a couple of couples looking for a low-key weekend by the sea. A short stroll to the main drag. Also available as a holiday rental (no breakfast).

## 🍴 Eating

### Café Lime CAFE $
(1/11 Goolwa Tce; meals $10-21; ☉9am-3pm) Pick up heat-and-eat gourmet dinners or a takeaway cone of salt-and-pepper squid with lime-salted fries. If you feel like lingering, nab a table for beer-battered Coorong mullet (not a description of a haircut at the pub), baguettes, curries, soups and pasta. Espresso perfecto.

### Hector's CAFE, MODERN AUSTRALIAN $$
(☑08-8555 5885; www.hectorsonthewharf.com; Goolwa Wharf; mains $10-32; ☉9am-3pm daily, 6pm-late Fri & Sat) Right on the Murray under the span of the Hindmarsh Island Bridge, eating at Hector's (festooned with fishing rods) is like hanging out in your mate's boathouse. Seafood chowder and spinach-and-fetta pie are sweetly complemented by jazzy tunes and local wines. There's good coffee, too.

## ❶ Information

**Goolwa Visitor Information Centre** (☑1300 466 592; www.visitalexandrina.com; 4 Goolwa Tce; ⊗9am-5pm Mon-Fri, 10am-4pm Sat & Sun) Inside an 1857 post office, with detailed local info (including accommodation).

## ❶ Getting There & Away

**Premier Stateliner** (www.premierstateliner. com.au) runs buses daily between Adelaide and Goolwa ($22, two hours, one to three daily).

See p87 for info on tourist steam trains running between Goolwa, Victor Harbor and the Adelaide Hills.

# KANGAROO ISLAND

From Cape Jervis, car ferries chug across the swells of the Backstairs Passage to Kangaroo Island (KI). Long devoid of tourist trappings, the island these days is a booming destination for wilderness and wildlife fans – it's a veritable zoo of seals, birds, dolphins, echidnas and (of course) kangaroos. Still, the island remains rurally paced and underdeveloped – the kind of place where kids ride bikes to school and farmers advertise for wives on noticeboards. Island produce is a highlight.

See www.tourkangarooisland.com.au.

## History

Many KI place names are French, attributable to Gallic explorer Nicholas Baudin who surveyed the coast in 1802 and 1803. Baudin's English rival, Matthew Flinders, named the island in 1802 after his crew feasted on kangaroo meat here. By this stage the island was uninhabited, but archaeologists think indigenous Australians lived here as recently as 2000 years ago. Why they deserted KI is a matter of conjecture, though the answer is hinted at in the indigenous name for KI: 'Karta', or 'Land of the Dead'. In the early 1800s an indigenous presence (albeit a tragically displaced one) was re-established on KI when whalers and sealers abducted Aboriginal women from Tasmania and brought them here.

## ✦ Activities

The safest **swimming** is along the north coast, where the water is warmer and there are fewer rips than down south. Try Emu Bay, Stokes Bay, Snelling Beach or Western River Cove.

For **surfing**, hit the uncrowded swells along the south coast. Pennington Bay has strong, reliable breaks; Vivonne Bay and Hanson Bay in the southwest also serve up some tasty waves. Pick up the *Kangaroo Island Surfing Guide* brochure from visitor information centres.

There's plenty to see under your own steam on KI. Check out www.tourkangaroo island.com.au/wildlife/walks.aspx for info on **bushwalks** from 1km to 18km.

The waters around KI are home to 230 species of fish, plus coral and around 60 shipwrecks – great **snorkelling** and **diving**! **Kangaroo Island Dive & Adventures** (☑08-8553 3196; www.kangarooislanddiveandad ventures.com.au; guided shore/boat dives from $195/320, snorkelling/diving equipment hire from $45/120) runs diving trips and offers gear hire.

Skidding down the dunes at **Little Sahara** is great fun. **Kangaroo Island Outdoor Action** (☑08-8559 4296; www.kioutdoorac tion.com.au; Jetty Rd, Vivonne Bay) rents out sandboards/toboggans ($29/39 per day), plus single/double kayaks ($39/69 for four hours).

There's plenty of good **fishing** around the island, including jetties at Kingscote, Penneshaw, Emu Bay and Vivonne Bay. Fishing charter tours (half-/full day from $100/200) include tackle and refreshments, and you keep what you catch. Try **Kangaroo Island Fishing Adventures** (☑08-8559 3232; www. kangarooislandadventures.com.au).

## ☞ Tours

See also Tours on p53. Stay at least one night on the island if you can (one-day tours are hectic). A few operators:

**Surf & Sun**                                        WILDLIFE
(☑1800 786 386; www.surfandsun.com.au) ✐ Two-day all-inclusive tours ex-Adelaide/KI ($445/309), with a strong focus on wildlife and activities.

**Kangaroo Island
Adventure Tours**                              GUIDED TOUR
(☑08-8202 8678; www.kiadventuretours.com. au) Two-day, all-inclusive tours ex-Adelaide ($389) with a backpacker bent and plenty of activities.

**Kangaroo Island Marine Tours**        WILDLIFE
(☑0427 315 286; www.kimarineadventures.com) ✐ Ninety-minute boat tours ($82.50) and longer half-day jaunts ($165), which include

### ALL CREATURES GREAT & SMALL

You bump into a lot of wildlife on KI (sometimes literally). Kangaroos, wallabies, bandicoots and possums come out at night, especially in wilderness areas such as Flinders Chase National Park. Koalas and the platypus were introduced to Flinders Chase in the 1920s when it was feared they would become extinct on the mainland. Echidnas mooch around in the undergrowth, while goannas and tiger snakes keep KI suitably scaly.

Of the island's 267 bird species, several are rare or endangered. One species – the dwarf emu – has gone the way of the dodo. Glossy black cockatoos may soon follow it out the door due to habitat depletion.

Offshore, dolphins and southern right whales are often seen cavorting in the waves, and there are colonies of little penguins, New Zealand fur seals and Australian sea lions here too.

swimming with dolphins, visiting seal colonies and access to remote areas of KI.

**Cruising Kangaroo Island** KAYAKING
(☑ 0439 507 018; www.cruisingkangarooisland.com; ☺ Oct-Apr) Two- to three-hour kayak paddles around choice KI coastal spots, from $80 per person.

**Alkirna Nocturnal Tours** WILDLIFE
(☑ 08-8553 7464; www.alkirna.com.au; ☺ Mar-Jan) Nightly two-hour, naturalist-led tours (adult/child $60/40) viewing nocturnal critters around American River.

**Sealink** SIGHTSEEING
(☑ 13 13 01; www.sealink.com.au) The ferry company runs a range of KI-highlight coach tours departing Adelaide (one/two days from $248/516). 4WD tours also available.

### 🛏 Sleeping

KI accommodation is expensive, adding insult to your wallet's injury after the pricey ferry ride. Self-contained cottages, B&Bs and beach houses charge from $150 per night per double (usually two-night minimum stay). There are some great camp sites around the island though, plus a few midrange motels. Quality caravan parks and hostels are scarce. Accommodation booking services include:

**Gateway Visitor Information Centre** ACCOMMODATION SERVICES
(☑ 1800 811 080; www.tourkangarooisland.com.au/accommodation)

**Kangaroo Island Holiday Accommodation** ACCOMMODATION SERVICES
(☑ 08 8553 9007; www.kangarooislandholidayaccommodation.com.au)

**Sealink** ACCOMMODATION SERVICES
(☑ 13 13 01; www.sealink.com.au/kangaroo-island-accommodation)

### ℹ Information

The main Gateway Visitor Information Centre (p94) is in Penneshaw. There are ATMs in Kingscote and Penneshaw. **Kangaroo Island Hospital** (☑ 08-8553 4200; www.countryhealthsa.sa.gov.au; The Esplanade; ☺ 24hr) is in Kingscote. Island mobile phone reception is patchy outside the main towns (best with Telstra). There are supermarkets at Penneshaw and Kingscote, and a general store at American River.

**Kangaroo Island Pass** (www.environment.sa.gov.au; adult/child/family $68/42/185) Covers all park and conservation area entry fees, and ranger-guided tours at Seal Bay, Kelly Hill Caves, Cape Borda and Cape Willoughby. Passes available online or at most sights.

### ℹ Getting There & Away

AIR

**Regional Express** (Rex; www.regionalexpress.com.au) flies daily between Adelaide and Kingscote (return from $220).

BUS

Sealink operates a morning and afternoon bus service between Adelaide Central Bus Station and Cape Jervis (return adult/child $50/26, 2¼ hours one way).

FERRY

**Sealink** (☑ 13 13 01; www.sealink.com.au) operates a car ferry between Cape Jervis and Penneshaw on KI, with at least three ferries each way daily (return adult/child from $96/48, bicycles/motorcycles/cars $22/58/280, 45 minutes one way). One driver is included with the vehicle price (cars only, not bikes).

# Kangaroo Island

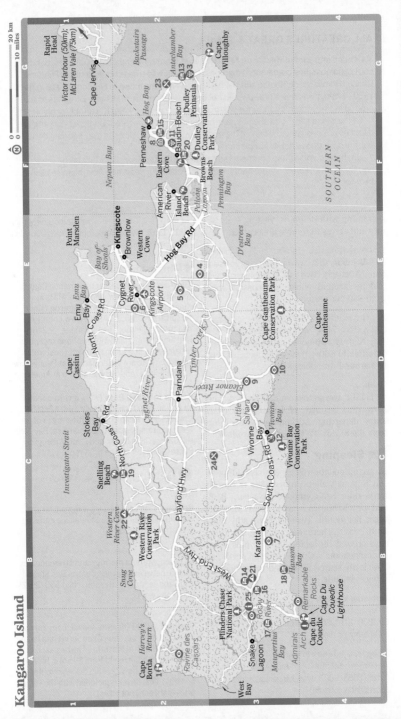

# Kangaroo Island

## ❶ Getting Around

There's no public transport anywhere on the island: take a tour or bring or hire some wheels. The island's main roads are sealed, but the rest are gravel, including those to Cape Willoughby, Cape Borda and the North Coast Rd (take it slowly, especially at night). There's petrol at Kingscote, Penneshaw, American River, Parndana and Vivonne Bay.

### TO/FROM THE AIRPORT

Kingscote Airport is 14km from Kingscote. **Kangaroo Island Transfers** (☑ 0427 887 575; www.kitransfers.com.au) connects the airport with Kingscote (per person $20, minimum two people), American River ($30) and Penneshaw ($40). Solo travellers pay double (eg Kingscote $40). Bookings essential.

### TO/FROM THE FERRY

Sealink (p91) runs a twice-daily shuttle between Penneshaw and American River (adult/child $14/7, 30 minutes) and Kingscote ($17/9, one hour). Bookings essential.

### CAR HIRE

Not all Adelaide car-rental companies will let you take their vehicles onto KI. **Budget** (www.budgetki.com) and **Hertz** (www.hertz.com.au) supply cars to Penneshaw, Kingscote and Kingscote Airport.

# Penneshaw & Dudley Peninsula

Looking across Backstairs Passage to the Fleurieu Peninsula, Penneshaw (population 300), on the north shore of the Dudley Peninsula, is the ferry arrival point. The passing tourist trade lends a certain transience to the businesses here, but the pub, hostel and general store remain authentically grounded. As do the resident little penguins. En route to American River, Pennington Bay has consistent surf.

## ◉ Sights & Activities

**Penneshaw Penguin Centre**                    ECOTOUR
(☑ 08-8553 1103; www.southaustralia.com/900 5545.aspx; cnr Middle Tce & Bay Tce, Penneshaw; adult/child/family $13/10/35; ☺ 6-9.30pm Mar-Jan) On the foreshore near the ferry terminal, this centre provides an unobtrusive view of the little local waddlers that nest here. Tours are included in admission; book ahead. Kids under seven free.

**Chapman River Wines**                          WINERY
(www.goodfoodkangarooisland.com/wine/chapmanriverwines.asp; off Cape Willoughby Rd, Antechamber Bay; ☺ 11am-4.30pm Thu-Mon Sep-Jun) Occupying a converted aircraft hangar, this

eccentric winery makes a mean merlot. The interior is festooned with art and quirky bits of salvage from churches, pubs and homesteads around SA. Good coffee, too.

### Penneshaw

#### Maritime & Folk Museum
MUSEUM

(www.nationaltrustsa.org.au; 52 Howard Dr, Penneshaw; adult/child/family $3/2/7; ⊙3-5pm Wed-Sun Sep-May) Displays artefacts from local shipwrecks and early settlement (check out those girthsome millstones!), plus endearingly geeky models of Flinders' *Investigator* and Baudin's *Geographe*.

#### Cape Willoughby Lightstation
LIGHTHOUSE

(www.environment.sa.gov.au; Cape Willoughby Rd; tours adult/child/family $14.50/9/38; ⊙tours 11.30am, 12.30pm, 2pm, 3pm & 4pm) About 28km southeast of Penneshaw (unsealed road), this lighthouse first shone in 1852 and is now used as a weather station. Lots of shipwreck info, plus basic cottage accommodation (doubles from $170; book through the DEWNR).

#### Kangaroo Island Farmers Market
MARKET

(www.goodfoodkangarooisland.com/tastingki/farmersmarket.asp; Lloyd Collins Reserve, Frenchmans Tce, Penneshaw; ⊙9am-1pm 1st Sun of the month) Baked goods, chutneys, seafood, olive oil, honey, eggs, cheese, yoghurt...and of course wine! Sealink (p91) sometimes offers dedicated passenger-only return tickets from the mainland if you'd just like to visit the market for the day.

#### Sunset Winery
WINERY

(www.sunset-wines.com.au; Penneshaw–Kingscote Rd; ⊙11am-5pm) Wow, what a view! If you can make it up the steep driveway, Sunset has brilliant sauvignon blanc and sparkling shiraz, and serves savoury platters to go with the panorama.

## 🛏 Sleeping & Eating

#### Antechamber Bay Ecocabins
CABINS $$

(☑08-8553 1557; www.kiecocabins.com; 142 Creek Bay Rd, Antechamber Bay; d from $140, extra adult/child $10/free) 🅿 Off Cape Willoughby Rd, these two eight-bed cabins are run by a couple of IT industry runaways. On 22 hectares behind the dunes, the cabins are rudimentary but perfectly comfortable, with roofless showers, self-composting toilets, and solar power and hot water. Kayaks and fishing gear available.

#### Kangaroo Island YHA
HOSTEL $

(☑08-8553 1344; www.yha.com.au; 33 Middle Tce, Penneshaw; dm $35, d without/with bathroom $75/110, f $220; ❇@🕏) Occupying an old '60s motel with faux-brick cladding, the island YHA has spacious, freshly painted rooms, mostly with en-suite bathrooms. There's a sunny communal kitchen, little lounge and laundry, and penguins at the bottom of the garden.

#### Wallaby Beach House
RENTAL HOUSE $$

(☑08-8362 5293; www.wallabybeachhouse.com.au; Browns Beach; d from $180, extra person $25; ❇) A secluded, self-contained three-bedroom beach house, 13km west of Penneshaw on unpeopled Browns Beach. Simple but stylish decor, with broad sunset views and passing seals, dolphins and penguins to keep you company. Sleeps six.

#### ★ Dudley Cellar Door
CAFE $$

(☑08-8553 1567; www.dudleywines.com.au; 1153 Cape Willoughby Rd, Cuttlefish Bay; mains $25-28; ⊙10am-5pm) KI's pioneering winery has a new cellar door, 12km east of Penneshaw. It's a fancy corrugated iron shed, with astonishing views back to the mainland and serving superb pizzas (try the King George whiting version), oysters and buckets of prawns – just perfect with a bottle of chardonnay on the deck.

#### Fish
SEAFOOD $

(☑0439 803 843; www.2birds1squid.com; 43 North Tce, Penneshaw; mains $13-18; ⊙dinner mid-Oct–May) Takeaway fish and chips like you ain't never had before – grilled, beer-battered or crumbed whiting and garfish – plus giant KI scallops, marron, lobster medallions, prawns and oysters. Dunk them in an array of excellent homemade sauces.

## ❶ Information

**Gateway Visitor Information Centre** (☑08-8553 1185; www.tourkangarooisland.com.au; Howard Dr; ⊙9am-5pm Mon-Fri, 10am-4pm Sat & Sun; 🕏) Just outside Penneshaw on the road to Kingscote, this centre is stocked with brochures and maps. Also books accommodation and sells park entry tickets and the Kangaroo Island Pass.

# American River

POP 230

Between Penneshaw and Kingscote on the way to nowhere in particular, American River squats redundantly by the glassy Pelican

Lagoon. The town was named after a crew of American sealers who built a trading schooner here in 1804. There's no such industriousness here today, just a general store and plenty of pelicans.

From the end of Scenic Dr, a **coastal walk** (2km one way) passes through natural scrub, sugar gums and she-oak en route to some old fish-cannery ruins.

## Sleeping & Eating

**All Seasons Kangaroo Island Lodge**                 MOTEL $$
(☑08-8553 7053, 1800 355 581; www.kilodge. com.au; Lot 2, Scenic Dr, American River; d incl breakfast $149-279; ✳@☎☀) Up-to-scratch motel suites overlooking either the pool or lagoon (the rammed-earth wing has the best rooms). The restaurant plates up plenty of local seafood (mains $20 to $30, serving 7.30am to 9am and 6pm to 8pm).

**Island Coastal Units**               MOTEL, CABINS $$
(☑08-8553 7010; www.kangarooislandcoastal units.com.au; Tangara Dr, American River; units/ cabins from $110/120, extra person $20) A low row of basic one- and two-bedroom motel-style units among trees opposite the foreshore, plus four beautiful self-contained cabins with solar hot water, gas cooktops and air-con (pay the extra $10!).

**American River Campsite**          CAMPGROUND $
(☑08-8553 4500; www.kangarooisland.sa.gov.au; Tangara Dr, American River; unpowered sites per 2 people $15, extra person $5) Shady, council-run camping beside the lagoon, with fire pits, showers and toilets. You will need to pay via self-registration.

**Oyster Farm Shop**                      SEAFOOD $
(☑08-8553 7122; www.goodfoodkangarooisland. com/food/kio_shop.asp; Tangara Dr; meals $8.50-21; ☺11am-3pm Mon-Fri) Operated by a local oyster farm, this little shack acts as an outlet for sustainable seafood producers from all over the island. Oysters, marron, abalone, King George whiting...even barramundi, cooked into meals or takeaway uncooked. A dozen fresh unshucked oysters are a paltry $8.50.

**American River General Store**  SELF-CATERING
(☑08-8553 7015; Scenic Dr; ☺7.30am-6pm) Packed to the northern hemisphere with provisions, bait and tackle, plus there's an amazing hardware 'cupboard', petrol and a bottle shop.

# Kingscote
POP 1700

Snoozy seaside Kingscote (pronounced 'kings-coat') is the main settlement on KI, and the hub of island life. It's a photogenic town with swaying Norfolk Island pines, a couple of pubs and some decent eateries.

## Sights & Activities

**Kangaroo Island Penguin Centre**   ECOTOUR
(www.kipenguincentre.com.au; Kingscote Wharf; adult/child/family $17/6/40, pelican feeding adult/ child $5/3; ☺tours 8.30pm & 9.30pm Oct-Jan & Mar, 7.30pm & 8.30pm Apr-Oct, closed Feb, pelican feeding 5pm) Runs one-hour tours of its saltwater aquariums and the local penguin colony, plus some stargazing if the sky is clear. It also runs informative (and comical) **pelican feeding** sessions at the adjacent wharf.

**Hope Cottage Museum**                  MUSEUM
(www.hopecottagemuseum.com; Centenary Ave; adult/child $6/2; ☺1-4pm daily Sep-Jul, Sat only Aug) Built on the hill in 1857, this cottage is now a fastidiously maintained National Trust museum decked out in period style, with a reconstructed lighthouse, an amazing old quilt, a tiny walled rose garden and KI's first piano.

**Kangaroo Island Spirits**             DISTILLERY
(KIS; www.kispirits.com.au; 856 Playford Hwy, Cygnet River; tastings free, bottles from $35; ☺11am-5pm Wed-Sun, daily during school holidays) This fiesty little moonshiner makes small-batch gin with KI native juniper berries, plus vodka, brandy and liqueurs (try the honey and walnut version, using organic KI honey).

**Island Beehive**                          APIARY
(www.island-beehive.com.au; 1 Acacia Dr, Kingscote; tours adult/child/family $4.50/3/13; ☺9am-5pm, group tours every 30min 9.30am-4pm) Runs factory tours where you can study up on passive, hard-working Ligurian bees and beekeeping, then stock up on by-products (bee-products?), including delicious organic honey and honeycomb ice cream. Tours for groups.

**Island Pure Sheep Dairy**               DAIRY
(www.islandpure.com.au; 127 Gum Creek Rd, Cygnet River; tours adult/child/family $6.50/5.50/22; ☺noon-4pm) Near Cygnet River, 12km from Kingscote, this dairy features 1500 sheep lining up to be milked (around 2pm daily). Take a tour of the factory, which includes

yoghurt and cheese tastings (the haloumi is magic).

### Kingscote Tidal Pool
SWIMMING

(www.kangarooisland.sa.gov.au/page.aspx?u=222; Chapman Tce; ⊙ daylight hours) FREE Kingscote beaches are lousy for swimming: locals usually head 18km northwest to Emu Bay, or to this 50m tidal swimming pool, which has a couple of pontoons and grassy banks to sun yourself on.

## 🍴 Sleeping & Eating

### Aurora Ozone Hotel
HOTEL $$

(☑ 08-8553 2011, 1800 083 133; www.aurora resorts.com.au; cnr Commercial St & Kingscote Tce; d pub/motel from $129/165, 1-/2-/3-bed apt from $190/340/540; ❋ @ � 🖥) Opposite the foreshore with killer views, the 100-year-old Ozone pub has quality pub rooms upstairs, motel rooms, and stylish deluxe apartments in a new wing across the street. The eternally busy bistro (mains $20 to $48) serves meaty grills and seafood, and you can pickle yourself on KI wines at the bar.

### Kangaroo Island
### Central Backpackers
HOSTEL $

(☑ 08-8553 2787; www.kicentralbackpackers.com; 19 Murray St, Kingscote; dm/d from $25/60; ❋ 🖥) Just a couple of blocks from Kingscote's main strip, this small, innocuous hostel is clean and affordable, and has a cosy lounge, lush lawns and a beaut en-suite double cabin out the back. It feels like staying at someone's house – good or bad, depending on how sociable you're feeling.

### Seaview Motel
MOTEL, GUESTHOUSE $$

(☑ 08-8553 2030; www.seaview.net.au; 51 Chapman Tce, Kingscote; guesthouse s/d $90/100, motel $146/156, extra adult/child $25/15; ❋ 🖥) It seems like this place is always full – surely a good sign! Choose from older-style 1924 guesthouse rooms with shared facilities (no air-con), or refurbished 1980s motel rooms. Family-owned, and quite affordable by KI standards.

### Kingscote Nepean
### Bay Tourist Park
CARAVAN PARK $

(☑ 08-8553 2394; www.kingscotetouristpark.com. au; cnr First & Third Sts, Brownlow; unpowered/powered sites $32/38, cabins/units from $90/135; ❋ 🖥) You'll find the standard gamut of caravan park delights behind the dunes in Brownlow, 3km southwest of Kingscote. You can walk back to Kingscote via a coastal walking trail. Better for camping than cabins.

### Yellow Ash 'n' Chili
MEXICAN $$

(59 Dauncy St, Kingscote; mains $16-22; ⊙ 10am-3pm & 6-8pm Tue-Sat, 10am-3pm Sun) Making a chilli-coloured splash on the KI foodie scene, this casual, brightly painted bungalow on Kingscote's main drag is run by a Californian who knows a thing or two about Mexican food. Expect simple but delicious tostadas, quesadillas, enchiladas etc, made with home-grown tomatoes and chillis and organic flour. Love the 'Day of the Dead' mural.

### Kangaroo Island Fresh Seafoods
SEAFOOD $

(www.goodfoodkangarooisland.com/eatingout/ kifreshseafood.asp; 26 Telegraph Rd, Kingscote; meals $8-16; ⊙ 8am-8pm Mon-Sat) This unassuming place attached to a petrol station has some of the best seafood you're ever likely to taste. A dozen fat oysters go for around a dollar each, then there are all manner of cooked and fresh KI seafood packs and combos. Superb!

### Bella
ITALIAN $$

(☑ 08-8553 0400; www.restaurantbella.com.au; 54 Dauncey St, Kingscote; pizzas $14-39, mains $26-32; ⊙ 9am-late Mon-Fri, 10am-late Sat, 11am-late Sun) Sit inside or sidewalk al fresco at Bella, a cheery Italian cafe/restaurant/pizza bar. Pizzas start at 11.30am (eat in or takeaway); dinner is à la carte, featuring American River oysters, Spencer Gulf king prawns, local roo and whiting.

## ℹ Information

**Natural Resources Centre** (Department of Environment, Water & Natural Resources; ☑ 08-8553 4444, accommodation bookings 08-8553 4410; www.environment.sa.gov.au; 37 Dauncey St, Kingscote; ⊙ 9am-5pm Mon-Fri) Sells the Kangaroo Island Pass and has info on national parks.

# North Coast Road

Exquisite beaches (calmer than the south coast), bushland and undulating pastures dapple the North Coast Rd, running from Kingscote along the coast to the Playford Hwy 85km west (the bitumen expires at Emu Bay). There's not a whole lot to do here other than swan around on the beach – sounds good!

About 18km from Kingscote, **Emu Bay** is a holiday hamlet with a 5km-long, white-sand beach flanked by dunes – one of KI's best swimming spots. Around 36km further west, **Stokes Bay** has a penguin rookery and broad rock pool you access by scrambling through a 20m tunnel in the cliffs at the bay's eastern end (mind your head!). Beware the rip outside the pool.

The view as you look back over **Snelling Beach** from atop Constitution Hill is awesome! Continue 7km west and you'll hit the turn-off to **Western River Cove**, where a small beach is crowded in by sombre basalt cliffs. The ridge-top road in is utterly scenic (and steep).

## 🛏 Sleeping & Eating

**Western River
Cove Campsite**                    CAMPGROUND **$**
(www.kangarooisland.sa.gov.au; unpowered sites per 2 people $15, extra person $5) This self-registration camp site is just a short walk from the beach and a footbridge over the river (it's so tempting to dangle a line). There's a toilet block and a barbecue hut but no showers.

**Emu Bay
Holiday Homes**            CABINS, RENTAL HOUSE **$**
(☑08-8553 5241; www.emubaysuperviews.com.au; 21 Bayview Rd, Emu Bay; cabins $90, holiday homes $115-145, extra person $20; ❄🗢) Great-value (if a little frilly) cabins and holiday homes in a large flower-filled garden on the hill above Emu Bay beach (great views!). The self-contained cabins (caravan-park cabins with a facelift, sans air-con) sleep four or six; the holiday homes sleep six or 10.

**Stone House**             RENTAL HOUSE **$$$**
(www.life-time.com.au; North Coast Rd, Snelling Beach; d from $410; ❄) It's pricey, but it's worth it: a gorgeous self-contained stone-and-timber house on the hillside above beautiful Snelling Beach (actually, it's not that pricey if there's a few of you: from $460 for six people in three bedrooms). Floor-to-ceiling windows, quirky artworks, a couple of decks and daisy-studded lawns.

**Rockpool Café**                  CAFE **$$**
(☑08-8559 2277; North Coast Rd, Stokes Bay; mains $15-27; ☉11am-5pm Tue-Sun, daily during school holidays) Don't worry about sandy feet at this casual, al fresco joint in Stokes Bay. 'What's the house special?', we asked. 'Whatever I feel like doin'!', said the chef (usually seafood, washed down with local wines and decent espresso).

# South Coast Road

The south coast is rough and wave-swept compared with the north.

## ◉ Sights & Activities

**Seal Bay Conservation Park**    NATURE RESERVE
(☑08-8553 4460; www.environment.sa.gov.au/sealbay; Seal Bay Rd; self-guided tours adult/child/family $15/9/40, guided $32/18/80, twilight $60/36/165; ☉tours 9am-4.15pm year-round, extra tours Dec-Feb) 🐾 'Observation, not interaction' is the mentality. Guided tours stroll along the beach (or boardwalk on self-guided tours) to a colony of (mostly sleeping) Australian sea lions. Twilight tours December and January. Bookings advised.

**Clifford's Honey Farm**              APIARY
(www.cliffordshoney.com.au; 1157 Elsegood Rd, Haines; ☉9am-5pm) It's almost worth swimming the Backstairs Passage for the honey ice cream (sourced from a colony of rare Ligurian bees) at this charming, uncommercial farm. A bit off the tourist radar (again, charming).

**Kelly Hill Conservation Park**    NATURE RESERVE
(☑08-8553 4464; www.environment.sa.gov.au; South Coast Rd; tours adult/child/family $15/9/40, caving $65/39/176; ☉tours 10.30am, then hourly 11.15am-4.15pm) This series of dry limestone caves was 'discovered' in the 1880s by a horse named Kelly, who fell into them through a hole. Take the standard **show cave tour**, or add on an **adventure caving tour** (following the 2.15pm standard tour; bookings essential). The **Hanson Bay Walk** (9km one way) runs from the caves through mallee scrub and past freshwater wetlands.

**Emu Ridge Farm
Eucalyptus Distillery**   DISTILLERY, GALLERY
(www.emuridge.com.au; 691 Willsons Rd, MacGillivary; admission free, self-guided tours adult/child $4.50/2; ☉9am-2pm) 🐾 A detour off Hog Bay or Birchmore roads takes you past this self-sufficient operation (all solar-, steam- and wind-powered) extracting eucalyptus oil from Kangaroo Island's narrow-leaf mallee. The attached craft gallery sells eucalyptus-oil products.

**Raptor Domain**                  AVIARY
(www.kangarooislandbirdsofprey.com.au; cnr South Coast Rd & Seal Bay Rd; birds of prey adult/child/family $15/10/45, reptiles $10/8/32; ☉10.30am-4pm) Check out some KI wedge-tailed eagles,

barn owls and kookaburras at a one-hour birds-of-prey display (11.30am and 2.30pm), or go scaly at a one-hour lizards and snakes show (1pm).

## 🛏 Sleeping & Eating

**Flinders Chase Farm**          HOSTEL, CABINS **$$**
(🖉 08-8559 7223; www.flinderschasefarm.com.au; 1561 West End Hwy; dm/cabins $25/70, d & tw with bathroom $110) A working farm with charm, a short drive from Flinders Chase National Park. Accommodation includes immaculate dorms, a couple of cosy cabins and ensuite rooms in a lodge. There's also a terrific camp kitchen, fire pits and 'tropical' outdoor showers.

**Western Kangaroo
Island Caravan Park**          CAMPGROUND **$**
(🖉 08-8559 7201; www.westernki.com.au; 7928 South Coast Rd, Flinders Chase; unpowered/powered sites $22/28, cabins $110-190; 🌢) A few minutes' drive east of Flinders Chase National Park, this friendly park has shady gums and resident roos. Check out the koala and lagoon walks, and the phone booth inside an old bakery truck. The shop sells groceries, homemade heat-and-eats and (for guests only) beer and wine.

**Kangaroo Island
Wilderness Retreat**          HOTEL, RESORT **$$**
(🖉 08-8559 7275; www.kiwr.com; Lot 1, South Coast Rd, Flinders Chase; d $176-360; 🌢@🛜) A low-key, log-cabin-style resort on the Flinders Chase doorstep with resident grazing wallabies. Accommodation ranges from basic motel-style rooms to flashy spa suites. There's a petrol pump, a bar and a restaurant here too, serving breakfast (mains $17 to $25, 7.30am to 9.30am) and dinner (mains $28 to $35, 6pm to 8.30pm).

**Marron Café**          MODERN AUSTRALIAN **$$**
(🖉 08-8559 4114; www.andermel.com.au/cafe.htm; 804 Harriet Rd, Central Kangaroo Island; mains $16-

38; ⊙ 11am-4.30pm) Around 15km north of Vivonne Bay you can check out marron in breeding tanks, then eat some! It's a subtle taste, not necessarily enhanced by the heavy sauces issued by the kitchen. There are steak and chicken dishes, for the crustacean-shy. Last orders 4pm.

# Flinders Chase National Park

Occupying the western end of the island, Flinders Chase National Park is one of SA's top national parks. Much of the park is mallee scrub, but there are some beautiful, tall sugar-gum forests, particularly around Rocky River and the Ravine des Casoars, 5km south of Cape Borda.

## ⊙ Sights & Activities

Once a farm, **Rocky River** is a rampant hotbed of wildlife, with kangaroos, wallabies and Cape Barren geese competing for your affections. A slew of good walks launch from behind the visitors centre, including the **Rocky River Hike** on which you might spy a platypus (9km loop, three hours).

From Rocky River, a road runs south to a remote 1906 **lighthouse** atop wild Cape du Couedic. A boardwalk weaves down to **Admirals Arch**, a huge archway ground out by heavy seas, and passes a colony of New Zealand fur seals (sweet smelling they ain't...).

At Kirkpatrick Point, a few kilometres east of Cape du Couedic, the much photographed **Remarkable Rocks** are a cluster of hefty, weather-gouged granite boulders atop a rocky dome that arcs 75m down to the ocean.

On the northwestern corner of the island, the 1858 **Cape Borda Lightstation** (🖉 08-8553 4465; www.environment.sa.gov.au/parks; admission free, tours adult/child/family $14.50/9/38; ⊙ 9am-5pm, tours 11am, 12.30pm & 2pm) stands

---

### SOUTHERN OCEAN LODGE

Millionaires, start your engines! The shining star in the SA tourism galaxy is **Southern Ocean Lodge** (🖉 08-9918 4355; www.southernoceanlodge.com.au; Hanson Bay; d per night from $1980; 🌢@🛜🌊), a sexy, low-profile snake tracing the Hanson Bay cliff-top – a real exercise in exclusivity. There's a two-night minimum stay; you get airport transfers, all meals and drinks and guided tours of KI.

If you want a sticky-beak, don't expect to see anything from the road: all you'll find is a steely set of gates and an unreceptive intercom: privacy is what guests are paying for here (Hey, wasn't that Teri Hatcher in that 4WD?). But you can catch a sneaky glimpse from Hanson Bay beach.

tall above the rippling iron surface of the Southern Ocean. There are walks here from 1.5km to 9km, and extra tours at 3.15pm and 4pm during summer holidays.

At nearby Harvey's Return a **cemetery** speaks poignant volumes about the reality of isolation in the early days. From here you can drive to **Ravine des Casoars** (literally 'Ravine of the Cassowaries', referring to the now-extinct dwarf emus seen here by Baudin's expedition). The challenging **Ravine des Casoars Hike** (7km return, three hours) tracks through the ravine to the coast

## 🛏 Sleeping & Eating

There are campgrounds at **Rocky River** (per person/car $9/27), **Snake Lagoon** (per person/car $7/13), **West Bay** (per person/car $7/13) and **Harvey's Return** (per person/car $7/13); book through the **Department of Environment, Water & Natural Resources** (DEWNR; ☑ 08-8553 4490; flinderschase@sa.gov.au).

There's also refurbished cottage accommodation at Rocky River – the budget **Postmans Cottage** (d $70) and family-friendly **Mays Homestead** (d $133) – and lightkeepers' cottages at **Cape du Couedic** and **Cape Borda** (basic huts to stone cottages, d $22-170). Book through the **Department of Environment, Water & Natural Resources** (☑ 08-8553 4410; kiparksaccom@sa.gov.au).

On the food front, the only option here if you're not self-catering is the **Chase Cafe** (☑ 08-8559 7339; www.thechasecafe.com.au; Flinders Chase Visitor Information Centre; meals $9-27; ☉ 9am-3.30pm) at the visitors centre, serving burgers, wraps, soup, coffee, and wines by the glass.

## ❶ Information

**Flinders Chase Visitor Information Centre**
(☑ 08-8559 7235; www.environment.sa.gov.au/parks; South Coast Rd, Flinders Chase; ☉ 9am-5pm) Info, maps and camping/accommodation bookings, plus a cafe and displays on island ecology.

# LIMESTONE COAST

The Limestone Coast – strung-out along southeastern SA between the flat, olive span of the lower Murray River and the Victorian border – is a curiously engaging place. On the highways you can blow across these flatlands in under a day, no sweat, but around here the delight is in the detail. Detour off-

road to check out the area's lagoons, surf beaches and sequestered bays. Also on offer are wine regions, photogenic fishing ports and snoozy agricultural towns. And what's *below* the road is even more amazing: a bizarre subterranean landscape of limestone caves, sinkholes and bottomless crater lakes.

Online, see www.thelimestonecoast.com.

## ❶ Getting There & Away

The Dukes Hwy (Rte A8) is the most direct route between Adelaide and Melbourne (729km), but the coastal Princes Hwy (Rte B1; about 900km) adjacent to the Coorong National Park is definitely more scenic.

**AIR**

**Regional Express** (Rex; www.regionalexpress.com.au) flies daily between Adelaide and Mount Gambier (one way from $160).

**BUS**

**Premier Stateliner** (www.premierstateliner.com.au) runs two bus routes – coastal and inland – between Adelaide and Mount Gambier ($73, seven hours). From Adelaide along the coast (Tuesday, Thursday, Friday and Sunday) via the Coorong you can stop at Meningie ($36, two hours), Robe ($64, 4½ hours) and Beachport ($68, 5¼ hours). The inland bus runs daily via Naracoorte ($71, five hours) and Penola ($70, 5¾ hours).

# Coorong National Park

The amazing **Coorong National Park** (www.environment.sa.gov.au) is a fecund lagoon landscape curving along the coast for 145km from Lake Alexandrina towards Kingston SE. A complex series of soaks and salt pans, it's separated from the sea by the chunky dunes of the **Younghusband Peninsula**. More than 200 species of waterbirds live here. *Storm Boy,* an endearing film about a young boy's friendship with a pelican (based on the novel by Colin Thiele), was filmed here.

In the 1800s the bountiful resources of the Coorong supported a large Ngarrindjeri population. The Ngarrindjeri are still closely connected to the Coorong, and many still live here.

At the edge of the Coorong on **Lake Albert** (a large arm of Lake Alexandrina), **Meningie** (population 900) was established as a minor port in 1866. These 'lower lakes' have returned to life recently, in the wake of the 2011 Murray River floods. Prior to this, the lakes were shrinking rapidly, and the entire Coorong ecosystem was under threat through salination and species decline. A momentary reprieve from climate change? Time will tell...

The Princes Hwy scuttles through the park, but you can't see much from the road. Instead, take the 13km, unsealed **Coorong Scenic Drive**. Signed as Seven Mile Rd, it starts 10km southwest of Meningie off the Narrung Rd, and takes you right into the landscape, with its stinky lagoons, sea mists, fishing shanties, pelicans and wild emus. The road rejoins the Princes Hwy, 10km south of Meningie.

It looks a little shabby, but **Camp Coorong** (☑ 08-8575 1557; www.ngarrindjeri.net; Princes Hwy; museum admission per car $5; ⊙ vary) – run by the Ngarrindjeri Lands and Progress Association and 10km south of Meningie – has a museum and is a great place to learn about Ngarrindjeri culture. Call ahead to make sure it's open.

With a 4WD you can access **Ninety Mile Beach**, a well-known surf-fishing spot. The easiest ocean access point is 3km off the Princes Hwy at 42 Mile Crossing, 19km south of Salt Creek.

On the southern fringe of the Coorong is **Kingston SE** (www.kingstonse.com.au) with a population of 2230. The town is a hotbed of crayfishing, and hosts the weeklong **Lobsterfest** in May. One of Australia's 'big' tourist attractions, the anatomically correct Larry the Lobster is a famed resident.

For a watery perspective, try Spirit of the Coorong (p89) in Goolwa, which runs ecocruises into the national park, including lunch and a guided walk. Adelaide bus connections available.

## 🛏 Sleeping & Eating

There are 11 bush **camp sites** (www.environ ment.sa.gov.au; per person/car $7/13) in the park, but you need a permit from the DEWNR, available from the Meningie visitor information centre or the Meningie petrol station. There are also 'honesty boxes' at some of the larger campgrounds.

★ **Dalton on the Lake**                        B&B **$$**
(☑ 08-8575 1162, 0428 737 161; admason@lm.net. au; 30 Narrung Rd, Meningie; d from $130; ❇) Generous in spirit and unfailingly clean, this lakeside B&B goes to great lengths to ensure your stay is comfortable. There'll be fresh bread baking when you arrive, jars of homemade biscuits, and bountiful bacon and eggs for breakfast. There's a modern self-

contained studio off to one side, or a renovated stone cottage – book either, or both.

**Lake Albert Caravan Park**          CARAVAN PARK **$**
(☑ 08-8575 1411; www.lakealbertcaravanpark.com. au; 25 Narrung Rd, Meningie; unpowered/powered sites from $23/30, cabins without/with bathroom from $70/95; ❇ 🐾) A breezy park with a beaut aspect overlooking pelican-prone Lake Albert (the best camp sites are absolute lakefront). The four deluxe two-bedroom cabins ($150) are the pick of the cabins.

**Coorong**
**Wilderness Lodge**          CAMPGROUND, CABINS **$$**
(☑ 08-8575 6001; www.coorongwildernesslodge. com; off Princes Hwy; unpowered/powered sites $15/30, dm/d/cabins, $40/90/200; ❇) At isolated Hack Point, 25km south of Meningie, this fish-shaped conference centre is run by a local Ngarrindjeri family. The bunkhouse and camp sites here are a bit ordinary, but the new kitchen-cabins are lovely. You can also book a bush-tucker walk ($30) or hire a kayak (half-/full day $40/60).

**Cheese Factory Restaurant**          PUB **$$**
(☑ 08-8575 1914; www.meningie.com.au; 3 Fiebig Rd, Meningie; mains $19-28; ⊙ noon-2pm Tue-Sun, 5.30-late Wed & Sun) In a converted cheese factory (you might have guessed), this outfit gives the Meningie pub a run for its money. Lean on the front bar with the locals, or munch into steaks, lasagne, mixed grills, Coorong mullet or a Coorong burger (with mullet!) in the cavernous dining room. The very lo-fi **Meningie Cheese Factory Museum** (www.meningiecheesefac torymuseum.com; admission $3; ⊙ 11am-5pm) is here too (butter churns, old typewriters, domestic knick-knackery)

## ❶ Information

**Meningie Visitor Information Centre** (☑ 08-8575 1770; www.meningie.com.au; 14 Princes Hwy; ⊙ 10am-4.30pm) Coorong camping permits and local info.

# Robe

POP 1130

Robe is a cherubic little fishing port that's become a holiday hot spot for Adelaidians and Melburnians alike. The sign saying 'Drain L Outlet' as you roll into town doesn't promise much, but along the main street you'll find quality eateries and boundless accommodation, and there are some magic beaches and lakes around town. Over Christmas and Easter, Robe is packed to the heavens – book *waaay* in advance.

## ⊙ Sights & Activities

Heritage-listed buildings dating from the late 1840s to 1870s litter the streets of Robe, including the upstanding little 1863 **Customs House** (www.nationaltrustsa.org.au; Royal Circus; adult/child $2/50¢; ⊙ 2-4pm Tue & Sat Feb-Dec, 2-4pm Mon-Sat Jan), now a nautical museum.

**Little Dip Conservation Park** (www.environment.sa.gov.au) runs along the coast for about 13km south of town. It features a variety of habitats including lakes, wetlands and dunes, and some beaut beaches, Aboriginal middens, walks and camping spots (per person/car $7/13). Access is via Nora Creina Rd.

The small town beach has safe swimming, while **Long Beach** (2km from town), is good for surfing, sailboarding and lazy days (safe swimming in some sections – ask at the visitors centre). **Steve's Place** (⊘ 08-8768 2094; stevesplace66@internode.on.net; 26 Victoria St; ⊙ 9.30am-5pm Mon-Fri, 9am-1pm Sat, 10am-1pm Sun) rents out boards/bodyboards/wetsuits (per day $40/20/20), and is also the best place for info on the annual **Robe Easter Classic** in April, SA's longest-running surf comp (since 1968).

## 🛏 Sleeping

Local rental agents with properties from as low as $80 per night in the off season include **Happyshack** (⊘ 0403 578 382, 08-8768 2341; www.happyshack.com.au), **SAL Real Estate** (⊘ 08-8768 2737; www.salrealestate.com.au; 25 Victoria St) and **Robe Lifestyle** (⊘ 1300 760 629; www.robelifestyle.com.au).

**Caledonian Inn**                               HOTEL $$
(⊘ 08-8768 2029; www.caledonian.net.au; 1 Victoria St; pub/cottage/villa d from $85/185/500; 🐾) This historic inn has it all under one roof (actually, several roofs). The half-dozen pub rooms upstairs share bathroom facilities but are bright and cosy, while the split-level, self-contained units – all rattan and white-painted wood – are sandwiched between the pub and beach. The plush villa sleeps eight. The pub grub is good, too (mains $18 to $36, serving noon to 2pm and 6pm to 8pm).

**Grey Masts**                                   B&B $$$
(⊘ 0411 627 146; www.greymasts.com.au; cnr Victoria & Smillie Sts; d from $200) A lovely, L-shaped, low-ceilinged 1850s stone cottage behind

the local bookshop. The two bedrooms sleep four, and there's a compact kitchen, welcoming lounge and flower-filled garden. The Savage family (Mr and Mrs Savage and their 12 sons!) once lived here.

**Lakeside Tourist Park**            CARAVAN PARK $
(⊘ 08-8768 2193; www.lakesiderobe.com.au; 24 Main Rd; unpowered/powered sites from $32/34, cabins/villas from $66/95; @ 🐾) Right on Lake Fellmongery (a 'fellmonger' is a wool washer, don't you know), this abstractly laid-out, rather boutique park has heritage-listed pine trees, plenty of grass, basic cabins and flashy villas.

**Robe Lakeview
Motel & Apartments**                      MOTEL $$
(⊘ 08-8768 2100; www.robelakeviewmotel.com.au; 2 Lakeside Tce; d/2-bedroom apt from $110/225, extra person $15; ❄ 🐾) Overlooking the water-skiing mecca Lake Fellmongery, the keenly managed Lake View is Robe's best motel. The decor is on the improve (slowly banishing the '90s), the rooms are roomy and immaculately clean, and the barbecue area pumps during summer.

## 🍴 Eating

**Union Cafe**                                   CAFE $
(⊘ 08-8768 2627; 4/17-19 Victoria St; mains $9-19; ⊙ 8am-4pm; 🐾) Robe's best coffee is at this curiously angled corner cafe with polished-glass fragments in the floor and improvised chandeliers on the ceiling. Unionise your hangover with big breakfasts (berry pancakes with bacon and maple syrup), stir-fries, pastas and risottos.

**Vic Street Pizzeria**                        PIZZA $$
(⊘ 08-8768 2081; www.vicstreet.com.au; 6 Victoria St; mains $10-21; ⊙ 11am-9pm) Vic Street is a high-energy, all-day cafe, serving good coffee and gourmet pizzas (we can recommend the 'Humdinger': ham, salami, chicken, red onion, olives, capsicum and pineapple). Mod-Asian interior touches, cool tunes on the stereo and local wines, too.

**Robe Providore**                              CAFE $
(⊘ 08-8768 2891; 4 Victoria St; mains $13-18; ⊙ 8am-late) A bit of 'big city' comes to Robe at this polished concrete-and-white eatery, serving good coffee, big breakfasts (eggs benedict, house-baked pastries), considered lunches (calamari salad) and wood-oven pizzas at night (try the pork-and-fennel sausage version). There are communal tables and bench seats.

## ⓘ Information

**Robe Visitor Information Centre** (☑08-8768 2465, 1300 367 144; www.robe.com.au; Mundy Tce, Public Library; ☉9am-5pm Mon-Fri, 10am-4pm Sat & Sun; 🛜) Displays, brochures and free internet. Look for *Scenic Drive, Heritage Drive* and *A Walk Through History* pamphlets.

# Beachport

POP 350

'See and be seen: headlights 24 hours!' say billboards on the way into Beachport. A town that's desperate to be noticed? A plaintive cry for attention? We like it the way it is: low-key and beachy, with aquamarine surf, the famous 800m-long jetty, staunch stone buildings and rows of Norfolk Island pines. Forget about being seen – your time here will be perfectly anonymous.

## ◉ Sights & Activities

**Old Wool & Grain Store Museum**  MUSEUM
(☑08-8735 8029; www.nationaltrust.org.au/sa; 5 Railway Tce; adult/child/family $5/2/10; ☉10am-4pm) In a National Trust building on the main street. Inside are relics from Beachport's whaling and shipping days, rooms decked out in 1870s style and a new display on the local Buandi people.

**Beachport Conservation Park**  NATURE RESERVE
(www.environment.sa.gov.au) There are some great walking tracks in the 710-hectare park, sandwiched between the coast and Lake George 2km north of town. Aboriginal middens, sheltered coves, lagoons and bush camping (per person/car $7/13).

**Pool of Siloam**  SWIMMING
(Bowman Scenic Dr) In the dunes on the western outskirts of town, the pool is great for swimming; the water is seven times saltier than the ocean. Ask at the vistor information centre for directions.

## 🍴 Sleeping & Eating

**Bompas**  HOTEL, CAFE $
(☑08-8735 8333; www.bompas.com.au; 3 Railway Tce; d without/with bathroom from $100/125; 🛜) In what was Beachport's first pub, Bompas is an all-in-one small hotel and licensed restaurant-cafe. Rooms upstairs are generously sized and strewn with modern art (shoot for room No 3 – more expensive, but worth it for the million-dollar views and deep balcony). Menu offerings downstairs

(mains $9 to $23, serving noon to 2pm and 6pm to 8pm, plus breakfast on weekends) include curries, schnitzels and pies, with local and imported beers.

**Southern Ocean Tourist Park**  CARAVAN PARK $
(☑08-8735 8153; sotp@bigpond.net.au; Somerville St; unpowered/powered sites $26/30, cabins from $105; ❄) This well-pruned, shady park is nooked into the base of a hill in the town centre. Facilities include a laundry, covered barbecues, crayfish cookers and a great little playground. The new kitchen cabins on the hilltop are lovely.

## ⓘ Information

**Beachport Visitor Information Centre**
(☑08-8735 8029; www.wattlerange.sa.gov.au; Millicent Rd; ☉9am-5pm Mon-Fri, 10am-4pm Sat & Sun) Info-packed, on the road into town. Look for the *Beachport's Bowman Scenic Drive* brochure.

# Mount Gambier

POP 24,900

Strung out along the flatlands below an extinct volcano, Mount Gambier is the Limestone Coast's major town and service hub. 'The Mount' sometimes seems a little short on urban virtues, but it's not what's above the streets that makes Mount Gambier special – it's the deep Blue Lake and caves that worm their way though the limestone beneath the town. Amazing!

## ◉ Sights & Activities

**Blue Lake**  LAKE
(John Watson Dr; ☉24hr) FREE Mount Gambier's big-ticket item is the luminous, 75m-deep lake, which turns an insane hue of blue during summer. Perplexed scientists think it has to do with calcite crystals suspended in the water, which form at a faster rate during the warmer months. Consequently, if you visit between April and November, the lake will look much like any other – a steely grey.

**Acquifer Tours**  (☑08-8723 1199; www.aquifertours.com; cnr Bay Rd & John Watson Dr; adult/child/family $9/4/25; ☉tours 9am-5pm Nov-Jan, 9am-2pm Feb-May & Sep-Oct, 9am-noon Jun-Aug) runs hourly tours, taking you down near the lake shore in a glass-panelled lift.

**Riddoch Art Gallery**  GALLERY
(www.riddochartgallery.org.au; 1 Bay Rd; ☉10am-5pm Mon-Fri, 11am-3pm Sat & Sun) FREE If the lake isn't blue, don't feel blue – cheer yourself

# PORT MACDONNELL

Around 30km south of Mt Gambier, snoozy crayfishing Port MacDonnell (population 700) is SA's southernmost town. It was once the second-busiest port in the state, which explains the handsome 1863 **Customs House** (☑08-8738 2475, 0418 854 595; www. thecustomshouse.com.au; 3 Charles St, Port MacDonnell; d from $260), now a B&B.

Around 40 ships have sunk along the coast near here since 1844. The **Port Mac-Donnell & District Maritime Museum** (www.dcgrant.sa.gov.au/page.aspx?u=449; 5-7 Charles St, Port MacDonnell; adult/child $5/3; ⊙9am-5pm Mon-Thu, 9am-8pm Fri, 10am-4pm Sat & Sun) is a barnacle-encrusted trove of artefacts recovered from the shipwrecks.

## Sleeping

**Park Hotel** (☑08-8725 2430; www.parkhotel.net.au; 163 Commercial St W; d from $140; ❄🔊) In Mount Gambier's western wastelands, this old corner pub has spent a fortune renovating its three upstairs rooms. Polished timber floors, double glazing, marble bathrooms and coffee-and-cream colour schemes – a really slick product.

**Colhurst House** (☑08-8723 1309; www.colhursthouse.com.au; 3 Colhurst Pl; d incl breakfast from $170; ❄) Most locals don't know about Colhurst – it's up a laneway off a sidestreet (Wyatt St) and you can't really see it from downtown Mt G. It's an 1878 mansion built by Welsh migrants, and manages to be old-fashioned without being twee. There's a wrap-around balcony upstairs with great views over the rooftops. Cooked breakfasts, too.

**Old Mount Gambier Gaol** (☑08-8723 0032; www.hmgetaway.com.au; 25 Margaret St; dm/tw/d from $26/60/80; 🔊) If you can forget that this place was a prison until 1995 (either that or embrace the fact), these refurbished old buildings make for an atmospheric and affordable stay. There's a regulation backpacker dorm in one building, or you can up the spooky stakes and sleep in a former cell. There's a bar with occasional live bands.

**Blue Lake Holiday Park** (☑08-8725 9856, 1800 676 028; www.bluelake.com.au; Bay Rd; unpowered/powered sites from $31/36, cabins/units/bungalows from $98/120/180; ❄@🔊🛏) Adjacent to the Blue Lake, a golf course and walking and cycling tracks, this amiable park has some natty grey-and-white cabins and well-weeded lawns. There are also spiffy contemporary, self-contained 'retreats' (from $200) that sleep four.

## Eating

**Yoeys** (www.yoeys.com.au; 32 James St; items $5-14; ⊙8.30am-5.30pm Mon-Fri, 8.30am-1.30pm Sat) What a find! A gourmet cafe-providore with shelves full of cakes, muffins, breads, chocolates, pasta and gourmet foodie hampers; a fabulous cheese fridge (rustic Italian goats' cheese anyone?); and the best coffee in town. Soups, pies and pasties, too.

**Bullfrogs** (☑08-8723 3933; www.bullfrogs.com.au; 7 Percy St; mains $11-32; ⊙11am-late) Spread over three floors of a fabulous old stone mill building, this is the place for beef and lamb grills, boutique beers, Coonawarra wines, cocktails, trusty coffee and occasional acoustic troubadours. Hard to beat.

**Banana Tree Cafe & Terrace** (☑08-8723 9393; www.bananatree.com.au; 53 Gray St; mains $16-33; ⊙11am-2pm & 6-9pm) Authentic Thai in Mount Gambier! Colourful and appropriately tacky (faux rattan, chandeliers, commercial FM), backstreet Banana Tree serves chilli-laden dishes like beef-and-basil stir-fry and a smokin' green chicken curry.

**Jens Town Hall Hotel** (☑08-8725 1671; 40 Commercial St E; mains $15-29; ⊙noon-2pm & 6-8pm) The most palatable place for a beer in the Mount (there are a lot of rambling old pubs here), the 1884 Jens has a vast dining room plating up equally large steaks, mixed grills, pastas, seafood and a damn fine lasagne. There are $12 lunch specials.

## Information

**Mount Gambier Visitor Information Centre** (☑08-8724 9750, 1800 087 187; www. mountgambiertourism.com.au; 35 Jubilee Hwy E; ⊙9am-5pm) has details on local sights, activities, transport and accommodation. **Lady Nelson Discovery Centre** (adult/child $2/1) is here too, featuring a replica of the historic brig *Lady Nelson*.

up at one of Australia's best regional galleries. There are three galleries (touring and permanent exhibitions, contemporary installations, community displays), plus heritage exhibits and a cinema screening local history flicks. Free tours 11am Thursday.

**Cave Gardens**                                        CAVE
(cnr Bay Rd & Watson Tce; ⊙24hr) FREE A 50m-deep sinkhole right in the middle of town, with the odd suicidal shopping trolley at the bottom. You can walk down into it, and watch the nightly Sound & Light Show (8pm) telling local Aboriginal Dreaming stories.

**Engelbrecht Cave**                                    CAVE
(☑08-8723 5552; www.mtgambiersa.com.au/attractions/engelbrecht-cave; Jubilee Hwy W, off Chute St; tours adult/child/family $12/8/34; ⊙tours hourly 9am-4pm, to 3pm winter) A meandering cave system running beneath Jubilee Hwy and 19 local houses! Tours last 45 minutes and take you down to an underground lake (call for cave-diving info). There's also a cafe here.

**Umpherston Sinkhole**                                 CAVE
(☑0429 349 328; 2160 Jubilee Hwy E; admission free, guided tours adult/child/family $9/4/20, self-guided tours adult/child $5/free; ⊙24hr, tours 9am-9pm summer, 10am-4pm winter) FREE Once 'a pleasant resort in the heat of summer' on James Umpherston's long since subdivided estate. It's free to check it out, or you can take a self-guided or guided tour.

# PENOLA & THE COONAWARRA WINE REGION

A rural town on the way up (what a rarity!), Penola (population 1670) is the kind of place where you walk down the main street and three people say 'Hello!' to you before you reach the pub. The town is famous for two things: first, for its association with the Sisters of St Joseph of the Sacred Heart, co-founded in 1867 by Australia's first saint, Mary MacKillop; and secondly, for being smack bang in the middle of the Coonawarra Wine Region.

## ◉ Sights & Activities

**Mary MacKillop Interpretive Centre** MUSEUM
(www.mackilloppenola.org.au; cnr Portland St & Petticoat La; adult/child $5/free; ⊙10am-4pm)

The centre occupies a jaunty building with a gregarious entrance pergola (perhaps not as modest as Saint Mary might have liked!). There's oodles of info on Australia's first saint here, plus the Woods MacKillop Schoolhouse, the first school in Australia for children from lower socioeconomic backgrounds.

**John Riddoch Centre**                               MUSEUM
(www.wattlerange.sa.gov.au/tourism; 27 Arthur St; ⊙9am-5pm Mon-Fri, 10am-4pm Sat & Sun) FREE In the visitor centre building, this museum casts a web over local history back to the 1850s, covering the local Pinejunga people and original Penola pastoralist Riddoch, who 'never gave in to misfortune' and was 'steady and persistent'. Closed for a refurbishment when we revisited.

**Petticoat Lane**                                     STREET
One of Penola's first streets. Most of the original buildings have been razed, but there are still a few old timber-slab houses, redgum kerbs and gnarly trees to see.

## 🛏 Sleeping & Eating

See www.coonawarradiscovery.com for B&B listings. Many local Coonawarra wineries also have restaurants.

**Must@Coonawarra**                              MOTEL $$
(☑08-8737 3444; www.mustatcoonawarra.com.au; 126 Church St; r from $165; ❋ 🔊) ⟋ On the way up the winery strip, plush Must is a newish option with jaunty roof curves reminiscent of a certain opera venue in Sydney. Accommodation ranges from studios to apartments, with sustainable features aplenty: rain-water showers, double glazing and insulation, solar hot water, natural cleaning products etc. Bike hire costs $20 per day.

**Heyward's Royal Oak Hotel**                         PUB $
(☑08-8737 2322; www.heywardshotel.com.au; 31 Church St; s $55, d & tw $88) The Royal Oak – a lace-trimmed, main-street megalith built in 1872 – is Penola's community hub. The rooms upstairs are a bit tatty and share bathrooms, but they're good bang for your buck. Downstairs the huge tartan-carpeted dining room (mains $20 to $33, open 11.30am to 2pm and 6pm to 8pm) serves classy pub food (roo fillets with pepper crust and cabernet glaze) and schnitzels as big as your head. There's a summery beer garden, too.

### Georgie's Cottage  B&B $$

(☑ 08-8737 3540; www.georgiescottage.com; 1 Riddoch St; d from $185; ❄) Feeling romantic? A short stroll from town on the road to Millicent, Georgie's is a cute little stone cottage fronted by blooming roses and hollyhocks. Gourmet provisions include chocolates and wine, which you may or may not feel like cracking into for breakfast.

### Pipers of Penola  MODERN AUSTRALIAN $$$

(☑ 08-8737 3999; www.pipersofpenola.com.au; 58 Riddoch St; mains $30-37; ⊙ 6-9pm Tue-Sat) A classy, intimate dining room tastefully constructed inside an old Methodist church, with friendly staff and seasonal fare. The menu is studded with words like 'galette', 'kromeski' and 'rotollo' – seriously gourmet indicators! The prices are getting up there, but quality is too. Superb wine list with lots of locals.

### diVine  CAFE $

(☑ 08-8737 2122; www.penola.org/divine.htm; 39 Church St; mains $10-19; ⊙ 9am-5pm) A bright, mod cafe serving baguettes, all-day breakfasts, great coffee and internationally inspired lunches (try the steamed Chinese pork buns). Nattering Penolans chew muffins and local cheeses, discussing the nuances of various vintages.

## ℹ Information

**Penola Visitor Information Centre** (☑ 08-8737 2855, 1300 045 373; www.wattlerange.sa.gov.au/tourism; 27 Arthur St; ⊙ 9am-5pm Mon-Fri, 10am-4pm Sat & Sun) Services the Coonawarra region, with info about local cycling routes and winery tours. The John Riddoch Centre is also here. Pick up the *Penola Cycle Trails* and *Walk With History* brochures.

# NARACOORTE CAVES NATIONAL PARK

About 10km southeast of Naracoorte township, off the Penola road, is the only World Heritage–listed site in SA. The discovery of an ancient fossilised marsupial in these limestone caves raised palaeontological eyebrows around the world, and featured in the BBC's David Attenborough series *Life on Earth*.

The park visitor centre doubles as the impressive **Wonambi Fossil Centre** (☑ 08-8762 2340; www.environment.sa.gov.au/naracoorte; Hynam-Caves Rd; adult/child/family $13/8/36; ⊙ 9am-5pm) – a re-creation of the rainforest that covered this area 200,000 years ago. Follow a ramp down past grunting, life-sized reconstructions of extinct

## COONAWARRA WINERIES

When it comes to spicy cabernet sauvignon, it's just plain foolish to dispute the virtues of the Coonawarra Wine Region (www.coonawarra.org). The *terra rossa* (red earth) soils here also produce irresistible shiraz and chardonnay. Five of the best:

**Zema Estate** (www.zema.com.au; Riddoch Hwy; ⊙ 9am-5pm) A steadfast, traditional winery started by the Zema family in the early '80s. It's a low-key affair with a handmade vibe infusing the shiraz and cab sav.

**Rymill Coonawarra** (www.rymill.com.au; Riddoch Hwy; ⊙ 10am-5pm) Rymill rocks the local boat by turning out some of the best sauvignon blanc you'll ever taste. The cellar door is fronted by a statue of two duelling steeds – appropriately rebellious.

**Majella Wines** (www.majellawines.com.au; Lynn Rd; ⊙ 10am-4.30pm) The family that runs Majella are fourth-generation Coonawarrans, so they know a thing or two about gutsy reds.

**Balnaves of Coonawarra** (www.balnaves.com.au; Riddoch Hwy; ⊙ 9am-5pm Mon-Fri, noon-5pm Sat & Sun) The tasting notes here ooze florid wine speak (dark seaweed, anyone?), but even if your nosing skills aren't that subtle, you'll enjoy the cab sav and chardonnay.

**Wynns Coonawarra Estate** (www.wynns.com.au; 2 Memorial Dr; ⊙ 10am-5pm) The oldest Coonawarra winery, Wynns' cellar door dates from 1896 and was built by Penola pioneer John Riddoch. Top-quality shiraz, fragrant riesling and golden chardonnay are the mainstays.

animals, including a marsupial lion, a giant echidna, *Diprotodon australis* (koala meets grizzly bear), and *Megalania prisca* – 500kg of bad-ass goanna.

The 26 limestone caves here, including Alexandra Cave, Cathedral Cave and Victoria Fossil Cave, have bizarre formations of stalactites and stalagmites. Prospective Bruce Waynes should check out the Bat Cave, from which thousands of endangered southern bentwing bats exit en masse at dusk during summer. You can see the Wet Cave by self-guided tour (adult/child/family $9/5.50/25), but the others require ranger-guided tours. Single-cave tours start at adult/child/family $20/12/55. There's also budget accommodation here at Wirreanda Bunkhouse ([☎]08-8762 2340; www.environment.sa.gov.au/naracoorte; dm/powered sites from $22/25), which is often full of school kids but can be booked by travellers.

For more local info and tips on places to stay, contact Naracoorte Visitor Information Centre ([☎]08-8762 1399; www.naracoortelucindale.com; 36 MacDonnell St; ⊙9am-5pm Mon-Fri, 10am-4pm Sat & Sun) in Naracoorte.

# MURRAY RIVER

On the lowest gradient of any Australian river, the slow-flowing Murray hooks through 650 South Australian kilometres. Tamed by weirs and locks, the Murray irrigates the fruit trees and vines of the sandy Riverland district to the north, and winds through the dairy country of the Murraylands district to the south. Raucous flocks of white corellas and pink galahs launch from cliffs and river red gums and dart across lush vineyards and orchards.

Prior to European colonisation, the Murray was home to Meru communities. Then came shallow-draught paddle steamers, carrying wool, wheat and supplies from Murray Bridge as far as central Queensland along the Darling River. With the advent of railways, river transport declined. These days, waterskiers, jet skis and houseboats crowd out the river, especially during summer. If your concept of riverine serenity doesn't include the roar of V8 inboards, then avoid the major towns and caravan parks during holidays and weekends.

Online, see www.themurrayriver.com.

## ◉ Sights & Activities

Houseboating is big business on the Murray. Meandering along the river is great fun – you just need to be over 18 with a current driving licence. Boats depart from most riverside towns; book ahead, especially between October and April.

The Houseboat Hirers Association ([☎]08-8231 8466, 1300 665 122; www.houseboatbookings.com) website has pictures of each boat and can make bookings on your behalf. For a three-night weekend, expect to pay anywhere from $670 for two people to $2700 for a luxury 10-bed boat. Most boats sleep at least two couples and there's generally a bond involved (starting at $200). Many provide linen – just bring food and fine wine. See also SA Tourism's *Houseboat Holidays* booklet for detailed houseboat listings.

## ℹ Getting There & Away

LinkSA (www.linksa.com.au) runs several daily bus services between Adelaide and Murray Bridge ($20, 1¼ hours), plus Adelaide to Mannum ($27, 2½ hours) from Monday to Friday (which involves a bus change at Mt Barker in the Adelaide Hills). Premier Stateliner (www.premierstateliner.com.au) runs daily Riverland buses from Adelaide, stopping in Waikerie ($42, 2½ hours), Barmera ($52, 3¼ hours), Berri ($52, 3½ hours) and Renmark ($52, four hours). Buses stop at Loxton ($52, 3¾ hours) daily, except Saturday.

---

### ROLLIN' ON THE RIVER

Until 2011, Old Man Murray was in dire straits, degraded by drought, salinisation, evaporation, upstream irrigation and the demands of servicing SA's domestic water requirements. Ecosystems were awry and many farmers faced bankruptcy. Debate raged over solutions: federal control of the Murray-Darling Basin? Stiffer quotas for upstream irrigators? A weir at Wellington? Opening the Goolwa barrages and letting salt water flood the lower lakes? Things were grim.

In 2011 the drought broke: flooding upstream in Queensland, New South Wales and Victoria and rains delivered by Tropical Cyclone Yasi got things flowing, purging the backlog of silt and salt, and filling wetlands with life. But what about the future? See www.savethemurray.com for the latest ideas on how to keep Old Man Murray a-flowin'.

# Murray Bridge

POP 18.370

SA's largest river town is a rambling regional hub (the fifth-biggest town in SA) with lots of old pubs but an underutilised riverfront, a huge prison and not a great deal of charm.

## ⊙ Sights

**Murray Bridge Regional Gallery**   GALLERY
(www.murraybridgegallery.com.au; 27 6th St; ⊙10am-4pm Tue-Sat, 11am-4pm Sun) FREE This is the town's cultural epicentre and houses touring and local exhibitions: painting, ceramics, glasswear, jewellery and prints.

**Monarto Zoo**   ZOO
(www.monartozoo.com.au; Princes Hwy, Monarto; adult/child/family $31.50/18/85; ⊙9.30am-5pm, last entry 3pm) About 14km west of town, the excellent open-range zoo is home to Australian and African beasts including cheetahs, rhinos and giraffes (and the cute offspring thereof). A hop-on/hop-off bus tour is included in the price; keeper talks happen throughout the day.

**Captain Proud Paddle Boat Cruises**   CRUISE
(✆0466 304 092; www.captainproud.com.au; Wharf Rd; 1/2/3hr cruises $25/45/49) River cruises from one-hour sightseeing to longer jaunts with lunch, high tea or drinks and cheese platters. Call for times and bookings.

## 🛏 Sleeping

**Adelaide Road Motor Lodge**   MOTEL $
(✆08-8532 1144; www.adelaiderdmotorlodge. com; 212 Adelaide Rd; d from $80, tr & q $130-215; ❄🛜🏊) If you're stuck for a bed here, your best bet is probably this funky '60s number with a 21st-century facelift – one of several motels on the road in from the Murray Bridge–Adelaide freeway.

## ❶ Information

**Murray Bridge Visitor Information Centre**
(✆1800 442 784, 08-8339 1142; www.murray bridge.sa.gov.au; 3 South Tce; ⊙9am-5pm) Stocks the *Murray Bridge Accommodation Guide* and *Eating Out in Murray Bridge* brochures, and has info on river-cruise operators.

# Mannum to Waikerie

Clinging to a narrow strip of riverbank 84km east of Adelaide, improbably cute Mannum (population 6750) is the unof-ficial houseboat capital of the world! The *Mary Ann*, Australia's first riverboat, was knocked together here in 1853 and made the first paddle-steamer trip up the Murray. The Mannum visitor information centre incorporates the **Mannum Dock Museum of River History** (www.psmarion.com; 6 Randell St, Mannum; adult/child $7.50/3.50), featuring info on local Ngarrindjeri Aboriginal communities, an 1876 dry dock and the restored 1897 paddle steamer *PS Marion,* on which you can occasionally chug around the river.

**Breeze Holiday Hire** (✆0438 802 668; www.murrayriver.com.au/breeze-holiday-hire-1052) hires out canoes and kayaks (per day $75), dinghies with outboards (per day $95) and fishing gear (per day $15), and can get you waterskiing too.

From Mannum to Swan Reach, the eastern riverside road often tracks a fair way east of the river, but various lookouts en route help you scan the scene. Around 9km south of Swan Reach, the Murray takes a tight meander called **Big Bend**, a sweeping river curve with pock-marked, ochre-coloured cliffs.

Sedentary old Swan Reach (population 850), 70km southwest of Waikerie, is a bit of a misnomer: an old pub and plenty of pelicans but not many swans.

A citrus-growing centre oddly festooned with TV antennas, Waikerie (population 4630) takes its name from the Aboriginal phrase for 'anything that flies'. There's plenty of bird life around here, with 180 species recorded at **Gluepot Reserve** (✆08-8892 9600; www.riverland.net.au/gluepot; Gluepot Rd; cars per day/overnight $5/10; ⊙8am-6pm), a mallee scrub area 64km north of Waikerie (off Lunn Rd) and part of Unesco's Bookmark Biosphere Reserve. Before you head off, check with Waikerie's Shell service station on Peake Tce to see if you'll need a gate key.

## ☞ Tours

**Jester Cruises**   CRUISE
(✆0419 909 116, 08-8569 2330; www.jestercruises. com.au; 1¾/2½hr tours $30/60) Cruise up and down the river from Mannum on the 40-seat Jester, running most days.

**Proud Mary**   CRUISE
(✆08-8406 444; www.proudmary.com.au; 1½hr tour adult/child $55/40) Lunch cruises on a big boat on the big river, departing from Mannum. Brush up on your Creedence Clearwater Revival lyrics.

## 🛏 Sleeping & Eating

**Mannum Motel**                    MOTEL **$$**
(📞 08-8569 1808; www.mannummotel.com.au; 76 Cliff St, Mannum; d/f from $130/150; ❄️ 🎨 📶) This unobtrusive brown-brick '80s number squats on a rise above the ferry crossing at Mannum. Some of the larger units have kitchenettes if you don't fancy the in-house bistro or a trip to the pub for dinner.

**Mannum Caravan Park**        CARAVAN PARK **$**
(📞 08-8569 1402; www.mannumcaravanpark.com.au; Purnong Rd, Mannum; unpowered/powered sites $25/29, cabins/villas from $64/120; ❄️ @ 📶) A clean-cut caravan park right on the river next to the Mannum ferry crossing. Ducks and water hens patrol the lawns, and there's a pool table in the games room if it's raining. Lots of shade-giving gums.

**Waikerie Hotel Motel**       HOTEL-MOTEL **$**
(📞 08-8541 2999; www.waikeriehotel.com; 2 McCoy St, Waikerie; d $79-139; ❄️ 📶) Waikerie's main-street pub has clean, affordable hotel rooms (all with bathroom, rather unusually) and updated motel rooms out the back. The oldest part of the pub burnt down in 2012, two days shy of its 100th birthday! The bistro does pub-grub classics (mains $16 to $35, serving noon to 2pm and 6pm to 8pm).

**Murray River Queen**          RIVERBOAT **$**
(📞 08-8541 2651; www.murrayriverqueen.com.au; Leonard Norman Dr, Waikerie; dm $30, d without/with bathroom from $55/90) When it's not cruising the Murray, this 1974 paddleboat

---

### ℹ️ DON'T PAY THE FERRYMAN

As the Murray curls abstractly across eastern SA, roads (on far more linear trajectories) invariably bump into it. Dating back to the late 19th century, a culture of free, 24-hour, winch-driven ferries has evolved to shunt vehicles across the water. Your car is guided onto the punts by burly, bearded, fluoro-clad ferrymen, who lock safety gates into position then shunt you across to the other side. There are 11 ferries in operation, the most useful of which are those at Mannum, Swan Reach and Waikerie. Turn off your headlights if you're waiting for the ferry at night so you don't bedazzle the approaching skipper.

---

berths at Waikerie and offers basic bunkrooms (a tad shabby and dim but undeniably novel) and more upmarket doubles. The onboard cafe is good for a light lunch (items $6 to $15, open 8.30am to 4pm Wednesday to Sunday). It's managed by the local caravan park.

**Pretoria Hotel**                    PUB **$$**
(📞 08-8569 1109; www.pretoriahotel.com.au; 50 Randell St, Mannum; mains $16-28; ⊙ noon-2pm & 6-8pm) The family-friendly Pretoria (built 1900) has a vast bistro and deck fronting the river, and plates up big steaks, roo fillets and parmas plus Asian salads and good seafood. When the 1956 flood swamped the town they kept pouring beer from the 1st-floor balcony!

## ℹ️ Information

**Mannum Visitor Information Centre** (📞 08-8569 1303, 1300 626 686; www.psmarion.com; 6 Randell St, Mannum; ⊙ 9am-5pm Mon-Fri, 10am-4pm Sat & Sun) Cruise and houseboat bookings, *Mannum Historic Walks* brochures and the **Museum of River History**.

---

# Barmera & Around

On the shallow shores of Lake Bonney (upon which world land-speed record-holder Donald Campbell unsuccessfully attempted to break his water-speed record in 1964), snoozy Barmera (population 4290) was once a key town on the overland stock route from NSW. These days the local passion for both kinds of music (country *and* western) lends a simple optimism to proceedings. Kingston-On-Murray (population 260; aka Kingston OM) is a tiny town en route to Waikerie.

## ⊙ Sights & Activities

The once ephemeral **Lake Bonney** has been transformed into a permanent lake ringed by large, drowned red gums, whose stark branches are often festooned with birds. If you're feeling uninhibited, there's a nudist beach at **Pelican Point Holiday Park** (www.riverland.net.au/pelicanpoint) on the lake's western shore.

There are wildlife reserves with walking trails and camping (per car $7) at Moorook on the road to Loxton, and Loch Luna across the river from Kingston-On-Murray. Loch Luna backs onto the Overland Corner Hotel. Both reserves have nature trails and are prime spots for birdwatching and canoeing. Self-register camping permits are available at reserve entrances.

There are also walking trails at the Overland Corner Hotel.

★ **Banrock Station Wine & Wetland Centre** WINERY
(www.banrockstation.com.au; Holmes Rd, Kingston OM; ⊙9am-4pm Mon-Fri, 9am-5pm Sat & Sun) 🌿 Overlooking regenerated, feral-proofed wetlands off the Sturt Hwy at Kingston OM, carbon-neutral Banrock Station Wine & Wetland Centre is a stylish, rammed-earth wine-tasting centre (love the tempranillo) and jazzy lunchtime restaurant (mains $17 to $25 – try the cumquat-glazed pork), using ingredients sourced locally. There are three wetland walks here: 2.5km and 4.5km ($3), and 8km ($5).

**Rocky's Hall of Fame Pioneers Museum** MUSEUM
(www.murrayriver.com.au/barmera/rockys-hall -of-fame-pioneers-museum; 4 Pascoe Tce, Barmera; adult/child $2/1; ⊙10am-noon & 1-3pm Wed-Mon) Country music is a big deal in Barmera, with the **South Australian Country Music Festival & Awards** (www. riverlandcountrymusic.com) happening here in June, and Rocky's Museum blaring sincere rural twangings down the main street from outdoor speakers. Don't miss the 35m Botanical Garden Guitar out the back, inlaid with the handprints of 160 country musos: from Slim Dusty to Kasey Chambers and everyone in between.

🛏 **Sleeping & Eating**

**Discovery Holiday Parks Lake Bonney** CARAVAN PARK $
(☑08-8588 2234; www.discoveryholidayparks. com.au; Lakeside Ave, Barmera; unpowered/powered sites from $22/29, cabins from $94; ❄🛜🏊) This keenly managed lakeside park has small beaches (safe swimming), electric barbecues, camp kitchen, laundry and plenty of room for kids to run amok. Plenty of trees; waterfront camp sites.

**Barmera Lake Resort Motel** MOTEL $
(☑08-8588 2555; www.barmeralakeresortmotel. com.au; Lakeside Dr, Barmera; d $90-145, f from $185; ❄🏊) Right across the road from the lake, this good-value motel has a barbecue, pool, laundry and tennis court. Rooms are nothing flash, but immaculate; most have lake views.

**Overland Corner Hotel** PUB $$
(☑08-8588 7021; www.murrayriver.com.au/ overland-corner; Old Coach Rd; mains $16-28; ⊙noon-2pm Tue-Sun, 6-8pm Thu-Sat) Off the Morgan Rd, 19km northwest of Barmera, this moody 1859 boozer is named after a Murray River bend where drovers used to camp. The pub walls ooze character and the meals are drover sized, plus there's a museum, a resident ghost and a beaut beer garden. An 8km self-guided **Overland Corner Walking Trail** leads to the river; pick up a brochure at the pub or Barmera visitor information centre.

ℹ **Information**

**Barmera Visitor Information Centre** (☑08-8588 2289, 1300 768 468; www.barmeratourism.com.au; Barwell Ave, Barmera; ⊙9am-5pm Mon-Fri, 10am-2pm Sat & Sun) Help with transport and accommodation bookings. Pick up the *Historic Overland Corner* walking trail brochure.

# Loxton

POP 4100

Sitting above a broad loop of the slow-roaming Murray, Loxton proclaims itself the 'Garden City of the Riverland'. The vibe here is low-key, agricultural and untouristy, with more tyre distributors, hardware shops and irrigation supply outlets than anything else.

◎ **Sights & Activities**

From Loxton you can canoe across to Katarapko Creek and the Katarapko Game Reserve in the **Murray River National Park** (www.environment.sa.gov.au); hire canoes from Loxton Riverfront Caravan Park.

**Tree of Knowledge** LANDMARK
Down by the river near the caravan park, the Tree of Knowledge is marked with flood levels from previous years. The bumper flows of 1931, '73, '74 and '75 and 2011 were totally outclassed by the flood-to-end-all-floods of 1956, marked about 4m up the trunk.

**Loxton Historical Village** MUSEUM
(www.loxtonhistoricalvillage.com.au; Allen Hosking Dr; adult/child/family $12/6/30; ⊙10am-4pm Mon-Fri, to 5pm Sat & Sun) The mildly kitsch (but nonetheless interesting) Loxton Historical Village is a re-created time warp of 45 dusty, rusty old buildings with costumed staff.

**ADELAIDE & SOUTH AUSTRALIA** LOXTON

## 🛏 Sleeping & Eating

**Harvest Trail Lodge**                    HOSTEL **$**
(📞 08-8584 5646; www.harvesttrail.com; 1 Kokoda
Tce; dm per night/week $45/125; ❄) Inside a
converted '60s waterworks office are four-
bed dorms with TVs and fridges, and a barbecue balcony to boot. Staff will find you
fruit-picking work, and shunt you to and
from jobs.

**Loxton Hotel**                    HOTEL-MOTEL **$$**
(📞 08-8584 7266, 1800 656 686; www.loxton
hotel.com.au; 45 East Tce; hotel s/d from $80/105,
motel from $120/135; ❄ 🛜 🏊) With all profits
siphoned back into the Loxton community,
this large complex offers immaculate rooms
with tasty weekend packages. The original
pub dates from 1908, but it has been relent-
lessly extended. Bistro meals are available
for breakfast, lunch and dinner (mains $17
to $28).

**Loxton Riverfront**
**Caravan Park**                    CARAVAN PARK **$**
(📞 08-8584 7862, 1800 887 733; www.lrcp.com.
au; Sophie Edington Dr; unpowered/powered sites
from $22/32, cabins without/with bathroom from
$62/75; ❄ 🛜) Situated on the gum-studded
Habels Bend, about 2km from town, this
affable riverside caravan park bills itself as
'The Quiet One'. You can hire a canoe (per
hour/day $11/55), and there's a free nine-
hole golf course (usually sandy, occasionally
flooded).

## ℹ Information

**Loxton Visitor Information Centre** (📞 08-
8584 8071, 1300 869 990; www.loxtontourism.
com.au; Bookpurnong Tce, Loxton Roundabout;
⊙ 9am-5pm Mon-Fri, 9am-4pm Sat, 10am-
4pm Sun) A friendly place for accommodation,
transport and national-park info, plus a small
art gallery. Look for the *Historic Walks of Loxton*
brochure.

---

# Berri

POP 7440

The name Berri derives from the Aboriginal
term *berri berri,* meaning 'big bend in the
river', and it was once a busy refuelling stop
for wood-burning paddle steamers. These
days Berri plays its role as an affluent re-
gional hub for both state government and
agricultural casual-labour agencies, and is
one of the better places to chase down casu-
al harvest jobs.

## ◉ Sights & Activities

Road access to the scenic Katarapko Creek
section of the **Murray River National Park**
(www.environment.sa.gov.au) is off the Stuart
Hwy between Berri and Barmera. This is a
beaut spot for bush camping (per car $7),
canoeing and birdwatching.

**Riverland Farmers Market**                    MARKET
(www.riverlandfarmersmarket.org.au; Crawford Tce,
Senior Citizens Hall; ⊙ 7.30-11.30am Sat) All
the good stuff that grows around here in
one place. A bacon-and-egg roll and some
freshly squeezed orange juice will right your
rudder.

**A Special Place for Jimmy James**    GARDENS
(Riverview Dr; ⊙ 24hr) A short amble from the
visitor centre, A Special Place for Jimmy
James is a living riverbank memorial to
the Aboriginal tracker who could 'read the
bush like a newspaper'. Whimsical tracks
and traces are scattered around granite
boulders.

**River Lands Gallery**                    GALLERY
(www.countryarts.org.au; 23 Wilson St; ⊙ 10am-
4pm Mon-Fri) As the murals and totem poles
around the base of Berri Bridge attest,
Berri is an artsy kinda town. This gallery
displays local, indigenous and travelling
painting, sculpture, weaving and digital
media exhibitions.

**BMS Tours**                    CRUISE
(📞 0408 282 300; www.houseboatadventure.com.
au/BMStours.php; tours from $60; 🚤) Murray
tours from Berri on an Everglades-style air-
boat called *Elka*.

## 🛏 Sleeping & Eating

**Berri Backpackers**                    HOSTEL **$**
(📞 08-8582 3144; www.berribackpackers.com.au;
1081 Old Sturt Hwy; dm per night/week $25/160;
@ 🛜 🏊) On the Barmera side of town, this
eclectic hostel is destination *numero uno*
for work-seeking travellers, who chill out
after a hard day's manual toil in quirky new-
age surrounds. Rooms range from messy
dorms to doubles, share houses, a tepee and
a yurt – all for the same price. The manag-
ers can hook you up with harvest work (call
in advance).

**Berri Resort Hotel**                    HOTEL-MOTEL **$$**
(📞 08-8582 1411, 1800 088 226; www.berri
resorthotel.com; Riverview Dr; hotel s & tw $75,
motel d $155-175; ❄ 🛜 🏊) This mustard-and-
maroon monolith across the road from the

river has hotel rooms (shared bathrooms) and a wing of spacious en-suite motel rooms. The cavernous bistro serves upmarket pub grub (mains $10 to $33, open for breakfast, lunch and dinner). A slick operation, albeit a bit Vegas.

**Sprouts Café**                              CAFE $
(☑ 08-8582 1228; www.sproutscafe.com.au; 28 Wilson St; mains $6-14; ⊙ 8.30am-4pm Mon-Fri, 9.30am-1pm Sat) A cheery new cafe on the hill a few blocks back from the river, with a natty lime-green colour scheme. Serves soups, quiches, burgers, curries, wraps and good coffee. There are homemade cakes and scones, too.

## ℹ Information

**Berri Visitor Information Centre** (☑ 1300 768 582, 08-8582 5511; www.berribarmera.sa.gov. au; Riverview Dr; ⊙ 9am-5pm Mon-Fri, 9am-2pm Sat, 10am-2pm Sun) Right by the river, with brochures, internet, maps, waterproof canoeing guides ($10) and cluey staff.

# Renmark

POP 9870

Renmark is the first major river town across from the Victorian border, about 254km from Adelaide. It's not a pumping tourist destination by any means, but has a relaxed vibe and grassy waterfront, where you can pick up a houseboat. This is the hub of the Riverland wine region: lurid signs on the roads into town scream 'Buy 6 Get 1 Free!' and 'Bulk port $4/litre!'.

## ◎ Sights & Activities

**Riverland Leisure Canoe Tours**      CANOEING
(☑ 08-8595 5399; www.riverlandcanoes.com.au; half-/full-day tours $75/120) Slow-paced guided canoe tours on the Murray, departing Paringa across the river from Renmark. Canoe/kayak hire (per day $65/55) and evening and moonlight tours also available.

**Chowilla Game Reserve**       NATURE RESERVE
(www.environment.sa.gov.au) Upstream from town, Chowilla Game Reserve is great for bush camping (per car $7), canoeing and bushwalking. Access is along the north bank from Renmark or along the south bank from Paringa. For more info, contact the **Department of Environment, Water & Natural Resources** (DEWNR; ☑ 08-8595 2111; 28 Vaughan Tce, Berri) in Berri.

## 🛏 Sleeping & Eating

**Renmark Hotel**                      HOTEL-MOTEL $$
(☑ 08-8586 6755, 1800 736 627; www.renmark hotel.com.au; Murray Ave; hotel/motel d from $90/110; ❀ @ 🛜 ☒ ) What a beauty! The sexy art-deco curves of Renmark's humongous pub are looking good these days, thanks to a $3.5-million overhaul. Choose from older-style hotel rooms and upmarket motel rooms. On a sultry evening it's hard to beat a cold beer and some grilled barramundi on the balcony at Nanya Bistro (mains $18 to $28, serving from noon to 2.30pm and 5.30pm to 9pm).

**Renmark Riverfront
Caravan Park**                     CARAVAN PARK $
(☑ 08-8586 6315, 1300 664 612; www.big4renmark. com.au; Sturt Hwy; unpowered/powered sites from $30/35, cabins $72-285; ❀ @ 🛜 ☒ ) Highlights of this spiffy riverfront park, 1km east of town, include a camp kitchen, canoe (single/double per hour $10/15), paddleboats (per hour $20) and absolute waterfront cabins and powered sites. The newish corrugated-iron cabins are top notch, and look a little 'Riviera' surrounded by scraggly palms. The waterskiing fraternity swarms here during holidays.

## ℹ Information

**Renmark Paringa Visitor Information Centre** (☑ 08-8586 6704, 1300 661 704; www.visit renmark.com; 84 Murray Ave; ⊙ 9am-5pm Mon-Fri, 9am-4pm Sat, 10am-4pm Sun) All the

---

### ℹ RIVERLAND FRUIT PICKING

The fruit- and grape-growing centres of Berri, Barmera, Waikerie, Loxton and Renmark are always seeking harvest workers. Work is seasonal but there's usually something that needs picking (stonefruit, oranges, grapes, apples...), except for mid-September to mid-October and mid-April to mid-May when things get a bit quiet. If you have a valid working visa and don't mind sweating it out in the fields, ask the local backpacker hostels about work. Also try **MADEC Jobs Australia Berri Harvest Labour Office** (☑ 1800 062 332; www.madec.edu.au; 3 Riverview Dr) and **National Harvest Information Service** (☑ 1800 062 332; www.jobsearch.gov.au/harvesttrail).

usual brochures and info, plus an interpretive centre and the recommissioned 1911 paddle steamer *PS Industry* (gold-coin donation). Rumoured to be relocating – call them if they're not where they're supposed to be.

# BAROSSA VALLEY

With hot, dry summers and cool, moderate winters, the Barossa is one of the world's great wine regions – an absolute must for anyone with even the slightest interest in a good drop. It's a compact valley – just 25km long – yet it manages to produce 21% of Australia's wine, and makes a no-fuss day trip from Adelaide, 65km to the southwest.

The local towns have a distinctly German heritage, dating back to 1842. Fleeing religious persecution in Prussia and Silesia, settlers (bringing their vine cuttings with them) created a Lutheran heartland where German traditions persist today. The physical remnants of colonisation – gothic church steeples and stone cottages – are everywhere. Cultural legacies of the early days include a dubious passion for oom-pah bands, and an appetite for wurst, pretzels and sauerkraut.

Online, see www.barossa.com.

## ☞ Tours

Wine-flavoured day tours departing from Adelaide or locally are bountiful. The Barossa visitor information centre makes bookings. Just a few of the many tours available:

**Barossa Epicurean Tours**     FOOD & WINE
(☑ 08-8564 2191; www.barossatours.com.au; full-/half-day tours $100/70) Good-value, small-group tours visiting the wineries of your choice and Mengler Hill Lookout.

**Barossa Classic Cycle Tours**     CYCLING
(☑ 0427 000 957; www.bccycletours.com.au; tours per person per day from $260) One- and two-day cycling tours of the valley, covering about 30km per day. Cheaper rates for bigger groups.

**Barossa Wine Lovers Tours**     WINE
(☑ 08-8270 5500; www.wineloverstours.com.au; tours incl lunch from $70) Minibus or car tours to wineries, lookouts, shops and heritage buildings...a good blend.

**Barossa Experience Tours**     SIGHTSEEING
(☑ 08-8563 3248; www.barossavalleytours.com; half-/full-day tours from $85/120) Local small-group operator whisking you around the major sites. The Food & Wine Experience ($240) includes lunch, cheese tastings and a glass of wine.

**Balloon Adventures**     BALLOONING
(☑ 08-8389 3195; www.balloonadventures.com.au; flights adult/child $300/195) Fly the Barossa sky in a hot-air balloon. One-hour flights depart Tanunda and include a champagne breakfast.

## ✦ Festivals & Events

**Barossa under the Stars**     MUSIC
(www.barossaunderthestars.com.au) Wine-slurping picnickers watch easy-listening crooners such as Chris Isaak and Sting in January.

**Barossa Vintage Festival**     FOOD & WINE
(www.barossavintagefestival.com.au) This week-long festival has music, maypole dancing, tug-of-war contests etc; around Easter in odd-numbered years.

**Barossa Gourmet Weekend**     FOOD & WINE
(www.barossagourmetweekend.com.au) Fab food matched with winning wines at select wineries; happens in late winter or early spring.

**A Day on the Green**     MUSIC
(www.adayonthegreen.com.au) A mature-age moshpit at Peter Lehmann Wines, with acts such as Simply Red and Diana Krall. Held in December.

## ❶ Getting There & Around

### BUS & TRAIN
**Adelaide Metro** (www.adelaidemetro.com.au) runs daily trains to Gawler ($4.90, one hour), from where **LinkSA** (www.linksa.com.au) buses run to Tanunda ($9.50, 45 minutes), Nuriootpa ($12, one hour) and Angaston ($14.50, 1¼ hours).

### TAXI
**Barossa Taxis** (☑ 0411 150 850) Taxis for up to nine people; 24-hour service.

# Tanunda
POP 4690

At the centre of the valley both geographically and socially, Tanunda is the Barossa's main tourist town. Tanunda manages to morph the practicality of Nuriootpa with the charm of Angaston without a sniff of self-importance. The wineries are what you're here for – sip, sip, sip!

# Barossa Valley

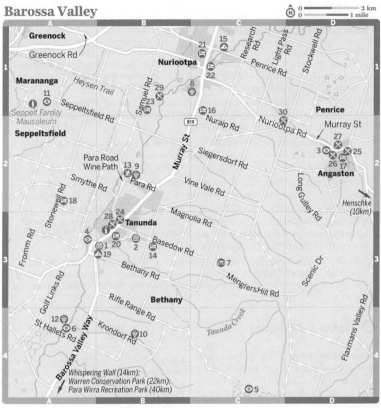

ADELAIDE & SOUTH AUSTRALIA TANUNDA

## Barossa Valley

### ◎ Sights
Barossa Farmers Market.............(see 30)
1 Barossa Museum...................................B3
2 Barossa Regional Gallery.....................B3
3 Barossa Valley Cheese
   Company.............................................D2
4 Goat Square...........................................A3
5 Kaiserstuhl Conservation Park............C4
6 Keg Factory............................................A4
7 Mengler Hill Lookout............................C3
8 Penfolds.................................................C1
9 Peter Lehmann Wines..........................B2
10 Rockford Wines.....................................B4
11 Seppeltsfield Road................................A1
12 St Hallett...............................................A4

### ☻ Activities, Courses & Tours
13 Para Road Wine Path............................B2

### ⊟ Sleeping
14 Barossa Backpackers............................B3

15 Barossa Valley Tourist Park.................C1
16 Doubles d'Vine.......................................C1
17 Marble Lodge.........................................D2
18 Stonewell Cottages...............................A2
19 Tanunda Caravan & Tourist
   Park.....................................................B3
20 Tanunda Hotel.......................................B3
21 Vine Court.............................................C1
22 Vine Inn.................................................C1
23 Whistler Farm........................................B1

### ⊗ Eating
24 1918 Bistro & Grill.................................B3
25 Angas Park.............................................D2
26 Angaston Hotel......................................D2
27 Blond Coffee..........................................D2
Die Barossa Wurst Haus
   Bakery............................................(see 28)
28 Ferment Asian.......................................B3
29 Maggie Beer's Farm Shop.....................B1
30 Vintners Bar & Grill...............................C2

**DON'T MISS**

## BAROSSA VALLEY WINERIES

The valley is best known for shiraz, with riesling the dominant white. There are around 80 vineyards here and 60 cellar doors, ranging from boutique wine rooms to monstrous complexes. The long-established 'Barossa Barons' hold sway – big, ballsy and brassy – while spritely young boutique wineries are harder to sniff out. Five of the best:

**Rockford Wines** (www.rockfordwines.com.au; Krondorf Rd, Tanunda; ⊙11am-5pm) This 1850s cellar door sells traditionally made, small-range wines, including sparkling reds. The Black Shiraz is a smooth and spicy killer.

**Henschke** (www.henschke.com.au; Henschke Rd, Keyneton; ⊙9am-4.30pm Mon-Fri, 9am-noon Sat) Henschke, about 10km southeast of Angaston in the Eden Valley, is known for its iconic Hill of Grace red, but most of the wines here are classics.

**Penfolds** (www.penfolds.com.au; 30 Tanunda Rd, Nuriootpa; ⊙10am-5pm) You know the name. Book ahead for the 'Make your own Blend' tour ($65) or 'Taste of Grange' tour ($150), which allows you to slide some Grange Hermitage across your lips.

**St Hallett** (www.sthallett.com.au; St Hallett Rd, Tanunda; ⊙10am-5pm) Reasonably priced but consistently good whites (try the Poacher's Blend) and the excellent Gamekeeper's Reserve Shiraz-Grenache. Unpretentious and great value for money.

**Peter Lehmann** (www.peterlehmannwines.com.au; Para Rd, Tanunda; ⊙9.30am-5pm Mon-Fri, 10.30am-4.30pm Sat & Sun) The multi-award-winning shiraz and riesling vintages here (oh, and the semillon) are probably the most consistent and affordable wines in the Barossa.

## ⦿ Sights & Activities

**Mengler Hill Lookout**　　　　　LOOKOUT
(Mengler Hill Rd; ⊙24hr) From Tanunda, take the scenic route to Angaston via Bethany for hazy valley views (just ignore the naff sculptures in the foreground). The road tracks through beautiful rural country, studded with huge eucalypts.

**Barossa Museum**　　　　　MUSEUM
(www.barossamuseum.com.au; 47 Murray St; adult/child $2/1; ⊙10am-5.30pm Tue-Fri, 9am-12.30pm Sat) Inside this 1856 post office building are displays of bone-handled cutlery, butter-making gear, photos of top-hatted locals, a re-created colonial bedroom and an amazing map of Germany pinpointing the homelands of Barossa settlers. The indigenous coverage could use a little help. Access via the bike-repair shop out the front.

**Goat Square**　　　　　HISTORIC SITE
(John St) Tanunda is flush with historic buildings, including the cottages around this square, on John St. This was the *ziegenmarkt,* a meeting and market place, laid out in 1842 as Tanunda's original town centre.

**Keg Factory**　　　　　FACTORY TOURS
(www.thekegfactory.com.au; Lot 10, St Hallett Rd; ⊙10am-4pm) **FREE** Watch honest-to-good-ness coopers make and repair wine barrels, 4km south of town.

**Barossa Regional Gallery**　　　　　GALLERY
(www.freewebs.com/barossagallery; 3 Basedow Rd, Soldiers Memorial Hall; ⊙11am-4pm Tue-Sun) **FREE** Has an eclectic collection of paintings, crafts and touring exhibitions, plus an impressive set of organ pipes at the back of the room.

**Whispering Wall**　　　　　INDUSTRIAL
(off Yettie Rd; ⊙24hr) About 7km southwest of Lyndoch, itself 13km south of Tanunda, the Barossa Reservoir dam is better known as the Whispering Wall. The huge concrete curve has amazing acoustics: whispers at one end of the wall can be heard clearly 150m away at the other. The perfect spot to propose?

## ⊨ Sleeping

**Tanunda Hotel**　　　　　PUB $
(⌨08-8563 2030; www.tanundahotel.com.au; 51 Murray St; d without/with bathroom $70/80, apt from $200; ❋) This boisterous ol' 1846 pub in the town centre is a real community hub. Pub rooms upstairs are good value and clean; out the back are nine ritzy mauve-coloured apartments. Downstairs, Duran Duran wails on the jukebox and schnitzels

fall off the edges of plates (mains $17 to $28, serving noon to 2pm and 6pm to 8pm).

**Barossa Backpackers**   HOSTEL **$**
(☑08-8563 0198; www.barossabackpackers.com.au; 9 Basedow Rd; unpowered sites/dm/d from $20/27/80; @ ☎) At last, a backpackers in the Barossa! Occupying a converted, U-shaped winery office building 500m from Tanunda's main street, it's a clean and ship-shape affair (if still a little office-like and spartan). Management can help you find picking/pruning work. Bike hire is $20 per day.

**Stonewell Cottages**   B&B **$$$**
(☑0417 848 977; www.stonewellcottages.com.au; Stonewell Rd; cottages d incl breakfast from $355; ✽) These romantic, waterfront spa retreats are surrounded by vines and offer unbeatable privacy, comfort and serenity. Pet ducks waddle around rusty old ploughs as waterbirds splash down in the reservoir. Pricey, but worth it (cheaper for online bookings).

**Tanunda Caravan & Tourist Park**   CARAVAN PARK **$**
(☑08-8563 2784; www.tanundacaravantouristpark.com.au; Barossa Valley Way; unpowered/powered sites from $33/36, cabins without/with bathroom from $77/108, villas from $285; ✽ @ ☎ ✾) This spacious park is dotted with mature trees offering a little shade for your hangover. Facilities include a playground, barbecues, laundry and bike hire for guests (per day $30). The flashy new villas sleep up to six and have a two-night minimum stay.

## ✖ Eating

**Ferment Asian**   SOUTHEAST ASIAN **$$**
(☑08-8563 0765; www.fermentasian.com.au; 90 Murray St; mains $22-26; ☺noon-2.30pm Tue-Sun, 6pm-9.30pm Wed-Sat) Having recently featured in the *Weekend Australian* magazine's 'Top 50 Restaurants' listings, Ferment is hot property right now. What sounds exotic is actually refreshingly simple: *goi bo den* = grilled Barossa Angus beef with herb salad; *ca ri vit* = red duck curry with lychees and pineapple. Modern Vietnamese in a lovely old stone villa.

**Die Barossa Wurst Haus Bakery**   BAKERY **$**
(86a Murray St; meals $4-18; ☺7am-4pm) This fast-not-flashy bakery serves *mettwurst* (Bavarian sausage) rolls, cheeses, pies, cakes, strudel and all-day breakfasts. It's hard to go past a trad German roll with kransky sausage, sauerkraut, cheese and mustard. An

emasculating display of phallic wursts dangles above the counter.

**1918 Bistro & Grill**   MODERN AUSTRALIAN **$$**
(☑08-8563 0405; www.1918.com.au; 94 Murray St; mains $27-35; ☺noon-2.30pm & 6.30-9pm) This enduring restaurant occupies a lovely old villa, set back from the street beneath a massive Norfolk Island pine. It's a sassy affair serving adventurous mains such as pork belly confit with braised cabbage and black-pudding crumble. Book a verandah table.

## ℹ Information

**Barossa Visitor Information Centre** (☑08-8563 0600, 1300 852 982; www.barossa.com; 66-68 Murray St, Tanunda; ☺9am-5pm Mon-Fri, 10am-4pm Sat & Sun; ☎) The lowdown on the valley, plus internet, bike hire and accommodation and tour bookings. Stocks the *A Town Walk of Tanunda* brochure.

# Nuriootpa
POP 5030

Along an endless main street at the northern end of the valley, Nuriootpa is the Barossa's commercial centre. It's not as endearing as Tanunda or Angaston, but has a certain agrarian appeal. Lutheran spirit runs deep in Nuri: a sign says, 'God has invested in you – are you showing any interest?'

## ◎ Sights & Activities

**Seppeltsfield Road**   STREET
(www.seppeltsfieldroad.com) An incongruous avenue of huge palm trees meandering through the vineyards behind Nuri. Beyond Marananga the palm rows veer off the roadside and track up a hill to the Seppelt Family Mausoleum – a Grecian shrine fronted by chunky Doric columns.

**Para Road Wine Path**   WALKING, CYCLING
(www.pararoadwinepath.com.au) Between Nuriootpa and Tanunda – a short-and-sweet walking/cycling trail passing four wineries.

## ⊨ Sleeping & Eating

**Doubles d'Vine**   COTTAGE **$**
(☑08-8562 2260; www.doublesdvine.com.au; cnr Nuraip Rd & Barossa Valley Way; lodge/cottage d $80/90; ✽ ☎) Affordable accommodation 1.5km south of Nuri, this is a self-contained cottage and separate 'lodge' (a renovated apricot shed) with two en-suite doubles and shared lounge and kitchen. Both have wood heaters, barbecues and access to the pool.

Reduced rates for two nights or more; bike hire for guests is $25 per day.

### Whistler Farm                              B&B $$
(☑ 0415 139 758; www.whistlerfarm.com.au; 616 Samuel Rd; d incl breakfast $195; ❀ 🛜) Surrounded by vineyards and native shrubs, this farmhouse B&B has a private guest wing with exposed timber beams, separate guest entry and two country-style rooms. Snooze on the wide verandah and contemplate a day's successful (or imminent) wine touring.

### Barossa Valley Tourist Park       CARAVAN PARK $
(☑ 08-8562 1404; www.barossatouristpark.com.au; Penrice Rd; unpowered/powered sites from $29/34, cabins without/with bathroom from $59/72; ❀ @ 🛜) There are at least six different kinds of cabin at this shady park, lined with pine trees next to the Nuriootpa football oval (go Tigers!). All cabins have TVs, fridges, cooking facilities and small balconies. Check out the 1930 Dodge 'House on Wheels' out the front – the seminal caravan?

### Vine Inn                               MOTEL $$
(☑ 08-8562 2133; www.vineinn.com.au; 14 Murray St; s/d/1-/2-bedroom from $95/105/155/210; ❀ 🛜 ▨) Regulation motel with swimming pool. The pub bistro (mains $15 to $30, serving 7am to 9am, noon to 2.30pm and 6pm to 8pm) serves pub grub amid bright lights, palms and pokies. Tandem business with

**Vine Court** (49 Murray St; ❀ 🛜) motel further up Murray St (same prices).

### Maggie Beer's Farm Shop              DELI $
(www.maggiebeer.com.au; 50 Pheasant Farm Rd; items $5-20; ☉ 10.30am-5pm) Celebrity SA gourmand Maggie has been hugely successful with her range of condiments, preserves and pâtés (and TV appearances!). The vibe here isn't as relaxed as it used to be, but stop by for some gourmet tastings, an ice cream, cooking demo or a hamper of delicious bites. Off Samuel Rd.

---

## Angaston
POP 1870

Photo-worthy Angaston was named after George Fife Angas, a pioneering Barossa pastoralist. An agricultural vibe persists, as there are relatively few wineries on the town doorstep: cows graze in paddocks down the ends of streets, and there's a vague whiff of fertiliser in the air. Along the main drag are two pubs, some terrific eateries and a few B&Bs in old stone cottages (check for double glazing and ghosts – we had a sleepless night!).

### ◎ Sights

**Barossa Valley
Cheese Company**                   CHEESE WRIGHT
(www.barossacheese.com.au; 67b Murray St; ☉ 10am-5pm Mon-Fri, 10am-4pm Sat, 11am-3pm

---

### BAROSSA REGIONAL PARKS

For a little grape-free time away from the vines, you can't beat the Barossa's regional parks, with walking tracks for everyone from Sunday strollers to hardcore bushwalkers. The Barossa visitor information centre (p115) can help with maps and directions.

**Kaiserstuhl Conservation Park** (☑ 08-8280 7048; www.environment.sa.gov.au; Tanunda Creek Rd, Angaston; ☉ daylight hours) Known for excellent walks, 390-hectare Kaiserstuhl is en route from Mengler Hill to Angaston. The Stringybark Loop Trail (2.4km) and Wallowa Loop Trail (6.5km) start at the entrance, and there are fantastic views from atop the Barossa Ranges. Look for Nankeen kestrels and western grey roos.

**Para Wirra Recreation Park** (☑ 08-8280 7048; www.environment.sa.gov.au; Humbug Scrub Rd, One Tree Hill; per person/car $4/10; ☉ 8am-sunset ) In the northern Mt Lofty Ranges, a 45km hook south of Tanunda – 1417 hectares of walking tracks, scenic drives, barbecues and tennis courts. Emus search hopefully around picnic areas; western grey roos graze in the dusk.

**Warren Conservation Park** (☑ 08-8280 7048; www.environment.sa.gov.au; Watts Gully Rd, Kersbrook; ☉ daylight hours) FREE Near Para Wirra – 363 tranquil hectares of wattles, banksias and spring heaths, plus pink, blue and statuesque river red gums. Steep tracks for experienced hikers.

Sun) The Barossa Valley Cheese Company is a fabulously stinky room, selling handmade cheeses from local cows and goats. Tastings are free, but it's unlikely you'll leave without buying a wedge of the Washington Washed Rind.

**Barossa Farmers Market**      MARKET
(www.barossafarmersmarket.com; cnr Stockwell & Nuriootpa Rds; ⊙7.30-11.30am Sat) Happens near Vintners Bar & Grill every Saturday. Expect hearty Germanic offerings and lots of local produce.

## 🛏 Sleeping & Eating

**Marble Lodge**      B&B $$
(☑08-8564 2478; www.marblelodge.com.au; 21 Dean St; d from $185; ❋@🖵) A grandiose 1915 Federation-style villa on the hill behind the town, built from local pink and white granite. Accommodation in two plush suites behind the house (high-colonial or high-kitsch, depending on your world view). Breakfast is served in the main house.

**Angaston Hotel**      PUB $$
(☑08-8564 2428; www.plushgroup.com/angaston.html; 59 Murray St; mains $13-24; ⊙noon-2pm & 6-8pm) The better looking of the town's two pubs, the friendly 1846 Angaston serves Barossa wines and the cheapest steaks this side of Argentina. Just try to ignore the *Triumph of Silenus* mural on the dining room wall ('Oh it's hideous!' says the barmaid). There's basic shared-bathroom pub accommodation upstairs (single/double $50/70).

**Blond Coffee**      CAFE $
(www.blondcoffee.com.au; 60 Murray St; mains $8-22; ⊙7.30am-5.30pm Mon-Fri, 8.30am-5.30pm Sat, 9am-5.30pm Sun) An elegant, breezy room with huge windows facing the main street, Blond serves nutty coffee and all-day cafe fare, including awesome pumpkin, capsicum and fetta muffins. There's also a wall full of local produce (vinegar, olive oil, biscuits and confectionery). Fake-blonde botoxed tourists share the window seats with down-to-earth regulars.

**Vintners Bar & Grill**      MODERN AUSTRALIAN $$
(☑08-8564 2488; www.vintners.com.au; cnr Stockwell & Nuriootpa Rds; mains $18-39; ⊙noon-2.30pm daily, 6.30-9pm Mon-Sat) One of the Barossa's landmark restaurants, Vintners stresses simple elegance in both food and atmosphere. The dining room has an open fire, vineyard views and bolts of crisp white linen; menus concentrate on local produce (pray the duck-leg curry is on the menu when you visit).

**Angas Park**      DELI $
(www.angaspark.com.au; 3 Murray St; ⊙9am-5pm Mon-Sat, 10am-5pm Sun) At the top end of the main street, Angas Park is an iconic SA company (recognise the little yellow bags?), selling mostly Australian-grown dried fruits, chocolates and nuts: brilliant for a picnic pick-me-up.

# CLARE VALLEY

Take a couple of days to check out the Clare Valley, two hours north of Adelaide. At the centre of the fertile Mid-North agricultural district, the skinny valley produces world-class rieslings and reds. This is gorgeous countryside, with open skies, rounded hills, stands of large gums and wind rippling over wheat fields. Towns here date from the 1840s, many built to service the Burra copper mines.

## 👉 Tours

Clare Valley tours also depart from Adelaide; see p61.

**Clare Valley Experiences**      SIGHTSEEING
(☑08-8842 1880; www.clarevalleyexperiences.com; tours from $75) 'Grape Express' half-day Clare tours and Riesling Trail rides; good rates for groups.

**Clare Valley Tours**      SIGHTSEEING
(☑0418 832 812, 08-8843 8066; www.cvtours.com.au; 4/6hr tours $86/100) Minibus tours taking in the Clare wineries, Martindale Hall and Burra.

**Swagabout Tours**      SIGHTSEEING
(☑0408 845 378; www.swagabouttours.com.au) Dependable, small-group full-day Clare Valley day trips (from $150).

## 🎉 Festivals & Events

**A Day on the Green**      MUSIC
(www.adayonthegreen.com.au) The Barossa's favourite festival comes to the Clare Valley in February. Lionel Ritchie, Crowded House, Daryl Braithwaite...

**Clare Valley Gourmet Weekend**      FOOD & WINE
(www.clarevalleywinemakers.com.au/gourmet.php) A frenzy of wine, food and music in May.

## THE RIESLING TRAIL

Following the course of a disused railway line between Auburn and Clare, the fabulous Riesling Trail is 24km of wines, wheels and wonderment. It's primarily a cycling trail, but the gentle gradient means you can walk or push a pram along it just as easily. It's a two-hour dash end to end on a bike, but why hurry? There are three loop track detours and extensions to explore, and dozens of cellar doors to tempt you along the way.

For bike hire, check out Clare Valley Cycle Hire (p120) or Riesling Trail Bike Hire in Clare, or Cogwebs (p118) in Auburn.

**Clare Show**  AGRICULTURAL
(www.sacountryshows.com) The largest one-day show in SA, held in October.

## ❶ Getting There & Around

### BICYCLE
In Auburn and Clare you can hire a bike to pelt around the wineries. Rates are around $25/40 per half/full day.

### BUS
**Yorke Peninsula Coaches** (📞08-8821 2755; www.ypcoaches.com.au) Adelaide to Auburn ($28, 2¼ hours) and Clare ($36, 2¾ hours), running Tuesday to Thursday and Sunday. Extends to Burra ($36, 3¼ hours) on Thursday.

### TAXI
**Clare Valley Taxi Service** (📞0419 847 900) Drop-off/pick-up anywhere along the Riesling Trail.

# Auburn

POP 320

Sleepy, 1849 Auburn – the Clare Valley's southernmost village – is a leave-the-back-door-open-and-the-keys-in-the-ignition kinda town, with a time-warp vibe that makes you feel like you're in an old black-and-white photograph. The streets are defined by beautifully preserved, hand-built stone buildings; cottage gardens overflow with untidy blooms. Don't forget to pick up a copy of the *Walk with History at Auburn* brochure from the Clare Valley visitor information centre.

Now on the main route to the valley's wineries, Auburn initially serviced bullockies and South American muleteers whose wagons – up to 100 a day – trundled between Burra's copper mines and Port Wakefield.

The brilliant 25km **Riesling Trail** starts (or ends) at the restored Auburn Train Station. **Cogwebs** (📞0400 290 687, 08-8849 2380; www.cogwebs.com.au; 30 Main North Rd; bike hire per half-/full day $25/40, tandems $35/65; ⊙8.30am-6pm Thu-Tue) has bike hire.

## 🛏 Sleeping & Eating

**Auburn Shiraz Motel**  MOTEL $
(📞08-8849 2125; www.auburnshirazmotel.com.au; Main North Rd; s/d/tr from $80/90/120; ❄🐾) This small motel on the Adelaide side of town has been proudly renovated with shiraz-coloured render and cabernet-coloured doors. There are nine bright units and friendly hosts. Bike hire $40 per day.

**Rising Sun Hotel**  PUB $$
(📞08-8849 2015; www.therisingsunhotel.com.au; 19 Main North Rd; mains $16-35; ⊙noon-2pm & 6-8pm; 🐾) This classic 1850 pub has a huge rep for its atmosphere, food and accommodation. The pub food is unpretentious (but unremarkable), with plenty of local wines to try. Accommodation takes the form of en-suite pub rooms and cottage mews rooms out the back (doubles from $90 and $125 respectively).

**Cygnets at Auburn**  CAFE $
(📞08-8849 2030; www.cygnetsatauburn.com.au; Main North Rd; mains $10-20; ⊙9.30am-4pm Fri-Mon) This gourmet cafe serves and stocks local produce, and has the best coffee in town. The scones with homemade raspberry jam steal the show ('Oh, so light!' says one happy customer). There's also cottage B&B accommodation out the back in the 1860 stables (doubles from $125).

# Mintaro

POP 230

Heritage-listed Mintaro (founded 1849) is a lovely stone village that could have been lifted out of the Cotswolds and plonked into the Australian bush. There are very few architectural intrusions from the 1900s – the whole place seems to have been largely left to its own devices. A fact for your next trivia night: Mintaro slate is used internationally in the manufacture of billiard tables. Pick up the *Historic Mintaro* pamphlet around the valley.

## ⊙ Sights

**Martindale Hall**                    HISTORIC BUILDING

(☑ 08-8843 9088; www.martindalehall.com; 1 Manoora Rd; adult/child $10/2.50; ⊘ 11am-4pm Mon-Fri, noon-4pm Sat & Sun) Martindale Hall is an astonishing 1880 manor 3km from Mintaro. Built for young pastoralist Edmund Bowman Jnr, who subsequently partied away the family fortune (OK, so drought and plummeting wool prices played a part... but it was mostly the partying), the manor features original furnishings, a magnificent blackwood staircase, Mintaro-slate billiard table and an opulent, museum-like smoking room. The hall starred as Appleyard College in the 1975 Peter Weir film *Picnic at Hanging Rock*. B&B and DB&B accommodation packages allow you to spend a spooky night here ($120 and $250 respectively). *Mirandaaa...*

**Mintaro Maze**                              MAZE

(www.mintaromaze.com; Jacka Rd; adult/child $10/7; ⊘ 10am-4pm Mon-Thu & school holidays)

Hedge your bets at Mintaro Maze as you try to find your way into the middle and back out again. There's a cafe here too.

## 🛏 Sleeping & Eating

**Reilly's**                        MODERN AUSTRALIAN $$

(☑ 08-8843 9013; www.reillyswines.com.au; cnr Hill St & Leasingham Rd; mains $16-28; ⊘ 10am-4pm) Reilly's started life as a cobbler's shop in 1856. An organic vegie garden out the back supplies the current restaurant, which is decorated with local art and serves creative, seasonal Mod Oz food (antipasto, rabbit terrine, spanikopita). The owners also rent out four gorgeous old stone cottages on Hill St (doubles from $145).

**Magpie & Stump Hotel**                   PUB $$

(☑ 08-8843 9014; www.mintaro.sa.au/eateries; Burra St; mains $12-26; ⊘ noon-2pm Tue-Sun, 6-8pm Mon-Sat) The old Magpie & Stump was first licensed in 1851, and was a vital rehydration point for the copper carriers travelling between Burra and Port Wakefield. Schnitzels and steaks, log fires, pool table, Mintaro-slate floors and a sunny beer garden out the front – the perfect pub?

---

**DON'T MISS**

### CLARE VALLEY WINERIES

The Clare Valley's cool micro-climates (around rivers, creeks and gullies) noticeably affect the wines, enabling local whites to be laid down for long periods and still be brilliant. The valley produces some of the world's best riesling, plus grand semillon and shiraz. Our favourite cellar doors:

**Skillogalee** (☑ 08-8843 4311; www.skillogalee.com.au; Trevarrick Rd, Sevenhill; ⊘ 10am-5pm) Skillogalee is a small family outfit known for its spicy shiraz, fabulous food and top-notch riesling. Kick back with a long, lazy lunch on the verandah (mains $20 to $30; book ahead).

**Pikes** (www.pikeswines.com.au; Polish Hill River Rd, Sevenhill; ⊘ 10am-4pm) The industrious Pike family set up shop in 1984, and have been producing show-stopping riesling ever since (and shiraz, sangiovese, pinot grigio, viognier...). It also bottles up the zingy 'Oakbank Pilsener' if you're parched.

**Knappstein** (www.knappstein.com.au; 2 Pioneer Ave, Clare; ⊘ 9am-5pm Mon-Fri, 11am-5pm Sat, 11am-4pm Sun) Taking a minimal-intervention approach to wine making, Knappstein has built quite a name for itself. Shiraz and riesling steal the show, but it also makes a mighty fine semillon sauvignon blanc blend (and beer!).

**Sevenhill Cellars** (☑ 08-8843 4222; www.sevenhill.com.au; College Rd , Sevenhill; ⊘ 9am-5pm Mon-Fri, 10am-5pm Sat & Sun) Want some religion with your drinking? This place was established by Jesuits in 1851, making it the oldest winery in the Clare Valley (check out the incredible 1866 St Aloysius Church). Oh, and the wine is fine too!

**Taylors Wines** (www.taylorswines.com.au; Taylors Rd, Auburn; ⊘ 9am-5pm Mon-Fri, 10am-5pm Sat, 10am-4pm Sun) Sure, it's a massive nationwide operation with a heinous mock-castle cellar door, but the wine here is fit for royalty (love the cab sav).

# Clare

POP 5460

Named after County Clare in Ireland, this town was founded in 1842 and is the biggest in the valley, but it's more practical than charming. All the requisite services are here (post, supermarket, fuel, internet etc), but you'll have a more interesting Clare Valley experience sleeping out of town.

## ⊙ Sights & Activities

**Riesling Trail Bike Hire**                BICYCLE HIRE
(✐0418 777 318; www.rieslingtrailbikehire.com.au; 10 Warenda Rd; bike hire per half-/full day $25/40, tandems $40/60) Quality two-wheelers (including two-seaters) right on the Riesling Trail itself.

**Clare Valley Cycle Hire**                BICYCLE HIRE
(✐0418 802 077, 08-8842 2782; www.clarevalley cyclehire.com.au; 32 Victoria Rd; bike hire per half/ full day $17/25) Also has baby seats and pull along buggies for the little 'uns.

**Spring Gully Conservation Park**        RESERVE
(www.environment.sa.gov.au; ⊙24hr) About 3km southwest of Sevenhill, the 400-hectare Spring Gully Conservation Park features blue-gum forest, red stringybarks and 18m-high winter waterfalls. There are plenty of bird twitters, critters and trails too.

**Old Police Station Museum**            MUSEUM
(www.nationaltrustsa.org.au; cnr Victoria & Neagles Rock Rd; adult/child $2/0.50; ⊙10am-noon & 2-4pm Sat & Sun) The 1850 cop shop and courthouse is now the Old Police Station Museum, displaying Victorian clothing, old photos, furniture and domestic bits and pieces.

# YORKE PENINSULA

A couple of hours west of Adelaide, boot-shaped Yorke Peninsula (better known as 'Yorkes') bills itself as 'Agriculturally Rich – Naturally Beautiful'. It does have a certain agrarian beauty – deep azure summer skies and yellow wheat fields on hazy, gently rolling hills – but if you're looking for cosmopolitan riches and tourist trappings, you won't find much to engage you.

That said, far-flung Innes National Park on the peninsula's southern tip is well worth visiting. The coastline here is gorgeous, with great surf, roaming emus, kangaroos, ospreys and sea eagles, and southern right whales and dolphins cruising by.

For history buffs, the peninsula's north has a trio of towns called the Copper Triangle: Moonta (the mine), Wallaroo (the smelter) and Kadina (the service town). Settled by Cornish miners, this area drove the regional economy following a copper boom in the early 1860s.

Online, see www.yorkepeninsula.com.au.

## ⌑ Tours

**Adjahdura Land**                        INDIGENOUS
(✐0429 367 121; www.adjahdura.com.au; half-/1-/2-day tours $65/130/320) ✐ Highly regarded Aboriginal cultural tours of the peninsula, exploring the incredibly long indigenous association with this country. Three- and five-day tours are also available.

## ⨅ Sleeping

There are 15 council-run **camp sites** (✐0408 170 414, 08-8832 0000; www.yorke.sa.gov.au; per night free-$10) around the peninsula. For holiday-house rentals from as little as $90 per night, try **Accommodation on Yorkes** (✐08-8852 2000; www.accommodationonyorkes. com.au) or **Country Getaways** (✐08-8832 2623; www.countrygetaways.info).

## ❶ Getting There & Around

BUS

**Yorke Peninsula Coaches** (✐08-8821 2755; www.ypcoaches.com.au) Daily buses from Adelaide to Kadina ($32, 2¼ hours), Wallaroo ($32, 2½ hours) and Moonta ($32, 3 hours), travelling as far south as Yorketown ($48, four hours, daily except Wednesday).

FERRY

**SEASA** (✐08-8823 0777; www.seasa.com. au; one-way per adult/child/car $35/10/140) Daily vehicle ferry between Wallaroo (Yorke Peninsula) and Lucky Bay (Eyre Peninsula) – a shortcut shaving 350km and several hours off the drive via Port Augusta. The voyage takes around 1¾ hours one way.

# West Coast

Fronting Spencer Gulf, the west coast has a string of shallow swimming beaches, plus the Copper Triangle towns, all a short drive from each other. **Kernewek Lowender** (www.kernewek.org), aka the Copper Coast Cornish Festival, happens around here in May in odd-numbered years.

# Kadina

POP 4030

Baking-hot, inland Kadina (ka-*dee*-na) has some impressive copper-era civic buildings and a slew of massive old pubs, car yards and petrol stations. The **Copper Coast Visitor Information Centre** (☑08-8821 2333, 1800 654 991; www.yorkepeninsula.com.au; 50 Moonta Rd; ☺9am-5pm Mon-Fri, 10am-4pm Sat & Sun) is here – the peninsula's main visitor centre. Behind it is an amazing collection of old farming, mining and domestic bits and pieces at the **Farm Shed Museum** (www.nationaltrust.org.au/sa; 50 Moonta Rd; adult/child/family $8/3/20; ☺9am-5pm Mon-Fri, 10am-3.30pm Sat & Sun), which gives an engaging insight into olden days and ways.

If you're just after a basic, clean place to rest your head, **Kadina Village Motel** (☑08-8821 1920; www.kadinavillagemotel.websyte.com. au; 28 Port Rd; s/d $80/90; ❄☎) is a retro, U-shaped joint on the road to Wallaroo.

# Wallaroo

POP 3050

Still a major wheat port, Wallaroo is a town on the up: the Eyre Peninsula ferry is running and the town is full of folks. There's a huge new subdivision north of town, and the shiny new **Copper Cove Marina** (www.coppercove.com.au) is full of expensive boats. The marina also hosts the nautical **Copper Cove Marina Festival** in October.

A stoic 1865 post office houses the **Heritage & Nautical Museum** (www.nationaltrust.org.au/sa; cnr Jetty Rd & Emu St; adult/child $6/3; ☺10am-4pm Mon-Fri, 2-4pm Sat & Sun), with tales of square-rigged English ships and George the pickled giant squid.

## 🛏 Sleeping & Eating

**Sonbern Lodge Motel**          HOTEL-MOTEL $
(☑08-8823 2291; www.sonbernlodgemotel.com. au; 18 John Tce; s/d/f from $75/90/125; ❄) Once a grand temperance hotel, Sonbern is an old-fashioned charmer, right down to the old wooden balcony and antique wind-up phone. There are basic pub-style rooms upstairs (with bathrooms), and newish motel units out the back.

**Wallaroo**
**Marina Apartments**     HOTEL, APARTMENTS $$
(☑08-8823 4068; www.wallarooapartments.com. au; 11 Heritage Dve; d/apt from $100/174; ❄) The new multistorey Wallaroo Marina Apartments at the marina on the northern edge of town has spiffy suites, plus cold beer, pub meals, marina views and the occasional live band downstairs in the **Coopers Alehouse** (☑08-8823 2488; www.wallaroomarina hotel.com/dining; mains $15-38; ☺noon-2.30pm & 6-8.30pm).

# Moonta

POP 3350

In the late 19th century, the Moonta copper mine was the richest in Australia. These days the town, which calls itself 'Australia's Little Cornwall', maintains a faded glory, with a couple of decent pubs, and shallow Moonta Bay 1km west of the town centre, with good fishing from the jetty and a netted swimming area.

**Moonta Visitor Information Centre** (☑08-8825 1891; www.moontatourism.org.au; Blanche Tce, Old Railway Station; ☺9am-5pm) has a smattering of history pamphlets, and details on the Moonta Heritage Site 1.5km east of town. The site includes the excellent **Moonta Mines Museum** (www.nationaltrust. org.au/sa; Verran Tce; adult/child $6/2; ☺1-4pm Sat-Thu, 10am-4pm Fri), once a grand school with 1100 pupils; the 1946 **Moonta Mines Sweet Shop** (Verran Tce; ☺10am-4pm) across the road; and a fully restored **Miner's Cottage** (Verco St; adult/child $3/1; ☺1.30-4pm Wed, Sat & Sun, daily during school holidays).

## 🛏 Sleeping & Eating

**Seagate Bistro Motel**          MOTEL $$
(☑08-8825 3270; www.seagatemoontabay.com. au; 171 Bay Rd; d from $170; ❄☎) The flashy Seagate is an octagonal (or is it a squashed dodecahedron?) motel right by Moonta Bay jetty. The pick of the rooms upstairs have sweeping oceanic views, as does the downstairs bistro (mains $18 to $37, open noon to 2pm and 6pm to 8pm), which serves better-than-average pub grub – perfect for a sunset beer.

**Moonta Bay Caravan Park**     CARAVAN PARK $
(☑08-8825 2406; www.yorkepeninsula.net.au; Foreshore, Moonta Bay; unpowered/powered sites from $30/32, cabins without/with spa from $107/145; ❄☎) This caravan park is handy to the beach and jetty, and has decent luxury cabins with spas. The grassy camping areas are almost on the beach (but wi-fi reception can be a bit patchy down here).

## BURRA

Bursting at the seams with historic sites, Burra (population 1110), 3km northeast of Clare, was a copper-mining boomtown between 1847 and 1877 with a burgeoning Cornish community. Towns like Mintaro and Auburn serviced miners travelling between Burra and Port Wakefield, from where the copper was shipped. The miners had it tough here, excavating dugouts for themselves and their families to live in.

**Burra visitor information centre** (☑ 08-8892 2154, 1300 775 540; www.visitburra. com; 2 Market St; ⊙ 9am-5pm Mon-Fri, 10am-4pm Sat & Sun) sells the self-guided **Burra Heritage Passport** (adult/child $25/free) giving access to eight historic sights and three museums. It also handles bike hire (half-/full day $20/35) and accommodation.

### Sleeping

**Bungaree Station** (☑ 08-8842 2677; www.bungareestation.com.au; Main North Rd; per person per night $44-99; ﹡) About 12km north of Clare is this beautiful 170-year-old homestead, still a working 3000-acre sheep and crop farm. It was once SA's northern-most settlement, with 50 staff, a church and a school. Accommodation is in simple, clean, renovated heritage buildings (one to four bedrooms, some with shared bathrooms). You can feed farm animals, take an audio tour (per person from $11) or have a dip in the pool.

**Battunga B&B** (☑ 08-8843 0120; www.battunga.com.au; Upper Skilly Rd, Watervale; d/q incl breakfast $195/315; ﹡) On an 80-hectare farm over the hills 2km west of Watervale (it's a little hard to find – ask for directions), Battunga has four modern apartments in two stone cottages with Mintaro-slate floors, barbecues, kitchenettes and wood fires. This is beautiful country – undulating farmland studded with huge eucalypts.

**Riesling Trail & Clare Valley Cottages** (☑ 0427 842 232; www.rtcvcottages.com.au; 9 Warenda Rd; 1-/2-/3-bed cottage d incl breakfast from $150/230/320; ﹡) A newish operation offering seven contemporary cottages, all encircled by country gardens and right on the Riesling Trail. Handily, the owners also run Riesling Trail Bike Hire.

**Clare Caravan Park** (☑ 08-8842 2724; www.clarecaravanpark.com.au; Main North Rd; unpowered/powered sites from $20/29, cabins from $89; ﹡ ⎙ ﹡) This huge, efficiently run park 4km south of town towards Auburn has secluded sites, all en-suite cabins, a creek and giant gum trees. There's also an inground pool for cooling off post-cycling, and it's a stone's throw from the Clare Valley visitor information centre.

### Eating

**Taminga Hotel** (☑ 08-8842 2808; www.tamingahotel.com.au; 302 Main North Rd; mains $16-30; ⊙ noon-2pm & 6-8pm) The most reliable of Clare's pubs when it comes to food, the tarted-up Taminga looks good. Pub classics are what you're here for: surf 'n' turf, steak-and-kidney pie and schnitzels.

**Wild Saffron** (☑ 08-8842 4255; www.wildsaffron.com.au; 288 Main North Rd; mains $7-18; ⊙ 8.30am-5.30pm Mon-Fri, 8.30am-12.30pm Sat & Sun) We're not sure how much wild saffron grows in the Clare Valley (most of it seems to be 'under vine', as they say), but this new cafe is hugely popular regardless. No surprises on the menu (focaccias, baguettes, BLTs, soup, homemade cakes), but it's simple stuff done well.

**Artisans Table** (☑ 08-8842 1796; www.artisanstable.com.au; Lot 3, Wendouree Rd; mains $28-32; ⊙ noon-3pm Sat & Sun, 6-9pm Wed-Sat) This mod, airy, hillside bar-restaurant has a broad, sunny balcony – perfect for a bottle of local riesling and some internationally inspired culinary offerings: a bit of Thai, a bit of Indian, a bit of Brazilian... Lots of seasonal and local produce, and surprisingly good seafood this far inland.

### Information

**Clare Valley Visitor Information Centre** (☑ 08-8842 2131, 1800 242 131; www. clarevalley.com.au; cnr Spring Gully & Main North Rd; ⊙ 10am-5pm Mon-Fri, 10am-4pm Sat & Sun) Local info, internet access and valley-wide accommodation bookings.

### Cornish Kitchen
FAST FOOD $

(10-12 Ellen St; items $4-8; ☺9am-4pm Mon-Fri, 9am-2pm Sat) After a hard day's copper mining, swing your shovel into the Cornish Kitchen for the ultimate Cornish pastie.

## Point Turton

For a far-flung Yorkes experience, try Point Turton (population 250) in the southwest. The breezy **Tavern on Turton** (☑08-8854 5063; www.tavernonturton.com; 154 Bayview Rd; mains $18-36; ☺9am-2pm & 6pm-8pm) is here, and the superfriendly **Point Turton Caravan Park** (☑08-8854 5222; www.pointturtoncp. com.au; Bayview Rd; unpowered/powered sites $22/29, cabins $55-150; ❄🐾), with lovely grassy sites and cabins overlooking the sea. You can learn to surf near here with **Neptunes Surf Coaching** (☑0417 839 142; www. neptunes.net.au; 2hr lessons from $45).

## East Coast

The east-coast road along Gulf St Vincent traces the coast within 1km or 2km of the water. En route, roads dart east to sandy beaches and holiday towns. Like the suburban Adelaide beaches across the gulf, this is prime crab-fishing territory.

Most of the coastal towns have a pub and a caravan park or camping ground, including unpretentious **Port Vincent** (population 480). The closest thing Yorkes has to a backpackers is the utilitarian **Tuckerway Hostel** (☑08-8853-7285; tuckerway14@bigpond.com; 14 Lime Kiln Rd, Port Vincent; dm from $21; ❄) – a concrete-block bunker uphill from the town containing simple dorms and a large kitchen.

Further south, **Edithburgh** (population 400) is roughly aligned with Adelaide's latitude, and has a **tidal swimming pool** in a small cove. From the cliff-tops, views extend offshore to sandy **Troubridge Island Conservation Park** (www.environment.sa.gov.au). You can stay the night at the **Troubridge Island Lighthouse** (☑08-8852 6290; www.light house.net.au; per adult/child incl transfers $80/30, min charge $320). It sleeps 10; BYO food and linen. Little penguins still live here, but the island is steadily eroding – what the sea wants, the sea will have...

Back on the mainland, the surprisingly hip **Tipper's B&B** (☑08-8852 6181; www.tip persedithburgh.com.au; 35 Blanche St; d from $150; ❄) is on Edithburgh's main street, with two suites occupying an ochre-coloured former blacksmiths (1890s).

# South Coast & Innes National Park

The peninsula's south coast is largely sheltered from the Southern Ocean's fury by Kangaroo Island, so there are some great swimming beaches along here. The surf finds its way through around Troubridge Point and Cape Spencer, where the **Cutloose Yorkes Classic** surf comp happens every October.

Cape Spencer is part of **Innes National Park** (☑08-8854 3200; www.environment.sa.gov. au; Stenhouse Bay Rd, Stenhouse Bay; per car $10; ☺visitor centre 10.30am-3pm Wed-Sun), where sheer cliffs plunge into indigo waters and rocky offshore islands hide small coves and sandy beaches. **Marion Bay** (www.marionbay. com.au), just outside the park, and **Stenhouse Bay** and **Pondalowie Bay**, both within the park, are the main settlements. Pondalowie Bay has a bobbing lobster-fishing fleet and a gnarly surf beach (keep one eye on the swell if you're swimming).

The rusty ribs of the 711-tonne steel barque *Ethel,* which foundered in 1904, arc forlornly from the sands just south of Pondalowie Bay. Follow the sign past the Cape Spencer turn-off to the ghost-town ruins of **Inneston**, a gypsum-mining community abandoned in 1930.

## 🛏 Sleeping & Eating

★ **Marion Bay Motel & Tavern**
MOTEL $$

(☑08-8854 4044; www.marionbaymotel.com.au; Jetty Rd, Marion Bay; s/d/tr $120/140/160; ❄🐾) This place is the highlight of tiny Marion Bay, with a wing of five spiffy motel rooms out the back (white walls, new TVs, nice linen). The glass-fronted tavern next door (mains $16 to $32, serving noon to 2pm and 6pm to 8pm) looks out over the bay and puts a southeast Asian spin on pub standards (try the Vietnamese chicken salad).

**Innes National Park**
CAMPGROUND, LODGE $

(☑08-8854 3200; www.environment.sa.gov.au; camping per person/car $5/16, lodges $100-170) Innes National Park has seven bushy camp sites. Our favourite spot is Pondalowie, or try Cable Bay for beach access, Surfers for surfing or Browns Beach for fishing. Alternatively, the heritage lodges at Inneston sleep four to 10 people and have showers and cooking facilities. Book ahead through the park visitor centre; BYO drinking water in summer.

### Rhino's Tavern & Innes Park Trading Post                    PUB $$

(☑08-8854 4078; www.rhinostavern.com.au; 1 Stenhouse Bay Rd, Stenhouse Bay; mains $18-30; ☺noon-2pm & 6-8pm) This is a one-stop shop for fuel, bait, groceries and takeaway food, or kick back with a beer and a pub meal (laksa and ribs!).

# EYRE PENINSULA & THE WEST COAST

The vast, straw-coloured triangle of Eyre Peninsula is Australia's big-sky country, and is considered by galloping gourmands to be the promised land of seafood. Meals out here rarely transpire without the option of trying the local oysters, tuna and whiting. Sublime national parks punctuate the coast, along with world-class surf breaks and lazy holiday towns, thinning out as you head west towards the Great Australian Bight, the Nullarbor Plain and Western Australia.

Eyre Peninsula's photogenic wild-western flank is an important breeding ground for southern right whales, Australian sea lions and great white sharks (the scariest scenes of *Jaws* were shot here). There are some memorable opportunities to encounter these submariners along the way.

Online, visit www.eyrepeninsula.info.

## ☞ Tours

### Wilderness Wanders                         WILDERNESS

(☑08-8684 5001; www.wildernesswanders.com. au) ✐ One- to eight-day Eyre Peninsula explorations ex-Port Lincoln, with lots of walking, wildlife and wilderness. The epic eight-day 'Walking on Eyre' tour ($2350) includes transport, accommodation, national park entry fees and most meals.

### Southern Blue Tours                       SIGHTSEEING

(☑08-8683 1330; www.southernblue.travel) Full-day tours to Lincoln National Park ($395), the Coffin Bay region ($245) and half-day Port Lincoln tours ($135).

## ❶ Getting There & Away

See p120 for info on the car ferry between Yorke Peninsula and Eyre Peninsula.

### AIR

**Regional Express** (Rex; www.regionalexpress. com.au) Daily flights from Adelaide to Whyalla (one way from $140), Port Lincoln (from $99) and Ceduna (from $180).

### BUS

**Premier Stateliner** (www.premierstateliner. com.au) Daily buses from Adelaide to Port Augusta ($54.50, 4¼ hours), Whyalla ($62, 5½ hours), Port Lincoln ($108.50, 9¾ hours), Streaky Bay ($113.50, 10 hours) and Ceduna ($126.50, 11¼ hours).

### TRAIN

The famous *Ghan* train connects Adelaide with Darwin via Port Augusta, and the *Indian Pacific* (between Perth and Sydney) connects with the *Ghan* at Port Augusta; see p283 for details. **Pichi Richi Railway** (☑1800 440 101; www.prr.org. au; one-way adult/child/family $52/19/122) runs between Port Augusta and Quorn (two hours) on Saturdays.

## Port Augusta

POP 13,900

At the head of Spencer Gulf, Port Augusta is having an identity crisis: is it the gateway to the outback, or the start of the southern Flinders Ranges? Is it the first town on the Eyre Peninsula, or the last big town until Kalgoorlie? The answer is all of the above. From the 'Crossroads of Australia', highways and railways roll west across the Nullarbor into WA, north to the Flinders Ranges or Darwin, south to Adelaide or Port Lincoln, and east to Sydney. Not a bad position!

The old town centre has considerable appeal, with some elegant old buildings and a revitalised waterfront: locals cast lines into the blue, and indigenous kids back-flip off jetties. The town has had problems with alcoholism (the streets are now a dry zone), but the vibe is rarely menacing.

## ◉ Sights & Activities

### Australian Arid Lands Botanic Garden                      GARDENS

(www.aalbg.sa.gov.au; Stuart Hwy; tours adult/ child $8/5.50; ☺9am-5pm Mon-Fri, 10am-4pm Sat & Sun, tours 10am Mon-Fri) **FREE** Just north of town, the excellent (and free!) botanic garden has 250 hectares of sand hills, clay flats and desert flora and fauna. Explore on your own, or take a guided tour. There's a cafe here, too.

# Eyre Peninsula & Yorke Peninsula

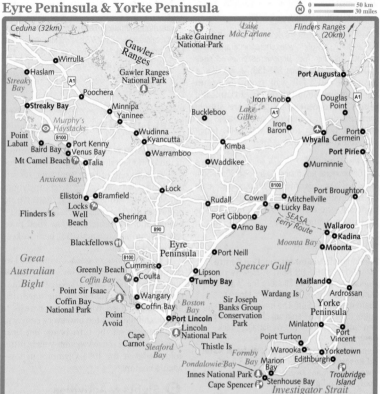

**Wadlata Outback Centre** MUSEUM
(www.wadlata.sa.gov.au; 41 Flinders Tce; adult/
child/family $16.50/10/38.50; ⏰9am-5.30pm
Mon-Fri, 10am-4pm Sat & Sun) The highlight
at this combined museum/visitor centre is
the 'Tunnel of Time', tracing local Aboriginal
and European histories using audio-visual
displays, interactive exhibits and a distress-
ingly big snake.

**Port Augusta Aquatic &
Outdoor Adventure Centre** OUTDOORS
(☑0427 722 450, 08-8642 2699; www.augustaout
doors.com.au; 4 El Alamein Rd; ⏰9am-4pm Mon-
Fri) Offers lessons and gear rental for kayaking, windsurfing, rock-climbing, abseiling,
snorkelling, bushwalking, sailing... Bike hire
is $55 per day.

## ☞ Tours

**Flinders & Outback Water Cruises** CRUISES
(☑0438 857 001; www.augustawestside.com.au; 3
Loudon Rd; adult/child $50/30) Two-hour morn-
ing eco-cruises to the top of the Gulf (any
dolphins?).

## 🛏 Sleeping & Eating

**Oasis Apartments** APARTMENTS $$
(☑08-8648 9000, 1800 008 648; www.majesti
chotels.com.au; Marryatt St, foreshore; apt $145-
215; ❋ 🛜 🏊) Catering largely to convention-
eers, this group of 75 luxury units (studios
to two-bedroom) with jaunty designs is
right by the water. All rooms have wash-
ing machines, dryers, TVs, fridges, micro-
waves, fortresslike security and flashy in-
terior design.

**Best Western Standpipe** MOTEL $$
(☑08-8642 4033; www.standpipe.com.au; cnr Stu-
art Hwy & Hwy 1; d/2-bedroom apt from $128/233;
❋ 🛜 🏊) The sprawling Standpipe attracts
government delegates and business types
with its 85 reasonably hip units – the best
motel in town, hands down. And the Indian

restaurant here (mains $18 to $38, open 5.30pm to 8pm) is unbelievable!

**Shoreline Caravan Park** CARAVAN PARK $
(☑08-8642 2965; www.shorelinecaravanpark.com.au; Gardiner Ave; unpowered/powered sites $30/33, dm $40, cabins $65-130; ❄❄) It's a dusty site and a fair walk from town (and the shoreline when the tide is out), but the cabins are decent, plus there are simple four-bed dorm units for backpackers. The cheapest beds in town if you don't fancy sleeping above a pub.

**Hot Peppers Cafe** CAFE $
(34 Commercial Rd; mains $7-16; ⊙8.30am-5pm Mon-Fri, 8.30am-1.30pm Sat) A buzzy little cafe on the main street serving salads, quiches, impressive homemade lasagne, baked potatoes and big sandwiches.

## ❶ Information

**Port Augusta Visitor Information Centre**
(☑1800 633 060, 08-8641 9193; www.port augusta.sa.gov.au; 41 Flinders Tce, Wadlata Outback Centre; ⊙9am-5.30pm Mon-Fri, 10am-4pm Sat & Sun) The major information outlet for the Eyre Peninsula, Flinders Ranges and outback. Part of the Wadlata Outback Centre.

**Department of Environment, Water & Natural Resources** (DEWNR; ☑08-8648 5300; www.environment.sa.gov.au; 9 Mackay St, 1st floor; ⊙9am-5pm Mon-Fri) Information, maps and road condition updates for the Flinders Ranges and outback.

## Whyalla

POP 21,130

An hour's drive south of Port Augusta is Whyalla – the third-biggest city in SA – with a deep-water port sustaining steel mills, oil and gas refineries and a morass of chugging chimneys, portworks and industrial estates. Ugly, yes, but the old town has some good pubs, well-preserved domestic architecture and migrating Giant Australian Cuttlefish in the waters offshore (May to August).

Whyalla Visitor Information Centre (☑08-8645 7900, 1800 088 589; www.whyalla.com; Lincoln Hwy; ⊙9am-5pm Mon-Fri, 9.30am-4pm Sat & Sun) can help with cuttlefish info and accommodation listings, or head straight for the utilitarian Foreshore Motor Inn (☑08-8645 8877; www.whyallaforeshore.com.au; Watson Tce; d/f from $145/170; ❄❄❄) down by the wide white sandy expanse of Whyalla's foreshore.

Next to the visitor centre is the Whyalla Maritime Museum (☑08-8645 8900; www.whyallamaritimemuseum.com.au; Lincoln Hwy; adult/child/family $12/7/31; ⊙10am-4pm, ship tours hourly 10am-2pm), which includes the HMAS *Whyalla*, allegedly the largest land-locked ship in Australia (...who keeps track of these things?).

## Port Lincoln

POP 15,000

Prosperous Port Lincoln, the 'Tuna Capital of the World', overlooks broad Boston Bay on the southern end of Eyre Peninsula. It's still a fishing town a long way from anywhere, but the vibe here is energetic (dare we say progressive!). The grassy foreshore is a busy promenade, and there are some good pubs, eateries and aquatic activities here to keep you out of trouble.

If not for a lack of fresh water, Port Lincoln might have become the South Australian capital. These days it's salt water (and the tuna therein) that keeps the town ticking. A guaranteed friend-maker here is to slip Dean Lukin's name into every conversation. Straight off the tuna boats, Big Dean won the Super Heavyweight weightlifting gold medal at the 1984 Olympics in LA – what a champ!

## ❍ Sights & Activities

The annual Tunarama Festival (www.tuna rama.net) on the Australia Day weekend in January celebrates every finny facet of the tuna-fishing industry.

There's good beginner/intermediate surfing at Fisheries Bay, Lone Pine and Wreck Beach. For info visit Lincoln Surf (☑08-8682 4428; 1 King St; ⊙9am-5.30pm Mon-Fri, 9am-2pm Sat). They're rumoured to be relocating, so phone them if they're not on King St.

If you'd rather be on the water rather than in it, the local fishing is outstanding. Ask Spot On Fishing Tackle (www.spoton fishing.com.au; 39 Tasman Tce; ⊙8.30am-5.30pm Mon-Fri, 8am-4pm Sat & Sun) about what's biting where.

**Adventure Bay Charters** ADVENTURE TOUR
(☑08-8682 2979; www.adventurebaycharters.com.au) ✿ Carbon-neutral Adventure Bay Charters takes you swimming with sea lions (adult/child $195/135) and Port Lincoln's famous tuna ($95/65), which you hand feed in

a fish-farm enclosure. Shark cage dives also available ($295).

### Swim With The Tuna ADVENTURE TOUR
(📞1300 788 378; www.swimwiththetuna.com.au; adult/child $80/55) Three-hour boat tours out to a floating tuna enclosure, where you can check out the big fish from an underwater observatory or jump into the brine with them.

### Calypso Star Charters ADVENTURE TOUR
(📞08-8682 3939, 1300 788 378; www.sharkcage diving.com.au; 1-day dive $420) Runs cage dives with great white sharks around Neptune Islands. Book in advance.

### Kuju Aboriginal Arts GALLERY
(www.visitaboriginalart.com; 30 Ravendale Rd; ⏰10am-5pm Mon-Fri) FREE Stocks exquisite indigenous artworks, and you can meet the artists who work on-site. Aboriginal owned and managed.

## 🛏 Sleeping & Eating

### ⭐ Tanonga B&B $$$
(📞0427 812 013; www.tanonga.com.au; Charlton Gully; d incl breakfast from $310, minimum 2-night stay; ❋) 🅿 Two plush, solar-powered, architect-designed ecolodges in the hills behind Port Lincoln. They're both super-private and surrounded by native bush, birdlife and walking trails. Roll in town for dinner, or DIY packs of local produce are available.

### Port Lincoln Hotel HOTEL $$
(📞08-8621 2000, 1300 766 100; www.portlin colnhotel.com.au; 1 Lincoln Hwy; d $139-250; ❋🛜🏊) Bankrolled by a couple of Adelaide Crows AFL footballers, this ritzy seven-storey hotel lifts Port Lincoln above the fray. It's a classy, contemporary affair with switched-on staff. Good on-site bars and eateries too, open all day – play 'Spot Mark Ricciuto' from behind your menu (mains $16 to $37).

### Port Lincoln YHA HOSTEL $
(📞08-8682 3605; www.yha.com.au; 24-26 London St; dm/d/f from $36/100/125; ❋@🛜) Run by a high-energy couple who have spent a fortune renovating the place, this impressive new 84-bed hostel occupies a 100-year-old house and the former squash courts behind it. Thoughtful bonuses include king-single beds, reading lights, a cafe/bar and power outlets in lockers (for phones!). Can help with booking activities, too.

### Pier Hotel PUB $
(📞08-8682 1322; www.portlincolnpier.com.au; 33 Tasman Tce; d/2-bedroom apt from $80/130; ❋) The old Pier has had a facelift, including the dozen en-suite rooms upstairs – bright and clean with polished floorboards and TVs. The bistro downstairs (mains $17 to $33, serving noon to 2pm and 6pm to 8pm) is big on local seafood: oysters, calamari and scallops reign supreme.

### Port Lincoln Tourist Park CARAVAN PARK $
(📞08-8621 4444; www.portlincolntouristpark. com.au; 11 Hindmarsh St; unpowered/powered sites $23/35, cabins & units $70-140; ❋@🛜) Lincoln's best caravan park is this breezy waterside operation, with some beaut executive cabins by the water and plenty of elbow room. You can fish from the jetty and swim at the beach. BYO linen in the basic cabins.

### GLO CAFE $
(📞08-8682 6655; www.goodlivingorganics.net; 23 Liverpool St; items $5-10; ⏰8.30am-5.30pm Mon-Fri, 9am-noon Sat; 🍴) 🅿 A local hang-out a block away from the beach (and thus not on many tourist radars), GLO (Good Living Organics) features cute staff in black T-shirts serving quiches, wraps, salads, falafels, couscous and Port Lincoln's best coffee.

## ℹ Information

**Port Lincoln Visitor Information Centre**
(📞08-8683 3544, 1300 788 378; www.visit portlincoln.net; 3 Adelaide Pl; ⏰9am-5pm) Books accommodation and has national parks information and passes, plus the *Port Lincoln & Districts Cycling Guide*. Ask about the local railway, maritime and heritage museums.

# Port Lincoln to Streaky Bay

## Around Port Lincoln

About 50km north of Port Lincoln, **Tumby Bay** (www.tumbybay.com) is a quiet little town with a beach, jetty, pub, caravan park and motel – serious holiday territory!

About 15km south of Port Lincoln is **Lincoln National Park** (www.environment.sa.gov. au; per car $10), with roaming emus, roos and brush-tailed bettongs, safe swimming coves and pounding surf beaches. Entry is via self-registration on the way in.

If you want to stay the night, the two-bedroom **Donnington Cottage** (per night

$85, 2-night minimum) at Spalding Cove, built in 1899, sleeps six and has photo-worthy views. Book through Port Lincoln visitor information centre; BYO linen and food. The visitor centre can also advise on **bush camping** (per car $17) in the park, including sites at Fisherman's Point, Memory Cove, September Beach and Surfleet Cove.

The Port Lincoln visitor information centre also sells permits to **Mikkira Station & Koala Sanctuary** (www.mikkirakoalas.com; Fishery Bay Rd; day permit/camping $15/25), Eyre Peninsula's first sheep station and home to the endemic Port Lincoln parrot (and some koalas); and **Whalers Way** (24hr pass per car incl 1 night camping $30), a super-scenic 14km coastal drive 32km southwest of Port Lincoln.

## Coffin Bay

POP 650

Oyster lovers rejoice! Deathly sounding Coffin Bay (named by Matthew Flinders after his buddy Sir Isaac Coffin) is a snoozy fishing village basking languidly in the warm sun...until a 2500-strong holiday horde arrives every January. Slippery, salty **oysters** from the nearby beds are exported worldwide, but you shouldn't pay more than $1 per oyster around town. Online, see www.coffinbay.net.

Along the ocean side of Coffin Bay there's some wild coastal scenery, most of which is part of **Coffin Bay National Park** (www.environment.sa.gov.au; per car $9), overrun with roos, emus and fat goannas. Access for conventional vehicles is limited: you can get to **Point Avoid** (coastal lookouts, rocky cliffs, good surf and whales passing between May and October) and **Yangie Bay** (arid-looking rocky landscapes and walking trails), but otherwise you'll need a 4WD. There are some isolated **camp sites** (per car $7) within the park, generally with dirt-road access.

**Coffin Bay Explorer** (☑ 0428 880 621, 1300 788 378; www.coffinbayexplorer.com; adult/child $85/45) runs half-day wildlife and seafood tours with plenty of oysters and dolphins. See also Earth Adventure (p53).

## 🛏 Sleeping & Eating

To rent out holiday shacks around town from $50 to $300 per night try **Coffin Bay Holiday Rentals** (☑ 0427 844 568; www.coffinbayholidayrentals.com.au) or **Flinders Keepers** (☑ 1300 986 849, 08-8685 4063; www.flinderskeepers.com.au).

**Coffin Bay Caravan Park**            CARAVAN PARK $
(☑ 08-8685 4170; www.coffinbay.net/caravanpark; 91 Esplanade; unpowered/powered sites $24/34, cabins without/with bathroom $75/105, villas $130; ❄) Resident cockatoos, galahs and parrots squawk around the shady she-oak sites here, and the cabins are a reasonable bang for your buck (BYO linen). Lovely two-bedroom family villas, too.

**Coffin Bay Hotel**            MOTEL $
(☑ 08-8685 4111; www.coffinbay.net/accommodation/hotel.html; cnr Jubilee Dr & Shepperd Ave; s/d $85/95; ❄) The sprawling local pub (built, it seems, to avoid any kind of view) has eight regulation units out the back (all brown brick and teak veneer), and plates up regulation counter meals (mains $16 to $27, serving noon to 2pm and 6pm to 8pm). What will emerge from the building site out the front?

**Oysterbeds**            SEAFOOD $$
(☑ 08-8685 4000; www.oysterbeds.com.au; 61 Esplanade; mains $18-28; ⏱ 10.30am-2pm Wed-Sun, 6-8pm Fri & Sat, closed Jun-Aug) A gregarious little food room – all tangerine, sea-blue and shiny liquor bottles – serving the pick of the local seafood. Takeaway oysters shucked/unshucked are $14/10 per dozen.

## Coffin Bay to Streaky Bay

There's reliable surf at **Greenly Beach** just south of Coulta, 40km north of Coffin Bay. There's also good salmon fishing along this wild stretch of coast, notably at **Locks Well**, where a long, steep stairway called the **Staircase to Heaven** (283 steps? Count 'em...) leads from the car park down to an awesome surf beach, the deep orange sand strewn with seashells.

About 15km further north, tiny **Elliston** (population 380; www.elliston.com.au) is a small fishing town on soporific Waterloo Bay, with a beautiful swimming beach and a fishing jetty (hope the whiting are biting). Waterside **Waterloo Bay Tourist Park** (☑ 08-8687 9076; www.visitelliston.net; 10 Beach Tce; unpowered/powered sites $25/29, cabins $60-110; ❄ 🛜) is a smallish operation with decent cabins (aim for one on top of the dunes) and fishing gear for sale.

Just north of Elliston, take the 10km detour to **Anxious Bay** for some anxiety-relieving ocean scenery (billed as Elliston's 'Great Ocean Tourist Drive'). En route you'll pass **Blackfellows**, which boasts some of the west coast's best surf. From here you can eyeball the 36-sq-km Flinders Island 35km offshore, where there's a sheep station and a self-contained, nine-bed holiday house (📞 0428 261 132; www.flindersgetaway.com; per person from $90). To get here you have to charter a plane from Port Lincoln or a boat from Elliston (additional to accommodation costs); ask for details when you book.

At Venus Bay there are sheltered beaches (and the not-so-sheltered Mount Camel Beach), a gaggle of pelicans, a small caravan park and the obligatory fishing jetty.

If you feel like taking a plunge and swimming with sea lions and dolphins, stop by Baird Bay and organise a tour with Baird Bay Ocean Eco Experience (📞 08-8626 5017; www.bairdbay.com; 4hr tours adult/child $140/70; ☉ Sep-May) 🎣. Accommodation is also available.

If you'd rather stay high-and-dry, the road to Point Labatt, 43km south of Streaky Bay, takes you to one of the few permanent sea-lion colonies on the Australian mainland; ogle them from the cliff-tops (with binoculars).

A few kilometres down the Point Labatt road are the globular Murphy's Haystacks, an improbable congregation of 'inselbergs' – colourful, weather-sculpted granite outcrops, which are millions of years old.

## Streaky Bay

POP 1150

This endearing little seasider (actually on Blanche Port) takes its name from the streaks of seaweed Matt Flinders spied in the bay as he sailed by. Visible at low tide, the seagrass attracts ocean critters and the bigger critters that eat them – first-class fishing. For tourist info, swing by the Streaky Bay Visitor Information Centre (📞 08-8626 7033; www.streakybay.com.au; 21 Bay Rd; ☉ 9am-12.30pm & 1.30-5pm Mon-Fri).

The Streaky Bay Museum (www.national trust.org.au/sa; 42 Montgomery Tce; adult/child $3.50/50c; ☉ 2-4pm Tue & Fri, 9am-noon Sat) is inside a 1901 school house, and features a fully furnished pug-and-pine hut, an old iron lung and plenty of pioneering history.

### 🛏 Sleeping & Eating

**Streaky Bay Hotel/Motel**          HOTEL-MOTEL $
(📞 08-8626 1008; www.streakybayhotel.com.au; 33 Alfred Tce; hotel s/d $50/65, motel d $110-135, all incl breakfast; ❄) The hotel rooms upstairs at this 1866 brick beauty have rip-snorting wa-

ter views and a large balcony from which to snort them. The downstairs rooms are sans views but perfectly decent. Motel rooms out the back are unglamorous but have more privacy. Breakfast, lunch and dinner happen in the bistro daily (mains $15 to $30, serving 7am to 9am, noon to 2pm and 6pm to 8.30pm).

**Foreshore Tourist Park**          CARAVAN PARK $
(📞 08-8626 1666; www.streakybayftpark.com. au; 82 Wells St; unpowered/powered sites from $23/28, cabins & units $85-110; ❄) Right on Doctors Beach just east of town, this sandy park is overrun with cavorting families in summer. Plenty of space and sea-based things to do.

★ **Mocean**          CAFE $$
(📞 08-8626 1775; www.moceancafe.com.au; 34b Alfred Tce; mains $16-32; ☉ 10am-3pm Tue-Sun, 6-8pm Thu-Sat) It looks like a big shipping container from the street, but this jaunty corrugated-iron-clad cafe is the town's social pacemaker, with murals, Moroccan lanterns and water views from the alfresco terrace. Dishes focus on scrumptious local seafood – try the chilli-and-lime squid. There's good coffee, too.

## Ceduna

POP 3800

Despite the locals' best intentions, Ceduna remains a raggedy fishing town that just can't shake its tag as a blow-through pit stop en route to WA. But the local oysters love it! Oysterfest (www.ceduna.net/site/page. cfm?u=167) in late September is the undisputed king of Australian oyster parties. And if you're heading west in whale season (May to October), Ceduna is the place for updates on sightings at Head of Bight.

For local info, swing by the Ceduna Visitor Information Centre (📞 08-8625 2780, 1800 639 413; www.cedunatourism.com.au; 58 Poynton St; ☉ 9am-5.30pm Mon-Fri, 9.30am-5pm Sat & Sun).

### ⊙ Sights

**Ceduna Museum**          MUSEUM
(www.nationaltrust.org.au/sa; 2 Park Tce; adult/child/family $3.50/2/7; ☉ 10am-noon Mon, Tue, Fri & Sat, 2-4pm Wed, 10am-4pm Thu) Little Ceduna Museum has pioneer exhibits, indigenous artefacts and a display on the tragic British nuclear tests at Maralinga.

Ceduna Aboriginal
Arts & Culture Centre                GALLERY
(www.visitaboriginalart.com; 2 Eyre Hwy; ⊙9am-
5pm Mon-Fri) FREE The sea-inspired works of
local indigenous artists from along the coast
steal the show at this casual arts centre.

## 🛏 Sleeping & Eating

Ceduna Foreshore Hotel/Motel       MOTEL $$
(☑08-8625 2008; www.cedunahotel.com.au; 32
O'Loughlin Tce; d $150-195, f $220; ❋🌐) The ren-
ovated 54-room Foreshore is the most luxu-
rious option in town, with water views and
a bistro zooming in on west-coast seafood
(mains $16 to $32, serving 6.30am to 9am,
noon to 2pm and 6pm to 8.30pm). Views
from the outdoor terrace look through Nor-
folk Island pines and out across the bay.

Ceduna Oyster Bar                   SEAFOOD $
(☑08-8626 9086; www.ceduna.net/site/page.
cfm?u=493; Eyre Hwy; 12 oysters $12; ⊙9.30am-
5pm Mon-Fri, 10am-4pm Sat) Pick up a box of
freshly shucked molluscs and head for the
foreshore, or sit by the highway-side here
and watch the road trains rumble past.
Hours can be sketchy – call in advance.

# Ceduna to the Western Australian Border

It's 480km from Ceduna to the WA border.
Along the stretch you can get a bed and a
beer at Penong (72km from Ceduna), Nun-
droo (151km), the Nullarbor Roadhouse
(295km) near Head of Bight, and at Border
Village on the border itself.

Wheat and sheep paddocks line the road
to Nundroo, after which you're in mallee
scrub for another 100km. Around 20km lat-
er, the trees thin to low bluebush as you en-
ter the true Nullarbor (Latin for 'no trees').
Road trains, caravans and cyclists of ques-
tionable sanity are your only companions as
you put your foot down and career towards
the setting sun.

Turn off the highway at Penong (popula-
tion 200), and follow the 20km dirt road to
Point Sinclair and Cactus Beach, which
has three of Australia's most famous surf
breaks. Caves is a wicked right-hand break
for experienced surfers (locals don't take
too kindly to tourists dropping in). There's
bush camping (per person from $10) on
private property close to the breaks; BYO
drinking water.

The viewing platforms at Head of Bight
(☑0407 832 297; www.yalata.org; adult $20, child
under/over 15 free/$15; ⊙8am-5pm) overlook
a major southern-right-whale breeding
ground. Whales migrate here from Ant-
arctica, and you can see them cavorting
from May to October. The breeding area is
protected by the Great Australian Bight
Commonwealth Marine Reserve (www.en
vironment.gov.au/coasts/mpa/gab), the world's
second-largest marine park after the Great
Barrier Reef.

Head of Bight is a part of the Yalata In-
digenous Protected Area. Pay your entry fee
and get the latest whale information from
the White Well Ranger Station on the way
in to the viewing area. The signposted turn-
off is 14km east of the Nullarbor Roadhouse.

While you're in the Head of Bight area,
you can also check out Murrawijinie Cave, a
large overhang behind the Nullarbor Road-
house, and have a look at the signposted
coastal lookouts along the top of the 80m-
high Bunda Cliffs.

If you're continuing west into WA, dump
all fruit, vegetables, cheese and plants at
Border Village (as per quarantine regula-
tions), and watch out for animals if you're
driving at night. Note that if you're driving
east rather than west, SA's quarantine check
point isn't until Ceduna.

## 🛏 Sleeping & Eating

Penong Caravan Park            CARAVAN PARK $
(☑08-8625 1111; www.nullarbornet.com.au/towns/
penong.html; 5 Stiggants Rd, Penong; unpowered/
powered sites $23/27, onsite vans/cabins from
$50/78; ❋) A short hop from Ceduna, this
well-kept park is rated by some travellers
as the best on the Nullarbor. The cabins are
in good shape, and the camping area has
a laundry and barbecues. Extra charge for
linen.

Fowlers Bay Caravan Park       CARAVAN PARK $
(☑08-8625 6143; www.nullarbornet.com.au/
towns/fowlersBay.html; Fowlers Bay; powered sites
$25, units $65-75; ❋) There's basic accommo-
dation, a shop and takeaway food in this
almost ghost town, plus heritage buildings,
good fishing and rambling dunes. Take the
Fowlers Bay turn-off 106km from Ceduna.

Nundroo Hotel/Motel                MOTEL $
(☑08-8625 6120; www.nundrooaccommodation.
com; Eyre Hwy, Nundroo; unpowered/powered sites
$8/20, d $90; ❋🌐) If you're heading west,
Nundroo has this decent hotel/motel and

the last mechanic until Norseman in WA, 1038km away. There's a very basic dorm, and worn but comfy motel rooms with updated bathrooms. There's a bar/restaurant onsite, open 11am until late (meals $15 to $35).

**Nullarbor Roadhouse** MOTEL $
(✆08-8625 6271; www.nullarbornet.com.au/towns/nullarbor.html; Eyre Hwy, Nullarbor; unpowered/powered sites $20/25, budget rooms s/d/tr $47/57/67, motel s/d/tr $125/145/165; ❄) Close to the Head of Bight whale-watching area, this roadhouse is a real oasis. The onsite bar/restaurant is open from 7am to 10pm (meals $15 to $30).

**Border Village Motel** MOTEL $
(✆08-9039 3474; www.nullarbornet.com.au/towns/borderVillage.html; Eyre Hwy, Border Village; unpowered/powered sites $15/20, budget rooms s/d/tr $40/60/70, motel s/d/f from $95/110/120; ❄@❄) Just 50m from the WA border, this motel has a variety of modern rooms and cabins and a licensed restaurant (meals $13 to $25, serving from noon to 2pm and 6pm to 8pm).

# FLINDERS RANGES

Known simply as 'the Flinders', this ancient mountain range is an iconic South Australian environment. Jagged peaks and escarpments rise up north of Port Augusta and track 400km north to Mt Hopeless. The colours here are remarkable: as the day stretches out, the mountains shift from mauve mornings to midday chocolates and ochre-red sunsets.

Before Europeans arrived, the Flinders were prized by the Adnyamathanha peoples for their red ochre deposits, which had medicinal and ritual uses. Sacred caves, rock paintings and carvings exist throughout the region. In the wake of white exploration came villages, farms, country pubs, wheat farms and cattle stations, many of which failed under the unrelenting sun.

The cooler Southern Ranges are studded with stands of river red gums and country hamlets with cherubic appeal. In the arid Northern Ranges, the desert takes a hold: the scenery here is stark, desolate and very beautiful.

Online, see www.flindersoutback.com.

##  Tours

See Heading Bush (p53).

**Bookabee Tours** INDIGENOUS
(✆0408 209 593, 08-8235 9954; www.bookabee.com.au; 2-/3-/4-day tours $995/1520/2025) ✎ Highly rated indigenous-run tours to the Flinders Ranges and outback, departing Adelaide, including quality accommodation, meals, cultural tours, activities and interpretation.

**Swagabout Tours** WILDERNESS
(✆0408 845 378; www.swagabouttours.com.au) Dependable Flinders Ranges trips including Quorn and Wilpena (plus Arkaroola on the four-day jaunt), and can be extended to Coober Pedy. Costs per day are around $300/500 with camping/hotel accommodation.

**Wallaby Tracks Adventure Tours** WILDERNESS
(✆0428 486 655; www.wallabytracks.com; 1-/4-day tours $250/1200) Small-group 4WD tours around the Ranges and Wilpena Pound. One-day tours ex-Quorn or Port Augusta; four-day tours ex-Adelaide.

**Adventure Tours Australia** WILDERNESS
(✆08-8132 8130, 1300 654 604; www.adventuretours.com.au) Popular small-group tours through the Flinders region and beyond; seven-day Adelaide to Alice Springs tours $1020.

**Groovy Grape** WILDERNESS
(✆08-8440 1640, 1800 661 177; www.groovygrape.com.au) Adelaide to Coober Pedy and back over four days, via the Flinders Ranges will cost $495.

## ❶ Getting There & Away

### BUS

**Premier Stateliner** (www.premierstateliner.com.au) Daily buses from Adelaide to Port Pirie ($43, 3¼ hours).
**Yorke Peninsula Coaches** (✆08-8821 2755; www.ypcoaches.com.au) Runs a Friday bus between Port Augusta and Quorn ($6, 40 minutes), and a Thursday bus between Port Pirie and Melrose ($6, 1¼ hours).

### TRAIN

Pichi Richi Railway (p124) has trains between Port Augusta and Quorn (two hours) every Saturday.

# Southern Ranges Towns

**Port Pirie** (population 13,200) is a big lead- and zinc-smelting town on the edge of the Southern Flinders. The Nyrstar smelter dominates the skyline, but the town itself has some pretty old buildings along Ellen St, and is a good spot to stock up on supplies before heading north. The **Port Pirie Regional Tourism & Arts Centre** (☑08-8633 8700, 1800 000 424; www.piriehasitall.com.au; 3 Mary Elie St; ☺9am-5pm Mon-Fri, 10am-4pm Sat & Sun) has local info.

You enter the Southern Ranges proper near Laura (population 550), emerging from the wheat fields like Superman's Smallville (all civic pride and 1950s prosperity). There's not a lot to do here, but the long, geranium-adorned main street has a supermarket, chemist, bakery, bank, post office...even a shoe shop!

The oldest town in the Flinders (1853) is Melrose (population 200), snug in the elbow of the 960m Mt Remarkable. It has the perfect mix of well-preserved architecture, a cracking-good pub, quality accommodation and parks with *actual grass*. Don't miss the decaying multistorey ruins of Jacka's Brewery (1878) on Mount St, which once employed 40 staff.

Online, see www.southernflindersranges.com.au.

## 🛏 Sleeping & Eating

**North Star Hotel**                      PUB $$
(☑08-8666 2110; www.northstarhotel.com.au; 43 Nott St, Melrose; d $110-225, trucks $160; ❋ 🛜) As welcome as summer rain, the North Star Hotel in Melrose is a fabulous 1854 pub renovated in city-meets-woolshed style. Sit under the hessian-sack ceiling and spinning fans for a fresh menu (mains $16 to $30, serving noon to 2pm and 6pm to 8pm), great coffee and cold beer. Accommodation ranges from rooms in Bundaleer Cottage next door (sleeps 16) to plush suites above the pub and surprisingly cool metal-clad cabins built on two old trucks out the back.

**Melrose Caravan Park**          CARAVAN PARK $
(☑08-8666 2060; www.members.westnet.com.au/venhoek/~melrose; Joe's Rd, Melrose; dm $20, unpowered/powered sites $20/25, cabins $60-120; ❋) A small, tidy park with five acres of bush campsites and self-contained cabins salvaged from the 2000 Sydney Olympics (all with TVs and cooking facilities – the cheaper ones are sans bathrooms). The 12km return hike up Mt Remarkable starts on the back doorstep. Next door is a converted agricultural shed with basic dorm facilities.

**Old Bakery**                        BAKERY $
(☑08-8663 2165; www.oldbakerystonehut.com.au; 1 Main North Rd, Stone Hut; items $4-10; ☺7am-

6pm) About 10km north of Laura in Stone Hut (population 290) is this amazing bakery, which makes legendary chunky beef pies, slices and quandong tart. There's cabin-style accommodation here too (doubles from $150).

# Mt Remarkable National Park

Bush boffins rave about the steep, jaggedy **Mt Remarkable National Park** (www.environment.sa.gov.au; per person/car $4/10) straddling the Southern Flinders. Wildlife and bushwalking are the main lures, with various tracks (including part of the Heysen Trail) meandering through isolated gorges.

From the car park at Alligator Gorge take the short, steep walk (2km, two hours) down into the craggy gorge (no sign of any 'gators), the ring route (9km, four hours), or walk to Hidden Gorge (18km, seven hours) or Mambray Creek (13km, seven hours). From Mambray Creek the track to Davey's Gully (2.5km, one hour) is (literally and metaphorically) a walk in the park. Peak baggers sweat up the track to the 960m-high summit of Mt Remarkable (12km, five hours); the trail starts behind Melrose Caravan Park.

Pay the park entry fee at the **Park Office** (☑08-8634 7068; www.environment.sa.gov.au) at Mambray Creek, off Hwy 1 about 21km north of Port Germein. On the inland route (Main North Rd between Melrose and Wilmington), there's an honesty box at Alligator Gorge. Both stations have park info brochures.

If you want to stay the night there's plenty of bush camping (per person/car $6/18), and two lodges: at Mambray Creek (sleeps 4, per night from $55) and Alligator Gorge (sleeps 10, per night from $150). Both are solar powered; Alligator Gorge has better cooking facilities and showers. Book through the Park Office.

# Quorn

POP 1210

Is Quorn a film set after the crew has gone home? With more jeering crows than people, it's a cinematographic little outback town. Wheat farming took off here in 1875, and the town prospered with the arrival of the Great Northern Railway from Port Augusta. Quorn (pronounced 'kworn') remained an

# Flinders Ranges

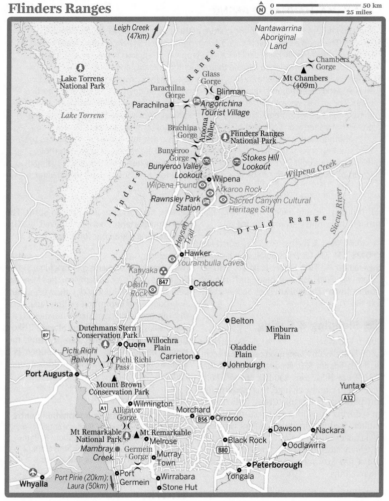

important railroad junction until trains into the Flinders were cut in 1970.

## Sights & Activities

Quorn's streetscapes, especially Railway Tce, are a real history lesson, and have featured in iconic Australian films such as *Gallipoli* and *Sunday Too Far Away*. Pick up the *Quorn Historic Buildings Walk* brochure from the visitor centre. A fragment of the long-defunct railway now conveys the Pichi Richi Railway (p124) between Port Augusta and Quorn.

Derelict ruins of early settlements litter the Quorn–Hawker road, the most impressive of which is **Kanyaka**, a once-thriving sheep station founded in 1851. From the homestead ruins (41km from Quorn) it's a 20-minute walk to a waterhole, loomed over by the massive **Death Rock**. The story goes that local Aborigines once placed their dying kinfolk here to see out their last hours.

**Pichi Richi Camel Tours**   CAMEL TOUR
(📱 0439 333 257, 08-8648 6640; www.pichirichi cameltours.com) Saddle up for two-hour sunset rides ($85), breakfast rides (55), or a longer

## ADNYAMATHANHA DREAMING

Land and nature are integral to the culture of the traditional owners of the Flinders Ranges. The people collectively called Adnyamathanha (Hill People) are actually a collection of the Wailpi, Kuyani, Jadliaura, Piladappa and Pangkala tribes, who exchanged and elaborated on stories to explain their spectacular local geography.

The walls of Ikara (Wilpena Pound), for example, are the bodies of two *akurra* (giant snakes), who coiled around Ikara during an initiation ceremony, eating most of the participants. The snakes were so full after their feast they couldn't move and willed themselves to die, creating the landmark. Because of its traditional significance, the Adnyamathanha prefer that visitors don't climb St Mary Peak, reputed to be the head of the female snake.

In another story another *akurra* drank Lake Frome dry, then wove his way across the land creating creeks and gorges. Wherever he stopped, he created a large waterhole, including Arkaroola Springs. The sun warmed the salty water in his stomach causing it to rumble, a noise which can be heard today in the form of underground springwater.

half-/full-day camel-back tour ($75/125) through the country around Quorn.

**Flinders Bikes & Bytes**     BICYCLE HIRE
(☑ 0428 838 737, 08 8648 6349; www.bikesandbytes.com.au; 43 First St; per hour $7; ⊙ 10am-5.30pm Wed-Sun) Hire a bike and ramble around town. There's internet access available too.

## 🛌 Sleeping & Eating

**Quorn Caravan Park**     CARAVAN PARK $
(☑ 08-8648 6206; www.quorncaravanpark.com.au; 8 Silo Rd; dm $20, unpowered/powered sites $23/29, van $65, cabins $90-120; ❄) ✔ Fully keyed in to climate change, this passionately run park on Pinkerton Creek is hell bent on reducing emissions and restoring native habitat. Features include spotless cabins, a backpacker cabin (sleeps eight), camp kitchen, shady sites, rainwater tanks everywhere and a few lazy roos lounging about under the redgums.

**Quandong Apartments**     APARTMENTS $$
(☑ 0432 113 473; www.quandongapartments.com; 31 First St; d $160; ❄) Next door to the Quandong Café (and run by the same folks), these two self-contained apartments have full kitchens, big TVs, quality linen and chintz-meets-Asian touches. Rates come down for stays of two nights or more.

**Austral Inn**     HOTEL-MOTEL $
(☑ 08-8648 6017; www.australinn.info; 16 Railway Tce; d motel/pub from $90/115; ❄) There's always a few locals here giving the jukebox a workout. The pub rooms are renovated – simple and clean with new linen (nicer than the motel rooms out the back). Try a kangaroo schnitzel in the bistro (mains $15 to $30,

serving noon to 2pm and 6pm to 8pm). The pub is purportedly above an old well, so if it's been raining watch out for mozzies.

**Quandong Café**     CAFE $
(www.quandongapartments.com/cafe.html; 31 First St; meals $4-15; ⊙ 8.30am-4pm mid-Mar–mid-Dec) A traditional country cafe with creaky floorboards and spinning ceiling fans, serving big breakfasts and light lunches. Try a generously adorned 'Railway Sleeper' (like a pizza sub), or a massive slab of lemon meringue or quandong pie (a quandong is a kind of native cherry). Good old-fashioned country value!

## ℹ️ Information

**Flinders Ranges Visitor Information Centre**
(☑ 08-8648 6419; www.flindersranges.com; Railway Tce, Quorn Railway Station; ⊙ 9am-5pm Mon-Fri, 9am-4pm Sat & Sun) Maps, brochures, internet access and advice.

# Hawker
POP 300

Hawker is the last outpost of civilisation before Wilpena Pound, 55km to the north. Much like Quorn, Hawker has seen better days, most of which were when the old *Ghan* train stopped here. These days Hawker is a pancake-flat, pit-stop town with an ATM and the world's most helpful petrol station.

## ⊙ Sights & Activities

It's not so much what's in Hawker that's interesting – it's more what's around it – but if you like your great outdoors inside (and a little bit eccentric), **Wilpena Panorama** (www.wilpenapanorama.com; cnr Wilpena

& Cradock Rds; adult/child $8/5.50; ⊘9am-5pm Mon-Sat, 9am-4pm Sat, 11am-2pm Sun, closed Jan & Feb) is a large circular room with a painting of Wilpena Pound surrounding you on all sides.

**Yourambulla Caves**, 12km south of Hawker, have detailed Aboriginal rock paintings (including emu tracks), with three sites open to visitors. **Yourambulla Peak**, a half-hour walk from the car park, is the most accessible spot to check out the paintings.

Around 40km north of Hawker towards Wilpena, **Arkaroo Rock** is a sacred Aboriginal site. The rock art here features reptile and human figures in charcoal, bird-lime and yellow and red ochre. It's a short(ish) return walk from the car park (2km, one hour).

## ☞ Tours

**Derek's 4WD Tours**                   DRIVING TOUR
(☑0417 475 770; www.dereks4wdtours.com; tours half-/full day from $115/170) These are 4WD trips with an environmental bent, including visits to Bunyeroo and Brachina gorges.

**Skytrek Willow Springs**              DRIVING TOUR
(☑08-8648 0016; www.skytrekwillowsprings.com. au) Six-hour self-drive tours on a working sheep station (per vehicle $65), or they can hook you up with a tour operator. Self-contained cabin accommodation is also available (doubles from $100).

## 🛏 Sleeping & Eating

**BIG4 Hawker Caravan Park**     CARAVAN PARK $
(☑08-8648 4006; www.hawkerbig4holidaypark. com.au; cnr Wilpena Rd & Chace View Tce; unpowered/powered sites $26/28, en-suite sites $39-45, cabins $96-162; ❄☞❄) At the Wilpena end of town, this upbeat, fastidiously maintained acreage has generous gravelly sites and a range of cabins. And there's a pool!

**Outback Motel &**
**Chapmanton Holiday Units**        MOTEL $$
(☑08-8648 4100; www.hawkersa.info/biz/out back.htm; 1 Wilpena Rd; s/d motel $110/125, units $120/150; ❄) Like a transplanted vision from Utah, this orange-brick, drive-up motel offers the best rooms in town. The two-bedroom units are good value for families.

**Flinders Ranges Accommodation**
**Booking Service**      ACCOMMODATION SERVICES $$
(FRABS; ☑08-8648 4022, 1800 777 880; www. frabs.com.au; d $75-225) Bookings for rural cottages and shearers quarters around Hawker.

**Old Ghan Restaurant**    MODERN AUSTRALIAN $$
(☑08-8648 4176; www.hawkersa.info/biz/ghan. htm; Leigh Creek Rd, Old Hawker Railway Station; mains $19-32; ⊘5.30-8pm Wed-Sat, closed Jan) In the *1884 Ghan* railway station on the outskirts of town, this rough-and-ready eatery is about as upmarket as Hawker gets. Expect mains such as kangaroo medallions with wattleseed and mustard, and beer-battered garfish.

## ⓘ Information

**Teague's Hawker Motors & Visitor Information Centre** (☑1800 777 880, 08-8648 4014; www.hawkervic.info; cnr Wilpena & Cradock Rds; ⊘7.30am-6pm) The town's petrol station (fill up if you're heading north) is also the visitor information centre.

# Flinders Ranges National Park

One of SA's most treasured parks, **Flinders Ranges National Park** (www.environment. sa.gov.au; per car $9) is laced with craggy gorges, saw-toothed ranges, abandoned homesteads, Aboriginal sites, native wildlife and, after it rains, carpets of wildflowers. The park's big-ticket drawcard is the 80-sq-km natural basin **Ikara (Wilpena Pound)** – a sunken elliptical valley ringed by gnarled ridges (don't let anyone tell you it's a meteorite crater!).

The Pound is only vehicle accessible on the Wilpena Pound Resort's **shuttle bus** (return adult/child/family $4/2.50/9), which drops you within 1km of the old Hills Homestead, from where you can walk to **Wangarra Lookout**. The shuttle runs at 9am, 11am, 1pm, 3pm and 5pm, dropping people off and coming straight back (so if you take the 5pm shuttle and want more than a cursory look around, you'll miss the return bus). Otherwise it's a three-hour, 8km return walk between the resort and lookout.

The 20km **Brachina Gorge Geological Trail** features an amazing layering of exposed sedimentary rock, covering 120 million years of the Earth's history. Grab a brochure from the visitors centre.

The **Bunyeroo–Brachina–Aroona Scenic Drive** is a 110km round trip, passing by Bunyeroo Valley, Brachina Gorge, Aroona Valley and **Stokes Hill Lookout**. There are plenty of short walks along the way; a stop at **Bunyeroo Valley Lookout** is mandatory. The drive starts north of Wilpena off the road to Blinman.

Just beyond the park's southeast corner, a one-hour, 1km return walk leads to the **Sacred Canyon Cultural Heritage Site**, with Aboriginal rock-art galleries featuring animal tracks and designs.

## ◎ Sights & Activities

**Bushwalking** in the Flinders is an unforgettable experience. Before you make happy trails, ensure you've got enough water, sunscreen and a hat, and tell someone where you're going and when you'll be back. Pick up the *Bushwalking in Flinders Ranges National Park* brochure/map from the visitors centre, detailing 19 park walks. Many of the walks kick off at Wilpena Pound Resort.

For a look at Wilpena, the walk up to **Tanderra Saddle** (return 15km, six hours) on the ridge of **St Mary Peak** on the Pound's rim is brilliant, though it's a thigh-pounding scramble at times. The Adnyamathanha people request that you restrict your climbing to the ridge and don't climb St Mary Peak itself, due to its traditional significance to them. If you have time, take the longer outside track for more eye-popping vistas. You can keep going on the round trip (22km, nine hours), camping overnight at Cooinda Camp.

The quick, tough track up to **Mt Ohlssen Bagge** (return 6.5km, four hours) rewards the sweaty hiker with a stunning panorama. Good short walks include the stroll to **Hills Homestead** (return 6.5km, two hours), or the dash up to the **Wilpena Solar Power Station** (return 500m, 30 minutes).

In the park's north (50km north of Wilpena Pound Resort), the **Aroona Ruins** are the launch pad for a few less-trampled walks. The **Yuluna Hike** (return 8km, four hours) weaves through a painterly stretch of the ABC Ranges. The challenging **Aroona– Youngoona Track** (one way 15.5km, seven hours) offers views of the Trezona and Heysen Ranges; cool your boots overnight at Youngoona camp site.

## ☞ Tours

Wilpena Pound Resort (half-/full day from $180/245) and Rawnsley Park Station (half-/full day from $135/225) both run **4WD tours**. There are also tour companies operating from Hawker.

**Air Wilpena Scenic Flights**    SCENIC FLIGHTS
(☑08-8648 0004; www.wilpenapound.com.au/scenic-flights; flights 20min/30min/1hr $165/190/299) Flights from Wilpena Pound Resort.

**Central Air Services**    SCENIC FLIGHTS
(☑08-8648 0040; www.centralairservices.com.au; flights 20min/30min/1hr $160/180/350) Scenic flights from Rawnsley Park Station.

## 🛏 Sleeping & Eating

Permits for **bush camping** (per person/car $7/13) within the national park (ie outside the resort) are available from either the visitor information centre or self-service booths along the way. Trezona, Aroona and Brachina East have creek-side sites among big gum trees; Youngoona in the park's north is a good base for walks. Remote Wilkawillina is certainly the quietest spot.

★**Wilpena Pound Resort**    RESORT $$$
(☑08-8648 0004, 1800 805 802; www.wilpenapound. com.au; Wilpena Rd via Hawker; unpowered/powered sites $22/32, permanent tent with/without linen $97/75, d $224-288; ❀@🛜🞉) Accommodation at this plush resort includes motel-style rooms, upmarket self-contained suites, and a great (although hugely popular) camp site. If you don't have your own camping gear, there are permanent tents sleeping five. Purchase your camping permit at the visitors centre, which also sells petrol and basic (and expensive) groceries. Don't miss a swim in the pool, happy hour at the bar (5pm to 6pm) and dinner at the excellent bistro (mains $19 to $29 – the roo is the best we've ever had!).

**Rawnsley Park Station**    RESORT $$
(☑08-8648 0030, caravan park 08-8648 0008, restaurant 08-8648 0126; www.rawnsleypark.com. au; Wilpena Rd via Hawker; unpowered/powered sites $22/33, hostel s/d/f from $50/75/95, cabins/ units/villas from $90/130/370; ❀@) This rangy homestead, 35km from Hawker just south of the national park, runs the accommodation gamut from tent sites to luxe eco-villas. There are also some caravan-park cabins set up as dorms, managed by the **YHA** (www.yha. com.au). Also on offer is a range of outback activities including mountain-bike hire (per hour $15), bushwalks (30 minutes to four hours), hot-air ballooning, 4WD tours and scenic flights. The Woolshed Restaurant (mains $10 to $40, open noon to 2pm and 6pm to 8pm) does bang-up bush tucker, plus curries, seafood and pizzas.

## ❶ Information

**Wilpena Pound Visitor Information Centre**
(☑08-8648 0048, 1800 805 802; www. wilpenapound.com.au; Wilpena Pound Resort;

⊙8am-5pm) Info on the park and district, internet access and bike hire (per half-/full day $20/40). Also does bookings for scenic flights and 4WD tours, and issues bushwalking advice. You can pay park entry fees here (per car $9).

# Blinman & Parachilna

North of Wilpena Pound on a sealed road, ubercute Blinman (population 30) owes its existence to the copper ore discovered here in 1859 and the smelter built in 1903. But the boom went bust and 1500 folks left town. Today Blinman's main claim to fame is as SA's highest town (610m above sea level).

Much of the old **Heritage Blinman Mine** (☑08-8648 4782; www.heritageblinmanmine. com.au; Main St, Blinman; tours adult/child/family $25/10/60; ⊙9.30am-5pm) has been redeveloped with lookouts, audio-visual interpretation and information boards. One-hour tours run at 10am, noon and 2pm (extra tours in winter).

Slate floors, old photos and colonial-style rooms collide at the renovated 1869 **North Blinman Hotel** (☑08-8648 4867; www.blinmanhotel.com.au; Mine Rd, Blinman; unpowered/powered sites $10/20, d motel/hotel $90/155; ❋🛜), which has tent sites out the back (...D'oh! They filled in the pool!). The bistro (mains $14 to $30, serving noon to 2pm and 6pm to 8pm) plates up pubby delights.

In an 1883 school building, **Wild Lime Café & Gallery** (☑08-8648 4679; www.wildlimecafe.com; Main St, Old Schoolhouse, Blinman; mains $8-20; ⊙9am-4pm daily Apr-Nov, closed Tue Dec-Mar) serves great coffee, soups, salads, pies, pasties, cakes and bush-inspired dishes such as red roo curry.

The road between Blinman and Parachilna tracks through gorgeous **Parachilna Gorge**, where you'll find free creek-side camping and chill-out spots. The northern end of the **Heysen Trail** starts/finishes here.

'Real people only, no Yuppies' is the slogan at **Angorichina Tourist Village** (☑08-8648 4842; www.angorichinavillage.com.au; Blinman–Parachilna Rd; unpowered/powered sites $22/26, dm $42, cabins from $120; ❋@), 17km west of Blinman in Parachilna Gorge. It's a rambling joint with a mix of accommodation; the store sells fuel. The **Blinman Pools Walk** (12km return, five hours) starts here, following a creek past abandoned dugouts, river red gums and cypress pines.

On the Hawker–Leigh Creek road, Parachilna (population somewhere between four and seven) is an essential Flinders Ranges destination. Aside from a few shacks, a phone booth and some rusty wrecks, the only thing here is the legendary **Prairie Hotel** (☑08-8648 4895, 1800 331 473; www.prairiehotel.com.au; cnr High St & West Tce, Parachilna; powered sites $32, cabins d/f from $80/180, hotel d $195-345; ❋🛜). It's a world-class stay with slick suites, plus camping and workers' cabins across the street. Don't miss a meal and a cold beer (or five) in the pub (mains $22 to $35, serving 11.30am to 3pm and 6pm to 8.30pm). Try the feral mixed grill (camel sausage, kangaroo fillet and emu). We arrived at 10.42am: 'Too early for a beer!? Whose rules are those?' said the barman.

# Leigh Creek & Copley

In the early 1980s, the previously nonexistent town of Leigh Creek (population 700) was built by the state government: blooming out of the desert, it's an odd, Canberra-like oasis of leafy landscaping and cul-de-sacs. It's a coal-mining town, supplying the Port Augusta power stations. The **Leigh Creek Visitor Information Centre** (☑08-8675 2315; www.loccleighcreek.com.au; Shop 2, Black Oak Dr, Leigh Creek; ⊙8.30am-5.30pm Mon-Fri, 8.30am-2pm Sat) is at Liz's Open Cut Cafe.

The hub of town life, the **Leigh Creek Tavern** (☑08-8675 2025; leighcreektavern@alintaenergy.com.au; Black Oak Dr, Leigh Creek; motel s/d $110/150, cabins s/d/f $90/100/130; ❋) offers jaunty '90s-style motel rooms, basic cabins a few hundred metres from the pub, and miner-sized bistro meals (mains $12 to $24, serving noon to 2pm and 6pm to 8pm).

About 6km north of Leigh Creek is the sweet meaninglessness of little Copley (population 80). **Copley Cabin & Caravan Park** (☑08-8675 2288; www.copleycaravan.com.au; Railway Tce W, Copley; unpowered/powered sites $25/28, cabins d $80-150; ❋) is a going concern: a small, immaculate park. Down the street is **Copley Bush Bakery & Quandong Cafe** (www.copleybushbakery.com.au; Railway Tce, Copley; items $4-6; ⊙8am-4pm), serving decent coffee and delicious quandong pies.

**Iga Warta** (☑08-8648 3737; www.igawarta.com; Arkaroola Rd; unpowered sites $36, dm & tents per person $36, cabins/safari tents d $104/150), 57km east of Copley on the way into Vulkathunha-Gammon Ranges National Park, is an indigenous-run establishment offering Adnyamathanha cultural experiences ($25 to $75) as well as 4WD and bushwalking tours ($52 to $228). The various onsite accommodation is open to all comers.

Immediately after Iga Warta just before the national park is Nepabunna, an Adnyamathanha community that manages the local land.

# Vulkathunha-Gammon Ranges National Park

Blanketing 1282 sq km of desert, the remote Vulkathunha-Gammon Ranges National Park (www.environment.sa.gov.au) has deep gorges, rugged ranges, yellow-footed rock wallabies and gum-lined creeks. Most of the park is difficult to access (4WDs are near compulsory) and has limited facilities. The rangers hang out at the Balcanoona Park Office (☑ 08-8648 4829, info line 08-8204 1910), 99km from Copley.

The area around Grindells Hut has expansive views and stark ridges all around. You can reach it on a 4WD track off the Arkaroola road, or by walking through Weetootla Gorge. It's a 13km return hike – you might want to stay the night at Grindells Hut. Check with the ranger before driving or walking into this area.

The park has six bush camping (per person/car $8/5) areas, including Italowie Gorge, Grindells Hut, Weetootla Gorge and Arcoona Bluff. Pick up camping permits at Balcanoona Park HQ. There are two huts that can be booked at the ranger's office: Grindells Hut (up to 8 people $145) and Balcanoona Shearer's Quarters (d/tr $40/65, exclusive use up to 18 people $265).

# Arkaroola

A privately operated wildlife reserve–resort 129km east of Copley on unsealed roads, Arkaroola Wilderness Sanctuary (☑ 08-8648 4848, 1800 676 042; www.arkaroola.com.au) occupies a far-flung and utterly spectacular part of the Flinders Ranges. The visitor information centre (☉ 9am-5pm) has displays on local natural history, including a scientific explanation of the tremors that often shake things up hereabouts.

The absolute must-do highlight of Arkaroola is the four-hour 4WD Ridgetop Tour (adult $120) through wild mountain country, complete with white-knuckle climbs and descents towards the freakish Sillers Lookout. Once you've extracted your fingernails from your seat, look for wedge-tailed eagles and yellow-footed rock wallabies. You can also book guided or tag-along tours (drives and walks) through the area. Most areas are accessible in a regular car, with some hiking to pump up your pulse.

The resort (Arkaroola Rd Camp; unpowered/powered sites $18/25, cabins $40, cottages $130-175, motel d $145-175; ❋ ❋ ) includes a motel complex and caravan park. Camp sites range from dusty hilltop spots to creekside corners; the comfortable cabins are a good budget bet. Other facilities include a woody bar-restaurant (mains $15 to $30, serving noon to 2pm and 6pm to 8pm), a supermarket and service station.

# OUTBACK

The area north of the Eyre Peninsula and the Flinders Ranges stretches into the vast, empty spaces of SA's outback. If you're prepared, travelling through this sparsely populated and harsh country is utterly rewarding.

Heading into the red heart of Australia on the Stuart Hwy, Woomera is the first pit stop, with its dark legacy of nuclear tests and shiny collection of left-over rockets. Further north, the opal-mining town of Coober Pedy is an absolute one-off: a desolate human aberration amid the blistering, arid plains. If you're feeling gung-ho, tackle a section of the iconic Oodnadatta Track, a rugged outback alternative to the Stuart Hwy tarmac. Along the way are warm desert springs, the gargantuan Lake Eyre and some amazing old outback pubs.

Online, see www.flindersoutback.com.

 Tours

For scenic outback flights, see the Coober Pedy, William Creek and Marree listings.

**Arabunna Tours**                    INDIGENOUS
(☑ 08-8675 8351; www.arabunnatours.com.au; 7-day tour ex-Adelaide $1695) Aboriginal-owned company offering cultural tours from Adelaide to the Flinders Ranges, Marree, Oodnadatta Track and Lake Eyre.

**Just Cruisin 4WD Tours**            INDIGENOUS
(☑ 08-8383 0962; www.justcruisin4wdtours.com.au; 5-day tour ex-Adelaide $3295) Aboriginal cultural tours visiting outback indigenous communities, sites and guides between Adelaide and Coober Pedy.

# ❶ Getting There & Around

AIR

**Regional Express** (Rex; www.regionalexpress.com.au) Flies most days between Adelaide and Coober Pedy ($235, two hours).

## BUS

**Greyhound Australia** (www.greyhound.com. au) Daily coaches from Adelaide to Alice Springs ($331, 19½ hours), stopping at Pimba ($122, seven hours), Glendambo ($153, 8¼ hours) and Coober Pedy ($197, 10½ hours). Online fares are cheaper.

## CAR

The Stuart Hwy is sealed from Port Augusta to Darwin. In SA, fuel and accommodation are available at Pimba (171km from Port Augusta), Glendambo (285km), Coober Pedy (535km), Cadney Homestead (689km) and Marla (771km). Pimba, Coober Pedy and Marla have 24-hour fuel sales. The Oodnadatta Track, Birdsville Track or Strzelecki Track are subject to closure after heavy rains – check conditions with the Royal Automobile Association in Adelaide, or online at www.dpti.sa.gov.au/OutbackRoads.

## TRAIN

The *Ghan* train runs through the SA outback between Adelaide and Alice Springs; see p283 for details.

# Woomera

POP 450

A 6km detour off the Stuart Hwy from Pimba (population 50; 485km from Adelaide), Woomera began in 1947 as HQ for experimental British rocket and nuclear tests at notorious sites like Maralinga. Local indigenous tribes suffered greatly from nuclear fallout. These days Woomera is an eerie, oddly artificial government town that's still an active Department of Defence test site.

Rocket into the **Woomera Heritage & Visitor Information Centre** (☑ 08-8673 7042; www.woomera.com.au; Dewrang Ave; museum adult/child $6/3; ⊙ 9am-5pm Mar-Nov, 10am-2pm Dec-Feb), with its displays on Woomera's past and present (plus a bowling alley!). Just across the car park is the **Lions Club Aircraft & Missile Park**, studded with jets and rocket remnants.

Built to house rocket scientists, the **Eldo Hotel** (☑ 08-8673 7867; www.eldohotel.com. au; Kotara Ave; d from $95; ❄) has comfortable motel-style rooms in a couple of 1960s buildings, and serves à la carte meals in an urbane bistro (mains $16 to $32, serving noon to 2pm and 6pm to 8.30pm). Try the kangaroo bratwurst snags!

Continue north through Woomera for 90km (sealed road) and you'll hit **Roxby Downs** (www.roxbydowns.com), population 4500, a bizarrely affluent desert town built to service the massive Olympic Dam Mine, which digs up untold amounts of copper, silver, gold and uranium.

# Woomera to Coober Pedy

Around 115km northwest of Pimba and 245km shy of Coober Pedy, middle-of-nowhere Glendambo (population 30) was established in 1982 as a Stuart Hwy service centre. This is the last fuel stop before Coober Pedy.

You can bunk down at the oasis-like **Glendambo Hotel-Motel** (☑ 08-8672 1030; Stuart Hwy; unpowered/powered sites $18/22, d $99-120; ❄ @ ☀), which has bars, a restaurant and a bunch of decent motel units. Outside are dusty camp sites; inside are meaty mains at the bistro ($16 to $30, serving noon to 2pm and 6pm to 8pm).

North of Glendambo the Stuart Hwy enters the government-owned Woomera Prohibited Area – the highway itself is unrestricted, but don't go a-wanderin' now, y'hear?

# Coober Pedy

POP 3500

Coming into Coober Pedy the dry, barren desert suddenly becomes riddled with holes and adjunct piles of dirt – reputedly more than a million around the township. The reason for all this rabid digging is opals, which have made this small town a mining mecca. This isn't to say it's also a tourist mecca – with swarms of flies, no trees, 50°C summer days, subzero winter nights, cavedwelling locals and rusty car wrecks in front yards, you might think you've arrived in a wasteland. But it sure is interesting!

> **ⓘ DESERT PARKS PASS**
>
> To explore the outback environment consider purchasing a **Desert Parks Pass** (☑ 1800 816 078; http://forms. bizgate.sa.gov.au/deh/parkspasses/desert. htm; per car $150), allowing access to seven outback parks (including camping), with a map and handbook. Pick one up from the DEWNR in Adelaide or Post Augusta, order one online and have it mailed to you (Australia only), or see www.environment.sa.gov.au/ parks/park_entry_fees/parks_pass_ outlets for regional pass agents in the Flinders Ranges and SA outback.

# Coober Pedy

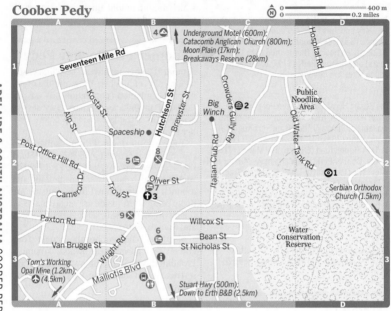

## Coober Pedy

Coober Pedy is actually very cosmopolitan, with 44 nationalities represented. Few locals make their living solely from mining, so there's a lot of 'career diversification' here (...the dude who drives the airport bus also loads the baggage, mans the hotel reception desk and works his opal claim on weekends).

The surrounding desert is jaw-droppingly desolate, a fact not overlooked by international filmmakers who've come here to shoot end-of-the-world epics like *Mad Max III*, *Red Planet*, *Ground Zero*, *Pitch Black* and the slightly more believable *Priscilla, Queen of the Desert*.

## ◉ Sights & Activities

### Opal Mining

There are hundreds of working opal mines around town, the elusive gems at the fore of everyone's consciousness. If you're keen for a fossick, tour operators or locals may invite you out to their claim to 'noodle' through the mullock (waste pile) for stones. Watch out for unmarked shafts, and never wander around the fields at night.

**Tom's Working Opal Mine** MINE
(www.tomsworkingopalmine.com.au; Lot 1993, Stuart Hwy; tours adult/child/family $25/10/55; ⊙ tours 8am, 10am, 2pm & 4pm) The best place to check out a working excavation is Tom's, 3km southwest of town: miners continue their search for the big vein while visitors noodle for small fortunes. Self-guided tours adult/child $10/5.

**Old Timers Mine** MUSEUM
(www.oldtimersmine.com; 1 Crowders Gully Rd; self-guided tours adult/child $15/1; ⊙9am-5pm) The interesting warren was mined in 1916 but was then hidden by the miners. The mine

was rediscovered when a dugout home punched through into the labyrinth of tunnels, which now makes a great tour. There's also a museum, a re-created 1920s underground home, and free mining-equipment demos daily (9.30am, 1.30pm and 3.30pm).

**Dugout Homes & Churches**
It gets hot here in summer – it makes sense to live underground! Even if it's a stinker outside, subterranean temperatures never rise above 23°C, and air-conditioning isn't necessary. The same goes for churches (miners are big on faith and hope).

**Faye's Underground**
**Display Home**                    UNDERGROUND HOME
(Old Water Tank Rd; adult/child $5/2.50; ⊙8am-5pm Mon-Sat Mar-Oct) Faye's was hand dug by three women in the 1960s. It's a little chintzy, but the living-room swimming pool is a winner!

**Serbian Orthodox Church**             CHURCH
(Saint Elijah Dr, off Flinders St; admission $5; ⊙24hr) The largest and most impressive underground church, with rock-wall carvings. It's about 8km south of town.

**St Peter & Paul Catholic Church**      CHURCH
(cnr Halliday Pl & Hutchison St; ⊙10am-4pm) FREE Coober Pedy's first church still has a sweet appeal.

**Catacomb Anglican Church**             CHURCH
(Catacomb Rd; ⊙24hr) FREE Remote sermons beamed onto a big screen.

**Other Sights**
You can't miss the **Big Winch**, from which there are sweeping views over Coober Pedy and towards the Breakaways. An optimistic 'if' painted on the side of the big bucket sums up the town's spirit.

Leftover sets and props from the movies that have been filmed here are littered around town. Check out the amazing **spaceship** from *Pitch Black*, which has crash landed outside the Opal Cave shop on Hutchison St.

## Tours

**Arid Areas Tours**                  WILDERNESS
(☑08-8672 3008; www.aridareastours.com; 2/4/6hr tours per 2 people $100/200/420) Offers 4WD tours around town, extending to the Painted Desert and the Breakaways.

**Desert Cave Tours**                SIGHTSEEING
(☑08-8672 5688; www.desertcave.com.au; 4hr tour per person $90) A convenient highlight

tour taking in the town, the Dog Fence, Breakaways and Moon Plain. Also on offer are four-hour 'Down 'N' Dirty' opal-digging tours (per person $105).

**Mail Run Tour**                    GUIDED TOUR
(☑08-8672 5226, 1800 069 911; www.mailruntour.com) Coober Pedy–based full-day mail-run tours through the desert and along the Oodnadatta Track to Oodnadatta and William Creek return ($195).

**Opal Air**                       SCENIC FLIGHTS
(☑08 8670 7997; www.opalair.com.au; flights per person from $470) Half-day scenic flights ex-Coober Pedy winging over Lake Eyre, William Creek and the Painted Desert.

**Oasis Tours**                      SIGHTSEEING
(☑08-8672 5169; 3hr tour adult/child $45/22.50) A good budget tour taking in the major town sights plus a little fossicking. Two-hour sunset Breakaways tours ($50/25) also swing by the Dog Fence and the Moon Plain. Run by BIG4 Oasis Coober Pedy caravan park.

**Coober Pedy Tours**                SIGHTSEEING
(☑08-8672 5223; www.cooberpedytours.com; 4hr tour adult/child $70/35) A wandering tour that includes an underground home, fossicking, the Breakaways, an underground church, the Dog Fence and an active opal mine. Stargazing and Breakaways sunset tours also available. Run by Radeka Downunder accommodation.

## Sleeping

**Down to Erth B&B**                     B&B $$
(☑08-8672 5762; www.downtoerth.com.au; Monument Rd; d incl breakfast $160, extra person $25; ❄) A real dugout gem 4km from town, where you can have your own subterranean two-bedroom bunker. There's a shady plunge pool for cooling off after a day exploring the Earth, and a telescope for exploring the universe.

**Underground Motel**                  MOTEL $$
(☑08-8672 5324; www.theundergroundmotel.com.au; Catacomb Rd; s/d/f incl breakfast from $125/135/182; ❄) Choose between standard rooms and suites (with separate lounge and kitchen) at this serviceable spot with a broad Breakaways panorama. It's a fair walk from town, but friendly and affordable.

**Desert Cave Hotel**                  HOTEL $$$
(☑08-8672 5688; www.desertcave.com.au; Lot 1 Hutchison St; s & d $250, extra person $35; ❄@🛜❄) For a much-needed shot of desert

luxury – plus a pool, gym, in-house movies, formidable minibar and the excellent Umberto's restaurant. Staff are supercourteous and there are plenty of tours on offer. Aboveground rooms also available.

**Riba's** CAMPGROUND $
(☑08-8672 5614; www.camp-underground.com. au; William Creek Rd; underground sites $30, above-ground unpowered/powered sites $20/28, s & d $60; @) Around 5km from town, Riba's offers the unique option of underground camping! Extras include an underground TV lounge, cell-like underground budget rooms and a nightly opal-mine tour (adult $22, free for campers).

**Mud Hut Motel** MOTEL $$
(☑08-8672 3003; www.mudhutmotel.com.au; St Nicholas St; d/2-bedroom apt $130/220; ❋ ☎) The rustic-looking walls here are actually rammed earth, and despite the grubby name this is one of the cleanest places in town. The two-bedroom apartments have cooktops and fridges. Central location.

**Radeka Downunder** HOSTEL $
(☑08-8672 5223, 1800 633 891; www.radeka downunder.com.au; 1 Oliver St; dm $35, d & tw $85, motel units $130; ❋ @ ☎) The owners started excavating this place in 1960 – they haven't found much opal, but have ended up with a beaut backpackers! On multiple levels down 6.5m below the surface are Coober Pedy's best budget beds, plus good individual rooms and motel units. The shared kitchen is handy for self-caterers, and there's a bar, barbecue, snooker room and laundry.

**BIG4 Oasis Coober Pedy** CARAVAN PARK $
(☑08-8672 5169; www.oasiscooberpedy.com. au; Seventeen Mile Rd; unpowered/powered sites $30/33, r/vans from $58/68, cabins $106-126; ❋ @ ☎ ❋) There are a few places to camp in Coober Pedy, but this place is reasonably central (a little way down the main street across from the drive-in cinema) and has the most shade, plus a swimming pool. An affordable tour runs daily.

## ✖ Eating

**John's Pizza Bar** ITALIAN $
(☑08-8672 5561; www.johnspizzabarandrestau rant.com.au; Shop 24, 1 Hutchison St; meals $7-31; ☺9am-10pm) Serving up table-sized pizzas, hearty pastas and heat-beating gelato, you can't go past John's. Grills, salads, burgers, yiros, and fish and chips also available. Sit inside, order some takeaways, or pull up a seat with the bedraggled pot plants by the street.

**Tom & Mary's Greek Taverna** GREEK $$
(☑08-8672 5622; Shop 4/2 Hutchison St; meals $15-25; ☺6-9pm) This busy Greek diner does everything from a superb moussaka to yiros, seafood, Greek salads and pastas with Hellenic zing. Sit back with a cold retsina as the red sun sets on another dusty day in Coober Pedy.

**Umberto's** MEDITERRANEAN $$$
(☑08-8672 5688; www.desertcave.com.au; Lot 1 Hutchison St; mains $28-46; ☺6-9pm) The Desert Cave Hotel's rooftop restaurant maintains the quality with first-class dishes such as wallaby shanks with vegetables and char-grilled tomato stew, and its 'Essential Tastes of the Outback' platter: char-grilled kangaroo, camel, emu and beef with bush chutney and hand-cut fries.

## ❶ Information

**Coober Pedy Visitor Information Centre**
(☑08-8672 4617, 1800 637 076; www.opalcap italoftheworld.com.au; Hutchison St, Council Offices; ☺8.30am-5pm Mon-Fri, 10am-1pm Sat & Sun) Free 30-minute internet access, history displays and comprehensive tour and accommodation info.

**Coober Pedy Hospital** (☑08-8672 5009; www.countryhealthsa.sa.gov.au; Lot 89 Hospital Rd; ☺24hr) Accident and emergency.

**24-hour Water Dispenser** (Hutchison St; per 30L 20c) Fill your canteens opposite the BIG4 Oasis Coober Pedy caravan park.

## ❶ Getting There & Around

**Budget** (☑08-8672 5333; www.budget.com. au; Coober Pedy Airport) Cars, 4WDs and camping vehicles from around $80 per day.

**Cedrent** (☑08-8672 3003; www.cedrent.com. au; St Nicholas St, Mud Hut Motel) Stationwagons, utes and 4WDs from $125 per day. Based at the Mud Hut Motel.

# Coober Pedy to Marla

The Breakaways Reserve is a stark but colourful area of arid hills and scarps 33km away on a rough road north of Coober Pedy – turn off the highway 22km west of town. You can drive to a lookout in a conventional vehicle and check out the white-and-yellow mesa called the Castle, which featured in *Mad Max III* and *Priscilla, Queen of the Desert*. Entry permits (per person $2.20) are available at the Coober Pedy visitor information centre.

An interesting 70km loop on mainly unsealed road from Coober Pedy takes in the

Breakaways, the Dog Fence (built to keep dingos out of southeastern Australia) and the table-like Moon Plain on the Coober Pedy–Oodnadatta Rd. If it's been raining, you'll need a 4WD.

If you're heading for Oodnadatta, turning off the Stuart Hwy at Cadney Homestead (151km north of Coober Pedy) gives you a shorter run on dirt roads than the routes via Marla or Coober Pedy. En route you pass through the aptly named Painted Desert (bring your camera).

Cadney Homestead (☑08-8670 7994; cadney@bigpond.com; Stuart Hwy; unpowered/powered sites $15/25, d cabin/motel $60/115; ✳@≋) itself has caravan and tent sites, serviceable motel rooms and basic cabins (no linen, shared facilities), plus petrol, puncture repairs, takeaways, cold beer, ATM, swimming pool…

In mulga scrub about 82km from Cadney Homestead, Marla (population 245) replaced Oodnadatta as the official regional centre when the *Ghan* railway line was rerouted in 1980. Marla Travellers Rest (☑08-8670 7001; www.marla.com.au; Stuart Hwy; unpowered/powered sites/cabins $15/25/40, d $100-120; ✳@≋) has fuel, motel rooms, camp sites, pool, a cafe and a supermarket.

Frontier-style Mintabie (population 250) is an opal field settlement on Aboriginal land 35km west of Marla – there's a general store, restaurant and basic caravan park here.

From Marla the NT border is another 180km, with a fuel stop 20km beyond that in Kulgera.

## Oodnadatta Track

The legendary, lonesome Oodnadatta Track is an unsealed, 615km road between Marla on the Stuart Hwy and Marree in the northern Flinders Ranges. The track traces the route of the old Overland Telegraph Line and the defunct Great Northern Railway. Lake Eyre (the world's sixth-largest lake and usually dry) is just off the road. The landscape here is amazingly diverse: floodplains south of Marla, saltbush flats around William Creek, dunes and red gibber plains near Coward Springs. Bring a 4WD – the track is often passable in a regular car, but it gets bumpy, muddy, dusty and potholed.

### ❶ Information

Before you hit the Oodnadatta – a rough, rocky and sandy track that's subject to closure after rains – check track conditions with the Coober Pedy visitor information centre, the Royal Automobile Association in Adelaide, or online at www.dpti.sa.gov.au/OutbackRoads.

If you're finding the dust and dirt heavy going, there are escape routes to Coober Pedy on the Stuart Hwy from William Creek and Oodnadatta. Fuel, accommodation and meals are available at Marla, Oodnadatta, William Creek and Marree.

See the *Oodnadatta Track – String of Springs* booklet from the South Australian Tourism Commission, and the *Travel the Oodnadatta Track* brochure produced by the Pink Roadhouse for detailed track info.

## Oodnadatta to William Creek

Around 209km from Marla, Oodnadatta (population 280) is where the main road and the old railway line diverged. Here you'll find the Pink Roadhouse (☑08-8670 7822, 1800 802 074; www.pinkroadhouse.com.au; ☺8am-5.30pm), a good source of track info and meals (try the impressive 'Oodnaburger'). The roadhouse also has an attached caravan park (unpowered/powered sites from $22/30, budget cabins d/f from $65/125, self-contained cabins d from $110; ✳@≋), which has basic camping through to self-contained cabins. Note that one of the roadhouse managers passed away in 2012 – at the time of writing the future of the business was uncertain.

In another 70km you'll hit William Creek (population six), best enjoyed in the weather-beaten William Creek Hotel (☑08-8670 7880; www.williamcreekhotel.net.au; William Creek; unpowered/powered sites $25/35, cabins s/d $35/70, hotel $110/140; ✳), an iconic 1887 pub festooned with photos, business cards, old licence plates and money stapled to the walls. There's also a dusty campground and modest cabins and motel rooms. Also on offer are fuel, cold beer, basic provisions, all-day meals (mains $16 to $32) and spare tyres.

William Creek is also a base for Wrightsair (☑08-8670 7962; www.wrightsair.com.au; William Creek), which runs scenic flights over Lake Eyre (per adult/child $260/234).

## Coward Springs to Marree

Some 130km shy of Marree, Coward Springs Campground (☑08-8675 8336; www.cowardsprings.com.au; unpowered sites adult/child $10/5) is the first stop at the old Coward

Springs railway siding. You can soak yourself silly in a natural hot-spring tub (per person $2) made from old rail sleepers, or take a six-day camel trek (per person $1500) to Lake Eyre from here.

Next stop is the lookout over Lake Eyre South, which is 12m below sea level. For a Lake Eyre water-level report, see www.lake eyreyc.com. About 60km from Marree is the Mutonia Sculpture Park (⊘24hr) FREE, featuring a jaunty car-engine hitchhiker and several planes welded together with their tails buried in the ground to form 'Planehenge'.

Marree (population 100) was once a vital hub for Afghan camel teams and the Great Northern Railway, and is the end (or start) of both the Oodnadatta Track and Birdsville Track. The big stone 1883 Marree Hotel (☑08-8675 8344; www.marreehotel.com.au; Railway Tce; unpowered sites free, pub s/d $90/110, cabins $110/130; ※ ) has decent pub rooms, brand new en-suite cabins and free camp sites! Marree is also a good place to organise scenic flights (1½ hours around $270): try GSL Aviation (☑1300 475 247; wwwgslaviation. com.au) or Aus Air Services (☑08-8675 8212; www.ausairservices.com.au).

From the air you'll get a good look at Marree Man, a 4.2km-long outline of a Pitjantjatjara Aboriginal warrior etched into the desert near Lake Eyre. It was only discovered in 1988, and no-one seems to know who created it. It's eroding rapidly these days.

From Marree it's 80km to Lyndhurst, where the bitumen kicks back in, then 33km down to Copley at the northern end of the Flinders Ranges.

## Birdsville Track

This old droving trail runs 517km from Marree in SA to Birdsville, just across the border in Queensland, passing between the Simpson Desert to the east and Sturt Stony Desert to the west. It's one of Australia's classic outback routes. For road conditions see www.dpti.sa.gov.au/OutbackRoads (...a 4WD is the best way to go, regardless).

## Strzelecki Track

Meandering through the sand hills of the Strzelecki Regional Reserve (www.environ ment.sa.gov.au), the Strzelecki Track spans 460km from Lyndhurst, 80km south of Marree, to the tiny outpost of Innamincka. Discovery of oil and gas at Moomba (a town closed to travellers) saw the upgrading of the road from a camel track to a decent dirt road, though heavy transport travelling along it has created bone-rattling corrugations. The newer Moomba–Strzelecki Track is better kept, but longer and less interesting than the old track, which still follows Strzelecki Creek. Accommodation, provisions and fuel are available at Lyndhurst and Innamincka, but there's nothing in between.

## Innamincka

POP 130

On Cooper Creek at the northern end of the Strzelecki Track, Innamincka is near where Burke and Wills' ill-fated 1860 expedition expired. The famous Dig Tree marks the expedition's base camp, and although the word 'dig' is no longer visible you can still see the expedition's camp number. The Dig Tree is over the Queensland border, though memorials and markers – commemorating where Burke and Wills died, and where sole survivor King was found – are downstream in SA. There's also a memorial where AW Howitt's rescue party made its base on the creek.

Cooper Creek only has water in it after heavy rains across central Queensland, but it has deep, permanent waterholes and the semipermanent Coongie Lakes, which are part of the Innamincka Regional Reserve (www.environment.sa.gov.au). Prior to European settlement the area had a large Aboriginal population, so relics such as middens and grinding stones can be seen around the area.

The Innamincka Trading Post (☑08-8675 9900; www.innaminckatp.com.au; South Tce; ⊘9am-4pm Mar-Nov, 10am-3pm Dec-Feb) sells fuel, Desert Parks passes, camping permits and provisions, including fresh bread and rolls.

The old-fashioned Innamincka Hotel (☑08-8675 9901; www.theoutback.com.au/in naminckahotel; 2 South Tce; s/d $130/155; ※ ) has decent motel-style rooms and hefty counter meals (mains $20 to $30, serving noon to 2pm and 6pm to 8pm).

There are plenty of shady bush camping sites (per car $25) along Cooper Creek – Innamincka Trading Post sells permits, or you can use a Desert Parks Pass. You can use the hot shower ($2) and toilet outside the Trading Post.

# Darwin to Uluru

## Includes ➡

## Best Places to Eat

➡ Saffrron (p166)

➡ Char Restaurant (p165)

➡ Litchfield Cafe (p177)

➡ Fernanda's Café & Restaurant (p201)

➡ Hanuman (p212)

## Best Places to Stay

➡ Kings Creek Station (p220)

➡ Ormiston Gorge Camping Ground (p219)

➡ Rum Jungle Bungalows (p176)

➡ Lakeview Park (p184)

➡ Mt Bundy Station (p177)

## Why Go?

From the tropics to the deserts, the Northern Territory (NT) is a splendid place to be during Australia's winter months. Access is easy, with good roads and air connections; however, the vast distances ensure a good dose of adventure accompanies every visit.

NT's tropical Top End has an undeniable wild side. Crocodiles lurk in the rivers, and the air is alive with birds. Here you will find unparalleled opportunities to experience timeless indigenous culture and behold ethereal rock art. The cosmopolitan capital of Darwin is Australia's doorstep to Asia and celebrates its multicultural mix with delicious fusion cuisine and a relaxed tropical vibe.

The Red Centre is Australia's heartland boasting the iconic attractions of Uluru and Kata Tjuta, plus an enigmatic central desert culture that continues to produce extraordinary abstract art. And delighting travellers with its eccentric offerings, pioneering spirit and weathered mountain setting, is Alice Springs, the city at the centre of a continent.

## When to Go
### Darwin

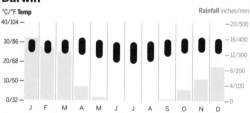

**Apr–Aug** Peak season with lower humidity up north and cooler temperatures in the Red Centre.

**Jun & Jul** Beanie Festival and Camel Cup in Alice, Beer Can Regatta and Fringe Festival in Darwin.

**Sep–Mar** Barramundi fishing heats up as the Wet turns the Top End into a watery wonderland.

# Darwin to Uluru Highlights

**1** Witness the wonderful **Uluru** (p227) and **Kata Tjuta** (p228) at sunset

**2** Paddle a canoe beneath soaring sandstone ramparts in **Nitmiluk (Katherine Gorge) National Park** (p193)

**3** Cruise with huge crocodiles at **Kakadu National Park** (p179)

**4** Sample a satay at **Mindil Beach Sunset Market** (p168)

**5** Hike past prehistoric ferns through bizarre rock formations to **Kings Canyon** (p220)

**6** Plunge into a crystal-clear rock pool at **Litchfield National Park** (p176)

Crocodiles inhabit rivers, billabongs and estuaries in tropical areas.

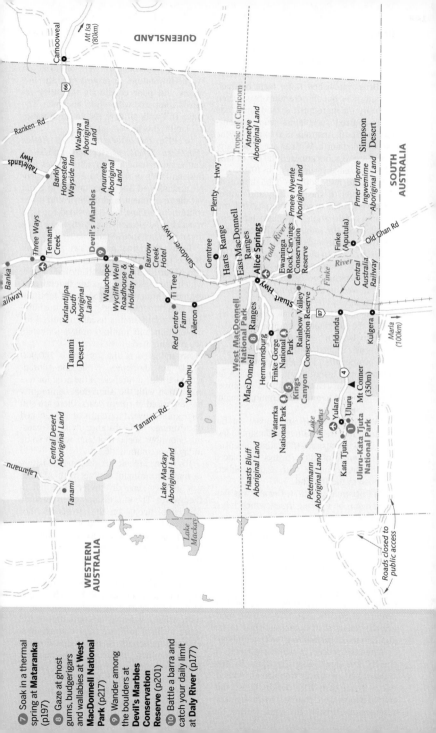

**QUEENSLAND**

Mt Isa (80km)

Camooweal

66

Ranken Rd

Tablelands Hwy

Barkly Homestead Wayside Inn

Wakaya Aboriginal Land

Anurrete Aboriginal Land

Tropic of Capricorn

Atnetye Aboriginal Land

Simpson Desert

**SOUTH AUSTRALIA**

Pmer Ulperre Ingwemirre Aboriginal Land

Plenty Hwy

Three Ways

Tennant Creek

Devil's Marbles

Barrow Creek Hotel

Plenty Hwy

Harts Range

East MacDonnell Ranges

**Alice Springs**

Pmere Nyente Aboriginal Land

Finke (Aputula)

Old Ghan Rd

Marla (100km)

Banka

Railway

Karlantipa South Aboriginal Land

Wauchope

Wycliffe Well Roadhouse & Holiday Park

Ti Tree

Red Centre Farm

Aileron

Gemtree

Sandover Hwy

Todd River

Ewaninga Rock Carvings Conservation Reserve

Finke River

Central Australia Railway

Stuart Hwy

Erldunda

Kulgera

87

Tanami Desert

Central Desert Aboriginal Land

Yuendumu

Tanami Rd

Tanami

Lake Mackay Aboriginal Land

West MacDonnell National Park

MacDonnell Ranges

Hermannsburg

Finke Gorge National Park

Rainbow Valley Conservation Reserve

Watarrka National Park

Kings Canyon

Lajamanu

Lake Mackay

Haasts Bluff Aboriginal Land

Kata Tjuta

Uluru-Kata Tjuta National Park

Yulara

Uluru

Lake Amadeus

Mt Conner (350m)

Petermann Aboriginal Land

**WESTERN AUSTRALIA**

Roads closed to public access

⑦ Soak in a thermal spring at **Mataranka** (p197)

⑧ Gaze at ghost gums, budgerigars and wallabies at **West MacDonnell National Park** (p217)

⑨ Wander among the boulders at **Devil's Marbles Conservation Reserve** (p201)

⑩ Battle a barra and catch your daily limit at **Daly River** (p177)

# History

Early attempts to settle the Top End were mainly due to British fears that the French or Dutch might get a foothold in Australia. The Brits established three forts between 1824 and 1838, but all were short-lived. Then the desire for more grazing land and trade routes spurred speculators from Queensland and South Australia (SA) to explore the vast untamed north. With an eye to development, SA governors annexed the NT in 1863 (it became self-governing only in 1978).

From the mid-1860s to 1895 hundreds of thousands of sheep, cattle and horses were overlanded to immense pastoral settlements. Dislocation and hardship were bedfellows of the industry, with Aborigines forced from their lands and pastoralists confronted by a swath of difficulties. Some Aborigines took employment as stockmen or domestic servants on cattle stations, while others moved on in an attempt to maintain their customary lifestyle.

In the early 1870s, during digging to establish the Overland Telegraph (from Adelaide to Darwin), gold was discovered. A minor rush ensued, with an influx of Chinese prospectors. Though the gold finds were relatively insignificant, the searches for it unearthed a wealth of natural resources that would lead to mining becoming a major economic presence in SA.

WWII had a significant impact on the Territory. Just weeks after the Japanese levelled Darwin causing 243 deaths, the entire Territory north of Alice Springs was placed under military control, with 32,000 soldiers stationed in the Top End.

On Christmas Eve 1974, Darwin was flattened again by Cyclone Tracy, which killed 71 people.

## Indigenous Darwin & Uluru

Australian Aborigines have occupied parts of the NT for around 60,000 years, although the central regions were not inhabited until about 24,000 years ago. The first significant contact with outsiders occurred in the 17th century when Macassan traders from modern-day Sulawesi in Indonesia came to the Top End to collect *trepang* (sea cucumber).

While the process of white settlement in the NT was slower than elsewhere in Australia, it had an equally troubled and violent effect. By the early 20th century, most Aboriginal people were confined to government reserves or Christian missions. During the 1960s Aboriginal people began to demand more rights.

In 1966 a group of Aboriginal stockmen, led by Vincent Lingiari, went on strike on Wave Hill Station, to protest over the low wages and poor conditions that they received compared with white stockmen. The Wave Hill walk-off gave rise to the Aboriginal land-rights movement.

In 1976 the *Aboriginal Land Rights (Northern Territory) Act* was passed in Canberra. It handed over all reserves and mission lands in the NT to Aboriginal people and allowed Aboriginal groups to claim vacant government land if they could prove continuous occupation – provided the land wasn't already leased, in a town or set aside for some other special purpose.

Today, Aboriginal people own about half of the land in the NT, including Kakadu and Uluru-Kata Tjuta National Parks, which are leased back to the federal government. Minerals on Aboriginal land are still government property, though the landowners' permission is usually required for exploration and mining, and landowners are remunerated.

Around 30% of the Territory's 200,000 people are Aborigines. While non-Aboriginal Australia's awareness of the need for reconciliation with the Aboriginal community has increased in recent years, there are still huge gulfs between the cultures. Entrenched disadvantage and substance abuse are causing enormous social problems within some indigenous communities.

It's often difficult for short-term visitors to make meaningful contact with Aborigines, as they generally prefer to be left to themselves. The impressions given by some Aboriginal people on the streets of Alice Springs, Katherine and Darwin, where social problems and substance abuse among a few people can present an unpleasant picture, are not indicative of Aboriginal communities as a whole.

Tours to Aboriginal lands (most operated by the communities themselves) and visits to arts centres are gradually becoming more widely available, as communities feel more inclined to share their culture. Benefits are numerous: financial gain through self-determined endeavour, and educating non-Aboriginal people about their culture and customs, which helps to alleviate the problems caused by the ignorance and misunderstandings of the past.

# National Parks

The NT is all about its national parks; it has some of the largest and most famous natural areas in Australia, including Kakadu, Uluru-Kata Tjuta and Nitmiluk. Parks Australia (p36) manages Kakadu and Uluru-Kata Tjuta, while the NT's Department of Natural Resources, Environment, the Arts and Sport (p150) manages the other parks and produces fact sheets, available online or from its various offices.

# 🏃 Activities

## Bushwalking

The Territory's national parks offer well-maintained tracks of different lengths and degrees of difficulty that introduce walkers to various environments and wildlife habitats. Carry plenty of water, take rubbish out with you and stick to the tracks.

Top bushwalks include the Barrk Sandstone Bushwalk in Kakadu National Park, the Jatbula Trail in Nitmiluk (Katherine Gorge) National Park, Ormiston Pound in the West MacDonnell Ranges, Trephina Gorge in the East MacDonnell Ranges, and the Valley of the Winds at Kata Tjuta.

## Fishing

No permit is required to fish the Territory's waterways, though there are limits on the minimum size and number of fish per person. Travel NT produces the excellent *The EsseNTial Fishing Travel Guide* booklet (free from information centres), and publishes some info online (www.travelnt.com). The **Amateur Fishermen's Association of the Northern Territory** (www.afant.com.au) also has online info.

The feisty barramundi lures most fisherfolk to the Top End, particularly to Borroloola, Daly River and Mary River. Increasingly, the recreational-fishing fraternity encourages catch and release to maintain sustainable fish levels. Loads of tours offer transport and gear and start at $250 per person.

## Swimming

The cool waterfalls, waterholes and rejuvenating thermal pools throughout the NT are perfect spots to soak. Litchfield National Park, in the Top End, and the West MacDonnell Ranges, in the Centre, are particularly rewarding.

Saltwater crocodiles inhabit both salt and fresh waters in the Top End, though there are quite a few safe, natural swimming holes. Before taking the plunge, be sure to obey the signs and seek local advice. If in doubt, don't risk it.

Box jellyfish seasonally infest the sea around Darwin; swimming at the city's beaches is safest from May to September.

## Wildlife Watching

The best places for guaranteed wildlife sightings, from bilbies to emus, are at the excellent Territory Wildlife Park outside Darwin and the Alice Springs Desert Park.

If you prefer to see wildlife in the wild, there are few guarantees; many of the region's critters are nocturnal. One exception is at Kakadu, where you'll certainly see crocodiles at Cahill's Crossing or Yellow Waters and numerous species of birds at its wealth of wetlands. In the arid Centre you'll see wallabies, reptiles and eagles. Good places to keep an eye out include the West MacDonnell Ranges and Watarrka (Kings Canyon) National Park.

# ☞ Tours

Even staunch independent travellers entrust some hard-earned time and money to a carefully selected tour. Tours can provide unmatched insights and access to the Territory, and they support local industry. Uluru Aboriginal Tours (p223) offer good tours of the famed rock.

**World Expeditions** ADVENTURE
(☑ 1300 720 000; www.worldexpeditions.com) Several Kakadu, Katherine Gorge and Arnhem Land trips ex-Darwin, and various options along the Larapinta Trail ex-Alice Springs.

**Kakadu Animal Tracks** INDIGENOUS
(www.animaltracks.com.au) Enviro-focused bush-tucker tour in Kakadu; profits support the local Buffalo Farm, which donates food to local communities.

**Conservation Volunteers Australia** VOLUNTEERING
(CVA; ☑ 1800 032 501; www.conservationvolun teers.com.au) Nature-based volunteer projects that double as tours: weeding, walking-track maintenance and wildlife surveys. Day trips are free; multiday projects cost from around $50 per night including meals, accommodation and travel.

**Magela Cultural & Heritage Tours** INDIGENOUS
(www.kakadutours.com.au) Aboriginal owned; runs tours into Arnhem Land and around Kakadu.

**Tiwi Tours**                    INDIGENOUS

Trips with local communities to the Tiwi Islands.

**Willis's Walkabouts**              BUSHWALKING

(✏08-8985 2134; www.bushwalkingholidays.com. au) Small-group multiday guided hikes, carrying your own gear, to Kakadu, Litchfield, Watarrka and the West MacDonnells.

## Seasonal Work

The majority of working-holiday opportunities in the NT for backpackers are in fruit picking, pastoral station work, labouring and hospitality.

Most work is picking mangoes and melons on plantations between Darwin and Katherine. Mango harvesting employs up to 2000 workers each season (late September to November). Station-work wannabes are generally required to have some skills (ie a trade or some experience), as with labouring and hospitality. Employers usually ask workers to commit for at least a month (sometimes three months).

## ❶ Information

RESOURCES

**Department of Natural Resources, Environment, the Arts and Sport** (✏08-8999 5511; www.nretas.nt.gov.au/national-parks-and -reserves/) Details on NT parks and reserves, including fact sheets.

**Exploroz** (www.exploroz.com) Handy user-generated site for fuel locations and pricing, weather forecasts, road conditions and more.

**Road Report** (www.ntlis.nt.gov.au/roadreport) Road-conditions report.

**Tourism Top End** (www.tourismtopend.com. au) Darwin-based tourism body.

**Travel NT** (www.travelnt.com) Official tourism site.

ABORIGINAL LAND PERMITS

Permits may be required to enter Aboriginal land, unless you are using recognised public roads that cross Aboriginal territory. Permits can take four to six weeks to be processed, although at the Injalak Arts Centre at Gunbalanya (Oenpelli) they are generally issued on the spot in Jabiru.

**Central Land Council** (www.clc.org.au) Alice Springs (p279); Tennant Creek (✏08-8962 2343; 63 Patterson St, Tennant Creek) Deals with all land south of a line drawn between Kununurra (Western Australia) and Mt Isa (Queensland).

**Northern Land Council** (www.nlc.org.au) Darwin (✏08-8920 5100; www.nlc.org.au; 45 Mitchell St); Jabiru (✏08-8979 2410; Flinders St, Jabiru; ⊗8am-4.30pm Mon-Fri); Katherine (✏08-8971 9802; 5 Katherine Tce) Responsible for land north of a line drawn between Kununurra (Western Australia) and Mt Isa (Queensland).

**Tiwi Land Council** (✏08-8919 4305; www.tiwi landcouncil.com) Permits for the Tiwi Islands.

## ❶ Getting There & Around

AIR

International and domestic flights arrive at and depart from **Darwin International Airport** (www.darwinairport.com.au; Henry Wrigley Dr, Marrara). There are also flights between Darwin, Alice Springs and Uluru. Airlines operating here include:

**Airnorth** (www.airnorth.com.au) To/from East Timor, and to Arnhem Land, Broome, Perth, Kununurra and the Gold Coast.

**Jetstar** (www.jetstar.com.au) Services most major Australian cities and several South-East Asian cities.

**Qantas** (www.qantas.com.au) To/from Asia and Europe, and servicing all major Australian cities.

**Virgin Australia** (www.virginaustralia.com) Direct flights between Darwin and Brisbane, Melbourne, Perth and Sydney.

BUS

**Greyhound Australia** (www.greyhound.com.au) regularly services the main road routes throughout the Territory, including side trips to Kakadu and Uluru.

An alternative is tour-bus companies such as AAT Kings, and backpacker buses that cover vast distances while savouring the sights along the way.

CAR

Having your own vehicle in the NT means you can travel at your own pace and branch off the main roads to access less-visited places. To truly explore, you'll need a well-prepared 4WD vehicle and some outback nous. The **Automobile Association of the Northern Territory** (AANT; www.aant.com.au; 79-81 Smith St, Darwin; ⊗9am-5pm Mon-Fri) can advise on preparation and additional resources; members of automobile associations in other states have reciprocal rights.

Many roads are open to conventional cars and campervans, which can be hired in Darwin and Alice Springs and can work out to be quite economical when split by a group.

Some driving conditions are particular to the NT. While traffic may be light and roads dead straight, distances between places are long. Watch out for the four great NT road hazards: speed (maximum speed on the open highway is now 130km/h), driver fatigue, road trains and animals (driving at night is particularly dangerous). Note that some roads are regularly closed during the Wet due to flooding.

Quarantine restrictions require travellers to surrender all fruit, vegetables, nuts and honey at the NT–Western Australia (WA) border.

### TRAIN

The famous interstate *Ghan* train is run by **Great Southern Rail** (www.gsr.com.au), grinding between Darwin and Adelaide via Katherine and Alice Springs. The *Ghan* is met in Port Augusta (SA) by the *Indian Pacific*, which travels between Sydney and Perth; and in Adelaide by the *Overland*, which travels to/from Melbourne.

The *Ghan* has three levels of sleeper berths plus a chair class.

# DARWIN

POP 127,500

Australia's only tropical capital, Darwin gazes out confidently across the Timor Sea. It's closer to Bali than Bondi, and many from the southern states still see it as some frontier outpost or jumping-off point for Kakadu National Park.

But Darwin is a surprisingly affluent, cosmopolitan, youthful and multicultural city, thanks in part to an economic boom fuelled by the mining industry and tourism. It's a city on the move but there's a small-town feel and a laconic, relaxed vibe that fits easily with the tropical climate. Here non-Aboriginal meets Aboriginal (Larrakia), urban meets remote, and industry meets idleness.

Darwin has plenty to offer the traveller. Boats bob around the harbour, chairs and tables spill out of streetside restaurants and bars, museums celebrate the city's past, and galleries showcase the region's rich indigenous art. Darwin's cosmopolitan mix – more than 50 nationalities are seamlessly represented here – is typified by the wonderful markets held throughout the dry season.

Nature is well and truly part of Darwin's backyard – the famous national parks of Kakadu and Litchfield are only a few hours' drive away and the unique Tiwi Islands are a boat-ride away. For locals the perfect weekend is going fishing for barra in a tinny with an esky full of cold beer.

## History

The Larrakia Aboriginal people lived for thousands of years in Darwin, hunting, fishing and foraging. In 1869 a permanent white settlement was established and the grid for a new town was laid out. Originally called Palmerston, and renamed Darwin in 1911, the new town developed rapidly, transforming the physical and social landscape.

The discovery of gold at nearby Pine Creek brought an influx of Chinese, who soon settled into other industries. Asians and Islanders came to work in the pearling industry and on the railway line and wharf. More recently, neighbouring East Timorese and Papuans have sought asylum in Darwin.

During WWII, Darwin was the frontline for the Allied action against the Japanese in the Pacific. It was the only Australian city ever bombed, and official reports of the time downplayed the damage – to buoy Australians' morale. Though the city wasn't destroyed by the 64 attacks, the impact of full-scale military occupation on Darwin was enormous.

More physically damaging was Cyclone Tracy, which hit Darwin at around midnight on Christmas Eve 1974. By Christmas morning, Darwin effectively ceased to exist as a city, with only 400 of its 11,200 homes left standing and 71 people killed. The town was rebuilt to a new, stringent building code and in the past decade has steadily expanded outwards and upwards, with the latest project the multimillion-dollar waterfront development at Darwin Harbour.

## ☉ Sights

### ◉ Central Darwin

**Crocosaurus Cove**        ZOO
(Map p156; www.croccove.com.au; 58 Mitchell St; adult/child $30/18; ⊙8am-6pm, last admission 5pm) If the tourists won't go out to see the crocs, then bring the crocs to the tourists. Right in the middle of Mitchell St, Crocosaurus Cove is as close as you'll ever want to get to these amazing creatures. Six of the largest crocs in captivity can be seen in state-of-the-art aquariums and pools. You can be lowered right into a pool with them in the transparent **Cage of Death** (1/2 people $150/220). If that's too scary, there's another pool where you can swim with a clear tank wall separating you from some mildly less menacing baby crocs. Other aquariums feature barramundi, turtles and stingrays, plus there's an enormous reptile house (allegedly

# Greater Darwin

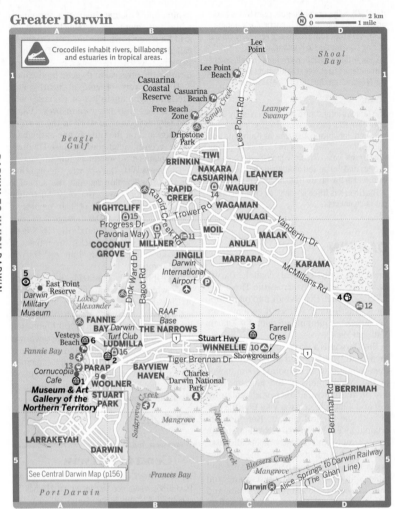

the greatest variety of reptiles on display in the country).

**Aquascene**                                          AQUARIUM
(Map p156; www.aquascene.com.au; 28 Doctors Gully Rd; adult/child $15/10; ⏰ high tide, check website) At Doctors Gully, an easy walk from the north end of the Esplanade, Aquascene runs a remarkable fish-feeding frenzy at high tide. Visitors, young and old can hand-feed hordes of mullet, catfish, batfish and huge milkfish. Check the website and tourism publications for feeding times.

**The Esplanade**                                      STREET
Darwin's Esplanade is a long, straight street with flashy hotels on one side and the lush waterside **Bicentennial Park** (Map p156; www.darwin.nt.gov.au; ⏰24hr) on the other. The park runs the length of the Esplanade from Doctors Gully to Lameroo Beach, a sheltered cove popular in the '20s when it housed the saltwater baths, and traditionally a Larrakia camp area. Shaded by tropical trees, the park is an excellent place to wander.

At the Herbert St end, there's a **ceno-taph** commemorating Australians' service to the country's war efforts. Also honoured

# Greater Darwin

are **200 Remarkable Territorians**: hand-painted tiles in panels dispersed intermittently along the Esplanade commemorate some of the Territory's 'quiet achievers', including pioneers, publicans and pastoralists.

**Lyons Cottage**                    HISTORIC BUILDING
(Map p156; www.aboriginalbushtraders.com; cnr Esplanade & Knuckey St; ⊙9am-3pm) FREE Just across the road from Bicentennial Park, Lyons Cottage was built in 1925. It was Darwin's first stone residence, formerly housing executives from the British Australian Telegraph Company (which laid a submarine cable between Australia and Java). Now it's a museum and retail outlet run by Aboriginal Bush Traders displaying Darwin in photos from the early days.

**Parliament House**                    NOTABLE BUILDING
(Map p156; ☎08-8946 1434; www.nt.gov.au/lant; ⊙8am-6pm) FREE At the southern end of Mitchell St is the elegant, box-like Parliament House, which opened in 1994. Reminiscent of Southeast Asian colonial architecture, it's designed to withstand Darwin's monsoonal climate. Attend a free tour exploring the cavernous interior on Saturday at 9am and 11am. No booking required. The building also houses the **Northern Territory Library**.

**George Brown Botanic Gardens**    GARDEN
(Map p156; www.nretas.nt.gov.au/national-parks-and-reserves/botanic; Geranium St, Stuart Park; ⊙7am-7pm, information centre 8am-4pm Mon-Fri, 8.30am-4pm Sat & Sun) FREE Named after the gardens' curator from 1971 to 1990, these 42-hectare gardens showcase plants from the Top End and around the world – monsoon vine forest, the mangroves and coastal plants habitat, boabs and a magnificent collection of native and exotic palms and cycads.

Many of the plants here were traditionally used by the local Aboriginal people, and self-guiding **Aboriginal plant-use trails** have been set up – pick up a brochure at the gardens' information centre near the Geranium St entry. You'll also find **birdwatching** brochures and garden maps here too.

The gardens are an easy 2km bicycle ride out from the centre of town along Gilruth Ave and Gardens Rd, or there's another entrance off Geranium St, which runs off the Stuart Hwy in Stuart Park. Alternatively, bus 7 from the city stops near the Stuart Hwy/Geranium St corner.

**Myilly Point Heritage Precinct**   HISTORIC SITE
(Map p156) At the far northern end of Smith St is this small but important precinct of four houses built between 1930–39 (which means they survived both the WWII bombings and Cyclone Tracy!). They're now managed by the National Trust. One of them, **Burnett House** (Map p156; www.nationaltrustnt. org.au; admission by donation; ⊙10am-1pm Mon-Sat), operates as a museum. There's a tantalising colonial high tea ($10) in the gardens on Sunday afternoon from 3.30pm to 6pm between April and October.

**Chinese Museum & Chung Wah Temple** MUSEUM, TEMPLE

(www.chungwahnt.asn.au; 25 Woods St; admission by donation; museum 10am-2pm, temple 8am-4pm) This excellent little museum explores Chinese settlement in the Top End. The adjacent temple has a hushed interior, punctuated by scarlet lanterns and smouldering incense sticks. The sacred tree in the grounds is rumoured to be a direct descendant from the Bodhi tree under which Buddha sat when he attained enlightenment.

## ◎ Darwin Waterfront Precinct

The bold redevelopment of the old Darwin Waterfront Precinct (www.waterfront.nt.gov.au) has transformed the city. The multimillion-dollar redevelopment features a cruise-ship terminal, luxury hotels, boutique restaurants and shopping, the Sky Bridge, an elevated walkway and elevator at the south end of Smith St, and a Wave Lagoon.

The old Stokes Hill Wharf (p164) is well worth an afternoon promenade. At the end of the wharf an old warehouse houses a food centre that's ideal for an alfresco lunch, cool afternoon beer or a seafood dinner as the sun sets over the harbour. Several harbour cruises and a jet boat also leave from the wharf.

**Wave & Recreation Lagoons** WATER PARK

(www.waterfront.nt.gov.au; Wave Lagoon adult/child half-day \$5/3.50, full day \$8/5; Wave Lagoon 10am-6pm) The hugely popular Wave Lagoon is a hit with locals and travellers alike. There are 10 different wave patterns produced (20 minutes on with a 10-minute rest in between) and there are lifeguards, a kiosk, and a strip of lawn to bask on. Adjacent is the Recreation Lagoon with a sandy beach, lifeguards and stinger-filtered seawater (although the nets and filters are not guaranteed to be 100% effective).

**WWII Oil-Storage Tunnels** TUNNELS

(Map p156; www.darwintours.com.au/tours/ww2tunnels.html; self-guided tour per person \$6; 9am-4pm May-Sep, 9am-1pm Oct-Apr) You can escape from the heat of the day and relive your Hitchcockian fantasies by walking through the WWII oil-storage tunnels. They were built in 1942 to store the navy's oil supplies (but never used), and they exhibit wartime photos.

**Indo-Pacific Marine Exhibition** AQUARIUM

(Map p156; www.indopacificmarine.com.au; 29 Stokes Hill Rd; adult/child \$22/10; 10am-4pm) This excellent marine aquarium at the Waterfront Precinct gives you a close encounter with the denizens at the bottom of Darwin Harbour. Each small tank is a complete ecosystem, with only the occasional extra fish introduced as food for some of the predators, such as stonefish or the bizarre angler fish.

Also recommended here is the Coral Reef by Night (adult/child \$110/55; 7pm Wed, Fri & Sun), which consists of a tour of the aquarium, seafood dinner (on biodegradable plates, no less!) and an impressive show of fluorescing animals.

## ◎ Fannie Bay

★ **Museum & Art Gallery of the Northern Territory** MUSEUM

(MAGNT; Map p152; www.magnt.nt.gov.au; Conacher St, Fannie Bay; 9am-5pm Mon-Fri, 10am-5pm Sat & Sun) FREE This superb museum and gallery boasts beautifully presented galleries

---

### DARWIN IN...

#### Two Days

Start with breakfast at **Four Birds** (p164)or **Roma Bar** (p164), while flipping through the *Northern Territory News*. Take a stroll downtown and through **Bicentennial Park** (p152). Don't miss the high-tide action at **Aquascene** (p152) and as the afternoon warms up, head down to the **waterfront precinct** (p154), stopping for a dip in the **Wave Lagoon** (p154). As the sun sets, make your way to **Mindil Beach Sunset Market** (p168), packed with food outlets, buskers and souvenirs.

On day two, hire a bike and head out to the **Museum & Art Gallery of the Northern Territory** (p154). Continue your coastal jaunt to the **East Point Reserve** (p155) and the **Darwin Military Museum** (p155). At night, hit the bars along Mitchell St, or find a quite waterfront restaurant at Cullen Bay and catch a movie under the stars at the **Deckchair Cinema** (p167).

of Top End–centric exhibits. The Aboriginal art collection is a highlight, with carvings from the Tiwi Islands, bark paintings from Arnhem Land and dot paintings from the desert.

An entire room is devoted to Cyclone Tracy, in a display that graphically illustrates life before and after the disaster. You can stand in a darkened room and listen to the whirring sound of Tracy at full throttle – a sound you won't forget in a hurry.

The cavernous Maritime Gallery houses an assortment of weird and wonderful crafts from the nearby islands and Indonesia, as well as a pearling lugger and a Vietnamese refugee boat.

Pride of place among the stuffed animals undoubtedly goes to Sweetheart: a 5m-long, 780kg saltwater crocodile. It became a Top End personality after attacking several fishing dinghies on the Finniss River.

The museum has a good bookshop, and the Cornucopia Cafe is a great lunch spot with views over the sea.

### Fannie Bay Gaol Museum    MUSEUM
(Map p152; www.ntretas.nt.gov.au/knowledge-and-history/heritage/visit/gaol; cnr East Point Rd & Ross Smith Ave; admission by donation; ☺10am-3pm) This interesting (if a little grim) museum represents almost 100 years of solitude. Serving as Darwin's main jail from 1883 to 1979, the solid cells contain information panels that provide a window into the region's unique social history. Lepers, refugees and juveniles were among the groups confined here, and you can still see the old cells and the gallows constructed for two hangings in 1952.

### East Point Reserve    GARDEN
(Map p152; ☺mangrove boardwalk 8am-6pm) North of Fannie Bay, this spit of land is particularly attractive in the late afternoon when wallabies emerge to feed and you can watch the sun set over the bay.

Lake Alexander, a small, recreational saltwater lake, was created so people could enjoy a swim year-round without having to worry about box jellyfish. There's a good children's playground here and picnic areas with BBQs. A 1.5km mangrove boardwalk leads off from the car park.

On the point's northern side is a series of WWII gun emplacements and the fascinating Darwin Military Museum.

### Darwin Military Museum    MUSEUM
(www.darwinmilitarymuseum.com.au; 5434 Alec Fong Lim Dr; adult/child $14/5.50; ☺9.30am-5pm)

## PARAP VILLAGE MARKET

Parap Village is a foodies heaven with several good restaurants, bars and cafes as well as the highly recommended deli, Parap Fine Foods (p166). However, it's the Saturday morning markets that attract locals like bees to honey. It's got a relaxed vibe as breakfast merges into brunch and then lunch. Between visits to the takeaway food stalls, mostly spicy southeast Asian snacks, shoppers stock up on interesting and amazing tropical fruit and vegetables – all you need to make your own laksa or rendang. The produce is local so you know it'll be fresh.

The Defence of Darwin Experience at the Darwin Military Museum is a sobering reminder of Australia's most significant wartime attack. It features personal accounts and an interactive light-and-sound show. Other museum exhibits include an assortment of military hardware. It's on the Tour Tub (p159) route.

### 24HR Art    ART GALLERY
(Map p152; www.24hrart.org.au; Vimy Lane, Parap Shopping Village; ☺10am-4pm Wed-Fri, 10am-2pm Sat) Changing and challenging exhibitions by the Northern Territory Centre for Contemporary Art.

## ⊙ Outer East

### Crocodylus Park    ZOO
(Map p152; www.crocodyluspark.com.au; 815 McMillans Rd, Berrimah; adult/child $35/17.50; ☺9am-5pm, tours 10am, noon, 2pm & 3.30pm) Crocodylus Park showcases hundreds of crocs and a mini-zoo comprising lions, tigers and other big cats, spider monkeys, marmosets, cassowaries and large birds. Allow about two hours to look around the whole park, and you should time your visit with a tour, which includes a feeding demonstration. Croc meat BBQ packs for sale!

The park is about 15km from the city centre. Take bus 5 from Darwin.

### Australian Aviation Heritage Centre    MUSEUM
(Map p152; www.darwinsairwar.com.au; 557 Stuart Hwy, Winnellie; adult/child $12/7; ☺9am-5pm) Darwin's aviation museum, about 10km from

DARWIN TO ULURU DARWIN

# Central Darwin

Crocodiles inhabit rivers, billabongs and estuaries in tropical areas.

71

Mindil Beach Reserve

Mindil Beach

*Fannie Bay*

Marina Blvd

50
36
24
7

Mandorah Ferry
20 Lock
17

Garden Park Golf Links

*Cullen Bay Marina*

*Cullen Bay*

Cullen Bay Cres

Stevens Tce

Mitchell St

Barossa St

Manoora St

Zealandia Cres

**LARRAKEYAH**

33

Larrakeyah Military Area

Allen Ave

Packard St

19

2

*Doctors Gully*

0 ——— 100 m
0 ——— 0.05 miles

Peel St
Smith St
Searcy St
Edmunds St
72
47
Litchfield St
21
52

Mitchell St

*Crocosaurus Cove*
1

65

46
25
Knuckey St
Cavenagh St

Chinese Museum & Chung Wah Temple

56
34
10
Shadforth La
53

Transit Centre
11
57
15
59
66
45
Smith St Mall
73
Austin La
49
Bennett St

13
23

38

West La
41

*Esplanade*
69
70
58
Darwinbus

6
42
Darwin Bus Terminus
Harry Chan Ave

37
55
Tourism Top End
61
Civic Square

Bicentennial Park

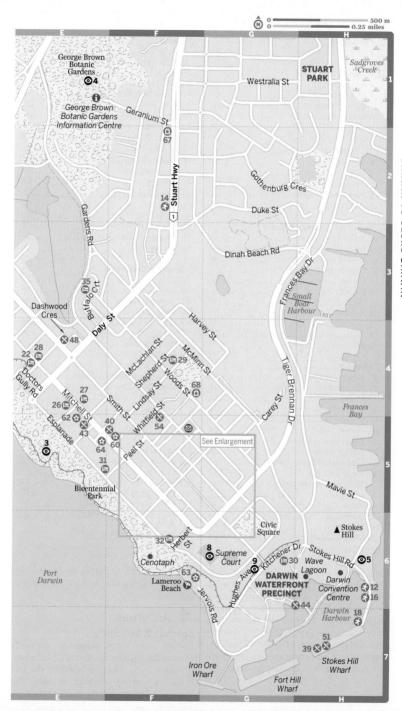

# Central Darwin

the centre, is one for military aircraft nuts. The centrepiece is a mammoth B52 bomber, one of only two of its kind displayed outside the USA, which has somehow been squeezed inside. It dwarfs the other aircraft, which include a Japanese Zero fighter shot down in 1942 and the remains of a RAAF Mirage jet that crashed in a nearby swamp. Free **guided tours** commence at 10am and 2pm.

Buses 5 and 8 run along the Stuart Hwy, and sometimes on the route of the Tour Tub (p159).

## 🏃 Activities

### Beaches & Swimming

Darwin is no beach paradise – naturally enough the harbour has no surf – but along the convoluted coastline north of the city centre is a string of sandy beaches. The most popular are **Mindil** and **Vestey's** on

Fannie Bay. Further north, a stretch of the 7km **Casuarina Beach** is an official nude beach. Darwin's swimming beaches tend to be far enough away from mangrove creeks to make the threat of meeting a crocodile very remote. A bigger problem is the deadly box jellyfish, which makes swimming decidedly unhealthy between October and March (and often before October and until May). You can swim year-round without fear of stingers in the western part of **Lake Alexander**, an easy cycle from the centre at East Point (p155), and at the Wave Lagoon (p154), the centre piece of the Darwin Wharf Precinct. Also at the wharf precinct is the Recreation Lagoon (p154), where filtered seawater and nets provides a natural seawater swim.

### Sailing

**Darwin Sailing Club**                 SAILING
(Map p152; ☑08-8981 1700; www.dwnsail.com.au) A good place to meet local yachties, and to watch the sunset over a beer. Although you can't charter boats here, there is a noticeboard advertising crewing needs and detailing the seasonal race program.

### Cycling

Darwin is great for cycling (in winter!). Traffic is light and a series of **bike tracks** covers most of the city, with the main one running from the northern end of Cavenagh St to Fannie Bay, Coconut Grove, Nightcliff and Casuarina. At Fannie Bay, a side track heads out to the East Point Reserve.

Consider heading for **Charles Darwin National Park** (Map p152; www.nt.gov.au/nreta/parks/find/charlesdarwin.html), 5km southeast of the city, with a few kilometres of path around the park's wetlands, woodlands and WWII bunkers.

Some hostels hire out bicycles for $15 to $25 per day for a mountain bike, or try:

**Darwin Scooter Hire**                 CYCLING
(Map p156; www.esummer.com.au; 9 Daly St; ☺8am-5pm Mon-Fri, 9am-3pm Sat) Mountain bikes for $20 a day ($100 deposit required).

**Darwin Holiday Shop**                 CYCLING
(Map p156; ☑08-8981 0277; www.darwinholidayshop.com.au; 88 The Esplanade, Shop 2, Mantra on the Esplanade; ☺9am-5pm Mon-Fri, 9am-1pm Sat) Mountain bikes per half-/full day $20/25.

### Rock Climbing

**The Rock**                 ROCK CLIMBING
(Map p156; www.rockclimbing.com.au; climbing incl equipment $25; ☺noon-9pm Tue, Thu & Sat,

noon-6pm Wed, Fri & Sun) Inside an old WWII oil-storage tank at Doctors Gully, The Rock is the place to chalk-up your fingers, defy gravity and dangle yourself off a climbing wall.

### Jetboating

**Oz Jet**                 JETBOATING
(Map p156; ☑1300 135 595; www.ozjetboating.com/darwin; 30min rides adult/child $55/30) If a harbour cruise is too tame, jump on Oz Jet for a white-knuckle ride around the harbour that'll test how long it's been since you had lunch. Departs from Stokes Hill Wharf. Bookings essential; closed during the Wet.

### Skydiving

**Top End Tandems**                 SKYDIVING
(☑0417 190 140; www.topendtandems.com.au; tandem jumps from $380) Has tandem skydives starting at Darwin Airport and landing at Lee Point Reserve.

## ☞ Tours

There are dozens of tours in and around Darwin, and lots of combinations covering Kakadu, Arnhem Land, Litchfield and further afield. Tourism Top End (p170) is the best place to start looking and asking questions. Remember that many tours run less frequently (or not at all) in the Wet.

### City Tours

**Darwin Walking & Bicycle Tours**                 WALKING, CYCLING
(☑08-8981 0227; www.darwinwalkingtours.com.au) ✎ Two-hour guided history walks around the city for $25 (children free), plus three-hour bike tours (adult/child $55/40) that take you out to Fannie Bay and East Point.

**Tour Tub**                 SIGHTSEEING
(☑08-8985 6322; www.tourtub.com.au; adult/child $45/20; ☺9am-4pm Apr-Sep) This open-sided hop-on, hop-off minibus tours all around Darwin's big-ticket sights throughout the day. Call for bookings, pick-up times and locations. Pay the driver onboard – cash only.

**Sea Darwin**                 ECOTOUR
(☑1300 065 022; www.seadarwin.com; tours adult/child from $35/20) ✎ One-, two-, or three-hour eco tours around the city and Darwin Harbour, checking out mangroves, a crocodile trap, a shipwreck and (if you're lucky) dugongs and dolphins.

## ABORIGINAL FESTIVALS & EVENTS

Most of the festivals in the Northern Territory's cities and towns have strong Aboriginal components, plus there's a bunch of annual Aboriginal celebrations to attend. Although these festivals are usually held on restricted Aboriginal land, permit requirements are generally waived for them; this applies to most of the festivals listed here. Bear in mind that alcohol is banned in many communities.

**Tiwi Grand Final** Held at the end of March on Bathurst Island, this sporting spectacular displays the Tiwis' sparkling skills and passion for Aussie Rules football. Thousands come from Darwin for the day, which coincides with the **Tiwi Art Sale** (www.tiwiart.com).

**Barunga Festival** (www.jawoyn.org/tourism/barunga-festival) For three days over a long weekend in mid-June, Barunga, 80km east of Katherine, displays traditional arts and crafts, dancing, music and sporting competitions. Bring your own camping equipment; alternatively, visit for the day from Katherine.

**Merrepen Arts & Sports Festival** (www.merrepenfestival.com.au) The Nauiyu community, on the banks of the Daly River, is the venue for this sporty arts festival on the first weekend in June. The Merrepen Arts Centre showcases its string bags, paintings and prints, while locals sweat it out in foot races and basketball and softball matches.

**Walking With Spirits** (www.djilpinarts.org.au/visit-us/walking-with-spirits) A two-day Indigenous cultural festival in July at Beswick Falls, 130km from Katherine. In a magical setting, traditional dance and music is combined with theatre, films and a light show. Camping is allowed at the site (only during the festival). A 4WD is recommended for the last 20km to the falls, or a shuttle bus runs from Beswick.

**Stone Country Festival** (www.injalak.com) This open day and cultural festival is held in August in Gunbalanya (Oenpelli) just outside Kakadu National Park. It has traditional music, dancing, and arts and crafts demonstrations, and is the only day you can visit Gunbalanya without a permit. Camping allowed; no alcohol.

**Garma Festival** (www.yyf.com.au) Also in August, a four-day festival in northeastern Arnhem Land. It's one of the most significant regional festivals, a celebration of Yolngu culture that includes ceremonial performances, bushcraft lessons, a *yidaki* (didgeridoo) master class and an academic forum. Serious planning is required to attend, so start early.

**Darwin Day Tours**  SIGHTSEEING
(Map p156; ☑1300 721 365; www.darwindaytours.com.au; afternoon city tour adult/child $69/55) Runs an afternoon city tour that takes in all the major attractions, including Stokes Hill Wharf, the Museum & Art Gallery and East Point Reserve, and can be linked with a sunset harbour cruise ($144/110).

### Harbour Cruises

Between April and October there are plenty of boats based at the Cullen Bay Marina and Stokes Hill Wharf to take you on a cruise of the harbour.

**Anniki Pearl Lugger Cruises**  SAILING
(☑0428 414 000; www.australianharbourcruises.com.au; tours adult/child $70/50) Three-hour sunset cruises on this historical pearling lugger depart at 4.45pm from Cullen Bay Marina and include sparkling wine and nibbles. You might recognise the ship from the film *Australia*.

**Sunset Sail**  SAILING
(Map p156; ☑0408 795 567; www.sailnt.com.au; tours adult/child $70/45) This three-hour afternoon cruise aboard the catamaran *Daymirri 2* departs from Stokes Hill Wharf. Refreshments are included but BYO alcohol.

**Darwin Harbour Cruises**  CRUISES
(Map p156; ☑08-8942 3131; www.darwinharbourcruises.com.au) Variety of cruises from Stokes Hill Wharf. The 20m schooner *Tumlaren* does a 'Tastes of the Territory' sunset cruise (adult/child $70/45), while the 30m schooner *Alfred Noble* has a full-dinner cruise departing at 5.30pm ($110/65).

### Spirit of Darwin
CRUISES

(Map p156; ☑ 0417 381 977; www.spiritofdarwin. com.au; tours adult/child $65/20) This fully licensed air-con motor-catamaran does a two-hour sightseeing cruise at 2pm and a sunset cruise at 5.30pm daily from Stokes Hill Wharf.

## Territory Trips

### Davidson's Arnhemland Safaris
INDIGENOUS

(☑ 08-8927 5240; www.arnhemland-safaris.com) ✔ Experienced operator based at Mt Borradaile, north of Oenpelli. Meals, guided tours, fishing and accommodation in the comfortable safari camp are included in the daily price of around $750; transfers from Darwin can be arranged.

### Tiwi Tours
INDIGENOUS

(☑ 1300 721 365; www.aussieadventures.com.au) Small-group cultural tours out to the nearby Tiwi Islands with indigenous guides (adult/child including flights $498/449). Kakadu and Litchfield tours also available through the company's other brands: Darwin Day Tours (p160) and Aussie Adventure.

### Adventure Tours
BACKPACKER

(Map p156; ☑ 08-8132 8230, 1800 068 886; www. adventuretours.com.au) Range of 4WD tours to suit the spirited backpacker crowd. Two-/three-day Kakadu tours $468/663, plus day tours to Litchfield ($119) and Katherine Gorge ($157). Longer tours available.

### Northern Territory
### Indigenous Tours
INDIGENOUS

(☑ 1300 921 188; www.ntitours.com.au) Upmarket indigenous tours to Litchfield National Park stopping off at Territory Wildlife Park (adult/child $249/124).

### Sacred Earth Safaris
WILDERNESS

(☑ 08-8981 8420; www.sacredearthsafaris.com.au) Multiday, small-group 4WD camping tours around Kakadu, Katherine and the Kimberley. Two-day Kakadu tour starts at $850; the five-day Top End tour is $2250.

### Kakadu Dreams
BACKPACKER

(Map p156; ☑ 1800 813 266; www.kakadudreams. com.au; 50 Mitchell St) Backpacker day tours to Litchfield ($119), and boisterous two-/three-day trips to Kakadu ($387/400).

### Wallaroo Tours
SIGHTSEEING

(☑ 08-8983 2699; www.litchfielddaytours.com) Small-group tours to Litchfield National Park ($130).

## ✦ Festivals & Events

### WordStorm
LITERARY

(www.wordstorm.org.au) The biannual NT Writers' Festival event, in May (even-numbered years), includes song, storytelling, visual-art collaboration, theatre, performance poetry, history, biography, poetry and fiction.

### Arafura Games
SPORTS

(www.arafuragames.nt.gov.au) A week-long multisport competition held in May in odd-numbered years, targeting up-and-coming athletes from the Asia-Pacific region. Athletics, basketball, cricket, soccer, swimming, volleyball...

### Darwin Blues Festival
MUSIC

(www.darwinbluesfestival.com) In late June, venues across Darwin charge up with live blues. Much beer and bending guitar strings.

### Beer Can Regatta
LOCAL CULTURE

(www.beercanregatta.org.au) An utterly insane and typically Territorian festival that features races for boats made out of beer cans. It takes places at Mindil Beach in July and is a good, fun day.

### Royal Darwin Show
AGRICULTURAL

(www.darwinshow.com.au) This agricultural show takes place at the showgrounds in Winnellie on the last weekend of July. Plenty of rides, demonstrations, competitions and pampered farm animals.

### Darwin Cup Carnival
HORSE RACING

(www.darwinturfclub.org.au) The Darwin Cup racing carnival takes place in July and August at the Darwin Turf Club in Fannie Bay. The highlight of the eight-day program is the running of the Darwin Cup, along with the usual fashion and frivolities.

### Darwin Aboriginal Art Fair
VISUAL ARTS

(www.darwinaboriginalartfair.com.au) Held at the Darwin Convention Centre, this two-day August festival showcases indigenous art from communities throughout the Territory.

### Darwin Festival
ARTS

(www.darwinfestival.org.au) This mainly outdoor arts and culture festival highlights the cultures of Darwin's large Aboriginal and Asian populations and runs for two weeks in August.

## 🛏 Sleeping

Darwin has a good range of accommodation, most of it handy to the CBD, but finding a

DARWIN TO ULURU DARWIN

bed in the peak May to September period can be difficult at short notice – book ahead, at least for the first night. Accommodation prices vary greatly with the season and demand. Prices given here are for high season, but expect big discounts between November and March, especially for midrange and top-end accommodation.

Backpacker hostels fluctuate the least, and prices differ little between places – concentrated as they are in a small stretch of bar-heavy Mitchell St. If you want a quieter stay, choose somewhere a bit further out – they're still within walking distance of the action. Hostel facilities usually include a communal kitchen, pool and laundry facilities and they all have tour-booking desks. Some offer airport, bus or train station pick-ups with advance bookings, and most give YHA/VIP discounts.

There are a few decent camping/caravan park options within 10km of the city centre. Some campervanners take their chances staying overnight at parking areas along the beach around Fannie Bay and East Point Reserve, but it's officially a no-no and council officers may move you on or dish out fines.

Darwin's larger hotels quote inflated rack rates, but there are all sorts of specials, including stand-by, weekend and internet rates. Most of the big hotels are gathered along the Esplanade.

## City Centre

### Frogshollow Backpackers HOSTEL $
(Map p156; 08-8941 2600, 1800 068 686; www.frogs-hollow.com.au; 27 Lindsay St; dm $24-30, d without/with bathroom $80/100; ❄@🛜≋) Presiding over a tranquil patch of parkland, Frogshollow is a chilled-out backpackers' choice. A relaxed Euro crew basks by the pool or kicks back in the park across the road. Afternoon balconies drip with pot-plant overflows as dorm-dwellers mooch around the kitchen. Some rooms have aircon; most have fans. Dorms can be a bit cramped.

### Dingo Moon Lodge HOSTEL $
(Map p156; 08-8941 3444; www.dingomoonlodge.com; 88 Mitchell St; dm $31-36, d & tw $100, all incl breakfast; ❄@🛜≋) Howl at the moon at the Dingo, a great addition to the Darwin hostel scene. It's a two-building affair with 65 beds – big enough to be sociable but not rowdy. A highlight is the pool, sparkling underneath a massive frangipani tree, and a great outdoor kitchen. No TV room – have a conversation instead.

### Melaleuca on Mitchell HOSTEL $
(Map p156; 1300 723 437; www.momdarwin.com.au; 52 Mitchell St; dm $31, d without/with bathroom $95/115; ❄@🛜≋) The highlight at this busy backpackers is the rooftop island bar and pool area overlooking Mitchell St – complete with waterfall spa and big-screen TV. Party heaven! The modern hostel is immaculate but a little sterile, with stark white walls and sparse rooms. Facilities are A1 though and it's very secure. The 3rd floor is female only.

### Chilli's HOSTEL $
(Map p156; 08-8980 5800, 1800 351 313; www.chillis.com.au; 69a Mitchell St; dm $32, tw & d without bathroom $100; ❄@🛜) Friendly Chilli's is a funky place with a small sundeck and spa (use the pool next door). There's also a pool table and a breezy kitchen/meals terrace overlooking Mitchell St. Rooms are compact but clean.

### Darwin YHA HOSTEL $
(Map p156; 08-8981 5385; www.yha.com.au; 97 Mitchell St; dm $33, d/f $115/145; ❄@🛜≋) The Darwin YHA is in a converted motel, so all 34 rooms (including dorms) have en suites, and they're built around a decent pool. The kitchen and TV room are tiny, but next door Globetrotters Bar has cheap meals and entertainment.

### Banyan View Lodge HOSTEL $
(Map p156; 08-8981 8644; www.banyanviewlodge.org.au; 119 Mitchell St; dm $27-29, s/d without bathroom from $68/78, d with bathroom from $110; ❄@≋) The Banyan View suits travellers who aren't into the party scene. It's a big, austere, office-block-looking YWCA that welcomes men too. Spacious rooms are clean and well kept – ask for one with a fan rather than air-con if you'd prefer. Bike hire available.

### Elkes Backpackers HOSTEL $
(Map p156; 1800 808 365; www.elkesbackpackers.com.au; 112 Mitchell St; dm $30, tw & d $85, tr $180; ❄@🛜≋) Elkes is a friendly, multilingual independent backpackers housed in a shambling cluster of rudimentary timber buildings punctuated by thick copses of vegetation. It's a good place to meet fellow travellers and chill out, but check the room thoroughly before settling in.

### Value Inn
HOTEL $$

(Map p156; ☑08-8981 4733; www.valueinn.com. au; 50 Mitchell St; d from $140; P❄☀) In the thick of the Mitchell St action but quiet and comfortable, Value Inn lives up to its name, especially out of season. En-suite rooms are small but sleep up to three and have fridge and TV.

### Palms City Resort
RESORT $$$

(Map p156; ☑08-8982 9200, 1800 829 211; www. citypalms.com; 64 The Esplanade; motel d $195, villas d $285; P❄☀☂) True to name, this centrally located resort is fringed by palm-filled gardens. If you covet a microwave and have space cravings, the superior motel rooms are worth a bit extra, while the Asian-influenced, hexagonal villas with outdoor spas are utterly indulgent. Butterflies and dragonflies drift between bougainvilleas in the knockout gardens.

### Medina Vibe
HOTEL $$$

(Map p156; ☑08-8941 0755; www.medina.com.au; 7 Kitchener Dr; d/studio from $215/235, apt from $335; P❄@☀☂) Two hotels in one building: standard doubles at Vibe, and studios and apartments next door at the Medina. Either way, you're in for an upmarket stay with friendly staff and a great location in the Darwin Waterfront Precinct. The Wave Lagoon is right next door if the shady swimming pool is too placid for you.

### ★Darwin Central Hotel
HOTEL $$$

(Map p156; ☑info 1300 364 263, 08-8944 9000; www.darwincentral.com.au; 21 Knuckey St; d from $180; P❄@☀☂; ☐4, 5, 8, 10) Right in the centre of town, this plush independent hotel oozes contemporary style and impeccable facilities, including an award-winning restaurant. There are a range of stylish rooms with excellent accessibility for disabled travellers. Rack rates are steep, but internet, weekend, and three-night-stay discounts make it great value.

### Argus
APARTMENTS $$$

(Map p156; ☑08-8925 5000; www.argusdarwin. com.au; 6 Cardona Ct; 1-/2-/3-bedroom apt from $280/360/590; P❄@☂) In a corner of town awash with apartment towers, the Argus stands out as a quality option. Apartments are *very* spacious, with lovely bathrooms, generous expanses of cool floor tiles, simple balcony living/dining spaces and snazzy kitchens with all the requisite appliances. The pool seems an afterthought, tucked into

a corner of the car park, but it's shady and welcoming on a sticky Top End afternoon.

### Novotel Atrium
HOTEL $$$

(Map p156; ☑08-8941 0755; www.novoteldarwin. com.au; 100 The Esplanade; d from $365, 2-bedroom apt from $485; P❄@☀☂) OK, OK, we know Novotel is a global chain and we've seen it all before, but what makes this one special are to-die-for ocean views and stylish standards above the norm: subtle lighting, fresh flowers and interesting indigenous art. Breathe the sea air on your balcony or descend into the kidney-shaped swimming pool, one of the best-looking puddles in Darwin. Off-season rates are a steal.

---

## 🛏 City Fringe & Suburbs

### Aurora Shady Glen Caravan Park
CARAVAN PARK $

(Map p152; ☑08-8984 3330, 1800 662 253; www. shadyglen.com.au; cnr Farrell Cres & Stuart Hwy, Winnellie; unpowered/powered sites $34/39, budget r $90, en suite cabins from $110; ❄☂) Well-treed caravan park with immaculate facilities, a camp kitchen, licensed shop and friendly staff. Public bus 8 rolls into downtown Darwin from the corner of the street.

### FreeSpirit Resort Darwin
CARAVAN PARK $

(☑08-8935 0888; www.darwinfreespiritresort.com. au; 901 Stuart Hwy, Berrimah; unpowered/powered sites $36/42, cabins & units $135-295; ❄@☀☂) An impressive highway-side park about a 10-minute drive from the city, with loads of facilities (including three pools). During the Dry there are regular nocturnal troubadours and activities including pancake breakfasts and water aerobics.

### Vitina Studio Motel
MOTEL $$

(Map p156; ☑08-8981 1544; www.vitinastudio motel.com.au; 38 Gardens Rd; d $149, ste $199; P❄@☀☂) Vitina is a convenient option providing bright, stylish accommodation in contemporary motel rooms as well as larger studios with kitchenettes. It's right on the city fringe convenient to the Gardens Park golf course, Botanic Gardens and Mindil Beach. Ask about discounts.

### Steeles at Larrakeyah
B&B $$

(Darwin City B&B; Map p156; ☑08-8941 3636; www. darwinbnb.com.au; 4 Zealandia Cres, Larrakeyah; d from $175, 1-/2-bedroom apt $250/270; ❄☂) Some B&Bs are business and others feel like you're staying with friends; Steeles is one of the latter. With a quiet residential location midway between the city centre, Cullen Bay and Mindil Beach, the three rooms in this pleasant Spanish Mission–style home are equipped with fridges, flat-screen TVs and private entrances. Breakfast happens in the tropical garden.

**Cullen Bay Resorts**     HOTEL, APARTMENTS **$$**
(Map p156; ☑ 08-8981 7999, 1800 625 533; www.cullenbayresortsdarwin.com.au; 26-32 Marina Blvd; hotel d $165-190, 1-/2-bed apt from $265/320; P ❋ 🛜 ☒ ) Cullen Bay is (or was, until the Waterfront Precinct came along) Darwin's prime waterfront location, and this pair of twin apartment towers boasts a million-dollar outlook over the marina and harbour. Interiors aren't super-flash, but the views are worth it.

**Grungle Downs B&B**     B&B **$$**
(Map p152; ☑ 08-8947 4440; www.grungledowns.com.au; 945 McMillans Rd, Knuckey Lagoon; d $140-165, cottage $400; ❋ ☒ ) Set on a two-hectare property, this beautiful rural retreat seems worlds away from the city (but it's only 13km). It's handy to Crocodylus Park and the airport, too. When it's hot outside, hang out in the guest lounge or by the pool. There are four lodge rooms (one with en suite) and a gorgeous two-bedroom cottage (which drops to $200 in the low season).

**Feathers Sanctuary**     BOUTIQUE HOTEL **$$$**
(Map p152; ☑ 08-8985 2144; www.featherssanctuary.com; 49a Freshwater Rd, Jingili; d incl breakfast $330; ❋ ☒ ) A sublime retreat for twitchers and nature lovers, Feathers has beautifully designed 'Bali-meets-bush' timber-and-iron cottages with semi-open-air bathrooms and luxurious interiors. The lush gardens have a private aviary breeding some rare birds, and a waterhole – more tropical birds than you're ever likely to see in one place again! Gangly free-roaming brolgas and jabirus steal the show.

# ✖ Eating

Darwin is the glistening pearl in the Territory's dining scene. Eateries make the most of the tropical ambience with alfresco seating, and the quality and diversity of produce tops anywhere else in the Territory.

Darwin has a growing number of cafes serving good coffee and grazing. The city's top restaurants will surprise with exotic and innovative fusion cuisine, while Darwin's famous markets sizzle and smoke with all manner of multicultural delights. Mitchell St pubs also entice backpackers off the pavement with free BBQs and cheap meals to soak up the beer.

On the edge of the CBD, Cullen Bay has a stylish waterfront dining scene with many options, while the food centre at the end of Stokes Hill Wharf provides cheap-and-cheerful fish and chips and Asian stir-fries, and there are also a few gems hidden in the suburbs north of the city.

# ✖ City Centre

There are two large supermarkets in downtown Darwin: **Coles** (Map p156; 55-59 Mitchell St, Mitchell Centre; ☺ 6am-10pm) and **Woolworths** (Map p156; cnr Cavenagh & Whitfield Sts; ☺ 6am-10pm)

**Four Birds**     CAFE **$**
(Map p156; 32 Smith St Mall, Shop 2, Star Village; items $4-8; ☺ breakfast & lunch Mon-Fri, plus Sat Jun-Aug) Nooked into the arcade on the site of the old Star Cinema (a '74 cyclone victim), this hole-in-the-wall does simple things very well: bagels, toasted sandwiches, muffins, paninis and coffee (we reckon it's the best in Darwin). Book-reading office types and travellers sit on stools scattered under a burgeoning frangipani tree.

**Roma Bar**     CAFE **$**
(Map p156; www.romabar.com.au; 9-11 Cavenagh St; mains $7-15; ☺ breakfast & lunch; 🛜 ) Roma is a local institution and meeting place for left-ies, literati and travellers. Well away from the craziness of Mitchell St, with free wi-fi, great coffee and juices, and you can get anything from muesli and eggs benedict for breakfast to excellent toasted focaccia and fish curry for lunch.

**Stokes Hill Wharf**     SEAFOOD, FAST FOOD **$**
(Map p156; www.darwinhub.com/stokes-hill-wharf; Stokes Hill Wharf; mains $8-16; ☺ lunch & dinner) Squatting on the end of Stokes Hill Wharf is a hectic food centre with half-a-dozen food counters and outdoor tables lined up along the pier. It's a pumping place for some fish and chips, oysters, a stir-fry, a laksa or just a cold sunset beer.

**Vietnam Saigon Star**     VIETNAMESE **$**
(Map p156; 21 Smith St, Shop 4; mains $12-18; ☺ lunch Mon-Fri, dinner daily; ☑ ) Darwin's speediest, shiniest Vietnamese restaurant serves up inexpensive rice-paper rolls, and beef, pork, chicken and seafood dishes with a multitude of sauces. Vegetarians are well

catered for and there are good-value lunch specials.

### Istanbul Cafe
TURKISH, FAST FOOD **$$**
(Map p156; 12 Knuckey St; mains $11-25; ⊙ breakfast, lunch & dinner) Inside Darwin's old Country Women's Association building (not a scone or pavlova in sight), this Turkish joint serves up quick takeaway kebabs, meaty grills, dip platters, kofte meatballs and kickarse Turkish coffee.

### ★Hanuman
INDIAN, THAI **$$**
(Map p156; 🖉08-8941 3500; www.hanuman.com.au; 28 Mitchell St; mains $16-38; ⊙lunch Mon-Fri, dinner daily; 🖉) Ask most locals about fine dining in Darwin and they'll usually mention Hanuman. Sophisticated but not stuffy, enticing aromas of innovative Indian and Thai Nonya dishes waft from the kitchen to the stylish open dining room and deck. The signature dish is oysters bathed in lemon grass, chilli and coriander, but the menu is broad, with exotic vegetarian choices and banquets also available.

### Go Sushi Train
JAPANESE **$$**
(Map p156; www.darwinhub.com/go-sushi-train; 28 Mitchell St, Shop 5; sushi $4.50-6.50, mains $25-38; ⊙lunch & dinner Tue-Sat; 🖉) Pull up a stool at this hip sushi circuit, hidden down a lane off Mitchell St. Despite the obscure location it's hugely popular, especially on 'Super Sushi Saturday' (all sushi $4 from 10.30am to 3.30pm). Can't get enough of those eel-and-cucumber rolls...

### ★Moorish Café
MIDDLE EASTERN **$$**
(Map p156; 🖉08-8991 0010; www.moorishcafe.com.au; 37 Knuckey St; tapas $4-12, mains $20-40; ⊙lunch & dinner Mon-Sat) Seductive aromas emanate from this divine terracotta-tiled cafe fusing North African, Mediterranean and Middle Eastern delights. The lunchtime crowd arrives for tantalising tapas and lunch specials, but it's an atmospheric place for dinner, too – order a tagine of NT prawns, apple cider, local jewfish coconut and lime, or the four-course banquet ($38 per person with a minimum of six diners; booking essential).

### Manolis Greek Taverna
GREEK **$$**
(Map p156; www.manolisgreektaverna.com.au; Shop 4, 64 Smith St; mains $18-30; ⊙lunch Tue-Fri, dinner Mon-Sat) Manolis boasts excellent Greek Island inspired dishes in a friendly, family-run restaurant with an unmistakable Greek ambience. There are blue-and-white table cloths and a fresh seafood-dominated menu that features small *mezethes* plates to share. Traditional favourites including fried cheese, lamb yiros, octopus, great salads and amazingly sweet desserts won't disappoint. There's boisterous live bouzouki music on Saturday nights.

### Crustaceans
SEAFOOD **$$**
(Map p156; 🖉08-8981 8658; Stokes Hill Wharf; mains $17-35; ⊙dinner Mon-Sat) This casual, licensed restaurant features fresh fish, bugs, lobster, oysters, even crocodile, as well as succulent steaks. The nerdy ordering forms detract from the romance, but it's the location, perched right at the end of Stokes Hill Wharf with sunset views over Francis Bay, plus the cold beer and a first-rate wine list that seals the deal.

### Tim's Surf 'n' Turf
STEAKHOUSE, SEAFOOD **$$**
(Map p156; 🖉08-8981 1024; www.timssurfandturf.com.au; 10 Litchfield St; mains $18-40; ⊙dinner daily) Squirrelled away on a city backstreet, Tim's is a long-standing locals' diner where you can enjoy good-value seafood, steak, schnitzels and pasta on a relaxed, leafy terrace (just ignore the faux waterfall). Mark what you want on the DIY ordering form with a pencil and hand it to the cashier.

### Ducks Nuts Bar & Grill
MODERN AUSTRALIAN **$$**
(Map p156; 🖉08-8942 2122; www.ducksnuts.com.au; 76 Mitchell St; mains $15-25; ⊙breakfast, lunch & dinner) An effervescent bar/bistro delivering a clever fusion of Top End produce with that Asian/Mediterranean blend we like to claim as Modern Australian. Great lunchtime burgers, light salads such as the warm Thai beef salad, and hearty mains such as lamb shanks. Good brekkies and caffeinated brews, too.

### Il Lido
ITALIAN **$$$**
(Map p156; 🖉08-8941 0900; www.illidodarwin.com.au; Wharf One, f3/19 Kitchener Dr, Waterfront Precinct; tapas $8-18, pizzas $17-27, mains $28-44) Taking pride of place in the Waterfront Precinct is this contemporary Italian restaurant developed by the folks that introduced Hanuman restaurant to Darwin two decades ago. Delightful breakfasts and a simply stunning balcony for sunset drinks and tapas.

### Char Restaurant
STEAKHOUSE **$$$**
(Map p156; 🖉08-8981 4544; www.charrestaurant.com.au; 70 The Esplanade; mains $28-54; ⊙lunch Wed-Fri, dinner daily) Housed in the grounds of the historic Admiralty House is Char, a

carnivore's paradise. The speciality here is chargrilled steaks – aged, grain-fed and cooked to perfection – but there's also a range of clever seafood creations on the associated 'Jellyfish' menu.

## City Fringe & Suburbs

**Parap Fine Foods**         SELF-CATERING **$**
(Map p152; www.parapfinefoods.com; 40 Parap Rd, Parap; ☺ 8am-6.30pm Mon-Fri, 8am-6pm Sat, 9am-1pm Sun) A gourmet food hall in the Parap shopping centre, stocking organic and health foods, deli items and fine wine – perfect for a picnic.

**Cyclone Cafe**         CAFE **$**
(Map p152; www.parapvillage.com.au; 8 Urquhart St, Parap; meals $7-14; ☺ breakfast & lunch Mon-Sat) Some of Darwin's best coffee is brewed at this unassuming Parap haunt. The decor is all rusty corrugated-iron (Cyclone Tracy's favourite projectile), the staff are upbeat, the coffee is strong and aromatic (try the triple-shot 'Hypercino'), and there's some great breakfast and lunch fare: croissants, burritos, cheese melts and bacon-and-egg rolls.

**Seadogs**         ITALIAN **$$**
(Map p156; ☎ 08-8941 2877; Marina Blvd, Cullen Bay; mains $15-27; ☺ lunch & dinner Tue-Sun) It may not front the marina, but the meals are cheaper at this popular local restaurant specialising in pizza, pasta, risotto and a few prawn and calamari dishes.

★**Saffrron**         INDIAN **$$**
(Map p152; ☎ 08-8981 2383; www.saffrron.com; 34 Parap Rd, Shop 14, Parap; mains $14-26; ☺ lunch Tue-Fri, dinner Tue-Sun, brunch Sun; ☏) ✐ Saffrron is Darwin's best Indian restaurant, a contemporary but intimate dining experience. The menu spans the subcontinent, from rich butter chicken masala to barramundi *mooli*. Sunday brunch is a South Indian taste adventure. There are plenty of vegetarian choices, traditional Indian sweets, and takeaways available. Rather progressively, it uses biodegradable furniture, cutlery, plates, bowls and takeaway containers.

**Nirvana**         THAI, INDIAN **$$**
(Map p156; ☎ 08-8981 2025; www.nirvanarestaurantdarwin.com; 6 Dashwood Cres; mains $15-30; ☺ dinner Mon-Sat; ☏) Excellent Thai, Malaysian and Indian dishes are only part of the story at Nirvana – it's also one of Darwin's best small live-music venues for jazz and

blues. It doesn't look much from the outside, but inside is an intimate warren of rooms with booth seating and Oriental decor. Enjoy a Thai green curry or fish masala with your tunes.

**Buzz Café**         MODERN AUSTRALIAN **$$**
(Map p156; ☎ 08-8941 1141; www.darwinhub.com/buzz-cafe; 48 Marina Blv, Cullen Bay; mains $18-40; ☺ lunch & dinner daily, breakfast Sun) This chic bar-restaurant furnished in Indonesian teak and Mt Bromo lava has a super multilevel deck overlooking the marina and makes a seductively sunny spot for a lazy lunch and a few drinks. Meals are Mod Oz, with some zingy salads and dishes to share. Aim for a deck table cantilevering out over the water.

## Drinking

Drinking is big business in tropical Darwin (cold beer and humidity have a symbiotic relationship), and the city has dozens of pubs and terrace bars that make the most of balmy evenings. Virtually all bars double as restaurants, especially along Mitchell St – a frenzied row of booze rooms full of travellers, all within stumbling distance of one another.

**Tap on Mitchell**         BAR
(Map p156; www.thetap.com.au; 51 Mitchell St) One of the busiest of the Mitchell St terrace bars, the Tap is always buzzing and there are inexpensive meals (nachos, burgers, calamari) to complement a great range of beer and wine.

**Darwin Ski Club**         SPORTS CLUB
(Map p152; www.darwinskiclub.com.au; Conacher St, Fannie Bay) Leave Mitchell St behind and head for a sublime sunset at this laid-back (and refreshingly run-down) water-ski club on Vestey's Beach. The view through the palm trees from the beer garden is a winner, and there are often live bands.

**Deck Bar**         BAR
(Map p156; www.thedeckbar.com.au; 22 Mitchell St) At the nonpartying parliamentary end of Mitchell St, the Deck Bar still manages to get lively with happy hours, pub trivia and regular live music. Blurring the line between indoors and outdoors brilliantly, the namesake deck is perfect for people-watching.

**Darwin Sailing Club**         SPORTS CLUB
(Map p152; www.dwnsail.com.au; Atkins Dr, Fannie Bay) More upmarket than the ski club, the sailing club is always filled with yachties enjoying a sunset beer overlooking the Timor Sea. Tunes on the sound system are surprisingly

un-yacht club (no Christopher Cross or Rod Stewart), and its waterfront bistro is a great place for dinner, too. Sign in as a visitor at the door (bring some ID).

**Shenannigans** PUB

(Map p156; www.shenannigans.com.au; 69 Mitchell St) It's a long way from Cork, but Darwin has a few Irish-theme pubs. Shenannigans mixes it up with a big Mitchell St terrace, hearty food and big party nights. Guinness aplenty, live music and rugby on the TV.

**Wisdom Bar & Grill** BAR

(Map p156; www.wisdombar.com.au; 48 Mitchell St) Bright blue walls, velour couches and a streetside terrace with a tree growing out of it add up to a more intimate version of the Tap on Mitchell.

**Ducks Nuts Bar & Grill** BAR

(www.ducksnuts.com.au; 76 Mitchell St) A big backlit cocktail bar, regular live music and the swanky vodka bar give the Ducks Nuts plenty of cred.

**Victoria Hotel** PUB

(The Vic; Map p156; www.thevic.com.au; 27 Smith St Mall) The venerable old Vic is a good place for a drink and where locals and travellers can mingle. Seemingly undergoing constant renovations, these days it's more of an all-round backpacker entertainment venue.

## ☆ Entertainment

Darwin's balmy nights invite a bit of late-night exploration and while there is only a handful of nightclubs, you'll find something on every night of the week. There's also a thriving arts and entertainment scene: theatre, film and concerts.

**Off the Leash magazine** (www.offtheleash. net.au) lists events happening around town, as does **Darwin Community Arts** (www.darwin communityarts.org.au). Keep an eye out for bills posted on noticeboards and telegraph poles that advertise dance and full-moon parties.

### Live Music

Just about every pub/bar in town puts on some form of live music, mostly on Friday and Saturday nights, and sometimes filling the midweek void with karaoke and DJs.

**Victoria Hotel** ROCK, DJS

(The Vic; Map p156; www.thevichotel.com; 27 Smith St Mall) The Vic has bags of history – the stone building dates from 1890 – but it's hard to see it these days. This is Darwin's favourite backpacker pub and goes off every night of the week. Dirt-cheap meals draw the travellers to the upstairs bar, and they stay for the pool tables, DJs and dance floor. Downstairs has a pub quiz on Monday, table dancing, live bands and DJs.

**Nirvana** JAZZ, BLUES

(Map p156; ☎ 08-8981 2025; www.nirvanarestaurant darwin.com; 6 Dashwood Cres) Behind an imposing dungeon-like doorway, this cosy restaurant-bar has live jazz/blues every Thursday, Friday and Saturday night and an open-mic jam session every Tuesday. And the Thai/Indian/Malaysian food here is magic.

### Clubs

**Discovery & Lost Arc** NIGHTCLUB

(Map p156; www.discoverydarwin.com.au; 89 Mitchell St; ☯9pm-4am Fri & Sat) Discovery is Darwin's biggest, tackiest nightclub and dance venue with three levels playing techno, hip hop and R&B. The Lost Arc is the neon-lit chill-out bar (undergoing renovations at the time of writing) opening on to Mitchell St, which starts to thaw after about 10pm.

**Throb** NIGHTCLUB

(Map p156; www.throbnightclub.com.au; 64 Smith St; ☯10pm-5am Fri & Sat) Darwin's premier gay- and lesbian-friendly nightclub and cocktail bar, Throb attracts party-goers of all genders and persuasions for its hot DJs and cool atmosphere. Hosts drag shows and touring live acts.

### Cinemas

★**Deckchair Cinema** OUTDOOR CINEMA

(Map p156; ☎ 08-8981 0700; www.deckchaircin ema.com; Jervois Rd, Waterfront Precinct; tickets adult/child $15/7; ☯box office from 6.30pm Apr-Nov) During the Dry, the Darwin Film Society runs this fabulous outdoor cinema below the southern end of the Esplanade. Watch a movie under the stars while reclining in a deckchair. There's a licensed bar serving food or you can bring a picnic (no BYO alcohol). There are usually double features on Friday and Saturday nights (adult/child $22/10).

**Birch Carroll & Coyle** CINEMA

(Map p156; www.eventcinemas.com.au; 76 Mitchell St; tickets adult/child $17/13) Darwin's mainstream cinema complex, screening latest-release films across five theatres. Head down on Tropical Tuesday for $12 entry (all day).

## DARWIN'S MAGICAL MARKETS

**Mindil Beach Sunset Market** (Map p156; www.mindil.com.au; off Gilruth Ave; ⊘5-10pm Thu, 4-9pm Sun May–Oct) As the sun heads towards the horizon on Thursday and Sunday, half of Darwin descends on Mindil Beach, with tables, chairs, rugs, grog and kids in tow. Food is the main attraction – Thai, Sri Lankan, Indian, Chinese and Malaysian to Brazilian, Greek, Portuguese and more – all at around $5 to $10 a serve. Don't miss a flaming satay stick from Bobby's brazier. Top it off with fresh fruit salad, decadent cakes or luscious crepes. But that's only half the fun – arts and crafts stalls bulge with handmade jewellery, fabulous rainbow tie-died clothes, Aboriginal artefacts, and wares from Indonesia and Thailand. Peruse and promenade, stop for a pummelling massage or to listen to rhythmic live music. Mindil Beach is about 2km from the city centre; an easy walk or hop on buses 4 or 6 which go past the market area.

Similar stalls (you'll recognise many of the stall holders) can be found at various suburban markets from Friday to Sunday.

**Parap Village Market** (Map p152; www.parapvillage.com.au; Parap Shopping Village, Parap Rd, Parap; ⊘8am-2pm Sat) This compact, crowded food-focused market is a local favourite with the full gamut of Southeast Asian cuisine, as well as plenty of ingredients to cook up your own tropical storm.

**Rapid Creek Market** (Map p152; www.rapidcreekshoppingcentre.com.au; 48 Trower Rd, Rapid Creek; ⊘6.30am-1.30pm Sun) Darwin's oldest market is another Asian marketplace, with a tremendous range of tropical fruit and vegetables mingled with a heady mixture of spices and swirling satay smoke.

**Nightcliff Market** (Map p152; www.nightcliffmarkets.com; Pavonia Way, Nightcliff; ⊘8am-2pm Sun) Another popular community market, north of the city in the Nightcliff Shopping Centre, where you will find lots of secondhand goods and designer clothing.

**Happy Yess Market** (Map p156; http://happyyess.tumblr.com; 56 Woods St; ⊘2-6pm 1st Sun each month) In association with the Darwin Visual Arts Association, this popular market is a great way to laze away a Sunday afternoon. The stalls are filled with secondhand treasures, tasty treats and whimsical stalls.

### Theatre

**Darwin Entertainment Centre** ARTS CENTRE (Map p156; ☑08-8980 3333; www.darwinentertainment.com.au; 93 Mitchell St; ⊘box office 10am-5.30pm Mon-Fri & 1hr prior to shows) Darwin's main community arts venue houses the Playhouse and Studio Theatres, and hosts events from fashion-award nights to plays, rock operas, comedies and concerts. Check the website for upcoming shows.

**Brown's Mart** ARTS CENTRE (Map p156; ☑08-8981 5522; www.brownsmart.com.au; 12 Smith St) This historic venue (a former mining exchange) features live theatre performances, music and short films.

## 🔒 Shopping

You don't have to walk far along the Smith St Mall to find a souvenir shop selling lousy NT souvenirs: tea towels, T-shirts, stubbie holders and cane-toad coin purses (most of it made in China). Also in oversupply are outlets selling Aboriginal arts and crafts (be informed about reliable operators). However, Darwin's fabulous markets sell unique handcrafted items such as seed-pod hats, shell jewellery, kites, clothing and original photos.

**Framed** ART, DESIGN (Map p156; www.framed.com.au; 55 Stuart Hwy, Stuart Park) Surrounded by sex shops, car yards and plumbing supply outlets, Frames presents a surprisingly classy range of NT arts and crafts. The eclectic and always changing range is typically tropical, and includes contemporary Aboriginal art, pottery, jewellery and some exquisitely carved furniture.

**Casuarina Square** MALL (Map p152; www.casuarinasquare.com.au; 247 Trower Rd, Casuarina) This massive shopping complex has 170 mainstream retail outlets, plus cinemas and a food court. Good air-con on sticky afternoons in the Wet. Buses 4 and 5 travel the 20 minutes north of Darwin.

**NT General Store**                    OUTDOOR GEAR
(Map p156; 42 Cavenagh St) This casual, corrugated-iron warehouse has shelves piled high with camping and bushwalking gear, as well as a range of maps.

### Arts & Crafts

**Aboriginal Fine Arts Gallery**        ART GALLERY
(Map p156; www.aaia.com.au; 1st fl, cnr Mitchell & Knuckey Sts; ⊙9am-5pm) Displays and sells art from Arnhem Land and the Central Desert region.

**Maningrida Arts & Culture**           ART GALLERY
(Map p156; www.maningrida.com; 32 Mitchell St, Shop 1; ⊙9am-5pm Mon-Fri, 11.30am-4.30pm Sat) 🍃 Features fibre sculptures, weavings and paintings from the Kunibidji community at Maningrida on the banks of the Liverpool River, Arnhem Land. Fully Aboriginal-owned.

**Mbantua Fine Art Gallery**            ART GALLERY
(Map p156; www.mbantua.com.au; 2/30 Smith St Mall; ⊙9am-5pm Mon-Sat) Vivid utopian designs painted on everything from canvasses to ceramics.

**Territory Colours**                   ART GALLERY
(Map p156; www.territorycolours.com; 46 Smith St Mall; ⊙10am-5pm Mon-Fri, 10am-3pm Sat & Sun) Contemporary paintings and crafts, including glass, porcelain and wood from local artists; features the work of contemporary indigenous artist Harold Thomas.

**Tiwi Art Network**                    ART GALLERY
(Map p152; www.tiwiart.com; 3/3 Vickers St, Parap; ⊙10am-5pm Wed-Fri, 10am-2pm Sat) 🍃 The office and showroom for three arts communities on the Tiwi Islands.

## ℹ Information

### EMERGENCY
**AANT Roadside Assistance** (☑13 11 11; www.aant.com.au)
**Ambulance** (☑000; www.stjohnnt.com.au)
**Fire** (☑000; www.nt.gov.au/pfes)
**Poisons Information Centre** (☑13 11 26; ⊙24hr) Advice on poisons, bites and stings.
**Police** (☑000; www.nt.gov.au/pfes)

### INTERNET ACCESS
Most accommodation in Darwin provides some form of internet access, and there is free wi-fi available in Smith Street Mall.
**Northern Territory Library** (☑1800 019 155; www.ntl.nt.gov.au; Mitchell St, Parliament House; ⊙10am-5pm Mon-Fri, 1-5pm Sat & Sun) Book in advance for free access. Wi-fi also available.

### MEDICAL SERVICES
**Royal Darwin Hospital** (☑08-8920 6011; www.health.nt.gov.au; Rocklands Dr, Tiwi; ⊙24hr) Accident and emergency services.
**Travellers Medical & Vaccination Centre** (☑08-8901 3100; www.traveldoctor.com.au; 43 Cavenagh St, 1st fl; ⊙8.30am-noon & 1.30-5pm Mon-Fri) GPs by appointment.

### MONEY
There are 24-hour ATMs dotted around the city centre, and exchange bureaux on Mitchell St.

**DARWIN TO ULURU** DARWIN

---

### BUYING ABORIGINAL ART

Taking home a piece of Aboriginal art can create an enduring connection with Australia. For Aboriginal artists, painting is an important cultural and economic enterprise. To ensure you're not perpetuating non-Indigenous cash-in on Aboriginal art's popularity, avoid buying cheap imported fridge magnets, stubbie holders, boomerangs or didgeridoos. Make sure you're buying from an authentic dealer selling original art, and if the gallery doesn't pay their artists upfront, ask exactly how much of your money will make it back to the artist or community.

A good test is to request some biographical info on the artists – if the vendor can't produce it, keep walking. An authentic piece will come with a certificate indicating the artist's name, language group and community, and the work's title, its story and when it was made.

You may also check that the selling gallery is associated with a regulatory body, such as the **Australian Commercial Galleries Association** (www.acga.com.au). Where possible, buy direct from Aboriginal arts centres or their city outlets (see www.ankaaa.org.au or www.aboriginalart.org); this is generally cheaper and ensures authenticity. You also get to view the works in the context in which they were created.

### POST

**General Post Office** (☑13 13 18; www.aus post.com.au; 48 Cavenagh St; ☺9am-5pm Mon-Fri, 9am-12.30pm Sat) Poste restante.

### TOURIST INFORMATION

**Tourism Top End** (☑08-8980 6000, 1300 138 886; www.tourismtopend.com.au; cnr Smith & Bennett Sts, Darwin, NT; ☺8.30am-5pm Mon-Fri, 9am-3pm Sat & Sun) Hundreds of brochures; books tours and accommodation.

## ❶ Getting There & Away

### AIR

Apart from the following major carriers arriving at Darwin International Airport (p150), smaller routes are flown by local operators; ask a travel agent.

**Airnorth** (www.airnorth.com.au) To/from East Timor, and to Broome, Perth, Kununurra and the Gold Coast.

**Jetstar** (www.jetstar.com) Direct flights to the eastern coast capitals and major hubs, as well as several Southeast Asian cities.

**Qantas** (www.qantas.com.au) Direct flights to Perth, Adelaide, Canberra, Sydney, Brisbane, Alice Springs and Cairns.

**Skywest** (www.skywest.com.au) Direct flights to Perth, Kununurra and Broome.

**Virgin Australia** (www.virginaustralia.com) Direct flights between Darwin and Brisbane, Broome, Melbourne, Sydney and Perth.

### BUS

**Greyhound Australia** (www.greyhound.com. au) operates long-distance bus services from the **Transit Centre** (69 Mitchell St). There's at least one service per day up/down the Stuart Hwy, stopping at Pine Creek ($75, three hours), Katherine ($94, 4½ hours), Mataranka ($132, seven hours), Tennant Creek ($290, 14½ hours) and Alice Springs ($391, 22 hours).

For Kakadu, there's a daily return service from Darwin to Cooinda ($87, 4½ hours) via Jabiru ($62, 3½ hours).

Backpacker buses can also get you to out-of-the-way places:

**Adventure Tours** (www.adventuretours. com.au)

**Oz Experience** (www.ozexperience.com)

### CAR & CAMPERVAN

For driving around Darwin, conventional vehicles are cheap enough, but most companies offer only 100km free, which won't get you very far. Rates start at around $40 per day for a small car with 100km per day.

There are also plenty of 4WD vehicles available in Darwin, but you usually have to book ahead and fees/deposits are higher than for 2WD ve-hicles. Larger companies offer one-way rentals plus better mileage deals for more-expensive vehicles. Campervans are a great option for touring around the Territory and you generally get unlimited kilometres even for short rentals. Prices start at around $50 a day for a basic camper or $80 to $100 for a three-berth hi-top camper, to $200-plus for the bigger mobile homes or 4WD bushcampers. Additional insurance cover or excess reduction costs extra.

Most rental companies are open every day and have agencies in the city centre. Avis, Budget, Hertz and Thrifty all have offices at the airport.

**Advance Car Rentals** (www.advancecar.com. au; 86 Mitchell St) Local operator with some good deals (ask about unlimited kilometres).

**Avis** (www.avis.com; 89 Smith St)

**Mighty Cars & Campervans** (www.mighty campers.com.au; 17 Bombing Rd, Winnellie) At the same depot as Britz, this is a budget outfit with small campers and hi-tops at reasonable rates.

**Britz Australia** (www.britz.com.au; 17 Bombing Rd, Winnellie) Britz is a reliable outfit with a big range of campervans and motorhomes, including 4WD bushcampers.

**Budget** (www.budget.com.au; cnr Daly St & Doctors Gully Rd)

**Europcar** (www.europcar.com.au; 77 Cavenagh St)

**Hertz** (www.hertz.com.au; 55–59 Mitchell St, Shop 41, Mitchell Centre)

**Thrifty** (www.rentacar.com.au; 50 Mitchell St)

**Travellers Autobarn** (www.travellers-autobarn. com.au; 13 Daly St) Campervan specialist.

**Wicked Campers** (www.wickedcampers.com. au; 75 McMinn St) Colourfully painted small campers aimed at backpackers.

### TRAIN

The legendary *Ghan* train, operated by **Great Southern Rail** (www.gsr.com.au), runs weekly (twice weekly May to July) between Adelaide and Darwin via Alice Springs. The Darwin terminus is on Berrimah Rd, 15km/20 minutes from the city centre. A taxi fare into the centre is about $35, though there is a shuttle service to/from the Transit Centre for $10.

## ❶ Getting Around

### TO/FROM THE AIRPORT

Darwin International Airport (p150) is 12km north of the city centre, and handles both inter-national and domestic flights. **Darwin Airport Shuttle** (☑08-8981 5066, 1800 358 945; www. darwin airportshuttle.com.au) will pick up or drop off almost anywhere in the centre for $15. When leaving Darwin book a day before depar-ture. A taxi fare into the centre is about $30.

## PUBLIC TRANSPORT

**Darwinbus** (www.nt.gov.au/transport) runs a comprehensive bus network that departs from the **Darwin Bus Terminus** (Harry Chan Ave), opposite Brown's Mart.

A $2 adult ticket gives unlimited travel on the bus network for three hours (validate your ticket when you first get on). Daily ($5) and weekly ($15) travel cards are also available from bus interchanges, newsagencies and the visitor information centre. Bus 4 (to Fannie Bay, Nightcliff, Rapid Creek and Casuarina) and bus 6 (Fannie Bay, Parap and Stuart Park) are useful for getting to Aquascene, the Botanic Gardens, Mindil Beach, the Museum & Art Gallery, Fannie Bay Gaol Museum, East Point Reserve and the markets.

Alternatively, the privately run Tour Tub (p159) is a hop-on, hop-off minibus touring Darwin's sights throughout the day.

## SCOOTER

**Darwin Scooter Hire** (www.esummer.com. au; 9 Daly St) Rents out mountain bikes/50cc scooters/motorbikes for $20/60/180 per day.

## TAXI

Taxis wait along Knuckey St, diagonally opposite the north end of Smith St Mall, and are usually easy to flag down. Call **Darwin Radio Taxis** (✆13 10 08; www.131008.com).

# AROUND DARWIN

## Mandorah

Mandorah is a low-key, relaxed residential beach suburb looking out across the harbour to Darwin. It sits on the tip of Cox Peninsula, 128km by road from Darwin but only 6km across the harbour by regular ferry. The main reason to visit is for the ferry ride across the harbour and a few drinks or dinner at the super-friendly pub. The nearby Wagait Aboriginal community numbers around 400 residents.

The **Mandorah Beach Hotel** (✆08-8978 5044; www.mandorahbeachhotel.bigpondhosting. com; d/f $88/110; ❀@☷) has sublime views over the beach and turquoise water to Darwin. All rooms in the refurbished motel have a fridge, TV and air-con. Even if you don't stay the night, the pub and restaurant (mains $13 to $26, open for lunch to 2pm, and dinner) food is great, and there's live music some weekends in season.

The **Mandorah Ferry** (www.fastferries.com. au; adult/child return $23/12) operates about a dozen daily services (adult/child return $25/12.50), with the first departure from the Cullen Bay Marina in Darwin at 6.30am and the last at 10pm (midnight on Friday and Saturday). The last ferry from Mandorah is at 10.20pm (12.20am Friday and Saturday). Bookings not required.

# Tiwi Islands

The Tiwi Islands – **Bathurst Island** and **Melville Island** – lie about 80km north of Darwin, and are home to the Tiwi Aboriginal people. The Tiwis ('We People') have a distinct culture and today are well known for producing vibrant art and the odd champion Aussie Rules football player.

Tourism is restricted on the islands and for most tourists the only way to visit is on one of the daily organised tours from Darwin.

The Tiwis' island homes kept them fairly isolated from mainland developments until the 20th century, and their culture has retained several unique features. Perhaps the best known are the pukumani (burial poles), carved and painted with symbolic and mythological figures, which are erected around graves. More recently the Tiwis have turned their hand to art for sale – carving, painting, textile screen-printing, batik and pottery using traditional designs and motifs. The Bima Wear textile factory was set up in 1969 to employ Tiwi women, and today makes many bright fabrics in distinctive designs.

The main settlement on the islands is **Nguiu** in the southeast of Bathurst Island, which was founded in 1911 as a Catholic mission. On Melville Island the settlements are **Pularumpi** and **Milikapiti**.

Most of the 2700 Tiwi Islanders live on Bathurst Island (there are about 900 people on Melville Island). Most follow a mainly nontraditional lifestyle, but they still hunt dugong and gather turtle eggs, and hunting and gathering usually supplements the mainland diet a couple of times a week. Tiwis also go back to their traditional lands on Melville Island for a few weeks each year to teach and to learn traditional culture. Descendants of the Japanese pearl divers who regularly visited here early this century also live on Melville Island.

Aussie Rules football is a passion among the islanders and one of the biggest events

# Around Darwin

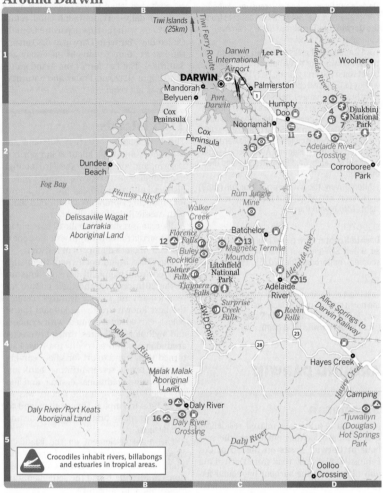

of the year (and the only time it's possible to visit without a permit or on a tour) is the Tiwi football grand-final day in late March. Huge numbers of people come across from the mainland for the event – book your tour/ferry well in advance.

## 🖝 Tours

There's no public transport on the islands, so the best way to see them is on a tour. You can catch the Tiwi Ferry over to Nguiu and have a look around the town without taking a tour or buying a permit, but if you want to explore further you'll need a permit from the Tiwi Land Council (p150).

**Tiwi Tours**         CULTURAL
(☑ 08-8923 6523, 1300 721 365; www.aussiead ventures.com.au; tour adult/child $465/418) Runs fascinating day trips to the Tiwis, although interaction with the local community is limited to your guides and local workshops and showrooms. A one-day tour to Bathurst Island includes a charter flight, permit, lunch, tea and damper with Tiwi women, craft workshops, and visits to the early Catholic-mission buildings, the Patakijiyali Museum

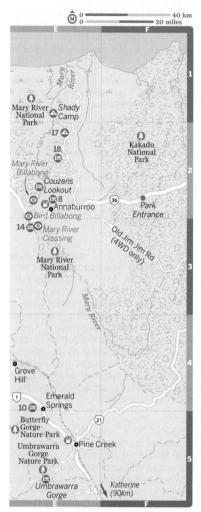

## Around Darwin

### ⊙ Sights

### ☉ Activities, Courses & Tours

### ⊟ Sleeping

### ⊗ Eating

---

and a pukumani burial site. Tours depart Monday to Friday from March to November.

**Tiwi Ferry** CULTURAL
(Map p156; ☑ 0418 675 266; www.tiwiferry.com.au; tour per person $149 plus ferry fare, ferry only return adult/child $180/120) Leaving from Cullen Bay ferry terminal at 7.30am and returning at 5pm, the boat trip takes about two hours, and you spend all of the land time in Nguiu, visiting the church, museum, Tiwi Design and Ngaruwanajirri Art Community. The ferry runs on Mondays, Wednesdays and Fridays.

## Arnhem Highway

The Arnhem Hwy (Route 36) branches off towards Kakadu 34km southeast of Darwin. About 10km along the road, in the small agricultural hub of Humpty Doo, the self-proclaimed 'world famous' **Humpty Doo Hotel** (☑ 08-8988 1372; humptydoohotel@hotmail.com; Arnhem Hwy; d/cabins $120/140; ✳ ☒) is a brawling kinda roadhouse, serving big meals (mains $17 to $30, lunch and dinner). There are unremarkable motel rooms and cabins out the back.

About 15km beyond Humpty Doo is the turn-off to the fecund green carpet of **Fogg Dam Conservation Reserve** (www. foggdamfriends.org). Bring your binoculars – there are ludicrous numbers of waterbirds living here. The dam walls are closed to walkers (due to crocs), but there are a couple of nature walks (2.2km and 3.6km) through the forest and woodlands. Bird numbers are highest between December and July. A further 8km beyond the Window on the Wetlands Visitor Centre is **Adelaide River Crossing**. It's from the murky waters of this river that large crocs are tempted to jump for camera-weilding tourists. See the boxed text (p175).

## Window on the
### Wetlands Visitor Centre  WILDLIFE RESERVE
(www.nretas.nt.gov.au/national-parks-andreserves/parks/windowwetlands; Arnhem Hwy; ⊘8am-7pm) **FREE** Three kilometres past the Fogg Dam turn-off is this dashing-looking structure full of displays (static and interactive) explaining the wetland ecosystem, as well as the history of the local Limilgnan-Wulna Aboriginal people. There are great views over the Adelaide River floodplain from the observation deck, and binoculars for studying the waterbirds on Lake Beatrice.

# Mary River Region

Beyond Adelaide River, the Arnhem Hwy passes through the Mary River region with the wetlands and wildlife of the Mary River National Park extending to the north.

**Bird Billabong**, just off the highway a few kilometres before Mary River Crossing, is a back-flow billabong, filled by creeks flowing off the nearby Mt Bundy Hill during the Wet. It's 4km off the highway and accessible by 2WD year-round. The scenic **loop walk** (4.5km, two hours) passes through **tropical woodlands**, with a backdrop of Mt Bundy granite rocks.

About another 2km along the same road is the emerald-green **Mary River Billabong**, with a BBQ area (no camping). From here the 4WD-only Hardies Track leads deeper into the national park to **Corroboree Billabong** (25km) and **Couzens Lookout** (37km).

Further along and north of the Arnhem Hwy, the partly sealed Point Stuart Rd leads to a number of riverside viewing platforms and to **Shady Camp**. The causeway barrage here, which stops freshwater flowing into saltwater, creates the ideal feeding environment for barramundi, and is the ideal fishing environment.

## 🛏 Sleeping & Eating

There are basic public **camping grounds** (adult/child/family $3.30/1.65/7.70) at Couzens Lookout and Shady Camp, where there are grassy camp sites under banyan trees. Come prepared to ward off armies of mosquitoes.

### Bark Hut Inn  HOTEL $
(☑08-8978 8988; unpowered/powered site $15/30, budget s/d $65/85, cabins $190) The Bark

Hut is a big barn of a place serving big beefy bistro meals (mains $15 to $26) and there's some interesting buffalo farming history on display. The budget rooms leave a bit to be desired.

### Mary River Wilderness Retreat  RESORT $$
(☑08-8978 8877; www.maryriverpark.com.au; Arnhem Hwy, Mary River Crossing; unpowered/powered sites $22/30, cabins $190-220; ❀ 🛜 ⊛) Boasting 3km of Mary River frontage, this bush retreat is heading steadily upmarket. The slick licensed restaurant (mains $12 to $30) has a wonderful deck to lounge about. There are 26 comfortable en-suite cabins complementing the grassy camping area down by the river. Go on a croc cruise ($45), hire a fishing boat, or ask about fishing charters; bookings essential.

## Point Stuart
### Wilderness Lodge  CAMPGROUND, HOTEL $$
(☑08-8978 8914; www.pointstuart.com.au; Point Stuart Rd; camping $34, d $120-170; ❀ ⊛) Accessible by 2WD and only 36km from the Arnhem Hwy, this remote-feeling lodge is part of an old cattle station and is ideal for exploring the Mary River region. Accommodation ranges from camp sites to budget rooms and decent lodge rooms. Wetland cruises on Rockhole Billabong per one/two/three hours cost $40/50/65, and boat hire is available. There's a bar/bistro here too, open for breakfast and dinner.

### Wildman Wilderness Lodge  RESORT $$$
(☑08-8978 8955; www.wildmanwildernesslodge.com.au; Point Stuart Rd; safari tent/cabin $490/630; ❀⊛) Wildman Wilderness Lodge is out-and-out an excellent upmarket safari lodge with a truly exceptional program of optional tours and fun activities. There are just 10 air-conditioned stylish cabins and 15 fan-cooled luxury tents to choose from and the daily tarriff includes breakfast and a three-course dinner.

# Stuart Highway to Litchfield National Park

## Territory Wildlife Park & Berry Springs Nature Park

The turn-off to the Territory Wildlife Park and Berry Springs is 48km down the Stuart Hwy from Darwin; it's then about 10km to the park.

## ⊙ Sights & Activities

★ **Territory Wildlife Park**    WILDLIFE PARK
(www.territorywildlifepark.com.au; 960 Cox Peninsula Rd; adult/child/family $26/13/45.50; ⊙8.30am-6pm, last admission 4pm) This excellent park showcases the best of Aussie wildlife. Highlights include the Flight Deck, where birds of prey display their dexterity (free-flying demonstrations at 11am and 2.30pm daily); the nocturnal house, where you can observe nocturnal fauna such as bilbies and bats; 11 different habitat aviaries; and a huge walk-through aviary, representing a monsoon rainforest. Pride of place must go to the aquarium, where a clear walk-through tunnel puts you among giant barramundi, stingrays, sawfish and saratogas, while a separate tank holds a 3.8m saltwater crocodile. To see everything you can either walk around the 4km perimeter road, or hop on and off the shuttle trains that run every 15 to 30 minutes and stop at all the exhibits.

**Berry Springs Nature Park**    NATURE RESERVE
(www.nretas.nt.gov.au/national-parks-and-reserves/parks/find/berrysprings; ⊙8am-6.30pm) Close by is this beautiful series of spring-fed swimming holes shaded by paperbarks and pandanus palms and serenaded by abundant birds. Facilities include a kiosk, a picnic area with BBQs, toilets, changing sheds and showers.

The turn-off to Berry Springs and Territory Wildlife Park is 48km down the Track from Darwin; it's then 10km to the park.

## Batchelor
POP 538

The government once gave Batchelor's blocks of land away to encourage settlement in the little town. That was before uranium was discovered and the nearby **Rum Jungle mine** developed (it closed in 1971 after almost 20 years). These days, Batchelor exists as a gateway and service centre for neighbouring Litchfield National Park, and is home to the **Batchelor Institute for Indigenous Education.**

Opposite the general store, a small, sporadically staffed **visitor information centre** (Tarkarri Rd; ⊙8.30am-5pm) is stocked with fliers, including national-parks info.

## 🛏 Sleeping & Eating

Although most travellers are naturally headed into Litchfield, this gateway town offers

### JUMPING CROCS

Few people seem to be able to resist the sight of a 3m-long saltwater crocodile launching itself out of the water towards a hunk of meat. Like a well-trained circus act, these wild crocs know where to get a free feed – and down on the Adelaide River, the croc-jumping show is guaranteed.

Jumping out of the water to grab prey is actually natural behaviour for crocs, usually to take surprised birds or animals from overhanging branches. They use their powerful tails to propel themselves up from a stationary start just below the surface, from where they can see their prey.

There are three operators at different locations along the Adelaide River. The modus operandi is pretty similar – a crew member (or nervous tourist) holds one end of a long stick that has a couple of metres of string attached to the other end. Tied to the end of the string is a very domesticated-looking pork chop – not exactly bush tucker, but the crocs love it. The whole thing is contrived, but it's still an amazing sight. And if you are lucky you will get to see one of the old denizens measuring over 5m. These old fellas aren't as spritely as their children but are a truly awesome sight.

**Adelaide River Cruises** (☎08-8983 3224; www.adelaiderivercruises.com.au; tours adult/child $35/25; ⊙9am, 11am, 1pm & 3pm May-Oct) On a private stretch of river past the Fogg Dam turn-off. Also runs small-group full-day wildlife cruises.

**Adelaide River Queen** (☎08-8988 8144; www.jumpingcrocodilecruises.com.au; tours adult/child $40/28; ⊙9am, 11am, 1pm & 3pm, for times Nov-Feb see website) Well-established operator on the highway just before Adelaide River Crossing.

**Spectacular Jumping Crocodile Cruise** (☎08-8988 9077; www.jumpingcrocodile.com.au; tours adult/child $35/20; ⊙9am, 11am, 1pm & 3pm) Along the Window on the Wetlands access road, this outfit runs one-hour tours. Ask about trips ex-Darwin.

some quality accommodation and a pub. The **Batchelor General Store** (cnr Tarkarri & Nurndina Rds; ⊙6am-6pm) has a well-stocked supermarket, takeaway shop, newsagent and post office.

**Rum Jungle Bungalows** B&B $$
(☑08-8976 0555; www.rumjunglebungalows.com. au; 10 Meneling Rd; d $160; ※☀) Bombarded by fluttering butterflies, these six olive-coloured bungalows are simple, elegant and immaculately clean. Each has a small fridge and en suite, and it's a short walk through tropical gardens (featuring native NT plants and herbs) to the private pool and breezy breakfast room (fresh seasonal fruit, local honey, homemade muesli and hot coffee).

**Batchelor Butterfly Farm** RESORT $$
(☑08-8976 0199; www.butterflyfarm.net; 8 Meneling Rd; d $110-160; ※@☎☀) This compact retreat divides itself between a low-key tourist attraction and friendly tropical-style resort. The kids will love the butterfly farm (adult/child $10/5) and mini zoo, which is free for staying guests. There are en suite cabins, a large homestay, and a busy all-day cafe/restaurant (mains $12 to $34), featuring Asian-inspired dishes. It's all a bit Zen with Buddha statues, chill music and wicker chairs on the shaded deck.

**Historic Retreat B&B** B&B $$
(☑08-8976 0554; www.historicretreat.com.au; 19 Pinaroo Cres; d incl breakfast $120-160; ※) The beautifully restored former home of Rum Jungle-mine managers is elevated (tropical-style) and has louvred windows, polished floorboards, vintage furniture and plenty of mine memorabilia. The five guest rooms share two bathrooms.

**Litchfield Tourist Park** CARAVAN PARK $
(☑08-8976 0070; www.litchfieldtouristpark.com. au; 2916 Litchfield Park Rd; unpowered/powered sites $24/32, bunkhouse $65, en-suite cabins $125-140; ※@☎☀) Just 4km from Litchfield, the standout feature of this attractive park is the two-bedroom ranch-style house that you can rent for $30. There's also a breezy, open-sided bar/restaurant here (mains $13 to $22, open breakfast and dinner) where you can get a beer, a burger or a real coffee.

**Batchelor Resort** RESORT $$
(☑08-8976 0123; www.batchelor-resort.com; 37-49 Rum Jungle Rd; unpowered/powered sites $30/38, cabins/motel d $130/170; ※☎☀) On the edge of town, this sprawling orange-brick complex has a caravan park with en suite sites and cabins, and a separate motel section. It's good for families, with bird feeding, two pools and two restaurants. There's also a bar and a grocery shop.

# Litchfield National Park

It may not be as well known as Kakadu, but many Territory locals rate Litchfield even higher. In fact, there's a local saying that goes: 'Litchfield-do, Kaka-don't'. We don't entirely agree – we think Kaka-do-too – but this is certainly one of the best places in the Top End for **bushwalking**, **camping** and especially **swimming**, with waterfalls plunging into gorgeous, safe swimming holes.

The 1500-sq-km national park encloses much of the spectacular Tabletop Range, a wide sandstone plateau mostly surrounded by cliffs. The waterfalls that pour off the edge of this plateau are a highlight of the park, feeding crystal-clear cascades and croc-free plunge pools.

The two routes to Litchfield (115km south of Darwin) from the Stuart Hwy join up and loop through the park. The southern access road via Batchelor is all sealed, while the northern access route, off the Cox Peninsula Rd, is partly unsealed, corrugated and often closed in the Wet.

About 17km after entering the park from Batchelor you come to what looks like tombstones. But only the very tip of these **magnetic termite mounds** is used to bury the dead; at the bottom are the king and queen, with workers in between. They're perfectly aligned to regulate temperature, catching the morning sun, then allowing the residents to dodge the midday heat. Nearby are some giant mounds made by the aptly named cathedral termites.

Another 6km further along is the turn-off to **Buley Rockhole** (2km), where water cascades through a series of rock pools big enough to lodge your bod in. This turn-off also takes you to **Florence Falls** (5km), accessed by a 15-minute, 135-step descent to a deep, beautiful pool surrounded by monsoon forest. Alternatively, you can see the falls from a lookout, 120m from the car park. There's a walking track (1.7km, 45 minutes) between the two places that follows Florence Creek.

About 18km beyond the turn-off to Florence Falls is the turn-off to the spectacular **Tolmer Falls**, which is for looking only. A

1.6km loop track (45 minutes) offers beautiful views of the valley.

It's a further 7km along the main road to the turn-off for Litchfield's big-ticket attraction, Wangi Falls (pronounced *Wong-guy*), 1.6km up a side road. The falls flow year-round, spilling either side of a huge orange-rock outcrop and filling an enormous swimming hole bordered by rainforest. Bring swimming goggles to spot local fish. It's immensely popular during the Dry (when there's a portable refreshment kiosk here), but water levels in the Wet can make it unsafe; look for signposted warnings.

The park offers plenty of bushwalking, including the Tabletop Track (39km), a circuit of the park that takes three to five days to complete depending on how many side tracks you follow. You can access the track at Florence Falls, Wangi Falls and Walker Creek. Overnight walkers should register (call ☑1300 650 730); camping fees apply. The track is closed September to March.

### ☞ Tours

There are numerous Litchfield tours ex-Darwin (p159).

### ⊫ Sleeping & Eating

There is excellent public camping (adult/child $6.60/3.30) within the park. Grounds with toilets and fireplaces are located at Florence Falls, Florence Creek, Buley Rockhole, Wangi Falls (better for vans than tents) and Tjaynera Falls (Sandy Creek; 4WD required). A visitor centre and cafe was being built at Wangi Falls at the time of writing. There are more-basic camp sites at Surprise Creek Falls (4WD required) and Walker Creek, with its own swimming hole, where camping involves bushwalking to a series of sublime, isolated riverside sites.

**Litchfield Safari Camp**    CAMPGROUND $
(☑08-8978 2185; www.litchfieldsafaricamp.com.au; Litchfield Park Rd; unpowered/powered sites $30/35, dm $30, d safari tents $130, extra person $10; ☀) Shady grassed sites make this a good alternative to Litchfield's bush camping sites, especially if you want power. The safari tents are great value as they comfortably sleep up to four folks. There's also a ramshackle camp kitchen, a kiosk and a pint-sized pool.

**★Litchfield Cafe**    CAFE $$
(www.litchfieldcafe.com.au; Litchfield Park Rd; mains $16-35; ⊘breakfast, lunch & dinner Apr-Sep, lunch only Oct-Mar) Filo parcels (try the chicken, mango and macadamia) make for a super lunch at this superb licensed cafe, or you could go for a meal of grilled local barra or roo fillet, topped-off with a good coffee and some wicked mango cheesecake.

# Adelaide River to Katherine

## Adelaide River
POP 238

Blink and you'll miss this tiny highway town, 111km south of Darwin, which was once an important point on the Overland Telegraph Line and supply depot during WWII. The Adelaide River War Cemetery (Memorial Tce) is an important legacy: a sea of brass plaques commemorating those killed in the 1942–43 air raids on northern Australia.

### ⊫ Sleeping & Eating

**Adelaide River Inn**    PUB $
(☑08-8976 7047; www.adelaideriverinn.com.au; 106 Stuart Hwy; unpowered/powered sites $18/25, budget/motel/cabin d $85/110/140; ☀☀) An affable little pub (mains $9 to $32, open breakfast, lunch and dinner) hiding behind the BP petrol station. On the corner of the bar stands Charlie the water buffalo, who lived here in relative obscurity until shooting to fame in *Crocodile Dundee*. When he died, the owner had him stuffed for posterity. There is a range of en-suite accommodation including neat cabins across the road.

**★Mt Bundy Station**    CAMPGROUND $
(☑08-8976 7009; www.mtbundy.com.au; Haynes Rd; unpowered/powered sites $22/26, s/d $50/85, cottage d $145, safari tent $202; ☀☀) If you're into horse riding, fishing and country-style hospitality, Mt Bundy Station is the perfect detour, 3km off the highway after Adelaide River. The original station buildings have become spotless guest accommodation, plus there are luxury safari tents. There are 4WD tours and plenty of animals on the property – guided horse rides cost $60 per hour, with overnight treks by arrangement.

## Daly River
POP 512

The Daly River is considered some of the best barramundi fishing country in the Territory and the hub is this small community

DARWIN TO ULURU ADELAIDE RIVER TO KATHERINE

117km southwest of Hayes Creek, reached by a narrow sealed road off the Dorat Rd (Old Stuart Hwy; Rte 23). Most of the population lives in the Nauiyu Nambiyu Aboriginal community, near the Daly River Crossing. A new bridge to replace the old causeway was under construction at the time of writing. There's a shop and fuel here and visitors are welcome without a permit, but note that this is a dry community (no alcohol).

Other than fishing, the main attraction here is Merrepen Arts (☑08-8978 2533; www. merrepenarts.com.au; ⊙10am-5pm) FREE, a gallery displaying locally made arts and crafts including etchings, screen printing, acrylic paintings, carvings, weaving and textiles. You can usually see artists at work in the mornings. Call in advance to check if they're open.

The Merrepen Arts & Sports Festival (www.merrepenfestival.com.au) celebrates arts and music from communities around the district, including Nauiyu, Wadeye and Peppimenarti, with displays, art auctions, workshops and dancing.

## 🛏 Sleeping & Eating

**Daly River Mango Farm** CAMPGROUND $
(☑08-8978 2464; www.mangofarm.com.au; unpowered/powered sites $30/35, d $100-175, 2-bedroom family cabin $350; ❄ 🖳) The camping ground here, on the Daly River 9km from the crossing, is shaded by a magnificent grove of near-century-old mango trees. Other accommodation includes budget and self-contained cabins. Guided fishing trips and boat hire available.

**Daly River Roadside Inn** PUB $
(☑08-8978 2418; dalyriverpub@bigpond.com; unpowered/powered sites $15/30, r $100-130; ❄) At Daly River itself is this rowdy pub with basic rooms, a small camping ground and meals (takeaway or pub food from $8 to $20) and fuel available.

**Perry's** CAMPGROUND $
(☑08-8978 2452; www.dalyriver.com; Mayo Park; unpowered/powered sites $28/24, unit $120; ❄🖳) A very peaceful place with 2km of river frontage and gardens where orphaned wallabies bound around. Dick Perry, a well-known fishing expert, operates guided trips, and boat hire is available. The self-contained unit has a deck with a BBQ and if you stay for seven nights you will only pay for six.

# Pine Creek
POP 381

A short detour off the Stuart Hwy, Pine Creek was once the scene of a frantic gold rush. The open-cut mine here closed in 1995, but today there's still gold and iron-ore mining and exploration nearby. A few of the 19th-century timber and corrugated-iron buildings still survive. The Kakadu Hwy (Rte 21) branches off the Stuart Hwy here, connecting it to Cooinda and Jabiru, making Pine Creek a useful base for exploring the region.

## ◉ Sights & Activities

**Railway Museum & Stream Train** MUSEUM
(Railway Tce; ⊙10am-2pm Mon-Fri May-Sep) FREE
Dating from 1889, the Railway Museum has a display on the Darwin-to-Pine Creek railway which ran from 1889 to 1976. The lovingly restored steam engine, built in Manchester in 1877, sits in its own enclosure next to the museum.

**Pine Creek Museum** MUSEUM
(www.nationaltrustnt.org.au; 11 Railway Tce; adult/child $2.20/free; ⊙11am-5pm Mon-Fri, 11am-1pm Sat) This museum is dedicated to the area's mining history and Chinese population. A one-time hospital, pharmacy and military communications centre, it's the oldest prefab corrugated iron building in Australia, made in England and shipped here in 1889.

**Umbrawarra**
**Gorge Nature Park** NATURE RESERVE
(www.nretas.nt.gov.au/national-parks-and-reserves /find/umbrawarragorge.html; campground adult/child $3.30/1.65) About 3km south of Pine Creek on the Stuart Hwy is the turn-off to pretty Umbrawarra Gorge, with a safe swimming hole, a little beach and a basic campground. It's 22km southwest on a rugged dirt road (just OK for 2WDs in the Dry; often impassable in the Wet). Bring plenty of water and mozzie repellent.

**Lookout** LANDMARK
Drive or walk up the short-but-steep hill off Moule St to the lookout over the old open-cut mine, now full of water (135m deep!).

## 🛏 Sleeping & Eating

**Lazy Lizard Tourist**
**Park & Tavern** CAMPGROUND $
(☑08-8976 1008; www.lazylizardpinecreek.com.au; 299 Millar Tce; unpowered/powered sites $17/25; 🖳) The small, well-grassed camping area at the

Lazy Lizard is really only secondary to the pulsing pub next door. The open-sided bar supported by carved ironwood pillars is a busy local watering hole with a pool table and old saddles slung across the rafters. The kitchen serves top-notch pub food (mains $16 to $30, open lunch and dinner), featuring big steaks and barra dishes.

**Emerald Springs Roadhouse** ROADHOUSE $
(☎08-8976 1169; www.emeraldsprings.com.au; Stuart Hwy; unpowered/powered sites $10/20, cabins from $65; ❋▨) About 25km north of Pine Creek, the excellent Emerald Springs Roadhouse (mains $16 to $32) makes an effort to provide more than a regulation roadhouse. You can still get a burger and a beer, but there's also a 'specials' blackboard with many wonderful choices. Out back there's decent accommodation and a great deck on which to sit, sip and savour your steak sanger or wok-tossed vegetables. And the homemade ice cream is awesome!

**Pine Creek Railway Resort** BOUTIQUE HOTEL $$
(☎08-8976 1001; www.pinecreekrailwayresort.com.au; s/d $85/110, cabins $130-150; ❋▨) This charming hotel uses raw iron, steel and wood in its stylish and modern rooms with options for singles, doubles and families. The dining area has been designed with romantic rail journeys of yore in mind and is a scene-stealer with pressed-tin ceilings and elaborate chandeliers. The menu is, however, modern with Asian-inspired dishes, pizzas and more.

# KAKADU & ARNHEM LAND

Kakadu and neighbouring Arnhem Land epitomise the remarkable landscape and cultural heritage of the Top End. Each is a treasure house of natural history and Aboriginal art, and both are significant homelands of contemporary indigenous culture.

## Kakadu National Park

Kakadu is a whole lot more than a national park. It's also a vibrant, living acknowledgment of the elemental link between the Aboriginal custodians and the country they have nurtured, endured and respected for thousands of generations. Encompassing almost 20,000 sq km (about 200km north–south

and 100km east–west), it holds in its boundaries a spectacular ecosystem and a mind-blowing concentration of ancient **rock art**. The landscape is an ever-changing tapestry – periodically scorched and flooded, apparently desolate or obviously abundant depending on the season.

In just a few days you can cruise on billabongs bursting with wildlife, examine 25,000-year-old rock paintings with the help of an indigenous guide, swim in pools at the foot of tumbling waterfalls and hike through ancient sandstone escarpment country.

If Kakadu has a downside – in the Dry at least – it's that it's incredibly popular. Resorts, camping grounds and rock-art sites can be very crowded, but this is a vast park and with a little adventurous spirit you can easily get off the beaten track and be alone with nature.

The Arnhem Hwy and Kakadu Hwy traverse the park; both are sealed and accessible year-round. The 4WD-only Old Jim Jim Rd is an alternative access from the Arnhem Hwy, joining the Kakadu Hwy 7km south of Cooinda.

Note that takeaway alcohol is hideously expensive anywhere in Kakadu – if you want a drink back at the camp site, stock up in Darwin.

### Geography

The circuitous Arnhem Land escarpment, a dramatic 30m- to 200m-high sandstone cliff line, forms the natural boundary between Kakadu and Arnhem Land and winds 500km through eastern and southeastern Kakadu.

Creeks cut across the rocky plateau and, in the wet season, tumble off it as thundering waterfalls. They then flow across the lowlands to swamp Kakadu's vast northern flood plains. From west to east, the rivers are the Wildman, West Alligator, South Alligator and East Alligator (the latter forming the eastern boundary of the park). The coastal zone has long stretches of mangrove swamp, important for halting erosion and as a breeding ground for bird and marine life. The southern part of the park is dry lowlands with open grassland and eucalypts. Pockets of monsoon rainforest crop up throughout the park.

More than 80% of Kakadu is savannah woodland. It has more than 1000 plant species, many still used by Aboriginal people for food and medicinal purposes.

# Kakadu National Park

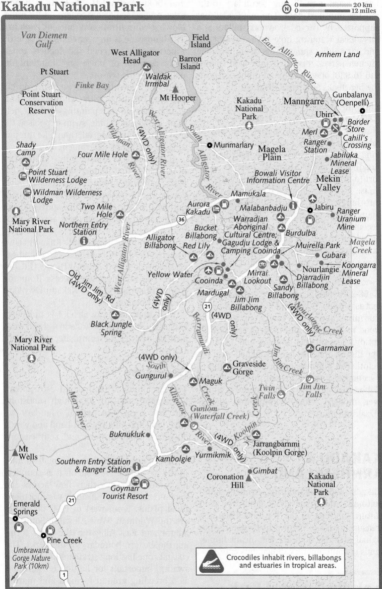

Crocodiles inhabit rivers, billabongs and estuaries in tropical areas.

## Climate

The average maximum temperature in Kakadu is 34°C, year-round. The Dry is roughly April to September, and the Wet, when most of Kakadu's average rainfall of 1500mm falls, is from October to March.

As wetlands and waterfalls swell, unsealed roads become impassable, cutting off some highlights such as Jim Jim Falls.

Local Aboriginal people recognise six seasons in the annual cycle:

Gunumeleng (October to December) is the build-up to the Wet. Humidity increases, the temperature rises to 35°C or more and mosquitoes reach near-plague proportions. By November the thunderstorms have started, billabongs are replenished, and waterbirds and fish disperse.

Gudjewg (January to March) is the Wet proper with violent thunderstorms, and flora and fauna thriving in the hot, moist conditions.

Banggerreng (April) is when storms (known as 'knock 'em down' storms) flatten the spear grass, which during the course of the Wet has shot up to 2m high.

Yegge (May to June) is the season of mists, when the air starts to dry out. The wetlands and waterfalls still have a lot of water and most of the tracks are open. The first firing of the countryside begins.

Wurrgeng (June to mid-August) is the most comfortable time, weather-wise, is the late Dry, beginning in July. This is when animals, especially birds, gather in large numbers around shrinking billabongs, and when most tourists visit.

Gurrung (mid-August to September) is the end of the Dry and the beginning of another cycle.

## Wildlife

Kakadu has more than 60 species of mammals, more than 280 bird species, 120 recorded species of reptile, 25 species of frog, 55 freshwater fish species and at least 10,000 different kinds of insect. Most visitors see only a fraction of these creatures (except the insects), since many of them are shy, nocturnal or scarce.

### Birds

Abundant waterbirds and their beautiful wetland homes are a highlight of Kakadu. This is one of the chief refuges in Australia for several species, including the magpie goose, green pygmy goose and Burdekin duck. Other fine waterbirds include pelicans, brolgas and the jabiru (or more correctly black-necked stork), Australia's only stork, with distinctive red legs and long beak. Herons, egrets, cormorants, wedge-tailed eagles, whistling kites and black kites are common. The open woodlands harbor rainbow bee-eaters, kingfishers and the endangered bustard. Majestic white-breasted sea eagles are seen near inland waterways. At night, you might hear barking owls calling – they sound just like dogs – or the plaintive wail of the bush stone curlew. The raucous call of the spectacular red-tailed black cockatoo is often considered the signature sound of Kakadu.

At Mamukala, 8km east of the South Alligator River on the Arnhem Hwy, is a wonderful observation building, plus bird-watching hides and a 3km walking track.

### Fish

You can't miss the silver barramundi, which creates a distinctive swirl near the water's surface. A renowned sportfish, it can grow to more than 1m in length and changes sex from male to female at the age of five or six years.

### Mammals

Several types of kangaroo and wallaby inhabit the park; the shy black wallaroo is unique to Kakadu and Arnhem Land – look for them at Nourlangie Rock, where individuals rest under rocky overhangs. At Ubirr, short-eared rock wallabies can be spotted in the early morning. You may see a sugar glider or a shy dingo in wooded areas in the daytime. Kakadu has 26 bat species, four of them endangered.

### Reptiles

Twin Falls and Jim Jim Falls have resident freshwater crocodiles, which have narrow snouts and rarely exceed 3m, while the dangerous saltwater variety is found throughout the park.

Kakadu's other reptiles include the frill-necked lizard, 11 species of goanna, and five freshwater turtle species, of which the most common is the northern snake-necked turtle. Kakadu has many snakes, though most are nocturnal and rarely encountered. The striking Oenpelli python was first recorded by non-Aboriginal people in 1976. The odd-looking file snake lives in billabongs and is much sought after as bush tucker. They have square heads, tiny eyes and saggy skin covered in tiny rough scales (hence 'file'). They move very slowly (and not at all on land), eating only once a month and breeding once every decade.

## Rock Art

Kakadu is one of Australia's richest, most accessible repositories of rock art. There are more than 5000 sites, which date from 20,000 years to 10 years ago. The vast majority of these sites are off limits or inaccessible, but two of the finest collections are the easily visited galleries at Ubirr and Nourlangie.

Rock paintings have been classified into three roughly defined periods: Pre-estuarine, which is from the earliest paintings up to around 6000 years ago; Estuarine, which covers the period from 6000 to around 2000 years ago, when rising sea levels brought the coast to its present level; and Freshwater, from 2000 years ago until the present day.

For local Aboriginal people, these rock-art sites are a major source of traditional knowledge and represent their archives. Aboriginal people rarely paint on rocks anymore, as they no longer live in rock shelters and there are fewer people with the requisite knowledge. Some older paintings are believed by many Aboriginal people to have been painted by mimi spirits, connecting people with creation legends and the development of Aboriginal lore.

As the paintings are all rendered with natural, water-soluble ochres, they are very susceptible to water damage. Drip lines of clear silicon rubber have been laid on the rocks above the paintings to divert rain. As the most accessible sites receive up to 4000 visitors a week, boardwalks have been erected to keep the dust down and to keep people at a suitable distance from the paintings.

## ☞ Tours

There are dozens of Kakadu tours on offer; book at least a day ahead if possible; operators generally collect you from your accommodation. There are plenty of tours departing from Darwin.

### Indigenous Tours & Sightseeing

**Kakadu Animal Tracks**               INDIGENOUS
(☑ 08-8979 0145; www.animaltracks.com.au; tours adult/child $205/135) ✐ Based at Cooinda, this outfit runs seven-hour tours with an indigenous guide combining a wildlife safari and Aboriginal cultural tour. You'll see thousands of birds, get to hunt, gather, prepare and consume bush tucker and crunch on some green ants.

**Magela Cultural &
Heritage Tours**                         INDIGENOUS
(☑ 08-8979 2548; www.kakadutours.com.au; tours adult/child $245/196) ✐ Aboriginal-owned and -operated 4WD day tour into northern Kakadu and Arnhem Land, including Injalak Hill and a cruise on Inkiyu billabong.

**Gagudju Adventure Tours**            SIGHTSEEING
(☑ 08-8979  0145;  www.gagudju-dreaming.com; tours adult/child $195/145) 4WD tours to Jim Jim and Twin Falls from April to October.

**Top End Explorer Tours**            SIGHTSEEING
(☑ 08-8979 3615, 1300 556 609; www.kakadutours. net.au; tours adult/child $195/150) 4WD tours to Jim Jim Falls and Twin Falls from Jabiru and Cooinda.

**Ayal Aboriginal Tours**              INDIGENOUS
(☑ 0429 470 384; www.ayalkakadu.com.au; tours adult/child $220/99) ✐ Full-day indigenous-run tours around Kakadu, with former ranger and local, Victor Cooper, shining a light on art, culture and wildlife.

**Kakadu Air**                     SCENIC FLIGHTS
(☑ 1800 089 113; www.kakaduair.com.au) Offers 30-minute/one-hour fixed-wing flights for $140/230 per adult. Helicopter tours, though more expensive, give a more dynamic aerial perspective. They cost from $210 (20 minutes) to $460 (45 minutes) per person. Also on offer are one- and two-day tours flying from Darwin that include land and wetland tours in Kakadu.

### Wetland & River Trips

**Yellow Water Cruises**          WILDLIFE CRUISES
(☑ 1800 500 401; www.gagudju-dreaming.com) Cruise the South Alligator River and Yellow Water Billabong spotting wildlife. Purchase tickets from Gagudju Lodge, Cooinda, where a shuttle bus will deliver you to the departure point. Two-hour cruises ($99/70 per adult/child) depart at 6.45am, 9am and 4.30pm; 1½-hour cruises ($68/47) leave at 11.30am, 1.15pm and 2.45pm.

**Guluyambi Cultural Cruise**          INDIGENOUS
(☑ 1800 895 175; www.kakaduculturaltours.com. au; adult/child $61/40; ☺ 9am, 11am, 1pm & 3pm May-Nov) ✐ Launch into an Aboriginal-led river cruise from the upstream boat ramp on the East Alligator River near Cahill's Crossing.

**Kakadu Culture Camp**                INDIGENOUS
(☑ night cruise 1800 811 633, overnight 0428 792 048; www.kakaduculturecamp.com) ✐ Aboriginal-owned and -operated cruises on the Djarradjin Billabong; three-hour night cruise (per adult/child $80/50), and five-hour cruise-plus-dinner tours ($260/180). Tours depart from Muirella Park campground.

## Ubirr & Around

It'll take a lot more than the busloads of visitors here to disturb Ubirr's inherent majesty and grace. Layers of rock-art paintings, in various styles and from various centuries, command a mesmerising stillness. Part of the main gallery reads like a menu, with images of kangaroos, tortoises and fish painted in x-ray, which became the dominant style about 8000 years ago. Predating these are the paintings of mimi spirits: cheeky, dynamic figures who, it's believed, were the first of the Creation Ancestors to paint on rock (...given the lack of cherry pickers in 6000 BC, you have to wonder who else but a spirit could have painted at that height and angle). Look out for the yam-head figures, where the head is depicted as a yam on the body of a human or animal; these date back around 15,000 years.

The magnificent Nardab Lookout is a 250m scramble from the main gallery. Surveying the billiard-table-green floodplain and watching the sun set and the moon rise, like they're on an invisible set of scales, is glorious, to say the least. Ubirr (⊙8.30am-sunset Apr-Nov, from 2pm Dec-Mar) is 39km north of the Arnhem Hwy via a sealed road.

On the way you'll pass the turn-off to Merl Camping Ground (p184), which is only open in the Dry and has an amenities block, and the Border Store (p184), selling groceries and takeaway food (no fuel).

## Activities

**Bardedjilidji Sandstone Walk** WALKING
Starting from the upstream picnic-area car park, this walk (2.5km, 90 minutes, easy) takes in wetland areas of the East Alligator River and some interesting eroded sandstone outliers of the Arnhem Land escarpment. Informative track notes point out features on this walk.

**Manngarre Monsoon Forest Walk** WALKING
Mainly sticking to a boardwalk, this walk (1.5km return, 30 minutes, easy) starts by the boat ramp near the Border Store and winds through heavily shaded vegetation, palms and vines.

**Sandstone & River Rock Holes** WALKING
This extension (6.5km, three hours, medium) of the Bardedjilidji Walk features

DARWIN TO ULURU KAKADU NATIONAL PARK

---

**URANIUM MINING**

It's no small irony that some of the world's biggest deposits of uranium lie within one of Australia's most beautiful national parks. In 1953 uranium was discovered in the Kakadu region. Twelve small deposits in the southern reaches of the park were worked in the 1960s, but were abandoned following the declaration of Woolwonga Wildlife Sanctuary.

In 1970 three huge deposits – Ranger, Nabarlek and Koongarra – were found, followed by Jabiluka in 1971. The Nabarlek deposit (in Arnhem Land) was mined in the late 1970s, and the Ranger Uranium Mine started producing ore in 1981.

While all mining in the park has been controversial, it was Jabiluka that brought international attention to Kakadu and pitted conservationists and indigenous owners against the government and mining companies. After uranium was discovered at Jabiluka in 1971, an agreement to mine was negotiated with the local Aboriginal peoples. The Jabiluka mine became the scene of sit-in demonstrations during 1998 that resulted in large-scale arrests. In 2003 stockpiled ore was returned into the mine and the decline tunnel leading into the deposit was backfilled as the mining company moved into dialogue with the traditional landowners, the Mirrar people.

In February 2005 the current owners of the Jabiluka mining lease, Energy Resources of Australia (ERA), signed an agreement that gave the Mirrar the deciding vote on any resumption of this controversial mining project. Under the deal, ERA is allowed to continue to explore the lease, subject to Mirrar consent. In 2011 the traditional owners of the Koongarra lease, near Nourlangie, rejected the promise of millions of dollars from French nuclear power conglomerate Areva and requested the land be integrated into the national park. The legal steps necessary for the inclusion of the lease into the park were well underway in 2012. Meanwhile, the Ranger mine – which is officially not part of the national park but is surrounded by it – was transitioning from an open-cut to an underground mine in late 2012. However, expansion of the mine is not guaranteed and under current legislation it is due to close in 2021, with rehabilitation complete by 2026.

sandstone outcrops, paperbark swamps and riverbanks. Closed in the Wet.

## 🛏 Sleeping & Eating

**Merl Camping Ground**   CAMPGROUND $
(adult/child $10/free) The turn-off to this national parks ground is about 1km before the Border Store. It is divided into a quiet zone and a generator use-zone, each with a block of showers and toilets. It can get mighty busy at peak times and be warned, the mosquitos are diabolical. The site is closed in the Wet.

**★ Border Store**   CAFE $$
(☑ 08-8979 2474; meals $6-26; ⊙ 8am-6pm Mon, 8am-8pm Tue-Sun Apr-Nov) The charming little Border Store is full of surprises, including real coffee, sweet cakes and delicious Thai-cooked Thai food. A real treat if you are camping at nearby Merl. You can book a Guluyambi Cultural Cruise on the East Alligator River or a tour to Arnhem Land, and watch local artists at work outside the cafe. Plans are in place for safari-tent and powered site accommodation.

## Jabiru

POP 1129

It may seem surprising to find a town of Jabiru's size and structure in the midst of a wilderness national park, but it exists solely because of the nearby Ranger uranium mine. It's Kakadu's major service centre, with a bank, newsagent, medical centre, supermarket, bakery and service station. You can even play a round of golf here.

## 🏃 Activities

**Ranger Uranium Mine Tour**   MINE TOUR
(☑ 1800 089 113; adult/child $30/10; ⊙ 9am, 11am & 1pm Mon-Sat) The Ranger Uranium Mine Tour is an opportunity to see one of the park's controversial mining projects up close and learn about some of the issues surrounding uranium mining. Guided tours leave from Jabiru airstrip, 8km east of town.

## 🛏 Sleeping & Eating

**★ Lakeview Park**   CABINS $$
(☑ 08-8979 3144; www.lakeviewkakadu.com.au; 27 Lakeside Dr; en suite powered sites $35, bungalows/d/cabins $120/130/235; ❄) Although there are no lake views as such, this Aboriginal-owned park is one of Kakadu's best with a range of tropical-design bungalows set in lush gardens. The doubles share

a communal kitchen, bathroom and lounge, and also come equipped with their own TV and fridge, while the 'bush bungalows' are stylish elevated safari designs (no air-con) with private external bathroom that sleep up to four. No pool, but one is planned and Jabiru public pool is only 50m away.

**Aurora Kakadu**
**Lodge & Caravan Park**   RESORT, CAMPGROUND $$$
(☑ 1800 811 154; www.auroraresorts.com.au; Jabiru Dr; unpowered/powered sites $26/38, cabins from $240; ❄ @ ❄) An impeccable resort/caravan park with shady, grassed sites and a lagoon-style swimming pool (movie nights by the pool on Fridays). Self-contained cabins sleep up to five people but are booked up well in advance. There's also a bar and bistro.

**Gagudju Crocodile Holiday Inn**   HOTEL $$$
(☑ 08-8979 9000; www.gagudju-dreaming.com; 1 Flinders St; d from $285; ❄ ❄ ❄) Known locally as 'the Croc', this hotel is designed in the shape of a crocodile, which, of course, is only obvious when viewed from the air or Google Earth. The rooms are clean and comfortable if a little pedestrian for the price (which drops considerably during the Wet). Try for one on the ground floor opening out to the central pool. The **Escarpment Restaurant** (mains $24-38; ⊙ breakfast, lunch & dinner) here is the best in Jabiru.

**Jabiru Sports & Social Club**   PUB $$
(☑ 08-8979 2326; Lakeside Dr; mains $16-32; ⊙ lunch & dinner daily) Along with the golf club, this low-slung hangar is the place to meet the locals over a beer. The bistro meals are surprisingly adventurous (try the tempura croc tail with bean salad and chilli ketchup), there's an outdoor deck overlooking the lake and sports on TV.

**Kakadu Bakery**   BAKERY $
(Gregory Pl; meals $5-17; ⊙ breakfast & lunch daily, dinner Mon-Sat) Superb made-to-order sandwiches on home-baked bread walk out the door, plus mean burgers, slices, breakfast fry-ups, pizzas, cakes and basic salads.

**Foodland**   SUPERMARKET $
(Jabiru Plaza; ⊙ 9am-5.30pm Mon-Fri, 9am-3pm Sat, 9am-1pm Sun) The local supermarket.

## Nourlangie

The sight of this looming outlier of the Arnhem Land escarpment makes it easy to understand its ancient importance to Aboriginal people. Its long red-sandstone bulk, striped in places with orange, white and black, slopes up from surrounding woodland to fall away at one end in stepped cliffs. Below is Kakadu's best-known collection of Aboriginal **rock art**.

The name Nourlangie is a corruption of *nawulandja,* an Aboriginal word that refers to an area bigger than the rock itself. The 2km looped walking track (open 8am to sunset) takes you first to the **Anbangbang Shelter**, used for 20,000 years as a refuge and canvas. Next is the **Anbangbang Gallery**, featuring Dreaming characters repainted in the 1960s. Look for the virile Nabulwinjbulwinj, a dangerous spirit who likes to eat females after banging them on the head with a yam. From here it's a short walk to **Gunwarddehwarde Lookout**, with views of the Arnhem Land escarpment.

Nourlangie is at the end of a 12km sealed road that turns east off Kakadu Hwy. About 7km south is the turn-off to **Muirella Park** (adult/child $10/free) camping ground at **Djarradjin Billabong**, with BBQs, excellent amenities and the 5km-return **Bubba Wetland Walk**.

## 🏃 Activities

### Nawurlandja Lookout WALKING
This is a short walk (600m return, 30 minutes, medium) up a gradual slope, but it gives excellent views of the Nourlangie rock area and is a good place to catch the sunset.

### Anbangbang Billabong Walk WALKING
This picturesque, lily-filled billabong lies close to Nourlangie, and the picnic tables dotted around its edge make it a popular lunch spot. The track (2.5km loop, 45 minutes, easy) circles the billabong and passes through paperbark swamp.

### Barrk Walk WALKING
This long day walk (12km loop, five to six hours, difficult) will take you away from the crowds on a circuit of the Nourlangie area. Barrk is the male black wallaroo and you might see this elusive marsupial if you set out early. Starting at the Nourlangie car park, this demanding walk passes through the Anbangbang galleries before a steep climb to the top of Nourlangie Rock. Cross the flat top of the rock weaving through sandstone pillars before descending along a wet-season watercourse. The track then

follows the rock's base past the Nanguluwur Gallery and western cliffs before re-emerging at the car park. Pick up a brochure from the Bowali Visitor Centre.

### Nanguluwur Gallery WALKING
This outstanding rock-art gallery receives far fewer visitors than Nourlangie simply because it's further to walk (3.5km return, 1½ hours, easy) and has a gravel access road. Here the paintings cover most of the styles found in the park, including very early dynamic style work, x-ray work and a good example of 'contact art', a painting of a two-masted sailing ship towing a dinghy.

## Jim Jim Falls & Twin Falls

Remote and spectacular, these two falls epitomise the rugged Top End. Jim Jim Falls, a sheer 215m drop, is awesome after rain (when it can only be seen from the air), but its waters shrink to a trickle by about June. Twin Falls flows year-round (no swimming), but half the fun is getting there, involving a little **boat trip** (adult/child $2.50/free, ⊙ running 7.30am to 5pm) and an over-the-water boardwalk.

These two iconic waterfalls are reached along a 4WD track that turns south off the Kakadu Hwy between the Nourlangie and Cooinda turn-offs. Jim Jim Falls is about 56km from the turn-off (the last 1km on foot), and it's a further five corrugated kilometres to Twin Falls. The track is open in the Dry only and can still be closed into late May; it's off limits to most rental vehicles (check the fine print). A couple of tour companies make trips here in the Dry and there's a camping area, **Garrnamarr** (adult/child $5/free) near Jim Jim Falls.

## Cooinda & Yellow Water

Cooinda is best known for the cruises (p182) on the wetland area known as Yellow Water, and has developed into a slick resort. About 1km from the resort, the **Warradjan Aboriginal Cultural Centre** (www.kakadu-attractions.com/warradjan; Yellow Water Area; ⊙9am-5pm) depicts Creation stories and has a great permanent exhibition that includes clap sticks, sugar-bag holders and rock-art samples. You'll be introduced to the moiety system (law of interpersonal relationships), languages and skin names, and there's a minitheatre with a huge selection of films from which to choose. A mesmeric soundtrack of chants and didgeridoos plays in the background. Warradjan is an easy 2km walk from the Cooinda resort.

**Gagudju Lodge & Camping Cooinda** (☑ 08-8979 0145, 1800 500 401; www.gagudju lodgecooinda.com.au; unpowered/powered sites $36/46, dm $57, budget/lodge r from $155/295; ✳@☒) is the most popular accommodation resort in the park. It's a modern oasis but, even with 380 camp sites, facilities can get very stretched. The budget air-con units share camping ground facilities and are compact and comfy enough (but for this money should be more than glorified sheds). The lodge rooms are spacious and more comfortable, sleeping up to four people. There's also a grocery shop, tour desk, fuel pump and the excellent open-air **Barra Bar & Bistro** (mains $15-36; ☺ breakfast, lunch & dinner) here too.

The turn-off to the Cooinda accommodation complex and Yellow Water wetlands is 47km down the Kakadu Hwy from the Arnhem Hwy intersection. Just off the Kakadu Hwy, 2km south of the Cooinda turn-off, is the scrubby **Mardugal camping ground** (adult/child $10/free)– an excellent year-round camping area with shower and toilets.

## Cooinda to Pine Creek

This southern section of the park sees far fewer tour buses. Though it's unlikely you'll have dreamy Maguk (Barramundi Gorge; 45km south of Cooinda and 10km along a corrugated 4WD track) to yourself, you might time it right to have the glorious natural pool and falls between just a few of you. Forty-odd kilometres further south is the turn-off to Gunlom (Waterfall Creek), another superb escarpment waterfall, plunge pool and camping area. It's located 37km along an unsealed road, again 4WD recommended. Walk the steep **Waterfall Walk** (1km, one hour) here, which affords incredible views.

Located just outside the park's southern boundary, the **Goymarr Tourist Resort** (☑ 08-8975 4564; Kakadu Hwy; unpowered/powered sites $20/30, dm $20, budget/motel d $65/125) has a variety of accommodation options, a bistro and a bar. If you are coming into Kakadu from the south, there's a small information office and art gallery housed in an orange shed where you can buy a park pass.

## 🏃 Activities

**Yurmikmik Walks**　　　　　　　　WALKING
On the road to Gunlom is the start of a series of interconnected walks leading first through woodlands and monsoon forest to **Boulder Creek** (2km, 45 minutes), then on to the **Lookout** (5km, 1½ to two hours), with views over rugged ridges, and **Motor Car Falls** (7.5km, four hours).

## ❶ Information

About 200,000 people visit Kakadu between April and October, so expect some tour-bus action at sites like Ubirr and Yellow Water. Consider spending some time bushwalking and camping in the south of the park – it's less visited but inimitably impressive.

Admission to the park is via a 14-day **Park Pass** (adult/child $25/free): pick one up (along with the excellent *Visitor Guide* booklet) from Bowali visitor information centre, Tourism Top End in Darwin, Gagudju Lodge Cooinda, Goymarr Tourist Resort, or Katherine visitor information centre. Carry it with you at all times, as rangers conduct spot checks (penalties apply for nonpayment). Fuel is available at Kakadu Resort, Cooinda, Goymarr Tourist Resort and Jabiru. Jabiru has a shopping complex with a supermarket, post office, a Westpac bank and newsagency.

Accommodation prices in Kakadu vary tremendously depending on the season – resort rates can drop by as much as 50% during the Wet.

The first-rate **Bowali Visitor Information Centre** (☑ 08-8938 1121; www.kakadunational parkaustralia.com/bowali_visitors_center.htm; Kakadu Hwy, Jabiru; ☺ 8am-5pm) has walk-through displays that sweep you across the land, explaining Kakadu's ecology from Aboriginal and non-Aboriginal perspectives. The helpful staffed info booth has details on walks and the plants and animals you might encounter along the way. The 'What's On' flier details where and when to catch a free and informative park ranger talk. The centre is about 2.5km south of the Arnhem Hwy intersection; a 1km walking track connects it with Jabiru.

The Northern Land Council issues permits (adult/child $16.50/free) to visit Gunbalanya (Oenpelli), across the East Alligator River.

## ❶ Getting There & Around

Many people choose to access Kakadu on a tour, which shuffles them around the major sights with the minimum of hassles. But it's just as easy with your own wheels, if you know what kinds of road conditions your trusty steed can handle (Jim Jim Falls and Twin Falls, for example, are 4WD-access only).

**Greyhound Australia** (www.greyhound.com. au) runs a daily return coach service from Darwin to Cooinda ($89, 4½ hours) via Jabiru ($65, 3½ hours).

# Arnhem Land

Arnhem Land is a vast, overwhelming and mysterious corner of the Northern Territory. About the size of the state of Victoria and with a population of only around 17,000, mostly Yolngu people, this Aboriginal reserve is one of Australia's last great untouched wilderness areas. Most people live on outstations, combining traditional practices with modern Western ones, so they might go out for a hunt and be back in time to watch the 6pm news. Outside commercial interests and visits are highly regulated through a permit system, designed to protect the environment, the rock art and ceremonial grounds. *Balanda* (white people) are unaware of the locations of burial grounds and ceremonial lands. Basically, you need a specific purpose for entering, usually to visit an arts centre, in order to be granted a permit. If you're travelling far enough to warrant an overnight stay, you'll need to organise accommodation (which is in short supply). It's easy to visit Gunbalanya (Oenpelli) and its arts centre, just over the border, either on a tour or independently. Elsewhere, it's best to travel with a tour, which will include the necessary permit(s) to enter Aboriginal lands.

## ☞ Tours

**Arnhemlander**
**Cultural & Heritage Tour**          SIGHTSEEING
(☑1800 895 179; www.kakaduculturaltours.com. au; adult/child $229/183) 4WD tours to the Mikinj (Crocodile Nest) Valley and Injalak Art Centre at Gunbalanya (Oenpelli).

**Davidson's Arnhemland Safaris** SIGHTSEEING
(☑08-8927 5240; www.arnhemland-safaris.com) Experienced operator taking tours to Mt Borradaile, north of Oenpelli. Meals, guided tours, fishing and safari camp accommodation are included in the daily price (from $750); transfers from Darwin can be arranged.

**Venture North Australia**          WILDERNESS
(☑08-8927 5500; www.northernaustralia.com; 4-/5-day tour $2290/2590) 4WD tours to remote areas; features expert guidance on rock art. It also has a safari camp near Smith Point on the Cobourg Peninsula.

**Lord's Kakadu &**
**Arnhemland Safaris**          SIGHTSEEING
(☑08-8948 2200; www.lords-safaris.com; tours adult/child $215/170) One-day trip into Arnhem Land (Gunbalanya) from Jabiru (or Darwin adult/child $245/195), visiting Oenpelli with an Aboriginal-guided walk around Injalak Hill rock-art site.

**Nomad Tours**          SIGHTSEEING
(☑08-8987 8085; www.banubanu.com; tours from 3-day $2188) Luxury small-group tours from Nhulunbuy including fishing charters, 4WD and cultural tours.

**Gove Diving & Fishing Charters**     FISHING
(☑08-8987 3445; www.govefish.com.au) Variety of fishing, diving and snorkelling, and wilderness trips from Nhulunbuy. Half-/full-day fishing trips costs $205/305.

## Gunbalanya (Oenpelli)
POP 1121
Gunbalanya is a small Aboriginal community 17km into Arnhem Land across the East Alligator River from the Border Store in Kakadu. The drive in itself is worth it with brilliant green wetlands and spectacular escarpments all around. Road access is only possible between May and October: check the tides at Cahill's Crossing on the East Alligator River before setting out so you don't get stuck on the other side.

A permit is required to visit the town, usually issued for visits to the **Injalak Arts & Crafts Centre** (www.injalak.com; ⊗ 8am-5pm Mon-Fri, 8.30am-2pm Sat). At this centre, artists and craftspeople produce traditional paintings on bark and paper, plus didgeridoos, pandanus weavings and baskets, and screen-printed fabrics, either at the arts centre or on remote outstations throughout Arnhem Land.

As you walk around the verandah of the arts centre to see the artists at work (morning only), peer out over the wetland at the rear to the escarpment and **Injalak Hill** (Long Tom Dreaming). Knowledgeable local guides lead tours to see the fine rock-art galleries here. The three-hour tours (bookings essential) cost from $150 per group. Although it may be possible to join a tour as a walk-in, it's generally best to book a tour from Jabiru or Darwin.

DARWIN TO ULURU ARNHEM LAND

The **Northern Land Council** (☎08-8938 3000, 1800 645 299; www.nlc.org.au; 3 Government Bldg, Flinders St, Jabiru; ◷8am-4.30pm Mon-Fri) issues permits (adult/child $16.50/free) to visit Injalak, usually on the spot. It also provides tide times for the East Alligator River, which is impassable at high tide.

## Cobourg Peninsula

The wilderness of this peninsula forms the **Garig Gunak Barlu National Park** (www.nretas.nt.gov.au/national-parks-and-reserves/parks/find/gariggunak) which includes the surrounding sea. In the turquoise water you'll likely see dolphins and turtles, and – what most people come for – a threadfin salmon thrashing on the end of your line.

On the shores of Port Essington are the stone ruins and headstones from Victoria settlement – Britain's 1838 attempt to establish a military outpost.

At Algarlarlgarl (Black Point) there's a **ranger station** (☎08-8979 0244) with a visitor information and cultural centre, and the **Garig Store** (☎08-8979 0455; ◷4-6pm Mon-Sat), which sells basic provisions, ice and camping gas.

Two permits are required to visit the Cobourg Peninsula: for a transit pass ($12.10 per vehicle) to drive through Aboriginal land contact the Northern Land Council (p150); for permission to stay overnight in the national park contact the **Cobourg Peninsula Sanctuary & Marine Park Board** (☎08-8999 4814; www.nretas.nt.gov.au/national-parks-and-reserves/parks/find/gariggunak). The overnight fee is $232.10 per vehicle, which covers up to five people for seven days and includes camping and transit pass.

There are two camping grounds in the park with shower, toilet, BBQs and limited bore water; generators are allowed in one area. Camping fees (per person per day $16.50) are covered by your vehicle permit, but if you fly in you'll have to pay them. Other accommodation is available in pricey fishing resorts.

### ⓘ Getting There & Away

The quickest route here is by private charter flight, which can be arranged by accommodation providers. The track to Cobourg starts at Gunbalanya (Oenpelli) and is accessible by 4WD vehicles only from May to October. The 270km drive to Black Point from the East Alligator River takes about four hours.

## Eastern Arnhem Land

The wildly beautiful coast and country of Eastern Arnhem Land (www.ealta.org) is really off the beaten track. About 4000 people live in the region's main settlement, Nhulunbuy, built to service the bauxite mine here. The 1963 plans to establish a manganese mine were hotly protested by the traditional owners, the Yolngu people; though mining proceeded, the case became an important step in establishing land rights. Some of the country's most respected art comes out of this region too, including bark paintings, carved mimi figures, *yidaki* (didgeridoo), woven baskets and mats, and jewellery.

**Nambara Arts & Crafts Aboriginal Gallery** (Melville Bay Rd, Nhulunbuy) sells art and crafts from northeast Arnhem Land and often has artists in residence. **Buku Larrnggay Mulka Art Centre & Museum** (www.yirrkala.com; Yirrkala; museum admission $2; ◷8am-4.30pm Mon-Fri, 9am-noon Sat), 20km southeast of Nhulunbuy in Yirrkala, is one of Arnhem Land's best. No permit is required to visit from Nhulunbuy or Gove Airport.

Overland travel through Arnhem Land from Katherine requires a permit (free) from the Northern Land Council (p150). The **Dhimurru Land Management Aboriginal Corporation** (☎08-8987 3992; www.dhimurru.com.au; Arnhem Rd, Nhulunbuy) issues recreation permits ($35/45 for seven days/two months) for visits to particular recreation areas in Eastern Arnhem Land – check the website for details.

### ⓘ Getting There & Away

**Airnorth** (☎1800 627 474; www.airnorth.com.au) and Qantaslink (p170) flies from Darwin to Gove (for Nhulunbuy) daily from $355 one way. Overland, it's a 10-hour 4WD trip and only possible in the Dry. The Central Arnhem Hwy to Gove leaves the Stuart Hwy (Rte 87) 52km south of Katherine.

# KATHERINE TO ALICE SPRINGS

The Stuart Hwy from Darwin to Alice Springs is still referred to as 'the Track' – it has been since WWII, when it was a dirt track connecting the Territory's two main towns, roughly following the Overland Telegraph Line. It's dead straight most of the way and gets drier and flatter as you head south, but there are a few notable diversions.

# Katherine

POP 9187

Katherine is considered a big town in this part of the world and you'll certainly feel like you've arrived somewhere after the long trip up the highway. Its namesake river is the first permanent running water on the road north from Alice Springs. In the Wet the river swells dramatically and has been responsible for some devastating floods – the worst in memory was Australia Day 1998, when rising waters inundated the surrounding countryside and left a mark up to 2m high on Katherine's buildings.

Katherine is probably best known for the Nitmiluk (Katherine Gorge) National Park to the east, and the town makes an obvious base, with plenty of accommodation and some decent restaurants. It also has quite a few attractions of its own, including a thriving indigenous arts community, thermal springs and a few museums.

The Katherine area is the traditional home of the Jawoyn and Dagoman Aboriginal people. Following land claims they have received the title to large parcels of land, including Nitmiluk National Park. You'll see a lot of Aborigines around town, in from outlying communities for a few days to meet friends and hang out. No one seems too bothered by the disconcerting mix of country and retro pop that pipes into the main street from loudspeakers day and night.

## ◎ Sights & Activities

**Katherine Low Level Nature Park**      PARK
(www.ourterritory.com/katherine_nt/low_level.htm) The park is a scenic spot on the banks of the babbling Katherine River, just off the Victoria Hwy (Rte 1) 4km from town. It has a popular dry-season swimming hole linked to crystalline **thermal pools** (access via Murray St) and the town by a tree-lined shared cycle way/footpath.

**Djilpin Arts**      ART GALLERY
(www.djilpinarts.org.au; Katherine Tce; ⊙9am-4pm Mon-Fri) This Katherine gallery is Aboriginal owned and represents art from the Ghunmarn Culture Centre, in the remote community of Beswick. Paintings, weavings and termite-bored didjeridoos.

**Top Didj Cultural Experience & Art Gallery**      ART GALLERY
(www.topdidj.com; cnr Gorge Rd & Jaensch Rd; cultural experience adult/child/family $50/28/140; ⊙9am-6pm May-Oct, cultural experience 9.30am & 2.30pm Sun-Fri, 9.30am & 1.30pm Sat) Run by the owners of the Katherine Art Gallery, this is a good place to see Aboriginal artists at work. The cultural experience is hands on with fire sticks, spear throwing, painting and basket weaving.

**Katherine Museum**      MUSEUM
(Gorge Rd; adult/child $7.50/3.50; ⊙9am-4pm) The museum is in the old airport terminal, about 3km from town on the road to the gorge. The original Gypsy Moth biplane flown by Dr Clyde Fenton, the first Flying Doctor, is housed here, along with plenty of interesting old rusty trucks. There's a good selection of historical photos, including a display on the 1998 flood.

**School of the Air**      SCHOOL
(☑08-8972 1833; www.schools.nt.edu.au/ksa; Giles St; adult/child $5/2; ⊙Mar-Nov) At the School of the Air, 1.5km from the town centre, you can listen into a class and see how kids in the remote outback are educated in the virtual world. Guided tours are held at 9am, 10am and 11am Monday to Friday; bookings preferred.

**Katherine Public Art & Craft Galley**      ART GALLERY
(www.ktc.nt.gov.au; Stuart Hwy, Civic Centre; ⊙8am-3pm Mon-Fri) FREE The low-key gallery is home to the Katherine Collection, a community-owned collection of interesting local art. There are a couple of amazing photos from the '98 flood here, too.

**Springvale Homestead**      HOMESTEAD
(www.travelnorth.com.au; Shadforth Rd) Alfred Giles established Springvale Homestead in 1879 after he drove 2000 cattle and horses and 12,000 head of sheep from Adelaide to the site in 19 months. It claims to be the oldest cattle station in the Northern Territory. The stone homestead still stands by the river, about 7km southwest of town, and the surrounding riverside property is now a caravan and camping resort. There's a free homestead tour at 3pm daily (except Saturday) from May to September. Canoe hire per hour/two hours/day costs $20/25/75. There's also accommodation here.

## ☞ Tours

**Gecko Canoeing & Trekking**      CANOEING, BUSHWALKING
(☑08-8972 2224, 1800 634 319; www.geckocanoeing.com.au) ✍ Offers some exhilarating

# Katherine

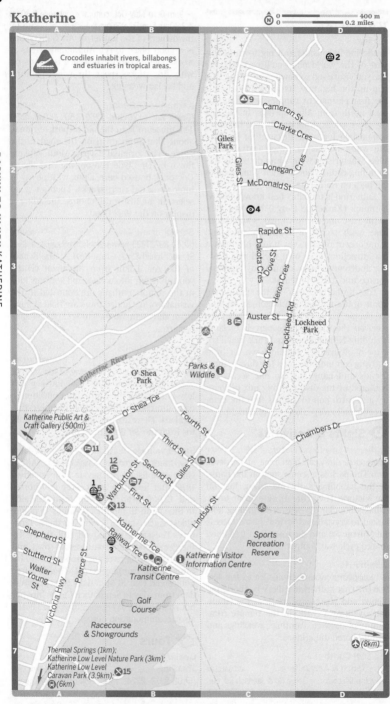

N

0            400 m
0            0.2 miles

Crocodiles inhabit rivers, billabongs and estuaries in tropical areas.

Cameron St
Clarke Cres
Giles Park
Giles St
Donegan Cres
McDonald St
Rapide St
Dakota Cres
Dove St
Heron Cres
Lockheed Rd
Auster St
Lockheed Park
Cox Cres
Katherine River
O' Shea Park
Parks & Wildlife
O' Shea Tce
Fourth St
Chambers Dr
Katherine Public Art & Craft Gallery (500m)
Third St
Giles St
Second St
Warburton St
First St
Katherine Tce
Lindsay St
Sports Recreation Reserve
Shepherd St
Stutterd St
Walter Young St
Railway Tce
Pearce St
Victoria Hwy
Katherine Transit Centre
Katherine Visitor Information Centre
Golf Course
Racecourse & Showgrounds

Thermal Springs (1km);
Katherine Low Level Nature Park (3km);
Katherine Low Level Caravan Park (3.9km);
(6km)

# Katherine

guided canoe trips on the more remote stretches of the Katherine River. Trips include three days ($810) on the Katherine River and six days ($1390) on the Daly and Flora Rivers. A five-day hike along the Jatbula Trail in Nitmiluk National Park costs $1290. Gecko can also shuttle Jatbula Trail hikers from Edyth Falls back to Katherine ($50) or Nitmiluk National Park HQ ($66). Minimum numbers apply.

**Crocodile Night Adventure**          CRUISE
(☑1800 089 103; www.travelnorth.com.au; cruises adult/child $69/45; ⊙6.30pm May-Oct) At Springvale Homestead, this evening cruise seeks out crocs and other nocturnal wildlife on the Katherine River. Includes BBQ dinner and drinks.

**Travel North**          SIGHTSEEING
(☑08-8971 9999, 1800 089 103; www.travelnorth. com.au; 6 Katherine Tce, Transit Centre) Katherine-based tour operator with a range of tours to Kakadu, Arnhem Land and Litchfield, and full-day Katherine town tours. Also booking agent for the *Ghan* and Greyhound.

## ✨ Festivals & Events

**Katherine Country Music Muster**          MUSIC
(www.kcmm.com.au) 'We like both kinds of music: country *and* western.' Plenty of live mu-

sic in the pubs and entertainment at the Tick Market Lindsay St Complex on a weekend in May or June. Check website for actual dates.

**Katherine District Show**          AGRICULTURAL
(www.katherineshow.org.au) Annual agricultural show at the Katherine Showgrounds, with the usual rides, stalls and pungent animals in July.

## ⌷ Sleeping

**Coco's International Backpackers** HOSTEL $
(☑08-8971 2889; www.21firstst.com; 21 First St; camping per person $18, dm $28) With travellers idly strumming on guitars and swapping outback tales, you'll feel like you've walked into an old Asian overland bolthole here. Coco's is a real backpackers and well-known to those on marathon cycling trips. It's a converted home where the owner chats with the guests and offers sage advice on didgeridoos from his tin shed gallery. Aboriginal artists are often here painting didgeridoos.

**Palm Court
Kookaburra Backpackers** HOSTEL $
(☑08-8972 2722, 1800 626 722; www.palmcourt backpackers.com; cnr Third & Giles Sts; dm $27, motel d $69, self-contained unit $89; ❋ @ ⊠) This well-equipped, welcoming backpackers occupies a retired motel, clad in faux stone in an attempt to resemble some kind of castle. Scruffy international knights and maidens enjoy rooms with bathrooms, fridges and TVs. It's a short walk to town or there's a free shuttle to the Transit Centre.

**Katherine Low
Level Caravan Park**          CARAVAN PARK $
(☑08-8972 3962; www.katherinelowlevel.com.au; Shadforth Rd; unpowered/powered sites $37/40, en suite cabin d $175; ❋ ⊛ ⊠) A well-manicured park with plenty of shady sites, a great swimming pool adjoining a bar and an excellent bistro (mains $20 to $25) that is sheltered by a magnificent fig tree. The amenities are first rate, making it the pick of the town's several caravan parks. It's about 5km along the Victoria Hwy from town and across the Low Level bridge.

**Springvale Homestead**   CARAVAN PARK, MOTEL $
(☑1800 089 103, 08-8972 1355; www.travelnorth. com.au; Shadforth Rd; unpowered/powered sites $20/27, d/f $69/79; ❋ ⊠) In a bushland setting by the Katherine River, about 7km west of town, this historic homestead is a lovely place to camp. There's plenty of space, a palm-shaded pool and a bistro open for breakfast

and dinner (mains $19 to $25). Rooms are motel-style (old but clean and good value), and there are free homestead tours at 3pm daily (except Saturday) in the Dry.

**Knott's Crossing Resort**  RESORT $$
(☑08-8972 2511, 1800 222 511; www.knottscrossing.com.au; cnr Cameron & Giles Sts; unpowered/powered sites $27/39, cabin/motel d from $99/149; ❄@🖥🌊) Knott's Crossing is more a motel and cabin resort than camping ground, but it's a great spot for caravans and campervans, too. Everything is packed pretty tightly into the tropical gardens here, but it's very professionally run and there's a bar and bistro.

**Katherine River Lodge Motel**  MOTEL $$
(☑08-8971 0266; www.katherineriverlodge.net; 50 Giles St; s/d from $95/105; ❄@🌊) One of Katherine's best-value motels (and definitely the friendliest), this large complex (three three-storey blocks) has spotless rooms in a tropical garden. The attached restaurant (mains $18 to $28) plates up filling meals nightly, or you can fire up the BBQ outside. You couldn't say the rooms are contemporary, but they're tidy and clean.

**Paraway Motel**  MOTEL $$
(☑08-8972 2644; www.parawaymotel.com.au; cnr First St & O'Shea Tce; d from $135; ❄🖥🌊) This smart motel is as neat as a pin, and its location is handy to the main street but quiet enough. Standard motel rooms are very clean, with typically tropical tile-and-floral-bedspread decor, plus there are spa rooms and a decent restaurant, too.

**St Andrews Apartments**  APARTMENTS $$$
(☑08-8971 2288, 1800 686 106; www.standrewsapts.com.au; 27 First St; apt $220-260; ❄🖥🌊) In the heart of town, these serviced apartments are great for families or if you're pining for a few home comforts. The two-bedroom apartments sleep four (six if you use the sofa bed), and come with fully equipped kitchen and lounge/dining area. Nifty little BBQ decks are attached to the ground-floor units.

## 🍴 Eating

**Coffee Club**  CAFE $
(www.coffeeclub.com.au; cnr Katherine Tce & Warburton St; meals $12-18; ⏱6.30am-5pm Mon-Fri, 7am-4pm Sat & Sun) Albeit a chain, the Coffee Club is the cafe of choice in Katherine, with huge gourmet breakfasts, decent coffee and plenty of options for a light or filling lunch.

**Katherine Country Club**  LICENSED CLUB $$
(www.katherinecountryclub.com.au; 3034 Pearce St; mains $15-25; ⏱10am-late) Overlooking Katherine's nine-hole golf course, this boozy bistro is a real locals' haunt. You don't have to be a club member (or even know how to swing a club) – just turn up and enjoy big steaks, burgers and schnitzels, and Aerosmith on the jukebox. 'The burgers are better at the Golfy!'

**Savannah Bar &
Restaurant**  MODERN AUSTRALIAN $$
(☑08-8972 2511; www.knottscrossing.com.au/restaurant; Knott's Crossing Resort, cnr Giles & Cameron Sts; mains $24-46; ⏱5.30pm-late) This intimate little bistro at Knott's Crossing Resort is a local fave. Wagyu beef, lobster and prawn pasta, crocodile spring rolls and grilled barramundi grace the menu, and you can eat inside or alfresco by the pool.

**Katherine Club**  LICENSED CLUB $$
(www.katherineclubinc.com; cnr Second St & O'Shea Tce; mains $19-32; ⏱11.30am-2pm Mon-Fri, 6.30-8.30pm Mon-Sat) Close to the town centre, the Club ain't fancy, but you can rely on satisfying bistro meals (steak, schnitzel and barra), and the kids are welcome. Tuesday is roast night, Wednesday is pizza and pasta, Thursday it's schnitzels. Sign in as a visitor at the fortress-like front desk, or find a member to tag along with.

## ℹ Information

**Katherine Art Gallery** (☑08-8971 1051; www.katherineartgallery.com.au; 12 Katherine Tce; ⏱9am-6pm daily May-Oct, 10am-5pm Mon-Fri, 10am-2pm Sat Nov-Apr) A commercial indigenous gallery doubling as an internet cafe.

**Katherine Hospital** (☑08-8973 9211; www.health.nt.gov.au; Giles St) About 3km north of town, with an emergency department.

**Katherine Visitor Information Centre** (☑1800 653 142; www.visitkatherine.com.au; cnr Lindsay St & Stuart Hwy; ⏱8.30am-5pm daily in the Dry, 8.30am-5pm Mon-Fri, 10am-2pm Sat & Sun in the Wet) Modern, air-con information centre stocking information on all areas of the Northern Territory. Pick up the handy *Katherine Region Visitor Guide*.

**Parks & Wildlife** (☑08-8973 8888; www.nt.gov.au/nreta/parks; 32 Giles St; ⏱8am-4.20pm) National park information and notes.

## ℹ Getting There & Around

Katherine is a major road junction: from here the Stuart Hwy tracks north and south, and the Victoria Hwy heads west to Kununurra in WA.

Greyhound Australia (www.greyhound.com. au) has regular services between Darwin and Alice Springs, Queensland or WA. Buses stop at **Katherine Transit Centre** (☑ 08-8971 9999; 6 Katherine Tce). One-way fares from Katherine include: Darwin ($94, four hours), Alice Springs ($315, 16 hours), Tennant Creek ($207, 8½ hours) and Kununurra ($146, 4½ hours).

The *Ghan* train, operated by **Great Southern Rail** (www.gsr.com.au), travels between Adelaide and Darwin twice a week, stopping at Katherine for four hours – enough for a whistlestop tour to Katherine Gorge! Katherine train station is off the Victoria Hwy, 9km southwest of town. Fares to/from Katherine are the same as per Darwin. **Nitmiluk Tours** (☑ 1300 146 743; www.nitmiluktours.com.au; Katherine Tce; ☺ 9am-5pm Mon-Sat) runs shuttles between the station and town.

# Around Katherine

## Cutta Cutta Caves Nature Park

About 30km south of Katherine, turn your back on the searing sun and dip down 15m below terra firma into this mazelike limestone cave system. The 1499-hectare Cutta Cutta Caves Nature Park (☑ 08-8972 1940; www.nretas.nt.gov.au/national-parks-and-reserves/ parks/find/cuttacuttacaves; tours adult/child $17/8.50; ☺ 8.30am-4.30pm, guided tours 9am, 10am, 11am, 1pm, 2pm & 3pm) has a unique ecology and you'll be sharing the space with brown tree snakes and pythons, plus the endangered ghost bats and orange horseshoe bats that they feed on. Cutta Cutta is a Jawoyn name meaning many stars; it was taboo for Aborigines to enter the cave, which they believed was where the stars were kept during the day. Admission by tour only.

## Nitmiluk (Katherine Gorge) National Park

Spectacular Katherine Gorge forms the backbone of the 2920-sq-km Nitmiluk (Katherine Gorge) National Park (www. nt.gov.au/nreta/parks/find/nitmiluk.html), about 30km from Katherine. A series of 13 deep sandstone gorges have been carved out by the Katherine River on its journey from Arnhem Land to the Timor Sea. It is a hauntingly beautiful place – though it can get crowded in peak season – and a mustdo from Katherine. In the Dry the tranquil river is perfect for a paddle, but in the Wet the deep still waters and dividing rapids are engulfed by an awesome torrent that churns through the gorge. Plan to spend at least a full day canoeing or cruising on the river and bushwalking.

The traditional owners are the Jawoyn Aboriginal people who jointly manage Nitmiluk with Parks & Wildlife. Nitmiluk Tours (p194) manages accommodation, cruises and activities within the park.

## ◎ Sights

**Leliyn (Edith Falls)**      NATURE RESERVE
Reached off the Stuart Hwy 40km north of Katherine and a further 20km along a sealed road, Leliyn is an idyllic, safe haven for swimming and hiking. The moderate **Leliyn Trail** (2.6km loop, 1½ hours) climbs into escarpment country through grevillea and spinifex and past scenic lookouts (Bemang is best in the afternoon) to the Upper Pool, where the moderate **Sweetwater Pool Trail** (8.6km return, three to five hours) branches off. The peaceful Sweetwater Pool has a small **camping ground** (per person $3.30, plus $50 refundable deposit); overnight permits are available at the kiosk.

The main Lower Pool – a gorgeous, mirror-flat swimming lagoon – is a quick 150m dash from the car park. The Parks & Wildlife **camping ground** (☑ 08-8975 4869; adult/child $12/6) next to the car park has grassy sites, lots of shade, toilets, showers, a laundry and facilities for the disabled. Fees are paid at the **kiosk** (☺ 8am-6pm May-Oct, 9.30am-3pm Nov-Apr), which sells snacks and basic supplies. Nearby is a picnic area with BBQs and tables.

## ☆ Activities

### Bushwalking
The park has around 120km of marked walking tracks, ranging from 2km stretches to 66km multinight hikes. Overnight hikers must register at the Nitmiluk Centre. There's a $50 refundable deposit for any overnight walk and a camping fee of $3.30 per person per night. The Nitmiluk Centre has maps and info on the full range of walks.

**Barrawei (Lookout) Loop**      BUSHWALKING
Starting with a short, steep climb this walk (3.7km loop, two hours, moderate difficulty) provides good views over the Katherine River.

**Butterfly Gorge**      BUSHWALKING
A challenging, shady walk (12km return, 4½ hours) through a pocket of monsoon

rainforest, often with butterflies, leads to midway along the second gorge and a deep-water swimming spot.

### Jawoyn Valley
BUSHWALKING

A difficult (40km loop, overnight) wilderness trail leading off the Eighth Gorge walk into a valley with rock outcrops and rock-art galleries.

### Jatbula Trail
BUSHWALKING

This renowned walk (66km one way, five days, difficult) to Leliyn (Edith Falls) climbs the Arnhem Land escarpment, passing the swamp-fed Biddlecombe Cascades, Crystal Falls, the Amphitheatre and the Sweetwater Pool. This walk can only be done one way (ie you can't walk from Leliyn to Katherine Gorge). It is closed from October to April, and a minimum of two walkers are required. A ferry service ($7) takes you across the gorge to kick things off.

### Canoeing

Nothing beats exploring the gorges in your own boat, and lots of travellers canoe at least as far as the first or second gorge. Bear in mind the intensity of the sun and heat, and the fact that you may have to carry your canoe over the rock bars and rapids that separate the gorges. Pick up the *Canoeing Guide* at the Nitmiluk Centre. If you want to use your own canoe you need to pay a registration fee of $5.50 per person, plus a refundable $50 deposit.

### Nitmiluk Tours
CANOEING

(☑ 08-8972 1253, 1300 146 743; www.nitmiluk tours.com.au) From April to November, Nitmiluk Tours hires out single/double canoes

for a half-day ($48/71, departing 8am and 1pm) or full day ($62/90, departing 8am), including the use of a splash-proof drum for cameras and other gear (it's not fully waterproof), a map and a life jacket. The half-day hire only allows you to paddle up the first gorge; with the full day you can get up as far as the third gorge depending on your level of fitness – start early. The canoe shed is at the boat ramp by the main car park, about 500m beyond the Nitmiluk Centre. There's a $50 deposit required for half-day hires.

You also can be a little more adventurous and take the canoes out overnight for $119/133 a single/double, plus $3.30 for a camping permit – there are camp sites at the fifth, sixth, eighth and ninth gorges. Bookings are essential as overnight permits are limited and there is a $60 deposit. Don't take this trip lightly though.

### Gorge Cruises

### Nitmiluk Tours
CRUISES

(☑ 08-8972 1253, 1300 146 743; www.nitmiluk tours.com.au; 2hr cruise adult/child $73/41, 4hr cruise $91/46, breakfast cruise $88/58, sunset cruise $142/126) An easy way to see far into the gorge is on a cruise. Bookings on some cruises can be tight in the peak season; make your reservation a day in advance. The two-hour cruise goes to the second gorge and visits a rock-art gallery (including 800m walk). Departures are at 9am, 11am, 1pm and 3pm daily year-round depending on river level. There's wheelchair access to the top of the first gorge only. The four-hour cruise goes to the third gorge and includes refreshments and a chance to swim. This

---

## GHUNMARN CULTURAL CENTRE

If you're interested in seeing genuine Aboriginal art produced by local communities, it's worth detouring off the Stuart Hwy to this remote cultural centre.

The small community of Beswick is reached via the sealed Central Arnhem Hwy 56km east of the Stuart Hwy on the southern fringes of Arnhem Land. Here you'll find the **Ghunmarn Culture Centre** (☑ 08-8977 4250; www.djilpinarts.org.au; Beswick; ☺ 9.30am-4pm Mon-Fri Apr-Nov), opened in 2007, and displaying local artworks, prints, carvings, weaving and didgeridoos from western Arnhem Land. The centre also features the Blanasi Collection, a permanent exhibition of works by elders from the western Arnhem Land region. Visitors are welcome to visit the centre without a permit – call ahead to check that it's open. If you can't get out here, drop in to Djilpin Arts (p189) in Katherine.

A very special festival at Beswick is Walking With Spirits (p160) – magical performances of traditional corroborees staged in conjunction with the Australian Shakespeare Company. It's held on the first weekend in August. Camping is possible at Beswick Falls over this weekend but advance bookings are essential.

cruise leaves at 9am daily from April to November, plus at 11am and 1pm May to August.

There's also a more leisurely two-hour breakfast cruise, leaving at 7am May to October and a sunset cruise, sailing at 4.30pm on Monday, Wednesday, Friday, Saturday and Sunday from May to December, with a candlelit buffet dinner and champagne.

### Scenic Flights

**Nitmiluk Tours** SCENIC FLIGHTS
(☑1300 146 743; www.nitmiluktours.com.au; flights from $85 per person) Nitmiluk Tours offers a variety of flights ranging from an eight-minute buzz over the first gorge (per person $85) to an 18-minute flight over all 13 gorges ($232). The Adventure Swim Tour ($449) drops you at a secluded swimming hole for an hour or so, and there are broader tours that take in Aboriginal rock-art sites and Kakadu National Park. Book at the Nitmiluk Centre.

### 🛏 Sleeping

There are bush-camping sites for overnight walkers throughout the park, and permanent camping grounds near the Nitmiluk Visitor Centre and at Leliyn (Edith Falls). The exciting new Cicada Lodge is due to open in 2013.

**Nitmiluk National Park Campground** CAMPGROUND $
(☑08-8972 1253, 1300 146 743; www.nitmiluktours. com.au; unpowered/powered sites $36/40, safari tents $124; ✹) Plenty of grass and shade, hot showers, toilets, BBQs, a laundry and a kiosk by the good-lookin' swimming pool. Wallabies and goannas are frequent visitors. There's a 'tent village' here with permanent safari tents sleeping two people. Book at the Nitmiluk Centre.

**Nitmiluk Chalets** CABINS $$
(☑08-8972 1253, 1300 146 743; www.nitmiluktours. com.au; 1-/2-bedroom cabins $195/245; ✹) Next door to the caravan park, these cabins are a serviceable choice if you'd rather have a solid roof over your head (and a flat-screen TV). Access to all the caravan park facilities (pool, BBQs, kiosk etc).

**Cicada Lodge** BOUTIQUE HOTEL $$$
(☑1300 146 743; www.cicadalodge.com.au; Nitmiluk National Park; d inc breakfast $645; ✹🛜✹) Under construction at the time of research, this luxury lodge, also near the visitor centre, has been architecturally designed to

meld modern sophistication and traditional Jawoyn themes. It will have just 18 luxury rooms overlooking the Katherine River. Packages including gorge and dinner cruises will be available.

### ℹ Information

The **Nitmiluk Centre** (☑08-8972 1253, 1300 146 743; www.nitmiluktours.com.au; ⊙7am-6pm) has excellent displays and information on the park's geology, wildlife, the traditional owners (the Jawoyn) and European history. There's also a restaurant here (snacks and meals $5 to $20), and a desk for **Parks & Wildlife** (☑08-8972 1886), which has information sheets on a wide range of marked walking tracks that start here and traverse the picturesque country south of the gorge. Registration for overnight walks and camping permits ($3.30 per night) is from 8am to 1pm; canoeing permits are also issued. Check at the centre for information on ranger talks.

### ℹ Getting There & Away

It's 30km by sealed road from Katherine to the Nitmiluk Centre, and a few hundred metres further to the car park, where the gorge begins and the cruises start.

Daily transfers between Katherine and the gorge are run by **Nitmiluk Tours** (☑08-8972 1253, 1300 146 743; www.nitmiluktours.com.au; 27 Katherine Tce, Shop 2, Katherine; adult/child return $27/19), departing from the Nitmiluk Town Booking Office and also picking up at local accommodation places on request. Buses leave Katherine at 7.30am, 12.15pm and 5pm, returning from Nitmiluk at 8am, 1.15pm and 5.30pm.

# Katherine to Western Australia

The sealed Victoria Hwy – part of the Savannah Way – stretches 513km from Katherine to Kununurra in WA. It winds through diverse landscapes, with extensive tracts annexed as cattle stations in the 1880s, which became the economy's backbone in the post-war recovery period of the 1950s.

A 4WD will get you into a few out-of-the-way national parks accessed off the Victoria Hwy, or you can meander through semiarid desert and sandstone outcrops until bloated boab trees herald your imminent arrival in WA. All fruits, vegetables, nuts and honey must be left at the quarantine-inspection post on the border. WA time is 1½ hours behind NT time.

## Flora River Nature Park

The irradescent bue-green water of the mineral-rich Flora River precipitates calcium carbonate onto roots and fallen branches creating limestone tufa (spongy rock) dams; the effect is a series of pretty cascades. Within Flora River Nature Park (www.nretas.nt.gov.au/national-parks-and-reserves/parks/find/florariver) there's a camping ground (adult/child $6.60/3.30) at Djarrung with an amenities block. The Flora River has crocs, so there's no swimming. The park will be known as Giwining in the near future.

The park turn-off is 90km southwest of Katherine; the park entrance is a further 32km along a passable dirt road (OK for 2WD cars in the Dry).

## Victoria River Crossing

The red sandstone cliffs surrounding this spot where the highway crosses the Victoria River (194km west of Katherine) create a dramatic setting. Much of this area forms the eastern section of Gregory National Park. The Victoria River Roadhouse Caravan Park (☑08-8975 0744; fax 08-8975 0819; Victoria Hwy; unpowered/powered sites $15/20, d $125), west of the bridge, has a shop, bar and meals ($12 to $29).

## Timber Creek

POP 231

Tiny Timber Creek is the only town between Katherine and Kununurra. It has a pretty big history for such a small place, with an early European exploration aboard the *Tom Tough* requiring repairs to be carried out with local timber (hence the town's name). The expedition's leader, AC Gregory, inscribed his arrival date into a boab; it is still discernable (and is explained in detail through interpretive panels) at **Gregory's Tree**, 15km northwest of town.

The town's Old Police Station Museum (www.nationaltrustnt.org.au; adult/child $4/free; ☉10am-noon Mon-Fri May-Oct), established to smooth relations with pastoralists and indigenous people, is now a museum displaying old police and mining equipment.

A highlight of Timber Creek is the Victoria River Cruise (☑08-8975 0850; www.victoriarivercruise.com; adult/child $85/45; ☉4pm Mon-Sat), which takes you 40km downriver, spotting wildlife and returning in time for a fiery sunset.

The town is dominated by the roadside Timber Creek Hotel & Circle F Caravan Park (☑08-8975 0722; www.timbercreekhotel.com.au; Victoria Hwy; unpowered/powered sites $25/27.50, budget r from $66, motel d $95; ❄ ≋). Enormous trees shade parts of the camping area, which is next to a small creek where there's croc feeding every evening (5pm). The complex includes the Timber Creek Hotel and Fogarty's Store.

## Gregory National Park

The remote and rugged wilderness of the little-visited Gregory National Park (www.nretas.nt.gov.au/national-parks-and-reserves/parks/find/gregory) will swallow you up. Covering 12,860 sq km, it sits at the transitional zone between the tropical and semiarid regions. The park, which will eventually be called Judbarra National Park, consists of old cattle country and is made up of two separate sections: the eastern (Victoria River) section and the much larger Bullita section in the west. While some parts of the park are accessible by 2WD, it's the rough-as-guts, dry-season-only 4WD tracks that are the most rewarding; for these you need to be self-sufficient and to register (call ☑1300 650 730).

Parks & Wildlife (☑08-8975 0888; ☉7am-4.30pm) in Timber Creek can provide park and 4WD notes, and a map to the various walks, camping spots, tracks and the historic homestead and ruggedly romantic original stockyards – a must before heading in. This is crocodile country; swimming isn't safe.

There's 2WD accessible bush camping at Big Horse Creek (adult/child $3.30/1.75), 7km west of Timber Creek.

## Keep River National Park

The remote Keep River National Park (www.nretas.nt.gov.au/national-parks-and-reserves/parks/find/keepriver) is noted for its stunning sandstone formations, beautiful desolation and rock art. Pamphlets detailing walks are available at the start of the excellent trails. Don't miss the rock-art walk (5.5km return, two hours) near Jarnem, and the gorge walk (3km return, two hours) at Jinumum.

The park entrance is just 3km from the WA border. You can reach the park's main points by conventional vehicle during the Dry. A rangers station (☑08-9167 8827) lies 3km into the park from the main road, and there are basic, sandstone-surrounded **camping grounds** (adult/child $3.30/1.65) at Gurrandalng (18km into the park) and Jarnem (32km). Tank water is available at Jarnem.

# Mataranka & Elsey National Park

POP 244

With soothing, warm thermal springs set in pockets of palms and tropical vegetation, you'd be mad not to pull into Mataranka for at least a few hours to soak off the road dust. The small settlement regularly swells with towel-toting visitors shuffling to the thermal pool or the spring-fed Elsey National Park. If you see Mataranka referred to as the 'capital of the Never Never', it's a reference to Jeannie Gunn's 1908 autobiographical novel *We of the Never Never*, about life as a pioneering woman on nearby Elsey Station – the deeds of title of which have since been returned to the Mangarayi indigenous owners.

## ◎ Sights & Activities

Mataranka's crystal-clear **thermal pool**, shrouded in rainforest, is 10km from town beside the Mataranka Homestead Resort. The warm, clear water dappled by filtered light leaking through overhanging palms rejuvenates a lot of bodies on any given day; it's reached via a boardwalk from the resort and can get mighty crowded. About 200m away (keep following the boardwalk) is the Waterhouse River, where you can rent canoes for $10 per hour. **Stevie's Hole**, a natural swimming hole in the cooler Waterhouse River, about 1.5km from the homestead, is rarely crowded.

**Elsey Station Homestead**   HISTORIC BUILDING
(admission by donation; ☉ daylight hours) Outside the Mataranka Homestead Resort entrance is a replica of the Elsey Station Homestead, constructed for the filming of *We of the Never Never*, which is screened daily at noon in the resort bar.

**Never Never Museum**   MUSEUM
(120 Roper Tce; adult/child $3.50/1.50; ☉ 9am-4.30pm Mon-Fri) Back in town, the Never Never Museum has displays on the northern railway, WWII and local history. Access via the Rural Transaction Centre next door.

**Elsey National Park**   NATURE RESERVE
(www.nretas.nt.gov.au/national-parks-and-reserves/parks/find/elsey) The national park adjoins the thermal-pool reserve and offers peaceful **camping**, **fishing** and **walking** along the Waterhouse and Roper Rivers. Bitter Springs is a serene palm-fringed thermal pool within the national park, 3km from Mataranka along the sealed Martin Rd. The almost unnatural blue-green colour of the 34°C water is due to dissolved limestone particles.

## 🛏 Sleeping & Eating

**Jalmurark Camping Area**   CAMPGROUND $
(John Hauser Dr; adult/child $6.60/3.30) Located at 12 Mile Yards in Elsey National Park, this scrubby camping ground has lots of shade, toilets and showers and access to the Roper River and walking trails. There's a kiosk here in the Dry from which you can hire canoes.

**Mataranka Homestead Resort**   CAMPGROUND $
(☎ 08-8975 4544; www.matarankahomestead.com.au; Homestead Rd; unpowered/powered site $24/29, dm/d/cabins $25/89/115; ❄ ⊛) Only metres from the main thermal pool and with a range of budget accommodation, this is a *very* popular option. The large camping ground is dusty but has a few shady areas and decent amenities. The fan-cooled hostel rooms are very basic (linen provided). The air-con motel rooms (also rudimentary) have fridge, TV and bathroom, while the cabins have a kitchenette and sleep up to six people. Book ahead.

**Mataranka Cabins**   CABINS $$
(☎ 08-8975 4838; www.matarankacabins.com.au; 4705 Martin Rd, Bitter Springs; unpowered/powered sites $25/30, cabins $120; ❄ @ 🛜) On the banks of the Little Roper River, only a few hundred metres from Bitter Springs thermal pool, this quiet bush setting has some amazing termite mounds adorning the front paddock. The TV-equipped, open-plan cabins have linen, bathrooms and kitchens, and two can accommodate up to five folks.

**Territory Manor Motel & Caravan Park**   CAMPGROUND, MOTEL $$
(☎ 08-8975 4516; www.matarankamotel.com; Martin Rd; unpowered/powered sites $26/30, s/d $100/115; ❄ @ ⊛) Mataranka's best caravan park with grassy, shaded sites and attractive rammed-earth motel units. Pet barramundi are hand fed in spectacular fashion twice a day. Their cousins are served up in the licensed

bistro (mains $20 to $35) along with steaks, salad etc.

**Stockyard Gallery**                    CAFE $
(www.stockyardgallery.com.au; Stuart Hwy; snacks $5-10; ⊗ breakfast & lunch daily May-Oct, lunch only Nov-Apr) This casual cafe is a little gem. There's a delicious range of homemade snacks (focaccia, sandwiches, cakes, muffins) plus fresh espresso coffee and divine mango smoothies. The art gallery here sells Aboriginal art, books, and souvenirs.

# Barkly Tableland & Gulf Country

East of the Stuart Hwy lies some of the Territory's most remote cattle country, but parts are accessible by sealed road and the rivers and inshore waters of the Gulf coast are regarded as some of the best fishing locales in the country.

## Roper Highway

Not far south of Mataranka on the Stuart Hwy, the mostly sealed single-lane Roper Hwy strikes 175km eastwards to Roper Bar, crossing the paperbark- and pandanus-lined Roper River where freshwater meets saltwater. It's passable only in the Dry. Keen fisherfolk stop here, with accommodation, fuel and supplies available at the **Roper Bar Store** (☑ 08-8975 4636; www.roperbar.com.au; unpowered site $20, s/d $95/115; ⊗ 9am-6pm Mon-Sat). Roper Bar is an access point to Borroloola. Head south along the rough-going Nathan River Rd through **Limmen National Park** (www.nt.gov.au/nreta/parks/find/limmen.html) – high-clearance with two spare tyres is required – and into southeastern Arnhem Land.

Continuing east along the highway for 45km leads to the Aboriginal community of Ngukurr, home to about 1000 people from nine different language groups and cultures. This cultural diversity informs the unique works on show and available to buy from the **Ngukurr Arts Centre** (www.ngukurrarts.com.au; ⊗ 9am-2pm Mon-Fri); no permit is required to visit the centre.

## Carpentaria & Tablelands Highways

Just south of Daly Waters, the sealed Carpentaria Hwy (Hwy 1) heads 378km east to Borroloola, near the Gulf of Carpentaria,

and one of the NT's top barramundi fishing spots. After 267km the Carpentaria Hwy meets the sealed Tablelands Hwy at Cape Crawford. At this intersection is the famous **Heartbreak Hotel** (☑ 08-8975 9928; unpowered/powered sites $16/26, s/d $70/80; ☀). Pitch the tent on the shaded grassy lawn and park yourself on the wide verandah with a cold beer. Breakfast, lunch and dinner (meals $15 to $30) are available.

**Cape Crawford Tourism** (☑ 0400 156 685; www.capecrawfordtourism.com.au) runs helicopter rides (from $100) to see the otherwise inaccessible Lost City sandstone formations.

From here it's a desolate 374km south across the Barkly Tableland to the Barkly Hwy (Rte 66) and the **Barkly Homestead Roadhouse** (☑ 08-8964 4549; www.barklyhomestead.com.au; unpowered/powered sites $20/28, cabins & motel d $140; ☀ ⊜), a surprisingly upbeat roadhouse. From here it's 210km west to Tennant Creek and 252km east to the Queensland border.

## Borroloola

POP 927

On the McArthur River close to the bountiful waters of the Gulf, Borroloola is big news for **fishing** fans, but unless you're keen on baiting a hook (the barramundi season peaks from February to April) or driving the remote (preferably 4WD) Savannah Way to Queensland, it's a long way to go for not much reward.

About three-quarters of the population of Borroloola is indigenous, and the town's colourful history is displayed at the **Borroloola Museum** (www.nationaltrustnt.org.au; Robinson Rd; admission $2; ⊗ 8am-5pm Mon-Fri May-Sep), inside the 1886 police station.

The **Savannah Way Motel** (☑ 08-8975 8883; www.savannahwaymotel.com.au; Robinson Rd; r $80-120, cabins $130; ☀ ⊜), on the main road through town, is clean and comfortable, with cabins, lodge rooms and tropical gardens. If you're with a group you can book the whole lodge for $440. There's a restaurant here, too.

There's also the **McArthur River Caravan Park** (☑ 08-8975 8712; mcarthurcaravanpark.com.au; Robinson Rd; unpowered/powered site $22/28, budget unit s/d $75/85, self-contained unit s/d $98/110), and meals available at the local pub: burgers, chops and mixed grills at the rowdy **Borroloola Hotel** (166 Robinson Rd; meals $10-28; ⊗ lunch & dinner), within a lounge bar reinforced with steel mesh.

# Mataranka to Tennant Creek

## Larrimah

POP 18

Once upon a time the railway line from Darwin came as far as Birdum, 8km south of tiny Larrimah, which itself is 185km south of Katherine. **Larrimah Museum** (Mahoney St; admission by donation; ⊘7am-9pm), in the former telegraph repeater station opposite the Larrimah Hotel, tells of the town's involvement with the railway, the Overland Telegraph and WWII. The town was built in 1940, essentially as life support for the nearby Gorrie Airfield.

Originally a WWII officers' mess, **Larrimah Hotel** (☑08-8975 9931; unpowered/powered sites $18/22, d $60-75; ❋❀) is a cheerfully rustic and quirky pub offering basic rooms, meals (mains $10 to $29) and a menagerie of animals. **Fran's Devonshire Teahouse** (Stuart Hwy; meals $4-15; ⊘8am-4pm) makes a great lunchtime pit stop. Try a legendary camel or buffalo pie, some roast lamb with damper, or just a Devonshire tea (a long way from Exeter) or fresh coffee.

## Daly Waters

POP 25

About 3km off the highway and 160km south of Mataranka is Daly Waters, an important staging post in the early days of aviation – Amy Johnson landed here on her epic flight from England to Australia in 1930. Just about everyone stops at the famous **Daly Waters Pub** (☑08-8975 9927; www.dalywaterspub.com; unpowered/powered sites $14/24, d $60-95, cabins $125-165; ❋❀). Decorated with business cards, bras, banknotes and memorabilia from passing travellers, the pub claims to be the oldest in the Territory (its liquor licence has been valid since 1893) and has become a bit of a legend along the Track, although it may be a bit too popular for its own good. Every evening from April to September there's the popular beef 'n' barra BBQ ($28). Otherwise, hearty meals (mains $10 to $25, open lunch and dinner), including the filling barra burger, are served. Beside the pub is a dustbowl camping ground with a bit of shade – book ahead or arrive early to secure a powered site. Accommodation ranges from basic dongas (small, transportable buildings) to spacious self-contained cabins.

## Daly Waters to Three Ways

Heading south, you encounter the fascinating ghost town of Newcastle Waters, 3km west of the highway. Its atmospheric, historic buildings include the Junction Hotel, cobbled together from abandoned windmills in 1932. South of the cattle town of Elliott, the land just gets drier and drier and the vegetation sparser. The mesmerising sameness breaks at Renner Springs, generally accepted as the dividing line between the seasonally wet Top End and the dry Centre, where there is a decent roadhouse.

**Banka Banka** (☑08-8964 4511; adult/child $10/5) is a historic cattle station 100km north of Tennant Creek, with a grassy camping area (no power), marked walking tracks (one leading to a tranquil waterhole) and a licensed bar and small kiosk selling basic refreshments.

Three Ways, 537km north of Alice Springs, is the junction of the Stuart and Barkly Hwys, from where you can head south to Alice, north to Darwin (988km) or east to Mt Isa in Queensland (643km). **Threeways Roadhouse** (☑08-8962 2744; www.threewaysroadhouse.com.au; Stuart Hwy; unpowered/powered sites $24/32, cabins d $90-113; ❋@❀) is a potential stopover with a bar and restaurant, but Tennant Creek is only 26km further south.

# Tennant Creek

POP 3061

Servicing a vast region of cattle stations and remote Aboriginal communities, roughly the size of the UK, Tennant Creek is the only town of any size between Katherine, 680km to the north, and Alice Springs, 511km to the south. It's a good place to break up a long drive and check out the town's few attractions.

Local legend speaks of Tennant Creek being founded on beer: first settled when the drivers of a broken-down beer-laden wagon settled in to consume the freight in the 1930s. The truth is far more prosaic: the town was established as a result of a small gold rush around the same time. While it was short-lived, gold-mining ventures have operated discontinuously depending on metal prices, and exploration continues in the region today.

Tennant Creek is known as Jurnkurakurr to the local Warumungu people and almost half of the population is of Aboriginal descent. When the town is in the news, it's often for the wrong reasons – mainly alcoholism and violence – but there is a lot that is positive happening here and it's worth a stop to experience the wealth of Aboriginal art and culture on offer.

## ◉ Sights & Activities

### Nyinkka Nyunyu                          ART GALLERY
(www.nyinkkanyunyu.com.au; Paterson St; tour guide $15; ☺ 8am-4pm Mon-Fri, 9am-4pm Sat & Sun) This innovative museum and gallery highlights the dynamic art and culture of the local Warumungu people. The absorbing displays focus on contemporary art, traditional objects (many returned from interstate museums), bush medicine and regional history. The diorama series, or bush TVs as they became known within the community, are particularly special. Nyinkka Nyunyu is located beside a sacred site of the spiky tailed goanna. Learn about bush tucker and Dreaming stories with your personal guide. There's also a gallery store and the lovely Jajjikari Café (☺ 8am-3pm), which serves espresso coffee and light meals.

### Julalikari Arts Centre                  ARTS CENTRE
(North Stuart Hwy; ☺ 8am-noon Mon-Thu) It's best to visit the 'Pink Palace', at the entrance to the Ngalpa Ngalpa community (also known as Mulga Camp), mid-morning when the artists are at work painting traditional and contemporary art. You can chat to the artists and purchase directly from them.

### Battery Hill Mining Centre              MINE
(Peko Rd; adult/child $25/15; ☺ 9am-5pm) Experience life in Tennant Creek's 1930s gold rush at this mining centre, which doubles as the Visitor Information Centre, 2km east of town. There are underground mine tours and audio tours of the 10-head battery. In addition there is a superb Minerals Museum and you can try your hand at gold panning. The admission price gives access to all of the above, or you can choose to visit the Minerals and Social History Museums only (adult/family $7/15), or just go panning (per person $2).

While you're here, ask for the key ($20 refundable deposit) to the old Telegraph Station, which is just off the highway about 12km north of town. This is one of only four of the original 11 stations remaining in the Territory. Just north of the Telegraph Station is the turn-off west to Kundjarra (The Pebbles), a formation of granite boulders like a miniature version of the better-known Devil's Marbles found 100km south. It's a sacred women's Dreaming site of the Warumungu.

### Kelly's Ranch                          HORSE RIDING
(☎ 08-8962 2045; www.kellysranch.com.au; 5 Fazaldeen Rd; trail rides per person $150, lesson per person $50) Experience the Barkly from the back of a horse with local Warumungu man Jerry Kelly. His two-hour trail rides start with a lesson and then a ride through some superb outback scenery with bush-tucker stops along the way. Jerry entertains with stories about Aboriginal culture and life on the cattle stations.

## 🛏 Sleeping & Eating

### Tourist's Rest Youth Hostel            HOSTEL $
(☎ 08-8962 2719; www.touristrest.com.au; cnr Leichhardt & Windley Sts; dm/d $26/56; ❄ @ ☒) This small, friendly and slightly ramshackle hostel has bright clean rooms, free breakfast and VIP discounts. The hostel can organise tours of the gold mines and Devil's Marbles and pick-up from the bus stop.

### Outback Caravan Park                   CAMPGROUND $
(☎ 08-8962 2459; Peko Rd; unpowered/powered sites $25/33, cabins $60-140; ❄ ☒) In a town that often feels parched, it's nice to be in the shade of this grassy caravan park about 1km east of the centre. There's a well-stocked kiosk, camp kitchen and fuel. You may even be treated to some bush poetry and bush tucker, courtesy of yarn spinner Jimmy Hooker, at 7.30pm ($5). There are discounts for bookings of more than three nights.

### Safari Lodge Motel                     MOTEL $
(☎ 08-8962 2207; safari@switch.com.au; Davidson St; s/d $90/100; ✚ ❄ @ ☎) You should book ahead to stay at this family-run motel where the owners have made steps to gain accreditation as environmentally friendly. Safari Lodge is centrally located next to the best restaurant in town and has clean, fairly standard rooms with phone, fridge and TV.

### Desert Sands                           MOTEL $$
(☎ 08-8962 1346; www.desertsands.com.au; 780 Stuart Hwy; s/d from $105/115, extra person $10; ❄ @ ☒) The Desert Sands offers enormous modern units (sleeping three to eight), each with a fully equipped kitchen, TV (with in-house movies) and bathroom with washing machine. The motel is at the southern

entrance to Tennant Creek, which makes for a decent walk if you don't have a car (plus it can get a bit rowdy at that end of town at night).

### Woks Up — CHINESE $$
(☑ 08-8962 3888; 108 Paterson St; mains $14-24; ⏱ 5pm-late) An unexpected gem, Woks Up is one of the Territory's best Chinese diners with an immense menu and generous portions in a bright and clean restaurant.

### ★ Fernanda's Café & Restaurant — MEDITERRANEAN $$
(☑ 08-8962 3999; 1 Noble St; mains $18-34; ⏱ 5.30-9.30pm Mon-Sat; ❄) Tucked inside the Tennant Creek squash courts (yes squash courts) is this surprising Mediterranean-inspired restaurant. A definite Tennant Creek highlight, it is run by the ebullient Fernanda, who serves up tantalising dishes such as Portuguese seafood hotpots.

### Tennant Food Barn — SUPERMARKET $
(185 Paterson St; ⏱ 8am-5pm) Opposite the post office, this supermarket has a pretty extensive selection and can supply your self-catering needs.

## ℹ Information

**Leading Edge Computers** (☑ 08-8962 3907; 145 Paterson St; per 20min $2; ⏱ 9am-5pm Mon-Fri, 9am-noon Sat) Internet access.

**Police Station** (☑ 08-8962 4444; Paterson St)

**Tennant Creek Hospital** (☑ 08-8962 4399; Schmidt St)

**Visitor Information Centre** (☑ 08-8962 3388; www.barklytourism.com.au; Peko Rd; ⏱ 9am-5.30pm) Located 2km east of town at Battery Hill.

## ℹ Getting There & Away

All long-distance buses stop at the **Transit Centre** (☑ 08-8962 2727; 151 Patterson St; 9am-5pm Mon-Fri, 8.30-11.30am Sat), where you can purchase tickets. **Greyhound Australia** (☑ 1300 473 946; www.greyhound.com.au) has regular buses from Tennant Creek to Alice Springs ($195, six hours), Katherine ($207, 8½ hours), Darwin ($282, 14 hours) and Mount Isa ($165, eight hours).

The weekly *Ghan* rail link between Alice Springs and Darwin can drop off passengers in Tennant Creek, although cars can't be loaded or offloaded. The train station is about 6km south of town so you will need a **taxi** (☑ 0432 289 369, 08-8962 3626; ⏱ 6am-5.30pm).

Car hire is available from **Thrifty** (☑ 08-8962 2207; Davidson St, Safari Lodge Motel), while for tyres and tyre repairs head to **Bridgestone Tyre Centre** (☑ 08-8962 2361; Paterson St).

# Tennant Creek to Alice Springs

The gigantic boulders in precarious piles beside the Stuart Hwy, 105km south of Tennant Creek, are called the Devil's Marbles. Karlu Karlu is their Warumungu name, and this registered sacred site has great cultural importance. The rocks are believed to be the eggs of the Rainbow Serpent.

According to scientists, the 'marbles' are the rounded remains of a layer of granite that has eroded over aeons. A 15-minute walk loops around the main site. This geological phenomenon is particularly beautiful at sunrise and sunset, when these oddballs glow warmly. The camping ground (adult/child $3.30/1.65) has remarkably hard ground, pit toilets and fireplaces (BYO firewood).

At Wauchope (*war*-kup), 10km south of the Devil's Marbles, you will find Bruce, the gregarious publican of the Wauchope Hotel (☑ 08-8964 1963; www.wauchopehotel.com.au; Stuart Hwy; unpowered/powered sites $14/20, budget s $45, en suite s/d $85/95; ❄✉). His budget rooms are dongas but the costlier rooms are more spacious, with bathrooms. Meals from the restaurant (mains $18-33) are more than satisfactory.

At the kooky Wycliffe Well Roadhouse & Holiday Park (☑ 1800 222 195, 08-8964 1966; www.wycliffe.com.au; unpowered/powered sites $34/35, budget s/d from $50/60, s/d cabins with bathroom $110/117; ⏱ 6.30am-9pm; ❄@✉), 17km south of Wauchope, you can fill up with fuel and food (mains $15 to $20) or stay and spot UFOs that apparently fly over with astonishing regularity. The place is decorated with alien figures and UFO newspaper clippings. The park has a lawn camp site, an indoor pool, kids' playground, a cafe and a range of international beer.

Heading south, you reach the rustic Barrow Creek Hotel (☑ 08-8956 9753; Stuart Hwy; powered camp sites $15, s/d $50/65; ⏱ 7am-11pm), one of the highway's eccentric outback pubs. In the tradition of shearers who'd write their name on a banknote and pin it to the wall to ensure they could afford a drink when next they passed through, travellers continue to leave notes and photos. Food and fuel are available and next door is one of the original Telegraph Stations on the Overland Telegraph Line.

The highway continues through Ti Tree, where you'll find a roadhouse and, off the highway, the Ti Tree Food Store, which has espresso coffee. About 12km south of Ti Tree, the Red Centre Farm (Shatto Mango; ☑ 08-8956 9828; www.redcentrefarm.com; Stuart Hwy; ⊙ 7am-7pm) sells unique Territory-style wine – made from mangoes. If that sounds a bit hard to swallow, try the other mango products, such as the delicious ice cream.

In the grand Australian tradition of building very big things by the side of the road to pull up drivers, Aileron, 135km north of Alice, has Naked Charlie Quartpot, the 12m Anmatjere (Anmatyerre) man, who cuts a fine figure at the back of the roadhouse along with his larger-than-life family. The Outback Art Gallery (☑ 08-8956 9111; Stuart Hwy; ⊙ 8am-5pm Mon-Sat, 10am-4pm Sun) sells inexpensive paintings by the local Anmatjere community, as well as works from the Warlpiri community of Yuendumu.

Aileron Hotel Roadhouse (☑ 08-8956 9703; www.aileronroadhouse.com.au; Stuart Hwy; unpowered/powered sites $10/12, dm $36, s/d $110/120; ⊙ 5am-9pm; ❋ ⌨) has camp sites (power available until 10pm), a 10-bed dorm and decent motel units. There's an ATM, bar, shop, a licensed restaurant (meals $10 to $25) and not forgetting Bozo the wedgetail eagle. The owner's large collection of Namatjira watercolours (at least 10 by Albert Namatjira) is displayed around the roadhouse's dining area.

About 70km north of Alice, the Plenty Hwy heads off to the east towards the Harts Range. The main reason to detour is to fossick in the gem fields about 78km east of the Stuart Hwy, which are well known for garnets and zircons. You're guaranteed to get lucky at the popular Gemtree Caravan Park (☑ 08-8956 9855; www.gemtree.com.au; Gemtree; unpowered/powered sites $22/30, cabins $85).

For a taste of desert life, time your visit with the annual Harts Range Races (last weekend in July), one of the Territory's best outback rodeos.

## The Tanami Road

Synonymous with isolated outback driving, the 1000km Tanami Rd connects Alice Springs with Halls Creek in WA and is essentially a short cut between central Australia and the Kimberley. In dry conditions it's possible to make it through the unsealed

dust and corrugations in a well-prepared 2WD. Stay alert, as rollovers are common, and stock up with fuel, tyres, food and water.

The NT section is wide and usually well graded, and starts 20km north of Alice Springs. The road is sealed to Tilmouth Well (☑ 08-8956 8777; www.tilmouthwell.com; unpowered/powered sites $25/35, cabins without bathroom $70; ❋ @ ⌨) on the edge of Napperby Station which bills itself as an oasis in the desert with a sparkling pool and lush, sprawling lawns.

The next fuel stop is at Yuendumu, the largest remote community in the region and home to the Warlpiri people who were made famous in Bush Mechanics (www.bushmechanics.com). It's worth popping in to the Warlukurlangu Art Centre (☑ 08-8956 4133; www.warlu.com; ⊙ 9am-5pm Mon-Fri), a locally owned venture specialising in acrylic paintings.

From here there is no fuel for another 600km until you cross the WA border and hit Billiluna (☑ 08-9168 8076; www.billiluna.org. au). Note, Rabbit Flat Roadhouse has closed permanently. Another 170km will have you resting your weary bones in Halls Creek.

## ALICE SPRINGS

POP 25,186

The Alice, as it's often known, sprang from humble beginnings as a lonely telegraph station on the continent-spanning Overland Telegraph Line (OTL) more than 140 years ago. Although still famous for its far-flung location, Alice Springs is no longer the frontier settlement of legend. Ignited by the boom in adventure tourism, the insatiable interest in contemporary Aboriginal art and improved access, the modernisation of Alice has been abrupt and confronting. Yet the vast surroundings of red desert and burnished ranges still underscore its remoteness.

This ruggedly beautiful town is shaped by its mythical landscapes, vibrant Aboriginal culture (where else can you hear six uniquely Australian languages in the main street?) and tough pioneering past. The town is a natural base for exploring central Australia, with Uluru-Kata Tjuta National Park a relatively close four-hour drive away. The mesmerising MacDonnell Ranges stretch east and west from the town centre, and you don't have to venture far to find yourself among ochre-red gorges, pastel-hued hills and ghostly white gum trees.

To the Arrernte people, the traditional owners of the Alice Springs area, this place is called Mparntwe. The heart of Mparntwe is the junction of the Charles (Anthelke Ulpeye) and Todd (Lhere Mparntwe) Rivers, just north of Anzac Hill (Untyeyetweleye). The topographical features of the town were formed by the creative ancestral beings – known as the Yeperenye, Ntyarlke and Utnerrengatye caterpillars – as they crawled across the landscape from Emily Gap (Anthwerrke), in the MacDonnell Ranges southeast of town. For many travellers, international and Australian, Alice Springs is their first encounter with contemporary indigenous Australia – with its enchanting art, mesmerising culture and present-day challenges.

## ⊙ Sights

**Alice Springs Desert Park**  WILDLIFE PARK
(www.alicespringsdesertpark.com.au; Larapinta Dr; adult/child $25/12.50; nocturnal tour adult/child $25/12.50; ⊘ 7.30am-6pm, last entry 4.30pm, birds of prey show 10am & 3.30pm, nocturnal tour 7.30pm) If you haven't managed to glimpse a spangled grunter or a marbled velvet gecko on your travels, head to the Desert Park where the creatures of central Australia are all on display in one place. The predominantly open-air exhibits faithfully re-create the animals' natural environment in a series of habitats: inland river, sand country and woodland.

Try to time your visit with the terrific **birds of prey show**, featuring free-flying Australian kestrels, kites and awesome wedge-tailed eagles. To catch some of the park's rare and elusive animals like the bilby, visit the excellent **nocturnal house**. If you like what you see, come back at night and spotlight endangered species on the guided **nocturnal tour** (booking essential).

To get the most out of the park pick up a free audioguide (available in various languages) or join one of the free ranger-led talks held throughout the day.

It's an easy 2.5km cycle out to the park. Alternatively, **Desert Park Transfers** (☑ 08-8952 1731, 1800 806 641; www.tailormadetours.com.au; adult/child $48/33) operates five times daily during park hours and the cost includes park entry and pick-up and drop-off at your accommodation.

**Araluen Cultural Precinct**  CULTURAL CENTRE
(Map p204; www.araluen.nt.gov.au; cnr Larapinta Dr & Memorial Ave; precinct pass adult/child $15/10)

You can wander around freely outside, accessing the cemetery and grounds, but the 'precinct pass' provides entry to the exhibitions and displays for two days (with 14 days to use the pass).

**Araluen Arts Centre**  ART GALLERY
(Map p204) For a small town, Alice Springs has a thriving arts scene and the Araluen Arts Centre is at its heart. There is a 500-seat theatre and four galleries with a focus on art from the central desert region.

The Albert Namatjira Gallery features works by the artist, who began painting watercolours in the 1930s at Hermannsburg. The exhibition draws comparisons between Namatjira and his initial mentor, Rex Battarbee and other Hermannsburg School artists. It also features 14 early acrylic works from the Papunya Community School Collection.

Other galleries showcase local artists, travelling exhibitions and newer works from Indigenous community art centres.

**Museum of Central Australia**  MUSEUM
(Map p204; ⊘ 10am-5pm, library 10am-4pm Mon-Fri) The natural history collection at this compact museum recalls the days of megafauna – when hippo-sized wombats and 3m-tall flightless birds roamed the land. Among the geological displays are meteorite fragments and fossils. There's a free audio tour, narrated by a palaeontologist, which helps bring the exhibition to life.

There's also a display on the work of Professor TGH Strehlow, a linguist and anthropologist born at the Hermannsburg Mission among the Arrernte people. During his lifetime he gathered one of the world's most documented collections of Australian Aboriginal artefacts, songs, genealogies, film and sound recordings. It's upstairs in the **Strehlow Research Centre** which has a library open to the public.

**Central Australia Aviation Museum** MUSEUM
(Map p204; Memorial Ave; ⊘ 9am-5pm Mon-Fri, 10am-5pm Sat & Sun) FREE Housed in the Connellan Airways Hangar, Alice's original aerodrome, there are displays on pioneer aviation in the Territory including Royal Flying Doctor (RFDS) planes.

Easily the most interesting exhibit is the wreck of the **Kookaburra**, a tiny plane that crashed in the Tanami Desert in 1929 while searching for Charles Kingsford Smith and his co-pilot Charles Ulm, who had gone down in their plane, the *Southern Cross*. The *Kookaburra* pilots, Keith

# Alice Springs

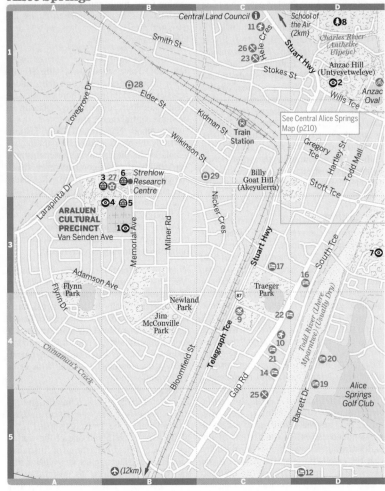

Anderson and Bob Hitchcock, perished in the desert, while Kingsford Smith and Ulm were rescued.

**Alice Springs Memorial Cemetery** CEMETERY
(Map p204) The cemetery is adjacent to the aviation museum and contains the graves of some prominent locals including Albert Namatjira (1902–59) and Harold Lasseter (1880–1931), the eccentric prospector whose fervent search for a folkloric reef of gold (Lasseter's Reef) claimed his life. Anthropologist Olive Pink (1884–1975), who campaigned for Aboriginal rights, is buried fac-

ing the opposite direction to the others – a rebel to the end.

**Telegraph Station
Historical Reserve**                   HISTORIC PARK
(Map p204; adult/child $9/4.50; ⊗8am-9pm, museum 9am-5pm) The old Telegraph Station, which used to relay messages between Darwin and Adelaide, offers a fascinating glimpse of the town's European beginnings. Built along the Overland Telegraph Line in the 1870s, the station continued to operate until 1932. It later served as a welfare home for Aboriginal children of mixed ancestry

It's an easy 4km walk or cycle north to the station from Todd Mall; follow the path on the western side of the riverbed.

### Royal Flying Doctor Service Base — MUSEUM

(RFDS; Map p210; www.flyingdoctor.net; Stuart Tce; adult/child $12/6; ☺9am-5pm Mon-Sat, 1-5pm Sun, cafe 9am-4.30pm Mon-Sat) This is the home of the Royal Flying Doctor Service, whose dedicated health workers provide 24-hour emergency retrievals across an area of around 1.25 million sq km. Entry to the visitor centre is by a half-hour tour that includes a video presentation, and a look at the operational control room as well as some ancient medical gear and a flight simulator. There's an adjoining giftshop and cafe.

### School of the Air — SCHOOL

(www.assoa.nt.edu.au; 80 Head St; adult/child $7.50/5; ☺8.30am-4.30pm Mon-Sat, 1.30-4.30pm Sun) Started in 1951, this was the first school of its type in Australia, broadcasting lessons to children over an area of 1.3 million sq km. While transmissions were originally all done over high-frequency radio, satellite broadband internet and web-cams now mean students can study in a virtual classroom. The guided tour of the centre includes a video. During school term you can view a live broadcast from 8.30am to 2.30pm Monday to Friday. The school is about 3km north of the town centre.

### Alice Springs Reptile Centre — ZOO

(Map p210; www.reptilecentre.com.au; 9 Stuart Tce; adult/child $14/7; ☺9.30am-5pm, handling demonstrations 11am, 1pm & 3.30pm) It may be small, but this reptile centre packs a poisonous punch with its impressive collection of venomous snakes, thorny devils and bearded dragons. Inside the cave room are 11 species of NT geckos, and outside there's Terry, a 3.3m saltwater croc plus Bub, a magnificent perentie, Australia's largest lizard. The enthusiastic guides will happily plonk a python around your neck during the handling demonstrations or let you pet a bluetongue lizard.

### Alice Springs Transport Heritage Centre — MUSEUM

At the MacDonnell siding, about 10km south of Alice and 1km west of the Stuart Hwy, are a couple of museums dedicated to big trucks and old trains. If you want to visit both the museums, consider the **half-day tour** (☑08-8955 5047; tours $55; ☺10am-2pm), which includes entry, a guide and lunch.

until 1963. The building has been faithfully restored and guided tours operate roughly on the hour between 9am and 4.30pm (April to October). Nearby is the original **'Alice' spring** (Thereyurre to the Arrernte Aboriginal people), a semipermanent waterhole in the Todd River after which the town is named.

It's all set in 450 hectares of shady parkland with free BBQs (alcohol permitted) and walking trails. The best is the 30-minute loop to **Trig Hill**, returning via the original station cemetery.

# Alice Springs

The **Old Ghan Rail Museum** (1 Norris Bell Ave; adult/child $10/6; ◎9am-5pm) has a collection of restored *Ghan* locos (originally called the Afghan Express after the cameleers who forged the route). There's also the Old Ghan Tea Rooms and an ad-hoc collection of railway memorabilia in the lovely Stuart railway station.

For a truckin' good time, head to the **National Road Transport Hall of Fame** (www.roadtransporthall.com; 2 Norris Bell Ave; adult/child $15/8; ◎9am-5pm) which has a fabulous collection of big rigs, including a few ancient road trains. Admission includes entry to the Kenworth Dealer Truck Museum. There are more than 100 restored trucks and vintage cars, including many of the outback's pioneering vehicles.

**Olive Pink Botanic Garden**    NATURE RESERVE
(Map p204; www.opbg.com.au; Tuncks Rd; admission by donation; ◎8am-6pm) A network of meandering trails leads through this lovely arid zone botanic garden, which was founded by the prominent anthropologist Olive Pink. The garden has more than 500 central Australian plant species and grows bush foods and medicinal plants like native lemon grass, quandong and bush passionfruit. There's a gentle climb up Meyers Hill with fine views over Alice and Ntyarlkarle

Tyaneme, one of the first sites created by the caterpillar ancestors.

The small visitor centre has various exhibitions during the year and the excellent **Bean Tree Cafe** (◎8am-3pm) is worth a trip to the gardens alone.

**Anzac Hill**    LANDMARK
(Map p204) For a tremendous view, particularly at sunrise and sunset, take a hike (use Lions Walk from Wills Tce) or a drive up to the top of Anzac Hill, known as Untyeyetweleye in Arrernte. From the war memorial there is a 365-degree view over the town down to Heavitree Gap and the Ranges.

**Heritage Walk**    NOTABLE BUILDINGS
(admission by donation) To get a feel for early Alice Springs, there are a number of historic-buildings-cum-mini-museums that you can pop into while wandering around town.

On Todd Mall is **Adelaide House** (Map p210; ◎10am-4pm Mon-Fri, 10am-noon Sat) built in the 1920s by the founding flying doctor Reverend John Flynn as the first hospital in central Australia. Enter a classroom from 1938 at the **Old Hartley Street School** (Map p210; 39 Hartley St; ◎10.30am-2.30pm Mon-Fri Feb-Nov) or take in the gracious beauty of the **Residency** (Map p210; 12 Parsons St; ◎10am-2pm Mon-Fri), built in 1927 and a symbol of the town's brief legislative independence from the rest of the NT.

#  Activities

## Ballooning

### Outback
BALLOONING

(☑1800 809 790; www.outbackballooning.com.au; 30/60min flight $290/385, mandatory insurance $25) Floating above Alice at sunrise is not an experience you will forget in a hurry (though the included picnic champagne breakfast may be). Hotel transfers are included in the price.

## Bowling

### Dust Bowl
BOWLING

(Map p204; ☑08-8952 5051; 29 Gap Rd; per game $11; ⊙10am-late) After the pins are scattered there's a bar serving drinks and a cafe serving burgers. In the same building, the Red Tomato has wood-fired pizzas.

## Bushwalking

Experience the bush around Alice with several easy walks radiating from the Olive Pink Botanic Garden and the Telegraph Station, which marks the start of the first stage of the Larapinta Trail.

### Alice Springs Bushwalkers Association
BUSHWALKING

(http://home.austarnet.com.au/longwalk) A group of local bushwalkers that schedules a wide variety of walks in the area, particularly the West MacDonnell Ranges, from March to November.

## Camel Riding

Camels played an integral part in pioneering central Australia before roads and railways, and travellers can relive some of that adventure.

### Pyndan Camel Tracks
CAMEL RIDING

(☑0416 170 164; www.cameltracks.com; Jane Rd) Local cameleer Marcus Williams offers one-hour rides (adult/child $50/25), as well as half-day jaunts (per person $95).

## Cycling & Mountain Bike Riding

Bikes are the perfect way to get around Alice Springs. There are cycle paths along the Todd River to the Telegraph Station, west to the Alice Springs Desert Park and further out to Simpsons Gap. For a map of cycling and walking paths pick up a copy of *Active in Alice* from the visitor information centre.

With its arid rangeland terrain and networks of single tracks, Alice Springs is getting a name for mountain bike riding, with the annual five-day MTB Enduro race a calendar highlight. Trails are easily accessed from town or meet up for a social sunset ride (☑08-8952 5800; centralaustralianrough riders.asn.au; Scout Hall, cnr Larapinta & Lovegrove Drs; ride $5; ⊙6pm Wed winter, 5pm summer) with the Central Australian Rough Riders' Club.

### Longhorn
BIKE HIRE

(☑0439 860 735; half-/full day $20/35) Drop-off/pick-up service with commuter, mountain and tandem bikes available as well as kids' bikes and baby seats.

### Ultimate Ride
BIKE SHOP

(Map p204; ☑08-8953 7297; 2/30 North Stuart Hwy; ⊙9am-6pm Mon-Fri, 9am-2pm Sat) Home of the Rough Riders, Ultimate Ride sells bicycles, stocks accessories and does repairs. It will also advise on bike tracks.

## Swimming

### Alice Aquatic & Leisure Centre
SWIMMING

(Map p204; ☑08-8953 4633; Speed St; adult/child $5/2.55; ⊙6am-7pm Mon-Fri, 9am-7pm Sat & Sun) With lots of grass for lounging about and views of the Ranges, the Leisure Centre makes a lovely alternative to your hotel pool. The solar-heated indoor pools are open year-round.

# ☞ Tours

## Around Alice & MacDonnell Ranges

### Alice Wanderer
OUTBACK

(Map p210; ☑1800 722 111; www.alicewanderer. com.au; Gregory Tce) Has the 'hop on, hop off' town tours aboard the Alice Explorer ($44), which continually loops around town stopping at the major sights. Also runs day tours into the West MacDonnell Ranges as far as Glen Helen Gorge, including morning tea and lunch (adult/child $117/72), and a half-day trip to Simpsons Gap and Standley Chasm ($68/42). The office is opposite the visitor information centre.

### Dreamtime Tours
INDIGENOUS

(☑08-8953 3739; www.rstours.com.au; adult/child $85/42, self-drive $66/33; ⊙8.30-11.30am) Runs the three-hour Dreamtime & Bushtucker Tour, where you meet Warlpiri Aboriginal people and learn a little about their traditions. As it caters for large bus groups it can be impersonal, but you can tag along with your own vehicle.

### ★ Foot Falcon
TOWN

(☑0427 569 531; www.footfalcon.com; tours $30; ⊙Mon & Thu 8.30am, Tue, Wed & Fri 4pm, Sun 3pm)

Local historian, author and teacher Linda Wells leads two-hour walks around town with insights into Alice's indigenous and pioneering history.

### L'Astragale                          TOWN
(☑ 08-8953 6293; eroullet@gmail.com; tours $27) Francophone Evelyne Roullet runs a local walking tour of Alice Springs (or customise tour to your interests) which leaves from the visitor information centre.

### Rainbow Valley Cultural Tours    INDIGENOUS
(☑ 1800 011 144; www.rainbowvalleyculturaltours.com; self-drive morning $50/25, afternoon $70/50) Tour beautiful Rainbow Valley with a traditional owner and visit rock-art sites not open to the general public. Sunset self-drive tours can include overnight camping and dinner for an extra $30/20.

### RT Tours                          FOOD
(☑ 08-8952 0327; www.rttoursaustralia.com; tours $150) Chef and Arrernte guide Bob Taylor runs a popular lunch and dinner tour at Simpsons Gap and the Telegraph Reserve where he whips up a bush-inspired meal. Other tours available.

### Trek Larapinta                    WALKING
(☑ 1300 133 278; www.treklarapinta.com.au; from 6 days $1895) 🏃 Guided multiday walks along sections of the Larapinta Trail. Also runs volunteer projects involving trail maintenance and bush regeneration on Aboriginal outstations.

#### Uluru, Kings Canyon & Palm Valley
### Emu Run Tours                     OUTBACK
(Map p210; ☑ 1800 687 220, 08-8953 7057; www.emurun.com.au; 72 Todd St) Operates day tours to Uluru ($215) and two-day tours to Uluru and Kings Canyon ($520). Prices include park entry fees, meals and accommodation. There are also recommended small-group day tours through the West MacDonnell Ranges ($110) or Palm Valley ($189), including morning tea, lunch and entrance fees.

### The Rock Tour                     OUTBACK
(☑ 1800 246 345; www.therocktour.com.au) Backpacker-friendly three-day (two nights) camping safari ($350) which visits Kings Canyon, Curtin Springs, the 'Rock' and Kata Tjuta. Leaves Alice daily at 6am.

### Wayoutback Desert Safaris          4WD
(☑ 08-8952 4324, 1300 551 510; www.wayoutback.com) Small group 4WD safari tours includ-

ing the excellent two-day Aboriginal-led Culture and Country trip ($670). There are also three-day safaris that traverse 4WD tracks to Uluru and Kings Canyon for $695, and five-day safaris that top it up with the Palm Valley and West MacDonnells for $1125.

## ★★ Festivals & Events

### Alice Springs Cup Carnival    HORSE RACING
(www.alicespringsturfclub.org.au) On the first Monday in May, don a hat and gallop down to the Pioneer Park Racecourse for the main event of this five-day carnival.

### Finke Desert Race              MOTOCROSS
(www.finkedesertrace.com.au) Motorcyclists and buggy drivers vie to take out the title of this crazy June race 240km from Alice along the Old South Rd to Finke; the following day they race back again. Spectators camp along the road to cheer them on.

### Alice Springs Beanie Festival     ARTS
(www.beaniefest.org) This four-day festival in June/July, held at the Araluen Art Centre, celebrates the humble beanie (knitted woollen hat) – handmade by women throughout the central desert.

### Camel Cup                     CAMEL RACING
(www.camelcup.com.au) A carnival atmosphere prevails during the running of the Camel Cup at Blatherskite Park in mid-July.

### Alice Springs Rodeo                RODEO
Bareback bull riding, steer wrestling and ladies' barrel races are on the bill at Blatherskite Park in August.

### Old Timers Fete                     FETE
Stock up on doilies and tea towels at this ode to granny arts, held on the second Saturday in August at the Old Timers Village.

### Alice Desert Festival               ARTS
(www.alicedesertfestival.com.au) A cracker of a festival, including a circus program, music, film, comedy and the highly anticipated Desert Mob art exhibition. It's held every September.

### Henley-on-Todd Regatta           REGATTA
(www.henleyontodd.com.au) These boat races in September on the dry bed of the Todd River are a typically Australian light-hearted denial of reality. The boats are bottomless; the crews' legs stick through and they run down the course.

# 🛏 Sleeping

If you are travelling in peak season (June to September) make sure you book ahead, but if you're trying your luck, check the internet for last-minute rates, which often bring top-end places into midrange reach.

### Alice Lodge Backpackers    HOSTEL $
(Map p204; ☑ 08-8953 1975, 1800 351 925; www.alicelodge.com.au; 4 Mueller St; dm $22-26, d/tr $65/80; ❄ @ 🛜 ⊠) Located in a lovely residential area across the Todd River, an easy 10-minute walk from town, this is a small, highly recommended, low-key hostel. The friendly staff are as accommodating as the variety of room options which include mixed and female, three-, four- and six-bed dorms, as well as comfortable doubles and twins built around a central pool.

### Pioneer YHA Hostel    HOSTEL $
(Map p210; ☑ 08-8952 8855; www.yha.com.au; cnr Leichhardt Tce & Parsons St; dm $24-31, tw & d $75; ❄ @ ⊠) This YHA is housed in the old Pioneer outdoor cinema and guests can still enjoy nightly screenings of movies under the stars. Location is the biggest bonus here but it's also friendly and well run. The comfortable doubles share bathrooms. There's a good-sized kitchen and a pleasant outdoor area around a small pool. Discounted weekly rates are available.

### Alice in the Territory    RESORT $
(Map p204; ☑ 08-8952 6100; www.alicent.com.au; 46 Stephens Rd; dm $22.50, s or d $89-99; ❄ @ 🛜 ⊠) This sprawling resort is the best bargain stay in town. The rooms, doubles or four-bed dorms, have tiny bathrooms, but otherwise are bright, spotless and comfortable and offer two free movie channels. The management is enthusiastic and eager to please, there's a great bar and multicuisine restaurant and the big pool sits at the foot of the Ranges.

### Alice's Secret Traveller's Inn    HOSTEL $
(Map p204; ☑ 08-8952 8686, 1800 783 633; www.asecret.com.au; 6 Khalick St; dm $23-26, s/d/tr $60/65/90; ❄ @ ⊠) Across the Todd River from town, this is a 'non-party' hostel where you can relax around the pool, puff on a didge, or lie in a hammock in the garden. Rooms in the dongas are a bit of a squeeze, and those in the house are simple, comfortable and clean.

### Toddy's Backpackers    HOSTEL $
(Map p204; ☑ 1800 027 027; www.toddys.com.au; 41 Gap Rd; dm $22-26, d $78; ❄ @ ⊠) Toddy's is a rambling place with a huge variety of rooms from dorms and budget doubles to a motel section. Toddy's is popular with groups and there's a party atmosphere, spurred on by the $8 meals and cheap jugs of beer at the outdoor bar every evening. Although there are plenty of beds, the motel-style rooms can be hard to get, so book ahead. Tariff includes a light breakfast.

### Annie's Place    HOSTEL $
(Map p204; ☑ 08-8952 1545, 1800 359 089; www.anniesplace.com.au; 4 Traeger Ave; dm $20, d & tw $55-75; ❄ @ ⊠) With its leafy beer garden, popular with travellers and locals, and great poolside area, Annie's is a lively place to hang out any night of the week. This is only a problem if you actually enjoy sleeping. The converted motel rooms (all with bathrooms and some with a fridge) are right on top of the bar and the new management should be on top of the old cleanliness issues.

### Heavitree Gap
### Outback Lodge    CARAVAN PARK $
(☑ 08-8950 4444, 1800 896 119; www.aurorar esorts.com.au; Palm Circuit; unpowered/powered sites $24/30, dm $26, d $130-180; ❄ @ 🛜 ⊠) At the foot of the Ranges and dotted with eucalypts and bounding rock wallabies, Heavitree makes a shady place to pitch or park. Alternatively, there are rooms: four-bed dorms, lodge and very basic kitchenette rooms that sleep six. The lodge offers a free shuttle into the town centre, which is about 4km away. The neighbouring tavern has live country music most nights of the week.

### MacDonnell Range
### Holiday Park    CARAVAN PARK $
(☑ 08-8952 6111, 1800 808 373; www.macrange.com.au; Palm Pl; unpowered/powered sites $39/45, cabins d $84-256; ❄ @ ⊠) Probably Alice's biggest and best kept secret, this park has grassy sites, spotless amenities and a variety of accommodation from simple cabins with shared bathroom to self-contained two-bedroom villas. Not the cheapest option, but you get what you pay for with a roster of daily activities from stargazing to pancake Sundays. Kids can cavort in the adventure playground, BMX track and basketball court, while adults can kick back around the pool.

### White Gum Motel    MOTEL $$
(Map p204; ☑ 08-8952 5144, 1800 624 110; www.whitegum.com.au; 17 Gap Rd; s/d/tr/q $100/115/130/145; ❄ 🛜 ⊠) This impeccable old-fashioned motel is located about 10 to

# Central Alice Springs

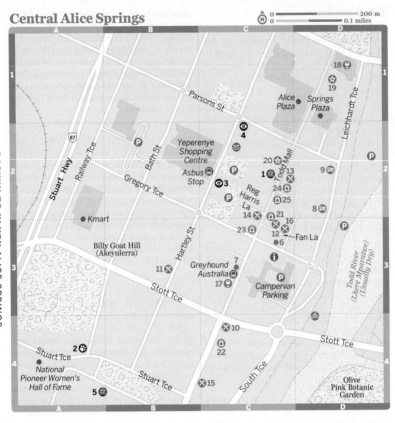

## Central Alice Springs

15 minutes' walk from the mall, and perfect if you want a reasonably priced room with your own full kitchen. The spacious rooms are self-contained, clean as a whistle, and ideal for families.

### Alice on Todd                    APARTMENTS $$

(Map p204; ☑08-8953 8033; www.aliceontodd. com; cnr Strehlow St & South Tce; studio $128, 1-/2-bedroom apt $156/195, deluxe 1-/2-bedroom apt $170/210; ✴@☎�) This attractive and secure apartment complex on the banks of the Todd River offers one- and two- bedroom self-contained units with kitchen and lounge. The balconied units sleep up to six so they're a great option for families. The deluxe apartments are a step up in decor and comfort. The landscaped grounds enclose a BBQ area, playground and a games room.

### Chifley Alice Springs          HOTEL $$

(Map p204; ☑08-8951 4545; www.chifleyhotels. com.au; 34 Stott Tce; standard/superior/deluxe d $140/190/250; ✴@☎☑) With a circle of double-storey buildings arranged around a swath of lawns and gum trees, the Chifley has a relaxed country-club vibe. Avoid the standard rooms and go for the recently refurbished superior and deluxe accommodation overlooking the Todd River. There's an attractive pool area with a swim-up bar, plus a seafood restaurant.

### All Seasons Oasis              HOTEL $$

(Map p204; ☑08-8952 1444; www.allseasons. com.au; 10 Gap Rd; d from $140; ✴@☎☑) With two swimming pools, the central one shaded by sails and surrounded with palm-shaded lawn, All Seasons convincingly re-creates the oasis experience. The rooms are conventional and comfortable enough to keep it busy with tour groups. There's a restaurant, a bar with a couple of pool tables and a happy hour that brings in the locals. The best rates are available from the website.

### Desert Palms Resort            HOTEL $$

(Map p204; ☑1800 678 037, 08-8952 5977; www. desertpalms.com.au; 74 Barrett Dr; villas $140; ✴@☑) This hotel has a relaxed island vibe with its shady palms, cascading bougainvil-lea and Indonesian-style villas. The rooms – which have cathedral ceilings, kitchenette, tiny bathroom, TV and private balcony are rather dated, though the island swimming pool is a big hit with kids.

### Alice Station Bed & Breakfast       B&B $$

(☑08-8953 6600; www.alicestation.com; 25 The Fairway; s/d/ste from $180/195/260; ✴@☎☑) The host of this lovely B&B, which backs on to the bush, really does have kangaroos in her backyard. Made out of old *Ghan* railway sleepers, the whimsically designed home has a relaxed atmosphere with a communal lounge and stylishly decorated rooms with local Aboriginal art on the walls. Continental breakfasts get the thumbs up, as do the homemade cakes and eight different types of tea.

### Crowne Plaza Alice Springs       HOTEL $$

(Map p204; ☑08-8950 8000, 1300 666 545; www. crowneplaza.com.au; Barrett Dr; d from $150, ste $188-328; ✴@☎☑) With its spacious resort-style facilities, this is widely considered Alice's top hotel. Choose from the garden-view rooms or the better mountain range-view rooms – they're decked out with floor-to-ceiling windows, cane furniture and pastel colours. There's a lovely pool and spa, well-equipped gym and sauna, tennis courts and a house peacock. Alice's best restaurant, Hanumans (p212), is in the lobby.

### Aurora Alice Springs           HOTEL $$$

(Map p210; ☑08-8950 6666, 1800 089 644; www. auroraresorts.com.au; 11 Leichhardt Tce; standard/deluxe/executive d $210/230/299; ✴@☎☑) Right in the town centre – the 'back' door opens out onto Todd Mall, the front door looks over the Todd River – this modern hotel has a relaxed atmosphere and a great restaurant, Red Ochre Grill (p212). Standard rooms are comfortable and well appointed with fridge, phone and free in-house movies.

### Bond Springs Outback Retreat     B&B $$$

(☑08-8952 9888; www.outbackretreat.com.au; cottage d $230; ✴☑) Experience a taste of outback station life at this retreat, about 25km from town. The private self-contained cottage is a refurbished stockman's quarters. A full breakfast is included but the rest is self-catering. Have a game of tennis or mooch around the enormous property including the original station school, which operated through the School of the Air (p205).

## ✖ Eating

### Kwerralye Cafe                    CAFE $

(Map p204; 6 South Tce; mains $6-12; ☺7.30am-3pm Mon-Fri) This excellent cafe is part of a program training young indigenous Territorians in all aspects of hospitality. There are excellent light breakfasts, homemade pies, gourmet salads and daily specials, plus espresso coffee.

### Bean Tree Cafe
CAFE $

(Map p204; Tuncks Rd, Olive Pink Botanic Garden; mains $9-12; ⊙8am-3pm) Breakfast with the birds at this superb outdoor cafe tucked away in the Olive Pink Botanic Garden. Service can be slow, but it's a relaxing place to sit and the wholesome home-style dishes such as the kangaroo burger and apple crumble are well worth the wait.

### Page 27 Cafe
CAFE $

(Map p210; Fan Lane; mains $9-16; ⊙7.30am-3pm Tue-Fri, 8am-3pm Sat & Sun; 🗷) Alice's locals duck down this arcade for great coffee or fresh juice and wholesome home-style breakfasts (eggs any style, pancakes), pita wraps, pies and salads. Excellent vegetarian menu.

### Water Tank Cafe
CAFE $

(Map p204; Hele Cres; mains $8-16; ⊙10am-3pm Mon-Fri, 9am-3pm Sat; 🗷) Tucked away in the Bloomin' Deserts nursery this friendly cafe serves up fresh salads, burgers and homemade cake. Locals sprawl out on the couches and beanbags, sipping potent coffee and making use of the free wi-fi.

### Tea Shrine
VEGAN $

(Map p210; 113 Todd St; mains $8-15; ⊙9am-4pm Mon-Sat; 🗷) Vegetarians may be forgiven for feeling a bit left out in meat-heavy Alice Springs, but not at the Tea Shrine, a vegan Asian restaurant and teahouse. Popular with hippies and health workers, this peaceful cafe has daily specials and a range of yum cha dishes.

### ★Hanuman Restaurant
THAI $$

(Map p204; 🗷08-8953 7188; Barrett Dr, Crowne Plaza Alice Springs; mains $18-36; ⊙12.30-2.30pm Mon-Fri, from 6.30pm daily; 🗷) You won't believe you're in the outback when you try the incredible Thai- and Indian-influenced cuisine at this stylish restaurant. The delicate Thai entrees are a real triumph as are the seafood dishes, particularly the Hanuman prawns. Although the menu is ostensibly Thai, there are enough Indian dishes to satisfy a curry craving. There are also several vegetarian offerings and a good wine list.

### Tinh & Lan Alice Vietnamese Restaurant
VIETNAMESE $$

(🗷08-8952 8396; 1900 Heffernan Rd; mains $16-30; ⊙11am-2pm & 5-10pm Tue-Sun) This atmospheric Vietnamese restaurant is set in a market garden illuminated with lanterns. All the favourites – rice paper rolls, pho, salt and pepper squid – are deliciously prepared and the ingredients, growing all around you, couldn't be fresher. Follow the signs off Colonel Rose Dr; it's about 14km south of town.

### Casa Nostra
ITALIAN $$

(Map p204; 🗷08-8952 6749; cnr Undoolya Rd & Sturt Tce; mains $14-28; ⊙6-10pm Mon-Sat) Step across the Todd River and into 1970s Italy at this old-school pizza and pasta joint. Madly popular on the weekends (bookings are recommended), it is wonderfully cosy with red and white checked tablecloths and plastic grape vines hanging from the ceiling. Order the famously delectable vanilla slice early as they run out the door. Note that it's BYO wine.

### Montes
MODERN AUSTRALIAN $$

(Map p210; cnr Stott Tce & Todd St; Mains $12-17; ⊙11am-late) A travelling circus meets outback homestead with a leafy beer garden (and range of beers) or intimate booth seating. Patio heaters keep patrons warm on a cool desert night. It's family friendly with a play area, and the food ranges from gourmet burgers, pizzas and tapas to curries and seafood.

### Thai Room
THAI $$

(Map p210; Fan Lane; mains $12-20; ⊙11am-2pm Mon-Fri, 6-10pm Mon-Sat) Head to this arcade restaurant for perky Thai dishes and quicker than average service. The modest menu mixes its signature spices with a variety of veggie, meat and seafood dishes. The lunch specials are a bargain and it's BYO.

### Soma
CAFE $

(Map p210; 64 Todd Mall; mains $12-17; ⊙8am-3pm; 🗷) There's excellent people-watching and even better eating to be had at this Todd Mall cafe which offers sophisticated dishes and great coffee. Breakfast is on all day and lunch ranges from a camel panini to a delicious vegan scrambled tofu. There is a focus on organic ingredients and there are a number of gluten-free options.

### Red Ochre Grill
MODERN AUSTRALIAN $$

(Map p210; Todd Mall; mains $14-32; ⊙6.30am-9.30pm) Offering innovative fusion dishes with a focus on outback cuisine, the menu usually features traditional meats plus locally bred proteins, such as kangaroo and emu, matched with native herbs: lemon myrtle, pepper berries and bush tomatoes. The all-day brunch in the courtyard turns out more predictable dishes including excellent eggs benedict.

**Overlanders Steakhouse** STEAKHOUSE $$$
(Map p210; ☑ 08-8952 2159; 72 Hartley St; mains $21-40; ☺ 6pm-late) The place for steaks, big succulent cuts of beef (and crocodile, camel, kangaroo or emu). Amid the cattle station decor (saddles, branding irons and the like) you can take the challenge of the Drover's Blowout, four courses including a platter of the aforementioned Aussie bush meats.

**Afghan Traders** HEALTH FOOD $
(Map p204; cnr Smith St & Helle Cres; ☺ 9am-6pm Mon-Fri, 9am-3pm Sat) Excellent range of organic and wholefoods.

# Drinking

**Annie's Place** BAR
(Map p204; 4 Traeger Ave; ☺ 5pm-late) Bustling backpackers bar. Decent music (sometimes live), leafy beer garden, cheap jugs and poolside drinking.

**Bojangles** BAR
(Map p210; 80 Todd St; ☺ 11.30am-late) Behind the swinging saloon doors is a 'Wild West meets Aussie outback' theme complete with cowhide seats, stockman regalia and a live 3m-long carpet python behind the bar. Bo's is beloved of backpacker groups and station ringers and is jumping most nights of the week.

**Montes** BAR
(cnr Stott Tce & Todd St) Most variety of beers on tap in Alice. Leafy street-front beer garden and plenty of cosy niches. Also good food (p212).

**Todd Tavern** PUB
(Map p210; www.toddtavern.com.au; 1 Todd Mall; ☺ 10am-midnight) This enduring, classically Aussie pub has a lively bar, pokies, decent pub grub and occasional live music on weekends.

# ☆ Entertainment

The gig guide in the entertainment section of the *Centralian Advocate* (published every Tuesday and Friday) lists what's on in and around town.

**Araluen Arts Centre** ARTS CENTRE
(Map p204; ☑ 08-8951 1122; www.araluen.nt.gov. au; Larapinta Dr) The cultural heart of Alice, the 500-seat Araluen Theatre hosts a diverse range of performers, from dance troupes to comedians, while the Art House Cinema screens films every Sunday evening at 7pm (adult/child $15/12). The website has an events calendar.

**Sounds of Starlight Theatre** LIVE MUSIC
(Map p210; ☑ 08-8953 0826; www.soundsofs tarlight.com; 40 Todd Mall; adult/family $30/90; ☺ 8pm Tue, Fri & Sat) This atmospheric 1½-hour musical performance evoking the spirit of the outback with didgeridoo, drums and keyboards, and wonderful photography and lighting is an Alice institution. Musician Andrew Langford also runs free didge lessons (10.30am and 2.30pm Monday to Friday).

**Alice Springs Cinema** CINEMA
(Map p210; ☑ 08-8952 4999; Todd Mall; adult/child $17/13, Tue all tickets $12) The place to go for latest-release Hollywood blockbusters.

# 🛍 Shopping

Alice is the centre for Aboriginal arts from all over central Australia. The places owned and run by community art centres ensure that a better slice of the proceeds goes to the artist and artist's community. Look for the black over red Indigenous Art Code (www. indigenousartcode.org) displayed by dealers dedicated to fair and transparent dealings with artists.

**Aboriginal Art World** INDIGENOUS ART
(Map p210; ☑ 08-8952 7788; www.aboriginalart world.com.au; 89 Todd Mall) Specialises in art from about 70 artists living in South Australia and NT central deserts, particularly Pitjant-jatjara lands. Most art pieces are sold with a DVD showing the artwork being created.

**Central Australian**
**Aboriginal Media Association** MUSIC STORE
(CAAMA; Map p210; ☑ 08-8951 9711; www.caama. com.au; 101 Todd St; ☺ 9am-5pm Mon-Fri) Here at the CAAMA studio, which has its own radio network (8KIN FM), you will find most of the CDs recorded by central Australia's Aboriginal musicians.

**Desert Dwellers** OUTDOOR GEAR
(Map p204; ☑ 08-8953 2240; www.desertdwellers. com.au; 38 Elder St; ☺ 9am-5pm Mon-Fri, 9am-2pm Sat) For camping and hiking gear, head to this shop, which has just about everything you need to equip yourself for an outback jaunt – maps, swags, tents, portable fridges, stoves and more.

**Mbantua Gallery**                    INDIGENOUS ART
(Map p210; ☑08-8952 5571; www.mbantua.com.au; 64 Todd Mall; ☺9am-6pm Mon-Fri, 9.30am-3pm Sat) This privately owned gallery includes a cafe and extensive exhibits of works from the renowned Utopia region, as well as watercolour landscapes from the Namatjira school. The upstairs Educational & Permanent Collection (admission free) is a superb cultural exhibition space with panels explaining Aboriginal mythology and customs.

**Papunya Tula Artists**               INDIGENOUS ART
(Map p210; ☑08-8952 4731; www.papunyatula.com.au; 63 Todd Mall; ☺9am-5pm Mon-Fri, 10am-2pm Sat) The Western Desert art movement began at Papunya Tula in 1971, and today this Aboriginal-owned gallery displays some of this most sought-after art. Papunya Tula works with around 120 artists, most painting at Kintore in the far west.

**Tjanpi Desert Weavers**              INDIGENOUS ART
(Map p204; ☑08-8958 2377; www.tjanpi.com.au; 3 Wilkinson St; ☺10am-4pm Mon-Fri) This small enterprise employs and supports Central Desert weavers from 18 remote communities. Their store is well worth a visit to see the magnificent woven baskets and quirky sculptures created from locally collected grasses.

**Todd Mall Market**                   MARKET
(Map p210; ☺9am-1pm 2nd Sun May-Dec) Buskers, craft stalls, sizzling woks, smoky satay stands, Aboriginal art, jewellery and knick-knacks make for a relaxed stroll.

## ℹ Information

### Dangers & Annoyances
Avoid walking alone at night anywhere in town but particularly around Gap Rd. Catch a taxi back to your accommodation if you're out late.

### Emergency
**Ambulance** (☑000)
**Police** (☑08-8951 8888, 000; Parsons St)

### Internet Access
**JPG Computers** (☑08-8952 2040; Bath St, Coles Complex; per hr $6; ☺9am-5.30pm Mon-Fri, 10am-2pm Sat)
**Water Tank Café** (Hele Cres) Free wi-fi at the Bloomin' Deserts nursery.

### Medical Services
**Alice Springs Hospital** (☑08-8951 7777; Gap Rd)

**Alice Springs Pharmacy** (☑08-8952 1554; 36 Hartley St, shop 19, Yeperenye Shopping Centre; ☺8.30am-7.30pm)

### Money
Major banks with ATMs, such as ANZ, Commonwealth, National Australia and Westpac, are located in and around Todd Mall in the centre.

### Post
**Main Post Office** (☑13 13 18; 31-33 Hartley St; ☺8.15am-5pm Mon-Fri) All the usual services are available here.

### Tourist Information
**Central Land Council** (☑08-8951 6211; www.clc.org.au; PO Box 3321, 31-33 Stuart Hwy, NT; ☺8.30am-noon & 2-4pm) For Aboriginal land permits and transit permits.
**Tourism Central Australia Visitor Information Centre** (☑08-8952 5199, 1800 645 199; www.centralaustraliantourism.com; 60 Gregory Tce; ☺8.30am-5pm Mon-Fri, 9.30am-4pm Sat & Sun) This helpful centre can load you up with stacks of brochures and the free visitors guide. Weather forecasts and road conditions are posted on the wall, and Mereenie Tour Passes ($3.50) and fossicking permits (free) are issued. National parks information is also available. Tourism Central Australia desks are also found at the airport and train station. Ask about their unlimited kilometre deals if you're thinking of renting a car.

### Websites
**Alice Online** (www.aliceonline.com.au) Wonderful stories, new and old, about central Australia.

## ℹ Getting There & Away

### AIR
Alice Springs is well connected, with **Qantas** (☑08-8950 5211, 13 13 13; www.qantas.com.au) operating daily flights to/from capital cities. Other airlines come and go but were not flying to Alice Springs at the time of research. Airline representatives are based at Alice Springs airport. One-way fares from Alice include Yulara (from $168), Adelaide (from $210), Darwin (from $300), Melbourne (from $280), Sydney (from $280), Brisbane (from $310) and Perth (from $350). Check websites for latest timetables and fare offers.

### BUS
**Greyhound Australia** (☑1300 473 946; www.greyhound.com.au; 113 Todd St, shop 3; ☺office 8.30-11.30am & 1.30-4pm Mon-Fri) has regular services from Alice Springs (check website for timetables and discounted fares). Buses arrive at, and depart from, the Greyhound office on Todd St.

| DESTINATION | ONE-WAY FARE ($) | TIME (HR) |
|---|---|---|
| Adelaide | 331 | 20 |
| Coober Pedy | 192 | 8 |
| Darwin | 391 | 22 |
| Katherine | 315 | 16½ |
| Tennant Creek | 195 | 6½ |

Emu Run (p208) runs the cheapest daily connections between Alice Springs and Yulara (adult/child $215/108) and between Kings Canyon and Alice Springs ($189/95). **Gray Line** (☏ 1300 858 687; www.grayline.com; Capricornia Centre 9 Gregory Tce) also runs between Alice Springs and Yulara (adult/child $226/113), and offers a one-way option ($156/113).

Backpacker buses roam to and from Alice providing a party atmosphere and a chance to see some of the sights on the way. **Groovy Grape Getaways Australia** (☏ 1800 661 177; www.groovygrape.com.au) plies the route from Alice to Adelaide on a seven-day, backpacker camping jaunt for $945.

### CAR & MOTORCYCLE

Alice Springs is a long way from everywhere. It's 1180km to Mt Isa in Queensland, 1490km to Darwin and 441km (4½ hours) to Yulara (for Uluru). Although the roads to the north and south are sealed and in good condition, these are outback roads, and it's wise to have your vehicle well prepared, particularly as you won't get a mobile phone signal outside Alice or Yulara. Carry plenty of drinking water and emergency food at all times.

All the major companies have offices in Alice Springs, and many have counters at the airport. Prices drop by about 20% between November and April but rentals don't come cheap, as most firms offer only 100km free per day, which won't get you far. Talk to the people at the **visitor centre** (☏ 08-8952 5199, 1800 645 199) about its unlimited kilometres deal before you book. A conventional (2WD) vehicle will get you to most sights in the MacDonnell Ranges and out to Uluru and Kings Canyon via sealed roads. If you want to go further afield, say to Chambers Pillar, Finke Gorge or even the Mereenie Loop Rd, a 4WD is essential.

**Alice Camp 'n' Drive** (☏ 08-8952 0098; www.alicecampndrive.com; 76 Hartley St) Provides vehicles fully equipped for camping with swags (or tents), sleeping bags, cooking gear, chairs etc. Rates include unlimited kilometres and vehicles can be dropped off at your accommodation.

**Avis** (☏ 08-8953 5533; www.avis.com.au; Crowne Plaza Hotel) Also has an airport counter.

**Britz** (☏ 08-8952 8814; www.britz.com.au; cnr Stuart Hwy & Power St) Campervans and cars; also at the airport. This is also the base for **Maui** (www.maui.com.au) and **Mighty** (www.mightycampers.com.au) campervans.

**Budget** (☏ 08-8952 8899, 13 27 27; www.budget.com.au; 79 Todd Mall & airport)

**Central Car Rentals** (☏ 08-8952 0098; www.centralcarrentals.com.au; 76 Hartley St) A local operator (associated with Alice Camp 'n' Drive) with 2WD and 4WD vehicles which can be equipped with camping gear. Unlimited kilometre rates are available.

**Europcar** (☏ 13 13 90; www.europcar.com.au; airport)

**Hertz** (☏ 08-8952 2644; www.hertz.com; 34 Stott Tce & airport)

**Territory Thrifty Car Rental** (☏ 08-8952 9999; www.rentacar.com.au; cnr Stott Tce & Hartley St)

### TRAIN

A classic way to enter or leave the Territory is by the *Ghan* which can be booked through **Great Southern Rail** (☏ 13 21 47; www.greatsouthernrail.com.au) or **Travelworld** (☏ 08-8953 0488; 40 Todd Mall). Discounted fares are sometimes offered, especially in the low season (February to June). Bookings are essential.

The train station is at the end of George Cres off Larapinta Dr.

## ❶ Getting Around

Alice Springs is compact enough to get to most parts of town on foot, and you can reach quite a few of the closer attractions by bicycle.

### TO/FROM THE AIRPORT

Alice Springs airport is 15km south of the town. It's about $40 by taxi. The **airport shuttle** (☏ 08-8952 2111; Gregory Tce; 1/2 persons one-way $18.50/30 plus $10 each additional person) meets all flights and drops off passengers at city accommodation. Book a day in advance for pick-up from accommodation.

### BUS

The public bus service, **Asbus** (☏ 08-8952 5611), departs from outside the Yeperenye Shopping Centre. Buses run about every 1½ hours from 7am to 6pm Monday to Friday, and from 9am to 12.45pm on Saturday. The adult/child fare for all routes is $2/0.50. There are three routes of interest to travellers: 400/401 has a detour to the cultural precinct, 100/101 passes the School of the Air, and 300/301 passes many southern hotels and caravan parks along Gap Rd and Palm Circuit. The visitor information centre has timetables.

The **Alice Explorer** (☑08-8952 2111, 1800 722 111; www.alicewanderer.com.au; adult/child $44/35; ☺9am-4pm) is a hop-on, hop-off sightseeing bus that covers 11 major sites, including the Telegraph Station, School of the Air, Old Ghan Rail Museum and Araluen. The ticket is valid for two days and the circuit runs every 70 minutes from opposite the visitor information centre on Gregory Tce. You can arrange to be picked up from your accommodation.

TAXI

Taxis congregate near the visitor information centre. To book one, call 13 10 08 or 08-8952 1877.

# MACDONNELL RANGES

The beautiful, weather-beaten MacDonnell Ranges, stretching 400km across the desert, are a hidden world of spectacular gorges, rare wildlife and poignant Aboriginal heritage all within a day's journey from Alice. There's no public transport to either the East or West MacDonnell Ranges; there are plenty of tours from Alice.

# East MacDonnell Ranges

Although overshadowed by the more popular West Macs, the East MacDonnell Ranges are no less picturesque and, with fewer visitors, can be a more enjoyable outback experience. The sealed Ross Hwy runs 100km along the Ranges, which are intersected by a series of scenic gaps and gorges. The gold-mining ghost town of Arltunga is 33km off the Ross Hwy along an unsealed road that is usually OK for 2WD vehicles, however access to John Hayes Rockhole (in Trephina Gorge Nature Park), N'Dhala Gorge and Ruby Gap is by 4WD only.

## Emily & Jessie Gaps Nature Park

Both of these gaps are associated with the Eastern Arrernte Caterpillar Dreaming trail. **Emily Gap**, 16km out of town, has stylised rock paintings and a fairly deep waterhole in the narrow gorge. Known to the Arrernte as Anthwerrke, this is one of the most important Aboriginal sites in the Alice Springs area; it was from here that the caterpillar ancestral beings of Mparntwe originated before crawling across the landscape to create the topographical features that exist today. The gap is a sacred site with some well-preserved paintings on the eastern wall. **Jessie Gap**, 8km further on, is equally scenic and usually much quieter. Both sites have toilets, but camping is not permitted. And both attract flocks of birds looking for a drink. An 8km unmarked bushwalk leads around the ridge between the two gaps.

## Corroboree Rock Conservation Reserve

Past Jessie Gap you drive over eroded flats before entering a valley between red ridges. Corroboree Rock, 51km from Alice Springs, is one of many strangely shaped dolomite outcrops scattered over the valley floor. Despite the name, it's doubtful the rock was ever used as a corroboree area, but it is associated with the Perentie Dreaming trail. The perentie lizard grows in excess of 2.5m, and takes refuge within the area's rock falls. There's a short walking track (15 minutes) around the rock.

## Trephina Gorge Nature Park

If you only have time for a couple of stops in the East MacDonnell Ranges, make Trephina Gorge Nature Park (75km from Alice) one of them. The play between the pale sandy river beds, the red and purple gorge walls, the white tree trunks, the eucalyptus-green foliage and the blue sky is spectacular. You'll also find deep swimming holes and abundant wildlife. The **Trephina Gorge Walk** (45 minutes, 2km) loops around the gorge's rim. The **Ridgetop Walk** (five hours, 10km one way) traverses the ridges from the gorge to John Hayes Rockhole; the 8km return along the road takes about two hours.

The delightful **John Hayes Rockhole**, 9km from the Trephina Gorge turn-off (the last 4km is 4WD only) has three basic **camping sites** (adult/child $3.30/1.65). From here, the gorgeous **Chain of Ponds Walk** (1½ hours, 4km loop) leads past rock pools and up to a lookout above the gorge.

There's a **rangers station** (☑08-8956 9765) and **camping grounds** (adult/child $3.30/1.65) with BBQs, water and toilets at Trephina Gorge and the Bluff.

## N'Dhala Gorge Nature Park

Shortly before the Ross River Resort, a strictly 4WD-only track leads 11km south to **N'Dhala Gorge**. More than 5900 ancient Aboriginal rock carvings and some rare endemic plants decorate a deep, narrow gorge, although the art isn't easy to spot. There's a small, exposed **camping ground** (adult/child $3.30/1.65) without reliable water.

## Ross River

About 9km past the Arltunga turn-off you come to the secluded **Ross River Resort** (📞 08-8956 9711; www.rossriverresort.com.au; unpowered & powered sites $36, bunkhouse $25, d/f cabin $120/150; ❄ ⊠ ), built around a historic stone homestead with basic timber cabins encircling a swimming pool. The stunning camp site is grassy and studded with gums. There's a store with fuel, and it's worth grabbing lunch (mains $15 to $20) or a beer in the Stockman's Bar.

## Arltunga Historical Reserve

Situated at the eastern end of the MacDonnell Ranges, 110km east of Alice Springs, is the old gold-mining ghost town of Arltunga (40km on unsealed road from the Ross Hwy). Its history, from the discovery of alluvial (surface) gold in 1887 until mining activity petered out in 1912, is fascinating. Old buildings, a couple of cemeteries and the many deserted **mine sites** in this parched landscape give visitors an idea of what life was like for the miners. There are walking tracks and old mines (with bats!) to explore, so bring a torch.

The unstaffed visitor information centre has old photographs of the gold-extracting process, plus a slide show on the area's history, and drinking water and toilets. There's no camping in the reserve itself.

From Arltunga it's possible to loop back to Alice along the Arltunga Tourist Dr, which pops out at the Stuart Hwy about 50km north of town. The road runs past the gracious **Old Ambalindum Homestead** (📞 08-8956 9993; www.oldambalindumhomestead.com.au; unpowered/powered sites $25/30, dm $75; ❄ ⊠ ) which offers self-catered accommodation for up to 12 people in the homestead and in the bunkhouse on a working cattle station. Bookings are essential and you need to bring your own food.

## Ruby Gap Nature Park

This remote park rewards visitors with wild and beautiful scenery. The sandy bed of the Hale River sparkles with thousands of tiny garnets. The garnets caused a 'ruby rush' here in the 19th century and some miners did well out of it until it was discovered that the 'rubies' were, in fact, virtually worthless. It's an evocative place and is well worth the considerable effort required to reach it – by high-clearance 4WD. The waterholes at **Glen Annie Gorge** are usually deep enough for a cooling dip.

**Camping** (adult/child $3.30/1.65) is permitted anywhere along the river; make sure to BYO drinking water and a camp cooker. Allow two hours each way for the 44km trip from Arltunga.

# West MacDonnell Ranges

With their stunning beauty and rich diversity of plants and animals, the West MacDonnell Ranges are not to be missed. Their easy access by conventional vehicle makes them especially popular with day-trippers. Heading west from Alice, Namatjira Dr turns northwest off Larapinta Dr 6km beyond Standley Chasm and is sealed all the way to Tylers Pass.

Most sites in the West MacDonnell Ranges lie within the West MacDonnell National Park, except for Standley Chasm, which is privately owned. There are ranger stations at Simpsons Gap and Ormiston Gorge.

## Larapinta Trail

The 230km Larapinta Trail extends along the backbone of the West MacDonnell Ranges and is one of Australia's great long-distance walks. The track is split into 12 stages of varying difficulty, stretching from the Telegraph Station in Alice Springs to the craggy 1380m summit of Mt Sonder. Each section takes one to two days to navigate and passes many of the attractions in the West MacDonnells:

**Section 1** Alice Springs Telegraph Station to Simpsons Gap (23.8km)

**Section 2** Simpsons Gap to Jay Creek (24.5km)

**Section 3** Jay Creek to Standley Chasm (13.6km)

**Section 4** Standley Chasm to Birthday Waterhole (17.7km)

**Section 5** Birthday Waterhole to Hugh Gorge (16km)

**Section 6** Hugh Gorge to Ellery Creek (31.2km)

**Section 7** Ellery Creek to Serpentine Gorge (13.8km)

**Section 8** Serpentine Gorge to Serpentine Chalet Dam (13.4km)

**Section 9** Serpentine Chalet Dam to Ormiston Gorge (28.6km)

**Section 10** Ormiston Gorge to Finke River (9.9km)

**Section 11** Finke River to Redbank Gorge (25.2km)

**Section 12** Redbank Gorge to Mt Sonder (15.8km return)

Trail notes and maps are available from **Parks & Wildlife** (www.nt.gov.au/nreta/parks/walks/larapinta/index.html). Walkers should register their names and itinerary at ☑1300 650 730. And don't forget to deregister.

There's no public transport out to this area, but transfers can be arranged through the **Alice Wanderer** (☑08-8952 2111, 1800 722 111; www.alicewanderer.com.au); see the website for the various costs. For guided walks, including transport from Alice Springs, go through Trek Larapinta (p208).

## Simpsons Gap

Westbound from Alice Springs on Larapinta Dr you come to the **grave of John Flynn**, the founder of the Royal Flying Doctor Service, which is topped by a boulder donated by the Arrernte people (the original was a since-returned Devil's Marble). Opposite the car park is the start of the sealed **cycling track** to Simpsons Gap, a recommended three- to four-hour return ride.

By road, Simpsons Gap is 22km from Alice Springs and 8km off Larapinta Dr. It's a popular picnic spot and has some excellent short walks. Early morning and late afternoon are the best time to glimpse black-footed rock wallabies. The visitor information centre is 1km from the park entrance.

## Standley Chasm (Angkerle)

About 50km west of Alice Springs is the spectacular **Standley Chasm** (☑08-8956 7440; adult/concession $10/8, family 2+2 $25, under 12 $5; ☺8am-5pm, last Chasm entry 4.30pm) which is owned and run by the nearby community of Iwupataka. This narrow corridor slices neatly through the rocky range and in places the smooth walls rise to 80m. The rocky path into the gorge (15 minutes) follows a creek bed lined with ghost gums and

cycads. You can continue to a second chasm (one hour return) or head up Larapinta Hill (45 minutes return) for a fine view. There's a cafe, picnic facilities and toilets near the car park.

## Namatjira Drive

Not far beyond Standley Chasm you can choose the northwesterly Namatjira Dr (which loops down to connect with Larapinta Dr west of Hermannsburg) or continue along Larapinta Dr. Namatjira Dr takes you to a whole series of gorges and gaps in the range like **Ellery Creek Big Hole**, 91km from Alice Springs, and with a large permanent waterhole – a popular place for a swim on a hot day (the water is usually freezing). About 11km further, a rough gravel track leads to narrow **Serpentine Gorge**, which has a waterhole blocking the entrance and a lookout at the end of a short, steep track, where you can view ancient cycads.

The **Ochre Pits** line a dry creek bed 11km west of Serpentine and were a source of pigment for Aboriginal people. The various coloured ochres – mainly yellow, white and red-brown – are weathered limestone, with iron-oxide creating the colours.

The car park for the majestic **Ormiston Gorge** is 25km beyond the Ochre Pits. It's the most impressive chasm in the West MacDonnells. There's a waterhole shaded with ghost gums, and the gorge curls around to the enclosed **Ormiston Pound**. It is a haven for wildlife and you can expect to see some critters among the spinifex slopes and mulga woodland. There are **walking tracks**, including the **Ghost Gum Lookout** (20 minutes), which affords brilliant views down the gorge, and the excellent, circuitous **Pound Walk** (three hours, 7.5km). There's a **visitor centre** (☑08-8956 7799) and a kiosk which is open 11am to 4pm (closed Wednesday).

About 2km further is the turn-off to **Glen Helen Gorge**, where the Finke River cuts through the MacDonnells. Only 1km past Glen Helen is a good lookout over Mt Sonder; sunrise and sunset here are particularly impressive.

If you continue northwest for 25km you'll reach the turn-off (4WD only) to multi-hued, cathedral-like **Redbank Gorge**. This permanent waterhole runs for kilometres through the labyrinth gorge, and makes for an incredible swimming and scrambling adventure on a hot day. Namatjira Dr then heads south and is sealed as far as **Tylers Pass Lookout**, which provides a dramatic view of **Tnorala** (Grosse Bluff), the legacy of an earth-shattering comet impact.

## 🛏 Sleeping & Eating

There are basic **camping grounds** (adult/child $3.30/1.65) at Ellery Creek Big Hole, Redbank Gorge and 6km west of Serpentine Gorge at Serpentine Chalet (a 4WD or high-clearance 2WD vehicle is recommended to reach the chalet ruins). The ritzy **camping area** (adult/child $6.60/3.30) at Ormiston Gorge has showers, toilets, gas barbecues and picnic tables.

**Glen Helen Resort**  HOTEL $
(☎ 08-8956 7489; www.glenhelen.com.au; Namatjira Dr; unpowered/powered sites $24/30, dm/r $30/160; ✳ ✳) At the edge of the national park is the popular Glen Helen Resort which has an idyllic back verandah overlooking the spectacular gorge. This comfortable retreat contains a busy restaurant-pub (breakfast and lunch $8 to $20, dinner $30 to $35) that serves hearty meals and showcases live music on the weekend. There are also 4WD tours available and helicopter flights ranging from $55 (five minutes) to $425, with the $145 Ormiston Gorge flight representing the best value for money.

# RED CENTRE WAY (MEREENIE LOOP)

The Red Centre Way is the 'back road' from Alice to the Rock. It incorporates an 'inner loop' comprising Namatjira (p218) and Larapinta Drive, plus the rugged Mereenie Loop Rd, the short cut to Kings Canyon. This dusty, heavily corrugated road is not to be taken lightly, and hire car companies won't permit their 2WD to be driven on it.

## Larapinta Drive

Continuing south from Standley Chasm, Larapinta Dr crosses the intersection with Namatjira Dr and the Hugh River before reaching the turn-off to the Western Arrernte community of **Wallace Rockhole**, 18km off the main road and 109km from Alice Springs.

You'll be virtually guaranteed seclusion at the **Wallace Rockhole Tourist Park** (☎ 08-8956 7993; www.wallacerockholetours.com.au; un-

powered/powered sites $20/24, cabins $130; ✳ ), which has a camping area with good facilities. Tours must be booked in advance and can include a 1½-hour rock-art and bush medicine tour (adult/child $15/13) with billy tea and damper.

About 26km from the Wallace Rockhole turn-off, continuing along Larapinta Dr, you will pass the lonely **Namatjira Monument**, which is about 8km from Hermannsburg.

## Hermannsburg

POP 625

The Aboriginal community of Hermannsburg (Ntaria), about 125km from Alice Springs, is famous as the one-time home of artist Albert Namatjira and the site of the Hermannsburg Mission.

The whitewashed walls of the **mission** (☎ 08-8956 7402; www.hermannsburg.com; adult/child $10/5; ⊙ 9am-4pm Mar-Nov, 10am-4pm Dec-Feb) are shaded by majestic river gums and date palms. This fascinating monument to the Territory's early Lutheran missionaries includes a school building, a church and various outbuildings. The 'Manse' houses an art gallery and a history of the life and times of Albert Namatjira as well as work of 39 Hermannsburg artists.

The **Kata-Anga Tea Room** (meals $8-12; ⊙ 9am-4pm), in the old missionary house, serves yummy apple strudel and Devonshire teas. Distinctive paintings and pottery by the locals is also on display here and is for sale.

West of Hermannsburg is **Namatjira's House**.

## Finke Gorge National Park

With its primordial landscape, the Finke Gorge National Park, south of Hermannsburg, is one of central Australia's premier wilderness reserves. The top-billing attraction is **Palm Valley**, famous for its red cabbage palms, which exist nowhere else in the world. These relics from prehistoric times give the valley the feel of a picture-book oasis.

Tracks include the **Arankaia walk** (2km loop, one hour), which traverses the valley, returning via the sandstone plateau; the **Mpulungkinya track** (5km loop, two hours), heading down the gorge before joining the Arankaia walk; and the **Mpaara track** (5km loop, two hours), taking in the Finke River, Palm Bend and a rugged amphitheatre (a semicircle of sandstone formations sculpted by a now-extinct meander of

Palm Creek). There's also a popular **camping ground** (adult/child $6.60/3.30).

Access to the park follows the sandy bed of the Finke River and rocky tracks, so a high-clearance 4WD is essential. If you don't have one, several tour operators go to Palm Valley from Alice Springs. The turn-off to Palm Valley starts about 1km west of the Hermannsburg turn-off on Larapinta Dr.

If you are well-prepared there's a challenging route through the national park along the sandy bed of the Finke River. This is a remote and scenic drive to the Ernest Giles Rd, from where you can continue west to Kings Canyon (and Uluru) or east back to the Stuart Hwy. It pays to travel in a convoy (getting bogged is part of the adventure) and get a copy of the *Finke River 4WD Route* notes (www.nretas.nt.gov.au).

# Mereenie Loop Road

From Hermannsburg you can continue west to the turn-off to Areyonga (no visitors) and then take the Mereenie Loop Rd to Kings Canyon. This is an alternative route from Alice to Kings Canyon. The NT Government is planning to seal the road but locals say they'll believe it when they see it. There are deep sandy patches and countless corrugations (call ☑1800 246 199 for latest road conditions) and it's best travelled in a high-clearance 4WD. Be aware that 2WD hire vehicles will not be covered by insurance on this road.

To travel along this route, which passes through Aboriginal land, you need a Mereenie Tour Pass ($3.50), which is valid for one day and includes a booklet with details about the local Aboriginal culture and a route map. The pass is issued on the spot (usually only on the day of travel) at the visitor information centre in Alice Springs, Glen Helen Resort, Kings Canyon Resort and Hermannsburg service station.

# Kings Canyon & Watarrka National Park

The main attraction along this route is one of the most spectacular sights in central Australia – the yawning chasm of **Kings Canyon** in Watarrka National Park. The other ways to get here include the unsealed Ernest Giles Rd which heads west off the Stuart Highway 140km south of Alice Springs, and the sealed Luritja Rd which detours off the Lasseter Hwy on the way to Uluru. The latter is the longest route but easily the most popular and comfortable.

Whichever way you get here you will want to spend some time shaking off the road miles and taking in the scenery. Walkers are rewarded with awesome views on the **Kings Canyon Rim Walk** (6km loop, four hours), which many travellers rate as a highlight of their trip to the Centre. After a short but steep climb (the only 'difficult' part of the trail), the walk skirts the canyon's rim before descending down wooden stairs to the **Garden of Eden**: a lush pocket of ferns and prehistoric cycads around a tranquil pool. The next section of the trail winds through a swarm of giant beehive domes: weathered sandstone outcrops, which to the Luritja represent the men of the Kuniya Dreaming.

The **Kings Creek Walk** (2km return) is a short stroll along the rocky creek bed to a raised platform with views of the towering canyon rim.

About 10km east of the car park, the **Kathleen Springs Walk** (one hour, 2.6km return) is a pleasant wheelchair-accessible track leading to a waterhole at the head of a gorge.

The **Giles Track** (22km one way, overnight) is a marked track that meanders along the George Gill Range between Kathleen Springs and the canyon; before starting out register with the **Overnight Walker Registration Scheme** (☑1300 650 730).

## ☞ Tours

Several tour companies depart from Alice and stop at Kings Canyon on the way to/from Uluru (see p208).

**Kings Creek Helicopters**     HELICOPTER FLIGHT
(☑08-8956 7083; www.kingscreekstation.com.au; flights per person $60-445) Flies from Kings Creek Station, including a breathtaking 30-minute canyon flight for $275.

**Professional Helicopter Services**     HELICOPTER FLIGHT
(PHS; ☑08-8956 7873; www.phs.com.au; flights per person $95-275) Picking up from Kings Canyon Resort, PHS buzzes the canyon for eight/15 minutes ($95/145).

## 🛏 Sleeping & Eating

**Kings Creek Station**     CABINS $$
(☑08-8956 7474; www.kingscreekstation.com.au; Luritja Rd; unpowered/powered sites $17/19, safari

# Kings Canyon

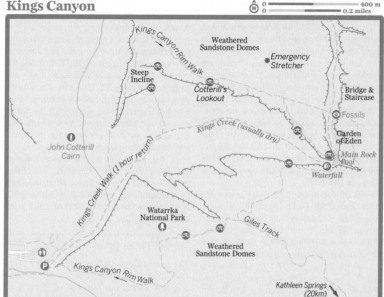

Kings Canyon Rim Walk

Weathered Sandstone Domes

Emergency Stretcher

Steep Incline

Cotterill's Lookout

Bridge & Staircase

Fossils

Kings Creek (usually dry)

Garden of Eden

John Cotterill Cairn

Kings Creek Walk (1 hour return)

Main Rock Pool

Waterfall

Watarrka National Park

Giles Track

Weathered Sandstone Domes

Kings Canyon Rim Walk

Kathleen Springs (20km)

cabins s/d incl breakfast $103/165; @ ⛱) Located 35km before the canyon, this family-run station offers a bush camping experience among the desert oaks. Cosy safari-style cabins (small canvas tents on solid floors) share amenities and a kitchen-BBQ area. You can tear around the desert on a quad bike (one-hour ride $93) or enjoy the more sedate thrills of a sunset camel ride (one-hour ride $60). Fuel, ice, beer, wine, BBQ packs and meals are available at the shop (open 7am to 7pm). Ask about **Conways' Kids** (www.conwayskids.org.au), a charitable trust set up by the owners to send local indigenous children to school in Adelaide.

**Kings Canyon Resort**      RESORT **$$$**
(☎1300 863 248; www.kingscanyonresort.com.au; Luritja Rd; unpowered/powered sites $38/42, dm $35, budget d $139, standard/deluxe spa d $279/339; ✲@⛱⛱) Only 10km from the canyon, this well-designed resort boasts a wide range of accommodation from a grassy camp area with its own pool and bar to deluxe rooms with an almost-outdoor spa. Eating and drinking options are as varied, with a cafe, a restaurant for buffet breakfasts and dinner, a bar with pizzas, an outback BBQ for big steaks and live entertainment. **Under the Desert Moon** ($160 per person; ☉ Apr-Oct) offers an exclusive six-course candlelit dinner around a campfire. There's a general store with fuel and an ATM at reception.

**Kings Canyon Wilderness Lodge** RESORT **$$$**
(☎1800 891 121; www.aptouring.com.au; Luritja Rd; tented cabins s/d $599/740; ✲) ☞ In a secret pocket of Kings Creek Station is this luxury retreat with 10 stylish tents offering private en-suite facilities and decks with relaxing bush views. Run by APT, independent travellers may find themselves squeezed in among tour groups. Tariff includes breakfast and dinner.

# SOUTH OF ALICE SPRINGS

## Old South Road

The Old South Road, which runs close to the old *Ghan* railway line, is pretty rough and really requires a 4WD. It's only 39km from Alice Springs to Ewaninga, where prehistoric Aboriginal petroglyphs are carved into sandstone. The rock carvings found here and at N'Dhala Gorge are thought to have been made by Aboriginal people who lived here before those currently in the region, between 1000 and 5000 years ago.

The eerie, sandstone Chambers Pillar, southwest of Maryvale Station, towers 50m above the surrounding plain and is carved with the names and visit dates of early explorers – and, unfortunately, some much less worthy modern-day graffiti. To the Aboriginal people of the area, Chambers Pillar is the remains of Itirkawara, a powerful gecko ancestor. Most photogenic at sunset and sunrise, it's best to stay overnight at the camping ground (adult/child $3.30/1.65). It's 160km from Alice Springs, and a 4WD is required for the last 44km from the turn-off at Maryvale Station.

Back on the main track south, you eventually arrive at Finke (Aputula), a small Aboriginal community 230km from Alice Springs. When the old *Ghan* was running, Finke was a thriving town; these days it seems to have drifted into a permanent torpor, except when the Finke Desert Race is staged. Fuel is sold at the Aputula Store (☑ 08-8956 0968; ⊙ 9am-noon & 2-4pm Mon-Fri, 9am-noon Sat), which is also an outlet for local artists' work.

From Finke, you can turn west along the Goyder Stock Rte to join the Stuart Hwy at Kulgera (150km), or east to Old Andado station on the edge of the Simpson Desert (120km). Just 21km west of Finke, and 12km north of the road along a signposted track, is the Lambert Centre. The point marks Australia's geographical centre and features a 5m-high version of the flagpole found on top of Parliament House in Canberra.

## Rainbow Valley Conservation Reserve

This series of freestanding sandstone bluffs and cliffs, in shades ranging from cream to red, is one of central Australia's more extraordinary sights. A marked walking trail takes you past claypans and in between the multihued outcrops to the aptly named Mushroom Rock. Rainbow Valley is most striking in the early morning or at sunset, but the area's silence will overwhelm you whatever time of day you are here.

The park lies 24km off the Stuart Hwy along a 4WD track that's 77km south of Alice Springs. It has a pretty exposed camping ground (adult/child $3.30/1.65) but the setting is perfectly positioned for sunset viewing.

## Stuarts Well

About 90km south of Alice Springs, drivers are urged to 'have a spell' at Stuarts Well. It's worth stopping in for a burger and a beer at Jim's Place (☑ 08-8956 0808; 08-8952 2111; unpowered/powered sites $20/25, budget r with own swag/supplied linen $15/30, cabins s/d $75/95; ❄ @ ☒) run by well-known outback identity Jim Cotterill, who along with his father opened up Kings Canyon to tourism. You might also catch a performance by Dinky the singing and piano-playing dingo.

If you would like to ride a camel, Camels Australia (☑ 08-8956 0925; www.camels-australia.com.au; ⊙ 7am-5pm) offers a short spin around the yard for adult/child $6/5, a 30-minute jaunt for $25/20 or a full hour ride for $45/35.

## Ernest Giles Road

The Ernest Giles Rd heads off to the west of the Stuart Hwy about 140km south of Alice and is a shorter but much rougher route to Kings Canyon only recommended for 4WD vehicles.

### HENBURY METEORITE CRATERS

About 11km west of the Stuart Hwy, a corrugated track leads 5km off Ernest Giles Rd to this cluster of 12 small craters, formed after a meteor fell to Earth 4700 years ago. The largest of the craters is 180m wide and 15m deep.

There are no longer any fragments of the meteorites at the site, but the Museum of Central Australia (p203) in Alice Springs has a small chunk that weighs 46.5kg.

There are also some pretty exposed camp sites (adult/child $3.30/1.65) available.

## Lasseter Highway

The Lasseter Hwy connects the Stuart Hwy with Uluru-Kata Tjuta National Park, 244km to the west from the turn-off at Erldunda. At Erldunda food, fuel and accommodation is available at the Desert Oaks Resort (☑ 08-8956 0984; www.desertoaksresort.com; Stuart Hwy, Erldunda; unpowered/powered sites $22/32, dm $18, motel s/d from $100/118; ❄ ☒).

**Mt Conner**, the large mesa (table-top mountain) that looms 350m out of the desert, is the outback's most photographed red herring – on first sighting many mistake it for Uluru. It has great significance to local Aboriginal people, who know it as Atila.

Curtin Springs Wayside Inn (📞08-8956 2906; www.curtinsprings.com; Lasseter Hwy; unpowered/powered sites free/$25, s/d $65/95, r with bathroom $150; ❂) is the last stop before Yulara about 80km away, and the closest alternative to staying at Ayers Rock Resort. You can pitch a tent for free (showers $3) or bed down in a well-maintained cabin. There's fuel, a store with limited supplies and takeaway and bistro meals (mains $20 to $32), plus a bar.

# ULURU-KATA TJUTA NATIONAL PARK

For many visitors, Australian and international, a visit to Uluru is high on the list of 'must-sees' and the World Heritage–listed icon has attained the status of a pilgrimage. But the park offers much more than just the multidimensional grandeur of Uluru. Along with the equally (some say more) impressive Kata Tjuta (the Olgas) the area is of deep cultural significance to the traditional owners, the Pitjantjatjara and Yankuntjatjara Aboriginal peoples (who refer to themselves as Anangu). The Anangu officially own the national park, which is leased to Parks Australia and jointly administered.

Although many of the 400,000 annual visitors whiz through here in 24 hours, it's recommended to spend at least the three days the entry pass allows. There's plenty to see and do: meandering walks, guided tours, desert culture and contemplating the many changing colours and moods of the great monolith itself.

The only accommodation is Ayers Rock Resort (p228) in the Yulara village, 20km from the Rock, where you can expect premium prices, reflecting the remote locale.

## ℹ Information

The **park** (www.environment.gov.au/parks/uluru; adult/child $25/free) is open from half an hour before sunrise to sunset daily (varying between 5am to 9pm November to March and 6am to 7.30pm April to October). Entry permits are valid for three days and available at the drive-through entry station on the road from Yulara.

**Uluru-Kata Tjuta Cultural Centre** (📞08-8956 1128; ⊙7am-6pm) is 1km before Uluru on the road from Yulara and should be your first stop. Displays and exhibits focus on tjukurpa (Aboriginal law, religion and custom) and the history and management of the national park.

The information desk in the Nintiringkupai building is staffed by park rangers who supply the informative *Visitor Guide*, leaflets and walking notes. During the week a local Anangu ranger runs a presentation at 10am each morning on bush foods and Aboriginal history.

The Cultural Centre encompasses the craft outlet **Maruku Arts** (📞08-8956 2558; www.maruku.com.au; ⊙8.30am-5.30pm), owned by about 20 Anangu communities from across central Australia (including the local Mutitjulu community), selling hand-crafted wooden carvings, bowls and boomerangs. **Walkatjara Art Centre** (📞08-8956 2537; ⊙9am-5.30pm) is a working art centre owned by the local Mutitjulu community. It focuses on paintings and ceramics created by women from Mutitjulu. **Ininti Cafe & Souvenirs** (📞08-8956 2214; ⊙7am-5pm) sells souvenirs such as T-shirts, ceramics, hats, CDs and a variety of books on Uluru, Aboriginal culture, bush foods and the flora and fauna of the area. The attached cafe serves ice cream, pies and light meals.

## ⌖ Tours

### Bus Tours

**Seit Outback Australia**　　　BUS TOURS
(📞08-8956 3156; www.seitoutbackaustralia.com.au) This small group tour operator has numerous options including a sunset tour around Uluru (adult/child $139/110), and a sunrise tour at Kata Tjuta for the same price including breakfast and a walk into Walpa Gorge.

**AAT Kings**　　　BUS TOURS
(📞08-8956 2171; www.aatkings.com) Operating the biggest range of coach tours, AAT offers a range of half- and full-day tours from Yulara. Check the website or enquire at the Tour & Information Centre in Yulara.

### Camel Tours

**Uluru Camel Tours**　　　CAMEL TOURS
(📞08-8956 3333; www.ulurucameltours.com.au; short rides adult/child $15/10; ⊙10.30am-2.30pm) View Uluru and Kata Tjuta from a distance atop a camel ($75, 1½ hours) or take the popular Camel to Sunrise and Sunset tours ($119, 2½ hours).

### Cultural Tours

★**Uluru Aboriginal Tours**　　　INDIGENOUS
(📞0447 878 851; www.uluruaboriginaltours.com.au; guided tours starting from $45 per person) Owned and operated by Anangu from the Mutitjulu community, this company offers a range of trips to give you an insight into the significance of the Rock through the eyes of the traditional owners. Tours operate

# South of Alice Springs

Tropic of Capricorn

Haasts Bluff

MacDonnell

Namatjira Dr

Tylers Pass

Tnorala
(Gosse Bluff)
Conservation
Reserve

Namatjira's
House

6

Hermannsburg

Haasts Bluff
Aboriginal Land

Mereenie Loop Rd

Kings Canyon
Resort

James Ranges

Palm Valley

Watarrka
National Park

George Gill Range

Walker Creek

Finke Gorge
National Park

McMinn

Kings
Canyon

Peterman Creek

Tempe
Downs

Kings Creek

Kings Creek
Station

Luritja Rd

6

Ernest Giles Rd

Waymour

Petermann
Aboriginal Land

Lake
Amadeus

Luritja Rd

Connellan
Airport

Katiti
Aboriginal
Land

Kernot

Mt Ebenezer
(700m)

4

Kata Tjuta
(The Olgas)

Lasseter Hwy

Yulara

Curtin
Springs

Range

Mt Ebenezer

4

Uluru
(Ayers Rock)

Mt Conner
Lookout

Uluru-Kata Tjuta
National Park

Mt Conner
(350m)

Britten Jones Creek

Mulga Park

Mulga Park Rd

**SOUTH AUSTRALIA**

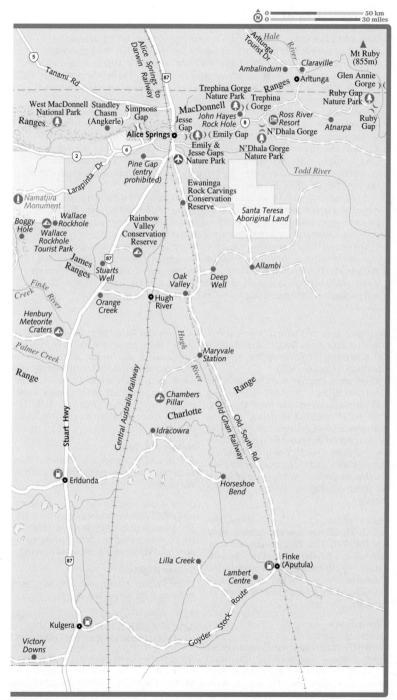

## A QUESTION OF CLIMBING

Many visitors consider climbing Uluru to be a highlight – even a rite of passage – of a trip to the centre. But for the traditional owners, the Anangu, Uluru is a sacred place. The path up the side of the rock is part of the route taken by the Mala ancestors on their arrival at Uluru and has great spiritual significance – and is not to be trampled by human feet. When you arrive at Uluru you'll see a sign from the Anangu saying 'We don't climb' and a request that you don't climb either.

The Anangu are the custodians of Uluru and take responsibility for the safety of visitors. Any injuries or deaths that occur are a source of distress and sadness to them. For similar reasons of public safety, Parks Australia would prefer that people didn't climb. It's a very steep ascent, not to be taken lightly, and each year there are several air rescues, mostly from people suffering heart attacks. Furthermore, Parks Australia must constantly monitor the climb and close it on days where the temperature is forecast to reach 36°C or strong winds are expected.

So if the Anangu don't want people to climb and Parks Australia would prefer to see it closed, why does it remain open? The answer is tourism. The tourism industry believes visitor numbers would drop significantly – at least initially – if the climb was closed, particularly from visitors thinking there is nothing else to do at Uluru.

The debate has grown louder in recent years and a commitment has been made to close the climb for good, but only when there are adequate new visitor experiences in place or when the proportion of visitors climbing falls below 20%. Until then, it remains a personal decision and a question of respect. Before deciding, visit the Cultural Centre and perhaps take an Anangu guided tour. You might just change your mind.

and depart from the Cultural Centre, as well as from Yulara Ayers Rock Resort (through AAT Kings) and from Alice Springs (through Adventure Tours Australia).

There are a range of tours including the New Dawn Rising tour, which includes bush skills demonstrations, like spear throwing, a hot buffet breakfast around a campfire, and unparalleled insights into traditional lore and legend from your local guide. There are also guided strolls down the Liru and Kuniya Walks, and more tours on offer depending on the season. Phone or email for the latest offerings of self-drive tours and packages.

**Desert Tracks**   CULTURAL TOURS
(☑ 0439 500 419; www.deserttracks.com.au; adult/child $249/199) This Pitjantjatjara-run company offers a full-day 4WD journey into the remote Pitjantjatjara Lands to meet the traditional owners of Cave Hill and view some spectacular rock art depicting the Seven Sisters story.

### Dining Tours
**Sounds of Silence**   DINING
(☑ 08-8957 7448; www.ayersrockresort.com.au/sounds-of-silence; adult/child $169/87) Waiters serve champagne and canapés on a desert dune with stunning sunset views

of Uluru and Kata Tjuta. Then it's a buffet dinner (with emu, croc and roo) beneath the southern sky, which, after dinner, is dissected and explained with the help of a telescope. If you're more of a morning person, try the similarly styled **Desert Awakenings 4WD Tour** (adult/child $158/122). Neither tour is suitable for children under 10 years.

### Motorcycle Tours
Sunrise and sunset tours to Uluru and Kata Tjuta can also be had on the back of a Harley Davidson.

**Uluru Motorcycle Tours**   MOTORCYCLE
(☑ 08-8956 2019; www.ulurucycles.com; rides $95-325) Motors out to Uluru at sunset ($170, 1½ hours) or rent your own bike if you're an experienced rider (from $290 for two hours).

### Scenic Flights
Prices are per person and include airport transfers from Ayers Rock Resort.

**Ayers Rock Helicopters**   HELICOPTER FLIGHTS
(☑ 08-8956 2077) A 15-minute buzz of Uluru costs $145; to include Kata Tjuta costs $275.

**Ayers Rock Scenic Flights**   SCENIC FLIGHTS
(☑ 08-8956 2345; www.ayersrockflights.com.au) Prices start from $100 for a 20-minute

flight over Uluru. Include Kata Tjuta and it's $200. For $495 you get a two-hour flight that also takes in Lake Amadeus and Kings Canyon.

# Uluru (Ayers Rock)

Nothing quite prepares you for the first sight of Uluru on the horizon – it will astound even the most jaded traveller. Uluru is 3.6km long and rises a towering 348m from the surrounding sandy scrubland (867m above sea level). If that's not impressive enough, it's believed that two-thirds of the rock lies beneath the sand. Closer inspection reveals a wondrous contoured surface concealing numerous sacred sites of particular significance to the Anangu. If your first sight of Uluru is during the afternoon, it appears as an ochre-brown colour, scored and pitted by dark shadows. As the sun sets, it illuminates the rock in burnished orange, then a series of deeper reds before it fades into charcoal. A performance in reverse, with marginally fewer spectators, is given at dawn.

## ✦ Activities

### Walking

There are walking tracks around Uluru, and ranger-led walks explain the area's plants, wildlife, geology and cultural significance. All the trails are flat and suitable for wheelchairs. Several areas of spiritual significance are off limits to visitors; these are marked with fences and signs. The Anangu ask you not to photograph these sites.

The excellent *Visitor Guide & Maps* brochure, which can be picked up at the Cultural Centre, gives details on a few self-guided walks.

**Base Walk**                                    WALKING
This track (10.6km, three to four hours) circumnavigates the rock, passing caves and paintings, sandstone folds and geological abrasions along the way.

**Liru Walk**                                    WALKING
Links the Cultural Centre with the start of the Mala walk and climb, and winds through strands of mulga before opening up near Uluru (4km return, 1½ hours).

**Mala Walk**                                    WALKING
From the base of the climbing point (2km return, one hour), interpretive signs explain the tjukurpa of the Mala (hare-wallaby people), which is significant to the Anangu, as well as fine examples of rock art. A ranger-guided walk (free) along this route departs at 10am (8am from October to April) from the car park.

## Uluru (Ayers Rock)

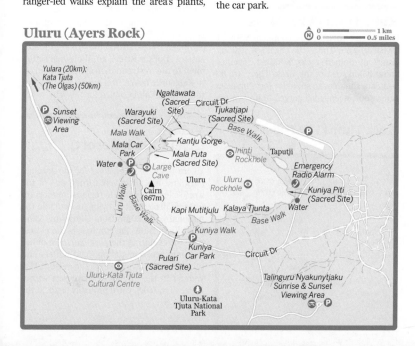

### Kuniya Walk
WALKING

A short walk (1km return, 45 minutes) from the car park on the southern side leads to the most permanent waterhole, Mutitjulu, home of the ancestral watersnake. Great birdwatching and some excellent rock art are highlights of this walk.

### Uluru Climb
WALKING

The Anangu ask that visitors respect Aboriginal law by not climbing Uluru. The steep and demanding path (1.6km return, two hours) follows the traditional route taken by ancestral Mala men. The climb is often closed (sometimes at short notice) due to weather and Anangu business. Between January and February the climb is closed at 8am.

### Sunset & Sunrise Viewing Areas

About halfway between Yulara and Uluru, the sunset viewing area has plenty of car and coach parking for that familiar postcard view. The Talnguru Nyakunytjaku sunrise viewing area is perched on a sand dune and captures both the Rock and Kata Tjuta in all their glory. It also has two great interpretive walks (1.5km) about women's and men's business. There's a shaded viewing area, toilets and a place to picnic.

## Kata Tjuta (The Olgas)

No journey to Uluru is complete without a visit to Kata Tjuta (the Olgas), a striking group of domed rocks huddled together about 35km west of the Rock. There are 36 boulders shoulder to shoulder forming deep valleys and steep-sided gorges. Many visitors find them even more captivating than their prominent neighbour. The tallest rock, **Mt Olga** (546m, 1066m above sea level) is approximately 200m higher than Uluru. Kata Tjuta means 'many heads' and is of great tjukurpa significance, particularly for men, so stick to the tracks.

The 7.4km **Valley of the Winds** loop (two to four hours) is one of the most challenging and rewarding bushwalks in the park. It winds through the gorges giving excellent views of the surreal domes and traversing varied terrain. It's not particularly arduous, but wear sturdy shoes, and take plenty of water. Starting this walk at first light often rewards you with solitude, enabling you to appreciate the sounds of the wind and bird calls carried up the valley.

The short signposted track beneath towering rock walls into pretty **Walpa Gorge** (2.6km return, 45 minutes) is especially beautiful in the afternoon, when sunlight floods the gorge.

There's a picnic and sunset-viewing area with toilet facilities just off the access road a few kilometres west of the base of Kata Tjuta. Like Uluru, Kata Tjuta is at its glorious, blood-red best at sunset.

## Heading West

A lonely sign at the western end of Kata Tjuta points in the direction of WA. If suitably equipped you can travel the 181km to Kaltukatjara (Docker River), an Aboriginal settlement to the west, and then about 1500km on to Kalgoorlie in WA. You need a permit from the Central Land Council for this trip.

## Yulara (Ayers Rock Resort)

POP 887

Yulara is the service village for the national park and has effectively turned one of the world's least hospitable regions into a comfortable place to stay. Lying just outside the national park, 20km from Uluru and 53km from Kata Tjuta, the complex is the closest base for exploring the park. Yulara supplies the only accommodation, food outlets and other services available in the region. If it weren't in the middle of the desert within cooee of the rock you'd probably baulk at the prices.

### Kata Tjuta (The Olgas)

> ### SUNSET WITH SOLITUDE
>
> Uluru at sunset is a mesmerising experience but it can be hard to escape the crowds and their cameras. Here park rangers share their secrets for a sunset with solitude.
>
> **Talinguru Nyakunytjaku** Wildly popular at dawn, but at sunset you'll have both Uluru and Kata Tjuta, in silhouette, in the same shot, all to yourself.
>
> **Kantju Gorge** Head to the end of the Mala Walk in time for a dazzling sunset on the walls of the Rock.
>
> **Kata Tjuta Sunset Viewing** Take a seat in a private area and watch the colours change to the deepest red.
>
> **Mutitjulu Waterhole** For profound peace follow the Kuniya Walk to this glorious waterhole.

## ⊙ Sights & Activities

The Ayers Rock Resort conducts numerous free activities throughout the day: from spear, boomerang and didgeridoo classes to dance programs. Pick up a program at your accommodation.

**Mulgara Gallery** ART GALLERY
(Sails in the Desert Hotel) Quality handmade Australian arts and crafts are displayed here. Each month brings a new artist in residence.

**Uluru Outback Sky Journey** STARGAZING
(☑08-8956 2563; Tour & Information Centre; adult/child $38/free; ⊙30 min after sunset) Takes an informative one-hour look at the startlingly clear outback night sky with a telescope and an astronomer. Tour starts at the Yulara Town Square.

## 🛏 Sleeping

All of the accommodation in Yulara, including the camping ground and hostel, is owned by the Ayers Rock Resort. And unless the free camping at Curtin Springs station outweighs the risk of driving in the dark for sunrise/sunset at Uluru, there's no other option. Even though there are almost 5000 beds, it's wise to make a reservation, especially during school holidays. Bookings can be made through **central reservations** (☑1300 134 044; www.ayersrockresort.com.au). Substantial discounts are usually offered if you book for two or three nights or more, and you can also save a reasonable amount through internet sites offering discount accommodation.

**Ayers Rock**
**Resort Campground** CAMPGROUND $
(☑08-8957 7001; camp.ground@ayersrockresort.com.au; unpowered/powered sites $36/41, cabins $150; ❄@☀) A saviour for the budget conscious, this sprawling campground is set among native gardens. There are good facilities, including a kiosk, free BBQs, a camp kitchen and a pool. During the peak season it's very busy and the inevitable pre-dawn convoy heading for Uluru can provide an unwanted wake-up call. The cramped cabins (shared facilities) sleep six people and are only really suitable for a family.

**Outback Pioneer Hotel & Lodge** HOSTEL $
(☑1300 134 044; dm $38-46, d $220-280; ❄@☀) With a lively bar, BBQ restaurant and musical entertainment, this is the budget choice for noncampers. The cheapest options are the 20-bed YHA unisex dorms and squashy four-bed budget cabins with fridge, TV and shared bathroom. There are also more spacious motel-style rooms that sleep up to four people. Children under 12 stay free, though anyone over 12 is an extra $50 a night.

**Emu Walk Apartments** APARTMENTS $$$
(☑1300 134 044; 1-/2-bedroom apt from $380/480; ❄) The pick of the bunch for families looking for self-contained accommodation, Emu Walk has comfortable, modern apartments, each with a lounge room (with TV) and a well-equipped kitchen with washer and dryer. The one-bedroom apartment accommodates four people, while the two-bedroom version sleeps six.

**Desert Gardens Hotel** HOTEL $$$
(☑1300 134 044; r $380-480; ❄@☀) One of Yulara's originals, the standard rooms, particularly the bathrooms, are looking dated but, at the time of research, a major renovation was planned for the near future. Currently the spacious deluxe rooms are the best option, featuring balconies with desert

# Yulara (Ayers Rock Resort)

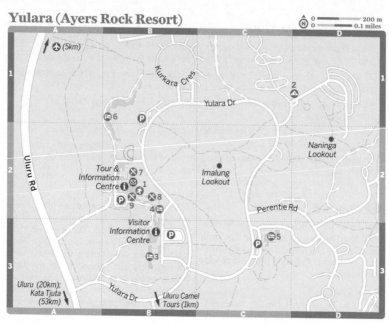

## Yulara (Ayers Rock Resort)

### ◎ Sights
Mulgara Gallery ...............................(see 6)

### ⊕ Activities, Courses & Tours
1 Uluru Outback Sky Journey ................. B2

### 🛏 Sleeping
2 Ayers Rock Resort Campground..........D1
3 Desert Gardens Hotel.........................B3
4 Emu Walk Apartments.........................B2
5 Outback Pioneer Hotel & Lodge ...........C3
6 Sails in the Desert .................................B1

### ✖ Eating
Arngulli Flame Grill .........................(see 3)

Bough House.....................................(see 5)
7 Geckos Cafe .........................................B2
Kuniya ............................................(see 6)
Outback Pioneer Barbecue............(see 5)
Pioneer Kitchen ..............................(see 5)
8 Red Rock Deli.......................................B2
Rockpool.........................................(see 6)
White Gums.....................................(see 3)
Winkiku ...........................................(see 6)
9 Yulara IGA Supermarket ......................B2

### ⊜ Drinking & Nightlife
Bunya Bar .......................................(see 3)
Pioneer Barbecue Bar....................(see 5)
Tali Bar............................................(see 6)

or Uluru views. A big buffet breakfast is served in the restaurant and there's a pleasant pool area shaded with gums.

**Sails in the Desert**　　　　　　HOTEL $$$
(☏1300 134 044; standard d $400, ste $780; ❄@🛜🏊) Although refurbished in 2011/12, the rooms still seem overpriced and by far the best part of this hotel is the lovely (and exclusive) pool and surrounding lawn shaded by sails and trees. There are also tennis courts, a health spa, several restaurants and a piano bar. The best rooms have balcony

views of the rock – request one when you make a booking.

## ✖ Eating

**Red Rock Deli**　　　　　　　　　DELI $
(Resort Shopping Centre; snacks $5-10; ⊙8am-4pm) Line up for steaming-hot espresso and croissants in the morning or grab filled paninis and wraps for lunch.

**Geckos Cafe**　　　　　　　MEDITERRANEAN $$
(Resort Shopping Centre; mains $18-28; ⊙11am-9pm; 🍴) For great value, warm atmosphere

and tasty food head to this buzzing licensed cafe, which, it says, 'cater for everyone'. The wood-fired pizzas, salads and pasta go well with a carafe of sangria, and the courtyard tables are a great place to enjoy the desert night air. There are several veggie and gluten-free options plus meals can be made to takeaway.

**Outback Pioneer Barbecue**       BBQ **$$**
(Outback Pioneer Hotel & Lodge; mains $20-35, salad only $16; ⊘6-9pm) For a fun, casual night out, this lively tavern is the popular choice for everyone from backpackers to grey nomads. Choose between kangaroo skewers, prawns, veggie burgers, steaks and emu sausages and grill them yourself at the communal BBQs. The deal includes a salad bar. In the same complex is the **Pioneer Kitchen** (meals $10-22; ⊘lunch & dinner), doing brisk business in burgers, pizza and kiddie meals.

**White Gums**       BUFFET **$$**
(☑08-8957 7888; Desert Gardens Hotel; buffet $27-33; ⊘6.30-10.30am) Hotel guests enjoy a big hot or cold buffet breakfast here.

**Arngulli Flame Grill**    MODERN AUSTRALIAN **$$**
(Desert Gardens Hotel; 2/3 courses $55/65; ⊘6.30-10.30pm) Featuring fusion cuisine with Asian, Mediterranean and Australian themes, the Arngulli Flame Grill specialises in meat and seafood dinners including Australian native meats such as kangaroo and crocodile.

**Rockpool**       TAPAS **$$$**
(Sails in the Desert; 3 tapas plates $45, plus dessert $50; ⊘11am-10pm) Beside the pool and under the sails, this casual eatery serves Mediterranean and Asian tapas-style dishes and some decadent desserts.

**Winkiku**       BUFFET **$$$**
(Sails in the Desert; breakfast/dinner buffet $38/70; ⊘6.30-10.30am & 6.30-9.30pm) In Yulara's five-star hotel, this casual-yet-stylish restaurant does extravagant seafood buffets with a meat carvery, and all the trimmings and desserts you can imagine. Kids eat free, so it can work out as good value for families. At the time of research a name change was being discussed.

**Bough House**       BUFFET **$$**
(Outback Pioneer Hotel & Lodge; breakfast/dinner buffets $30/52; ⊘6.30-10am & 6.30-9.30pm) This family-friendly, country-style place overlooks the pool at the Outback Pioneer and has buffet spreads for breakfast and dinner. The 'Tastes of Australia' dinner features outback tucker – kangaroo, emu, crocodile and barramundi. Kids under 12 eat free, making this popular with families.

**Kuniya**       MODERN AUSTRALIAN **$$$**
(☑08-8956 2200; Sails in the Desert; mains $45-60; ⊘6.30-9.30pm) Yulara's most sophisticated restaurant, Kuniya is the place for romantic dinners and special occasions. The walls are adorned with contemporary Australian art and the inspired menu features Aussie cuisine infused with native ingredients that complement the extensive Australian wine list. Reservations are essential.

**Yulara IGA Supermarket**       SUPERMARKET **$**
(Resort Shopping Centre; ⊘8am-9pm) This well-stocked supermarket has a delicatessen and sells picnic portions, fresh fruit and vegetables, meat, groceries, ice and camp supplies.

 **Drinking**

**Pioneer Barbecue Bar**       PUB
(Outback Pioneer Hotel & Lodge; ⊘10am-midnight) This rowdy bar is lined with long benches, with plenty of chances to meet other travellers. It has pool tables and live music nightly (usually a touch of twang).

**Tali Bar**       BAR
(Sails in the Desert; ⊘11am-midnight) The cocktails ($18 to $21) at this bar include locally inspired mixes like Desert Oasis. The piano gets a workout most nights during the season from 8pm.

**Bunya Bar**       BAR
(Desert Gardens Hotel; ⊘10.30am-10pm) This is a rather characterless hotel lobby bar, but it knows the importance of well-chilled beer, and the cocktails are several dollars cheaper than at Tali Bar.

**❶ Information**

The useful *Welcome to Ayers Rock Resort* flier is available at the Visitor Information Centre and at hotel desks. Most of the village's facilities are in the shopping centre, including a post office and a local job vacancies board.

**ANZ bank** (☑08-8956 2070) Currency exchange and 24-hour ATMs.

**Emergency** (☑ambulance 0420 101 403, police 08-8956 2166)

**Internet Cafe** (Outback Pioneer Hotel; per 10min $2; ⊘5am-11pm) In the backpacker common room. Internet access is also available at the Tour & Information Centre and all accommodation.

**Post Office** (☎08-8956 2288; Resort Shopping Centre; ⊗9am-6pm Mon-Fri, 10am-2pm Sat & Sun) An agent for the Commonwealth and NAB banks. Pay phones are outside.

**Royal Flying Doctor Service Medical Centre** (☎08-8956 2286; ⊗9am-noon & 2-5pm Mon-Fri, 10-11am Sat & Sun) The resort's medical centre and ambulance service.

**Tour & Information Centre** (☎08-8957 7324; Resort Shopping Centre; ⊗8am-8pm) Most tour operators and car-hire firms have desks at this centre.

**Visitor Information Centre** (☎08-8957 7377; ⊗8.30am-4.30pm) Contains displays on the geography, wildlife and history of the region. There's a short audio tour ($2) if you want to learn more. It also sells books and regional maps.

## Getting There & Away

### AIR

Connellan airport is about 4km north of Yulara. **Qantas** (☎13 13 13; www.qantas.com.au) has direct flights from Alice Springs, Melbourne, Perth, Adelaide and Sydney. **Virgin Australia** (☎13 67 89; www.virginaustralia.com) has daily flights from Sydney.

### BUS

Daily shuttle connections (listed as mini tours) between Alice Springs and Yulara are run by **AAT Kings** (☎1300 556 100; www.aatkings.com) and cost adult/child $150/75. Emu Run (p208) runs the cheapest daily connections between Alice Springs and Uluru ($215/108).

### CAR & MOTORCYCLE

One route from Alice to Yulara is sealed all the way, with regular food and petrol stops. It's 200km from Alice to Erldunda on the Stuart Hwy, where you turn west for the 245km journey along the Lasseter Hwy. The journey takes four to five hours.

Renting a car in Alice Springs to go to Uluru and back is a reasonably priced option if you make the trip in a group.

## Getting Around

A free shuttle bus meets all flights and drops off at all accommodation points around the resort; pick-up is 90 minutes before your flight. Another free shuttle bus loops through the resort – stopping at all accommodation points and the shopping centre – every 15 minutes from 10.30am to 6pm and from 6.30pm to 12.30am daily.

**Uluru Express** (☎08-8956 2152; www.uluru express.com.au) falls somewhere between a shuttle-bus service and an organised tour. It provides return transport from the resort to Uluru (adult/child $50/30, $60/30 for the sunrise and sunset shuttles). Morning shuttles to Kata Tjuta cost $80/45; afternoon shuttles include a stop at Uluru for sunset and cost $90/45. There are also two-day ($170/90) and three-day ($195/90) passes which allow unlimited use of the service. Fares do not include the park entry fee.

Hiring a car will give you the flexibility to visit the Rock and the Olgas whenever you want. **Hertz** (☎08-8956 2244) has a desk at the Tour & Information Centre, which also has direct phones to the **Avis** (☎08-8956 2266) and **Thrifty** (☎08-8956 2030) desks at Connellan Airport.

Bike hire is available at the **Ayers Rock Resort Campground** (☎08-8957 7001; per hr $7, per half-/full day $15/20; ⊗7am-8pm).

# Understand Central Australia

# Central Australia Today

Central Australia is so geographically, socially and climatically diverse, it's little wonder there are all kinds of things causing a ruckus around here at the moment. But despite the ongoing national shame of indigenous welfare and the usual swag of regional political gripes, it's fair to say that the mood here is on the up. GFC concerns linger, but major projects, water in the Murray River and a new, subtle appreciation for the uncrowded wide-open spaces here are keeping locals smiling.

## Best in Film

**The Adventures of Priscilla, Queen of the Desert** (Director Stephan Elliott; 1994) Sequinned Sydney drag queens road-trip to Alice Springs.
**Samson & Delilah** (Director Warwick Thornton; 2009) A devastating portrait of life in a remote outback indigenous community.
**Storm Boy** (Director Henri Safran; 1976) A young boy, his dad and a pelican living in the Coorong.
**Crocodile Dundee I & II** (Directors Peter Faiman/John Cornell; 1986/88) Central Australia hits the cinematic jackpot.
**Australia** (Director Baz Luhrmann; 2008) Kidman goes to the Kimberley (and Darwin).

## Best in Print

**Adelaide** (Kerryn Goldsworthy; 2011) Eccentric, personal biography of Adelaide.
**The Dog Fence** (James Woodford; 2004) Outback life, people and dingoes.
**All Things Bright and Beautiful: Murder in the City of Light** (Susan Mitchell; 2004) Repressed evils beneath Adelaide's famed piety.
**We of the Never Never** (Jeannie Gunn; 1908) Autobiographical account of Gunn's 1902 Top End experiences.

## Murray River Flows

South Australia – Australia's driest state – is still feeling the flow-on effects from incredible flooding across Queensland, New South Wales and Victoria catchments in 2010 and 2011. The mighty River Murray, Australia's version of the Mississippi, is flowing freely again after years of salination and habitat degradation. Riverland irrigators, lower-lakes farmers and environmentalists remain locked in ongoing battles with the Murray-Darling Basin Authority, state and federal governments over water allocations within SA and upstream, but it seems Adelaide's water supply is assured for the moment. So confident in the revitalised Murray is the SA government that the $1.83 billion Adelaide Desalination Plant south of the city, commissioned at the height of the drought and within sight of being fully functional, has been mothballed (for locals, it's a case of 'It's nice to know it's there...').

## Darwin on the Rise

International tourism has taken a downturn in Darwin of late (the GFC is still biting into Top End tourism), but Darwin itself is revelling in real boom-town mood. The city's breezy, multicultural vibe has long been a hit with locals (sunset drinks, markets, Asian food, balmy weather – what's not to like?) but add the new Waterfront Precinct to the mix (restaurants, bars, hotels and a wave pool!) and you've got a potent place to be. It seems the locals are having too much fun to worry about tourism, as numerous new high-rent apartment towers scrape the sky behind them. The newly elected conservative Country Liberal Party territory government will be praying the current $34 billion Icthys export natural gas project continues long-term, firming up the city's economy and cementing its economic ties with Asia.

## Outback Indigenous Issues

Substance abuse, domestic violence, suicide and infant mortality rates in indigenous communities – particularly in the Northern Territory which has such a high indigenous population percentage – remain significantly higher than in the non-indigenous Australian community. Furthermore, indigenous Australians can expect to live for around 10 years less than non-indigenous Australians. In the wake of the Howard government's controversial 'intervention' policies of the mid-2000s, the NT government announced measures to help stem juvenile crime in Alice Springs, including the creation of a youth detention centre and 'safe houses' where young people can go. Indeed – and in spite of booming desert arts commerce – Alice Springs is still a town that survives on the Aboriginal services industry. Even with all the social workers and government funding here, Alice is feeling a little sad, with quite a few empty shopfronts along Todd St.

## Kangaroo Island Fishing Rights

The South Australian state government has proposed a series of marine parks with 'no-take' fish sanctuary zones around the state's coastline – including four around Kangaroo Island – aimed at preserving fish stocks and, in KI's case, its iconic status as wildlife haven. Claiming a lack of consultation and a devastating impact on the island's large net-fishing economy, the KI council (along with 1500 protestors on Kingscote wharf) are up in arms. The number of spray-painted banners around the island seems inversely proportionate to the actual percentage of ocean that will be covered by the scheme (around 6% of SA's ocean territory). But, as any local businessperson will tell you, island economies are fragile things...

## Adelaide Oval Redevelopment

The gorgeous old 1871 Adelaide Oval, oft touted as one of the most picturesque sporting arenas in the world, is undergoing a $575-million facelift. The idea was to reinvigorate the old dame, bringing AFL football to the venue and linking it more easily to the city via a River Torrens footbridge. Gone are the picturesque old stands, making way for two new sexy, scalloproofed southern and eastern stands, plus restaurants, bars and a very corporate vibe. Fortunately, the grassy 'hill' area and magnificent old heritage scoreboard have dodged the wrecking ball, and the excellent Don Bradman Museum will return. Pessimists say it just won't be the same, but many locals think 'different' will also mean 'better'.

POPULATION: **1.88 MILLION**

AREA: **2,332,611 SQ KM**

GDP: **$103.2 BILLION**

GDP GROWTH: **2.4%**

INFLATION: **1.9%**

UNEMPLOYMENT: **4.5%**

## if Central Australia were 100 people

**95** would be non-indigenous
**5** would be indigenous

## where people live
(% of population)

65 Adelaide
7 Darwin
2 Alice Springs
1 Mt Gambier
1 Whyalla
24 other

## population per sq km

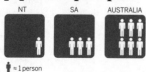

NT · SA · AUSTRALIA

≈ 1 person

# History

In many ways, the history of central Australia, from civilised Adelaide to frontier Darwin, is a distillation of a broader Australian history. Far-reaching indigenous heritage collides with European ambitions, settlements rise and fall, resources and politics intertwine... Presiding over it all, the harsh environment has proved an indomitable force.

## Aboriginal Settlement

For a timely account of central Australian indigenous history, check out the SBS TV series *First Australians* (2008; www.sbs.com.au/firstaustralians), or the accompanying book, edited by Rachel Perkins and Marcia Langton.

Human contact with Australia began around 60,000 years ago, when Aboriginal people journeyed across the straits from what is now Indonesia and Papua New Guinea – the beginning of the world's longest continuous cultural history.

Within a few thousand years, Aboriginal people populated much of Australia. In South Australia (SA), the earliest known Aboriginal relics are rock carvings near Olary, dated at 43,000 years – around the same era as the paintings in the Cave of El Castillo in northern Spain. In Kakadu National Park in the Northern Territory (NT), the oldest rock-art sites date back 20,000 years; further east in Arnhem Land, evidence suggests that rock art was being produced as far back as 60,000 years ago. Central Australia was occupied about 24,000 years ago.

Aboriginal peoples traded goods, items of spiritual significance, songs and dances across central Australia and beyond, using routes that followed the paths of ancestors from the Dreaming, the complex system of country, culture and beliefs that defines indigenous spirituality. An intimate understanding of plant ecology and animal behaviour ensured that food shortages were rare. Even central Australia's hostile deserts were occupied year-round, thanks to scattered permanent wells. Firestick farming was practised in forested areas to the south and north of the deserts, involving the burning of undergrowth and dead grass to encourage new growth, to attract game and reduce the threat of bushfires.

## Early Contact

The Chinese eunuch Admiral Cheng Ho (Zheng He) may have been the first non-Aboriginal visitor to northern Australia. He reached Timor in

| TIMELINE | 60,000 BC | AD 1627 | 1836 |
|---|---|---|---|
| | Experts say that Aboriginal people settled in Australia around this time. Evidence suggests the oldest rock-art sites in the NT are 60,000 years old; those in SA date from 43,000 years. | Dutch captain Francois Thijssen, aboard the *Gulden Zeepaard,* is the first European to spy the coast of SA. The French follow in the 1700s, the British in the 1800s. | The Province of South Australia is proclaimed. The first official settlement at Kingscote on Kangaroo Island is soon replaced by Adelaide, on the advice of Colonel William Light. |

the 15th century, and some suggest he also made it to Australia. In 1879, a small, carved figure of the Chinese god Shao Lao was found lodged in the roots of a banyan tree in Darwin. That's the clincher, the pro-Zheng camp says: the carving apparently dates from the Ming Dynasty (1368–1644).

There's evidence to suggest that the Portuguese were the first Europeans to sight Australia's northern coast, sometime during the 16th century, followed promptly by the Dutch. Famed Dutch navigator Abel Tasman charted the north coast, from Cape York to the Kimberley in Western Australia, in 1664.

Other 17th-century visitors to the north were Macassan traders from the island of Celebes (today's Sulawesi in Indonesia), who set up seasonal camps to gather *trepang* (sea cucumber). Interracial relationships were common, with some local Aboriginal people journeying to Celebes to live.

Down south, the Dutch ship *Gulden Zeepaard* made the first European sighting of the SA coast in 1627. The French ships *Recherche* and *L'Esperance* followed in 1792, while the first British explorer on the scene was Lieutenant James Grant in 1800. In 1802 Englishman Matthew Flinders charted Fowlers Bay, Spencer and St Vincent Gulfs and Kangaroo Island on his ship the *Investigator*.

## Europeans Move In

In 1829 Captain Charles Sturt headed inland from Sydney and fell into the Murray River, floating downstream to Lake Alexandrina (in today's SA). His glowing reports inspired the National Colonisation Society to propose a utopian, self-supporting South Australian colony founded on planned immigration with land sales, rather than convict-based grants. The British Parliament then passed the *South Australian Colonisation Act* in 1834, making SA the only Australian colony established entirely by free colonists (a distinction most South Australians happily highlight).

The first official settlement was established in 1836 at Kingscote on Kangaroo Island, before colonial surveyor-general Colonel William Light

Colonel William Light, celebrated planner of Adelaide, died from tuberculosis in 1839, aged 54. Dogged by criticism and character slurs, he passed away before his vision for the city could fully be appreciated.

HISTORY EUROPEANS MOVE IN

### WHAT LIES BENEATH

In 2005, making way for the billion-dollar Darwin City Waterfront development, Darwin Harbour was dredged for unexploded Japanese bombs. The harbour was peppered with 60kg bombs during WWII, sinking eight ships and damaging many more. Some estimates placed 160 unexploded bombs lying latent at the bottom of the harbour.

With the developers wringing nervous hands, scans detected 230 metal chunks in the mud. Disposal experts were called in, but turned up little more than a brass fuse, a Chinese jug and some remnants of the sunken ship MV *Neptuna*. No bombs, but we suggest you don't go poking around in the sludge...

| 1862 | 1869 | 1894 | 1901 |
| John McDouall Stuart makes the first south–north crossing of the continent from SA into the NT, the highlight of his many epic explorations. | After three other NT colonies all fail to take hold, Palmerston (renamed Darwin in 1911) is established by George Goyder, South Australia's Surveyor-General. | South Australian women are the first in the British Empire permitted to vote, and the first in the world eligible to stand for parliament. | With the federation of the disparate Australian colonies, South Australia becomes a state of the Commonwealth of Australia. |

chose Adelaide as the site for the capital. The first governor, Captain John Hindmarsh, landed at present-day Glenelg on 28 December 1836, and proclaimed the Province of South Australia.

In the NT, early European attempts at settlement – on Melville Island in 1824, Raffles Bay in 1829 and the Cobourg Peninsula in 1838 – all failed in the face of indigenous resistance, disease and climate, until the settlement of Palmerston (renamed Darwin in 1911) was established in 1869.

Conflict marked the arrival of European cattle farmers across central Australia. The Arrernte (*uh*-rahn-da) people defended their lands and spiritual heritage, spearing cattle for food as farmers had destroyed many of their hunting grounds. In return, those waterholes not already ruined by cattle were poisoned, and reprisal raids saw many massacres.

> During the 1850s gold rush in Victoria, thousands of Chinese miners dodged the Victorian government's $10-per-head tax by landing at Robe in SA, then walking 400km to Ballarat: 10,000 arrived in 1857 alone. But the loophole closed when the SA government instituted its own tax on the Chinese.

## Immigration & Exploration

The first immigrants to SA were poor, young English, Scots and Irish. About 12,000 landed in the first four years of settlement, followed by 800 German farmers and artisans between 1838 and 1841 – mainly Lutherans fleeing religious persecution. Around 5400 more Germans arrived by 1850; many more followed during the next decade. They settled mainly in the Adelaide Hills and the Barossa Valley, their vineyards forming the beginning of the SA wine industry. Thousands of Cornish people also came to SA following the discovery of copper in the 1840s, many of them jumping ship to Victoria in the 1850s when gold was discovered there.

In the NT, the discovery of gold and copper south of Darwin (then Palmerston) attracted miners, and settlers with cattle moved into the NT from SA and northern Queensland. In 1877 the first Lutheran mission was established at Hermannsburg; Catholic and Methodist missions followed elsewhere.

Successive waves of immigration fuelled the search for new arable land. Between 1839 and 1841 Edward John Eyre made the first traverse of the Flinders Ranges in SA. In 1839, Charles Bonney drove the first herd of cattle from Melbourne to Adelaide via Mt Gambier.

---

### DINNER ON KI

British explorer Matthew Flinders bumped into Kangaroo Island on 2 March 1802. His crew of hungry sailors stormed ashore in search of sustenance – their eyes boggled at the thousands of kangaroos bouncing around on the beach. Flinders described the inevitable feeding frenzy in his journal: 'The whole ship's company was employed this afternoon in the skinning and cleaning of kangaroos. After four months' privation they stewed half a hundred weight of heads, forequarters and tails down into soup for dinner... In gratitude for so seasonable a supply, I named this south land 'Kangaroo Island'.'

---

| 1942 | 1974 | 1978 | 1980 |
|---|---|---|---|
| Darwin is bombed by the Japanese during WWII – 243 people lose their lives in 64 raids. A mass exodus cripples the Top End economy. | Cyclone Tracy tears through Darwin on Christmas Eve, demolishing 70% of the city's buildings and killing 65 people. Much of the city was rebuilt (more strongly) within four years. | The Northern Territory is granted legislative self-government, but remains under the constitutional auspices of the federal government (and does to this day). | The rickety, washout-prone old *Ghan* railway line through the Flinders Ranges and Oodnadatta is replaced by a new, more reliable standard gauge line 160km further west. |

Five years later, Charles Sturt set off from Adelaide towing a whale-boat to find the mythical central Australian inland sea, but after 18 months of hardship he abandoned it in a waterless red expanse of stones and sandhills. If nothing else, he had discovered the Simpson Desert.

In 1844 Prussian scientist Ludwig Leichhardt set off from Queensland to blaze an overland route into the NT. The party reached the Gulf of Carpentaria and headed northwest. Leichhardt was afforded hero status for his efforts, but his route was too difficult for regular use and no promising grazing areas were discovered.

The hard-drinking John McDouall Stuart made several epic forays into central Australia between 1858 and 1862. His successful south–north crossing of the continent led to SA wresting governmental control of the NT from NSW in 1863. The Stuart Hwy, from Port Augusta in SA to Darwin, is named in his honour.

## Wheat, Sheep, Copper & Gold

By 1865 SA was growing half of Australia's wheat. Overcropping in the Adelaide Hills and Fleurieu Peninsula led to more land being opened up in the mid-north and Flinders Ranges. A 'wheat boom' ensued. Enthusiastic trumpeting of 'a rich golden harvest' extending into the NT continued until drought struck in the mid-1880s.

Sheep farmers also helped to open up SA, but a tendency to overestimate carrying capacity led to overstocking, and with no pasture kept in reserve, the 1880s drought ruined many. The SA breeders survived by developing a strain of merino sheep suited to semiarid conditions.

By the 1870s SA had replaced Cornwall as the British Empire's leading copper producer, making many South Australians wealthy and leaving a legacy of fine public buildings in mining towns such as Burra.

The NT was opened up with the discovery of gold at Yam Creek, 160km south of Darwin. The find fired up local prospectors, and it wasn't long before other discoveries at Pine Creek, south of Darwin, sparked a minor rush. The SA government built a railway line in 1883 from Darwin to Pine Creek, but the gold rush was soon over. Subsequent government-backed NT projects such as sugar, tobacco and coffee plantations, peanut farming, pearling and crocodile- and snakeskin trading either failed completely or provided only minimal returns.

## Finding Federation

When parliament sprang up in 1856, SA began with the most democratic constitution of any colony. Before that it was governed by representatives from the SA Board of Commissioners and the British government.

Fighting off recession, transport and communications systems grew rigorously in SA. By 1890 railways connected Adelaide with Melbourne,

In 1865 Surveyor-General George Goyder drew an imaginary line across SA: drought-prone land to the north, viable wheat-growing land to the south. Over time, the famed Goyder's Line has proved reliable. But Goyder was pre-climate change: where would he draw the line today?

GOYDER

DOCO DALFIANO / GETTY IMAGES

**1982**
Blaming a dingo, Lindy Chamberlain is jailed for the murder of her baby daughter Azaria at Uluru in 1980. She is finally exonerated in 2012.

**1986**
Paul Hogan stars as Mick 'Crocodile' Dundee and launches Kakadu National Park (in the NT's Top End) onto the world cinematic stage.

➜ The Ghan (p283)

Oodnadatta in the outback, and Cockburn on SA's border with NSW. There were also 3200km of sealed roads and 100-plus steamboats trading on the Murray River. The SA parliament established Australia's first juvenile court in 1890, and granted free education in 1891. In 1894 SA became the first Australian colony to recognise women's right to vote in parliamentary elections, and the first place in the world to allow women to stand for parliament.

With federation in 1901 – the amalgamation of disparate colonies into the states of the Commonwealth of Australia – SA experienced slow but steady growth, but South Australian speculators and investors in the NT were getting cold feet. Soon after federation the South Australian government threw in the towel, offering control of the ugly NT duckling back to the federal government.

## Twentieth-Century Trials

After federation, manufacturing and heavy engineering became important in SA. The Port Pirie smelter was enlarged during WWI, and was soon producing 10% of the world's lead, as well as silver and zinc.

WWI was a time of division in SA. Before 1914 the state had many German place names, but in a fit of anti-German zeal many of these were replaced. Most were reinstated during the 1936 centennial celebrations, when the German settlers' huge contribution to SA's development was officially recognised.

In 1872 Adelaide became the first Australian capital to be connected by telegraph with London, slashing communication times from six months to seven hours.

The early 1920s brought prosperity across Australia, before a four-year drought led into the Great Depression. All states suffered during this period, but SA fared worst of all: in 1931 more than 70,000 people out of a population of 575,000 were dependent on welfare.

Industrial development in SA quickened during WWII – water-pipeline construction, ship building and coal mining all took off – but people in the NT had more pressing issues to contend with. At 9.57am on 19 February 1942, nearly 200 Japanese aircraft bombed Darwin's harbour and the RAAF base at Larrakeyah. Darwin was attacked 64 times during the war and 243 people lost their lives; it was the only place in Australia to suffer prolonged attacks. In March 1942 the entire NT north of Alice Springs was placed under military control and by December there were 32,000 troops stationed in the Top End.

After WWII, the Australian government launched an ambitious scheme to attract immigrants. Thousands of people from Britain, Greece, Italy, Serbia, Croatia, the Netherlands, Poland, Turkey, Malta and Lebanon took up the offer of government-assisted passage. The immigration boom fuelled growth in SA, which shifted from a rural economy to a predominantly industrial one. In the NT the urban areas of Darwin and Alice Springs also grew.

| 1995 | 1998 | 1998 | 2000 |
|---|---|---|---|
| After 10 noisy years, Adelaide hosts the Australian Formula One Grand Prix for the last time. Bon Jovi closes the show with some raucous, pyrotechnic cock rock. | The NT returns a negative result in a referendum on whether it should become a state rather than federally administered territory. The result surprises many. | Ross Fargher stubs his toe on the world's oldest vertebrate fossil on his Flinders Ranges property in SA. At 560 million years old, it beats the previous oldest find by 30 million years. | Mandatory sentencing laws and zero-tolerance policing in the NT increase the jailing of Aboriginal people for trivial offences, causing national outrage. The laws are repealed in 2001. |

# LAND RIGHTS IN CENTRAL AUSTRALIA

Britain colonised Australia on the legal principle of 'terra nullius', meaning the country was unoccupied. Early colonists could therefore take land from Aboriginal peoples without signing treaties or providing compensation. This principle remained legally potent until the landmark Mabo High Court decision in 1992, which voided the presumption of terra nullius and officially recognised native title as a traditional connection to or occupation of Australian lands.

Preceding the Mabo decision, in 1966 the South Australian government made the first move of any Australian state to give Aboriginal peoples title to their land. The Aboriginal Lands Trust was created, vesting title to the missions and reserves still operating in South Australia. These lands are leased back to their Aboriginal occupants, who have repeated rights of renewal. The South Australian parliament then passed two pieces of legislation, the *Prohibition of Discrimination Act* and the *Aboriginal Affairs Act,* giving South Australian Aboriginal peoples the right to run their own communities.

In 1981 the *Pitjantjatjara Land Rights Act* was drawn, granting freehold title to an area of northwest SA to the Anangu-Pitjantjatjara. Another 76,000 sq km, occupied by the federal government as part of the Maralinga project, was returned to traditional owners in 1984. Land held under Aboriginal freehold title cannot be sold or taken back into public ownership, and no development can begin without permission of traditional owners.

A more convoluted land-rights path has been navigated in the Northern Territory. In 1962 a bark petition was presented to the federal government by the Yolngu peoples of Yirrakala, in northeast Arnhem Land, demanding the government recognise Aboriginal peoples' occupation and ownership of Australia since time immemorial. The petition was ignored, so the Yolngu peoples took the matter to court – and lost.

But the wheels had begun to turn, and under increasing pressure the federal government passed the *Aboriginal Land Rights (Northern Territory) Act* in 1976, establishing three Aboriginal land councils empowered to claim land on behalf of traditional owners.

Under the act, the only claimable land is crown land outside town boundaries that no one else owns or leases – usually semidesert or desert. So when the Anangu, Uluru's traditional owners, claimed ownership of Uluru and Kata Tjuta, their claim was overruled because the land was within a national park. It was only by amending two acts of parliament that Uluru-Kata Tjuta National Park was handed back to its traditional owners providing it was leased back to the federal government as a national park.

Around half of the NT has been claimed, or is under claim. The native-title process is tedious and can take years to complete, often without success. Many claims are opposed by state and territory governments, and claimants are required to prove they have continuous connection to the land and are responsible for sacred sites under Aboriginal law. If a claim is successful, Aboriginal peoples have the right to negotiate with mining interests and ultimately accept or reject exploration and mining proposals. This right is often opposed by Australia's mining lobby, despite traditional Aboriginal owners in the NT rejecting only about a third of such proposals outright.

| 2001 | 2004 | 2007 | 2007 |
|---|---|---|---|
| The federal government incarcerates asylum seekers at the Baxter Detention Centre in SA's outback. Some Adelaidians display signs 'Asylum seekers welcome here' in their windows; others go to jail for protesting. | After a 70-year wait, the *Ghan* passenger train runs from Adelaide to Darwin, finally linking the Top End with the southern states. | The federal government's 'Intervention' policy in NT indigenous communities is controversially received in both black and white communities. | Causing general public outrage, the NT government introduces speed limits of 130km/h on the Stuart, Victoria, Arnhem and Barkly Highways. |

The 1960s and '70s were difficult times in SA – economic and population growth were stagnating, and overseas competition heightened a deepening industrial recession. Socially, however, SA premier Don Dunstan's progressive Labor government was kicking goals, passing an act prohibiting racial discrimination (the first in Australia), and creating the South Australian Film Corporation (1972).

The NT was also ailing economically, and the good citizens of Darwin were soon brought to their knees once more. On Christmas Eve 1974, Cyclone Tracy ripped through the city, killing 71 people and destroying more than 70% of Darwin's buildings.

From the late '70s into the 1990s, mining dug a tunnel to economic recovery. In SA, huge deposits of uranium, copper, silver and gold were found at Roxby Downs, plus oil and gas in the Cooper Basin. In the NT, copper and gold were unearthed at Tennant Creek, and oil and gas in the Amadeus Basin. Bauxite was found at Gove, manganese at Groote Eylandt, and uranium at Batchelor and (more controversially) Kakadu.

In the aftermath of Cyclone Tracy in 1974, an exodus saw Darwin's population fall from 45,000 to just 11,000. These days it's bounced back to a cosmopolitan 127,500.

## These Days

Today, mining continues to drive the economies of SA and the NT (and Australia's as a nation), but tourism is the big success story in central Australia. SA has an extremely well-oiled governing tourist body extolling the virtues of the state's diverse regions. In the NT the tourist magnets of Uluru and Kakadu each receive more than half a million visitors per year. At the end of WWII the population of Alice Springs (Uluru's main access point) was around 1000; today it's around 25,000 – a direct result of selling the central Australian outback as 'the real-deal Aussie experience'. The rise in environmental awareness and ecotourism has also boosted Kakadu's popularity.

Across the region, major issues spark and fade and spark again – most notably the aftermath of the 2007 *Northern Territory National Emergency Response* (aka 'The Intervention'), heavily criticised as a backward step in Aboriginal reconcilliation; and in SA, the water levels in the Murray River – but in the big cities daily life continues uninterrupted. Adelaide retains its barrage of quality festivals dappling the calendar: this is a city of substance, grace and poise. Shedding its redneck skin (well, mostly), contemporary Darwin is vibrant, multicultural and increasingly urbane. Although legislative self-governance was granted to the NT in 1978, the federal government retains arm's-length control. Is Darwin the teenage city that will never quite leave home?

| 2011 | 2012 | 2012 | 2013 |
|---|---|---|---|
| Cyclone Yasi and monumental rainfalls across Queensland and NSW bring relief to the drought-stricken Murray River in SA. | Coroner deems that a dingo did in fact kill baby Azaria Chamberlain at Uluru in 1980. Lindy Chamberlain states, 'We live in a beautiful country but it is dangerous.' | The NT elects a new conservative Country Liberal Party government. Incoming Chief Minister Terry Mills is thirsty: 'It's waiting in the fridge... so I'm going to finish [his victory speech] shortly.' | 2010 Tour de France winner Andy Schleck is announced as a starter in the annual Tour Down Under race in SA (who needs Lance Armstrong...). |

# Aboriginal Australia

**Aboriginal culture has evolved over thousands of years with strong links between the spiritual, economic and social lives of the people. This heritage has been kept alive from one generation to the next by the passing of knowledge and skills through rituals, art, cultural material and language.**

## Aboriginal Culture

Aborigines originally had an oral tradition, therefore language played an extremely important part in maintaining and preserving Aboriginal cultures through the passing of knowledge. Today there is a national movement to revive Aboriginal languages and there remains a strong Aboriginal art sector. Traditional knowledge is being implemented in science, natural resource management and government programs. Aboriginal culture was never static but evolved with the changing times and environment. New technologies and mediums are now used to tell their stories, and cultural tourism and hospitality ventures, where visitors can experience an Aboriginal perspective, have been established. You can learn all about ancestral beings at particular natural landmarks, look at rock art that is thousands of years old, taste traditional indigenous foods or attend an Aboriginal festival or performance. There are so many opportunities on offer and many activities opened to the public are advertised in both Aboriginal and mainstream media.

Support for cultural programs is sporadic and depends on the political climate at the time. However, Aboriginal people are determined to maintain their links with the past and to also use their cultural knowledge to shape a better future.

### Land

Aboriginal land ethic was based on humans fitting into the ecology and not outside of it. Everything was connected and not viewed as just soil and rocks but as a whole environment that sustained the spiritual, economic and cultural lives of the people. In turn, Aboriginal people sustained the land by conducting ceremonies, rituals, songs and stories. This interrelation was

## KEY EVENTS

### 1920s
Anthony Martin Fernando, the first Aboriginal activist to campaign internationally against racial discrimination in Australia, was arrested for protesting outside Australia House in London in 1928. He wore a large overcoat with little skeletons pinned to it. His placard read 'This is all that is left of my people.'

### 26 Jan 1938
To mark the 150th anniversary of the arrival of the British, The Aborigines Progressive Association held a meeting in the Australia Hall at 150 Elizabeth St, Sydney, called 'A Day of Mourning and Protest'. The meeting was one of the first known civil rights meetings.

### 15 Aug 1963
A bark petition was presented to the House of Representatives from the people of Yirrikala in the Northern Territory. Written in their own language on a length of stringy bark, the petition objected to mining on their land, which the federal government had approved without consulting the people who lived there.

### 27 May 1967
A federal referendum allowed the Commonwealth to make laws on Aboriginal issues and include them in the census. They would now have the same rights as other Australians.

### 12 Jul 1971
The Aboriginal flag first flew on National Aborigines Day in Adelaide. Designed by Central Australian man, Harold Thomas, the flag has become a unifying symbol of identity for Aboriginal people.

developed and practised over thousands of years. For Aboriginal people land is intrinsically connected to identity and spirituality. All land in Australia is reflected in Aboriginal lore but particular places may be significant for religious and cultural beliefs. Some well-known sites are The Three Sisters in the Blue Mountains and Warreen Cave in Tasmania with artefacts dated around 40,000 years old.

Sacred sites can be parts of rocks, hills, trees or water and are associated with an ancestral being or an event that occurred. Often these sites are part of a Dreaming story and link people across areas. The ranges around Alice Springs are part of the caterpillar Dreaming with many sites including Akeyulerre (Billy Goat Hill), Atnelkentyarliweke (Anzac Hill) and rock paintings at Emily Gap. The most well known are Uluru and Kata Tjuta which is the home of the snake, Wanambi. His breath is the wind that blows through the gorge. Pirla Warna Warna, a significant site in the Tanami Desert for Warlpiri people, is 435km northwest of Alice and is where several Walpiri Dreaming stories meet.

Cultural tours offer visits to Aboriginal sites, learning about plants and animals, hunting and fishing expeditions and even workshops on bushfood or learning to dance.

Please note that many Aboriginal sites are protected by law and are not to be disturbed in any way.

## The Arts

### Visual Arts

It is difficult to define Aboriginal art as one style because form and practice vary from one area to another. From the original art forms of rock art, carving and body decoration, a dynamic contemporary art industry has grown into one of the success stories of Aboriginal Australia.

### Music

Music was always a vital part of Aboriginal culture. Songs were important for teaching and passing on knowledge and musical instruments were often used in healing, ceremonies and rituals. The most well known instrument is the Yadaki or didgeridoo which was only played by men

The *Koori Mail* is an Aboriginal-owned national newspaper. Set up by several Aboriginal communities in 1991 to give a voice to Aboriginal people, it provides news and information on politics, sport, social and cultural life from communities across Australia. It is published fortnightly and can be purchased at most newsagencies.

## THE IMPORTANCE OF STORYTELLING

Aboriginal people had an oral culture so storytelling was an important way to learn. Stories gave meaning to life and were used to teach or translate the messages of the spirit ancestors. Although beliefs and cultural practices vary according to region and language groups, there is a common world-view that these ancestors created the land, the sea and all living things. This is often referred to as the Dreaming and Aboriginal people attribute their origins and existence to these ancestors. Through stories, the knowledge and beliefs are passed on from one generation to another and set out morals and values and rules to live by. They also recall events from the past. Today artists have continued this tradition but are using new mediums like film and writing. The first Aboriginal writer to be published was David Unaipon, a Ngarrindjeri man from South Australia who was a writer, scientist and advocate for his people. Born in 1872, he published *Aboriginal Legends* in 1927 and *Native Legends* in 1929.

Other early writers were Oodgeroo Noonuccal, Kevin Gilbert and Jack Davis. All have works published. Contemporary writers of note are Alexis Wright, Kim Scott, Anita Heiss and Ali Cobby Eckerman. Award-winning novels to read are Kim Scott's *Deadman Dancing* (Picador Australia) and *Benang* (Fremantle Press), Alexis Wright's *Carpentaria* (Giramando) and Ali Cobby Eckerman's *Little Bit Long Time* (Picaro Press) and *Ruby Moonlight* (Magabala Books).

in northern Australia. Other instruments included clapsticks, rattles and boomerangs and in southern Australia, animal skins were stretched across the lap to make a drumming sound.

This rich musical heritage continues today with a very strong contemporary music industry. Like other art forms, Aboriginal music has developed into a fusion of new ideas and styles mixed with strong cultural identity and a few musicians have been successful in mainstream music. Contemporary artists like Dan Sultan and Jessica Mauboy have crossed over successfully into the mainstream winning major music awards and seen regularly on popular programs and at major music festivals. Aboriginal radio is the best and most accessible way to hear Aboriginal music.

## Performing Arts

Dance and theatre are a vital part of social and ceremonial life and important elements in Aboriginal culture. Dances often told stories for passing on knowledge. Styles varied from one nation to the next and depended on whether it was for social or ritual reasons. Imitation of animals, birds and the elements was common across Australia but dance movements like set arm, leg and body movements differed greatly. Ceremonial or ritual dances were highly structured and distinct from the dancing that people did socially at corroborrees. Like other art forms, dance has adapted to the modern world and contemporary dance companies and groups have merged traditional forms into a modern interpretation. The most well known dance company is the internationally acclaimed company Bangarra Dance Theatre.

Theatre also draws on the storytelling tradition. Currently there are two major Aboriginal theatre companies, Ilbijerri in Melbourne and Yirra Yakin in Perth. In addition there are several mainstream companies that specialise in Aboriginal stories. These companies have had several successes with productions here and overseas. Australia has a thriving Aboriginal theatre industry and many Aboriginal actors and writers work in or collaborate with mainstream productions. Traditionally drama and dance came together in ceremonies or corroborees and this still occurs in many contemporary productions.

## TV, Radio & Film

Aboriginal people have quickly adapted to electronic broadcasting and have developed an extensive media network of radio, print and television services.

There are more than 120 Aboriginal radio stations and programs operating across Australia in cities, rural areas and remote communities. Program formats differ from location to location. Some broadcast only in Aboriginal languages or cater to a specific music taste.

There is a thriving Aboriginal film industry and in the last few years feature films like *The Sapphires*, *Bran Nue Day* and *Samson and Delilah* have had mainstream

### 26 Jan 1972
The Aboriginal Tent Embassy was set up on the lawns of Parliament House in Canberra to oppose the treatment of Aboriginal people and the government's recent rejection of a proposal for Aboriginal Land Rights.

### 10 Aug 1987
A Royal Commission into Aboriginal Deaths in Custody investigated the high number of Aboriginal deaths in gaols. Aboriginal people are still over represented in the criminal system.

### 26 Jan 1988
As Australia celebrated its bicentenary, more than 40,000 Aboriginal people and their supporters marched in Sydney to mark the 200-year anniversary of invasion.

### 3 Jun 1992
The previous legal concept of *terra nullius* was overturned by the Australian High Court in its landmark decision in the Mabo Case, declaring Australia was occupied before British settlement.

### 28 May 2000
Over 300,000 people walked across Sydney Harbour Bridge to highlight the need for reconciliation between Aboriginal people and other Australians.

### 21 Jun 2007
The federal government suspended the Racial Discrimination Act to implement a large-scale intervention – the Northern Territory Emergency Response – to address child abuse in Northern Territory Aboriginal communities. Extended to 2022 it heavily regulates lives, including mandatory income management.

success. Since the first Aboriginal television channel, NITV, was launched in 2007, there has been a growth in the number of filmmakers wanting to tell their stories.

# History of Aboriginal Australia

Before the coming of Europeans to Australia, culture was the common link for Aboriginal people across Australia. There were many aspects that were common to all groups in Australia and it was through these commonalities that Aboriginal people were able to communicate and interact with each other. In post colonial Australia, it is also the shared history that binds Aboriginal people. Here is a brief description of the major events of that history.

Most Australians celebrate 26 January as Australia Day in recognition of British settlement but for Aboriginal people it is known as 'Invasion Day,' 'Survival Day' or 'Day of Mourning.'

## First Australians

Although academics believe Aboriginal people came from somewhere else, there has never been enough evidence to verify these claims. Over the years, various theories have been presented but have always been challenged. Scientific evidence places Aboriginal people on the continent at least 40,000 to 50,000 years ago. This means that Aboriginal people were here during the ice age and in the megafauna period.

At the time of European contact the Aboriginal population was grouped into 300 or more different nations with distinct languages and land boundaries. Most Aboriginal people did not have permanent shelters but moved within their territory and followed seasonal patterns of animal migration and plant availability. The diversity of landscapes in Australia meant that each nation varied in their lifestyles and cultures. Although these nations were distinct cultural groups, there were also many common elements. Each nation had several clans or family groups

## THE STOLEN GENERATION

When Australia became a Federation in 1901, a set of government polices known as the 'White Australia Policy' was put in place. These were implemented to restrict nonwhite immigration to Australia but the policy also impacted on Aboriginal Australia. Assimilation into the broader society was 'encouraged' by all sectors of government with the intent to eventually fade out the Aboriginal race. A policy of forcibly removing Aboriginal and Torres Strait Islander children from their families was official from 1909 to 1969 although the practice was happening before and after those years. There is no real estimate of how many children were taken as few records remain. It is estimated that around 100,000 Aboriginal children (or one in three children) were taken from their families.

A special government agency, The Aborigines Protection Board, was set up to manage the policy and had the power to remove children without consent from families or without a court order. Many of the children never saw their families again and those that did manage to find their way home often found it difficult to maintain relationships. The generations of children who were taken from their families became known as the stolen generations.

In the 1990s the Australian Human Rights Commission held an inquiry into the practice of removing Aboriginal children. The 'Bring Them Home' report was tabled in parliament in May 1997 and told of the devastating impact that these polices had on the children and their families. Governments, churches and welfare bodies all took part in the forced removal. Sexual and physical abuse and cruelty was common in many of the institutions where children were placed. Today many of the stolen generations still suffer trauma associated with their early lives.

On 13 February 2008, the then prime minister of Australia, Kevin Rudd, offered a national apology to the stolen generations. For many Aboriginal people it was the start of a national healing process and today there are a number of programs and organisations working with the stolen generations.

who were responsible for looking after specific areas. For thousands of years Aboriginal people lived within a complex kinship system that tied them to the natural environment. From the desert to the sea Aboriginal people shaped their lives according to their environments and developed different skills and a wide body of knowledge on their territory.

## Colonisation
The effects of colonisation started immediately after the Europeans arrived. Right from the start was the appropriation of land and water resources and an epidemic of diseases. Small pox killed around 50% of the Sydney Harbour natives. A period of resistance occurred as Aboriginal people fought back to retain their land and their way of life. As violence and massacres swept the country, many Aboriginal people were pushed further and further away from their traditional lands. In a period of 100 years, the Aboriginal population was decimated by 90%.

In the late 1800s most of the fertile land had been taken and most Aboriginal people were living in poverty on the fringes of settlements or on land unsuitable for settlement. Aboriginal people had to adapt to the new culture but were treated like second-class citizens. Employment opportunities were scarce and most people worked as labourers or domestic staff. This disadvantage has continued and even though successive government policies and programs have been implemented to assist Aboriginal people most have not made much impact on improving lives.

## Rights & Reconciliation
The relationship between Aboriginal people and other Australians hasn't always been an easy one. This history of forced resettlement, removal of children and the loss of land and culture cannot be erased, even with governments addressing certain issues. The impact of this discrimination is still evident today. Standards of education, employment status, health and living conditions are still poor compared to the mainstream population. Life expectancy is 10 to 12 years less than other Australians and Aboriginal people are over represented in the criminal justice system. Current policies are focused on 'closing the gap' and centre on better delivery of essential services to improve lives but without real engagement and consultation and a resolution to Aboriginal demand for land and cultural rights, these policies will not succeed.

Aboriginal people have been at the whim of continuous unworkable government policies but have managed to maintain their identity and link to country and culture. Aboriginal struggle for legal and cultural rights continues today and are always at the forefront of politics. Although there is a growing recognition and acceptance of Aboriginal people's place in this country, there is still a long way to go before Aboriginal people are treated the same as other Australians. There is no real political or economic wealth and high unemployment rates. Despite these problems Aboriginal people have never stopped campaigning for their rights. Any gains for Aboriginal people have been hard won and initiated by Aboriginal people themselves in bringing the issues to public notice.

**13 Feb 2008**
The prime minister Kevin Rudd made a national apology to Aboriginal people for the forced removal of their children and the injustices that occurred.

**10 Jul 2010**
Aboriginal leader Yagan was put to rest in a Perth park bearing his name. Murdered in 1833, his head was sent to England. Aboriginal people have campaigned for decades to repatriate their peoples' remains.

After many years of lobbying to have their language and culture reflected in the media landscape, NITV hit the airwaves with the launch in 2007. The TV channel broadcasts news, views and current affairs but also produces programs for children, documentaries and sports programs. The channel is free to air on the SBS network.

ABORIGINAL AUSTRALIA HISTORY OF ABORIGINAL AUSTRALIA

# Indigenous Visual Arts

**Although there is no word in indigenous Australian languages for 'art', visual imagery is a fundamental part of indigenous culture and life: a connection between the past, present and future, and between indigenous people and their traditional homelands. The earliest forms of indigenous visual cultural expression were rock carvings (petroglyphs) and paintings on rock galleries, body painting and ground designs, with the earliest engraved designs known to exist dating back at least 40,000 years, perhaps older.**

Rock Art Sites from NT: Ubirr; Nourlangie – Nanguluwur Gallery; Arnhem Land/Gunbalanya (Oenpelli) – Injalak Hill. From SA: Yourambulla Peak; Arkaroo Rock; Flinders Ranges: Sacred Canyon Cultural Heritage Site.

Visual art, including painting, sculpture and *tjanpi* (weaving) in central Australia has flourished to such a degree that it is now a substantial source of income for many communities. It has also been an important educational tool for children, through which they can learn different aspects of spiritual and ceremonial knowledge. In the past decade or so women have played a huge role in the visual-arts movement, with some of the most innovative work being created by women artists, working equally alongside their male counterparts. More recently, significant efforts have been made to involve youth in cultural maintenance and revival projects, as well as contemporary art production to ensure continuity of art centres and local culture.

Indigenous art, with some notable exceptions, was either largely disregarded by nonindigenous people or viewed in an ethnographic context, with most examples of indigenous material culture placed in natural-history museums, as opposed to fine-art museums. The first exception to this was the acquisition of a work of Aboriginal art by a fine-art museum in 1939, when the Art Gallery of South Australia bought a watercolour by Western Arrernte artist Albert Namatjira (1902–59). Other state galleries followed suit, developing similarly themed collections.

## Papunya Tula Art

In 1971 an event took place that would challenge nonindigenous perceptions about indigenous art. At the remote government-established community of Papunya, 240km northwest of Alice Springs, a group of senior men from the community – led by Kaapa Mbitjana Tjampitjinpa (Anmatyerre/Arrernte people; 1925–89), along with Long Jack Phillipus Tjakamarra (Pintupi/Luritja/Warlpiri people) and Billy Stockman Tjapaltjarri (Anmatyerre people), all elders of the community and employed as groundsmen at the Papunya school – were encouraged to paint a mural on one of the school's external walls by art teacher Geoffrey Bardon (1940–2003), who was instrumental in the genesis of the Papunya Tula Artists movement. Shortly after painting commenced, other members of the community became enthused by the project and joined in creating the mural *Honey Ant Dreaming*. Government regulations later saw the mural destroyed, but its effect on the community was profound. Images of spiritual significance had taken on a permanent and very public form. Notwithstanding the debate the mural caused at Papunya, other members of the community expressed a desire to paint. Initially the paintings were executed on smallish boards, but within a short time larger canvases were used.

Although indigenous artists were working in other regions throughout the country, this fraught beginning in a remote Aboriginal community arguably instigated the commencement of the contemporary indigenous art movement in Australia. That it developed in Papunya is not without irony, since the community was established in 1960 under the auspices of the Australian government's cultural assimilation policy.

In the four decades since the genesis of Papunya Tula Art a diversity of contemporary visual art and culture has blossomed across the Northern Territory and South Australia, with myriad art centres being established to represent the breadth of this creativity, supported by advocacy organisations, state and territory public art museums, and commercial galleries.

With the growing importance of art as both an economic and a cultural activity, an association was formed to help the artists from Papunya community sell their work. Papunya Tula Artists Pty Ltd in Alice Springs is the longest-running Aboriginal-owned and -directed gallery in the country, and operates from a stylish contemporary gallery space in Todd Mall, Alice Springs.

When in Adelaide, a must-visit venue for people interested in indigenous culture is the Tandanya National Aboriginal Cultural Institute. Tandanya comes from the local Kaurna people's word for Red Kangaroo Dreaming (Tarndanyangga/ Tarndanya).

# Rock Art of Arnhem Land & Kakadu

Arnhem Land, in the Top End of the NT, is an area of abundant, diverse artistic and cultural heritage. Recent scientific discoveries have confirmed that rock paintings were being produced as long as 28,000 years

## DJAMBAWA MARAWILI AM

Djambawa Marawili, a senior leader of the Madarrpa clan, received the Order of Australia medal in 2010 for service to the arts as a sculptor and painter, to the preservation of indigenous culture, to arts administration, and as a mentor of emerging artists. Living at Yilpara, in Arnhem Land's Blue Mud Bay, Djambawa is a lifelong cultural activist and a renowned artist. For him 'the production of art is a small part of a much bigger picture'.

He is a custodian for the spiritual/cultural welfare of his own and other related clans, and is an activist and manager at the metaphorical border between non-indigenous people and the Yolngu (Aboriginal) people of northeast Arnhem Land. Djambawa's visual culture is steeped in the traditions of the Ancestral Stories, including that of Baru, the ancestral crocodile, and the fire that the crocodile carried into the water of Blue Mud Bay. On being awarded the Order of Australia, Djambawa stated:

'...the main thing I'd like Ngapaki (non-indigenous people) to understand is that our art, the beautiful paintings, prints and sculptures people buy or see at galleries around the world – this art is informed by our ancient traditions and culture that is our life... Our homelands and art centres are our universities and art academies, though they have almost no funding for this role. It's where our young people learn our culture, all our songs, clan designs and patterns, dances, kinship, names and stories. Our homelands are where we hold Ngarra, holy ceremonies that honour our spiritual foundation on our land and sea country. These are really big gatherings that bring together people from many clans. It is where we go much more deeply into our sacred places and lands. These ceremonies are what feeds our art, makes it strong and lets it speak of what I am, who we are.

People can feel this in our art. The land cannot talk, but we can speak for it through our artwork and reach across cultures. I hope this award will help to strengthen the support and understanding of our artists, our traditions and our culture and bring all Australians closer together.'

Djambawa Marawili is chairperson of Association of Northern, Kimberley and Arnhem Aboriginal Artists (ANKAAA); chairperson of Buku Larrnggay Mulka, Yirrkala; Director of Arnhem Land Region, ANKAAA.

ago, possibly up to 60,000 years, and some of the rock art galleries in the huge sandstone Arnhem Land plateau are at least 18,000 years old.

The rock art (pictographs, petroglyphs, stencils, prints, beeswax and geoglyphs) of Arnhem Land depicts ancestral stories for the many language groups and clans of the region, with stylised designs, often hatched and *rarrk* (cross-hatched), of ancestral beings, spirits, totems, and cultural exchanges with Macassans. The Macassans were Indonesian mariners from Sulawesi who regularly visited the north coast for at least three centuries until their visits were banned by South Australian (as the region was then known as the Northern Territory of South Australia) government regulations in 1906.

The paintings contained in the Arnhem Land rock-art sites constitute one of the world's most significant and fascinating rock-art collections. They provide a wonderful record of changing environments and lifestyles over millennia.

There is a plethora of publications on the market but a key resource is *One sun, one moon: Aboriginal art in Australia* (2007, Sydney: Art Gallery of New South Wales).

In some places they are concentrated in large galleries, with paintings from more recent eras sometimes superimposed over older paintings. Some sites are kept secret – not only to protect them from damage, but also because they are private or sacred to the Aboriginal owners. Some are believed to be inhabited by malevolent spirit beings sometimes known as Namorrodo, who must not be approached by those who are ignorant of the indigenous customs of the region. However, two of the finest sites have been opened up to visitors, with access roads, walkways and explanatory signs. These are Ubirr and Nourlangie in Kakadu National Park, although a terrible irony is that the original custodians no longer paint at these sites, though descendants ensure cultural maintenance and management to the sites as part of their ongoing cultural obligations through work at the park.

The rock paintings show how the main styles succeeded each other over time. The earliest hand-prints were followed by a 'naturalistic/figurative' style, with large outlines of people or animals filled in with colour. Some of the animals depicted, such as the thylacine (Tasmanian tiger), have long been extinct on mainland Australia.

After the naturalistic style came the 'dynamic', in which motion was often depicted (a dotted line, for example, to show a spear's path through the air). In this era the first ancestral beings appeared, with human bodies and animal heads.

The next style mainly showed simple human silhouettes, and was followed by the curious 'yam figures', in which people and animals were drawn in the shape of yams. Other painting styles, including the 'X-ray' style, which displays the internal organs and bone structure of animals, also appeared around this time.

By about 1000 years ago many of the salt marshes had turned into freshwater swamps and billabongs. The birds and plants that provided new food sources in this landscape appeared in the art of this time.

From around 400 years ago, indigenous artists also depicted the human newcomers to the region – Macassan traders and, more recently, Europeans and other nonindigenous people – and the things they brought, or their modes of transport such as ships and horses, and species such as cattle and buffalo, which severely impacted upon the environment.

There are a number of cultural tours owned and managed by local traditional custodians, such as Magela Cultural and Heritage Tours in Kakadu National Park. Key visual arts communities across Arnhem Land include Gunbalanya/Oenpelli in western Arnhem Land, Maningrida, Milingimbi and Ramingining in central Arnhem Land, and Yirrkala in northeast Arnhem Land. The Tiwi Islands of Bathurst and Melville Islands are also home to a number of art centres.

# Dot Painting

Western Desert painting, also known as 'dot' painting, evolved from 'ground, or sand paintings', which formed the foundation of ceremonial practices. These were made from diverse media including pulped plant material, natural pigments and feathers, with the designs created on the ground and/or body using particles (dots) of this material. Dots, or stippling effects, were also used in other ways: to outline objects in rock paintings and to highlight geographical features or vegetation.

While these paintings may look abstract, they depict ancestral Tjukurrpa/Jukurrpa (Dreaming) stories, and can be read in many ways, including as aerial, topographical and underground geographical maps, though not always literally. Many paintings feature the tracks of birds, animals and humans, often identifying key ancestral beings. Subjects may be depicted by the imprint they leave in the sand – a simple arc depicts a sitting person, a *coolamon* (wooden carrying dish) is shown by an oval shape, a digging stick by a single line, a campfire by a circle. Men or women are identified by the objects associated with them – gathering tools and objects for women, hunting tools and objects for men. Concentric circles generally depict ancestral sites, or places where ancestors paused in their journeys.

Although these symbols are widely used, only the artist knows their meaning in each individual painting and the people closely associated with his or her story – either by clan or by the Tjukurrpa/Jukurrpa – since different clans apply different interpretations to each painting's subject matter. In this way sacred stories can be publicly portrayed, as the deeper meaning is not revealed to uninitiated viewers, but coded by layers of stippled acrylic paint, literally and metaphorically concealing sacred information from uninitiated people. Many recent works are far more coded in their imagery with few or no figurative symbols, using colour and application to achieve optical effects denoting the power inherent in the stories portrayed.

# Bark Painting

It is difficult to establish when bark was first used, partly because it is perishable, so the oldest pieces in existence date from the late 19th century and none of the early works were created in the format that we know today. The paintings were never intended to be permanent records but were painted on the bark shelters in much the same way as the art on rock galleries. Nonindigenous explorers travelling through the region in the early 19th century observed the practice of painting the inside walls of bark shelters, and later in the 19th century and early in the 20th century the trade in examples of bark paintings brought them to the notice of natural history/ethnographic museums around the world.

One of the main features of Arnhem Land bark paintings is the use of *rarrk* designs. These designs identify particular clans, and are based on body paintings handed down through generations. More recently, senior artists are recognised by their specific stylistic signature, while retaining communal clan designs. The paintings can also be broadly categorised by their regional styles. In the region's west the tendency was towards naturalistic and figurative images and plain backgrounds, although many renowned artists from Western and Central Arnhem Land cover the entire surface of the bark or carving in intricate line work to create a sense of power emanating from the imagery depicted. To the east, the use of geometric, abstract designs is more common, with the artists of northeast Arnhem Land renowned for their use of *kaolin* (white) in their ever-innovative paintings and sculpture.

INDIGENOUS VISUAL ARTS DOT PAINTING

JAGAMARRA

In the 1980s acclaimed Papunya Tula artists were invited to submit works for the new Parliament House in Canberra. Michael Nelson Jagamarra's *Possum and Wallaby Dreaming* is embedded in the mosaic forecourt: www.papuny atula.com.au

The art reflects themes from ancestral times that vary by region. In eastern and central Arnhem Land the most prominent ancestral beings are the Djan'kawu Sisters, who travelled the land with their elaborate dillybags (string carry bags) and digging sticks (for making waterholes); and the Wagilag/Wawilak Sisters, who are associated with snakes and waterholes and the creation of the clans of the regions. In western Arnhem Land, the significant being (according to some clans) is Yingarna, the Rainbow Serpent, as is one of her offspring, Ngalyod. Other groups paint Nawura as the principal ancestral being – he travelled through the rocky landscape creating sacred sites and giving people the attributes of culture. Another powerful ancestral being is Namarrkon, the Lightning Man, associated with the monsoon season.

The Mimi spirits are another feature of western Arnhem Land art, on both bark and rock. These mischievous spirits are attributed with having taught the indigenous people of the region many things, including hunting, food-gathering and painting skills. More recently, many of the most senior artists have become renowned for their highly innovative depictions of ancestral stories with works of art held in major national and international public and private collections. The Museum & Art Gallery of the Northern Territory, on the gorgeous location of Bullocky Point, Darwin, presents changing displays from its extensive collection of work from communities across the NT.

## Contemporary Art

The *art+soul* DVD series (2011, Sydney: ABC Sales & Hibiscus Films) is produced by one of Australia's most respected indigenous curators and educators, Hetti Perkins. The series covers a diversity of artists who have had a significant impact on the development of the contemporary indigenous art scene over the past two decades.

Since the early 1970s there have been burgeoning centres of creativity throughout remote regions, often where clan connections cross government borders, particularly throughout the Anangu/Pitjantjatjara/Yankunytjatjara (APY) Lands, which include parts of SA, NT and WA. In the late 1980s to mid-1990s critical and popular focus centred on artists and work from the communities of Utopia, Haasts Bluff, Papunya and Yuendumu in central Australia, and Ngukurr in southeast Arnhem Land. In the 1990s, work being created in communities across Arnhem Land gained national and international acclaim.

The most significant developments over the past three decades have come from urban and rural-based artists, living in the regions that have experienced the longest impact of colonisation. Their individual and collective contributions challenged the status quo of the time, being that 'authentic' Aboriginal art could only be created by artists from remote communities – those regions that supposedly were more 'traditional'. This misconception overlooked the strong cultural connections held by Aboriginal people whose families and communities had been moved off their customary homelands, had children forcibly removed and placed in government and church-operated institutions, lost access to language and customs, yet intrinsically retained a sense of indigenous identity, which was represented – overtly or subtly – in the work they created.

Much of this work was created by artists/activists living, studying and working in major metropolitan centres across Australia such as Sydney, Brisbane, Melbourne, Adelaide and Perth. Artist-run initiatives such as Boomalli Aboriginal Artists Co-operative in Sydney in 1987, Dumbartung in Perth (1989), Tandanya National Aboriginal Cultural Centre in Adelaide in 1989, and Campfire Group (later Fireworks Gallery) in Brisbane in 1990, were established as a political response to the exclusive nature of the contemporary mainstream art scene, and the impact of these venues and the artists involved on the uninformed art world continues to resonate nearly three decades later.

Subject matter ranged from identity politics, land and cultural rights, stolen generations and cultural revival, and the media included paintings, sculpture, textiles, photo-media and film, new media and installation and conceptual work. Works on paper have long been created by artists from all regions across the country – urban, rural and remote – with many art centres producing their own works on paper or working with specialist organisations. Fine art prints are now produced by many artists and communities, assisted by master print-makers and organisations such as Northern Editions at the Charles Darwin University. These works of art are sought after due to their affordability.

Discussion has long surrounded the 'contemporary' vs 'traditional' debate, but perhaps the biggest change has been the involvement of indigenous curators of Aboriginal and Torres Strait Islander art working in artist-run spaces, state and federal public art galleries and museums, which ensures that visual art and culture is presented from an indigenous perspective.

There are many wonderful opportunities to view the latest developments in contemporary Aboriginal art. See the Major Indigenous Art Festivals boxed text, below.

Emily Kame Kngwarreye (c 1910–96), an Anmatyere elder, was an incredibly prolific artist and a supernova on the contemporary art scene. Kngwarreye is represented in every major public collection in Australia and in 1997 she posthumously represented Australia at the Venice Biennale with Yvonne Koolmatrie and Judy Watson.

## Artefacts & Contemporary Objects

Objects traditionally made for utilitarian or ceremonial practices, such as weapons, hunting and gathering tools and musical instruments, often feature intricate and symbolic decoration. In recent years many communities have also developed nontraditional forms of weavings and objects that have generated cultural revival and pride, employment and income. In central Australia, artists have created idiosyncratic works such as *mu*

### MAJOR INDIGENOUS ART FESTIVALS

#### The Telstra

In August each year, the **Telstra National Aboriginal & Torres Strait Islander Art Award** (the Telstra; www.artsandmuseums.nt.gov.au/museums/natsiaa) is a major event on the national visual arts calendar. In 2013 it will celebrate its 30th anniversary, making it the longest running indigenous art prize in the country. Held at the Museum & Art Gallery of the Northern Territory in Darwin, the exhibition showcases contemporary art by indigenous artists from all over Australia. It runs to the end of October each year.

#### Desert Mob

Smaller than the Telstra, the Desert Mob exhibition packs a whole lot of (he)art and soul into its annual showcase of contemporary work from central Australia. Hosted by the Araluen Arts Centre in Alice Springs, **Desert Mob** (www.desertmob.nt.gov.au) has grown from somewhat humble beginnings to an exciting event involving artists from up to 40 Desert member art centres. Calendar events include a one-day symposium where artists share stories, images and films, and a weekend marketplace where visitors have the chance to meet artists and works can be acquired for incredibly reasonable prices. A central event of the Alice Desert Festival, the exhibition is on from September until late October.

#### Our Mob

South Australia's **OUR MOB** (www.adelaidefestivalcentre.com.au), held in October, is the new annual exhibition kid on the block. First held in 2005, it's quickly blossomed into an exciting event bringing South Australian indigenous artists and their work together at the Adelaide Festival Centre Gallery on the banks of the Torrens River. Works of all mediums are represented, with art centres from the APY Lands showing alongside artists from the west coast, Riverland and Coorong regions, as well as urban-based artists. The public program includes talks by artists, curators and arts workers. It runs from October until early December.

*kata* (beanies or hats), *tjanpi* (woven natural grasses, brightly coloured wool, seeds and beads) objects ranging from birds, animals and humans to the more quirky – the near life-size *Tjanpi Toyota* by Tjanpi Desert Weavers, which won the overall Telstra NATSIAA in 2005 and is on permanent display at the Museum & Art Gallery of the NT in Darwin.

The depiction of ancestral beings in indigenous art is a signifier of respect and cultural connection to specific regions and language groups. For example, the Nyoongar people's Wagyl (Waugal or Waagal) in southern WA is similar to the Rainbow Serpent Ngalyod or Yingarna in parts of Arnhem Land. Every community and nation has their respective ancestral beings and totemic spirit beings.

### Didgeridoo

The most widespread craft objects seen for sale these days are didgeridoos. There has been a phenomenal boom in their popularity and they can be found in outlets around the country, although not always made by an indigenous artisan. A hollow drone instrument, the didgeridoo is played by a musician who has mastered the art of circular (nonstop) breathing and is now used by indigenous and nonindigenous musicians due to its unique and amazingly diverse sound. It has been used in traditional, crossover, country, rock and classical music.

Although it is often considered a universal Aboriginal musical instrument, the didgeridoo originates from Yolngu culture in northeast Arnhem Land, where it remains a revered cultural object and is known as the *yidaki*. For more information on the cultural protocols for use of the didgeridoo see www.didgefestival.com/about-the-didge.

## Buying Aboriginal Art Ethically

The rising interest in Aboriginal art in Australia and overseas over the past decade or so has been accompanied by an increase in unethical actions by individuals who have not always had the rights of the artists and their communities as a priority.

Very few galleries in SA or the NT are owned and directed by indigenous people, but there are many Aboriginal art centres that are governed by Aboriginal people. The best place to buy art is either directly from the communities that have art collectives, or from galleries and outlets that are operated or supported by indigenous arts and advocacy groups. In most major cities and towns there are also commercial galleries that have established long-term relationships with artists and communities. These usually display a notice stating they are a member of the Australian Commercial Galleries Association (ACGA) and/or the Indigenous Art Code.

### Art Centres & Advocacy Groups

The following art centres provide useful information on their websites:

➡ **Association of Northern, Kimberley & Arnhem Aboriginal Artists** (ANKAAA; www.ankaaa.org.au), based in Darwin, is the peak advocacy and support agency for Aboriginal artists and art centres in Arnhem Land, Tiwi Islands, Darwin/Katherine and the Kimberley in north Western Australia. ANKAAA recently celebrated its 25th anniversary.

➡ **Desart Inc** (www.desart.com.au) is the key support agency in Central Australia. Based in Alice Springs, it is the major advocacy agency for at least 45 central Australian art centres across three borders (NT, SA and WA).

➡ **Ananguku Arts & Culture Aboriginal Corporation** (www.anangukuarts.com.au), over the border in South Australia, was established in 1997 by women artists at Ernabella to cover the Anangu Pitjantjatjara Yankunytjatjara (APY) Lands. Ananguku Arts now provides services to more than 460 artists at seven Aboriginal-owned and -governed art centres in far northwest SA.

➡ **Tiwi Art Network** (www.tiwiart.com) is an alliance between the three art centres on the Islands: Munupi Arts & Crafts, Tiwi Design and Jilamara Arts & Crafts.

# The Outback Environment

Parts of the Australian outback are among the world's oldest land surfaces. Australia's last great mountain-building events took place more than 300 million years ago, and it's hard to believe that Uluru was once part of a mountain range that would have rivalled the Andes in height. Erosion and the relentless cycle of drought and flood have leached the nutrients away from Australia's ancient soils and prevented the creation of new soils, resulting in the vast sandy plains of the Australian outback.

## The Land

The Stuart Hwy passes through some of the lowest, flattest and driest parts of Australia, but there are numerous ranges and individual mountains scattered through the outback. At 1531m, Mt Zeil is not remarkable by world standards, but it is the highest mountain west of the Great Dividing Range. The rocky ranges of the outback provide important refuges for a diverse collection of plants and animals, and are significant in the ancient song lines and *stories* (accounts of the Dreaming that link into the law) of the traditional Aboriginal custodians of these areas.

In the outback you will drive past huge salt or clay pans that rarely fill with water. These may be dry for years, but when there is an abundance of rain they become important arid wetland systems: they hold water long after the surrounding landscape has dried out and are crucial to the survival of many plants and animals, especially those that require inundation during their life cycles.

While spectacular geological formations are characteristics of the south and central deserts, it is the extensive river systems and wetlands that herald your arrival in the Top End. The sandstone escarpment and plateau of western Arnhem Land is a magnificent sight, but the life-sustaining floodplains at its base are just as impressive.

SA's low and unreliable rainfall has resulted in water from the Murray River being piped over long distances to ensure the survival of many communities, including Adelaide. More than 50% of South Australians depend entirely on the Murray for their water supply, and this figure can rise to 90% in drought years.

## The Land & Indigenous Peoples
*by Dr Irene Watson*

The earth is our sacred relative; it is a relationship that is based on nurturing, caring and sharing. From birth we learn of the sacredness of all living things. Every aspect of the natural world is honoured and respected, and we learn to tread lightly on the earth.

The spirit of creation is in all things, for all life forms are related. The philosophy of respect for all living things is an idea central to Aboriginal spirituality and is an idea that nurtured and kept the land in a pristine state prior to colonisation.

**THE OUTBACK ENVIRONMENT THE LAND & INDIGENOUS PEOPLES**

## The Spirit in the Land

The land is sacred because the essence of our spirituality lies in the earth; our spirit guides are resting in the mountains, in the rocks and in the rivers, and they are everywhere in the land. The land is sacred because it carries the footsteps of our spirit ancestors as they walked every part of it, laying tracks and spiritual songs across the country. The ancestors lie sleeping deep in the earth and we are responsible for the care of their places of rest, for their creative powers are alive and influence all things still in the natural world.

If these spirits are disturbed, so too are the natural order and cycles of life. Where sacred sites are destroyed we believe the ancestors are disturbed and will no longer protect or provide for the people. As a result of damaged or destroyed sacred sites, natural disasters and sickness may occur and afflict communities who have not fulfilled their cultural obligations as custodians. By neglecting our spiritual and cultural obligations we bring disharmony to the country and the community.

## The Relationship to the Land

The idea of the land being *terra nullius*, or a vast empty space across which we range sporadically, is a myth. We know the land intimately: every rock and every river has a name and is remembered in the Dreaming, as it is still remembered today.

To own the land as a piece of real estate, as a 'property', is an idea remote to Aboriginal people. Our relationship to the land is considerably more complex. The land cannot be treated as a consumable, which can be traded or sold. We believe the land cannot be sold.

We have always lived as a part of the natural world, and we take from the environment only what is needed to sustain life; we nurture the land as we do ourselves, for we are one.

The land is both nurturer and teacher from which all life forms grow; all life is inseparably linked. The Aboriginal relationship to the land carries with it both obligations and rights. The relationship to land is at once one of traditional owner and of custodian. It is a relationship that is difficult to explain in a foreign language, because the term 'owner' has different meanings across cultures. Ownership is not viewed in relation to ownership of material goods, but is more accurately viewed as in possession of other values: knowledge, culture and law business, a relationship, a problem, a dispute, a ceremony.

The idea of Aboriginal ownership is not exclusive, and it does not define the owned object as a commodity. Instead, that which is owned is defined as the concern of a limited group of people who stand in a

Established in the 1800s, Goyder's Line marks the 250mm rainfall isobar as the recommended northern limit for cropping in SA. With the increase in temperature and reduction in rainfall, there have been suggestions that the line should shift as far south as the Clare Valley.

particular relationship to the owner, and whose various responsibilities depend on that relationship.

## Managers & Bosses

There are both managers and bosses for country, and each party has a different responsibility or right. The manager is the custodian and the boss is the owner. Naming the parties a manager or a boss is simply a way of discerning between custodian and owner, although in reality these two roles are not always strictly separate and are often merged to become one.

Some of these responsibilities are made known to the members of an Aboriginal community through songs and ceremonies. For example, there may be a particular obligation not to kill the females of a certain animal, in order to preserve the species.

When traditional custodians and/or owners approach their country they will talk to the spirit ancestor of the place. They will tell them who they are and also who they may have brought with them to the place. When food is taken from the land, thanks are given to the ancestors. Nothing is assumed or taken for granted, not even the next meal. We are always seeking permission from the spirit world for our actions.

The boundaries between different Aboriginal clans or nations are sometimes marked. These boundaries are not straight lines but may be determined by the footsteps and tracks of the ancestors, by bends in the creek or the river, the rain shadow, trees or rocks. Some regions were shared between different Aboriginal peoples and some were restricted, with strict rules for obtaining permission to travel across the country.

A visit to the 200-hectare Australian Arid Lands Botanic Garden, on the Stuart Hwy in Port Augusta, is a great way to see a range of different arid-zone plants in one place. Check out the website at www.australian-aridlands-botanic-garden.org.

# Wildlife

The timing of your visit to central Australia will determine the variety and types of wildlife you are likely to see. In January, a flooded wetland in the north will be teeming with wildlife, whereas a searing hot January day in the desert may leave you wondering if anything lives there at all apart from flies and ants.

## Feathers & Scales

The rivers and wetlands of both South Australia (SA) and the Northern Territory (NT) are home to an incredible variety of birds, as well as hosting great flocks of migratory birds from other parts of Australia and the world. In Kakadu look out for regal pairs of Jabiru storks and brolgas among the massive flocks of magpie geese.

Away from the wetlands, birdwatchers will need to put in more time and effort, as the birds of the dry desert regions are generally more mobile, only visiting waterholes for a quick drink before disappearing into the void. The waterholes of the MacDonnell Range can teem with colourful and noisy zebra finches and budgerigars only to be abandoned a few minutes later. Keep an eye out for emus near the road around Coober Pedy – even at the hottest time of the day!

## VOLUNTEERING FOR THE ENVIRONMENT

Want to get you hands dirty? Conservation Volunteers Australia (p272) is a not-for-profit organisation focusing on practical conservation projects such as tree planting, walking-track construction, and flora and fauna surveys. You'll meet like-minded people and get to visit interesting areas of the country. Most projects are either for a weekend or a week and all food, transport and accommodation is supplied in return for a small contribution to help cover costs.

## ABORIGINAL LAND MANAGEMENT

For more than 50,000 years Aboriginal and Torres Strait Islander peoples have occupied the full range of environments within Australia. Indigenous people have successfully utilised and renewed the country, using an accumulated intimate knowledge of the land, and have implemented innovative management regimes with traditional customs to keep the country healthy and productive.

Through this long-term use and occupation, indigenous people developed an intimate understanding of the environment including the flora and fauna, and the environmental conditions. This knowledge was crucial for long-term survival in a land that can be harsh and uninviting at the best of times. The land has always nurtured and provided for indigenous people, through meats like kangaroo and emu or vegetables like yams and sweet potatoes. However, the land means a great deal more than that – it also provides spiritual strength. Through *story* places (where special Dreaming events occurred) and Dreaming tracks throughout the landscape, our attachment to land provides us with our identity – where we come from as Aboriginal people, who we are, where our land is, our languages and our social structure.

The land is all important. However, with invasion many Aboriginal people were denied access to their land – they were killed, dispersed or taken away to Aboriginal missions. This has had a variety of effects on Aboriginal people, including separation from family, loss of identity and the myriad social problems that accompany these things, such as alcohol abuse and unemployment.

Nevertheless, Aboriginal occupation and day-to-day use have been, and in many places continue to be, significant factors in maintaining the landscape. Firestick farming (burning off) is a well-documented technique Aboriginal people used to renew and manage the land. In most areas burning off the country with fire was, and in some areas continues to be, an annual occurrence. In the north of Australia it is carried out at the beginning of the cool Dry season. Firestick farming serves two main purposes. One is to decrease the chance of a bushfire by reducing the vegetation build-up after a wet season. This vegetation could be fuel for a major fire. Secondly, fire is used to clear the country and encourage new growth. This new growth attracts wildlife such as kangaroos and other species, which are drawn to nibble on the soft, new shoots that sprout after the fire.

Although much of the special knowledge of the environment has been lost due to the various impacts upon traditional culture, a great deal still exists. Aboriginal people's special attachment to land is tied to their social, cultural and economic wellbeing. Understanding this attachment can provide a good insight into the way Aboriginal people used and continue to use the land, and their aspirations for looking after their 'country'. Many Aboriginal and Torres Strait Islander people want to play a role in managing their country. Since invasion, Australia has lost a large percentage of its native vegetation and many native species are in danger of extinction. For Australia to maintain its unique environmental credentials, it needs Aboriginal people and their knowledge to play a role in environmental management.

*Barry Hunter, Indigenous Land Management Facilitator, Balkanu Cape York Development Corporation in Queensland*

Early morning and late afternoon are the best times for birdwatching. Some species are rarely seen, while others hang around in flocks so large that you can't possibly miss them. Australia is in fact the perfect place for lazy birdwatchers because many of our birds are noisy and easily identifiable, such as pink cockatoos, red-tailed black cockatoos, sulphur-crested cockatoos, galahs, kookaburras, parrots and corellas. Australia's majestic wedge-tailed eagles are a common sight along the Stuart Hwy and you will often hear a whistling kite before you see it.

Despite their abundance in central Australia, most reptiles are difficult to observe because many of them are inactive during hot summer days and hibernate during winter. Snakes tend to move around more between October and April, when you may spot a large, active daytime predator such as a large perentie, python or a sand goanna. In southern and central Australia, following an ant trail in the red desert sand may lead you to a small thorny devil taking lunch. The camouflaged, thorny coat of this lizard features a decoy 'head' behind the real head to fool predators.

In the tropical woodlands of the Top End, the well-known frill-necked lizards spend most of their days in trees eating insects and termites. When a 'frilly' is frightened or defending its territory, its defensive strategy is to open its mouth, widen its impressive frill and hiss. This menacing show is all bluff and a frilly will generally run very fast on its two hind legs in the opposite direction when the show is over. In June and July, when many other reptile species are hibernating, Australia's best-known reptiles – the freshwater and estuarine crocodiles – can be seen warming themselves on the banks of Top End rivers.

## Marsupials Rule

Of the larger marsupials, you are most likely to see mobs of Australia's unique marsupial macropods, either bounding away from you, grazing quietly with ears twitching or resting in the shade of a tree. Look for a joey poking out from the female's pouch. In southern and central Australia, the most common macropod species is the red kangaroo, the world's largest marsupial. Males are a reddish brown colour and can grow to 2m, while females are smaller with blue grey colouring. Robust euros (or wallaroos) can be seen around Alice Springs and yellow-footed rock wallabies are making a comeback in the Flinders Ranges, thanks in part to a feral-animal eradication program. In the north, the most common macropod species is the agile wallaby, which grows to about 1m and has a distinct white line from the tip of its nose to its eye.

Not all Australian mammals have pouches. You may see the occasional solitary dingo; usually slinking away annoyed at being discovered. But many of Australia's mammals are small, secretive and nocturnal, so you're unlikely to see them in the wild unless you go spotlighting with a knowledgeable guide or visit one of the excellent wildlife parks in Alice Springs and Darwin.

If you stay overnight in Alice Springs, a visit to Simpsons Gap just before dark is your best bet for seeing black-footed rock wallabies in their natural environment.

### The Ferals

The introduction of animals from other countries in the last 200 years has contributed significantly to the fragmentation of ecosystems and the extinction of native animals in Australia. Introduced species include foxes, rabbits, cats, pigs, goats, donkeys, horses, camels, starlings, sparrows, cane toads, mosquitofish and carp. They each bring a unique suite of problems as they carve out a niche for themselves in their new environment – some as predators of native animals, others as competitors for the limited resources of food, water and shelter.

## JOEY FACTORIES

A kangaroo's breeding cycle will be suspended during periods of severe drought. In a good year, however, a doe may have an unweaned joey on foot, one suckling from inside the pouch and a dormant embryo in the uterus. The embryo is prevented from developing by the suckling of the joey in the pouch, but it's ready for birth within a day of that joey's departure. Each of the offspring feeds only from one teat and each teat supplies a different mix of nutrients depending on the age of the young.

THE OUTBACK ENVIRONMENT WILDLIFE

WALLABIES

## Plants & Habitats

There is a great diversity of vegetation between Adelaide and Darwin, reflecting the sweeping range in climate and rainfall. Much of the Top End receives an annual rainfall of around 1600mm, while the desert regions of SA receive less than 150mm (median) of annual rainfall.

*Field Guide to Australian Birds* by Michael Morcombe is a well-designed field guide, with beautiful colour illustrations and just the right amount of detail.

Known as wattles in Australia, acacia species dominate the woodlands occupying large areas of the arid zone, with mulga varieties having by far the largest representation. Mulga has varying forms, from a multi-branched shrub of 1m to an erect tree of 7m. Once used by Aboriginal people to make spear throwers and long, narrow shields, the wood is extremely hard and today it is used for turning, craftwork and fence posts. Gidgee is another acacia that covers large areas of central Australia.

Some of the deserts of southern and central Australia are surprisingly well vegetated, usually with tough, dry chenopod shrublands (such as saltbush) and spinifex-dominated hummock grasslands. After heavy rains, seeds that have been lying dormant are triggered into life and the desert is then blanketed in wildflowers. The brightly coloured poached-egg daisy is one of the most abundant and conspicuous wildflowers.

You'll see a wide variety of eucalypt species, from multistemmed mallee to giant, shade-giving river red gums, such as those majestic specimens lining the Todd River in Alice Springs and the creeks of the Flinders Ranges. These massive, spreading trees offer refuge to a variety of wildlife, such as bats, birds, small mammals, lizards and insects. The glossy green leaves and stark white bark of the ghost gum are another common sight in central Australia, and it's around Alice that they've achieved most of their fame, largely through the work of artists such as Albert Namatjira. The impressive river red gums line the creeks of the Flinders Ranges and the dry riverbeds of central Australia.

One of the dominant Top End eucalypts is the Darwin woollybutt, a tall tree that produces large clusters of bright orange flowers (usually from May to August). Whether flowering or not, it is easily recognisable by the 'stocking' of rough, dark-coloured bark on its lower trunk, which is in stark contrast to the smooth, white upper trunk and branches. This is the tree's inbuilt protection from grass fires. Many a termite-eaten woollybutt ends up as a didgeridoo.

### Plant Invaders

Weed infestations can destroy wildlife habitats and make pastoral and cropping land unusable – the cost in environmental and economic terms is incalculable.

In northern Australia, weeds such as para grass, mimosa and salvinia have invaded floodplains and choked out native vegetation, while gamba grass has devastated large areas of native woodlands. In the sandy riverbeds of central and southern Australia, buffel grass is threatening entire ecosystems. Add fire to the mix and you have a recipe for disaster for native vegetation, as weeds such as buffel and gamba are highly flammable and recover quickly after being burnt; they are thus able to regenerate faster than the native plants in the area.

# Survival Guide

# Directory A–Z

## Accommodation

As well as the usual slew of hotels, motels, caravan parks and youth hostels, central Australia offers some truly Aussie ways to spend the night. Roll out your swag under the desert stars, park your campervan at a remote cattle station, dream shiraz-coloured dreams in a plush wine region B&B or blow a small fortune on a luxury 'tent' with views of Uluru.

**Seasons** In southern South Australia (SA), prices peak during summer (December to February) and school and public holidays. Outside these times discounts and lower walk-in rates can be found. Winter is peak season in the Flinders Ranges and outback areas of northern SA. In the Northern Territory (NT) peak season (the Dry) is June to September, plus school and public holidays. April to May and October to November are quieter shoulder seasons up north, and summer (the Wet in the Top End) is the low season – prices can drop by as much as 30%. Book accommodation in advance in peak periods.

## B&Bs

The atmosphere and privacy of B&Bs can be hard to top. Most B&Bs are 'self-catering', meaning breakfast provisions are provided for you to cook. Rates are typically $100 to $180, though they can climb higher.

The South Australian Tourist Commission (SATC) publishes a B&B booklet. Online resources include the following:

➡ www.babs.com.au

➡ www.australianbedand breakfast.com.au

➡ www.ozbedandbreakfast. com

➡ www.bandbfsa.com.au

## Camping

Bush camping at remote sites or in national parks is a highlight of any central Australian trip. In the desert, where rain and mosquitoes are often not an issue, you don't even need a tent – just slip into a swag.

**Costs** Payment is often made into honesty boxes (around $7 to $15 per person per night).

**Facilities** There are plenty of free camping places out here, including roadside rest areas. In national parks camping is usually only permitted in designated areas, where facilities can range from a fireplace and simple pit toilet to hot showers and free gas barbecues.

## Caravan Parks

**Costs** Central Australia's caravan parks are excellent value, charging from $20 to $30 for two people camping, slightly more for a powered site. Most have basic cabins with shared facilities (from around $60) and en-suite cabins with cooking facilities ($80 to $140). Book ahead for powered sites and cabins in peak season.

**Facilities** Most parks have a camp kitchen, laundry, barbecues and a shop or kiosk, and all offer toilets and hot showers. If the gods are smiling there might even be a swimming pool.

## Farm & Station Stays

For a true country experience, stay on a farm or working cattle station.

---

### SLEEPING PRICE RANGES

In this book the following price ranges refer to a double room with bathroom in high season. Unless otherwise indicated, unpowered/powered camp site prices are for two people.

| | |
|---|---|
| $ | less than $100 |
| $$ | $100 to $200 |
| $$$ | more than $200 |

Some let you kick back and watch workers raise a sweat; others rope you in to day-to-day chores. Most accommodation is very comfortable – B&B-style in the main homestead (dinner on request), or in self-contained cottages. Some farms also provide budget outbuildings or shearers' quarters. Online, see the following:

➡ www.farmstaycamping australia.com.au

➡ www.stayz.com.au/farm -accommodation

➡ www.bandbfsa.com.au

➡ www.frabs.com.au

## Hostels

Hostels are a highly social and low-cost fixture of the central Australian accommodation scene.

**Costs** A dormitory bed costs around $22 to $30, and most also have comfortable private rooms from around $60 ($70 to $90 with en suite).

**Facilities** Most hostels have kitchens with fridges, stoves, microwaves and cooking utensils, communal areas with TV, a laundry, internet access (including wi-fi), travellers' noticeboards and tour-booking services.

### HOSTEL ORGANISATIONS

There are several Australia-wide backpacker organisations that run hostels around the country (Base, Nomads etc), but in central Australia, your best bet is the ever-reliable **YHA** (📞08-8981 6344; www.yha.com.au) chain, which runs 11 hostels in SA and the NT. A Hostelling International membership costs $42/80 for one/two years, slightly less if you're younger than 26.

### INDEPENDENT HOSTELS

Central Australia (particularly SA) has numerous independent hostels, competition for the backpacker dollar prompting fairly high

standards and enticements such as free breakfasts and courtesy buses. Places range from rundown pubs trying to fill empty rooms, to converted motels where dorm units have a fridge, TV and bathroom. Prices mimic those in the larger hostel organisations.

## Motels

For comfortable midrange accommodation, motels are the way to go. They proliferate in cities and smaller towns, and many outback roadhouses also have motel rooms out the back.

**Costs** Expect to pay at least $90 for a double and up to $150 for more upmarket places.

**Facilities** The average motel is a modern (but anonymous) low-rise affair with parking and tidy rooms that have a bathroom, tea/coffee making facilities, TV, telephone, air-con, a fridge humming in the corner and, if the gods are smiling, a swimming pool.

## Hotels

Fancy hotels and resorts are all around SA but are limited to Darwin, Alice Springs, Yulara, Kings Canyon and Kakadu in the NT. Most have fabulous facilities and locations, but more than a few five-star places are clinical and corporate in atmosphere. Although rack rates are high, discounts and deals mean you'll rarely pay full price except in peak season.

## Pubs

For the budget traveller, pubs ('hotels' that serve beer) are

cheap, central options. Many pubs were built during boom times, so they're often the largest, most extravagant buildings in town.

**Costs** Pub singles/doubles with shared facilities start around $40/60, more if you want a private bathroom. Few have a separate reception area – just ask at the bar.

**Facilities** Some pubs have been restored as heritage buildings, but generally rooms remain small and old fashioned, with an amble down the hall to the bathroom. If you're a light sleeper, avoid booking a room above the bar, and be aware that pub rooms don't always have air-con.

## Rental Accommodation

Serviced apartments and holiday flats resemble motels but usually contain cooking facilities – good value for longer stays. This kind of accommodation is usually found in beachy holiday areas, while you'll find serviced apartments in Darwin and Adelaide. In some holiday accommodation you provide your own sheets and bedding; others are fully equipped.

# Customs Regulations

When entering Australia you can bring most articles in free of duty, provided customs is satisfied they're for personal use and that you'll be taking them with you when you leave. Duty-free per-adult quotas:

→ **Alcohol** 2.25L

→ **Cigarettes** 50

→ **Dutiable goods** Up to the value of A$900

Narcotics, of course, are illegal, and customs inspectors and their highly trained hounds are diligent in sniffing them out. Quarantine regulations are strict, so you must declare all goods of animal or vegetable origin – wooden spoons, straw hats, the lot. Fresh food, particularly meat, cheese, fruit, vegetables and flowers, is also prohibited. There are disposal bins located in the airport where you can dump any questionable items if you don't want to bother with an inspection.

For more information:

→ **Australian Quarantine & Inspection Service** (☑02-6272 3933, 1800 020 504; www.daff.gov.au)

→ **Australian Customs Service** (☑02-9313 3010, 1300 363 263; www.customs.gov.au)

## Discount Cards

### Seniors Card

The **Seniors Card** (www.seniorscard.com.au) is available to permanent residents over the age of 60, giving discounts on everything from accommodation and tours to car hire and meals (with participating businesses, of course). The card is free; apply online. Even without a card, seniors with proof of age receive a discount on admission to many attractions in central Australia.

### Student Cards

A student card entitles you to a wide range of discounts – from transport and tour charges to admission fees. The most common is the **International Student Identity Card** (ISIC; www.isiccard.com). To get one you need proof of full-time student status.

The same organisation also produces the **International Youth Travel Card** (IYTC) with benefits equivalent to the ISIC, issued to people between 12 and 26 years of age and not full-time students. Another similar card is the **International Teacher Identity Card** (ITIC), available to teaching professionals.

All three cards are issued by student unions, hostelling organisations and student-travel companies.

## Electricity

240V/50Hz

## Embassies & Consulates

The principal diplomatic representations to Australia are in Canberra in the ACT; some countries also have consular representation in Adelaide and Darwin:

**Canadian Embassy** (☑02-6270 4000; www.australia.gc.ca; Commonwealth Ave, Yarralumla, ACT)

**Chinese Embassy** (☑02-6273 4780; http://au.china-embassy.org/eng; 15 Coronation Dr, Yarralumla, ACT)

**Dutch Consulate** (☑08-8232 3855; www.netherlands.org.au; L1, 147 Frome St, Adelaide, SA)

**Dutch Embassy** (☑02-6220 9400; www.netherlands.org.au; 120 Empire Circuit, Yarralumla, ACT)

**French Embassy** (☑02-6216 0100; www.ambafrance-au.org; 6 Perth Ave, Yarralumla, ACT)

**German Embassy** (☑02-6270 1911; www.canberra.diplo.de; 119 Empire Circuit, Yarralumla, ACT)

**Indonesian Consulate** (☑08-8943 0200; http://darwin.kemlu.go.id; 20 Harry Chan Ave, Darwin, NT)

**Indonesian Embassy** (☑02-6250 8600; www.deplu.go.id/canberra; 8 Darwin Ave, Yarralumla, ACT)

**Irish Embassy** (☑02-6214 0000; www.embassyofireland.au.com; 20 Arkana St, Yarralumla, Canberra, ACT)

**Japanese Embassy** (☑02-6273 3244; www.au.emb-japan.go.jp; 112 Empire Circuit, Yarralumla, ACT)

**Malaysian Embassy** (☑02-6120 0300; www.malaysia.org.au; 7 Perth Ave, Yarralumla, ACT)

**New Zealand Embassy** (☑02-6270 4211; www.nzembassy.com; Commonwealth Ave, Yarralumla, ACT)

**Singaporean Embassy** (☑02-6271 2000; www.mfa.gov.sg/canberra; 17 Forster Cres, Yarralumla, ACT)

**Thai Embassy** (☑02-6206 0100; 111 Empire Circuit, Yarralumla, ACT)

**UK Consulate** (☑08-8941 6130; www.ukinaustralia.fco.gov.uk; 30 The Mall, Darwin, NT)

**UK Embassy** (☑02-6270 6666; www.ukinaustralia.fco.gov.uk; Commonwealth Ave, Yarralumla, ACT)

**US Embassy** (☑02-6214 5600; http://canberra.usembassy.gov; 1 Moonah Pl, Yarralumla, ACT)

## Food

Eating in central Australia can be as pricey or prudent as you like: A roadhouse hamburger can taste just as good as a fine-dining morsel in a haughty winery bistro. For the SA foodie low-down, check out the South Australian Wine & Food chapter (p39).

## Gay & Lesbian Travellers

**South Australia** Attitudes towards homosexuality in SA are fairly relaxed, but as you'd expect, homophobia does rear its ugly head the further you travel into the outback. Adelaide has plenty of gay-friendly venues, and a dedicated annual gay and lesbian cultural festival, **Feast** (www.feast.org.au), held over three weeks in November. For info on the G&L scene, pick up a copy of **Blaze** (www.gaynewsnetwork. com.au) magazine, available around Adelaide, or contact the **Gay & Lesbian Counselling Service SA** (☑08-8193 0800; www.glcssa.org.au).

**Northern Territory** In the NT you'll find active gay and lesbian communities in Alice Springs, though homophobic attitudes do exist beyond the main towns.

**Resources** For general information, check out the **Gay & Lesbian Tourism Australia** (www.galta.com. au), which has information on gay-friendly businesses, places to stay and nightlife. See also www.gaystayaustralia.com.

## Health

by Dr David Millar

Healthwise, Australia is a remarkably safe country in which to travel, considering that such a large portion of it lies in the tropics. Few travellers to central Australia will experience anything

### EATING PRICE RANGES

In this book the following price ranges refer to a standard main course:

| | |
|---|---|
| **$** | less than $15 |
| **$$** | $15 to $32 |
| **$$$** | more than $32 |

worse than sunburn or a bad hangover and, if you do fall ill, the standard of hospitals and health care is high.

### Vaccinations

➡ Since most vaccines don't produce immunity until at least two weeks after they're given, visit a physician four to eight weeks before departure. Ask your doctor for an International Certificate of Vaccination (otherwise known as 'the yellow booklet'), which will list all the vaccinations you've received.

➡ If you're entering Australia within six days of having stayed overnight or longer in a yellow fever–infected country, you'll need proof of yellow fever vaccination. For a full list of these countries, visit **Centers for Disease Control & Prevention** (www. cdc.gov/travel).

➡ The **World Health Organization** (WHO; www. who.int/wer) recommends that all travellers be covered for diphtheria, tetanus, measles, mumps, rubella, chicken pox and polio, as well as hepatitis B, regardless of their destination. The consequences of these diseases can be severe and, while Australia has high levels of childhood vaccination coverage, outbreaks of these diseases do occur.

### Availability & Cost of Health Care

**Facilities** Australia has an excellent health-care system. It's a mixture of privately run medical clinics and hospitals alongside a system of public hospitals funded by the Aus-

tralian government. There are also excellent specialised public-health facilities for women and children in major centres.

**Medicare** The Medicare system covers Australian residents for some health-care costs. Visitors from countries with which Australia has a reciprocal health-care agreement are eligible for benefits specified under the Medicare program. Agreements are currently in place with Finland, Italy, Malta, the Netherlands, Norway, Sweden and the UK – check the details before departing these countries. For further details, visit www.medicare australia.gov.au/public/ migrants/visitors.

**Over-the-counter Medications** Widely available at chemists throughout Australia. These include painkillers, antihistamines for allergies, and skincare products.

**Prescriptions** You may find that medications readily available over the counter in some countries are only available in Australia by prescription. These include the oral contraceptive pill, some medications for asthma and all antibiotics.

### Health Care in Remote Areas

**Distance** In remote central Australian locations, it's possible there'll be a significant delay in emergency services reaching you in the event of a serious accident or illness. Don't underestimate the vast distances between most major outback towns. An increased level of self-

## PRACTICALITIES

⇒ **DVDs** Australian DVDs are encoded for Region 4, which includes Mexico, South America, Central America, New Zealand, the Pacific and the Caribbean.

⇒ **Newspapers** The main newspapers are the *Advertiser* (SA), the *NT News* (Darwin) and the *Centralian Advocate* (Alice Springs). The *Age, Sydney Morning Herald* and *Australian* newspapers are readily available.

⇒ **Radio** Tune in to Triple J (ABC youth radio station) and the multicultural SBS National Radio.

⇒ **Smoking** Banned on public transport and in pubs, bars and eateries.

⇒ **TV** On TV you'll find the government-sponsored ABC, the multicultural SBS, Imparja (an Aboriginal-owned station), the three major commercial stations: Seven, Nine and Ten; plus additional digital channels.

⇒ **Weights & Measures** Australia uses the metric system.

reliance and preparation is essential. The **Royal Flying Doctor Service** (RFDS; www.flyingdoctor.net) provides an important back-up for remote communities.

**First Aid** Consider taking a wilderness first-aid course, such as those offered by **Wilderness First Aid Consultants** (www.wfac.com.au). Take a comprehensive first-aid kit appropriate for the activities planned.

**Communication** Ensure you have adequate means of communication. Australia has extensive mobile-phone coverage, but additional radio communication is important for remote areas.

## Bites & Stings

### MARINE ANIMALS

**Stings** Stings from jellyfish (box jellyfish, irukandji) occur in Australia's tropics, particularly during the Wet season (November to April). Warning signs and stinger nets exist at popular affected beaches. Never dive into water unless you've checked that it's safe. First aid consists of washing the skin with vinegar followed by

transfer to a hospital; anti-venin is available.

**Spikes & Spines** Marine spikes found on sea urchins, stonefish, scorpion fish and stingrays can cause severe local pain. If this occurs, immerse the affected area in hot water (as high a temperature as possible). Keep topping up with hot water until the pain subsides and medical care is reached. Stonefish antivenin is available.

### CROCODILES

The risk of crocodile attack in tropical northern Australia is real but predictable and largely preventable. Discuss the local risk with police or tourist agencies in the area before swimming in rivers, waterholes (even far inland) and in the sea, and always heed warning signs.

### SHARKS

Despite extensive media coverage (SA in particular has a bad rep), the risk of shark attack in Australian waters is no greater than in other countries with expansive coastlines. That said, check with

local surf life-saving groups and surfers about risks.

### SNAKES

**Risks** Australian snakes have a fearful reputation, but the actual risk to travellers and locals is low. Snakes are usually quite timid and, in most instances, will move away if disturbed. Prevent bites by wearing protective clothing (such as gaiters) around the lower legs when bushwalking.

**Treatment** If bitten, prevent the spread of venom by applying pressure to the wound and immobilising the area with a splint or sling before seeking medical attention. Firmly wrap an elastic bandage (or a T-shirt) around the entire limb, but not so tight as to cut off the circulation.

### SPIDERS

Australia has several poisonous spiders. In central Australia, redback spider bites cause increasing pain at the site, profuse sweating, muscular weakness and nausea. If bitten, apply ice or cold packs to the bite then transfer to hospital.

## Heat Exhaustion, Heatstroke & Dehydration

**Heat Exhaustion** Heat exhaustion occurs when fluid intake does not keep up with fluid loss. Symptoms include dizziness, fainting, fatigue, nausea or vomiting, and pale, cool and clammy skin. Treatment consists of rest in a cool, shady place and fluid replacement with water or diluted sports drinks.

**Heatstroke** Heatstroke is a severe form of heat illness that occurs after fluid depletion or extreme heat challenge from heavy exercise. Extreme heatstroke is a true medical emergency, with heating of the brain leading to disorientation, hallucinations and seizures.

**Dehydration** A number of unprepared travellers die

from dehydration each year in outback Australia – preventable by following these simple rules:

➡ Carry sufficient water for any trip, including extra in case of vehicle breakdown.

➡ Always let someone, such as the local police, know where you are going and when you expect to arrive.

➡ Carry communications equipment.

➡ Stay with the vehicle rather than walking for help.

## Insect-Borne Illnesses

Various insects can be a source of irritation and, in central Australia, may be the source of specific diseases (eg Ross River fever). Protection from mosquitoes, sandflies, ticks and leeches can be achieved by a combination of the following strategies:

➡ Wear light, loose-fitting, long-sleeved clothing.

➡ Apply 30% DEET to all exposed skin and repeat every three to four hours.

➡ Impregnate clothing with permethrin (an insecticide that kills insects but is believed to be safe for humans).

## Sunburn

Ultraviolet (UV) exposure is greatest between 10am and 4pm, so avoid skin exposure during these times. Always use SPF 30+ sunscreen, apply it 30 minutes before going into the sun and repeat application regularly.

## Traveller's Diarrhoea

**Water** Tap water is usually safe in central Australia. All other water should be boiled, filtered or chemically disinfected (with iodine tablets) to prevent traveller's diarrhoea and giardiasis (giardia).

**Treatment** If you develop diarrhoea, drink plenty of fluids – preferably an oral rehydration solution containing lots of salt and sugar. You should also begin taking an antibiotic (usually a quinolone drug) and an antidiarrhoeal agent (such as loperamide). If diarrhoea is bloody, persists for more than 72 hours or is accompanied by fever, shaking chills or severe abdominal pain, seek medical attention.

## Medical Checklist

➡ antibiotics

➡ antidiarrhoeal drugs (eg loperamide)

➡ acetaminophen (paracetamol) or aspirin

➡ anti-inflammatory drugs (eg ibuprofen)

➡ antihistamines (for hay fever and allergic reactions)

➡ antibacterial ointment for cuts and abrasions

➡ steroid cream or cortisone (for allergic rashes)

➡ bandages, gauze, gauze rolls

➡ adhesive or paper tape

➡ scissors, safety pins, tweezers

➡ thermometer

➡ pocketknife

➡ DEET-containing insect repellent for the skin

➡ permethrin-containing insect spray for clothing, tents and bed nets

➡ sunscreen

➡ oral rehydration salts

➡ iodine tablets or water filter (for water purification)

# Insurance

Worldwide travel insurance is available at www.lonely planet.com/travel_services. You can buy, extend and claim online anytime – even if you're already on the road.

**Level of Cover** A good travel insurance policy covering theft, loss and medical problems is essential. Some policies specifically exclude designated 'dangerous activities' such as scuba diving, motorcycling and even bushwalking. Make sure the policy you choose fully covers you for your activity of choice.

**Health** You may prefer a policy that pays doctors or hospitals directly rather than requiring you to pay on the spot and claim later. If you have to claim later make sure you keep all documentation. Check that the policy covers ambulances and emergency medical evacuations by air.

**Car** For information on insurance matters relating to cars that are bought or rented, see p280.

# Internet Access

## Access Points

**Libraries** Most public libraries have internet access, but generally they're provided for research needs, not for travellers to check their emails – so book ahead or tackle an internet cafe.

**Internet Cafes** You'll find plenty of these in Adelaide, Darwin, Alice, larger towns and pretty much anywhere that travellers congregate. The cost ranges from less than $6 an hour to $10 an hour. Most youth hostels can hook you up, as can many hotels and caravan parks.

## Hooking Up

**ISPs** If you're bringing your palmtop or laptop, check with your Internet Service Provider (ISP) for access numbers you can dial into in central Australia. Most international ISPs have numbers for Adelaide and Darwin. Some major Australian ISPs:

➡ **Dodo** (www.dodo.com)

➡ **iPrimus** (www.iprimus.com.au)

➡ **Optus** (www.optus.com.au)

➡ **Telstra BigPond** (www.bigpond.com)

**Plugs** Australia primarily uses the RJ-45 telephone plugs although you may see Telstra EXI-160 four-pin plugs – electronics shops such as Tandy and Dick Smith can help.

**Wi-fi** Wireless connections are increasingly popular throughout Australia, but don't count on wi-fi being available. To find locations visit www.freewifi.com.au.

**Modem** Keep in mind that your PC-card modem may not work in Australia. The safest option is to buy a reputable 'global' modem before you leave home or buy a local PC-card modem once you get to Australia.

## Legal Matters

Most travellers will have no contact with Australia's police or legal system; if you do, it's most likely to be while driving.

**Driving** There's a significant police presence on central Australian roads; police have the power to stop your car, see your licence (you're required to carry it), check your vehicle for roadworthiness, and insist that you take a breath test for alcohol (and sometimes illicit drugs).

**Drugs** First-time offenders caught with small amounts of illegal drugs are likely to receive a fine rather than go to jail, but the recording of a conviction against you may affect your visa status.

**Visas** If you remain in Australia beyond the life of your visa, you'll officially be an 'overstayer' and could face detention and expulsion, then be prevented from returning to Australia for up to three years.

**Arrested?** It's your right to telephone a friend, lawyer or relative before questioning begins. Legal aid is available only in serious cases; for Legal Aid office info see www.nla.aust.net.au. However, many solicitors do not charge for an initial consultation.

## Maps

### Touring & 4WD Maps

➡ **Royal Automobile Association of South Australia** (RAA; Map p56; ☑08-8202 4600; www.raa. net; 41 Hindmarsh Sq, Adelaide; ⊙8.30am-5pm Mon-Fri, 9am-noon Sat)

➡ **Automobile Association of the Northern Territory** (AANT; ☑08-8925 5901; www. aant.com.au; 79-81 Smith St, Darwin, NT)

➡ **Hema** (☑07-3340 0000; www.hemamaps.com.au)

➡ **Westprint** (☑03-5391 1466; www.westprint.com.au)

### Bushwalking Maps
**Geoscience Australia** (☑1800 800 173; www.ga.gov. au) publishes large-scale topographic sheet maps for bushwalking and 4WD explorations. See also the Map Shop, following.

**City Street Guides UBD Gregory's** (☑02-9857 3700; www.hardiegrant.com.au) produces Adelaide and Darwin street directories (around $35).

**GPS** In SA, GPS systems and topographic maps are available from **Carto Graphics** (☑08-8357 1777; www.cartographics.com.au; 147 Unley Rd, Unley, SA) and the **Map Shop** (Map p56; www. mapshop.net.au; 6-10 Peel St; ⊙9.30am-5pm Mon-Fri, 9am-12.30pm Sat). You can also hire a GPS in Alice Springs at **Central Comms** (☑08-8952 2388; www.central comms.com.au; cnr Stuart Hwy & Wills Tce, Alice Springs, NT), or rent one from the major car-hire companies (Darwin and Adelaide only, subject to availability).

## Money

### Currency

Australia's currency is the Australian dollar, comprising 100 cents. There are 5c, 10c, 20c, 50c, $1 and $2 coins,

and $5, $10, $20, $50 and $100 notes. In this book, unless otherwise stated, prices listed are in Australian dollars.

See p17 for exchange rates and costs.

### ATMs & Eftpos

**ATMs** There are 24-hour ATMs in most substantial towns in SA and the NT (including Yulara at Uluru and Jabiru and Cooinda in Kakadu National Park). All accept cards from other Australian banks, and most are linked to international networks. Stuart Hwy roadhouses also have ATMs.

**Eftpos** Most service stations and supermarkets have Electronic Funds Transfer at Point of Sale (Eftpos) facilities allowing you to make purchases and even draw out cash with your credit or debit card.

### Credit Cards

Credit cards (especially Visa and MasterCard) are widely accepted throughout central Australia. A credit card is essential if you want to hire a car, and can also be used for cash advances at banks and from ATMs (depending on the card). Diners and AmEx cards are not widely accepted.

Lost credit card contact numbers:

➡ **American Express** (☑1300 132 639)

➡ **Diners Club** (☑1300 360 060)

➡ **MasterCard** (☑1800 120 113)

➡ **Visa** (☑1800 450 346)

### Debit Cards

A debit card allows you to draw money directly from your home bank account using ATMs, banks or Eftpos machines. Any card connected to the international banking network – Cirrus, Maestro, Plus and Eurocard – should work with your PIN (Personal Identification Number). Expect substantial fees.

Companies such as Travelex offer debit cards (Travelex calls them 'Cash Passport' cards) with set withdrawal fees and a balance you can top-up from your personal bank account while on the road.

## Taxes & Refunds

**Goods & Services Tax** The GST is a flat 10% tax on all Australian goods and services, with some exceptions such as basic food items (milk, bread, fruit and vegetables etc). By law, the tax is included in the quoted or shelf prices. All prices in this book are GST inclusive.

**GST Refund** If you purchase new or secondhand goods with a minimum value of $300 from any one supplier within 30 days of departure from Australia, you're entitled to a refund of GST paid under the Tourist Refund Scheme (TRS). Contact the **Australian Customs Service** (☎02-9313 3010, 1300 363 263; www.customs.gov.au) for more details.

## Tipping

Tipping is far from ingrained in Australian society, and most people in the outback don't bother. The only place where tipping is considered normal is restaurants, where 10% of the bill is reasonable for good service. Taxi drivers also appreciate you rounding up the fare.

## Travellers Cheques

➡ The ubiquity and convenience of internationally linked credit and debit card facilities in Australia means that travellers cheques are virtually redundant.

➡ AmEx and Travelex will exchange their associated travellers cheques, and major banks will also change travellers cheques.

➡ In all instances you'll need to present your passport for identification when cashing them.

# Opening Hours

**Banks** 9.30am to 4pm Monday to Thursday; until 5pm on Friday.

**Cafes** All-day affairs opening from around 7am until around 5pm, or continuing their business into the night.

**Petrol stations & roadhouses** Usually open 8am to 10pm. Some urban service stations open 24 hours.

**Post offices** 9am to 5pm Monday to Friday; some from 9am to noon on Saturdays. You can also buy stamps from newsagents and delis.

**Pubs** Usually serving food from noon to 2pm and from 6pm to 8pm. Pubs and bars often open for drinking at lunchtime and continue well into the evening, particularly from Thursday to Saturday.

**Restaurants** Open around noon for lunch and from 6pm for dinner, typically serving until at least 2pm and 8pm respectively, often later. Adelaide and Darwin eateries keep longer hours.

**Shops & businesses** 9am to 5pm or 6pm Monday to Friday, until either noon or 5pm on Saturday. In Adelaide and Darwin on Friday, doors stay open until 9pm.

**Supermarkets** Generally open from 7am until at least 8pm; some open 24 hours. Delis (general stores) also open late.

# Public Holidays

National and statewide public holidays observed in SA and the NT:

**New Year's Day** 1 January
**Australia Day** 26 January
**Easter** Good Friday to Easter Monday inclusive; March/April
**Anzac Day** 25 April
**May Day** 1st Monday in May (NT only)
**Adelaide Cup Day** 3rd Monday in May (SA only)
**Queen's Birthday** 2nd Monday in June
**Picnic Day** 1st Monday in August (NT only)
**Labour Day** 1st Monday in October (SA only)
**Christmas Day** 25 December
**Boxing Day** 26 December (NT only)
**Proclamation Day** 28 December (SA only)

# Safe Travel
## Animal Hazards

➡ For around half the year (at least – generally from September to May) you'll have to cope with those two banes of the Australian outdoors: the fly and the mosquito (mozzie).

➡ Insect repellents such as Aerogard and Rid deter mosquitoes, and try to keep your arms and legs covered as soon as the sun sets.

➡ See p266 for info on sharks, snakes, spiders, jellyfish, crocodiles and stinging marine animals.

## Bushfires

➡ In hot, dry and windy weather, be extremely careful with any naked flame (including cigarette butts) and make sure your fire's out before you decamp.

➡ On Total Fire Ban days it's forbidden even to use a camping stove in the open – penalties are harsh.

➡ Campfires are banned in conservation areas during the Fire Danger Period (FDP), which is usually from 1 November to 31 March (30 April in some places).

➡ Postpone your bushwalk if a Total Fire Ban is in place.

## Crime

Central Australia is a relatively safe place to visit but you should still take reasonable precautions:

➡ Lock hotel rooms and cars, and don't leave your

valuables unattended or visible through car windows.

➟ Avoid walking alone in unlit areas at night, especially in Darwin, Alice Springs and Katherine.

➟ Refuse drinks offered by strangers in bars, and drink bottled alcohol rather than from a glass.

## On the Road

➟ Road distances are HUGE out here: take regular breaks to avoid fatigue.

➟ Avoid outback driving at night: animals straying onto the road are a serious hazard, particularly kangaroos but also livestock and camels.

➟ Do some careful planning and preparation before you go: driving on dirt roads can be tricky if you're not used to them, and travellers regularly encounter difficulties in the harsh outback conditions.

➟ Always carry plenty of water and tell someone where you're going.

## Swimming

➟ Popular beaches are patrolled by surf lifesavers; safe areas are marked by red-and-yellow flags.

➟ Undertows (or 'rips') at surf beaches are a problem. If you find yourself being carried out by a rip, don't panic or swim against the current – swim parallel to the shore to escape the rip and then make your way

back to the beach. Raise your arm (and yell!) if you need help.

➟ A number of people are paralysed every year by diving into waterholes or waves in shallow water and hitting the bottom – look before you leap.

# Telephone

Australia's main telecommunication companies:

➟ **Telstra** (www.telstra.com.au) The main player – landline and mobile phone services.

➟ **Optus** (www.optus.com.au) Telstra's main rival – landline and mobile phone services.

➟ **Vodafone** (www.vodafone.com.au) Mobile phone services.

➟ **Virgin** (www.virginmobile.com.au) Mobile phone services.

## Information & Toll-Free Calls

➟ Numbers starting with 190 are usually recorded information services, costing anything from 35c to $5 or more per minute (more from mobiles and payphones).

➟ Many businesses have either a toll-free 1800 number, dialled from anywhere within Australia for free, or a 13 or 1300 number, charged at a local call rate. None of these numbers can be dialled from outside Australia.

➟ To make a reverse-charge (collect) call from a public or private phone, dial 1800 738 3773 or 12 550.

## International Calls

➟ You can make international ISD (International Subscriber Dialling) calls from most phones, but the cheapest deals come through phonecards where calls to the UK and USA can be as low as 5c per minute.

➟ To call overseas from Australia, dial the international access code from Australia (0011 or 0018), the country code, the area code (minus the initial '0'), then the local phone number.

➟ Dialling Australia from overseas, use the 61 country code, then the state/territory STD area code (minus the initial '0'), then the local phone number.

## Local Calls

Local calls cost 50c from public phones; 25c from private phones – there are no time limits. Calls to/from mobile phones cost more and are timed.

## Long-distance Calls

Australia uses four Subscriber Trunk Dialling (STD) area codes for long-distance calls, which can be made from public phones. Long-distance calls are timed; rates vary depending on distance, service provider and time of day – they're cheaper off-peak (usually between 7pm and 7am).

### STD AREA CODES

➟ New South Wales & ACT 02

➟ Victoria & Tasmania 03

➟ Queensland 07

➟ South Australia, Northern Territory & Western Australia 08

## Mobile (Cell) Phones

**Numbers** Australian mobile-phone numbers have the prefixes 04xx.

## GOVERNMENT TRAVEL ADVICE

The following government websites offer travel advisories and information on current hot spots.

➟ **Australian Department of Foreign Affairs** (www.smartraveller.gov.au)

➟ **British Foreign Office** (www.fco.gov.uk)

➟ **Foreign Affairs & International Trade Canada** (www.voyage.gc.ca)

➟ **US State Department** (http://travel.state.gov)

**Reception** Australia's mobile networks service more than 90% of the population but leave vast tracts of the country uncovered. Adelaide, Darwin and most of central Australia's settled areas get good reception, but as the towns thin out, so does the service. Don't rely on coverage in outback areas.

**Networks** Australia's digital network is compatible with GSM 900 and 1800 (used in Europe), but isn't compatible with the systems used in the USA or Japan.

**Providers** It's easy and cheap to get connected short term – the main service providers all have prepaid mobile systems.

## Phonecards

A range of phonecards ($10, $20, $30 etc) is available from newsagencies and post offices, and can be used with any public or private phone by dialling a toll-free access number and then the PIN on the card. Rates vary from company to company – shop around.

## Time

➡ SA and the NT are on Central Standard Time, half an hour behind the eastern states (Queensland, New South Wales, Victoria and Tasmania), and 1½ hours ahead of Western Australia.

➡ Central Standard Time is 9½ hours ahead of GMT/UTC (London), 13½ hours ahead of New York, 15½ hours ahead of LA, 2½ hours ahead of Jakarta and 2½ hours behind Wellington (New Zealand).

➡ 'Daylight Savings' does not apply in the NT, Western Australia or Queensland during summer, so from October to March (approximately), most eastern states are 1½ hours ahead of NT time, and SA is one hour ahead of NT time.

## Toilets

➡ Toilets in central Australia are sit-down western style (...though you mightn't find this prospect too appealing in some remote outback pit-stops).

➡ See www.toiletmap.gov.au for public toilet locations.

## Tourist Information

Almost every decent-sized central Australian town has a visitor information centre of some description, with a proliferation of brochures and maps. They're usually staffed by volunteers (some with sketchy knowledge of tourism).

**South Australian Visitor Information Centre** (Map p56; ☏1300 764 227; www.southaustralia.com; 108 North Tce, Adelaide, SA; ☺9am-5pm Mon-Fri, 9am-2pm Sat, 10am-3pm Sun) Abundantly stocked with info (including fab regional booklets) on Adelaide and SA.

**Tourism Australia** (www.australia.com) The main government tourism site with visitor info.

**Tourism NT** (www.travelnt.com) Bountiful info on the Northern Territory outback. Also produces *The Essential NT Drive Guide*, a great booklet with driving distances, national parks, and outback info and advice for 2WD and 4WD travellers.

**Tourism Top End** (☏08-8980 6000, 1300 138 886; www.tourismtopend.com.au; cnr Smith & Bennett Sts, Darwin, NT; ☺8.30am-5pm Mon-Fri, 9am-3pm Sat & Sun) Hundreds of brochures; books tours and accommodation.

## Travellers with Disabilities

Disability awareness in central Australia is pretty high and getting higher. New accommodation must meet accessibility standards, and discrimination by tourism operators is illegal. Many key attractions provide access for those with limited mobility, and sometimes for those with visual or aural impairments; contact attractions in advance.

Long-distance bus travel isn't viable for wheelchair users, but the *Ghan* train has disabled facilities (book ahead). Some car-rental companies (Avis, Hertz) offer rental cars with hand controls at no extra charge for pick-up at the major airports (advance notice required).

### Resources

**Deaf CanDo** (Royal South Australian Deaf Society; ☏08-8100 8200, TTY 08-8340 1654; www.deafcando.com.au)

**Deafness Association of the Northern Territory** (☏08-8945 2016; www.connectingup.org/organisation/deafness-association-of-north ern-territory-inc)

**Disability Information & Resource Centre** (DIRC; Map p56; ☏08-8236 0555, 1300 305 558; www.dircsa.org.au; 195 Gilles St; ☺9am-5pm Mon-Fri) Info on accommodation, venues and travel for people with disabilities.

**Easy Access Australia** (www.easyaccessaustralia.com.au) A publication by Bruce Cameron available from various bookshops. Details accessible transport, accommodation and attraction options.

**Guide Dogs SA.NT** (☏08-8203 8333; www.guidedogs.org.au)

**National Information Communication & Awareness Network** (NICAN; www.nican.com.au) Australia-wide directory providing information on access issues, accessible accommodation, sporting and recreational activities, transport and specialist tour operators.

**South Australian Royal Society for the Blind** (☑08-8417 5599; www.rsb.org.au)

**Vision Australia** (☑1300 847 466; www.visionaustralia.org.au)

## Visas

➜ All visitors to Australia need a visa – only New Zealand nationals are exempt, and even they sheepishly receive a 'special category' visa on arrival.

➜ There are several different visas available, depending on your nationality and what kind of visit you're contemplating.

➜ See the website of the **Department of Immigration & Citizenship** (☑13 18 81; www.immi.gov.au) for info and application forms (also available from Australian diplomatic missions overseas and travel agents), plus details on visa extensions, Working Holiday Visas (417) and Work & Holiday Visas (462).

### eVisitor

Many European passport holders will find themselves eligible for a free eVisitor visa, allowing stays in Australia for up to three months within a 12-month period. eVisitor visas must be applied for online (www.immi.gov.au/e_visa/evisitor.htm). They are electronically stored and linked to individual passport numbers, so no stamp in your passport is required. It's advisable to apply at least 14 days prior to the proposed date of travel to Australia.

### Electronic Travel Authority (ETA)

Passport holders from eight countries which aren't part of the eVisitor scheme – Brunei, Canada, Hong Kong, Japan, Malaysia, Singapore, South Korea and the USA – can apply for either a visitor or business ETA. ETAs are valid for 12 months, with stays of up to three months on each visit. You can apply for the ETA online (www.eta.immi.gov.au), which attracts a nonrefundable service charge of $20.

### Tourist Visas (676)

If you're from a country not covered by the eVisitor and ETA, or you want to stay longer than three months, you'll need to apply for a Tourist Visa. Standard Tourist Visas (AUD$115) allow one (in some cases multiple) entry, for a stay of up to 12 months, and are valid for use within 12 months of issue. Online, see www.immi.gov.au/e_visa/e676.htm.

## Volunteering

Lonely Planet's *Volunteer: A Traveller's Guide to Making a Difference Around the World* provides useful information about volunteering.

**Australian Volunteers International** (AVI; ☑03-9279 1788, 1800 331 292; www.australianvolunteers.com) The AVI places skilled volunteers into Aboriginal communities in northern and central Australia (mostly long-term placements). There are occasional short-term unskilled opportunities too, helping out at community-run roadhouses.

**Conservation Council of SA** (☑08-8223 5155; www.conservationsa.org.au) Offers South Australian volunteer opportunities including restoration of swamps, grasslands and other natural habitats, and recovery programs to help threatened bird species.

**Conservation Volunteers Australia** (CVA; ☑03-5330 2600, 1800 032 501; www.conservationvolunteers.com.au) A nonprofit organisation that is involved in tree planting, walking-track construction, and flora and fauna surveys.

**Nature Conservation Society of South Australia** (☑08-7127 4630; www.ncssa.asn.au) Survey fieldwork volunteer opportunities in SA.

## Women Travellers

Travelling in central Australia is generally safe for women, but both sexes should exercise some basic common sense.

➜ Avoid walking alone at night and be wary of stopping for anyone on the highway.

➜ Sexual harassment is rare though some macho (and less enlightened) Aussie males still slip – particularly when they've been drinking.

➜ Hitching is not recommended for anyone. Even when travelling in pairs, exercise caution at all times.

➜ Lone women should also be wary of staying in basic pub accommodation unless it looks safe and well managed.

➜ The Adelaide-based **Women's Information Service** (Map p56; ☑08-8303 0590, 1800 188 158; www.wis.sa.gov.au; Ground Fl, 91-97 Grenfell St, Chesser House; ⊙10am-4pm Mon, Tue, Thu & Fri) provides information, advice and referrals.

## Work

**Work Visas** If you come to Australia on a tourist visa then you're not allowed to work for pay: you'll need a Working Holiday Visa (417) or Work & Holiday Visa (462) – visit www.immi.gov.au for details.

**Finding Work** Backpacker magazines, newspapers and hostel noticeboards are usually excellent places to help source local work opportunities. In SA, seasonal fruit picking and vineyard work abounds.

## Resources

**Career One** (www.careerone.com.au) General employment site; good for the cities.

**Gumtree** (www.gumtree.com.au) Classified site with jobs, accommodation and items for sale.

**Harvest Trail** (www.jobsearch.gov.au/harvesttrail) Harvest jobs around Australia.

**MyCareer** (www.mycareer.com.au) General employment site; good for metropolitan areas.

**National Harvest Labour Information Service** (☎1800 062 332) Info on when and where you're likely to pick up harvest work.

**Seek** (www.seek.com.au) General employment site; good for metropolitan areas.

**Travellers at Work** (www.taw.com.au) Excellent site for working travellers in Australia.

**Workabout Australia** (www.workaboutaustralia.com.au) State-by-state breakdown of seasonal work opportunities.

**Viterra** (www.viterra.com.au) Seasonal grain harvest jobs in Victoria and South Australia (October to January).

# Transport

## GETTING THERE & AWAY

Australia is a long way from just about everywhere – getting there usually means a long-haul flight. If you're short on time on the ground, consider internal flights – they're affordable (compared with petrol and car-hire costs), can usually be carbon offset, and will save you some *looong* days in the saddle. Flights, tours and rail tickets can be booked online at lonelyplanet.com/bookings.

## Entering Australia

Provided your visa is in order, arrival in Australia is straightforward, with the usual customs declarations.

### Passports

There are no restrictions regarding citizens of foreign countries entering Australia. If you have a current passport and visa (p272), you should be fine.

## Air

### Airports & Airlines

Some airlines fly directly into **Adelaide Airport** (ADL; ☎08-8308 9211; www.adelaide airport.com.au) and **Darwin Airport** (www.darwinairport. com.au; Henry Wrigley Dr, Marrara), but most utilise east-coast hubs (Sydney, Melbourne, Brisbane) from where you can book domestic flights to Adelaide, Darwin and regional centres.

Australia's international carrier **Qantas** (☎13 13 13; www.qantas.com.au) has an outstanding safety record (...as Dustin Hoffman said in *Rainman*, 'Qantas never crashed'). Other airlines that fly in and out of Australia include the following:

**Air Canada** (www.aircanada. com)

**Air New Zealand** (www. airnewzealand.com)

**Air Pacific** (www.airpacific. com)

**American Airlines** (www. aa.com)

**British Airways** (www. britishairways.com)

**Cathay Pacific** (www.cathay pacific.com)

**Emirates** (www.emirates. com)

**Garuda Indonesia** (www. garuda-indonesia.com)

**Japan Airlines** (www.jal. com)

**Jetstar** (www.jetstar.com.au)

**KLM** (www.klm.com)

**Korean Air** (www.koreanair. com)

**Lufthansa** (www.lufthansa. com)

**Malaysia Airlines** (www. malaysiaairlines.com)

**Royal Brunei Airlines** (www.bruneiair.com)

---

### CLIMATE CHANGE & TRAVEL

Every form of transport that relies on carbon-based fuel generates $CO_2$, the main cause of human-induced climate change. Modern travel is dependent on aeroplanes, which might use less fuel per kilometre per person than most cars but travel much greater distances. The altitude at which aircraft emit gases (including $CO_2$) and particles also contributes to their climate change impact. Many websites offer 'carbon calculators' that allow people to estimate the carbon emissions generated by their journey and, for those who wish to do so, to offset the impact of the greenhouse gases emitted with contributions to portfolios of climate-friendly initiatives throughout the world. Lonely Planet offsets the carbon footprint of all staff and author travel.

**Singapore Airlines** (www.singaporeair.com.au)

**South African Airways** (www.flysaa.com)

**Thai Airways** (www.thaiairways.com)

**Tiger Airways** (www.tigerairways.com)

**United Airlines** (www.unitedairlines.com)

**Virgin Atlantic** (www.virgin-atlantic.com)

**Virgin Australia** (☑13 67 89; www.virginaustralia.com)

# Land

If you're a keen driver, central Australia was made for you! There's not much traffic here, roads are in good condition, and there are plenty of opportunities for off-road exploration.

**South Australia** Bitumen highways link the huge distances between Adelaide in SA and other Australian cities, including the Stuart Hwy which runs north–south across the entire country to Darwin.

**Northern Territory** Getting to the NT overland means a lot of travel through empty country, but there's no better way to appreciate Australia's vastness. The nearest state capital to Darwin is Adelaide (a tick over 3000km), while Perth and Sydney are both around 4000km away, about the same distance as New York to Los Angeles and more than 2½ times the drive from London to Rome!

## Border Crossings

➡ The main routes into SA include Hwy 1 from Western Australia (across the Nullarbor Plain), and the Stuart Hwy from the NT (via Alice Springs).

➡ From Victoria, there are two main crossings: the Princes Hwy (via Mt Gambier and/or Great Ocean Rd), and the more direct (but more dull) Dukes Hwy (via Bordertown and Victoria's Western Hwy).

## INTERSTATE QUARANTINE

Within Australia, there are restrictions on carrying fruit, plants and vegetables across state and territory borders. This is in order to control the movement of disease or pests – such as fruit fly, cucurbit thrips, grape phylloxera and potato cyst nematodes – from one area to another.

Most quarantine control relies on honesty and quarantine posts at the state/territory borders are not always staffed. However, the Western Australia border is permanently manned and sometimes uses dogs to sniff out offending matter. This may seem excessive, but it's taken very seriously. It's prohibited to carry fresh fruit and vegetables, plants, flowers, and even nuts and honey across the Northern Territory–Western Australia border in either direction. The controls with South Australia, Victoria, New South Wales and Queensland are less strict – there's usually an unmanned honesty bin for disposal. Check at the borders.

➡ Outback 4WD tracks aside, there are three main (sealed) roads into the NT: the Victoria Hwy from WA (via Kununurra), the Barkly Hwy from Queensland (via Mt Isa), and the Stuart Hwy from SA (via Coober Pedy).

## Bus

Many travellers prefer to access central Australia by bus because it's one of the best ways to come to grips with the area's size – also the bus companies have far more comprehensive route networks than the railway system (and they have good air-con!). Discounts are available for backpacker associations/international student ID card holders. See p277 for info on bus passes.

Major long-haul operators include the following:

**Firefly Express** (☑1300 730 740; www.fireflyexpress.com.au) Buses between Adelaide and Melbourne (from $65, 11 hours), continuing to Sydney.

**Greyhound Australia** (☑1300 473 946; www.greyhound.com.au) Services between Adelaide and Melbourne, Sydney and Alice Springs, connecting to Darwin.

**V/Line** (☑03-9697 2076, 13 61 96; www.vline.com.au) Combined bus/train services between Adelaide and Melbourne (the Melbourne–Bendigo leg is via train).

## Car & Motorcycle

See p277 for info on driving (or riding) in central Australia.

# Sea

There are no scheduled international passenger-ferry services to/from SA or the NT, but it's possible – with a bit of graft and fortune – to sail to northern Australia from Asia by hitching rides or crewing on yachts. Ask around at harbours, marinas or yacht clubs. Darwin is a good place to try to hitch a ride to Indonesia, Malaysia or Singapore. Try contacting the **Darwin Sailing Club** (Map p152; ☑08-8981 1700; www.dwnsail.com.au) at Fannie Bay, or the **Darwin Port Corporation** (☑08-8922 0660; www.darwinport.nt.gov.au).

# GETTING AROUND

## Air

### Airlines in Australia

➡ Flying around Australia is the fastest, safest and often cheapest way to get from state to state or city to city.

➡ The major Australian domestic carriers **Qantas** (☑13 13 13; www.qantas. com.au) and **Virgin Australia** (☑13 67 89; www. virginaustralia.com) fly all over Australia, operating flights between Adelaide and Darwin (via Melbourne in Virgin's case) and other centres. Qantas also flies to Alice Springs and Uluru; Virgin flies to Uluru from Sydney.

➡ See regional chapters for scenic flight listings. Other regional A-to-B airline options include:

**Airnorth** (☑1800 627 474; www.airnorth.com.au) Small NT-based airline with flights from Darwin to Broome and Kununurra in WA, and Mt Isa and Townsville in Queensland. Also connects Darwin with Gove, Maningrida and Groote Eylandt.

**Air South** (☑1300 247 768; www.airsouth.com.au) Adelaide-based charter flights around SA.

**Altitude Aviation** (☑1800 747 300; www.altitudeavia tion.com.au) Charter flights (including helicopters) to/ from pretty much anywhere in central Australia.

**Jetstar** (☑13 15 38; www. jetstar.com.au) Services capital cities (including Adelaide and Darwin) and key holiday destinations.

**Regional Express** (Rex; ☑13 17 13; www.regionalex press.com.au) Flies between Adelaide and Kingscote on Kangaroo Island, Coober Pedy, Ceduna, Mt Gambier, Port Lincoln and Whyalla.

**Tiger Airways** (☑03-9999 2888; www.tigerairways.com)

Connects Adelaide with Melbourne.

### Air Passes

➡ **Qantas** (☑13 13 13; www. qantas.com.au) offers a discount-fare **Walkabout Air Pass** for passengers flying into Australia from overseas with Qantas or American Airlines. The pass allows you to link up around 80 domestic Australian destinations (including Adelaide, Uluru, Alice Springs and Darwin) for less than you'd pay booking flights individually.

## Bicycle

**South Australia** SA is a great place for cycling. There are some excellent bike tracks in Adelaide, thousands of kilometres of quiet, flat country roads, converted railway tracks in wine regions and the **Mawson Trail** (www.southaustraliantrails. com), an 800km mountain-bike track from Adelaide to Parachilna Gorge in the Flinders Ranges.

**Northern Territory** Darwin also has a network of bike tracks, and Katherine and Alice Springs have plenty of pancake-flat riding opportunities. However, actually using a bicycle as your mode of transport in the NT is another matter. Dehydration and the availability of drinking water are the main concerns. It can be a long way between towns and roadhouses, and those isolated bores, creeks and tanks shown on your map may be dry or undrinkable.

Make sure you've got the necessary spare parts and bike-repair knowledge. Carry a good map and let someone know where you're headed before setting off. Check road conditions and weather forecasts, and make conservative estimates of how long your journey will take. Beware of road trains: if you hear one coming, get right off the road. No matter how fit you are,

take things slowly until you're used to the heat, wear a hat and plenty of sunscreen, and drink *lots* of water.

### Bike Hire

➡ In SA you can hire bikes in Adelaide, McLaren Vale, Victor Harbor, the Barossa and Clare Valleys and the Flinders Ranges.

➡ In the NT you can hire bikes in Darwin, Alice Springs, Yulara and Wauchope.

➡ Costs start at around $25 per day, usually including helmet, lights and lock.

### Buying a Bike

➡ If you want to buy a reliable new road or mountain bike, your absolute bottom-level starting point is $500 to $650. Throw in all the requisite on-the-road equipment (panniers, helmet etc), and your starting point becomes $1500 to $2000.

➡ Secondhand bikes are worth checking out in the cities, as are the post-Christmas sales and midyear stock takes, when newish bicycles can be heavily discounted.

➡ To sell your bike, try hostel noticeboards or online at www.tradingpost.com.au.

### Legalities

➡ Bike helmets are compulsory in all states and territories, as are white front lights and red rear lights for riding at night.

### Transport

➡ If you're coming to central Australia specifically to cycle, it makes sense to bring your own bike – check with your airline for costs and the degree of dismantling/ packing required.

➡ While you can load your bike onto a bus to skip the boring/difficult bits, bus companies require you to dismantle your bike, and some don't guarantee that it will travel on the same bus as you.

## Resources

**Bicycle SA** (☑08-8168 9999; www.bikesa.asn.au; 111 Franklin St, Adelaide, SA) Information on bike touring around SA, plus the excellent (and free!) Adelaide City Bikes scheme (see p60).

**Northern Territory Cycling Association** (☑08-8945 6012; www.nt.cycling.org.au) Information and links to local clubs and events.

**South Australian Trails** (www.southaustraliantrails.com) Detailed SA bike-track info plus links to cycling organisations, clubs and maps.

## Boat

**South Australia** The only passenger ferries in this region of SA are between Cape Jervis and Kangaroo Island, run by **SeaLink** (☑13 13 01; www.sealink.com.au); and across Spencer Gulf between Wallaroo on the Yorke Peninsula and Lucky Bay on the Eyre Peninsula, run by **Sea SA** (☑08-8823 0777; www.seasa.com.au). Both are smooth, efficient operations (if a little pricey).

**Northern Territory** In the NT passenger ferries operate under the umbrella of **Tiwi Ferry** (☑0499 675 266, 0418 675 266; www.tiwiferry.com.au), chugging between Darwin and Mandorah and the Tiwi Islands.

## Bus

Bus transport in central Australia is regular, safe, efficient and (usually) cost-effective. Regional services within SA and the NT are as follows:

### South Australia

➡ In SA, Adelaide's **Central Bus Station** (☑08-8221 5080; www.cityofadelaide.com.au; 85 Franklin St, Adelaide, SA) has ticket offices and terminals for all major statewide and interstate services, including long-distance operators

**Greyhound Australia** (☑13 14 99; www.greyhound.com.au), **Firefly Express** (☑1300 730 740; www.fireflyexpress.com.au) and **V/Line** (☑03-9697 2076, 13 61 96; www.vline.com.au).

➡ For online bus timetables see www.bussa.com.au.

➡ Within SA the main service provider is **Premier Stateliner** (☑08-8415 5555; www.premierstateliner.com.au), which runs to destinations including McLaren Vale, Victor Harbor, Mt Gambier, Port Augusta, Port Pirie, Naracoorte and Penola, among many others.

➡ Other regional SA bus companies include:

**Link SA** (☑08-8532 2633; www.linksa.com.au) Servicing towns around the lower Murray River (Murray Bridge, Mannum, Berri, Swan Reach), Barossa Valley (Tanunda, Angaston, Nuriootpa) and parts of the Adelaide Hills.

**SeaLink** (☑13 13 01; www.sealink.com.au) The Kangaroo Island ferry company also runs buses between Adelaide and Cape Jervis, the mainland ferry departure point.

**Southlink** (☑08-8186 2888; www.southlink.com.au) Services the Fleurieu Peninsula and Adelaide's far northern suburbs, working in conjunction with Adelaide Metro services.

**Yorke Peninsula Coaches** (☑08-8821 2755; www.ypcoaches.com.au) Services the Clare Valley, Yorke Peninsula and southern Flinders Ranges towns.

### Northern Territory

➡ In Darwin, interstate and intra-NT buses use the **Transit Centre** (www.enjoy-darwin.com/transit-bus.html; 69 Mitchell St).

➡ **Greyhound Australia** (☑1300 473 946; www.greyhound.com.au) runs the major long-distance regional routes in the NT, including Alice Springs to Uluru and

Kings Canyon; Alice to Darwin via Katherine and Tennant Creek; and Darwin to Kakadu.

## Bus Passes

If you're planning on doing a lot of travel in central Australia, a **Greyhound Australia** (☑1300 473 946; www.greyhound.com.au) bus pass will save you money. Bus-pass discounts of 10% apply to backpacker- and student-card holders, and children under 14.

**Kilometre Passes** Under the banner of 'Oz-Flexi Travel', these are the simplest passes, giving you specified amounts of travel starting at 500km ($108), going up in increments of 1000km to 20,000km ($2254), with a maximum of 25,000km ($2600). Passes are valid for 12 months (90 days for 500km and 1000km passes), and you can travel where and in what direction you please, stopping as many times as you like. Use the online kilometre chart to figure out which pass suits you. Phone at least a day ahead to reserve your seat.

**Micro Passes** In the 'Oz-Choice Travel' pass category, another option are these set-route passes, allowing you to travel a designated route over 10 to 14 days, with a rest stop or two along the way. In central Australia there's the 10-day 'Opal Stopover' ($226) which runs in either direction between Adelaide and Alice Springs via Coober Pedy; and the 14-day 'Croc Stopover' ($255) which runs between Alice Springs and Darwin in either direction, with three stops permitted en route.

## Car & Motorcycle

The ultimate freedom within central Australia is to have your own wheels. Driving distances are long, but you can take it at your own pace and branch off the main roads

## ROAD DISTANCES (KM)

| | Adelaide | Adelaide River | Alice Springs | Barrow Creek | Coober Pedy | Darwin | Elliot | Erldunda | Glendambo | Katherine | Kulgera | Larrimah | Marla | Pimba/Woomera | Port Augusta | Port Pirie |
|---|---|---|---|---|---|---|---|---|---|---|---|---|---|---|---|---|
| Adelaide River | 2903 | | | | | | | | | | | | | | | |
| Alice Springs | 1524 | 1379 | | | | | | | | | | | | | | |
| Barrow Creek | 1808 | 1095 | 284 | | | | | | | | | | | | | |
| Coober Pedy | 835 | 2068 | 689 | 973 | | | | | | | | | | | | |
| Darwin | 3020 | 117 | 1496 | 1212 | 2185 | | | | | | | | | | | |
| Elliot | 2284 | 619 | 760 | 476 | 1449 | 736 | | | | | | | | | | |
| Erldunda | 1324 | 1579 | 200 | 484 | 489 | 1696 | 960 | | | | | | | | | |
| Glendambo | 590 | 2313 | 934 | 1218 | 245 | 2430 | 1694 | 734 | | | | | | | | |
| Katherine | 2702 | 201 | 1178 | 894 | 1867 | 318 | 418 | 1378 | 2112 | | | | | | | |
| Kulgera | 1250 | 1653 | 274 | 558 | 415 | 1770 | 1034 | 74 | 660 | 1452 | | | | | | |
| Larrimah | 2522 | 381 | 998 | 714 | 1687 | 498 | 238 | 1198 | 1932 | 180 | 1272 | | | | | |
| Marla | 1068 | 1835 | 456 | 740 | 233 | 1952 | 1216 | 256 | 478 | 1634 | 182 | 1454 | | | | |
| Pimba/Woomera | 485 | 2418 | 1039 | 1323 | 350 | 2535 | 1799 | 839 | 105 | 2217 | 765 | 2037 | 583 | | | |
| Port Augusta | 300 | 2603 | 1224 | 1508 | 535 | 2720 | 1984 | 1024 | 290 | 2402 | 950 | 2222 | 768 | 185 | | |
| Port Pirie | 225 | 2678 | 1299 | 1583 | 610 | 2795 | 2059 | 1099 | 365 | 2477 | 1025 | 2297 | 843 | 260 | 75 | |
| Tennant Creek | 2032 | 871 | 508 | 224 | 1197 | 988 | 252 | 708 | 1442 | 670 | 782 | 490 | 964 | 1547 | 1732 | 1807 |

to places public transport doesn't go. Shared between three or four people the cost of hiring a car or campervan is reasonable but, before you drive off into the sunset, you need to know a few things about outback travel (see p35).

**2WD or 4WD?** To truly explore outback areas you'll need a well-prepared 4WD vehicle, but there are plenty of routes open to a conventional (2WD) vehicle. Even the legendary Oodnadatta Track can, in theory, be tackled in a 2WD, but we wouldn't recommend it.

**Motorcycle** Born to be wild? The central Australian climate is good for bikes for much of the year, particularly in SA, and the many small tracks from the road into the bush lead to perfect spots to spend the night.

➡ A fuel range of 350km will cover fuel stops along the Stuart Hwy.

➡ The long, open roads are really made for large-capacity machines above 750cc.

➡ Contact the **Motorcycle Riders Association of SA** (☑ 0408 607 788; www.mrasa. asn.au) for info.

## Aboriginal Land Permits

If you wish to travel through the outback independently, particularly in the NT, you may need special permits if you're passing through Aboriginal land or visiting a community. Generally, such land has government-administered reserve status or it may be held under free-hold title vested in an Aboriginal land trust and managed by a council or corporation.

**Exclusions** In some cases permits won't be necessary if you stick to recognised public roads that cross Aboriginal territory, but as soon as you leave the main road by more than 50m you

may need a permit (Arnhem Land is a good example). If you're on an organised tour the operator should take care of permits – check before you book.

In the NT a transit permit is required for the Yulara–Kaltukatjara (Docker River) Rd, but not for either the Tanami Track or the Sand-over Hwy where these cross Aboriginal land. Travellers may camp overnight without a permit within 50m of the latter two routes.

**Applications** The easiest way to apply for a permit is to download a form from the relevant land council and send it by email. Alternatively you can send it by post or fax. Allow plenty of time: transit permits can be approved within 24 hours, but others can take 10 working days. Keep in mind that your application may be knocked back for a number of reasons, including the risk of interference with sacred sites or disruption of ceremonial business. Also, some communities simply may not want to be bothered by visitors without good reason.

The following places issue permits:

**Northern Land Council**
(☑08-8920 5100; www.nlc.
org.au) Servicing northern NT, with offices in Darwin, Katherine, Jabiru and Tennant Creek.

**Central Land Council**
(☑08-8951 6211; www.clc.org.
au) Covering the southern half of the NT; main office in Alice Springs.

**Tiwi Land Council** (☑08-8919 4305; www.tiwilandcoun cil.com) Permits for the Tiwi Islands.

## Automobile Associations

Official automobile associations offer emergency breakdown services and useful advice on motoring, including road safety, local regulations and buying/selling a car. The following organisations have reciprocal arrangements with similar organisations overseas and interstate.

**Royal Automobile Association of South Australia**
(RAA; ☑08-8202 4600; www.
raa.net; 55 Hindmarsh Sq, Adelaide, SA)

**Automobile Association of the Northern Territory**
(AANT; ☑08-8925 5901; www.
aant.com.au; 79-81 Smith St, Darwin, NT)

## Driving Licences

Foreign driving licences are valid in Australia as long as they are in English or are accompanied by a translation. You can also get an **International Driving Permit** from automobile associations in your own country.

## Fuel

➡ Unleaded, diesel and LPG fuel are available from urban service stations and highway roadhouses.

➡ Distances between fill-ups can be long in the outback, so check locations and

opening times of service stations and carry spare fuel.

➡ Prices vary from place to place depending on how remote they are, but fuel in outback central Australia is some of the most expensive in the country: at the time of writing unleaded petrol prices were hovering around $1.45 in Adelaide, $1.60 in Darwin, and climbing to $1.80 in remote areas. Regardless, expect to pay 20% more in Darwin than in the east coast capitals, and up to 50% more in small outback towns.

## Hire

There are plenty of car-rental companies ready and willing to put you behind the wheel. Competition is fierce so rates vary and special deals pop up and disappear again. The main thing to remember when assessing your options is distance – if you want to travel far, you need unlimited kilometres. The major companies offer this, or 100km a day free plus however many cents per kilometre beyond 100km (make sure you do your sums!).

**Age** You must be at least 21 years old to hire from most firms – if you're under 25 you may only be able to hire a small car or have to pay a surcharge.

**One-way Hire** One-way hire into or out of the NT and SA may be subject to a hefty repositioning fee; however, some big rental firms offer good deals from Alice Springs to Adelaide or Adelaide to Melbourne. Ask about this before deciding on one company over another.

**Relocations** For budget car-hire experience, relocations can often work well: when a rental company requires a certain vehicle to be moved to a certain location, they'll sometimes offer a cheap rate for someone to drive it there. Lucky you! **Relocations2Go** (☑1800 735 627;

www.relocations2go.com) is a good place to look.

**Insurance & Excess** Most car-rental companies include insurance in the price, but in the event of an accident the hirer is still liable for a sometimes-hefty excess. Most offer an excess-reduction daily rate on top of the base rental rate. Most firms won't let you drive after dark in the outback due to the risk of hitting kangaroos – read the fine print.

**Costs** Daily rates, including insurance and taxes, are typically about $40 to $70 a day for a small car (Toyota Yaris, Hyundai i20), $70 to $90 a day for a medium car (Holden Cruze, Toyota Corolla) or $90 up to $100 a day for a big car (Holden Commodore, Hyundai i45). Local firms are almost always cheaper than the big boys – sometimes half-price – but cheaper hire often comes with crippling restrictions. It's cheaper if you rent for a week or more and there are often low-season and weekend discounts.

The main players:

**Avis** (☑13 63 33; www.avis.
com.au)

**Budget** (☑13 27 27; www.
budget.com.au)

**Europcar** (☑1300 131 390;
www.europcar.com.au)

**Hertz** (☑13 30 39; www.hertz.
com.au)

**Thrifty** (☑1300 367 227;
www.thrifty.com.au)

### CAMPERVANS

Many people find a campervan is the best way to explore the outback, and it's hard to disagree. From a two-berth to a full-blown family camper, they offer a home on wheels, allowing you to pull up anywhere, save on accommodation costs and crank up the AC/DC as loud as hell! Most have some sort of cooking facilities and there are a few 4WD models. They typically cost from $90 to $150 a day.

The following companies have fitted-out vans and 4WDs, offer one-way rental and have offices in the major cities around Australia, including Alice Springs:

**Apollo** (☑1800 777 779; www.apollocamper.com)

**Britz** (☑1800 331 454; www.britz.com.au)

**Maui** (☑1300 363 800; www.maui.com.au)

**Mighty Cars & Campers** (☑1800 670 232; www.mightycampers.com.au)

**Wicked Campers** (☑1800 246 869; www.wickedcampers.com.au) Funkily painted backpacker vans (Jimi Hendrix, Alice Cooper, Bob Marley etc).

### 4WDS

Having a 4WD vehicle is essential for off-the-beaten-track driving into the outback. And there might even be room to sleep in the back! The major car- and campervan-hire companies also offer 4WDs.

**Costs** Renting a 4WD vehicle is affordable if a few people get together: something like a Nissan X-Trail (which can get you through most, but not all, tracks) costs around $100 to $150 per day; for a Toyota Landcruiser you're looking at around $150 up to $200, which should include unlimited kilometres.

**Exclusions** Check the insurance conditions, especially the excess, as they can be onerous and policies might not cover damage caused when travelling off-road.

### Insurance

**Excess** Rather than risking paying out thousands of dollars if you do have a crash, you can take out comprehensive insurance on the car or pay an additional daily amount to the rental company for an 'insurance excess reduction' policy. This reduces the excess (the amount of money for which you're liable before

the insurance kicks in) from between $2000 and $5000 to a few hundred dollars, though it pushes the rental cost up.

**Exclusions** Be aware that if you're travelling on dirt roads you often won't be covered by insurance unless you have a 4WD – in other words, if you have an accident you'll be liable for all costs involved. Also, most companies' insurance won't cover the cost of damage to glass (including the windscreen) or tyres. Similarly, because of the risk of hitting an animal, most companies void your insurance if you travel outside city limits between dusk and dawn. Always read the small print.

## Purchase

Buying your own vehicle to travel around in gives you the freedom to go where and when the mood takes you, and may work out cheaper than renting in the long run. Some dealers will sell you a car with an undertaking to buy it back at an agreed price, but don't accept verbal guarantees – get it in writing. It's your responsibility to ensure the car isn't stolen and that there's no money owing on it: check the car's details with the **Personal Property Securities Register** (☑1300 007 777; www.ppsr.gov.au).

### WHAT TO LOOK FOR

It's prudent to have a car checked by an independent expert – automobile associations (p279) offer vehicle checks, and road transport authorities (p281) have lists of licensed garages – but if you're flying solo, things to check include the following:

➡ tyre tread

➡ number of kilometres

➡ rust damage

➡ accident damage

➡ oil should be translucent and honey-coloured

➡ coolant should be clean and not rusty in colour

➡ engine condition; check for fumes from engine, smoke from exhaust while engine is running and engines that rattle or cough

➡ exhaust system should not be excessively noisy or rattle when engine is running

➡ windscreen should be clear with no cracks or chip marks.

When test-driving the car, also check the following:

➡ listen for body and suspension noise and changes in engine noise

➡ check for oil and petrol smells, leaks and overheating

➡ check instruments, lights and controls all work: heating, air-con, brake lights, headlights, indicators, seatbelts and windscreen wipers

➡ brakes should pull the car up straight, without pulling, vibrating or making noise

➡ gears and steering should be smooth and quiet.

### WHERE TO BUY

If buying a second-hand vehicle, keep in mind the hidden costs: stamp duty, registration, transfer fee, insurance and maintenance.

### ONLINE

Private and dealer car sales are listed online on websites such as **Car Sales** (www.carsales.com.au) and **Trading Post** (www.tradingpost.com.au).

### PRIVATE ADS

Buying privately can be time consuming, and you'll have to travel around to assess your options. But you should expect a lower price than that charged by a licensed dealer. The seller should provide you with a roadworthy certificate (if required in the state you're in), but you won't get a cooling-off period or a statutory warranty.

## BACKPACKERS & RIDE-SHARING

**Backpackers** Hostel notice-boards and online notice-boards such as those on www.taw.com.au and the Thorn Tree travel forum at www.lonelyplanet.com are good places to find vehicles for sale.

**Ride-sharing** A good way to split costs and environmental impact with other travellers. Hostel noticeboards are good places to find ads, as well as online classified sites like www.catchalift.com and www.needaride.com.au.

## DEALERS

Buying from a licensed dealer gives you some protection. They are obliged to guarantee that no money is owing on the car and you're usually allowed a cooling-off period (usually one day). Depending on the age of the car and the kilometres travelled, you may also receive a statutory warranty. You will need to sign an agreement for sale; make sure you understand what it says before you sign.

## PAPERWORK

When you buy a vehicle in Australia, you need to transfer the vehicle registration into your own name within 14 days. Each state has slightly different requirements and different organisations to do this. Similarly, when selling a vehicle you need to advise the state or territory road transport authority.

Some considerations:

**Transfer of Registration Form** In the NT, you and the seller need to complete and sign this form. In SA there is no form, but you and the seller need to complete and sign the reverse of the registration certificate.

**Roadworthy Certificate** In the NT and SA you don't need to provide a roadworthy certificate when selling a vehicle.

**Changing State of Registration** Note that registering a vehicle in a different state to the one it was previously registered in can be difficult, time consuming and expensive.

## REGISTRATION

'Rego' is usually renewed annually Australia-wide. This generally requires no more than payment of the registration fee, but SA and the NT have some extra considerations to think about:

➡ **SA** You can pay for three, six, nine or 12 months registration.

➡ **NT** Vehicle roadworthy inspections are required once the vehicle is three years old. Vehicles older than three years, but less than 10 years old, require a roadworthy inspection every two years until they reach their 10th year. Vehicles over 10 years old require an annual roadworthy inspection.

## ROAD TRANSPORT AUTHORITIES

For more information about processes and costs in central Australia:

**Department of Planning, Transport & Infrastructure SA** (☑13 10 84; www.dpti.sa.gov.au)

**Department of Transport NT** (☑1300 654 628; www.transport.nt.gov.au)

# Road Conditions, Hazards & Parking

**Sealed Roads** In SA, all major highways into Adelaide are bitumen in good condition. Further north in the outback, the Stuart Hwy and the main roads into Lyndhurst, Roxby Downs and Wilpena Pound are the only bitumen roads – the rest are unsealed. In the NT, the Stuart Hwy into Darwin is sealed, as is the loop road through Kakadu and the main highways into WA and Queensland.

**Unsealed Roads** Driving on unsealed roads requires special care, as cars perform differently when braking and turning on dirt. Conditions vary from well-maintained gravel to rough corrugations, deep sand and dust. Heavy rain will quickly turn some roads into muddy skating rinks, many impassable when wet. If a road is officially closed because of heavy rain, you can be fined up to $1000 per wheel for travelling on it. Under no circumstances exceed 80km/h on dirt roads; if you go faster you won't have time to respond to a sharp turn, stock on the road or an unmarked gate or cattle grid. Take your time and don't try to break the land-speed record.

**Road Condition Reports** For up-to-date SA road conditions, call 1300 361 033 or check www.dpti.sa.gov.au/outbackroads; in the NT call 1800 246 199 or check www.roadreport.nt.gov.au.

**Animal Hazards** Collisions with kangaroos, cattle, camels, brumbies and emus can be a real hazard. The result of a collision with an animal at high speed in a car can be disastrous. Kangaroos are most active around dawn and dusk, and often travel in groups. If you see one hopping across the road in front of you, slow right down – its friends are probably just behind it. If one hops out right in front of you, hit the brakes and only swerve to avoid the animal if it is safe to do so. If possible, avoid travelling at night on the highway.

**Road Trains** Road trains are a prime mover truck with two or three trailers stretching for as long as 50m. On dual-lane highways they pose few problems, although you need some distance and plenty of speed to overtake. On single-lane bitumen roads you should get right off the road if one approaches. On dirt roads you also need to pull over, and often stop altogether while you wait for the dust cloud to clear.

**Fatigue** Driving long distances (particularly in hot weather) can send you to sleep at the wheel. On a long haul, stop and rest every two hours or so – stretch, do some exercise, change drivers or have a coffee.

**Hitchers** A couple of incidents in recent years have led to warnings against stopping for people, or vehicles, on isolated stretches of road – even if they wave you down.

**Parking** We've used the parking 'P' icon in this book only for Sleeping listings in Adelaide and Darwin, to indicate where parking is available. Elsewhere it's rarely an issue.

### OUTBACK DRIVING

**Resources** The **RAA** (RAA; ☎08-8202 4600; www.raa.net; 55 Hindmarsh Sq, Adelaide, SA) and **AANT** (AANT; ☎08-8925 5901; www.aant.com.au; 79-81 Smith St, Darwin, NT) can advise on preparation, and supply maps and track notes.

**Preparations** Apart from being well prepared with spare parts and tyres, plenty of water (5L per person per day and extra for the radiator) and a basic knowledge of outback driving (things such as deflating tyres to get through deep sand), an extra safety net is to carry a high-frequency (HF) radio transceiver or satellite phone to contact Royal Flying Doctor Service bases, a Global Positioning System (GPS) unit and/or an emergency position-indicating radio beacon (EPIRB). **Central Comms** (☎08-8952 2388; www.cen tralcomms.com.au; cnr Stuart Hwy & Wills Tce, Alice Springs, NT) in Alice Springs hires out sat phones and EPIRBs for around $100 a week. The big car-hire companies also hire out GPS units from around $60 a week.

**Seasons** It's wise not to attempt tough tracks during the heat of summer (November to March) when the dust can be severe and water scarce, making a breakdown more dangerous. Travel during the Wet (November to April) in the north may be hindered by flooding and impassable mud.

**Tell Someone** There are still many unsealed roads in central Australia where the official recommendation is that you report to the police before you leave, and again when you arrive at your destination. If not the police, tell friends, family and/or your car-hire company what you're up to.

**In Trouble?** If you do run into trouble in the back of beyond, always stay with your car. It's easier to spot a car than a human being from the air, and you wouldn't be able to carry a heavy load of water very far anyway. Police suggest that you carry two spare tyres (for added safety) and, if stranded, set fire to one of them (let the air out first) – the pall of smoke will be seen for miles.

### Road Rules

Australians drive on the left-hand side of the road.

**Give Way** When driving, 'give way to the right', meaning that if an intersection is unmarked (common in the outback, but not in cities), you *must* give way to vehicles entering the intersection from your right.

**Speed Limits** The general speed limit in built-up areas is 50km/h (25km/h or 40km/h near schools at certain times – look for the signs), and 110km/h on highways in SA. In the NT, the speed limit on the open highway is either 110km/h or 130km/h.

**Seat Belts** Seat belts must be worn by law.

**Drink Driving** You must not drive with a blood-alcohol content 0.05% or more.

**Mobile Phones** Talking on a mobile phone while driving is illegal in Australia (excluding hands-free technology).

## Hitching

Hitching (or picking up hitchers) is never entirely safe – we do not recommend it. Hitching to or from SA across the Nullarbor is definitely not advisable as waits of two or three days are common. People looking for travelling companions for the long car journeys interstate often leave notices on boards in hostels and backpacker accommodation: ask around.

## Local Transport

In SA, Adelaide has an extensive public bus network, a not-so-extensive public train system and one tram line (which is surprisngly useful). All are run by **Adelaide Metro** (☎1300 311 108; www.adelaidemetro.com.au).

In the NT, Darwin and Alice Springs have handy public bus networks run by the **Department of Transport** (☎08-8924 7666; www.transport.nt.gov.au/public/bus/darwin).

## Tours

Backpacker-style and more formal bus tours offer a convenient way to get from A to B and see the sights on the way. Operators include the following:

**AAT Kings** (☎1300 556 100; www.aatkings.com) Big coach company (popular with the older set) with myriad tours in the NT and SA, including Uluru, Alice Springs, the Barossa Valley and Kangaroo Island.

**Adventure Tours Australia** (☎1300 654 604; www.adventuretours.com.au) Two- to 24-day tours taking in Uluru, Alice Springs, Darwin and Kakadu in the NT, and Adelaide, Barossa Valley and Kangaroo Island in SA. A 14-day Adelaide to Darwin trip via Alice Springs costs $2114; two days taking in Alice Springs and Uluru costs $490.

**Autopia Tours** (☑03-9419 8878, 1800 000 507; www.autopiatours.com.au) Small-group, three-day Melbourne–Adelaide tours along Great Ocean Rd ($425 including dorm accommodation and most meals).

**Bookabee Tours** (☑08-8235 9954; www.bookabee.com.au) Aboriginal-run, two-to five-day Flinders Ranges explorations, ex-Adelaide.

**Groovy Grape** (☑1800 661 177; www.groovygrape.com.au) Small-group tours including a three-day trip from Melbourne to Adelaide via the Great Ocean Road ($425), and seven days from Adelaide to Alice Springs via the Flinders Ranges, Coober Pedy and Uluru ($975). Includes meals, camping and national park entry fees. Kangaroo Island and Barossa Valley tours are also available.

**Heading Bush** (☑1800 639 933; www.headingbush.com) Rugged, small-group, 10-day Adelaide to Alice Springs expeditions are $1995 all-inclusive. Stops include the Flinders Ranges, Coober Pedy, Simpson Desert, Aboriginal communities, Uluru and West MacDonnell Ranges. Yorke Peninsula and dedicated Flinders Ranges tours are also available.

**Oz Experience** (☑1300 300 028; www.ozexperience.com) Hop-on–hop-off backpacker network with frequent buses looping around eastern Australia including Darwin, Adelaide and the east coast. There's a range of passes (valid for 12 months). The Sydney to Darwin 'Fish Hook' pass via Melbourne, Adelaide and Alice Springs costs $2465.

**The Rock Tour** (☑1800 246 345; www.therocktour.com.au) Three-day/two-night tours to Uluru, Kata Tjuta and Kings Canyon, departing Alice Springs. Combo tour/transport tickets with Qantas and Greyhound are also available.

**Wildlife Tours** (☑1300 661 730 ; www.wildlifetours.com.au) Two- or three-day, small-group Melbourne–Adelaide tours along Great Ocean Rd (from $239).

## Train

The famous *Ghan* train connects Adelaide with Darwin via Alice Springs. From Adelaide there are rail connections with Sydney and Perth on the *Indian Pacific* and Melbourne on the *Overland*. You can also join the *Ghan* at Port Augusta, the connection point on the Sydney–Perth *Indian Pacific* route.

➡ From Adelaide, the *Ghan* departs Adelaide for Alice Springs on Sunday and

Wednesday (18 hours), continuing on to Darwin arriving on Tuesday and Friday (another 24 hours). It reverses from Darwin to Alice Springs on Wednesday and Saturday, continuing to Adelaide arriving on Friday and Monday.

➡ From Melbourne, the *Overland* has day trains to Adelaide (10 hours) on Tuesday, Thursday and Saturday, returning on Monday, Wednesday and Friday.

➡ From Sydney, the *Indian Pacific* departs on Wednesday (plus Saturday in September and October) for Adelaide (25 hours, arriving Thursday), continuing to Perth (another 40 hours, arriving Saturday). The return leg chugs out of Perth on Sunday (plus Wednesday in September and October),

## Costs & Classes

**Classes** The *Ghan* and *Indian Pacific* offer 'daynighter' seats and more comfortable sleeper classes; the *Overlander* has two classes of seats. With a daynighter you get a reclining seat in an open carriage, foldaway table and access to a licensed lounge car serving light meals and drinks. Sleeper classes involve cabins with all kinds of foldaway seats and beds. Pricier sleepers have en suites and private restaurant-car dining.

### STANDARD ADULT/CHILD TRAIN FARES

| JOURNEY | SEAT | STANDARD SLEEPER | 1ST-CLASS SLEEPER | MOTORAIL |
| --- | --- | --- | --- | --- |
| Adelaide–Alice Springs | $431/202 | $1190/882 | $2290/2290 | $615 |
| Adelaide–Darwin | $862/403 | $2290/1582 | $3390/3390 | $800 |
| Adelaide–Perth | $553/310 | $1750/1202 | $2850/2850 | $615 |
| Darwin–Alice Springs | $431/202 | $1190/882 | $2290/2290 | $204 |
| Melbourne–Adelaide | from $116/60 | n/a | n/a | $143 |
| Sydney–Adelaide | $375/213 | $850/688 | $1350/1350 | $286 |

**Discounts & Passes** Booking some months ahead will often secure a discount on the prices listed here (up to 25% off). Backpacker discounts apply to all fares (up to 50% off!). International visitors (only) can take advantage of a **Rail Explorer Pass** (3/6 months $450/590) allowing unlimited travel for three or six months in daynighter seat class on all three routes; present your passport to qualify.

**Motorail** The Motorail service allows you to put your vehicle on the train.

## Reservations

Book tickets through **Great Southern Rail** (☏13 21 47; www.gsr.com.au). Advance bookings are recommended in peak season (June to September), especially for Motorail spaces.

# Behind the Scenes

## SEND US YOUR FEEDBACK

We love to hear from travellers – your comments keep us on our toes and help make our books better. Our well-travelled team reads every word on what you loved or loathed about this book. Although we cannot reply individually to postal submissions, we always guarantee that your feedback goes straight to the appropriate authors, in time for the next edition. Each person who sends us information is thanked in the next edition – the most useful submissions are rewarded with a selection of digital PDF chapters.

Visit **lonelyplanet.com/contact** to submit your updates and suggestions or to ask for help. Our award-winning website also features inspirational travel stories, news and discussions.

Note: We may edit, reproduce and incorporate your comments in Lonely Planet products such as guidebooks, websites and digital products, so let us know if you don't want your comments reproduced or your name acknowledged. For a copy of our privacy policy visit lonelyplanet.com/privacy.

## OUR READERS

**Many thanks to the travellers who used the last edition and wrote to us with helpful hints, useful advice and interesting anecdotes:**
Stuart Babbage, Colin Davies, Lisa & Lynn Frankes, Luke Gellard, Ronan Gough, Tony Henshaw, Ursula Hickey, Andrew Hunt, Jane Luckraft, John May, Wout De Nooij, Joshua Radke, Rosemary Royle, Marianne Schmid, Claudia Speck-Grimme, Anne-Marie Sutcliffe, Jim Thiselton, Janice Worland.

## AUTHOR THANKS

### Charles Rawlings-Way

Huge thanks to Maryanne for the gig, and to our highway-addled co-author Lindsay, who covered a helluva lot of kilometres in search of the perfect review. Thanks also to the all-star in-house LP production staff, particularly the Lords of Christo (you know who you are). Special thanks to Meg, my road-trippin' sweetheart, and our fab travelling companions – our daughters Ione and Remy – who provided countless laughs, unscheduled pit-stops and ground-level perspectives along the way.

### Meg Worby

Grateful thanks to Maryanne for the gig: it's always good working with you. Cheers to the in-house team in Footscray for all their hard work. Thanks to Brother Dave, Mike Stewart and Zsa Zsa for insider tips on Adelaide and sharing an SA table or two. A shout out to our little back-seaters, Ione and Remy, who make travelling more challenging and more rewarding than ever. Huge thanks, as ever, to Charles – away and at home, you make hard work seem easy.

### Lindsay Brown

Thanks to Lizzie and Phoebe in Alice, and Jenny, Sinead and Pat at home. Cheers to all the national parks rangers that put up with my questions, and the great staff at all the Northern Territory visitor centres. Finally, thanks to Meg, Charles and Maryanne for getting this whole show on the road.

## ACKNOWLEDGMENTS

Cover photograph: Uluru; redbrickstock.com/Alamy

# THIS BOOK

This 6th edition of Lonely Planet's *Central Australia: Adelaide to Darwin* guidebook was researched and written by Charles Rawlings-Way, Meg Worby and Lindsay Brown. Lindsay also updated The Outback Environment chapter originally written by Dave Fuller, Kylie Strelan and Dr Irene Watson. The previous edition was also written by the same team, with the added assistance of Paul Harding. This guidebook was commissioned in Lonely Planet's Melbourne office, and produced by the following:

**Commissioning Editor** Maryanne Netto

**Coordinating Editor** Justin Flynn

**Coordinating Cartographer** Corey Hutchison

**Coordinating Layout Designer** Mazzy Prinsep

**Managing Editors** Sasha Baskett, Barbara Delissen

**Managing Cartographer** Diana Von Holdt

**Managing Layout Designer** Jane Hart

**Assisting Editors** Susie Ashworth, Jenna Myers

**Assisting Cartographers** Jeff Cameron, Csanad Csutoros

**Cover Research** Brendan Dempsey

**Internal Image Research** Aude Vauconsant

**Thanks to** Ryan Evans, Larissa Frost, Mark Griffiths, Genesys India, Jouve India, Trent Paton, Raphael Richards, Gerard Walker

# Index

# Map Legend

## Sights
- Beach
- Bird Sanctuary
- Buddhist
- Castle/Palace
- Christian
- Confucian
- Hindu
- Islamic
- Jain
- Jewish
- Monument
- Museum/Gallery/Historic Building
- Ruin
- Sento Hot Baths
- Shinto
- Sikh
- Taoist
- Winery/Vineyard
- Zoo/Wildlife Sanctuary
- Other Sight

## Activities, Courses & Tours
- Bodysurfing
- Diving/Snorkelling
- Canoeing/Kayaking
- Course/Tour
- Skiing
- Snorkelling
- Surfing
- Swimming/Pool
- Walking
- Windsurfing
- Other Activity

## Sleeping
- Sleeping
- Camping

## Eating
- Eating

## Drinking & Nightlife
- Drinking & Nightlife
- Cafe

## Entertainment
- Entertainment

## Shopping
- Shopping

## Information
- Bank
- Embassy/Consulate
- Hospital/Medical
- Internet
- Police
- Post Office
- Telephone
- Toilet
- Tourist Information
- Other Information

## Geographic
- Beach
- Hut/Shelter
- Lighthouse
- Lookout
- Mountain/Volcano
- Oasis
- Park
- Pass
- Picnic Area
- Waterfall

## Population
- Capital (National)
- Capital (State/Province)
- City/Large Town
- Town/Village

## Transport
- Airport
- Border crossing
- Bus
- Cable car/Funicular
- Cycling
- Ferry
- Metro station
- Monorail
- Parking
- Petrol station
- Subway station
- Taxi
- Train station/Railway
- Tram
- Underground station
- Other Transport

## Routes
- Tollway
- Freeway
- Primary
- Secondary
- Tertiary
- Lane
- Unsealed road
- Road under construction
- Plaza/Mall
- Steps
- Tunnel
- Pedestrian overpass
- Walking Tour
- Walking Tour detour
- Path/Walking Trail

## Boundaries
- International
- State/Province
- Disputed
- Regional/Suburb
- Marine Park
- Cliff
- Wall

## Hydrography
- River, Creek
- Intermittent River
- Canal
- Water
- Dry/Salt/Intermittent Lake
- Reef

## Areas
- Airport/Runway
- Beach/Desert
- Cemetery (Christian)
- Cemetery (Other)
- Glacier
- Mudflat
- Park/Forest
- Sight (Building)
- Sportsground
- Swamp/Mangrove

*Note: Not all symbols displayed above appear on the maps in this book*